Liliana E. Popa



# Patterns of Treaty Interpretation as Anti-Fragmentation Tools

## A Comparative Analysis with a Special Focus on the ECtHR, WTO and ICJ

Springer

Liliana E. Popa
School of Law
University of Essex
Colchester, United Kingdom

ISBN 978-3-030-09741-7 ISBN 978-3-319-65488-1 (eBook)
DOI 10.1007/978-3-319-65488-1


Softcover re-print of the Hardcover 1st edition 2018


Printed on acid-free paper

This Springer imprint is published by Springer Nature
The registered company is Springer International Publishing AG
The registered company address is: Gewerbestrasse 11, 6330 Cham, Switzerland

# Patterns of Treaty Interpretation as Anti-Fragmentation Tools

*To the loving memory of my father:*
*Valeriu Popa*

The original version of the book back matter has been revised. The new version of the bibliography has been inserted in the back matter.

# Acknowledgments

In this book, I offer some arguments developed during my doctoral research at the University of Essex. Much of what I have written in the book was inspired by the view of international law as a 'moral project'. However, it is one thing to draw up a concept in general terms and quite another thing to elaborate it into precise expression. That process has taken some time in my case, and it was inspired by the teachings of two great international law Professors: Francis A. Boyle and Dan Ciobanu, as well as by the teachings of a great philosophy Professor: Petru Sitov, all with whom I had the honor to study. I am grateful to all of them. The ideas presented in this book have been developed in reaction to what pre-eminent jurists have written on the subject and took shape during many discussions with my supervisors at Essex, Professors David Ong and Karen Hulme. I could have not started this project or developed it without Professor David Ong's endorsement, his feedback, guidance and faith in this project. I could have not accomplished it without Professor Karen Hulme's constant guidance, feedback and insights on various drafts of this research project. This book reflects my supervisors' well-considered and thoughtful criticism, and I express my gratitude to both of them for all their valuable feedback and support. If the arguments developed in this book sometimes sound more conclusive than they should, I hope that it is because I have tried to state them as clearly as I could and not because I have discounted the thoughtful criticism of my supervisors. I would also like to extend my gratitude to Dr. Darren Calley at Essex for his important feedback, continuous support, as well as for his belief in this project. The book as it stands could have not been written without the feedback of Professor Malgosia Fitzmaurice from Queen Mary and of Dr. Scott Sheeran from Essex, who made various suggestions for the improvement of the initial PhD thesis that forms the substance of this book. Their writings on the subject inspired me to nuance my takes on the topics covered by this book, and I would like to express my gratefulenss to both of them for their generosity and valuable feedback.

I am grateful to Liviu, my husband, for his unwavering moral support and encouragement, to my mother for believing in me, and to my siblings for all their support and for being there to fill with joy my few moments of break during this extensive journey.

Finally, I am indebted to my editor at Springer, Anke Seyfried, for her endorsement and for making a complex editorial system as easily as possible.

I dedicate this book to the memory of my father, who prematurely passed away long before I started this journey. His teachings were never forgotten. May God rest him in peace!

# Contents

# Table of Cases

## I.C.J.

*Access of Polish War Vessels to the Port of Danzig*, Advisory Opinion No. 22, 11 December 1931, P.C.I.J., Ser. A/B, No. 43.

*Aegean Sea Continental Shelf Case* (Greece v. Turkey), Judgment of 19 December 1978, I.C.J.

*Ambatielos Case* (Greece v. United Kingdom), Preliminary Objections, Judgment of 1 July 1952, I.C.J. Rep.

*Anglo-Norwegian Fisheries Case* (United Kingdom v. Norway), Merits, Judgment, 18 December 1951, I.C.J. Rep. 142.

*Appeal Relating to the Jurisdiction of the ICAO Council* (India v. Pakistan), Order of 18 August 1972, I.C.J. Rep. 46.

*Application of the Convention on the Prevention and Punishment of the Crime of Genocide* (Bosnia and Herzegovina v. Serbia and Montenegro), Judgment of 26 February 2007, I.C.J. Rep.

*Application of the Convention on the Prevention and Punishment of the Crime of Genocide* (Bosnia and Herzegovina v. Yugoslavia), Judgment of 10 August 1993, I.C.J. Rep.

*Application of the Interim Accord of 13 September 1995* (The Former Yugoslavia Republic of Macedonia v. Greece), Judgment of 5 December 2011, I.C.J. Rep.

*Arbitral Award Made by the King of Spain on 23 December 1906*, Judgment of 18 November 1960, I.C.J. Rep.

*Arbitral Award of 31 July 1989* (Guinea-Bissau v. Senegal), Judgment of 12 November 1991, I.C.J. Rep. 53, ICGJ 90 (ICJ 1991).

*Armed Activities on the Territory of the Congo* (Democratic Republic of Congo (DRC) v. Uganda), Merits, Judgment of 19 December 2005, I.C.J. Rep. 168.

*Asylum Case* (Colombia v. Peru), Judgment of 20 November 1950, I.C.J. Rep. 266.

*Avena and Other Mexican Nationals* (Mexico v. the United States of America), Judgment of 31 March 2004, I.C.J. 12.

*Barcelona Traction, Light and Power Co. Ltd.* (Belgium v. Spain), Judgment of 5 February 1970, I.C.J. Rep. 3.

*Border and Transborder Armed Actions* (Nicaragua v. Honduras), Jurisdiction and Admissibility, Judgment of 20 December 1988, I.C.J. Rep. 69.

*Payment in Gold of Brazilian Federal Loans Contracted in France* (France. v. Brazil), Judgment of 12 July 1929, P.C.I.J., Series A, No. 21.

*Case Concerning Ahmadou Sadio Diallo* (Republic of Guinea v. Democratic Republic of Congo), Merits, Judgment 30 November 2010, I.C.J. Rep. 639.

*Case Concerning Gabcikovo-Nagymaros Project* (Hungary v. Slovakia), Judgment of 25 September 1997, I.C.J. Rep. 7.

*Case of S.S. Wimbledon* (United Kingdom v. Germany), Judgment of 28 June 1923, P.C.I.J., Ser. A., No. 1.

*Case Concerning Legality of Use of Force* (Serbia and Montenegro v. United Kingdom), Preliminary Objections, 2004, I.C.J. Reports.

*Case Concerning Military and Paramilitary Activities in and Against Nicaragua* (Nicaragua v. United States of America), Jurisdiction of the Court and Admissibility of the Application, Judgment of 26 November 1984, I.C.J. Reports.

*Case Concerning Military and Paramilitary Activities in and Against Nicaragua* (Nicaragua v. United States of America), Merits, Judgment of 27 June 1986, I.C.J. Reports.

*Case Concerning Oil Platforms* (Islamic Republic of Iran v. United States of America), Preliminary Objections, 12 December 1996, I.C.J.

*Case Concerning Rights of United States in Morocco* (France v. United States of America), Judgment of 27 August 1952, I.C.J. Reports.

*Case Concerning the Territorial Dispute* (Libyan Arab Jamahirya v. Chad), Judgment of 3 February 1994, I.C.J. Rep.

*Certain German Interests in Polish Upper Silesia* (Germany v. Poland), P.C.I.J., Rep. Series A No. 7, 1926.

*Certain Expenses of the United Nations* (Article 17, Paragraph 2, of the Charter), Advisory Opinion, I.C.J. Reports 1962.

*Competence of the International Labour Organization in Regard to International Regulation of the Conditions of Labour of Persons Employed in Agriculture*, Advisory Opinion, P.C.I.J., Ser. B, Nos. 2 and 3, 1922.

*Competence of the General Assembly for the Admission of a State to the United Nations* (Second Admissions Case), Advisory Opinion, 3 March 1950, I.C.J. Rep. 4.

*Constitution of the Maritime Safety Committee of the Inter-Governmental Maritime Organization*, Advisory Opinion of 8 June 1960, I.C.J. Rep. 150.

*Condition of Admission of a State to Membership in the United Nations (Article 4 of the Charter)*, Advisory Opinion of 28 May 1948, I.C.J. Rep. 57.

*Competence of the ILO to Regulate the Personal Work of the Employer*, P.C.I.J., Series B, No. 13, 1926.

*Competence of the ILO to Regulate Agricultural Labour*, P.C.I.J., Series B, Nos. 2 and 3, 1922.

*Corfu Channel* (United Kingdom of Great Britain and Northern Ireland v. Albania), Merits, Judgment of 9 April 1949, I.C.J. Rep. 4.
*Corfu Channel* (United Kingdom of Great Britain and Northern Ireland v. Albania), Preliminary Objection, Judgment of 25 March 1948, I.C.J. Rep. 15.
*Dispute Regarding Navigational and Related Rights* (Costa Rica v. Nicaragua), Judgment of 13 July 2009, I.C.J.
*Elettronica Sicula S.P.A. (ELSI)* (United States of America v. Republic of Italy), Judgment of 20 July 1989, I.C.J. Rep. 15.
*Exchange of Greek and Turkish Population (Lausanne Convention VI, 30 January 1923, Article 2)*, Advisory Opinion, P.C.I.J., Series B, No. 10, 1925.
*Fisheries Case* (United Kingdom v. Norway), Judgment of 18 December 1951, I.C.J. Rep. 116.
*Fisheries Case* (United Kingdom v. Iceland), Judgment of 2 February 1973, I.C.J. Rep. 3.
*Free Zones of Upper Savoy and District of Gex* (France. v. Switzerland), Order of 19 August 1929, P.C.I.J., Series A, No. 22.
*Frontier Dispute* (Burkina Faso v. Mali), Provisional Measures, Order of 10 January 1986, I.C.J. Rep. 3.
*Haya de la Torre* (Colombia v. Peru), Merits, Judgment of 13 June 1951, I.C.J. Rep. 71.
*Interpretation of Article 3, Para. 2, of the Treaty of Lausanne*, P.C.I.J., Advisory Opinion of 21 November 1925, Series B, No. 12.
*Interpretation of Peace Treaties with Bulgaria, Hungary and Romania* (Second Phase), Advisory Opinion of 18 July 1950, I.C.J. Rep. 221.
*Interpretation of Article 3, Paragraph 2, of the Treaty of Lausanne*, Advisory Opinion of 21 November 1925, P.C.I.J., Ser. B, No 12.
*Jurisdiction of the ICAO Council* (India v. Pakistan), Order of 18 August 1972, I.C.J. Rep. 46.
*Kasikili/Sedudu* (Botswana v. Namibia), Judgment of 13 December 1999, I.C.J. Rep. 1045.
*LaGrand* (Germany v. United States of America), Merits, Judgment of 27 June, 2001, I.C.J. Rep. 466.
*Land, Island and Maritime Frontier Dispute* (El Salvador/Honduras: Nicaragua Intervening), Judgment of 11 September 1992, I.C.J. Rep. 351.
*Land and Maritime Boundary Between Cameroon and Nigeria* (Cameroon v. Nigeria), Provisional Measures, Order of 15 March 1996, I.C.J.
*Legal Consequences for States of the Continued Presence of South African Namibia* (South West Africa) *Notwithstanding SC Resolution* 276, Advisory Opinion of 21 June 1971, I.C.J. Rep. 16.
*Legal Consequences of the Construction of a Wall in the Occupied Palestinian Territory*, Advisory Opinion of 9 July 2004, I.C.J. Rep. 136.
*Maritime Delimitation in the Black Sea* (Romania v. Ukraina), Judgment of 3 February 2009, I.C.J. Rep. 61.
*Maritime Delimitation and Territorial Questions Between Qatar and Bahrain* (Qatar v. Bahrain), Jurisdiction and Admissibility, Judgment of 1 July 1994, I.C.J. Rep. 112.

*Maritime Delimitation in the Indian Ocean* (Somalia v. Kenya), Preliminary Objections, Judgment of 2 February 2017.

*Mavrommatis Palestine Concessions Case* (Greece v. Britain), Judgment of 30 August 1924, P.C.I.J., Ser. A, No. 2.

*Minority Schools in Albania*, Advisory Opinion, 1935, P.C.I.J., Series A/B No. 64.

*North Sea Continental Shelf Cases* (F.R.G./Den. v. F.R.G./Neth.), Judgment of 20 February 1969, I.C.J. Rep. 3.

*Nuclear Tests* (Australia v. France), Interim Protection, Order of 22 June 1973, I.C.J. Rep. 99.

*Nuclear Tests* (New Zealand v. France), Interim Protection, Order of 22 June 1973, I.C.J. Rep. 135.

*Polish Upper Silesia Case* (Germany v. Poland), 1926, P.C.I.J., Rep. Series A No. 7.

*Reservations to the Convention on the Prevention and Punishment of the Crime of Genocide*, Advisory Opinion, I.C.J., Advisory Opinion, 1951, I.C.J. Rep. 15.

*Rights of Nationals of the United States of America in Morocco* (France v. United States of America), Judgment of 27 August 1952, I.C.J. Rep. 176.

*Rights of Minorities in Upper Silesia (Minority Schools)*, Judgment of 26 April 1928, P.C.I.J., Series A 15.

*Settlers of German Origin in Poland*, Advisory Opinion of 10 September 1923, P.C. I.J., Series B, No. 6.

*Sovereignty over Pulau Ligitan and Pulau Sipadan* (Indonesia v. Malaysia), Merits, Judgment of 17 December 2002, I.C.J. Rep. 625.

*Sovereignty over Certain Frontier Land* (Belgium v. Netherlands), Merits, Judgment of 20 June 1959, I.C.J. Rep. 209.

*South West Africa Cases* (Second Phase) (Ethiopia v. South Africa, Liberia v. - South Africa), Judgment of 18 July 1966, I.C.J. Rep. 6.

*South West Africa Cases* (Ethiopia v. South Africa, Liberia v. South Africa), Judgment of 21 December 1963, I.C.J. Rep. 310.

*Tehran Hostages Case* (United States v. Iran), Judgment of 24 May 1980, I.C.J. Rep. 3.

*Temple of Preah Vihear* (Cambodia v. Thailand), Merits, Judgment of 15 June, I.C.J. Rep. 6.

*Territorial Dispute* (Libyan Arab Jamahiriya v. Chad), Merits, Judgment 3 February 1994, I.C.J. Rep. 6.

*The Legality of the Threat of Use of Nuclear Weapons*, Advisory Opinion of 8 July 1996, I.C.J. Reports 226.

*Treatment of Polish Nationals and Other Persons of Polish Origin or Speech in the Danzing Territory*, Advisory Opinion of 4 February 1932, P.C.I.J., Series A/B 44.

*Question Concerning the Acquisition of Polish Nationality*, Advisory Opinion of 15 September 1923, Series B, P.C.I.J., No. 7.

# ECtHR

*Ahmet Özkan and Others v. Turkey*, No. 21689/93, §§ 85–90, 309–320 and 326–330, 6 April 2004.

*Al-Adsani v. The United Kingdom*, Appl. No. 35763/97, Judgment, Strasbourg, 21 November 2001.

*Airey v. Ireland*, App. No. 6289/73, Series A, No. 32, Judgment, Strasbourg, 9 October 1979.

*Al-Skeini and Others v. United Kingdom* (App. No. 55721/07), Judgment, Strasbourg, 7 July 2011.

*Artico v. Italy* (App. No. 6694/74), Judgment, Strasbourg, 13 May 1980.

*Austin and Others v. the United Kingdom* [GC], Nos. 39692/09, 40713/09 and 41008/09, § 54, Strasbourg, 15 March 2012.

*Banković and Others v. Belgium and Others* [GC] (Dec.), No. 52207/99, § 66, ECHR 2001-XII.

*Behrami and Behrami v. France* and *Saramati v. France, Germany and Norway* (App. Nos. 71412/01 and 78166/01), ECHR, Decision on May 2007.

*Belilos v. Switzerland* (App. No. 10328/83), Judgment of 29 April 1988, ECHR, Series A, Vol. 132.

*Buckley v. United Kingdom* (Merits) (App. No. 20348/92), Case No. 23/1995/529/615, ECHR 1996-IV [1996] ECHR 39 (1997) 23 EHRR 101, IHRL 3110, ECHR.

*Case 'Relating to Certain Aspects of the Laws on the Use of Languages in Education in Belgium' v. Belgium* (App. Nos. 1474/62, 1677/62, 1691/62, 1769/63, 1994/63, 2126/64), Judgment, Strasbourg, 9 February 1967.

*Case Relating to Certain Aspects of the Laws on the Use of Languages in Education in Belgium v. Belgium* (Merits) (Appl. Nos. 1474/62, 1677/62, 1691/62, 1769/63, 1994/63, 2126/64), Judgment, Strasbourg, 23 July 1968.

*Catan and Others v. Moldova and Russia* (App. Nos. 43370/04, 8252/05 and 18454/06), Judgment, Strasbourg, 19 October 2012.

*Christine Goodwin v. the United Kingdom* [GC] (App. No. 28957/95, § 74), ECHR 2002-VI.

*Cyprus v. Turkey* [GC] (App. No. 25781/94, § 278), ECHR 2001-IV.

*Cudak v. Lithuania* [GC] (App. No. 15869/02), Judgment, Strasbourg, 23 March 2010.

*Delcourt* (Delcourt v. Belgium) (App. No. 2689/65), Judgment, Strasbourg, 17 January 1970.

*Demir and Baykara v. Turkey* [GC] (App. No. 34503/97, § 67), Strasbourg, 2 November 2008.

*De Wilde, Ooms and Verssyp ('Vagrancy') v. Belgium* (Article 50) (Merits) (App. Nos. 2832/66, 2835/66, 2899/66), Judgment, Strasbourg, 10 March 1972.

*Fabris v. France*, Judgment (Merits) (Appl. No. 16574108), Strasbourg, 7 February 2013.

*Folgerø and Others v. Norway* [GC] (App. No. 15472/02, § 84), Judgment, Strasbourg, 29 June 2007.

*Golder v. United Kingdom* (App. No. 4451/70), Judgment, Strasbourg, 21 February 1975.

*Handyside v. the United Kingdom* (App. No. 5493/72), Judgment, Strasbourg, 7 December 1976.

*Hertel v. Switzerland* (Appl. No. 25181/94), Judgment (Chamber), Strasbourg, 25 August 1998, Reports 1998-VI.

*Hirsi Jamaa and Others v. Italy* (App. No. 27765/09), Judgment, Strasbourg, 23 February 2012.

*Ilascu and Others v. Moldova and Russia* [GC] (App. No. 48787/99), Judgment, Strasbourg, 8 July 2004.

*Ireland v. United Kingdom* (App. 5310/71), Judgment, Strasbourg, 18 January 1978.

*Isayeva v. Russia* (App. No. 57950/00, §§ 180 and 210), Judgment, Strasbourg, 24 February 2005.

*Ivatoc and Others v. Moldova and Russia* (App. No. 23687/05), Judgment, Strasbourg, 15 November 2011.

*James and Others v. the United Kingdom* (App. No 8793/79), Judgment, 21 February 1986.

*Johnston and Others v. Ireland* (App. No. 9697/82), Judgment, Strasbourg, 18 December 1986.

*Kanlibaş v. Turkey* (App. No. 32444/96, §§ 39–51), Judgment, Strasbourg, 8 December 2005.

*Kjeldsen, Busk Madsen and Pedersen v. Denmark* (Application Nos. 5095/71, 5920/72, 5926/72), Judgment, Strasbourg, 7 December 1976.

*Klass and Others v. Germany* (App. No. 5029/71), Judgment, Strasbourg, 6 September 1978.

*Lautsi and Others v. Italy* [GC] (App. No. 30814/06, § 60), Judgment [GC], Strasbourg, 18 March 2011.

*Lawless v. Ireland* (No. 3) (Application No. 332/57), Judgment (Merits), Strasbourg, 1 July 1961.

*Lingens v. Austria* (App. No. 9815/82), Judgment, Merits and Just Satisfaction, Strasbourg, 8 July 1986.

*Lithgow and Others v. the United Kingdom* (App. Nos. 9006/80, 9262/81, 9263/81, 9265/81, 9266/81, 9313/81, 9405/81), Judgment, Strasbourg, 8 July 1986.

*Loizidou Case* (Loizidou v. Turkey), Preliminary Objections (Application No. 15318/89), Judgment, Strasbourg, 23 March 1995.

*M. and Others v. Italy and Bulgaria* (Appl. No. 40020/03), Judgment, Strasbourg, 31 July 2012.

*Mamatkulov and Askarov v. Turkey* (App. Nos. 46827/99 and 46951/99), Judgment, Strasbourg, 4 February 2005.

*Manoilescu and Dobrescu v. Romania and Russia* (Appl. No. 60861/00), Judgment, Strasbourg, 3 March 2005.

*Matznetter v. Austria* (App. No. 2178/64), Judgment, Strasbourg, 10 November 1969.

*Nada v. Switzerland* (Appl. No. 10593108), Judgment, Strasbourg, 12 September 2012.

*Neumeister v. Austria* (Merits) (App. No. 1936/63 (A/8)), Judgment, Strasbourg, 27 June 1968.

*Oleynikov v. Russia* (Appl. No. 36703104), Judgment, Strasbourg, 14 March 2013.
*Observer and Guardian v. the United Kingdom* (App. No. 13585/88), Judgment, Strasbourg, 26 November 1991.
*Raban v. Romania* (App. No. 25437/08), Judgment, Strasbourg, 26 October 2010.
*Rantsev v. Cyprus and Russia* (App. No. 25965/04, §§ 273–274), Judgment, Strasbourg, 2010.
*Saadi v. the United Kingdom* [GC] (App. No. 13229/03, § 62), Judgment, Strasbourg, 2008.
*Selmouni v. France 9* (App. No. 25803/940), Judgment, Strasbourg, 28 July 1999.
*Soering v. the United Kingdom* (Application No. 14038/88), Judgment, Strasbourg, 7 July 1989.
*Stec and Others v. the United Kingdom* (Dec.) [GC], App. Nos. 65731/01 and 65900/01, § 48), ECHR 2005-X.
*Steel and Morris v. the United Kingdom* (App. No. 68416/01, § 87), ECHR 2005-II.
*Stoll v. Switzerland* [GC] (Appl. No. 69698/01), Judgment, Strasbourg, 10 December 2007.
*Streletz, Kessler and Krenz v. Germany* [GC] (App. Nos. 34044/96, 35532/97 and 44801/98 § 90), ECHR 2001-II.
*Sunday Times v. the United Kingdom* (App. No. 6538/74, A/30) [1979] ECHR 1.
*Tyrer v. the United Kingdom* (App. No. 5856/72), Judgment, Strasbourg, 25 April 1978.
*Wemhoff v. Germany* (App. No. 2122/64), Judgment, Strasbourg, 27 June 1968.
*Winterwerp v. the Netherlands* (Application No. 6301/73), Judgment, Strasbourg, 24 October 1979.
*Witold Litwa v. Poland* (App. No. 26629/95), Judgment, Strasbourg, 4 April 2000.
*Vo v. France* [GC] (App. No. 53924/00, § 82), ECHR 2004-VIII.

## WTO

*Brazil Export Financing Programme for Aircraft (Brazil – Aircraft)*, WT/DS 46/AB/R, 2 August 1999.
*Brasil – Export Financing Programme for Aircraft (Brazil – Aircraft)*, Second Recourse by Canada to Article 21.5 of the DSB, WT/DS46/RW/2, 26 July 2001.
*Canada Term of Patent Protection (Canada – Patent Term)*, WT/DS170/R, Panel Report adopted 12 October 2000, upheld by Appellate Body Report WT/DS170/AB/R, DSR 2000:XI, 5121.
*Canada – Measures Affecting the Importation of Milk and the Exportation of Dairy Products (Canada – Dairy)* WT/DS103/AB/R, WT/DS113/AB/R, adopted 27 October 1999.
*Canada – Measures Affecting the Export of Civilian Aircraft (Canada – Aircraft)*, 2 August 1999, WT/DS70/AB/R, DSR 1999: III, 1377.
*Canada – Measures Affecting Exports of Unprocessed Herring and Salmon*, Panel Report adopted 22 March 1988 (L/6268 – 35S/98).

*Certain Measures Affecting Imports of Poultry from China (US – Poultry)*, WT/DS392/R, Panel Report adopted 29 September 2010.

*China – Measures Related to the Exportation of Various Raw Materials (China – Raw Materials)*, WT/D394/AB/R, WT/D395/AB/R, WT/DS398/AB/R, 30 January 2012.

*China – Measures Related to the Exportation of Various Raw Materials (China – Raw Materials)*, WT/DS394/R, WT/DS395/R, WT/DS398/R, Panel Report adopted 5 July 2011.

*Chile – Measures Affecting the Transit and Importation of Swordfish (Chile – Swordfish)*, WT/DS183/1, 19 April 2000.

*European Communities – Measures Affecting Trade in Large Civil Aircraft (EC and Certain Member States – Large Civil Aircraft*), WT/DS316/R, Panel Report, 30 June 2010.

*European Communities – Customs Classification of Certain Computer Equipment (EC – Computer Equipment)*, T/DS62/AB/RWT/DS67/AB/R, WT/DS68/AB/R, 5 June 1998.

*European Communities – Measures Affecting the Importation of Certain Poultry Products (EC – Poultry)*, WT/DS69/AB/R, 13 July 1998.

*European Communities – Anti-Dumping Duties on Malleable Cast Iron Tube or Pipe Fittings from Brazil*, WT/DS219/AB/R, adopted as modified by Appellate Body 18 August 2003.

*European Communities – Measures Affecting the Approval and Marketing of Biotech Products (EC – Approval and Marketing of Biotech Products)*, WT/DS291/R, WT/DS292/R, WT/DS293/R, Panel Reports adopted 21 November 2006.

*European Communities – Measures Affecting the Approval and Marketing of Biotech Products*, WT/DS291-293/INTERIM, issued 7 February 2006.

*European Communities – Measures Concerning Meat and Meat Products (Hormones)*, 1998, WT/DS26/AB/R, WT/DS48/AB/R, adopted 13 February 1998, DSR. 1998:I.

*European Communities – Measures Concerning Meat and Meat Products (Hormones)*, WT/DS26/AB/R, WT/DS48/AB/R, adopted 16 January 1998, DSR 1998:I.

*Guatemala – Definitive Anti-Dumping Measures on Grey Portland Cement from Mexico (Guatemala –Cement I)*, WT/DS60/R, circulated 24 October 2000.

*India – Patent Protection for Pharmaceutical and Agricultural Chemical Products (India – Patents (US))*, WT/DS50/AB/R, adopted 16 January 1998, DSR 1998:I.

*Italian Discrimination Against Imported Agricultural Machinery* (*Italy – Agricultural Machinery*), Panel Report adopted 23 October 1958 (L/833-7S/60).

*Korea – Definitive Safeguard Measure on Imports of Certain Dairy Products* (*Korea – Dairy*), WT/DS98R, WT/DS98/AB/R, circulated 14 December 1999.

*Korea – Measures Affecting Government Procurement (Korea – Procurement)*, WT/DS163/R, Panel Report adopted 19 June 2000.

*Korea – Measures Affecting Imports of Fresh Chilled and Frozen Beef (Korea – Various Measures on Beef)*, WT/DS161/AB/R, WT/DS169/AB/R, 11 December 2000.

*Thailand – Restrictions on the Importation of and Internal Taxes on Cigarettes (Thailand – Cigarettes)*, DS10/R-37S/200, Panel Report adopted 7 November 1990.

*United States Antidumping Act of 1916, Complaint by the European Communities (US – 1916 Act (EC))*, WT/DS136/R (adopted 26 September 2000, upheld by Appellate Body Report WT/DS136/AB/R, WT/DS162/AB/R, DSR 2000: X, 4593).

*United States – Anti-Dumping Duty on Dynamic Random Access Memory Semiconductors (DRAMS) of One Megabit or Above from Korea (US – DRAMS)*, WT/DS99/R, Panel Report adopted 19 March 1999.

*United States – Countervailing Duties on Certain Corrosion-Resistant Carbon Steel Flat Products from Germany (US – Carbon Steel)*, WT/DS213/R and Corr. 1, 3 July 2002, as modified by Appellate Body Report WT/DS213/AB/R, DSR 2002:IX, 3833.

*United States – Final Countervailing Duty to Determination with Respect to Certain Softwood from Canada (US – Softwood Lumber IV*, AB-2003-6, January 2004), WT/DS257/AB/R, adopted 17 February 2004, DSR 2004:II.

*United States – Prohibition of imports of Tuna and Tuna Products from Canada (Canadian – Tuna)*, Panel Report adopted on 22 February 1982 (L/5198-29S/91).

*United States – Import Prohibition of Certain Shrimp and Shrimp Products (US – Shrimp)*, WT/DS58/AB/R, 12 October 1998.

*United States Countervailing Measures Concerning Certain Products from the European Communities (US – Countervailing Measures on Certain EC Products)*, WT/DS212/R, 31 July 2002.

*United States Gambling and Betting Services (US – Gambling)*, 1, WT/DS285/AB/R, 7 April 2005.

*United States – Section 211 Omnibus Appropriation Act of 1998 (US – Section 211 Appropriations Act)*, WT/DS176/R, 6 August 2001.

*United States – Taxes on Automobiles (US – Taxes on Automobiles)*, DS31/R, 11 October 1994, Panel Report circulated on 11 October 1994, not adopted.

*United States – Restrictions on Imports of Tuna, 'Son of Tuna-Dolphin' ('Son of Tuna/Dolphin')*, DS29/R, Panel Report circulated on 16 June 1994, not adopted.

*United States – Restrictions on Imports of Tuna, the 'Tuna-Dolphin' ('Tuna-Dolphin')*, DS21/R –39S/155, Panel Report circulated on 3 September 1991, not adopted.

## ICC

*Prosecutor v. Omar Hassan Ahmad Al Bashir*, Judgment on the Appeal of the Prosecutor Against the Decision on the Prosecution's Application for Warrant of Arrest Against Omar Hassan Ahmad Al Bashir (ICC-02/05-01/09, P.T.C.I.), Appeals Chamber, 3 February 2010.

## IACtHR

*Velasquez Rodriguez v. Honduras*, IACtHR, Judgment of 29 July 1989, Series C No. 4, 28 ILM 291.

## ITLOS

*MOX Plant Case (Ireland v. United Kingdom),* Request for Provisional Measures, 41 I.L.M. 405, ITLOS, Case No. 10, Order of 3 December 2001.

*Southern Bluefin Tuna Case (Australia v. New Zealand/Japan), Award on Jurisdiction and Admissibility* (constituted under Annex VII of the United Nations Convention on the Law of the Sea ('UNCLOS')), 4 August 2000.

# Chapter 1
# Introduction

*Interpretation* in philosophy and in law is a venerable topic, older than two millennia.[1] In spite of the arguments exchanged by philosophers and jurists alike during those millennia, not all the issues related to 'interpretation' could be settled definitively.[2] In law, from the nineteenth century onwards, and with the advancement of modern civil codes in municipal law of continental Europe, the topic of 'interpretation' has received renewed consideration (Koskenniemi 2001). Initially, general rules of interpretation were laid down in the nineteenth century following Roman law ideas.[3] As national laws evolved and diversified, ideas about legal interpretation also evolved so in the twentieth century legal scholars were able to provide a more nuanced picture of the concept of 'interpretation' (Pound 1923; Curtis 1949). Meanwhile, on the international arena, several developments have made even more visible the potential of 'legal interpretation' to operate as one of the cornerstones of the international legal system. Thus, after the end of World War II, a complex array of international organisations was created, and numerous treaties were adopted. Later, after the end of the Cold War and with the advancement of a globalised world, characterised by a pluralistic legal order, this picture complicated further as the number of international judicial bodies,[4] and the treaties

[1]See e.g. Ramberg and Gjesdal (2009)—tracing the roots of hermeutics to Plato, and for a useful historical overview of the links between hermeneutics and interpretation of texts; Stein (1994)—for an overview of the Roman jurists schools of though positions relatively to legal texts interpretation at the beginning of the Roman Empire; Morigiwa et al. (2011).

[2]See, e.g., Endicott (2000)—for a discussion on 'legal interpretation' that deals with legal indeterminacy. In the author's view, 'the law is indeterminate in virtue of any indeterminacy in the rules of the language' and legal interpretation does not resolve or eliminate all indeterminacies in the application of legal rules.

[3]See, e.g., Stein (1994).

[4]Examples of *adjudicative* and *non adjudicative* bodies emerged after the Cold War: North American Commission on Environmental Cooperation (1993); NAFTA Dispute Settlement Panels (1994); Common Court of Justice and Arbitration of the Organization for the Harmonization of Corporate Law in Africa (1997); Arbitration and Mediation Center of the World Intellectual



L.E. Popa, *Patterns of Treaty Interpretation as Anti-Fragmentation Tools*,
DOI 10.1007/978-3-319-65488-1_1

that they were entrusted with, multiplied apace. It is not surprising then that, in this intellectual milieu, one of the problematic topics of international law, especially in the past two decades, has been whether the multiplication of international judicial bodies leads to the fragmentation of international law. Accordingly, the topic of *treaty interpretation* has received in the last decade a great deal of attention, especially in relation to the issues of the possible fragmentation of international law that may result from the proliferation of international adjudication *fora*. Thus, how *treaty interpretation* is undertaken by international bodies, in particular by specialised adjudicatory bodies, is perceived in the scholarship as one of the most salient topics of international law.[5]

Although the academic literature on treaty interpretation topic is too wide to be cited even cursorily in this introduction, several studies on this subject deserve attention as they constitute an important frame of reference for this book. The first such research belongs to the late Jonathan I. Charney, who in 1998 was already asking, in the course he held at The Hague Academy of International Law, whether fragmentation of international law occurs as a result of multiplication of international judicial bodies (Charney 1998). Analysing the International Court of Justice and specialised courts' case law on various substantive matters of international law (e.g., treaty interpretation and reservation, compensation for violations of international legal obligations, nationality, state responsibility, sources of international law: customary law and general principles of international law), Charney observed that although some variations on various matters of international law among the international courts and tribunals occur, such variations do not affect fundamentally international law so its fragmentation does not materialize.[6] This early contribution was followed by a special conference in 1998, convened at New York University, where a select group of scholars discussed the topic of possible fragmentation of international law as a result of multiplication of international courts and tribunals (Kingsbury 1998). Most notably, the United Nations decided in 2003 that the topic of fragmentation of international law as a result of multiplication of international judicial bodies deserved attention and entrusted the International Law Commission

---

Property Organization (1994); Eritrea-Ethiopia Claims Commission (2000); International Tribunal for the Law of the Sea (1996); World Trade Organization Appellate Body (1995); Court of Justice of the European Union (2010); Common Court of Justice and Arbitration of the Organization for the Harmonization of Corporate Law in Africa (1997); East African Court o Justice (2001); Court of Justice of the Economic Community of West African States (ECOWAS) (2001); International Criminal Court—ICC (2004); International Criminal Tribunal for the Former Yugoslavia—ICTY (1993); International Criminal Tribunal for Rwanda—ICTR (1995); Serious Crimes Panels in the District Court of Dili, East Timor (2000–2005); Panels in the Courts of Kosovo (2001); War Crimes Chamber of the Court of Bosnia-Herzegovina (2005); Special Court for Sierra Leone (2002); Extraordinary Chambers in the Courts of Cambodia (2006); Special Tribunal for Lebanon (2009), etc.

[5]See e.g. ILC Report (2006), Simma and Pulkowski (2006), Jackson (1998), Kelly (2001), Jennings (2004), Van Damme (2010), Lennard (2002).

[6]Charney (1998). Such comparative analyses dedicated to substantive international law fields are treated in a more illustrative way, using one or more cases succinctly analysed.

(ILC) with the task of writing a report on this matter.[7] The ILC, under the direction of Martti Kosekenniemi, named as Special Rapporteur, delivered the report in 2006, concluding in principle that fragmentation is not likely to occur as a result of the proliferation of international judicial bodies (ILC Report 2006).

Though extremely important, inasmuch as the ILC gives us a detailed taxonomy and description of the means by which the adjudicative bodies apply general international law and fill the 'gaps' in the texts of the treaties, the ILC Study Report did not have the purpose of dealing directly and in detail with the ways in which the international specialised bodies apply general international law but instead clarified the main substantive issues of 'fragmentation' in international law. Moreover, the ILC Study did not focus on the application of treaty interpretation by a specific specialised court or tribunal in a comparative analysis with the International Court of Justice (ICJ). The ILC touched the subject of application of general international law by various courts and tribunals when analysing the ways in which the 'gaps' of treaties are filled by reference to (general) international law (ILC Report 2006). In doing so, the ILC Report strove to offer a legal conceptual framework of 'fragmentation', and, as the new regimes derive their binding force from the law of treaties, the framework and focus of the ILC inquiry was the *1969 Vienna Convention on the Law of the Treaties* (VCLT) (ILC Report 2006, p. 6). While the ILC considered the topic of fragmentation closed after the delivery of the report, the scholarship on this topic has continued apace.[8] And given the limitations of the ILC framework, the continuous scholarly attention to the ways in which the various international judicial bodies interpret treaties is not surprising.

Overall, the understanding of *interpretation* within particular international law topics has tremendously improved in the recent years as a result of academic contributions such as those provided by Linderfalk (2007), Letsas (2007; 2010), Gardiner (2008), Orakhelashvili (2008), Kamminga and Scheinin (2009), Fitzmaurice et al. (2010), Merkouris (2010), Van Damme (2010), Forowicz (2010), Pauwelyn and Elsig (2011), Cannizzaro and Arsanjani (2011), Sheeran (2014), Bjorge (2014), to name just a few. Nevertheless, still missing in the general scholarship on the topic are comparisons between the ICJ (which has greatly contributed to the development and clarification of the rules and principles of international law)[9] and the international specialised courts in respect of their application of the customary rules of treaty interpretation. Consequently, there is relatively little analysis of the manner in which the specialised courts' interpretative

[7] Fifty-fifth Session, Supplement No. 10 (A/55/10), The fourth session (2002) decided to include the topic 'Risk ensuing from fragmentation of international law' in its program of work. From the fifty-fifth (2003) to fifty-seventh (2005) session of the Commission, the Study Group was successively reconstituted under the chairmanship of Mr. Martti Koskenniemi and carried out several tasks upon the methodology to be adopted for the study of fragmentation of international law.

[8] See e.g. Gardiner (2008), Carozza (2008), Mavroidis (2008), Scheinin (2009), Kamminga and Scheinin (2009), Tzevelekos (2009), Van Damme (2010), Fitzmaurice et al. (2010), Letsas (2010), Pauwelyn and Elsig (2011), McInerney-Lankford (2012), Bjorge (2014).

[9] Lauterpacht (1982), p. 282. See also on this aspect Waldock (1964).

practices diverge or not from the general (customary) rules of treaty interpretation, respectively from the standard provided by the Vienna Convention's universal methodology of interpretation. Yet such comparison between general and specialised courts would allow for a better understanding of how interpretation works at international courts generally, as also for a better assessment of the issue of 'fragmentation'/'unity' of international law from the perspective of treaty interpretation. In particular, it may allow for a better understanding of the issue of fragmentation in international law that might happen as a result of treaty interpretative practice at international specialised judicial bodies.

Thus, one major objective of this work is to analyse whether the practice of treaty interpretation of two of the foremost specialised international courts, the *European Court of Human Rights* (ECtHR) and the *World Trade Organization* (WTO) (adjudicative bodies), often perceived in scholarship as 'self-contained' regimes that promote a more radical process of functional specialisation than other international regimes (courts and tribunals), is consistent with the general methodology of treaty interpretation provided by the 1969 VCLT. Specifically, this work attempts to investigate whether treaty interpretation practice at these specialised courts could constitute a tool of unification of an alleged fragmented international law, or, otherwise, these courts' interpretative practices contribute to, or exacerbate the fragmentation of international law, thus rendering these courts part of the 'fragmentation' problem. For this purpose, the practice of the ICJ on treaty interpretation will be taken as the comparator since the ICJ is known as a general court with a general jurisdiction; its practice on treaty interpretation being considered the major source of inspiration for the ILC in drawing the rules of interpretation that found formulation in the 1969 VCLT.[10] As it has recently concluded by Judge Guillaume, one of the foremost recent presidents of the World Court, of crucial importance for 'fragmentation' not to happen is *the creation of a dialogue among judicial bodies.*[11]

Because the specialised courts have to interpret distinct treaties, sometimes considered as *lex specialis*, this book attempts to determine whether the ECtHR and WTO use *patterns of treaty interpretation* that are also *common* to the ICJ when they interpret *lex specialis*. The book especially attempts to determine whether the ECtHR and WTO's adjudicative bodies apply interpretative patterns akin to those deployed by the ICJ when they are confronted with analogous difficulties in the construction of the texts of treaties, such as *insufficient clear*, *inconsequent*, *ambiguous*, *doubtful*, *obscure*, *vague or silent* language of the text. The selection of

[10]See e.g. Waldock (1964).

[11]See Guillaume (1995; 2000a, b; 2004; 2011). In the author's view, such utilisation of the precedent is a guarantor of certainty and foreseeability in the application of law by any dispute settlement system (Guillaume 2011, p.7). Guillaume suggests in his Address to the UN General Assembly, in 2000 that in order to reduce the risks of conflicting interpretations of international law, and thus of fragmentation in international law, other international courts should seek the opinion of the ICJ on doubtful or important points of general international law raised in cases before them.

cases at both general (the ICJ) and specialised (the ECtHR and WTO) courts provided in this book has the benefit of enabling the comparisons of interpretation of entirely different treaties. Thus, the comparisons provided could be significant for showing the existence of homogeneous tendencies (preferences) observable at these courts in respect of their application of general rules of treaty interpretation. By providing a critical analysis of these three regimes, this book will attempt to highlight in particular the tendencies of the ECtHR and WTO to interpret their treaties in ways that would reconcile the customary rules of interpretation with their specific (autonomous) interpretative means ('doctrines'/'techniques'). The book will further attempt to assess on this basis what are the implications (impact) of such tendencies vis-à-vis international law and thus to address the missing scholarly comparative analysis of patterns of treaty interpretation indicated above.

However, even if the nature of the treaties interpreted by the ICJ is generally different from the nature of treaties interpreted by the specialised international courts, such a comparison is both possible and necessary. This comparison is arguably necessary if one wishes to have a better perspective of how international law is applied by the international specialised bodies and to respond to the more general question of whether their specialised practice deviates from international law. Thus, unlike a majority of writings, which do not offer a cross-cutting view among the international courts on matters related strictly to treaty interpretation, this book explores in depth specific cases at the ICJ, ECtHR and WTO, starting with their earliest practice up till the present. It also provides a more detailed account of these courts' techniques/patterns of approaching the general rules and methods of interpretation of treaties. By considering more cases of these courts and analysing them in more depth and comparatively than they are usually analysed in scholarly writings, and by putting these cases in a time perspective, this book attempts to identify possible *common patterns of treaty interpretation* in these courts' practices.

What this work attempts to achieve becomes even clearer if one accepts that she could conceive the concept of *fragmentation* (of international law) as having to do with the *coherence of interpretative approach* of a given court, on three dimensions. A *first dimension* of coherence will be thus *historical*, prior to and after a given time point, which, in the case of treaty interpretation, is the adoption of the *1969 Vienna Convention on the Law of Treaties*. 'Fragmentation' in this case will imply that a court approaches the interpretation of treaties in a different way prior to the adoption of the VCLT than it approaches interpretation after the entry into force of the VCLT. A *second dimension* of coherence will be *internal* to any given court and could be determined by observing whether that given court does in carrying out its interpretation what it states it does. Fragmentation in such a case could occur if one particular court is inconsistent with its own approach in a given case and frequently does something different than what it declares or suggests it does when applying the customary rules of interpretation. Finally, a *third dimension* of coherence will be *comparative* and will consist of the determination of similar or dissimilar approaches to treaty interpretation based on general rules of interpretation adopted by the ECtHR, WTO and ICJ. Since all these courts have to interpret treaties, it could be assumed that they encounter similar difficulties in interpreting the text of treaties such as ambiguity, insufficient clarity, obscurity in treaty language, or silence in treaty text in regard to a specific circumstance of a given case. Thus *such common difficulties could be conceptualised as a sort of prism through which the interpretative patterns of various courts can be assessed and compared*. 'Fragmentation' in this dimension of coherence will arguably not occur if the interpretative patterns detected in international courts' practices are similar or, conversely, will occur if these patterns diverge.

Summing up, many authors approached the issue of 'fragmentation' by looking at the ways in which various substantive matters of international law (e.g., treaty interpretation, state responsibility, nationality, citizenship, aliens, state immunities, exhaustion of domestic remedies) are interpreted by various international courts and tribunals. Eventually, they approached 'fragmentation' by comparing succinctly the ICJ's and one or more specialised courts' approaches on various substantive international law matters, in order to test whether there are differences (variations) between courts in approaching those matters. Such an approach could eventually determine the existence/non-existence of fragmentation in international law from the perspective of what I have called above: the 'third dimension' of coherence (comparative dimension) of legal interpretation at international courts. In this book, a different perspective is applied, starting from the observation that the cohesion of treaty interpretation could be analysed on the three levels mentioned above and that the absence of cohesion on any such level might lead to some sort of 'fragmentation' in international law. In principle, this book will investigate whether the general rules and methods of treaty interpretation used by the ICJ diverge or not in fundamental ways when they are being applied in the specific context of the ECtHR and WTO. While investigating whether the two specialised courts, ECtHR and WTO, which regulate human rights and international trade, respectively (*lex specialis*), use the customary rules of treaty interpretation in similar patterns/techniques to resolve treaty interpretative difficulties, the book will also inquire whether these specialised adjudicative bodies' practice are influenced by the ICJ's methods and techniques of treaty interpretation and whether they use the ICJ's precedents.

The methodology of this work is informed by a logical, doctrinal and systematic perspective,[12] and it is broadly comparative, insofar as this work is not confined to an analysis of an individual court, but it examines two different international

[12]See for explanation on this type of methodology, e.g., Van Hoecke (2011).

specialised courts (the ECtHR and WTO) in relation to a general one (the ICJ). The two specialised courts included in this analysis were not chosen randomly, but specifically because of their importance among the international specialised courts, and because of the possibility to generalise in some degree the findings derived from a qualitative analysis of case law at these courts to other similar specialised international judicial bodies. Since the ECtHR was the first human rights court in the international arena to develop a substantive body of HR case law, and its case law and interpretative doctrines were used in the development of specific doctrines of the other foremost human rights courts (e.g., the Inter-American Court of Human Rights, African Court of Human and People's Rights), it could be used as a comparator unit of analysis, from which qualitative generalisations could be made with respect to international human rights regimes. Similarly, the WTO could be used in making generalisations derived from qualitative research applicable to international economic regimes. Although there are other important specialised economic courts, more notably the Court of Justice of the European Union (CJEU), the WTO represents arguably a more representative international judicial body than the CJEU for the analysis of the specialised judicial forums entrusted with the interpretation of trade treaties.

Moreover, the reason for selecting these particular dispute settlement regimes is that they are by far the most active international courts, adjudicating a large caseload annually. Though relatively new in comparison with PCIJ/ICJ, both the ECtHR and WTO (which functioned first through the filter of a Commission in the case of the ECtHR and in the case of the WTO as panels) have developed the most intensive interpretative practices in the history of international dispute settlement and thus an extensive jurisprudence. In addition, in the context of the 'proliferation/fragmentation' discourse, the ECtHR and WTO dispute settlement regimes have generated controversial debates, being perceived by an increasing number of scholars as 'subsystems', or 'autonomous systems decoupled from general international law'. Having their own specific procedures, or rules of adjudication, they are thought to promote 'self-contained regimes', as well as an even 'more radical process of functional specialisation' than other 'subsystems' (Simma and Pulkowski 2006, p. 11). As such, they represent ideal *loci* where the issue of 'fragmentation of international law' could be investigated, respectively whether it is likely or not to occur. To round up such an investigation, as mentioned above, it is necessary to take as a comparator the ICJ's practice on treaty interpretation, since the ICJ has contributed mostly since its inception to the development of the canons of interpretation, from which the International Law Commission had drawn the customary rules of interpretation as they stand today codified in the 1969 VCLT. Thus, at the empirical level, this book discusses extensively and comparatively cases of treaty interpretation at the ICJ (Chap. 4) and at the ECtHR and WTO (Chaps. 5 and 6), bringing new insights on the theory of *treaty interpretation* and subsequently assessing the 'fragmentation'/'unity' of international law from this perspective.

To make the analysis of the techniques and patterns of interpretation at the international courts easier to follow, the number of courts analysed and cases presented had to be limited, and the selection of the cases based on their value in demonstrating the interpretative methodology applied by the courts had to be adopted. Because of this limitation, objections could be raised to the selection made or to any of the case analysis or to the number of cases taken into analysis at all of the three selected courts (in part II of the book). So it is worth clarifying in this respect that, according to Robert K. Yin, 'case studies like experiments are generalisable to theoretical propositions and not to populations of universes. In this sense, *the case study, like experiment, does not represent a "sample", and in doing a case study [the] goal will be to expand and generalise theories (analytic generalisation) and not to enumerate frequencies (statistical generalisation)*'.[13] Thus, the selection of case law will allow this work to identify the similarities and differences in the application of the customary rules of treaty interpretation (as reflected in the VCLT general methodology of interpretation) by the ICJ, ECtHR, WTO (panels and the Appellate Body). By providing an empirical based response to the question of whether treaty interpretative approaches at the ECtHR and WTO could constitute 'part' of the 'fragmentation' problem, a time perspective and in-depth analyses on the courts' case law (prior to, and after the 1969 VCLT up to the present), the analysis provided in this book is intended to contribute to expanding the general knowledge within a much-debated theory of 'fragmentation' of international law as a result of 'proliferation' of international forums, as also to the general theory on interpretation in international law. More specific research of the type attempted in this book are called to improve our knowledge about the works of specialised international courts on matters of treaty interpretation and their practices' impact on international law. Therefore, the analysis in this book could open the possibility of further inquiries to establish general criteria that can be further used for large data set analyses of case law to investigate the phenomenon of 'fragmentation' versus 'unification' (of international law) at other specialised international courts.

The underlying assumption followed in this book is based on the ILC Report of 2006. According to this ILC Report, the general methodology of treaty interpretation formulated in Articles 31, 32 and 33 of the 1969 Vienna Convention on the Law of Treaties provides both a unifying framework of developments of international law, legal institutions and spheres of legal practice and a framework for analysing the problem of fragmentation of international law (ILC 2006, p. 6). However, since the issue of application by the specialised bodies (in particular, the ECtHR and WTO) of the general rules of treaty interpretation is controversial, further assumptions had to be adopted in this book. It is admitted in the scholarship that the specialised judicial bodies (such as the ECtHR and WTO) have developed their own special 'rules' and 'techniques' of interpretation, often called 'doctrines', and have relied on them in interpreting their own *lex specialis*, so a distinction between what a 'method' is and what a 'doctrine' is should be made here. Thus, another important assumption underlying this work is that there is a fundamental difference

[13]See Yin (2003), p. 11 (emphasis added). See also McConville and Chui (2007).

between 'method' and 'doctrine' (i.e., 'doctrines' elaborated by international judicial bodies adjudicating special regimes), and this difference is reflected in the way in which the 'fragmentation/unity' of international law could be assessed.

The term 'method', according to the *Oxford Dictionary of English*, is defined as '1: a procedure or process for attaining an object: a) (1): a systematic procedure, technique, or mode of inquiry employed by or proper to a particular discipline or art, (2): a systematic plan followed in presenting material for instruction; b (1): a way, technique, or process of or for doing something, (2): a body of skills or techniques; 2: a discipline that deals with the principles and techniques of scientific inquiry; 3: a) orderly arrangement, development, or classification; b) the habitual practice of orderliness and regularity'.[14] Thus, 'method' such as is the general method of interpretation of treaties provided by the 1969 VCLT is what all the international judicial bodies generally employ as basis (procedure) of attaining the interpretation of their treaties.

On the other hand, 'doctrine' is defined as 'a: something that is taught; b: a principle or position or the body of principles in a branch of knowledge or system of belief, c: a principle of law established through past decisions'.[15] A 'doctrine' is admitted as rather particular to a special regime, for example, the 'living instrument', 'practical and effective rights', 'autonomous concepts', 'margin of appreciation', 'evolutive interpretation', 'dynamic interpretation'—elaborated by ECtHR—or specific to the WTO regime, for example, the doctrine of 'mandatory/discretionary' law, 'product process', 'Special and Differential Treatment' of developing countries. The main implication of this distinction is that a 'method' (as is the VCLT general method of interpretation of treaties) can be common and extended to all the courts, whereas a doctrine cannot be extended, in principle, since the latter is often particular to a specific regime and developed by it. Thus, the ECtHR and WTO could not rely solely on autonomous 'doctrines' in resolving difficulties encountered in their interpretation of treaties (the ECHR and WTO Agreements). And this is so because such doctrines address a strictly normative, thus a different interpretative/analytical level, compared with the VCLT general methodology of treaty interpretation, which functions as a base guideline, indicating *how the judge should argue to arrive at a conclusion about the meaning of the interpreted treaty provision.*[16] In principle, the VCLT universal methodology of interpretation helps the judge to analyse the internal structure/construction of the treaty text (its elements), notably *the conventional meanings of the terms use in the treaty*, and to *determine what the parties to the treaty intended at the time they concluded it.*[17]

[14]Stevenson (2010).

[15]Also according to *Black Dictionary*, '*doctrine*' is defined as '[a] rule, principle, theory, or tenet of the law'.

[16]See on this argument Linderfalk (2007).

[17]*Id.*

In pursuing the objective of a comparative analysis of the practices of treaty interpretation between the ICJ and ECtHR, on one hand, and the ICJ and WTO, on the other hand, the framework of comparison is therefore given by the general methodology of treaty interpretation reflected in *Articles 31 to 33 of the VCLT*. In the attempt to provide a better understanding of the positions of the two specialised dispute settlement regimes (ECtHR and WTO) in relation to international law, the theoretical parts of Chap. 5 (treaty interpretation at the ECtHR) and Chap. 6 (treaty interpretation at the WTO) will succinctly capture the disagreement among scholars as to the compatibility of the *lex specialis* (the European Convention of Human Rights and WTO Agreement) with the general rule of interpretation provided by the Vienna Convention on the Law of Treaties (*lex generalis*). Key to the background of the 'fragmentation' issue is the recognition of the phenomenon of proliferation of international adjudicative bodies and the acknowledgment of the fear that each judicial body may interpret treaty rules differently, and hence create a fragmented body of international law with the rules being differently applied, depending on the body adjudicating. Thus, the analysis of the 'proliferation' phenomenon helps in understanding the doctrinal framework in which the issue of 'fragmentation' arises as it aids in answering the general question of whether the creation of multiple international judicial *fora* is a source, or is likely to be a source, or, indeed, a cause of the fragmentation of international law.

The book is divided into seven chapters, which include Introduction (Chap. 1) and Conclusions (Chap. 7) of the book. The theoretical part of the book comprises Chaps. 2 and 3 and the empirical part: Chaps. 4–6. Chapter 2 presents the general background related to the proliferation of judicial bodies and the question of fragmentation of international law as a result of such proliferation. It includes a critical review of some of the key concepts utilised in this work such as 'international judicial body', 'international law', 'unity of international law', 'fragmentation of international law', 'proliferation of international judicial bodies', '*lex specialis/lex generalis*', '*self-contained regime*'. It is followed in Chap. 3 by a doctrinal discussion of ideas on 'treaty interpretation', which includes the concepts of 'interpretation', 'legal reasoning', 'legal interpretation', as well as an analysis of the rules (canons) of treaty interpretation in their historical development and their formulation in various drafts, including in the 1969 Vienna Convention's 'general rule of interpretation', in order to set the present work in context.

The discussion on the proliferation of international judicial courts and tribunals and fragmentation of international law in Chap. 2, together with the discussion on 'interpretation' in Chap. 3, constitutes a necessary theoretical framework for approaching the analysis of treaty interpretation (as a matter of general international law) at the ICJ, ECtHR and WTO (Chaps. 4–6). Thus, having laid the theoretical foundation in the first part of the book, the second part moves to an examination of the practice on treaty interpretation at the ICJ, ECtHR and WTO. The main focus of this examination is to discover whether the treaty interpretative practice of two prominent specialised courts, the ECtHR and WTO, is consistent with the universal methodology of treaty interpretation (general rules and principles of interpretation), as also whether there is any resemblance between these specialised courts and the

ICJ in their manner of approaching the same general methodology of interpretation and what could be inferred from such findings. To this purpose, I will analyse whether the ICJ's practice on treaty interpretation has influence upon the ECtHR's human rights and WTO's trade adjudication, cementing the relationship between these different 'worlds' and consequently contributing to the coherence and unity of international law. The book will also investigate whether the ECtHR and the WTO specialised adjudicative bodies make a clear admission of the general methodology of treaty interpretation provided by the 1969 VCLT beyond their own special interpretative means, respectively whether these courts reconcile the general rules of treaty interpretation with their own specific 'rules' (doctrines) of interpretation and, if it is so, how they do this. Each chapter's findings will be summarised in a conclusion, and then general conclusions of this book will be provided separately in a final chapter (Chap. 7). Ultimately, this analysis attempts to respond to a more general question of whether the practices of international specialised bodies on application of general international law within their special context might affect the coherence and unity of international law, contributing to its fragmentation.

## References

Bjorge, E. (2014). *The evolutionary interpreation of treaties*. Oxford: Oxford University Press.

Cannizzaro, E., & Arsanjani, M. H. (2011). *The law of treaties beyond the Vienna convention*. Oxford: Oxford University Press.

Carozza, P. G. (2008). Human dignity and judicial interpretation of human rights: A reply. *European Journal of International Law, 19*(5), 931–944.

Charney, J. I. (1998). Impact on the international legal system of the growth of international courts and tribunals. *New York University Journal of International Law and Politics, 31*, 697.

Curtis, C. P. (1949). Better theory of legal interpretation. *Vanderbilt Law Review, 3*, 407.

Endicott, T. A. O. (2000). *Vagueness in law*. Oxford, England: Oxford University Press.

Fitzmaurice, M., Elias, O. A., & Merkouris, P. (Eds.). (2010). *Treaty interpretation and the Vienna Convention on the Law of Treaties: 30 years on* (Vol. 1). Leiden, The Netherlands: Brill.

Forowicz, M. (2010). *The reception of international law in the European court of human rights*. USA.: Oxford University Press.

Gardiner, R. K. (2008). *Treaty interpretation*. Oxford, England: Oxford University Press.

Guillaume, G. (1995). The future of international judicial institutions. *International and Comparative Law Quarterly, 44*(4), 848–862.

Guillaume, G. (2000a, October 27). *The proliferation of international judicial bodies: The outlook for the international legal order*. Speech by his excellency Judge Gilbert Guillaume, President of the International Court of Justice, to the Sixth Committee of the General Assembly of the United Nations.

Guillaume, G. (2000b, October 26). Address by HE Judge Gilbert Guillaume, President of the International Court of Justice to the United Nations General Assembly, New York. Retrieved from http://www.icj-cij.org/court/index.php?pr=84&pt=3&p1=1&p2=3&p3=1

Guillaume, G. (2004). Advantages and risks of proliferation: A blueprint for action. *Journal of International Criminal Justice, 2*, 300.

Guillaume, G. (2011). The use of precedent by international judges and arbitrators. *Journal of International Dispute Settlement, 2*(1), 5–23.

International Law Commission. (2006). *Fragmentation of international law: Difficulties arising from the diversification and expansion of international law*. Geneva, Switzerland: United Nations.

Jackson, J. H. (1998). Fragmentation or unification among international institutions: The World Trade Organization. *New York University Journal of International Law and Politics, 31*, 823.

Jennings, M. (2004, June). The WTO and international law. In *ANZSIL conference*.

Kamminga, M. T., & Scheinin, M. (Eds.). (2009). *The impact of human rights law on general international law*, Oxford, England: Oxford University Press.

Kelly, J. P. (2001). Judicial activism at the World Trade Organization: Developing principles of self-restraint. *Northwestern Journal of International Law & Business, 22*, 353.

Kingsbury, B. (1998). Foreword: Is the proliferation of international courts and tribunals a systemic problem. *New York University Journal of International Law and Politics, 31*, 679.

Koskenniemi, M. (2001). *The gentle civilizer of nations: The rise and fall of international law 1870–1960 (Hersch Lauterpacht memorial lectures)*. Cambridge, England: Cambridge University Press.

Lauterpacht, H. (1982). *The development of international law by the international court* (p. 282). Cambridge, England: Cambridge University Press.

Lennard, M. (2002). Navigating by the stars: Interpreting the WTO agreements. *Journal of International Economic Law, 5*(1), 17–89.

Letsas, G. (2007). *A theory of interpretation of the European convention on human rights*. Oxford: Oxford University Press.

Letsas, G. (2010). Strasbourg's interpretive ethic: Lessons for the international lawyer. *European Journal of International Law, 21*(3), 509–541.

Linderfalk, U. (2007). *On the interpretation of treaties: The modern international law as expressed in the 1969 Vienna Convention on the law of treaties* (Vol. 83). Springer Science & Business Media.

Mavroidis, P. C. (2008). No outsourcing of law? WTO law as practiced by WTO courts. *American Journal of International Law, 102*, 421–474.

McConville, M., & Chui, W. H. E. (Eds.). (2007). *Research methods for law*. Edinburgh University Press.

McInerney-Lankford, S. (2012). Fragmentation of international law redux: The case of Strasbourg. *Oxford Journal of Legal Studies, 32*(3), 609–632.

Merkouris, P. (2010). Introduction: Interpretation is a science, is an art, is a science. In *Treaty interpretation and the Vienna Convention on the Law of Treaties: 30 years on* (pp. 1–14). Leiden, The Netherlands: Brill.

Morigiwa, Y., Stolleis, M., & Halpérin, J. L. (Eds.). (2011). *Interpretation of law in the age of enlightenment: From the rule of the king to the rule of law* (Vol. 95). Springer Science & Business Media.

Orakhelashvili, A. (2008). *The interpretation of acts and rules in public international law*. Oxford University Press.

Pauwelyn, J., & Elsig, M. (2011). *The politics of treaty interpretation: Variations and explanations across international tribunals*. https://ssrn.com/abstract=1938618 or https://doi.org/10.2139/ssrn.1938618.

Pound, R. (1923). The theory of judicial decision. *Harvard Law Review, 36*, 802.

Ramberg, B., & Gjesdal, K. (2009). *"Hermeneutics", the Stanford Encyclopedia of Philosophy* (E. N. Zalta, Ed.). Retrieved December 2012, from http://plato.stanford.edu/archives/sum2009/

Scheinin, M. (2009). Impact on the law of treaties. In M. T. Kamminga & M. Scheinin (Eds.), *The impact of human rights law on general international law* (p. 33). Oxford: OUP.

Sheeran, S. (2014). The relationship of international human rights and general international law: A hermeneutic constraint, or pushing the boundaries? In S. Sheeran & N. Rodley (Eds.), *Routledge handbook of international human rights law*. London: Routledge.

Simma, B., & Pulkowski, D. (2006). Of planets and the universe: Self-contained regimes in international law. *European Journal of International Law, 17*(3), 483–529.

Stein, P. (1994). Interpretation and legal reasoning in Roman law. *Chicago-Kent Law Review, 70*, 1539.

Stevenson, A. (Ed.). (2010). *Oxford Dictionary of English* (3rd ed.). Oxford, England: Oxford University Press.

Tzevelekos, V. P. (2009). Use of Article 31 (3)(C) of the VCLT in the case law of the ECtHR: An effective anti-fragmentation tool or a selective loophole for the reinforcement of human rights teleology-between evolution and systemic integration. *Michigan Journal of International Law, 31*, 621.

Van Damme, I. (2010). Treaty interpretation by the WTO appellate body. *European Journal of International Law, 21*(3), 605–648.

Van Hoecke, M. (Ed.). (2011). *Methodologies of legal research: Which kind of method for what kind of discipline?* Hart Publishing.

Waldock, H. (1964). Third report on the law of treaties, by Sir Humphrey Waldock, Special Rapporteur. *Yearbook of the International Law Commission, 2*, 49.

Yin, R. K. (2003). *Case study research design and methods, Applied social research methods series* (Vol. 5, 3rd ed.). Thousand Oaks, CA: Sage Publications.

# Chapter 2
# Does Proliferation of International Judicial Bodies Lead to the Fragmentation of International Law?

## 2.1 Introduction

While after the Second World War a revival and enhancement of the role of the judiciary in municipal law took place in Western Europe and elsewhere in the world, there was no similar development of the international judiciary in the first few decades after the war.[1] However, this situation was beginning to change slowly in the last decades of the twentieth century as a result of a combination of several developments in the international arena: the multiplication of actors on the international scene,[2] the multiplication of treaties concluded by state actors and the need to have the disputes arising from the application of these treaties adjudicated by independent judicial bodies,[3] the multiplication of the fields of international law

[1]As this trend is multifaceted, the literature of the subject is too extensive as to be referenced in this context. Suffice it to mention here, e.g., Tate and Vallinder (1995)—for the political implications of the advent of the courts in the second half of the twentieth century; Sweet (2000)—for a European paradigm; Baudenbacher (2003)—for what is going on at more global level. In retrospect, taking into consideration where the courts started at the end of WWII on the 'political' spectrum, see e.g. Curran (2001).

[2]As a result of the appearance of new states due to the process of decolonisation taking place in the fourth, fifth and sixth decades of the past century.

[3]There are many examples of *international judicial bodies* having emerged in the last three decades, as courts and tribunals, quasi- judicial bodies, other dispute settlement bodies, which could be divided in *adjudicative* and *non-adjudicative* mechanisms. Examples of *adjudicative bodies* such as courts and tribunals: Court of Arbitration for Sport (1984); North American Commission on Environmental Cooperation (1993); NAFTA Dispute Settlement Panels (1994); Common Court of Justice and Arbitration of the Organization for the Harmonization of Corporate Law in Africa (1997); Arbitration and Mediation Center of the World Intellectual Property Organization (1994); the Iran–USA Claims Tribunal(1980); Marshall Islands Nuclear Claims Tribunal (1983); Eritrea-Ethiopia Claims Commission (2000); International Tribunal for the Law of the Sea (1996); World Trade Organization Appellate Body (1995); Court of Justice of the European Union (2010); Common Court of Justice and Arbitration of the Organization for the Harmonization of Corporate Law in Africa (1997); East African Court o Justice (2001); Court of

 
L.E. Popa, *Patterns of Treaty Interpretation as Anti-Fragmentation Tools*,
DOI 10.1007/978-3-319-65488-1_2

and the emergence of new directions of development for international law, the globalisation process, to name but a few. As the developments accelerated, towards the end of the twentieth century and into the first decades of the present century, both scholars and the international community became concerned with the possible implications of the phenomenon of the multiplication of international judicial bodies for the international legal order. The subsequent debate, which has arisen out of this concern, strove to conceptualise the dimensions of the international judiciary and to anticipate the consequences for the international legal system of this multiplication of judicial bodies and legal regimes.

The ongoing debate on the features and implications of the multiplication of international specialised judicial bodies and legal regimes is important for understanding the shape that international law is taking. Because the views expressed in the scholarship are far from converging as different agendas and assumptions have been advanced on this topic, an examination of the scholarship on multiplication of international judicial forums may warrant a better understanding of this phenomenon and its major implication: the fragmentation of international law. This analysis constitutes the theoretical basis for investigation of the subject of this book: whether the practice of treaty interpretation of two relatively new specialised courts, respectively the ECtHR and WTO (adjudicative bodies) often seen as promoting 'self-contained' regimes, will contribute to, or exacerbate, the fragmentation of international law, or otherwise such practices will constitute a tool for keeping the coherence and unity of international law. In this scope, the practice of the ICJ on treaty interpretation is taken as the comparator.

This chapter is divided into two parts (Sects. 2.2 and 2.3), which are structured in sections and subsections. The first part (Sect. 2.2) analyses the 'proliferation' phenomenon, which begins with a brief explanation of what is an 'international judicial body' and 'proliferation' (Sects. 2.2.1 and 2.2.2). Further section will attempt to capture the main arguments expressed in the scholarship concerning the phenomenon of proliferation of international judicial forums and its positive implications for international law and the international legal system (Sect. 2.2.3). Since the question of whether the multiplication of judicial bodies could lead to 'fragmentation' of international law is doctrinally important for this work, the second part (Sect. 2.3) of this chapter will examine the issue of 'fragmentation' as one of the major concerns among international law scholars. In order to accomplish this, the second part of the chapter will begin with a brief analysis of the key concepts of 'international law', 'unity of international law' (Sect. 2.3.1) and 'fragmentation of international law' (Sect. 2.3.2) necessary for a better

---

Justice of the Economic Community of West African States (ECOWAS) (2001); International Criminal Court—ICC (2004); International Criminal Tribunal for the Former Yugoslavia—ICTY (1993); International Criminal Tribunal for Rwanda—ICTR (1995); Serious Crimes Panels in the District Court of Dili, East Timor (2000–2005); Panels in the Courts of Kosovo (2001); War Crimes Chamber of the Court of Bosnia-Herzegovina (2005); Special Court for Sierra Leone (2002); Extraordinary Chambers in the Courts of Cambodia (2006); Special Tribunal for Lebanon (2009).

understanding of the doctrinal framework in which the issue of 'fragmentation' arises. The focus of the second part will be on the scholarly debate related to the implications of the increasing numbers of international courts and tribunals, in particular on those theories that advocate both a restrained fear for 'fragmentation' (Sect. 2.3.2.2) and those considering it a serious threat for international law (Sect. 2.3.3). In addition, a brief discussion of some of the risks associated with the continuing expansion and diversification of international adjudication forums will be provided (Sect. 2.3.4). The chapter will conclude with an assessment of whether the creation of multiple international judicial forums is a source, or is likely to be a source or a cause of fragmentation in international law.

This analysis is intended to offer the theoretical perspective and the necessary background for the empirical examination undertaken in the later chapters (Chaps. 4–6). Here, the empirical analysis will be applied in order to investigate whether the techniques of application of the general rules of treaty interpretation by two prominent, specialised adjudicative bodies, the ECtHR and WTO, are similar to the techniques applied by the ICJ in respect of the same (general) rules of interpretation when dealing with similar interpretative difficulties of interpreting the text of treaties, or are different, and what the implications of such findings are vis-à-vis the unity of international law.

## 2.2 Proliferation

Since international society has continuously evolved compared with its origins centuries ago, a lot more states and non-state actors have to deal with an increasingly broad spectrum of instruments due to this 'diversity'. Consequently, this international 'diversity' has changed the nature of the law itself in comparison with what is called the traditional 'international core' (Nicolaidis and Tong 2003, p. 1352). In this context, international dispute settlement systems needed to evolve and accommodate the increasing numbers of international actors.[4] It appears that a new generation of institutions emerges to protect and enforce agreements made under the auspices of international law, albeit in a context that lacks centralised authorities to enforce international obligations as in national law (Charney 1998a, p. 700). An international community that absorbs international organisations, corporations, non-governmental organisations (NGOs), intergovernmental organisations (IGOs), domestic organisations, individuals and other private actors exercising their rights under international law appears to inevitably shape international law (Reed and Jacovides 2002, pp. 228–229). Given this perspective, questions persist in the legal scholarship such as whether there is and should be an international legal system, whether unification is a desirable aim or what specific doctrines and practices might be elaborated to ameliorate the problems that emerged from the

[4]Nicolaidis and Tong (2003), p. 1352.

proliferation of international judicial institutions,[5] and also whether the proliferation of international courts and tribunals in a horizontal legal arrangement, lacking in hierarchy or in any formal structure or links among them, leads to fragmentation of international law or, on the contrary, to building on international law.[6] These are questions to which international legal scholars, lawyers and political scientists have different standpoints when asked ultimately 'whether this diversity is good or bad, or it should be promoted or counteracted' (Nicolaidis and Tong 2003, p. 1352).

Since different agendas and assumptions are advanced by scholars in respect of the proliferation of international judicial bodies, the following section of this part will attempt to capture the main arguments relating to the implications of 'proliferation' for the international legal system. Beforehand, however, an explanation of the concepts of 'international judicial body' and 'proliferation of judicial bodies' is needed.

### 2.2.1 What Is an 'International Judicial Body'?

Since there is no universally accepted definition of what an 'international judicial body' is,[7] and not much focus on this topic in the scholarship, of great help in drawing out the meaning of this concept is Romano's influential analysis of the 'multiplication of international judicial bodies' phenomenon (Romano 2011). Since Romano's analysis offers a comprehensive and updated chart of international judicial bodies, instructive here is his important distinction between the categories of *non-adjudicative means* (counting 75 bodies),[8] namely judicial bodies sharing

[5]Charney (1998a).

[6]*Id.*

[7]The term is similar in literature to 'international judicial institution', 'international judicial organ' or 'international tribunal'.

[8]Romano (2011). According to Romano, all bodies in the class of *Non-Adjudicative Bodies* (Mechanisms or Means) share the trait of producing outcomes that are not binding, called 'reports' or 'recommendations'. These bodies are composed of States' representatives and not independent experts and because they issue non-binding reports. For example: the UN Human Rights Council, or the United Nations Educational, Scientific and Cultural Organization (UNESCO) Committee on Conventions and Recommendations; Human Rights Bodies (e.g. the Inter-American Commission of Human Rights); International Review, Accountability, Oversight and Audit Mechanisms; Compliance Mechanisms of Multilateral Environmental Agreements; Bodies with Universal Scope (ILO Commission of Inquiry; ILO Committee of Experts on the Application of Conventions and Recommendations; ILO Conference Committee on the Application of Conventions; (UN) Commission on the Status of Women; ILO Governing Body Committee on Freedom of Association; (UN) Committee on the Elimination of Racial Discrimination; (UN) Human Rights Committee, UNESCO); Bodies with Regional Scope (Europe # Council of Europe; European Committee for the Prevention of Torture and Inhuman or Degrading Treatment or Punishment; European Commission Against Racism and Intolerance; European Committee of Social Rights; Council of Europe European Commissioner for Human Rights; Committee of Expert on Issues Pertaining to the Framework Convention for the Protection of National Minorities; European

the trait of producing outcomes that are not binding and *adjudicative means* that includes judicial bodies that produce binding outcomes (counting 142 bodies and procedures).[9] In regard to the 'International Adjudicative Means', Romano suggests that this category be further divided into at least three distinct orders: (1) international courts and tribunals, (2) arbitral tribunals and (3) international claims and compensations bodies.[10] Most helpful in this context is Romano's basic criteria for determining the conditions for an *international judicial body* to be included within the order of 'International Court' and 'International Tribunal'. He mentions in this respect seven criteria:

1. have been established by an international legal instrument;
2. rely on international law as applicable law;
3. decide cases on the basis of predetermined rules of procedure;
4. are composed of independent members/judges;
5. only hear cases in which at least one party is a state or an international organisation;
6. issue legally binding judgments;
7. are permanent.[11]

Also, Romano observes that scholars who resort to the term 'International Tribunal' tend to include in their writings about this subject both ad hoc arbitral tribunals as well as tribunals with permanent jurisdictions (Romano 1998, p. 715). With respect to the 'permanency', as a trait of a court or tribunal, according to the same author, international courts and tribunals are permanent when judges are not

Ombudsman; Inter-American Commission of Women; Inter-American Commission on Human Right; Committee on the Elimination of All Forms of Discrimination against Persons; African Commission on Human and Peoples' Rights; The African Committee of Experts on the Rights and Welfare of the Child; Arab Commission of Human Rights; Arab Human Rights Committee; ASEAN Intergovernmental Commission on Human Rights etc).

[9] *Id* (updated 2011). See for more examples of adjudicative bodies, *supra* note 3. The Orders of the class of *International Adjudicative Means* provided by Romano:

A. *International Courts and Tribunals* (a. State-only Courts; b. Administrative Tribunals; c. Human Rights Courts; d. Courts of Regional Economic and/or Political Integration Agreements; e. International Criminal/Humanitarian Law).
B. *Arbitral Tribunals* (e.g. Permanent Court of Arbitration (1899), International Joint Commission (1909), Bank for International Settlements Arbitral Tribunal (1930), International Civil Aviation Organization Council (under the 1944 Chicago Convention the ICAO Council has certain dispute settlement competences) (1944), International Centre for the Settlement of Investment Disputes (1966), Gulf Cooperation Council Commission for the Settlement of Disputes (1981), Court of Arbitration for Sport (1984), North American Commission on Environmental Cooperation (1993), NAFTA Dispute Settlement Panels (1994))
C. International Claims and Compensations Bodies (e.g. Iran-United States Claims Tribunal (1980), Marshall Islands Nuclear Claims Tribunal (1983), Eritrea-Ethiopia Claims Commission (2000)).

[10] *Id.*

[11] *Id.*

selected ad hoc by parties in any given case.[12] Thus, the ad hoc criminal tribunals instead, such as the ICTY, ICTR and the hybrid criminal tribunals (e.g., Sierra Leone), are temporary institutions with a temporary mandate.[13] However, such tribunals are perceived as permanent in the sense that judges have been appointed to decide a long series of cases relating to the same situation.[14]

In addition, besides permanent international judicial bodies (established either on the basis of an international convention or established by the U.N. Security Council), which according to the former ICJ Judge Mosler were clearly defined by the PCIJ in 1925 as '[bodies] already constituted and as having [their] own rules or organizations and procedures', there are other international judicial bodies that may possess characteristic traits of a court, and they are *arbitral tribunals* (Mosler 1980, p. 434). According to Mosler, these 'arbitral tribunals' are either ad hoc bodies (in the case of a particular dispute) or bodies established on the basis of a general arbitration treaty or of a compromissory clause providing for arbitration of a dispute.[15]

Since notions such as 'international judicial bodies', 'international judicial *fora*', 'international judicial forums', 'law-based forums', 'judicial bodies', which encompass *international adjudicative bodies*, are referred in this book, the above brief analysis helps in clarifying the distinction between such notions and others (e.g., '*fora*', 'forums', 'legal *fora*', 'international *fora*', 'international bodies'), which may be used in reference to both *adjudicative* and *non-adjudicative bodies* taken together.[16] Specifically, when referring further to notions such as 'international court' or 'international tribunal', 'international specialised body' or 'specialised court', Romano's criteria described above ('the order of "International Court" and "International Tribunal"') will be taken into consideration.

### 2.2.2 Defining 'Proliferation'

According to the *Oxford English Dictionary*, the term 'proliferation' is defined as 'rapid increase in the number or amount of something'. Many authors who

[12]Romano (1998), p. 715.

[13]*Id.*

[14]*Id* (as Romano notes, judges are not ad hoc appointed to hear a particular case in ad hoc criminal tribunals).

[15]Mosler (1980), p. 434. Mosler adds that an essential aspect of an 'international body' is the procedure on which it should be established: either on the basis of an international convention (such as the previous international courts—e.g. the PCIJ/ICJ, or established by the U.N. Security Council through a Chapter VII resolution of the U.N. Charter (e.g. the ICTY and ICTR). The author finds common criteria for judicial and arbitral settlement such as: (1) independence from the government and the parties; (2) equality of the parties in the proceedings; (3) objective rules to guide the judge in determining the law.

[16]Many authors often resort to the expression: 'international courts and tribunals' when discussing 'proliferation' and its related 'fragmentation' issue, also in reference to all international judicial bodies.

examined this phenomenon have attempted to define proliferation in various ways. For example, Simma sees proliferation as an expansion and diversification of international law matters 'through development of new fields in the law that go their own way' (Simma 2009, p. 270). He explains that the choice of the word 'proliferation' must have been born out of concerns for 'the proliferation and diversity (not of the substance of international law itself), but of international courts and tribunals – as a challenge' to the 'systemic coherence of international law' and so as an 'accelerant of fragmentation'.[17] In Simma's view, 'proliferation' occurs because 'the jurisdiction of most international tribunals is limited to the rules established by the treaty instruments which set them up, i.e., that such tribunals are not normally mandated to apply "general" international law, at least not in express terms'.[18] Also, Simma refers to the 'proliferation of judicial bodies' phenomenon as an 'explosion of international litigation and arbitration'.[19]

Similarly, Spelliscy defines 'proliferation' as the creation of many new tribunals in the latter half of the twentieth century, particularly as an 'upswing' in the number of international tribunals in the last decade (Spelliscy 2001, p. 150). The author considers that the expansion of dispute settlement mechanisms is 'an attempt by States to maintain the viability of the international judicial system in the light of the increased complexity of international relations' between states after the end of the Cold War.[20] He sees it as an answer to 'the need for specialised expertise in new and developing areas of international law'.[21] Also, for Brown, the proliferation of international judicial bodies means 'the establishment of new *fora* for third party dispute settlement' (Brown 2002, pp. 253–254). In the same vein, Buergenthal refers to the proliferation of judicial bodies as 'a viable, effective means of international dispute resolution' (Buergenthal 2001, p. 267). The former president of the ICJ, Judge Schwebel, also considers that '[t]he creation of new legal *fora* indicates that the effectiveness of international law can be increased by ensuring that legal obligations are equipped with means for their determination and application' (Schwebel 2011, p. 3).

### 2.2.3 Implications of the Proliferation of International Judicial Bodies: Positive Aspects

The complexity of the international community requires the creation of specialised courts and tribunals to adapt to the normative diversification. The 'proliferation' phenomenon is generally thought of in the academic literature to appear to be

[17]Simma (2009), p. 278.

[18]*Id.*

[19]*Id.*

[20]Spelliscy (2001), p. 150.

[21]*Id.*

suggesting that the old established international judicial bodies cannot resolve all the emerging legal issues in the best interests of the international judicial system as a whole (Spelliscy 2001, p. 3). Indeed, the *United Nations Charter* clearly envisaged the proliferation, or at least development, of other international judicial tribunals (Han 2006, p. 104). Thus, by means of Article 95 of the U.N. Charter, '[n]othing in the present Charter shall prevent Members of the United Nations from entrusting the solution of their differences to other tribunals by virtue of agreements already in existence or which may be concluded in the future'.[22] As one commentator exemplifies in this regard, the fact that the states parties and members of the UNCLOS and the WTO have accepted the establishment and the development of their own tribunals, it underlines the acceptance and political support for 'proliferation' rather than 'unification' under the ICJ or vesting appellate standing in the ICJ (Han 2006, p. 104). Furthermore, Article 33 of the U.N. Charter enables states to resort to the peaceful settlement of disputes and goes on to list many methods of dispute settlement that do not involve the ICJ, such as negotiation, enquiry, mediation and conciliation.[23]

Many scholars preoccupied with the proliferation of international judicial bodies generally admit this phenomenon to be both healthy and necessary. For example, an important argument in favour of such 'proliferation' brought by Han is that since the ICJ could not deal with every international dispute efficiently, and is unable to solve highly specialised issues, it results that 'proliferation' may play in general a positive role for international law.[24] However, as rightly admitted by Han, the new international specialised bodies address, adopt or improve upon the ICJ's experience.[25] From a practitioner's perspective, Judge Higgins concludes that the new tribunals come as a necessity because of 'certain decentralization of some of the topics with which the ICJ can in principle deal to new highly specialised bodies whose members are experts in a subject matter'.[26] So these specialised bodies are necessary since they can respond more rapidly and efficiently to specialised issues of international law.

A number of scholars defend the 'proliferation' phenomenon by considering it as a promoter of law, a progressive tool in international relations. In addition, many authors share the opinion that the increasing number of judicial adjudication possibilities leads to an improvement in the quality of judgments and reports among the tribunals.[27] One of the most prominent scholars, who analysed in depth the impact of the multiplication phenomenon on international law, is Charney, who claims that 'proliferation' is not a problem and that a positive impact of the multiplication of international tribunals is that it permits a degree of

---

[22]Article 95 of the Charter of the United Nations (1945).

[23]U.N. Charter (1945), Art. 33, paragraph 1.

[24]Han (2006), p. 105.

[25]*Id*, p. 104.

[26]Rao (2003), p. 946 (commenting on various opinions of the ICJ's judges on 'proliferation').

[27]*Id.*

experimentation and exploration that can, actually, lead to improvements in international law (1999, pp. 705–706). Similarly, Pauwelyn and Salles rightly assume that the competition among courts and tribunals is a positive aspect since it 'may improve the quality of rulings and expediency of proceedings'.[28] And this is so because a tribunal, by 'keeping a critical eye over another, finally, offer a welcome level of control over international tribunals and indirectly enhance their legitimacy' (Pauwelyn and Salles 2009, p. 77). In this sense, interestingly, even if various courts may differ, as Charney points out, it will be constructive for the international legal community to discover what might be the most acceptable interpretations of international law.[29] Moreover, seeing the proliferation of new courts definitively as important for the international law's development, Simma admits that '[t]he more international courts apply a specific rule of international law in the same manner, the more legitimacy it will be accorded, and the more can we be certain about its normative strength. On the other hand, if various international courts do disagree on a point of law, the ensuing judicial dialogue may possibly further progressive development of the law' (Simma 2009, p. 279). In the same vein, by focusing on the implications stemming from diversification and expansion of international law, the ILC Study Report of 2006 finds that if the existence of various legal regimes does not lead to a fundamental transformation of international law as there is a common ground on which these regimes operate, then the creation of third-party forums as arbiters of disputes arising from such regimes could rather have a positive impact on the international legal system.[30]

From the perspective that various third-party international judicial forums come to decide questions of international law by resolving more international disputes, Kingsbury, for example, concludes that the preponderant view expressed by Charney, Dupuy, Abi-Saab and several others is that 'proliferation' has a positive impact (Kingsbury 1998, p. 686). He states that, in the view of these legal scholars, 'proliferation has been the only way, and perhaps a very good way, to increase third-party settlement of international disputes through law-based forums' (Kingsbury 1998, p. 686) and that, in this way, such a 'proliferation' would make 'more disputes judiciable in practice' and 'future adjudicative decisions more predictable'.[31]

Regarding the implications that the proliferation of international judicial bodies may have for the maintenance of the *coherence* of international law, Wellens, for example, correctly assumes that *consistency in the case law ultimately gives*

---

[28]Charney (1998a), pp. 705–706.

[29]Charney et al. (2002), p. 369. Charney assumes that the more states and other actors involved in disputes that exist, the more they will negotiate solutions that take account of law without instituting formal proceedings or before a final third-party decision is reached.

[30]ILC (2006), p. 247. The ILC Study notes that the VCLT constitutes the main tool of unification of such regimes. And that such regimes being created as a result of treaties to which the Vienna Convention applies, they are bound together and coordinated by the Convention and General Principles of International Law.

[31]Kingsbury (1998), p. 686.

*coherence to international law* (Wellens 2003, p. 1159). And importantly, this consistency could be seen more or less as a counterbalance of any process of fragmentation of international law.[32] However, according to Wellens, the hypothesis that the specialised tribunals could develop greater variation in their determination and application of general international law that could damage the coherence of the international legal system is not to be excluded.[33] Nevertheless, cases of 'deviation' from general international law, according to Simma, 'remain the exception, and actually courts have gone to great lengths to avoid contradicting each other'; thus, not any significant contradictory jurisprudence of international courts has been registered (Simma 2009, p. 273). Moreover, as the same author claims, 'if an international court relies on the case law of other such courts, applies and maybe develops it, without, however, changing it fundamentally', it will 'obviously add to the legitimacy of a judgment',[34] and this aspect will definitively have an important impact in keeping a coherent international law. Finally, regarding the *coherence* of international law in the given context of 'proliferation', Abi-Saab observes that what is important for specialised tribunals is to keep a proper balance among their holdings since more 'specialisation' implies a greater need for the preservation of the *unity* of the whole legal system, *unity* being what actually makes specialisation possible and meaningful (Abi-Saab 1998, p. 925). However, Spelliscy admits that faith in the formal structure of the international judiciary is not needed because international tribunals often listen to what other tribunals have said and maintain a de facto coherent system, even if such coherence is not *de jure* required.[35]

Another positive implication of the 'proliferation' phenomenon discussed in the scholarship is that a degree of judicial dialogue takes place among international judicial bodies (Charney 1998b). This phenomenon is generally known as 'cross-fertilization', which means the reception by one such body of the case law (resort to precedents) of other international judicial bodies.[36] Since international law continues to expand, the questions about the interaction between the fields of international law gain more space in the legal scholarship. In this regard, by relying on an ample research on the decisions of various courts and tribunals, Charney concludes that a multiplicity of tribunals allows for 'creativity' and 'iterative development of the law' through dialogue among them (Charney 1998a, p. 700). For example, the Inter-American Court's decisions are used as a source and guide for constitutional adjudication (Basch 2007, p. 195). Also, as observed by the president of the Inter-American Commission of Human Rights, Judge Carozza, the European Human

[32]Wellens (2003), p. 1159. The author gives as example the role of the case law of the International Administrative Tribunals; the ICJ; ECtHR; CJEU (Court of Justice of the European Union), and domestic courts.

[33]*Id.*

[34]Simma (2009), p. 279.

[35]Spelliscy (2001), pp. 174–175. The author mentions, for example, the decision of the Appeals Chamber of the ICTY in the *Tadic* case.

[36]See e.g. Jacobs (2003).

Rights system, 'not surprisingly', served as a role model to the American system in respect of its institutional design, proceedings and case law (Carozza 2009).

Regarding legal opinions provided by the various tribunals, Charney, similarly to Simma, observes that the major divergences between these tribunals in applying specific matters of international law are hardly a cause of alarm.[37] In his observation, although differences between tribunals exist, they are engaged in the same dialectics, and therefore the fundamentals of general international law remain the same regardless of which tribunal decides the case.[38] That such differences between tribunals should not be a cause of concern is also underlined by Kingsbury, who admits that in fact these divergences reflect largely the differences in *purpose* and *subject matter* between general and special regimes (Kingsbury 1998, p. 683). Given the particular features and specialised interests, according to Spelliscy, the international specialised forums often have unavoidable disagreements between them, or the same court may overturn its own position with the majority supporting a new position.[39] On one hand, as the author underlines, disagreements could not to be ignored as they constitute the most dangerous factor among international tribunals when faced with a clearly enunciated general principle of international law.[40] On the other hand, such disagreements may be generally considered healthy for the development of international law as a system, as long as they are related to differences in perception about the applicable principles and exceptions that apply within the same system (Charney 1998a, pp. 705–706).

If at the end of the twentieth century it was clear that the multiplication of international legal regimes and international judicial bodies was a new trend emerging in the international law arena that could no longer be ignored, for many scholars it was less clear whether this trend was a positive one. As some still would argue, since international law and the international legal order appear as menaced by the multiplication of international judicial bodies, which implies risks such as forum shopping, overlap of legal rules or jurisdictions and normative conflicts, the 'proliferation' phenomenon should be seriously considered and investigated in order to reveal its possible destructive implications for international law.

## 2.3 Fragmentation

The preceding part analysed the *proliferation of international judicial bodies*. Since the rapid expansion of many international judicial forums, especially specialised ones, could lead to the *fragmentation of international law*, the second part of this chapter examines this issue. The opinions of scholars who opposed the

[37]Charney (1998a), p. 700.

[38]*Id.*

[39]Spelliscy (2001), p. 170.

[40]*Id.*

multiplication of international courts and tribunals are mainly based on theoretical and normative grounds since a number of features of the international adjudicative system are perceived as presenting intrinsic risks of fragmentation of international law. Successive ICJ presidents have criticised the proliferation of international tribunals and posited its main negative implication: *substantive fragmentation of international law*.[41] Thus, the question that inevitably arose among legal practitioners and scholars is whether the variations among tribunals deciding questions of international law would be so significant as to affect the coherence and unity of international law as a system, and thus its legitimacy.

### 2.3.1 Understanding the 'Fragmentation of International Law'

The discussion related to the 'fragmentation of international law' is necessary for clarifying this issue that is sometimes a little vague in the scholarship. It also helps to determine subsequently what type of 'fragmentation' could occur at the ECtHR and WTO specialised adjudicative bodies as a result of their application of the general rules of treaty interpretation of public international law in their specialised context. It could be argued that the boundaries of macro 'fragmentation' (which may occur at the level of the international legal system among international judicial bodies)[42] are blurred and intertwined with those of micro 'fragmentation' (which may occur because of the activity of a specific court, within its context), thus making the discussion on 'fragmentation' rather abstract and rendering difficult a clear assessment of this phenomenon. However, as this book moves in the second part towards an empirical examination of 'fragmentation' at the micro-level (at particular courts: the ICJ, ECtHR, WTO), and also at the macro-level between the courts (the ECtHR and ICJ, the WTO and ICJ), assessing these levels and possible types of fragmentation is necessary in this chapter. The aim of this discussion is to provide a theoretical foundation for evaluating the impact of the ECtHR and WTO's treaty interpretative practice upon the coherence and unity of international law.

For a closer examination of and to expand the understanding of the 'fragmentation of international law' issue as result of proliferation of international judicial bodies, a brief explanation of the key concept of 'international law' is first needed. Particularly, since the empirical part of this study deals with the application of

[41] See e.g. Guillaume (2000)—commenting on various opinions of the ICJ's judges on 'proliferation'; or Charney (1998a)—referring to Judge Oda as a scholar and a negotiator of the Law of the Sea Convention.

[42] I.e., as result of the overlapping jurisdictions, forum shopping, etc.

*customary rules of treaty interpretation* of public international law in both general (ICJ) and specialised contexts (ECtHR and WTO), a contextualisation of the *general (customary) rules of interpretation* and of *treaties* in international law as a whole will be necessary for a better understanding of those rules' nature as *customary* (how they developed to become customary rules, and codified in the 1969 Vienna Convention on the Law of Treaties will be analysed in more detail in Chap. 3) and their role in the interpretation of treaties of both general and special characters. Defining *international law* is crucially important, especially since the application of the customary rules of treaty interpretation at both general and specialised international courts implies, *inter alia*, a resort to other rules and principles of general international law (under the 'systemic integration' principle as reflected in Article 31(3)(c) of the VCLT). Generally, by knowing *how* and *why* rules and principles of international law have developed is necessary for understanding *how* such rules and principles *should be interpreted.* In addition, an examination of the notion of *international law* will allow for a better assessment of the relation between *lex generalis* and *lex specialis* in the context of the discussion related to the fragmentation/unity of international law.

#### 2.3.1.1 Defining 'International Law'

One of the leading scholars who provide an analytical introduction to the subject of *international law*, Mark Janis, traces the origins of *international law* 'deep in history' to the ancient Roman belief in *ius gentium* as the law 'common to all men' (Janis 1999, p. 11). According to Janis, in the seventeenth century, the sovereign states of Europe established 'a set of mutually agreed-upon rules respecting the nature of . . . states and their fundamental rights and obligations *inter se*'.[43] The Dutch jurist Hugo Grotius claimed that certain fundamental legal principles governed the relations among states.[44] In essence, *international law* has maintained this past legacy in the modern and contemporary eras, and authoritative works of eminent legal scholars, as well as the practice of courts and tribunals, stand as evidence of this legacy.[45]

Nowadays there are various views and theories in the scholarship discussing the concept of international law or whether international law really *is* law 'properly called' (Payandeh 2010, p. 969). Since there are many approaches regarding what

[43]Janis (1999), p. 11; see also Janis (2010), p. 127. Janis points out that 'International Law in the meaning of the term as used in modern times did not exist during antiquity and the first part of the Middle Ages. It is in its origin essentially a product of Christian civilization, and began gradually to grow from the second half of the Middle Ages. But it owes its existence as systematized, body of rules to the Dutch jurist and statesman Hugo Grotius'.

[44]*Id.*

[45]In the narrowest sense, for example, 'international law' was stated by the PCIJ in the *Lotus* case (1927): *as governing relations between independent States.*

international law is, some denying the validity of it[46] or others not fully denying it,[47] an elaborate review of theories on this topic is beyond the scope of the study. Thus, only some of the views that are useful for the perspective of *coherence* and *unity* of international law (treated in the next section) and its related *fragmentation* issue will be addressed in this section. It will address, in particular, notions such as *sources* (of international law), *hierarchy* of sources (or lack of it), *subjects* (of international law), *system* (of international law), *jus cogens* and *erga omnes* rules, as they constitute the theoretical framework of analysing the practice of the ICJ, ECtHR and WTO on treaty interpretation (application of general rules of international law) *vis-à-vis* the issue of 'fragmentation'/'unity' of international law.

Oppenheim, for example, whose work remains of reference on this topic, speaks about *international law* as the *Law of Nations (jus gentium).*[48] He defines international law as 'the name for the body of *customary* and *conventional rules* which are considered legally binding by civilised States in their relations with each other'.[49] Oppenheim mentions three elements as necessary to form a *law*: *a community*, *a body of rules* for human conduct within a community and *the enforcement* by external power of these rules that are common for an 'international law'.[50] As explained by the author, the existence of *law* is not reduced to a community of states (e.g., 'a confederation of states'), but it appears everywhere where there is a 'community' as is, for example, a 'community of individual men'.[51] Later, Verdross appears to nuance even more this definition of international law, admitting it as 'that legal order which regulates the relations between all the sovereign legal communities', where the notion of *communities* refers to independent states and certain other sovereign communities, such as the Catholic Church, recognised belligerents, ecclesiastical communities, different churches, as also the conduct of certain individuals (Verdross 1949, p. 435). And what is essentially important in respect of all these members of the community is that, as subjects of duties, they are *equally subordinated to international law.*[52] Thus, *states* are no longer solely and exclusively *subjects of international law* since non-states actors like *individual human beings* and *international organisations* also have become increasingly subjects of international law.[53]

---

[46]E.g. Austin (1995).

[47]E.g. Morgenthau (1940, 1948) and Slaughter and Ratner (1999).

[48]Oppenheim (1912), para 13. It was considered the law between States and not above them.

[49]*Id*, para 1. (emphasis added).

[50]*Id*, para 5. The concept of *community* in the view of the author covers not only a community of individual men, but also a community of individual communities such as individual states (i.e. a confederation of states is a community of states).

[51]*Id.*

[52]*Id.*

[53]See for this discussion, e.g., An introduction to subjects of international law for students (available at: https://ruwanthikagunaratne.wordpress.com/2011/03/26/1-2-an-introduction-to-subjects-of-international-law/). Some argue that international non-governmental organisations and multinational companies also fall into the category of subjects of international law.

In spite of the definitions and explanations provided in the legal scholarship, the concept of *international law* is still perceived as insufficiently analysed. Kamminga, for example, observes that 'general international law' is a concept that is often used but rarely defined (Kamminga 2008, p. 2). He remarks that *general international law* is the opposite of *special international law* (*lex specialis*) that governs particular topics.[54] As to the question of whether international law is a *system*, most scholars claim that it is a system that regulates the relations between states and/or international intergovernmental organisations. However, Detter claims that it is unacceptable to use such parameters for an international legal system (Detter 1994, p. 1). She explains that we cannot propose that *international law* emanates from states since from the states emanates only their own legal system.[55] Thus, in Detter's view, what characterises international law is the *interest* criterion that remains valid, notably that international law regulates *matters of concern and interest to international society*, encompassing rules of both *public* and *private international laws*.[56]

A more complex approach to the concept of 'international law' and international law as a *system* is offered by H.L.A. Hart in his *The Concept of Law*, Chapter X. While Hart's theory of law and international law is not free from criticism, it remains influential and attractive for it goes to the nature of 'law' and 'international law'. Elaborating a comprehensive model for the *sources* of international law, Hart classifies these sources as 'primary' and 'secondary' rules of law (Hart et al. 1994, p. 92). He explains that '[r]ules of the first type impose duties; rules of the second type confer powers, public or private. Rules of the first type concern actions involving physical movement or change; rules of the second type provide for operations which lead not merely to physical movement or change, but to the creation or variation of duties or obligations.'[57] Thus, the primary rules are concerned with the actions that individuals *must* or *must not do*.[58] They lay down rights and obligations for members of the community or society (material rules), while secondary rules 'specify the ways in which the primary rules may be conclusively ascertained, introduced, eliminated, varied, and the fact of their violations conclusively determined' (seen more as procedural rules).[59] For example, the customary rules of interpretation set forth in the 1969 Vienna Convention on the Law of Treaties, which will be discussed in detail in the next chapter, are admitted in the scholarship as belonging to the type of 'secondary rules'.

In *The Concept of Law*, Hart questions whether *international law* is sufficiently analogous to the municipal legal order to be qualified as a legal system and argues that it is indeed law, however differing in some important respect from municipal

[54]Kamminga (2008), p. 2.

[55]Detter (1994), p. 1.

[56]*Id.*

[57]Hart et al. (1994), p. 92.

[58]*Id.*

[59]*Id.*

law. Considering the idea that the 'legal system is a complex union of primary and secondary rules', for a legal system to exist, Hart admits that it must meet two minimum necessary conditions (Hart et al. 1994, p. 116). First, those rules of behavior which are valid must be generally obeyed', and second, it is necessary that the 'rules of recognition specifying the criteria of legal validity and its rules of change and adjudication must be effectively accepted as common public standards of official behavior by its officials'.[60] Thus, in Hart's view, the primary rules of international law are only 'binding if they are accepted and function as such'.[61]

While stressing that 'the most fruitful way of regarding a legal system' is to look at it as the union of *primary* and *secondary rules*, Hart, however, perceives international law as consisting mainly of primary rules.[62] He expresses doubts as to whether any *secondary rules* actually exist at the international law level since their existence depends on whether they are accepted or not in practice as rules of a general standard of legal validity.[63] In principle, Hart sees international law as simply consisting of a set of rules, which does not constitute a system.[64] However, in this respect, it is worth mentioning that Hart's view of *international law* as 'law' but not as a 'legal system' is generating confusion (Payandeh 2010, p. 967). While not contesting Hart's important contribution to understanding the concept of *international law*, Payandeh, in contrast with Hart, strengthens the argument that *international law is a legal system*.[65] Thus, contrary to Hart, who claims, in principle, the absence of a uniform rule of recognition, seen as a rule that determines which rules are binding, Payandeh rightly admits that the international legal practice accepts international law as consisting also of 'secondary rules' of recognition, change and adjudication.[66] Furthermore, Payandeh insists that 'legal norms are considered normatively valid when they come into being in the generally recognised procedures provided by Article 38(1) of the ICJ's Statute', which encompasses *sources* of public international law.[67] Moreover, in his view, it should not be problematic to recognise sources of international law other than those encompassed in Article 38 of the ICJ's Statute (conventions, customary international law, general principles of law, judicial decisions and scholarly opinions).[68]

---

[60]*Id.*

[61]*Id*, p. 235.

[62]*Id* (emphasis added) Hart explains in the 'The concept of law' that the legal system is characterised by duality. He states in this regard: 'The assertion that a legal system exists is therefore a Janus-faced statement looking both towards obedience by ordinary citizens and the acceptance by officials of secondary rules as critical common standard of official behaviour.'

[63]Hart et al. (1994), pp. 116–117. Thus for Hart, the basic rule of recognition of the primary rules is that they are 'binding if they are accepted and function as such'.

[64]*Id*, p. 236.

[65]Payandeh (2010), p. 994. The author claims that international legal order is built on an international legal system 'just as the national polity is governed by a municipal legal system'.

[66]*Id.*

[67]*Id.*

[68]*Id*, p. 989.

So whether legal norms are subsequently implemented or adhered to is a question that, in Payandeh's view, does not have any influence on the normativity or legal validity of norms.[69]

In addition to the issue related to what *is international law*, questions such as *how* international law was created, *what* was the reason for creating it or how the validity of international law can be proven—have also attracted the attention of many distinguished legal scholars and practitioners. For example, in his investigation into the nature of law, Kelsen concisely defines the term *sources* of law as designating not only the different methods of creating *law* but also the methods of applying law and ascertaining its *raison d'etre*.[70] According to the author, *lato* sensu, since there is a principle that *law*, in general, regulates its own creation, this principle applies also to *international law* where 'every legal norm is a source of that other norm, the creation of which it regulates'.[71] However, s*tricto* sensu, the norms created upon the provisions of another norm become, in Kelsen's opinion, the *source* of the inferior legal norm.[72] Thus, the *source of law* appears to impose naturally a *hierarchy* of norms since the norm that regulates the creation of another norm is 'superior' to the norms that are created according to the former.[73]

With respect to the creation of norms, it is widely admitted that *custom* is the older and original source of international law and of *law* in general.[74] Oppenheim, for example, succinctly explains the creation of *custom* when 'a clear and continuous habit of doing certain actions has grown up under the aegis of the conviction that these actions are legally necessary or legally right' (Oppenheim 1912, para 17). Thus, when a great number of states adopt such a conduct, the rule that may be deduced from it is a rule of *customary international law*.[75] And importantly, according to Brierly, a customary norm is observed not because it had been consented to but because it is believed to be binding. So its binding force does not depend on the approval of the individual or the state to which customary rule is addressed (Brierly 1955, p. 53). Therefore, an important characteristic of *custom* is that it is unconscious and unintentional lawmaking, as observed by Kelsen, since individuals or states do not necessarily intend to create law. This unintentional character is what distinguishes *custom* from *legislation*, where legislation is lawmaking by a special organ.[76]

---

[69]*Id.*

[70]Kelsen (2003), p. 303. Also in a wider sense (*lato* sensu), by 'sources', Kelsen admits all those ideas which actually influence the law creating organs (e.g. moral norms, political principles, legal doctrine, the *opinio juris* of jurists, experts, etc), however they do not have character of law and thus binding force.

[71]*Id.*

[72]*Id.*

[73]*Id.*

[74]See e.g. Oppenheim (1912), para 17; Kelsen (2003), p. 307; Verdross (1949), p. 435; Brierly (1955).

[75]Oppenheim (1912), para 17.

[76]Kelsen (2003), p. 308. According to Kelsen, customary law has binding force which relies precisely on the hypostudy that international custom is a law-creating fact.

However, as observed by Ciobanu, the simple repetition of a practice is not sufficient in itself to create a *custom*.[77] Hence, in order to be a *custom*, a practice reflecting an unwritten rule of behaviour needs to meet certain conditions: (1) the repetition for a long time of an established practice (*longa diuturna inveterata consuetudo*), (2) the belief that this practice reflects a rule of law (*opinio juris sive necesitatis*),[78] (3) the need for such practice to be uniform in respect of the same social relation.[79] A non-uniform practice as to the same social relation, in the same region/place, cannot lead to the formation of a *custom*.[80] It is to be noted that the need to state with precision the content of *customary* law and to prove its existence had led those who believe that *customary international law* played an important role in the creation of international law to contemplate the codification of *custom*.[81] According to Ciobanu, a *custom* is thought to be proven through a multilateral (general) convention (treaty), decisions of international courts and tribunals (e.g., the advisory opinions of the PCIJ/ICJ) and publications (official or unofficial) consisting of the *opinio juris* of qualified jurists, publicists of various nations, with regard to the existence and content of that custom.[82]

Further, what the basis of our knowledge is regarding the formation of *customary law* and its scope is a puzzling subject that continues to generate disagreements among international scholars. For example, in a recent study on the nature of *customary law*, Kammerhofer claims that sometimes law cannot be concretised in a sufficient manner as to make it work in practice, so to a degree it remains uncertain (Kammerhofer 2004, p. 16). Distinguishing between the two elements necessary for a rule to be *custom* (the *objective*: what states do, their behaviour, and the *subjective*: the will or belief of states), Kammerhofer concludes that 'the only

[77]See *North Sea Continental Shelf Cases* (Germany v. Denmark and the Netherlands, 1969, Judgment of 20 February 1969, ICJ, Reports, p. 3), p. 45, para 77.

[78]Ciobanu (1991), p. 20. See *Fisheries Case* (United Kingdom v. Iceland), Judgment of 2 February 1973, ICJ; also *North Sea Continental Shelf Cases*, *supra* note 77.

[79]*Id.*

[80]*Id.* As observed by Ciobanu *customs* are thought to be: general, regional and local, depending of the region which generates them, and also of the number of participants of the custom's formation. He mentions, for example, that until the codification of diplomatic law in 1961 by the Vienna Convention, many of the rules codified by this Convention, such as those regulating diplomatic immunity, consisted in general customs. Diplomatic asylum in Latin countries is seen by some writers as based on a regional custom.

[81]Ciobanu (1991), p. 23. It is known that the ILC, as a principal organ of the U.N., established in 1947 by the General Assembly, was charged with promoting the progressive development of international law and its codification. According to Ciobanu, all modern conventions of customary law codification contain elements of progressive development of those rules content. For example, the author mentions those progressive developments of the content of customary rules (which are reaffirmed in writing) that could be tracked back to the years preceding the adoption of the Napoleonic Code (1804): in the writings of the members of the codification commission, and, in special, in the writings of Pothier, the president of that commission. The author makes clear that the customary rules codified in conventions are not to be seen identical with the unwritten rules (customs), which formed the object/source of codification.

[82]*Id.*

way either states behaviour or the views of states can be discovered is through what states *do* or *not do*, and that such a distinction might be an essential element of custom formation'.[83] Nevertheless, in Kammerhofer's view, uncertainty still exists in respect of *custom* as no one imposes exact limits on the amount of state practice needed to create law.[84] So it appears impossible or impractical to determine the quantity of acts necessary for a practice to become customary, though a large number of precedents become highly relevant in practice for establishing a law.[85]

Moving to *treaty*—as another major source of international law—it is to be mentioned that *treaty law* derives from *custom.*[86] Kelsen, for example, defines *treaty* as 'an international agreement between two or more states by which the expression of their common consent concerning a mutual behaviour is established'.[87] Unlike *customary law*, the nature of *treaties* as a source of international law is thought to be 'quite unambiguous and uncontroversial' (Hoof 1983, p. 117). According to Hoof, this is because in comparison with *customary law*, the *law of treaties* has been 'well developed and well demonstrated in time', now finding regulation in the *1969 Vienna Convention on the Law of Treaties.*[88] In principle, a *treaty* creates and imposes obligations only upon the contracting parties (states) in relation to their mutual behaviour upon which they agree.[89] Based on the rule of customary international law—*pacta sunt servanda*—a treaty achieves binding force upon the parties to it.[90] Thus, *customary international law* is admitted as the basis of *conventional international law (treaty law).*[91] Further, *treaties* may be concluded for innumerable purposes.[92] When *treaties* can stipulate new rules for future international conduct or confirm, define or abolish existing customary or conventional rules, they are called lawmaking treaties, and thus they are a source of international law, admittedly the most important one.[93] Contrary to customary law, *treaties* imply conscious and deliberate lawmaking, but not by special organs (Kelsen 2003, p. 308). Because this process develops relatively quick, exclusively being directed towards the scope of creating international law rules, it is easy to be demonstrated, unlike customary law (Hoof 1983, p. 117).

---

[83]Kammerhofer (2004), p. 3 (emphasis added).

[84]*Id*, p. 16.

[85]*Id.*

[86]Oppenheim (1912), para 18.

[87]Kelsen (2003), p. 314.

[88]Hoof (1983), p. 117.

[89]*Id.*

[90]*Id.* According to the author, *pacta sunt servanda* constitutes the source of all the law created by treaties, notably the 'conventional law'.

[91]*Id.*

[92]It is well known that states transact a vast amount of work and interests by using the means of treaties: disputes, peace, wars, territory delimitation or acquired, special interests between states, creation of international institutions and adjudicative mechanism, etc.

[93]Oppenheim (1912), para 18. The author notes that treaties create law for the contracting parties only, and, however, their law achieve universal character when all the members of the Family of Nations are parties to those treaties.

Finally, since reference to *other sources* of international law will often be made in the empirical part of the book, which analyses in detail the practice of the ICJ, ECtHR and WTO on treaty interpretation, a brief discussion on these sources is also necessary. Thus, other sources of international law are accepted as important and separate from *custom* and *treaty* such as *general principles of law*, *judicial decisions* and *scholarly opinions*. Often writers limit themselves to enumerating such other sources or giving little explanation of their content.[94] In these sources' respect, Shaw, for example, provides a good discussion. He states that the provision of 'the general principles of law recognised by civilised nations' was inserted in Article 38 of the ICJ's Statute with the idea to provide rules that govern new situations, precisely to fill gaps that might be uncovered in international law—a problem known as *non liquet* (Shaw 2008, p. 98). Relying on the jurisprudence of the ICJ,[95] Shaw observes that by virtue of judicial discretion, this Court applies *principles of international law* in particular circumstances, when *customary* and *treaty law* are unable to provide the required solution.[96] Among the most important of such sources, Shaw specifies *pacta sunt servanda*, good faith, equity, rules generally accepted by municipal legal systems, the principle of estoppel, *res judicata* and elementary principles of humanity.[97] In addition, Shaw points out that the decisions of arbitral tribunals and municipal courts, as also those of the highest municipal courts, have all contributed to developing principles of international law.[98]

Nevertheless, on what grounds principles of international law have developed and how they become generally accepted still remain crucial questions. Recently, Dworkin, for example, by asking what the grounds of international law are, he observes that if enough states forming 'the international community of States' have recognised fundamental rules as peremptory and non-negotiable, it means that these rules are peremptory and non-negotiable for the whole international community (Dworkin 2013, p. 5). Dworkin's interesting view rejects the idea that the basic ground of international law is the self-limiting consent of sovereign nations, admitting instead that a more basic principle provides, or is thought to provide, that basic ground.[99] Preoccupied with 'a scheme for identifying international law, as a way of persuading anyone to accept that law',[100] Dworkin comes to the

[94]According to Oppenheim other sources of international law such as opinions of famous writers on international law, decisions of courts, arbitral awards, instructions issued by various States for guidance of their diplomatic and other organs, State papers concerning foreign politicians, certain municipal laws, decisions of municipal courts.

[95]The ICJ is thought to be contributed more than any other court to developing principles of international law, as well as to confirming other sources of international law.

[96]Shaw (2008), p. 105. This aspect will be illustrated inter alia in Chap. 3 of this book.

[97]*Id*, pp. 99–112.

[98]*Id*, p. 112.

[99]Dworkin (2013), p. 5. If no state can be forced to cooperate, according to Dworkin, then 'they will all have a reason not to participate'. Thus, 'consent' in Dworkin's view 'is neither a necessity nor a sufficient ground of legitimacy' for international law.

[100]*Id*, p. 13.

conclusion that the 'principle of salience' works in this respect. This principle provides, according to the author, a better and persuasive account of *the moral foundation of international law* than is provided by the theory of *consent*, as well as a compelling justification for the conventional sources of international law.[101] So as more nations recognise *a duty* to accept and follow widely accepted principles of international law, then 'those even more widely accepted principles *have greater moral gravitational force*'.[102] In brief, by defending 'the moralized approach to international law', Dworkin admits that the helpful strategy in finding the grounds of international law is one based not on 'consent' but on 'the legitimacy account'.[103] Importantly, the author proposes an *interpretative conception of international law doctrine* by virtue of which the legitimacy of international arrangements could be improved.[104] So by knowing *how* and *why* rules and principles (set out in the international documents, which constitute 'some kind of legal system') are developing is crucially important because 'how these rules and principles should be *interpreted*, hinges on it'.[105]

In addition, there are *subsidiary sources* that are often used in the determination of rules of law such as *opinions of writers* and the *teaching of the most qualified publicists of the various nations*, which add to clarifying the direction and purpose of international law rules (Shaw 2008, p. 113). According to Shaw, *scholarly works* as subsidiary sources are used as methods of discovering what the law is on any particular point; in elucidating the nature, history and practice of rules of law; in stimulating thoughts, suggestions as to the value and scope of international law; or in revealing the strengths and limits of the international legal system.[106] Also, Shaw admits that other possible *subsidiary sources* are to be considered such as *declarations* and *resolutions of the General Assembly (of the UN)*, as well as draft articles and drafts statutes prepared by the International Law Commission, to which the International Court of Justice often refers.[107]

---

[101] *Id*, p. 20. According to the author the principle of salience implies a duty of states to subscribe to an agreed code of practice developed either by treaties or by other form of coordination by a significant number of states, encompassing a significant population.

[102] *Id* (emphasis added). Based on the salience principle, Dworkin provides the example of the moral obligation to treat the Charter of the U.N.O. as law that 'is created not by consent but by the moral force of salience as a route to a satisfactory international order'. Or, also the Geneva Conventions or the Treaty of Rome (ICC) that are international law not just for the signatory states, but for all. The author notes that such grow in recognition of these principles strengthens international order.

[103] *Id*, p. 21. Dworkin claims that the sources of international law (Article 38 of the ICJ Statute) flow, not from *consent*, but 'from the moral demands, on which the legitimacy of an international system depends'.

[104] *Id*, p. 26.

[105] *Id*, p. 3 (emphasis added).

[106] Shaw (2008), p. 113.

[107] *Id*, p. 120. Shaw notes that the ILC drafts are important source of international law since: it is involved in at least two major sources of law, its drafts may form the bases of international treaties; its work is part of the whole range of state practice, which can lead to new customary law; its drafts may constitute evidence of custom, contribute to the corpus of usages which may create new law and evidence the *opinio juris*.

The rules of international law compiled in Article 38 of the Statute of the International Court of Justice[108] are recognised as *sources* of public international law and are enumerated as *conventions*, *customary international law*, *general principles* of law, *judicial decisions* and *scholarly opinions* (Shaw 2008, p. 6). Admittedly, since these sources exist in a hierarchy, certain relations among them exist. However, the notion of *hierarchy* is controversial and has generated a large volume of literature, from which only one or two points need be briefly addressed here, inasmuch as they shed light on the 'fragmentation'/'unity' of international law discussion. Although the ILC does not view the main sources of international law set forth in Article 38 of the ICJ Statute in a hierarchical relationship inter se, it admits that norms exist at higher and lower hierarchical levels (ILC 2006, p. 614). Thus, some rules are admitted to be of more importance than others due to their content, as well as their universal acceptance as superior. Such norms are designated as 'fundamental', as expressions of 'elementary considerations of humanity' or as 'intransgressible principles of international law'.[109] For example, *jus cogens* norms ('compelling law', referred to as peremptory norms from which one cannot derogate) are widely admitted as norms of duty and not as norms of 'optimal' rights, holding the highest hierarchical position among all other norms and principles.[110] In the *jus cogens* category can be reminded, for instance, those norms prohibiting aggression (unlawful use of force), genocide, slavery and slave trading, piracy, racial discrimination, torture, apartheid; the basic rules of international humanitarian law applicable in armed conflict; the right to self-determination.[111] The *jus cogens* character of such norms has been confirmed by various sources as are the

[108]Art. 38 of the ICJ provides: '1. The Court, whose function is to decide in accordance with international law such disputes as are submitted to it, shall apply:

a. international conventions, whether general or particular, establishing rules expressly recognized by the contesting states;

b. international custom, as evidence of a general practice accepted as law;

c. the general principles of law recognized by civilized nations;

d. subject to the provisions of Article 59, judicial decisions and the teachings of the most highly qualified publicists of the various nations, as subsidiary means for the determination of rules of law.

2. This provision shall not prejudice the power of the Court to decide a case *ex aequo* et *bono*, if the parties agree thereto.'

[109]ILC Conclusions of the Work of the Study Group on the Fragmentation of International Law: Difficulties Arising from the Diversification and Expansion of International law (2006) adopted by the ILC. The Study Group's Conclusions appear at Rep. of the Int'l L. Comm'n, 58th Sess, May 1–June 9, July 3–Aug. 11, 2006, pp. 407–423, U.N. Doc. A/61/10; GAOR, 61st Sess., Supp. No. 10 (2006), paras 31–32.

[110]Bassiouni (1996), p. 67. The author claims that some scholars see *jus cogens* sources and customary international law as the same.

[111]ILC Conclusions (2006), para 33.

statutes of international courts, international law documents, conventions,[112] as well as the practice of the PCIJ/ICJ.[113] According to the ILC, by virtue of a treaty provision, a rule can also be superior to other rules. For example, Article 103 of the Charter of the U.N. establishes a hierarchy of norms when it provides that in the case of conflict between obligations of the Members of the U.N. under the Charter and their obligations under any other international agreement, the obligations under the Charter prevail.[114] An important conclusion of the ILC in this respect is that 'a rule conflicting with a norm of *jus cogens* becomes thereby *ipso facto* void', and, indeed, it becomes void when conflicting with Article 103 of the U.N. Charter.[115] Also, Article 53 of the 1969 Vienna Convention on the Law of Treaties provides for peremptory norms of international law,[116] although it does not specify which norms

---

[112]Bassiouni (1996), p. 68. Bassiouni gives examples of sources in which *jus cogens* is stated: The 1993 International Tribunal For the Former Yugoslavia and the 1994 International Tribunal for Rwanda statutes (the Statute of the International Tribunal for the Former Yugoslavia, U.N. SCOR, 48th Sess., 3217th mtg., at 1, U.N. Doc. S/RES/827 (1993) and the Statute for the International Tribunal for Rwanda, U.N. SCOR, 49th Sess., 3453rd mtg., at 1, U.N. Doc. S/RES/955 (1994)), address Genocide, Crimes Against Humanity, and War Crimes. The 1996 Code of Crimes includes these three crimes plus Aggression. See, e.g., Draft Code of Crimes Against Peace and Security of Mankind: Titles and Articles on the Draft Code of Crimes Against Peace and Security of Mankind adopted by the International Law Commission on its Forty-Eighth Session, U.N. GAOR, 51st Sess., U.N. Doc. A/CN.4L.532 (1996), revised by U.N. Doc. A/CN.4L.532/Corr. 1, and U.N. Doc. A/CN.41.532/Corr. 3; Crimes Against U.N. Personnel, in M. Cherif Bassiouni, International criminal law conventions (1997 in print). Also the 1969 Vienna Convention on the Law of the Treaties has given the recognition of the norms of *jus cogens* in Article 53.

[113]For a discussion on the PCIJ/ICJ's recognition of the *jus cogens* norms, see, e.g., cases such as: *Oscar Chinn Case*, 1934, PCIJ, S.AB 63, 12 December, 1934; For the opinion of the ICJ, see, e.g. *Reservation to the Convention on the Prevention and Punishment of the Crime of Genocide*, 1951, I.C.J., 15 (May 28); *Application of the Convention of 1902 Governing the Guardianship of Infants* (Neth. v. Swed.), 1958, I.C.J. 55 (Nov. 28) (separate opinion of Judge Quintana); *Right of Passage Over Indian Territory* (Port. v. India) 1960 I.C.J. 6 (Apr. 12) (separate opinion of Judge ad hoc Fernandes); *South West Africa Case*, Second Phase (Eth. v. S. Afr.; Liber. v. S. Afr.) 1966, I.C.J. 6 (July 18) (separate opinion of Judge Tanaka); *North Sea Continental Shelf Cases* (F.R.G./Den. v. F.R.G./Neth.) 1969, I.C.J. 3 (Feb. 20) (separate opinion of Judge Nervo); *Military and Paramilitary Activities in and against Nicaragua* (Nicar. v. U.S.), 1986, ICJ (Jun. 27); *Application of the Convention on the Prevention and Punishment of the Crime of Genocide* (Bosn. and Herz. v. Serb. And Mont.), 2007, I.C.J. (Febr. 26).

[114]ILC Conclusions (2006), para 35.

[115]*Id*, para 41.

[116]Article 53 of the VCLT provides: 'Treaties conflicting with a peremptory norm of general international law (*jus cogens*)':

> A treaty is void if, at the time of its conclusion, it conflicts with a peremptory norm of general international law. For the purposes of the present Convention, a peremptory norm of general international law is a norm accepted and recognized by the international community of States as a whole as a norm from which no derogation is permitted and which can be modified only by a subsequent norm of general international law having the same character.

have the character of *jus cogens*.[117] The origin of *jus cogens* is believed to be in municipal legal systems, where the application of some rules cannot be set aside by the will of the parties to a contract.[118] Despite the recognition of *jus cogens* only in 1969, in the VCLT, this concept of *ordre public* existing in municipal systems has been advocated for a very long time in international law[119]; however, it remains a controversial subject.

In a recent, interesting study on *jus cogens*, Petsche admits that the concept of *jus cogens* as codified in the VCLT is far from being clear and is even of limited relevance for the actual practice of international law.[120] He argues that by providing rather a procedural connotation as to how *jus cogens* norms can be determined, the VCLT definition of this concept omits specific and fundamental values (interests) of the international community such as peace, security and the protection of human rights.[121] The author further observes that the *jus cogens* concept is applied to certain overriding principles of international law. He suggests that *jus cogens* should be viewed as *a basic idea* or *principle*, which has exercised a continuous influence on the international lawmaking process, and not as a norm of international law in its true meaning.[122] So relying on fundamental values that exist in a hierarchy, *jus cogens* should be perceived as 'not entirely dependent on the consent of the subjects of international law'.[123] However, as Petsche observes, there is a progressive acceptance among scholars of the idea that *jus cogens* norms, which govern the conduct of international relations between states, ultimately affect individuals.[124] Here, the author underlines the necessity of prioritising human rights

[117]See Verdross (1966), p. 57 on this point. According to the author, the ILC refrained to include any examples of *jus cogens* norm, for two reasons: first because it may lead to misunderstanding as the position of others possible cases; and second, because a complete list of such rules was impossible without a prolonged study on this matter. He states that some members of the Commission considered that 'no definition is necessary, because the idea of *jus cogens* is clear in itself'.

[118]Schwelb (1967), p. 948. According to Schwelb, it was Gerald Fitzmaurice and Humphrey Waldock who introduced the concept of consistency with a general rule or principle of international law having the character of *jus cogens*, which Hersh Lauterpach proposed for codification in the law of treaties.

[119]*Id.* According to Schwelb, it was Gerald Fitzmaurice and Humphrey Waldock who introduced the concept of consistency with a general rule or principle of international law having the character of *jus cogens*, which Hersh Lauterpach proposed to codification in the law of treaties.

[120]Petsche (2010), p. 237. In the author's view, *jus cogens* definition in the VCLT is 'at best useless and at worst harmful', even giving rise to serious difficulties in its application in the practical conduct of international relations.

[121]*Id*, p. 242.

[122]Petsche (2010), p. 237. Petsche notes that *jus cogens* was fundamental in creation and justification of international tribunals, i.e., Tokyo and Nuremberg Tribunals—which mission implied a violation of the cardinal criminal law principle of *nullum crimen, nulla poena sine lege* (no crime, no penalty without law).

[123]*Id*, p. 272. Here, the author underlines the idea that the initial State centered approach of peremptory norms of international law, which focus of the vital State interest's preservation, 'has given way to a more individual-centered notion of *jus cogens*'.

[124]*Id.*

values in an existing hierarchy of international law norms, *jus cogens* thus aiming essentially to protect individual rights.[125]

Since various academic writers have been given great attention to *jus cogens*, in particular to *jus cogens* norms underlying the protection of specific individual rights as *jus cogens*, it is worth mentioning in this context Verdross' comprehensive and highly influential views on the *jus cogens* concept, expressed before the codification of this concept in the 1969 VCLT. Verdross admits *jus cogens* norms as those *exceptions* to the principle that states can enter into international agreements on any subject, whatever this subject might be.[126] While distinguishing *jus cogens* rules from general international law rules, which are not imperative (*jus dispositivum*) but relative,[127] Verdross defines *jus cogens* as those rules that exist to satisfy not the interests of the individual states but a *higher interest of the international community*. So *jus cogens* rules must be admitted as *absolute*.[128] In essence, in Verdross' view, a norm of *jus cogens* can practically be created only by a norm of general customary law or by a general or multilateral convention.[129] The author divides the rules having the character of *jus cogens* into groups: (1) all norms created for a humanitarian purpose, in the highest interest of humanity as a whole[130]; (2) humanitarian principles included in conventions as basic principles of international law[131]; (3) rules forbidding the use of force, introduced by the United Nations Charter (Article 2, para 4, and Article 51)[132]; and (4) rules forbidding war crimes.[133] As admitted in the scholarship, Verdross' influential views paved the way to nowadays a general admission that *jus cogens* norms are rules that correspond to the fundamental norms of public international policy and cannot be altered unless a subsequent norm of the same standard is established (Hossain 2005).

---

[125]*Id*, p. 269. As an example, the author mentions the possibility to try and prosecute authors of international crimes, according to the principle of universal jurisdiction: to punish serious violations of individual rights, to some extent without the will of the States concerned (when i.e. States unduly acquit the alleged offender(s)).

[126]Verdross (1966), p. 56. Verdross shares the opinion of those writers who defend the idea that all treaties against the public order of international community are null and void (e.g., an agreement defending slavery, preventing the development of individual liberty, etc).

[127]*Id*. According to Verdross the rights and obligations created by *jus dispositivum* rules concern only individual States inter se. The author cites the advisory opinion in the *Genocide* case (1950), where the ICJ recognised these two categories of rules.

[128]*Id*, p. 58.

[129]*Id*, p. 60.

[130]*Id*. Verdross mentions in this regard norms of *jus cogens* existent in those treaties concluded in violation of the conventions concerning slavery, traffic of women and children, rights of prisoners of wars are void.

[131]*Id*. The author refers here to those principles already existent before the Second World War, affirming 'faith in fundamental human rights of men and women', enshrined in the U.N. Charter, as the most important part of the constitutional law of the present international community.

[132]*Id*. See Article 2 (4) and Article 51 Charter of the U.N.O.

[133]*Id*, pp. 58–61.

Therefore, *jus cogens* are to be founded on fundamental principles deeply rooted in the international community.[134]

In addition to *jus cogens* rules, there are obligations *erga omnes* (towards all)[135] that derive from *jus cogens* (e.g., the prohibition of acts of aggression, the prohibition of genocide, obligations concerning the protection of basic human rights).[136] These *erga omnes* obligations enjoy a special status due to the universal scope of their applicability (i.e., when a state has obligations towards the international community as a whole).[137] Bassiouni, for example, gives a succinct explanation of such an *erga omnes* norm, when he describes it as being 'a consequence of a given international crime having risen to the level of *jus cogens*' (Bassiouni 1996). However, the ILC finds that not all *erga omnes* obligations are established by peremptory norms of general international law, as are, for example, certain obligations under the principles and rules concerning the basic rights of the human person or some obligations related to global commerce.[138] In addition, the concept of *erga omnes* has been applied to treaty obligations that a state owes to all other states parties or to non-party states, as third-party beneficiaries.[139]

According to Shaw, the hierarchy of international law sources is even more complicated due to the proliferation of international courts and tribunals that exist in a non-hierarchical structure and, indeed, due to the significant expansion of international law (Shaw 2008, pp. 123–124). Dupuy, who admits that we clearly witness an expansion of international law, regards this development as due to the growing necessity of international cooperation that urges international law to cover now almost every field of human activity—political, social, economic, scientific and technical[140]—which actually contributes to enriching international law.[141]

---

[134]Hossain (2005).

[135](Meaning from Latin: 'towards all') *Erga omnes* obligations are defined in Article 1 of the Resolution of the Institute of International Law, Fifth Commission, Obligations and rights *erga omnes* in international law, Rapporteur M. Giorgio Gaja, 2005.

[136]The *obligatio erga omnes* concept is held by the ICJ in e.g. *Barcelona Traction, Light and Power Co. Ltd.* (Belgium v. Spain), 1970, I.C.J. 3, 32 (Feb 5). The ICJ stated in *Barcelona* (1970), that the first criterion of an obligation rising at the level of erga omnes is 'the obligation of a state towards the international Community as a whole'. Also in *Reservation to the Convention on the Prevention and Punishment of the Crime of Genocide*, 1951; *South West Africa Cases* (Ethiopia v. South Africa; Liberia v. South Africa), 1963, I.C.J Rep. 310 (Dec. 21).

[137]ILC Conclusions (2006), para 37.

[138]*Id.*

[139]*Id.* The ILC gives as example boundary and territorial treaties, regarding the issues of territorial status.

[140]Dupuy (1998), p. 791. For example, Dupuy mentions the growing role of non-State actors, such as non-governmental organisations (NGOs), and the effort to improve the efficiency of public international obligations, with the establishment of some 'follow-up machineries', in particular, in the fields of human rights, international economic law, international trade law, and international environmental law.

[141]*Id* (Dupuy mentions, e.g., international criminal law that has known an expansion, focusing on the essential rights of human beings; human rights law has brought a radical change from the traditional laws which protect individuals, and individuals can enjoy 'rights' direct from international law).

However, since potential conflicts between norms will arise in this 'proliferation' context, as observed by Sands, the relationship between and the hierarchy among different norms of international law certainly play a basic role in resolving such conflicts (Sands 1998, p. 85). Importantly in this respect, as according to Sheeran, is that human rights, in particular, have fundamentally influenced the development of the concepts of *erga omnes* and *jus cogens*, consequently introducing a hierarchy of norms that certainly 'altered the structural fabric of international law' (Sheeran 2014, p. 94). However, such a change in the structural fabric of what can be called the old or traditional international law should not be seen as creating chaos. As observed by Koskenniemi in his comment on the ILC Study's findings, '[l]aw has integrity as a system', and the ILC made clearly that *international law is a legal system* (Koskenniemi 2007, p. 18). Thus, since meaningful relationships between rules and principles exist, as also concluded by the ILC Study Group (ILC 2006, p. 614), it could be implied that international law functions as a *system*, and it is endowed with a kind of *unity* that characterises it as a whole.[142]

It can be summed up that *international law* should be perceived as a *system*, consisting in a *set of rules* existing in meaningful relationships between each other and endowed with *unity*. *International law* is, nevertheless, as concisely put by Shaw, the product of its own environment and of the network of relationships existing primarily, if not exclusively, between states that recognise certain *common principles* and modalities of resolving issues among them (Shaw 2008, pp. 123–124). As an international legal order, *international law* is perceived as an accumulation of legal regimes or as a *system* that is composed of sub-systems (Prost 2012, p. 10).

#### 2.3.1.2 Unity of International Law

When speaking in general about fragmenting a thing (object, process or phenomenon), one makes an assumption about the 'unity' of that thing as a *whole*. In this case, the 'whole' is *international law*. Thus, one cannot tackle the notion of 'fragmentation' *vis-à-vis* international law without considering the concept of *unity of international law*. Despite that *unity* of international law is thought to be 'more assumed than explained', and even 'under-theorised in analytical jurisprudence at large',[143] there have been authors preoccupied with the structures of international law and with what gives coherence to the multitude of norms constituting international law. Arguably, such authors provide sufficient ideas as to form an understanding of what *unity* of international law could signify. Kelsen, for example, asks what constitute *the unity* of a multitude of norms since the law could be seen as a normative order organised around 'a system of norms that regulates the behaviour of men' (Kelsen 1970, p. 193). He asserts that since the reason for the validity of a norm can only be the validity of another norm, it is then

[142]See also, e.g., Simma (2009) for remarks on this point.

[143]Prost (2012), p. 13.

this latter norm, the basic norm, that provides for '*the unity* in the multitude of norms that belong to this order'.[144] On this premise Kelsen explains international law as a system of norms, and as a (unified) normative order.[145] Moreover, he admits that the *unity* is reflected in that legal order, respectively that this 'unity' 'may be described in rules of law that do not contradict each other'.[146] That it is so is due to the existence of a meaningful (interdependence) relationship between rules or, as explained by Kelsen, because the lower norm has the reason for its validity in the higher norm. In other words, there cannot be conflict between a higher norm and a lower norm since one norm's creation is dependent on the existence of another norm.[147]

Extending Kelsen's view on the 'unity' of international law, authors Prost and Clark link the idea of *unity* to that of *legitimacy* of international law. They consider that while international law exists 'as a legal order worthy of its name', and is no longer questioned as such in the academic literature, its unity, nonetheless, constitutes a subject of continuous inquiry (Prost and Clark 2006). This continuous questioning is due, according to the authors, in principle to the contemporary expansion of 'normative specificity' of international law and to the proliferation of judicial and non-judicial international bodies that occurred without specific means to hold the international law system together. Such changes are generally perceived as a threat to the existing body of international law norms, since they can lead to a formation of 'more or less coherent set of "normative islands" constituted by partial autonomous and perhaps "self-contained" or "legal sub-systems"' (Prost and Clark 2006). For example, some authors admit that the development of human rights (sub-system), in particular, constitutes one of the principal causes that make international law to be seen as fragmented. In this connection, in an interesting study on unity and pluralism in international law, Casanovas and La Rosa observe that there are two factors that determine the unity of international law (as it has been conceived traditionally) to be questioned in the legal scholarship: 'one is the specific characteristics of the treaty rules for the international protection of human rights, and the other, the existence of international rules concerning human rights of universal application' (Casanovas and La Rosa 2001, p. 154).

Nevertheless, the idea that the 'unity' of international law could be undermined by the continuous expansion of 'self-contained' sub-systems of international law is also developed by the work of the International Law Commission. And up till now, as correctly admitted by Simma, the most direct contribution of the ILC to the *unity* and *coherence* of international law remains 'the 2006 (final) Report of Martti Koskenniemi's Study Group on Fragmentation, with its "tool box" of ways and

[144]Kelsen (1970), p. 205.

[145]*Id*, p. 197. In this respect Kelsen adds: 'The basic norm is the common source for the validity of all norms that belong to the same order', so the fact that 'a certain norm belongs to a certain order is based on the circumstances that its last reason of validity is the basic norm of this order'.

[146]*Id*.

[147]*Id*, p. 205.

means to cope with the undesirable effects of our phenomenon' of 'fragmentation' as results of diversification and expansion of international law (Simma 2009, p. 271). In Simma's view, this ILC Study Report is of immense value because it 'attempts to assemble the totality of international law's devices available to counter the negative aspects of fragmentation'.[148] Relying on the ILC Study Group's findings in 2006, Koskenniemi observes that because international law has became so diversified, such change in the international law landscape has determined international lawyers to speculate on the 'danger' of incoherence, 'forum shopping' and 'loss of overall control' in international law, a picture that did not point precisely to *unity* in international law (Koskenniemi 2007, p. 4). However, the gist of Koskenniemi's view regarding 'fragmentation' is that because *law is a whole* and *has integrity as a system*, when the rules run out or specialised regimes fail, such regimes could not function but within the frame of general international law to which they always relate, by resorting back to this framework.[149] Important to be recalled in this context is the conclusion of the ILC on *lex specialis* (Article 55) formulated in the draft's Articles on *Responsibility of States for Internationally Wrongful Acts*. According to the ILC, these Articles 'do not apply where and to the extent that the conditions for the existence of an international wrongful act of its legal consequences are determined by special rules of international law'.[150] This conclusion, which reflects a perceived consensus among international lawyers that *international law* is, as succinctly expressed by Pulkowsky, 'a *unified* and, to a certain extent, hierarchical legal order', appears to be a 'logical candidate for tying *special regimes* to *general international law*'.[151] Such conclusion could certainly strengthen the belief of legal scholars and practitioners that disagreements on the interaction between norms from different regimes (sub-systems) can find solution within the framework of general international law, which points directly to the international law's unity. Moreover, according to a recent study on the *unity* of international law, Schemers and Blokker conclude that the proliferation of both judicial and non-judicial bodies does not constitute a threat to the *unity* of international law (Schermers and Blokker 2011, p. 27). These authors observe that even at the level of non-judicial international bodies, for example, certain rules of procedure applied by international organisations and international conferences 'have achieved near universal application and may well by now have the status of customary international law'.[152] Similarly, the general rules concerning treaties to which international organisations are parties,[153] or the draft rules on responsibility

[148]Simma (2009), p. 271.

[149]Koskenniemi (2007), pp. 17–18.

[150]See for commentaries on Article 55: Draft Articles on Responsibility of States for Internationally Wrongful Acts, with commentaries (2001)—as part of Commission's report covering the work of that session (A/56/10).

[151]Pulkowski (2005), p. 3 (emphasis added).

[152]Schermers and Blokker (2011), p. 27.

[153]*Id.* Schermers and Blokker refer to The 1986 Vienna Convention on the Law of Treaties between States and International Organisations or between International Organisations.

of international organisations adopted on first reading by the ILC in 2009, have achieved such universal character.[154]

In the context of the scholarly debate on *unity* versus *fragmentation of international law*, it is worth mentioning furthermore Pulkowsky's observation that the discourse on *fragmentation* is based on the assumption of a *unified legal order*, which is especially concerned with the structures of international law (Pulkowski 2005, p. 10). However, Pulkowsky asks whether such a concern is not excessive and questions the 'political projects' behind the quest for *unity*.[155] He observes, for example, that the scholars discussing 'fragmentation' attempt to elucidate the structure of law 'by organising the often chaotic and disparate legal practice' and systematising international law 'by fitting it into certain meta-categories', such as the concept of a *unified legal order*.[156] Pulkowsky avoids such pitfalls when he offers a new perspective on the concept of *unity* of international law, which focuses on the universal/particular rapport to explain the dialectic between 'system' and its elements ('sub-systems', 'regimes'). Analysing some special regimes' practice (especially the WTO's and the ECtHR's), Pulkowsky observes, for example, that international legal discourse 'continuously oscillate between the two extremes, and re-positions itself in an attempt to make a convincing argument on the relationship between norms from different regimes'.[157] In order to be convincing, as the author points out, every legal argument should necessarily relate to the universal system (public international law) while taking account of the particularity of the regime (e.g., trade, human rights, environment, etc). Thus, *unity* and *particularity* should only constitute 'categories that help jurists negotiate the balance between effectiveness and legitimacy'.[158] So in order for international legal sub-systems to remain effective and gain normative strength and legitimacy, their rules need to remain connected with the universal legal order, assuming there is a *unified legal order*.[159]

Furthermore, in a recent study on the concept of *unity* of international law, Prost observes that the notion of *unity* has been usually admitted to mean 'coherence among rules of international law', where this *coherence* is referred to the existence of 'identical or comparable rules', to 'the uniform development of jurisprudence' and to 'judicial harmony'.[160] But most frequently, *unity* has been understood as 'the

---

[154] *Id.*

[155] Pulkowski (2005), p. 13.

[156] *Id*, p. 10.

[157] *Id*, p. 13.

[158] *Id*, p. 11. The author claims that the quest for unity can be interpreted as 'a quest for containment of power', 'a quest for universality, denying the existence of the particular'.

[159] *Id*, p. 3. According to Pulkowski, while universalists suggest that the quest for a unified international law is motivated by a 'fear of power structures separated from the imperfect, yet comforting and familiar processes of international law as we know it', however, 'particularists may object that the erection of meta structures (such as the concept of a unified legal order) risk to blur and conceal the true struggle of interests, power and identities in which international law is situated'.

[160] *Id*, p. 48.

absence of conflict between norms, regimes or decisions', a definitively important aspect, in Prost's view, when talking about *unity* of international law, but not sufficiently comprehensive in its respect.[161] Contextualising the scholarly debate on 'unity' and 'fragmentation' of international law, Prost aptly observes that while *unity* of international law is generally contested in the legal scholarship, paradoxically the discourses on 'fragmentation' that are necessarily contingent find justification (Prost 2012, p. 1). As the author further notes, however, most discussions about *unity/fragmentation* provide actually no definition of *unity* at all.[162] Thus, the concept of *unity* imposes to be analysed with much more force since 'each branch of the law, each special regime has started debating its own fragmentation'.[163] Unlike other authors who admit that *fragmentation* discourse relies on the assumption of a unified legal order, Prost correctly assumes that the source of disagreement in the scholarship over the issue of fragmentation can, actually, be traced back to the '*unresolved disagreements over the meaning of unity*'.[164] In his opinion, the unity of international law can be 'graded', since unity possesses various 'semantic layers', and also 'dynamic', because it relies on the dynamics of forces that are 'sometimes compatible and sometimes at odds with one another'.[165] Prost identifies three fundamental dimensions on *unity*: *the substantial unity*, which refers to the 'uniformity and formal coherence of "positive" international law'; *the cultural unity*, which 'is premised on a concept of international law as an intellectual project and as a form of argument'; and the *logical unity*, which 'considers international law as a rational (epistemological unity) or as a value system (axiological unity)'.[166] However, in Prost's view, no perspective is self-evident or intrinsically right, and the subjective element of choice is always involved when references to *unity* are made.[167]

Analysing the *unity of international law* from the perspective of fragmentation, also Dupuy suggests that in order to diminish the risk of fragmentation of international law, specialised judges should accept that *lex specialis* exists and must be read in the light of general international law (Dupuy 2007, p. 11). Similarly to other authors,[168] Dupuy rightly considers that the *unity* of international law could only be guaranteed by a harmonised application and interpretation of the rules of international law. But most importantly, in his view, this *unity* can be guaranteed by the (legal) culture of international judges and by the extent to which these judges understand their adjudicatory activity to be part of one and the same international

[161] *Id*, p. 30.

[162] Prost (2012), p. 1.

[163] *Id*, p. 9.

[164] *Id*, p. 14 (emphasis added).

[165] *Id*, p. 17.

[166] *Id*, p. 31.

[167] *Id*, p. 30.

[168] See e.g. Wellens (2003), Abi-Saab (1998), van Eikema Hommes (1978), Simma (1985), Spelliscy (2001).

legal order, although this is a subjective, fragile element, as Dupuy himself stresses.[169] Borrowing from Hart's theory of legal order, Dupuy draws the conclusion that the international 'legal order', seen as a system of norms binding on determined subjects, has two kinds of unity: *formal* and *substantial* (Dupuy 1998, p. 791). The *formal unity of international law* is given by what Hart calls 'secondary rules'. As discussed in the above section, Hart defined in *The Concept of Law* the 'primary rules' (imposing duties) as rules according to which human beings are required to do or abstain from certain actions. By contrast, the 'secondary rules' (conferring power) were defined as those rules by which 'human beings may, by doing or saying certain things, introduce new rules of the primary type, extinguish or modify old ones, or in various ways determine their incidence or control their operations' or 'norms of adjudication' (e.g., rules of international responsibility for wrongdoings, establishing the conditions under which an injured state may have recourse to countermeasures, the general rules of interpretation of treaties, etc).[170] Contrary to Hart, however, Dupuy sees international law as endowed with a full set of secondary rules, and on this basis he identifies the *formal unity of international law*. Nevertheless, adopting the meaning provided by Hart for 'primary rules', Dupuy concludes that these rules were used to establish a body of general customary principles (admitted as having a 'constitutional' character since the adoption of the Charter of the United Nations), some of them of peremptory nature and qualified as *erga omnes* rules (e.g., rules prohibiting the use of force, outlawing genocide, the basic/essential rights of the people, the basic/essential rights of a human person).[171] So it is this set of rules composed of substantial rules (and not of formal ones) that, in Dupuy's view, provides the *public international law* with the *substantial unity*.[172]

These scholarly analyses of *unity* and *coherence of international law* are further augmented and nuanced in the legal scholarship. Simma, for example, admits that among the most important pillars in keeping the *unity* and *coherence* of universal international law are the *International Law Commission* and the *International Court of Justice*, the two judicial authorities that introduced a normative hierarchy in international law (Simma 2009). Despite the fact that the ICJ has not yet raised its voice specifically on the international law *unity* challenge, as according to Simma, 'certain recent judgments do offer insights in the Court's perception of the *coherence* and *unity* of international law and the ways to preserve these qualities'.[173] Regarding the position of the ICJ in relation to other international judicial forums, Dupuy warns that this Court must not hope to be granted 'a formal

[169] *Id.*

[170] Dupuy (1998), p. 791.

[171] *Id.*

[172] *Id.*

[173] Simma (2009), p. 277 (emphasis added). E.g. *Application of the Convention of the Prevention and Punishment of the crime of genocide* (Bosnia Herzegovina v. Serbia and Montenegro), Judgment of 26 February, 2007; *Legal Consequences of the Construction of a wall in the Occupied Palestinian Territory*, Advisory Opinion of 9 July 2004, ICJ Reports 136. This aspect will be further discussed in Chap. 3 of this book.

authority over other courts, but rather to reinforce its moral authority by pronouncing itself on, and advancing the scope and interpretation of international law, at every opportunity' (Dupuy 2007, p. 1). How other international courts, especially those specialised ones, apply international law definitively remains important in determining the *coherence* and *unity* of international law. In principle, as concisely captured by Simma, '[*t*]*he more international courts apply a specific rule of international law in the same manner, the more legitimacy it will be accorded, and the more can we be certain about its normative strength*'.[174] Moreover, as mentioned earlier in the chapter, the reliance of international courts on the case law of other international courts and the coherent application and development of such case law add to the legitimacy of such courts' judgments, directly contributing to the preservation of the *coherence* and *unity of international law*.[175]

Another important aspect to keep in mind when inquiring about the *unity of international law* is, according to Finnis, that as long as the 'law' has distinctive devices such as defining terms, specifying rules, with sufficient and necessarily artificial clarity, predictability and definiteness,[176] the international law's core values can be preserved and thus its 'fragmentation' impeded. As Prost and Clark aptly state, there is only in the theory that some authors express their concern about the dangers of incoherent case law, while others, however, contest even 'the idea of the unity of international law' (Prost and Clark 2006). And this is so because the authors who express such views do not check if in reality such incoherency in case law is perpetuated. They usually base their analysis on only one precedent, which has become famous for this reason in the context of 'fragmentation' discussion, without checking if such 'fragmentation' has actually arisen in the recent past.[177] This aspect will be illustrated later, in the empirical part of this book (Chaps. 4–6).

Similarly to Simma, also Eikema-Hommes suggests that a crucial contingent aspect to bear in mind when analysing the concept of 'unity' of international law is that in a multiplicity of legal rules, *the necessity of systematic interpretation and of unity in adjudication is of the essence for the general principle of legal unity*.[178] From this perspective, it will be analysed in the empirical part of this book the *coherence* in adjudication (approaches to treaty interpretation) of three different courts (at micro- and macro-levels, as explained in the introduction of the book). These courts, despite the differences they present in the *context*, *object and purpose*, *subsequent practice* and *parties participating in this practice*, as well as *travaux preparatoires* of

[174] *Id*, p. 279 (emphasis added).

[175] *Id*.

[176] Finnis (1992), p. 153. What keeps a legal system to be legally in shape, as Finnis claims, is the Rule of Law, which involves 'certain qualities of process which can be systematically secured only by institutions of judicial authority ... and its exercise by persons professionally equipped and motivated to act according to law'.

[177] Prost and Clark (2006).

[178] Van Eikema Hommes (1978), p. 43.

the treaties they are called to adjudicate, employ the same general rules of interpretation as basis for interpreting their treaties. More specifically, it will be analysed comparatively *how* the ICJ, ECtHR and WTO employ *the general rules of treaty interpretation* (prior to and post the 1969 VCLT's adoption periods) when dealing with similar difficulties in interpreting the text of treaties. This analysis will then be able to show whether these courts' treaty interpretative practices may constitute a tool either for unifying (keeping the *coherence* and *unity* of) international law or for fragmenting international law.

## 2.3.2 *Implications of the Proliferation of Judicial Bodies: The 'Fragmentation' Issue*

### 2.3.2.1 Defining 'Fragmentation'

Since the international society continuously diversifies, it urges international law to cover almost every field of human activity (political, social, economic, scientific or technical), diversifying itself as well (Simma 2009, p. 271). This alleged 'fragmentation' of the international society has become a source of concern for many scholars and lawyers preoccupied to identify in what forms this phenomenon manifests *vis-à-vis* general international law. However, the 'fragmentation' phenomenon, seen sometimes as a split of international law into highly 'specialised boxes' that claim relative autonomy from each other and from general law, can be analysed from a wide range of perspectives (McInerney-Lankford 2012, p. 610). Or, in other words, both *fragmentation* and *unity* are matters of 'narrative perspective' (Koskenniemi 2007, p. 25).

Thus, when analysing the 'fragmentation' of international law, what is seen as diversification reflected in a continuous emergence of new fields, legal regimes or rules can appear from one angle as a chaotic image, but from another angle it may appear as a complex reflection of a deeper unity.[179] Koskenniemi, for example, sees this diversification from the latter perspective when he perceives, in principle, international law not in danger to be fragmented. According to him, 'fragmentation' is 'after all, the result of a *conscious* challenge to the unacceptable features of that general law and the powers of the institutions that apply it'.[180] For this reason, there will be no conflicts and hierarchy between the various regimes (i.e., between trade and human rights) because there is no 'nation state' or 'meta-rationality' to allocate to each of the regimes its respective place.[181] From the latter perspective, however, Crawford observes that the root of fragmentation of international law is to be found in international law system itself. He sees 'fragmentation' as 'the product of a

[179]Koskenniemi (2007), p. 25.

[180]*Id*, p. 19.

[181]*Id*, p. 23.

system of laws that, by and large, lacks a sense of vertical integration, of hierarchy' (Crawford 2014, p. 211).

Furthermore, we should also consider that, while many interpretations of the terminology exist in respect of 'fragmentation', two of them are generally admitted as a potential threat for international law (Rayfuse 2005, pp. 688–689). One such interpretation of 'fragmentation' is *substantive*, relating to the matter of consistency and continuity in the development and application of legal principles, while the other is *procedural*, relating to the matter of the availability and appropriateness of the dispute settlement forums.[182] Despite the fact that these types of fragmentation are distinct in many respects, according to Rayfuse they are interrelated in the sense that a 'choice of a forum may have implications for the characterization of a dispute and *vice-versa*, which in turn have implications for the substantive resolution of the dispute'.[183]

Finally, an important and broad perspective of understanding the 'fragmentation' issue is provided by the ILC Study Group in 2006. This Study considers 'fragmentation' as reflecting the rapid expansion of international legal activity into various new specialised fields, each of them generating new technical and functional requirements, its own principles and its own form of expertise (ILC 2006, pp. 11–14). Based on an ample study on diversification and expansion of international law, the Study finds three types of 'fragmentation': (1) through conflicting interpretations of general law, (2) through the emergence of special law as an exception to the general law and (3) through conflict between different types of special laws.[184] Nevertheless, since multiplication of international judicial bodies and diversification of international law imply risks as building up conflicting jurisprudence, the emergence of 'self-contained' regimes, forum shopping or loss of legal security that could lead to the erosion of coherent and consistent legal rules of international law,[185] further discussion with a focus on these aspects is needed. This discussion is important as it provides the theoretical basis to respond to the question of this book: how specialised adjudicative forums such as the ECtHR and WTO apply general international law in their specific context, respectively how their treaty interpretation practices contribute to keeping the unity of international law or, otherwise, to fragmenting it. Before proceeding in more detail with an analysis of the risks of 'fragmentation', a brief review of the main theories regarding the fragmentation of international law will be provided.

---

[182]Rayfuse (2005), pp. 688–689.

[183]*Id.*

[184]ILC (2006), p. 15.

[185]*Id*, p. 11.

#### 2.3.2.2 Theories That Advocate a Restrained Fear for 'Fragmentation of International Law'

Since states and other members of the international community have now a greater range of third-party dispute settlement forums than had before to resolve their disputes, this aspect has raised the concern that the proliferation of such forums will lead to the *fragmentation of international law* or, at least, to *the fragmentation of the interpretation of its norms* (Dupuy 1998, p. 792). According to the ILC Report Study's findings, some critics of the multiplication of settlement forums in international law have seen in the 'fragmentation' phenomenon an erosion of general international law, the emergence of conflicting jurisprudence, forum shopping and loss of legal security.[186] Nevertheless, other scholars considered that the 'fragmentation' issue is merely a technical problem that has naturally emerged with the increase of international legal activity (ILC 2006, p. 11). So if this is a natural phenomenon, as the ILC underlines, then 'fragmentation' could not be considered a 'danger' for international law as to affect its coherency.[187] And this can be so because in dealing with conflicts between legal rules and principles, there are techniques in the traditional law that can be used and adapted to particular conflicts.[188] In this regard, a different study conducted by the Netherlands Yearbook of International Law in 1995, which focuses on the 'secondary rules' within special regimes, has reached an optimistic result (Wellens 1994, p.28). This study has concluded that as far as the 'secondary rules' are concerned within special regimes (such as is the diplomatic law, law of war, human rights law, environmental law, GATT/WTO law, space law and European Community law), they have been applied in a way that promoted and guaranteed at the same time 'the growing effectiveness of their own particular set of primary rules, without putting in jeopardy the unity or coherence of the international legal order'.[189]

Commenting on the issues surrounding the 'fragmentation' phenomenon underlined in the ILC Study, authors such as Spelliscy justly see that only a preservation of a consistent and continuous body of international law, of certain core norms as a minimum on which states can rely, would warrant the legitimacy of the international judicial system (Spelliscy 2001, pp. 151–152). Thus, it could be said that a uniform interpretation and application of the general international law works against its fragmentation. In the same vein, the former judge of the ICTY, Abi-Saab, rightly assumes that the unity of the interpretation of law and the cohesion of international law as a system could only be maintained if the judges of specialised tribunals are always mindful of the functioning of 'the overarching principles' that sustain international law's normative edifice and keep it together

[186]Dupuy (1998), p. 792.

[187]ILC (2006), p. 15.

[188]*Id.*

[189] Wellens (1994), p.28. (emphasis added).

and also if they keep a proper balance among their holdings (Abi-Saab 1998, p. 926).

Similarly to Abi-Saab, or to Charney before him, Rao observes that some international law judges share the opinion that the ICJ could play a pivotal role in this effort by earning a status of primus inter pares, which would be followed 'not out of legal compulsion, but through *recognition of and deference to its intrinsic authority and the quality of its legal reasoning and findings*' (Rao 2003, p. 929). On this latter aspect, Dupuy too agrees that states, as well as the new specialised judicial bodies, need guidance from the ICJ in interpreting the *substance and scope of the basic principles of international law* as the number of international jurisdictions increase (Dupuy 1998, p. 807). However, in relation to how basic principles of international law can be preserved (even without a direct 'intervention' from the ICJ), a useful assumption derived from the idea underlined by Finnis in his *Natural Theory of Law* is, according to Han, that since international law is fluid in nature, then some divergences in narrow interpretations are acceptable as long as the core values are respected and not disputed (Han 2006, p. 119). Han assumes that 'some fragmentation and uncertainty resulting from a decentralised and proliferated system may not greatly hurt states' respect for international law'.[190]

A further nuance into the discussion of fragmentation in international law is added by Koskenniemi and Leino, who observe that the core of this issue consists 'not so much in the emergence of the sub-systems but in the use of general law by new bodies representing interests or views that are not identical with those represented in old ones' (Koskenniemi and Leino 2002, p. 561). These authors assume that the problems that arise as a result of the multiplication of judicial bodies can be regarded 'as effects of politics and not as technical mistakes or unfortunate side-effects of some global logic'.[191] Thus, excessive worries over 'fragmentation' are not warranted because 'fragmentation' could be seen as expression of political pluralism in the international field.[192] In expanding this point, Koskenniemi and Leino assume that if a human rights body (e.g., IACHR or ECtHR) or a WTO panel applies the 1969 VCLT when interpreting the relevant treaties or reinforcing that body's jurisdiction and as result it deviates from the standard of treaty interpretation, then 'this is bound to weaken the authority of that standard of interpretation and to buttress the interests or objectives represented by the human rights body or the WTO panel'.[193] This issue constitutes a main theme of exploration of this book, which will be further examined in detail, in the empirical part (Chaps. 5 and 6).

---

[190]Han (2006), p. 119.

[191]Koskenniemi and Leino (2002), p. 561. For more on this view, see, e.g., Benvenisti and Downs (2007).

[192]*Id*, p. 553. Koskenniemi and Leino bring further cultural arguments to this context, but such arguments are not necessary to be discussed since they are outside the scope of an introduction to 'fragmentation'.

[193]*Id*, pp. 561–562.

To sum up this discussion, it could therefore be said that the notion of 'fragmentation' could have many interpretations and assumptions depending on the angle from which this issue is approached. Or, as better put by Koskenniemi and Leino, while 'fragmentation' is seen in international law as new, diversification, specialisation, challenging accustomed ways of thinking and organising the world, the problem of *fragmentation* and *coherence* remains, actually, in 'the eye of the beholder'.[194]

### 2.3.3 'Fragmentation': Viewed as a Problem

Irrespective of the influential views of those considering multiplication of international judicial bodies as a desirable phenomenon, the assumption expressed in the scholarship that the mere emergence of new judicial bodies could lead automatically to *fragmentation* of *international law* appears to be a strong one. Similarly strong appears the interrelated assumption that, eventually, such result would prejudice the basic *unity* of the international legal order. Accordingly, the 'fragmentation of international law' as a cause of conflicts between normative systems has become one of the major concerns among public international lawyers and the subject of an ongoing debate. In this regard, the ILC stresses that a number of conflicts between legal regimes and enforcement machineries, between Charter rules and other rules, between immunity and human rights, between environment and trade, between law of the sea and new fisheries treaties are likely to occur.[195] According to the ILC Report's findings, the cause of such potential conflicts could be seen in the fact that 'specialised law-making and institution-building tends to take place with relative ignorance of legislative and institutional activities in the adjoining fields and of the general principles and practices of international law' (ILC 2006, p. 11). This process, moreover, could have as possible results 'conflicts between rules or rule-systems', 'deviating institutional practices' and 'the loss of an overall perspective on the law'.[196]

---

[194]*Id.*

[195]Report of International Law Commission, Fifty-fifth session, Supplement No. 10 (A/58/10), 2003, p. 17. This study is of great importance in the process of understanding the fragmentation of international law phenomenon, by analysing the difficulties arising from the diversification and expansion of international law. Further, the ILC focused on the 'Function and scope of the *lex specialis* rule and the question of "self-contained regimes"' (2004). The Study Group found of significant importance to their analysis: 'The Interpretation of Treaties in the light of any relevant rules of international law applicable in relations between parties' (article 31(3)(c) of the Vienna Convention on the Law of Treaties); 'the modification of multilateral treaties between certain of the parties only (article 41 of the Vienna Convention on the Law of the Treaties) as well as the final report on "Hierarchy in International Law: *jus cogens*, obligations *erga omnes*, Article 103 of the Charter of the United Nations as conflict rules"'. This is a report of the Study Group produced in the course of 4 years of work (2003–2006).

[196]ILC (2006), p. 11.

Prior to this ILC Study, Charney had also expressed concern in respect of 'deviating institutional practices', although he advocated the view that the major divergences between specialised courts and tribunals in applying general international law are not a serious cause of alarm (Charney 1998a, p. 700). He referred to the potential confusion that might derive from those interpretations of international law (e.g., rules of treaty interpretation, customary law, principles of international law) by various courts and tribunals, which could diverge fundamentally from the current international law doctrine.[197] In order to avoid this from happening, Charney considered the ICJ's pronouncements on questions of general international law as particularly significant.[198] He admitted, however, that significant variations in (general) international law, caused by specialised courts and tribunals in the absence of a centralised authority and the power and independence of judicial entities, could lead to a narrowing in the scope and role of international law.[199]

From a different angle, in a recent study on the 'fragmentation' topic, Martineau sees 'fragmentation' as a play between *unity* and *diversity*, a matter of 'political interpretation', a 'powerful rhetoric' or a disagreement among lawyers who assess international law differently, a disagreement that in fact existed in each period of the development of international law. In Martineau's opinion, a supporter of the 'old' unity of international law sees 'fragmentation' as a threat to such 'unity'.[200] For example, the former ICJ president, Judge Guillaume, expresses his concern that 'specialised courts are inclined to favour their own disciplines' (Guillaume 2000). Although Guillaume has pronounced in favour of proliferation of judicial forums, as he himself put it that '[t]he international community needs courts' and that '[t]he proliferation of courts should be a source of enrichment, not of anarchy', he actually has averted 'the danger of fragmentation in law', recommending the use of *the ICJ's advisory opinions* to avoid it, as also crucially important: *the creation of a dialogue*

[197] Charney (1998a), p. 700.

[198] *Id*, p. 134. For example, Charney illustrates variations in approaches on particular areas of international law (which are observed by the author not as discontinuities or radical deviations from the traditional international law doctrine), less resolved or explored at the following courts: the Court of Justice of European Union, which had numerous opportunities to apply general principles of international law, and on other occasions it has identified novel general principles, which however may have limited value, not creating incoherence with the substance of general principles of law; at the *Iran-United States Claims* Tribunal, which had the occasion to explore two areas of contemporary international law in greater depth than other tribunals (i.e. compensation for takings and dual nationality), but the tribunal adhered to the body of substantive international law; at the European Court of Human Rights the determination that territorial reservation to the Court's jurisdiction in the *Loizidou* case (1995) was considered severable, since Turkey' s consent to the compulsory jurisdiction was validated by the ECtHR. To the question whether the ECtHR applied a different approach in matter of 'territorial reservation', deviating from the jurisprudence of the ICJ on this matter, Charney notes that the ICJ had not clearly elucidated this issue, for the ECtHR to be consistent with.

[199] *Id*.

[200] Martineau (2009), p. 3.

*among judicial bodies.*[201] However, when analysing these concerns, Koskenniemi and Leino emphasise that such statements of presidents of the ICJ might be seen as 'defensive moves in a changing political climate, which further other interests than those of traditional principles of diplomatic law represented by the ICJ' (Koskenniemi and Leino 2002, p. 562). These authors explain by analogy that if 'specialised courts are inclined to favour their own disciplines', it should also be valid to the ICJ.[202] And indeed, if a president of a court suggests that other courts should request advisory opinions from his court, this appears just as an effort to ensure the preservation of his institution at the top of the hierarchy.[203]

Since one of the main risks posed by the increasing multiplication of international judicial bodies is 'forum shopping' and its related 'overlapping jurisdictions', which is thought to be leading to the fragmentation of international law, a further discussion on this topic is needed.

## 2.3.4 *Is 'Fragmentation' Imminent?*

### 2.3.4.1 Forum Shopping

Among the risks posed by the increasing multiplication of international judicial bodies that may lead to 'fragmentation', 'forum shopping' has been perceived in the scholarship as the most salient. 'Forum shopping' is seen as the situation when litigants have alternative forums that permit them to choose the most suitable one to proceed with their dispute. It is considered as one of the most serious disadvantages to international law as each judicial forum could issue multiple interpretations on the same legal issue. As observed by Linton and Tiba, some authors consider that in choosing the most 'appropriate' forum, the parties are guided by factors such as the favourability of the applicable law of the forum to their case, tactical considerations of the particular judicial system that might give parties an advantage over the other side, considerations of access to the court or tribunal, the procedural rules or the court's composition (Linton and Tiba 2009, p. 407).

Some legal theorists and practitioners perceive 'forum shopping' as posing a serious problem for international law, while others take this concern as exaggerated. From a practitioner's perspective, Judge Guillaume, for example, sees 'forum shopping' in a more negative light, as a 'way for applicant States to seek out those courts which they believe, rightly or wrongly, to be more amenable to their arguments' (Guillaume 2000). He considers that 'forum shopping' generates unwanted confusion as it 'can distort the operation of justice, which should not

[201] Guillaume (2000).

[202] Koskenniemi and Leino (2002), p. 562.

[203] *Id.*

be made subject to the law of the marketplace'.[204] Also, Judge Oda, as a scholar and negotiator of the Law of the Sea Convention, is less enthusiastic about the positive aspect of 'forum shopping'. He refers, for example, to the creation of the International Tribunal for the Law of the Sea (ITLOS), which in his view would prove to be a big mistake because it would constitute a second court with overlapping jurisdiction in parallel with the ICJ, which has a long tradition as the principal organ of the United Nations and a solid history of dealing with law of the sea disputes (Charney et al. 2002, p. 371).

Other scholars, although not denying the risks of 'forum shopping', see those risks as being limited. For example, Charney observes that by taking into account the consent requirements and limitations on the ability of different types of legal actors to appear before different tribunals, 'forum shopping' may have a limited risk.[205] By responding to Judge Oda's opinion in respect of the ITLOS, Charney claims that which forum the disputants prefer may actually show an indication about what forums the parties believe are most suitable in providing the most acceptable rules of law.[206] As other authors admit, the risk of 'forum shopping' is attenuated, moreover, because governments have facilitated the creation of forum selection agreements by means of international agreements on the allocation of jurisdiction (Petersmann 2006, p. 273). So given such agreements, the judicial bodies tend in general to show an increasing respect for the selection of the forum by the parties that seek a solution to their disputes.[207] In addition, many authors claim that there are rules and principles of international law that may prevent and manage the issue of engaging multiple institutions on the same dispute,[208] such as the principles known as *electa una* via,[209] *lis alibi pendens*[210] and *res judicata*.[211] However, 'forum shopping' is seen as having negative implications upon the unity of international law, eventually leading to 'fragmentation', due to the fact that the overwhelming majority of the forums exercise a 'compulsory jurisdiction' so that litigation is triggered only unilaterally (Romano 2006, p. 792).

---

[204]Guillaume (2000). The author states that overlapping jurisdiction also exacerbates the risk of conflicting judgments, as a given issue may be submitted to two courts at the same time, and they may hand down inconsistent judgments.

[205]Charney et al. (2002), p. 371.

[206]*Id.* See for an illustration of this point, e.g., The *Southern Bluefin Tuna* case (Australia and New Zealand/Japan), (Jurisdiction and admissibility constituted under annex VII of the United Nations Convention on the Law of the Sea) Award of 4 August 2000.

[207]Petersmann (2006), p. 273.

[208]Linton and Tiba (2009), p. 407.

[209]*Electa una* via, *non datur recursus ad alteram*, is translated by the legal dictionary as 'When there is concurrence of means, he who has chosen one cannot have recourse to another' (10 Toull. n. 170).

[210]Called *litispendence*—when two courts were to hear the same dispute, it is possible they would reach inconsistent decisions.

[211]Principle of finality—when there has been issued a final judgment upon a dispute, and it is no longer subject to appeal.

As one of the few scholars who approached this topic in more depth, Romano observes the negative implication of 'forum shopping' for international adjudicative bodies, claiming that such bodies 'are activated not only frequently and unilaterally but often simultaneously or serially to litigate essentially the same disputes'.[212] This argument does not go without contentions. From the perspective that each judicial forum could issue multiple interpretations on the same legal issue, according to Brown, some scholars remind us that from the mere fact that different international courts and tribunals could reach different decisions, we cannot draw the inference that international law is being 'fragmented' (Brown 2002, p. 463). Brown informs us further that such scholars suggest that when speaking of 'fragmentation', attention should be paid to the fact that *'fragmentation' only occurs if the same rule is applied differently* and not if a rule that may be *lex specialis* just differs from another rule.[213] However, since 'forum shopping' is not the final issue related to 'fragmentation of international law' addressed in the scholarship, for a more rounded perspective on the risks of 'fragmentation', other aspects that concern the substantive issues will be next addressed.

### 2.3.4.2 Is the Fear of 'Fragmentation' Really Justified?

As shown above, the possible/potential *institutional conflicts* are only one aspect resulting from the proliferation of international judicial bodies analysed in the scholarship. Other aspects, concerning *the substantive* issues that might occur in the context of the 'proliferation' phenomenon, also have received attention in the academic literature. Such substantive issues are, for example, those related to conflict of norms and conflict of interpretations, emergence of special law as an exception to the general law, conflicts between different types of special law and 'self-contained regimes'. Although an extended analysis of all these issues

[212]Romano (2006), p. 798. See more on this point, e.g., Romano (2001)—for a discussion on the *Southern Bluefin Tuna* case (*Australia and New Zealand/Japan*), (Jurisdiction and admissibility constituted under annex VII of the United Nations Convention on the Law of the Sea) Award of 4 August 2000. In short, the applicants had a choice of judicial *fora* to initiate proceedings: before an ad hoc Arbitral tribunal constituted under Article 16 of the 1993 Convention; before the ICJ; or before the dispute settlement procedures of the UNCLOS. *Southern Bluefin Tuna* is an unprecedented instance of deviation from what has been in the past seemed a fundamental principle of the privacy of arbitration proceedings. Also *Chile – Measures Affecting the Transit and Importation of Swordfish* (*European–Community v. Chile*), WT/DS183/1, 19 April 2000. This case is considered in the literature as likely to make history, for the reason that it is an exception to the traditional custom of resorting to arbitration only by mutual agreement, and because it is one of the first cases after UNCLOS's entry into force in which the parties could made a choice of forum on the same dispute matter. Or, t*he MOX Plant* case (*Ireland. v. United Kingdom*), Request for Provisional Measures, 41 I.L.M.405, ITLOS, Case No. 10, Order of Dec. 3, 2001. This case shows a situation that involved three different international adjudicative bodies seized by Ireland, and thus three different institutional procedures.

[213]Brown (2002), p. 463.

discussed in the scholarship is beyond the purpose of this study, the next two sections will try to succinctly capture some of the most important aspects of the scholarly debate on these themes. This analysis will complement the theoretical framework of 'fragmentation' provided earlier in this chapter, which constitutes the basis for assessing the ways in which the ECtHR and WTO perform the application of the same general rules of treaty interpretation in their specialised contexts, respectively whether 'fragmentation' at these specialised courts really occurs from the perspective of treaty interpretation (Chaps. 5 and 6).

#### 2.3.4.2.1 Lex Generalis/Lex Specialis

The ideas related to *lex specialis* appear in the scholarship in the context of 'fragmentation' discussion and are often used for evaluating the activity of interpretation of treaties performed by international courts. In this context, the core issue of 'fragmentation' is generally perceived in the scholarship in relation to *the use of general law by new bodies representing interests or views that are not identical with those represented in old ones* (Koskenniemi and Leino 2002, p. 560). By splitting up the law into 'highly specialised 'boxes' that claim relative autonomy from each other and from the general law,'[214] questions are imposed such as: what are the substantive effects of such specialisation, and how should the relationship between such 'boxes' be conceived (Michaels and Paulwelyn 2011, p. 237)? According to the ILC Study Report, this claimed relative autonomy of specialised bodies sometimes leads to conflicts between special sets of rules and the general law, as well as between different sets of specialised rules.[215]

However, the ILC Study Report provides important key findings on the issue of substantive 'fragmentation', which solve the apparent paradoxes resulting from the uses of *lex specialis* in the interpretation of general (international) law by new international bodies, underlined by the scholars fearing the multiplication of international bodies. The ILC Study solves these paradoxes by considering the interpretative techniques/tools around the *lex specialis/lex generalis* (as a more specific

---

[214]ILC (2006), pp. 12–13.

[215]*Id*, p. 614. The ILC Study gives examples of conflict of norms such as *lex specialis* and *lex generalis* in *The Legality of the Threat or Use of Nuclear Weapons*, Advisory opinion, ICJ Reports 1996, where the ICJ had to decide between different set of rules, and none of these could fully extinguish the other. The Court held that human rights law continued to apply within armed conflict. Humanitarian law as *lex specialis* did not suggest that human rights to be abolished. Also, in t*he Case Concerning Gabcikovo-Nagymaros Project* (*Hungary v. Slovakia*), ICJ Report, 1977, the Court considered the 1977 Treaty (as *lex specialis*) on a superior position, which led to the Court's setting aside other treaty and general law. Or, when conflict exists between *lex specialis norms*, such as in *European Communities-Measures Concerning Meat and meat Products (Hormones)* (*United States v. European Communities*), WT/DS26/AB. WT/DS48/AB/R, 13 February 1998. In this case the Appellate Body of the WTO concluded that whatever the status of the principle 'under international environmental law', it had not been binding upon the WTO. The ILC points out that 'environmental law' and 'trade law' might be governed by different principles.

norm regulates the matter more efficiently) utilised by various international judicial bodies. These interpretative techniques are considered by the authors of the ILC Study as crucially important for the examination of both positive and negative consequences of the possible fragmentation of international law.[216] As a tool used in the context of 'fragmentation' discussion, the *lex specialis* is also thought by other authors to be better able to accommodate particular circumstances while providing a comparison and connection between 'traditional' international law and the 'new' sub-systems of international law (Simma and Pulkowski 2006).

Furthermore, in applying international law, the ILC Study Group Report on the fragmentation of international law finds that it is often necessary to determine the precise relation between two or more rules and principles (norms) that are both valid and applicable to a given situation (ILC 2006, p. 408). For this purpose, the Study divides this relationship into two: one relating to *interpretation*, where one norm assists in the interpretation of another norm, and the other relating to *conflict*, where two norms that are both valid and applicable point to incompatible decisions, so that a choice between them must be made.[217] Most importantly, this ILC Study develops the idea that in the resolution of normative conflicts as between two or more norms, the basic rules are to be found in the 1969 VCLT.[218] In particular, the relationship of norms 'should be interpreted in accordance with or analogously to the VCLT and especially the provisions of its Articles 31-33 having to do with the interpretation of treaties'.[219]

The ILC Study recognises the principle *lex specialis derogat lex generalis* as an accepted technique of interpretation and conflict resolution in international law.[220] According to the Study's findings, this principle suggests that 'whenever two or more norms deal with the same subject matter, priority should be given to the norm that is more specific'.[221] This principle could be clearly illustrated, for example, in the ICJ's judgment in the *North Sea Continental Shelf* cases (1969),[222] where the Court held that 'it is well understood that, in practice, rules of [general] international law can, by agreement, be derogated from in particular cases or as between particular parties'.[223] Noteworthy is that, in accordance with the principle of

[216]See, e.g., ILC (2006), p. 614; Simma (2009), p. 275.

[217]ILC (2006), p. 408.

[218]*Id.*

[219]*Id.*

[220]*Id.*

[221]*Id.*

[222]*North Sea Continental Shelf* (*Federal Republic of Germany/Denmark*; *Federal Republic of Germany/Netherland*), ICJ Reports, 1969, p. 42, para 72.

[223]ILC (2006), p. 45. See also *Military and Paramilitary Activities in and against Nicaragua* (*Nicaragua v. United States of America*), Merits, ICJ Reports 1986, p. 137, para 274. The ICJ held in *Nicaragua* that: '[i]n general, treaty rules being *lex specialis*, it would not be appropriate that a State should bring a claim based on a customary rule if it has by treaty already provided means for settlement of such a claim'. Or, in *Amoco International Finance Corporation v. Iran* (*Amoco v. Iran*), Iran–US CTR., vol. 15, 1987-II, p. 222—where the US Claims Tribunal held that, despite

harmonisation,[224] the ILC Study suggests that *lex generalis* (general law) continues to give direction for the interpretation and application of the relevant *lex specialis* (special law), filling the gaps when a matter is not regulated by *lex specialis*; *lex specialis* is silent on situations not provided by it; or in case of failure of special regimes, when a special law has no reasonable prospect of appropriately addressing their intended objectives.[225] To test whether a rule is seen as an 'application', 'modification' or 'exception' to another rule, as the ILC points out, it depends on how those rules are viewed in the context in which they are applied, considering their object and scope.[226] Although priority is given to the norm that is more specific when two or more norms deal with the same matter, *jus cogens* is admitted as being expressly non-derogable since its content is universally accepted as superior to other rules.[227]

More recently, an interesting view that captures well the relation between *lex specialis*/*lex generalis* in international law is offered by Michaels and Pauwelyn. Rather than addressing the ontological question of whether international law is a 'system', these authors proceed to examine the adequacy of different sets of rules for different types of conflicts of public international law (Michaels and Paulwelyn 2011, p. 375). If the distinction between *lex specialis* and *lex generalis* makes more sense in municipal law, as these authors assume, it becomes more complicated and problematic in the international law arena.[228] And this is so because conflicts of norms emerge between branches (or sub-systems) of international law, respectively between general international law and these branches (sub-systems), and also within one branch.[229] From the perspective of international law's fragmentation, Michaels and Pauwelyn claim that the most pressing problems are provided by conflicts between sub-systems or branches of international law—the inter-systemic type of conflicts (e.g., as between trade and environment, financial and human rights, etc)—since each sub-system claims to have its own specific body of norms and no hierarchy between them exists.[230] Given this, the *lex posterior*

---

recognising *lex specialis* the Treaty as superseding the *lex specialis*, 'the rules of customary law may be useful in order to fill in possible lacunae of the Treaty . . .'.

[224]Under Article 31(3)(c) of the Vienna Convention on the Law of Treaties, which will be discussed in the next chapter.

[225]ILC (2006), pp. 408–409. According to the ILC, the principle of harmonisation 'is a generally accepted principle that when several norms bear on a single issue they should, to the extent possible, be interpreted as to rise to a single set of compatible obligations'.

[226]*Id*, p. 53. The ILC Study identifies four different situations of *lex specialis*' operationalisation: (a) within a single instrument; (b) between two different instruments; (c) between a treaty and a non–treaty standard; and (d) between two non-treaty standards.

[227]ILC Conclusions (2006), para 32.

[228]Michaels and Paulwelyn (2011), p. 375.

[229]*Id*, p. 368 (The authors identified the inter-systemic type of conflicts, as between UN and EC treaties, EC law and ECHR, UNCLOS and WTO).

[230]*Id*, p. 357.

rule[231] does not work between sub-systems or branches (e.g., interactions between UN and EC treaties, EC law and ECHR, UNCLOS and WTO).[232] The assumption is that when regulating a specific area, a lawmaker wants to create special rules that trump the general rules in the field so that 'the latest/or more specific legislative expression matters and prevails'.[233] Since each of the branches has its own rules dealing with conflicts that often differ, Michaels and Pauwelyn consider that there is little point in trying to define the *lex specialis*.[234] For example, in the interaction between trade agreements and environmental agreements, from the perspective of trade agreements, the trade rule will be more specific, and from the environmental viewpoint, the environmental rule will be consequently more specific.[235] Arguably, an implication of Michaels and Pauwelyn's argument is that, even if we characterise, for example, human rights as *lex specialis*, there could be no reason why the application of human rights norms by a human rights court should be similar to the application of human rights by an international economic court. If this is the case, then, on what basis is there to decide that a treaty or specific norm is 'more specific'?[236] Or which rules work best for different contexts ('conflict of norms' or 'conflict of laws')?[237] These are key questions that Michaels and Pauwelyn are attempting to respond to in their argument dealing with the *unity* of international law *vis-à-vis* the 'fragmentation' issue. A good solution to attenuate conflicts between sub-systems (e.g., trade and human rights), and thus to reduce the risks of 'fragmentation' or anarchy in international law, could be, as the authors suggest, a rational balancing that courts and tribunals can consider more.[238] And this rational balancing should imply an application and good coordination of the intra-systemic conflict rules that could be developed from private international law rules such as *lex superior*, *lex specialis*, *lex posterior*, notably, whichever regime is more appropriate to be applied to the particular fact pattern (the proper law).[239]

---

[231]*Id*, p. 354.

[232]*Id*, p. 336.

[233]*Id*. The authors mention, i.e., GATT Article XXIV which provides that trade agreements such as NAFTA are subject to certain GATT principle, setting up the GATT as *lex superior*, and on the other side, Article 103 of NAFTA states that in the event of conflict between GATT and NAFTA, NAFTA prevails.

[234]*Id*, p. 367.

[235]*Id*.

[236]*Id*, p. 366.

[237]*Id*, p. 363. (the authors refer to 'conflict of laws'- as conflict between legal systems).

[238]*Id*.

[239]*Id*, p. 368. As the authors interestingly propose, this rational balancing could be attained on the basis of connecting factors (as in the international private law), pointing towards one branch of international law rather than the other.

However, if the ILC's view is to be admitted, notably that the international legal system, as a dynamic system,[240] is fragmented into technical 'regimes' (e.g., environmental, human rights, criminal, trade laws) and that this fragmentation is not so different from what could be termed 'traditional fragmentation' into more or less autonomous territorial regimes (called 'national legal systems'), then the techniques existent in the traditional law must be considered useful and could be adapted to solve particular conflicts (between legal rules and principles) when dealing with regimes or sub-systems in the international arena.[241] To sum up this discussion, it could be stated that while *lex specialis* may be used to apply, clarify, update or modify, as well as set aside general law, nevertheless, general law will remain valid and applicable with regard to any special regime.[242] Thus, general (international) law continues to give directions for the interpretation and application of the relevant special law and will become fully applicable in situations not provided for the special law (*lex specialis*).[243]

Nonetheless, since the ECtHR and WTO specialised adjudicative bodies are often seen as promoters of 'self-contained' regimes (human rights law and, respectively, trade law as sub-systems of international law system), a general discussion on what is a 'self-contained' regime is further necessary. In this scope, it is helpful to place the concept of 'self-contained regime' into a broader perspective offered by the views on 'fragmentation' and then on this basis to assess further, in the empirical part of this work, whether the practice of the ECtHR and WTO on treaty interpretation might contribute to the unification of international law or, conversely, to the fragmentation of it, as some scholars have claimed.[244]

##### 2.3.4.2.2 'Self-Contained' Regime Versus *Lex Generalis*

When debating the issue of fragmentation of international law, special attention is reserved in the scholarship to the so-called 'self-contained regime' concept. This concept could be useful when attempting to determine whether the process of 'fragmentation' really happens, in particular for the situations when a strong form of *lex specialis* could exclude the application of general international law, as is thought by some scholars in respect of the ECtHR and WTO international specialised bodies.

The concept of a 'self-contained' international regime has become the subject of debate among scholars, especially when such a regime is seen as an entirely autonomous legal sub-system. According to Simma and Pulkowski, the controversial character of the discussion addressing the alleged self-containment of legal

[240] ILC Conclusion (2006), para 21.

[241] ILC (2006), p. 15.

[242] *Id*, para 9.

[243] *Id*.

[244] See for example authors mentioned in Sect. 2.3, part II of this chapter.

sub-systems is, actually, due to the lack of uniform terminology around it.[245] These authors claim that the various levels of autonomy have been associated with the notion of 'self-contained regimes', especially since the *Tehran Hostages* case.[246] Relying on Article 55 of the ILC Report in explaining what is actually a 'self-contained' regime, Simma and Pulkowski observe that a 'strong' form of *lex specialis* may be designed to exclude completely, for example, the application of the general international law of state responsibility, either by explicit provision or by implication, on the ground that it is by virtue of a regime's particular structure or of its object and purpose.[247] However, a 'weak' form of *lex specialis* is thought to be able to only modify the general regime on a specific point.[248] According to the ILC Report, Article 55 of the Draft Articles on Responsibility of States for Internationally Wrongful Acts (2001), which reflects the maxim *lex specialis derogat lex generalis*, is designed to cover 'both "strong" forms of *lex specialis*, including what are often referred to as self-contained regimes, as well as a "weaker" form'.[249] The *Tadic* case (1996) at the ICTY, for example, illustrates well this explanation, as it recalls one of the meanings of the term 'fragmentation', referring to the division of international law into 'regional or functional regimes with special interests and ethos' (ILC 2006, p. 11). The *Tadic* case is considered in the scholarship as a deviation from the 'effective control' test used by the ICJ in the *Nicaragua* case (1986) (Teitel and Howse 2008, p. 5). In principle, *Tadic* is thought as an 'obvious and dramatic flashpoint for "fragmentation" anxiety, concerning tribunalization', since the Appellate Chamber rejected the ICJ's interpretation of certain rules of state responsibility.[250] As it was observed in this case, the ICTY

---

[245]Simma and Pulkowski (2006), p. 491. The authors state in this regard: 'Social system cannot exist in splendid isolation from their environment. This point is conceded even by ardent proponents of regime specialization. According to Niklas Luhann's System theory, for example, all systems are to some extend interlinked by structural coupling. Similarly, legal subsystems coexisting in isolation from the remaining bulk of international law are inconceivable.'

[246]*Id.* The authors refer to the '*Tehran Hostages*' *case* (United States Diplomatic and Consular Staff in Tehran), ICJ Reports (1980). The ICJ ruled in this case that the 'diplomatic law constitutes a self-contained regime'.

[247]*Id.*

[248]*Id.*

[249]Draft Articles on Responsibility of States for Internationally Wrongful Acts (2001, p. 140, paras 2 and 5). The ILC admits that Article 55 constitutes an important indication (although it is one of a number of possible approaches) for 'determining which of several rules potentially applicable is to prevail or whether the rules simply coexist'. Article 55 (Lex specialis) provides:

> These articles do not apply where and to the extent that the conditions for the existence of an internationally wrongful act or the content or implementation of the international responsibility of a State are governed by special rules of international law.

[250]Teitel and Howse (2008), p. 5. See also on this case discussion: ILC (2006), p. 31. Examining the judgment in *Nicaragua* (ICJ, 1986), the ICTY held in *Tadic* that the 'effective control' was a too high threshold for holding an outside power legally responsible for domestic unrest. For the ICTY, it was sufficient that the power had 'a role in organizing, coordinating, or planning the military actions of the military group, so that the power exercised "overall control" over the military for the conflict to be an "international conflict"'.

alluded to itself as being a 'self-contained' regime in the international law system when holding that:

> International law, because it lacks a centralised structure, does not provide for an integrated judicial system operating an orderly division of labour among a number of tribunals, where certain aspects as a power could be centralized or vested in one of them but not the others. In international law, every tribunal is a self-contained system.[251]

However, relying on case studies the ILC has found three somewhat different ways in which the term 'self-contained regimes' was used by the courts. This ILC Study refers to two 'strong forms' of *lex specialis* in the PCIJ's judgment of the *S.S. Wimbledon* (1923) case,[252] which coined for the first time the term 'self-contained regime', and to another one, in the ICJ's judgment of the *Hostages* (1980) case.[253] In the *Wimbledon* case, the ICJ applied the concept of 'self-contained' regime to solve a question of treaty interpretation concerning the relation between two sets of primary international obligations (Simma and Pulkowski 2006, p. 491). In this case, the Court was confronted with the question of whether the provisions of the Treaty of Versailles relating generally to German waterways also applied to the Kiel Canal.[254] Thus, at issue was the determination of the status of the Kiel Canal, which was covered by both general law on internal waterways and special rules on the Canal as laid down in the 1919 Treaty of Versailles. In this regard, the ILC Study Report makes clear that the PCIJ could not mean more by 'self-contained' expression in the *Wimbledon* case than simply that, in order to interpret certain expressions in a treaty, it was unnecessary to refer to external sources.[255]

In the more recent *Teheran Hostages* case (1980), the ICJ interpreted the concept of 'self-contained regime' in reference to diplomatic law, seen at the level of secondary norms, and as a subcategory of *lex specialis* within the law of state responsibility (claiming primacy to the general rules concerning consequences of a violation).[256] The ICJ argued in this case that the regime of specific legal consequences contained in the *1961 Vienna Convention on Diplomatic Relations* was a self-contained regime *vis-à-vis* the customary international law of state responsibility.[257] The Court held that in the event of violation of the Vienna Convention, no resort may be had to any remedies provided for by general international law since 'diplomatic law by itself provides necessary means of defense against, and sanction for, illicit activities by members of diplomatic or consular missions'.[258] However, the definition of 'self-

---

[251] *Id* (in the *Prosecutor v. Tadic* case (Jurisdiction), 1996, 35 ILM 32, p. 39).

[252] *S.S. Wimbledon*, PCIJ, Ser. A, No. 1, 1923, p. 23.

[253] ILC (2006), p. 31. See the *'Tehran Hostages'* case (1980), p. 38.

[254] *S.S. Wimbledon* (1923). The Court held in 'S.S. *Wimbledon*' that: 'The provisions relating to the Kiel Canal in the Treaty of Versailles are therefore self-contained; if they had to be supplemented and interpreted by the aid of those referring to the navigable waterways of Germany in the previous Section of Part II, they would lose their "*raison d'etre*"...'.

[255] ILC (2006), p. 67.

[256] *Id*, pp. 66–68.

[257] *Id*.

[258] *Tehran Hostages* (1980).

contained regime' given by the Court in *Tehran Hostages*, as one commentator observes, is far from being exhaustive as it is discussed only in the context of 'state responsibility', where the Court demanded a narrow interpretation.[259] Nevertheless, there is a perception among scholars that since the decision in *Tehran Hostages*, the notion of 'self-contained' regime has been specifically related to the 'completeness of a subsystem's secondary rules', and thus it refers to those regimes that 'embrace a full exhaustive and definitive set of secondary rules' (Pulkowski 2005, p. 12).

Further, according to the ILC Study, the notion of 'self-contained' regime has an even broader connotation than those mentioned above. It is sometimes attributed to whole fields of functional specialisation or teleological orientation, which are thought to modify rules of general international law, deviate from these rules (through their interpretative guidance and direction) or even exclude them in their administration.[260] Such fields are 'human rights law', 'WTO law', 'European law/EU law', 'humanitarian law', 'space law',[261] all regarded in the scholarship and practice as (special) 'branches of international law', having their own (special) rules/principles, institutions, teleology and techniques of interpretation and administration (Koskenniemi and Leino 2002, p. 571).

Considered more controversial than others, the WTO is, for example, examined in the ILC Study as a 'self-contained' regime from the perspective provided by Article 23 of the Dispute Settlement Understanding (of the WTO Agreement). This article excludes unilateral determinations of breach or countermeasures outside the 'specific subsystem' of the WTO regime (ILC 2006, p. 71). The same Study observes that the academic debate is divided with respect to the extent to which the WTO law is a 'self-contained' regime, when it comes to reception of law from other special regimes, such as environmental law, or non-WTO treaties into its trade context.[262] A conflict between different types of special law, for example between 'trade law' and 'environmental law', illustrated in the controversial *Beef Hormones* case (1998) at the WTO, can suggest that these two different regimes might be governed by different principles, and hence they could be seen as 'self-contained' (ILC 2006, p. 34). The Appellate Body in this case held that, while the so-called precautionary principle might have been 'crystallized into a general principle of customary environmental law', it was not clear whether this principle had become a part of general customary law.[263] Thus, the WTO Body did not admit the

---

[259]Runersten (2008), p. 12. See also for this argument ILC (2006), p. 289. The ILC points out that States were entitled to set up self-contained regimes on State responsibility, but such regimes, actually, have never been considered as to form 'closed legal circuits'.

[260]ILC (2006), pp. 68–70. For example, the ILC quoting Simma (1985), pp. 115–116, notes that *subsystems* are seen as self-contained when, for example, intent to 'exclude more or less totally the application of general legal consequences of wrongful acts, in particular the application of the counter measures normally at the disposal of an injured party'.

[261]*Id*. See also on this point Koskenniemi and Leino (2002).

[262]*Id*, p. 88.

[263]*Id*, pp. 47–48, paras 123–125.

'precautionary principle' as binding for the WTO Agreements.[264] However, the ILC Study acknowledges that the WTO adjudicative bodies (panels and the Appellate Body) have resorted to international customary law and general principles very widely—a view that is not shared by some scholars.[265]

Although the WTO is considered a coherent body of procedural and substantive laws, there are tensions between those who praise the achievements of this regime and those who criticise it. Thus, while some scholars see the WTO as an innovative dispute settlement mechanism in general, others point, particularly, only to the consequences of interpretation of particular agreements (McRae 2004, p. 3). For example, on matters related to 'remedies', the Appellate Body is criticised because, sometimes, it exceeds its interpretative function by creating new rights or imposing new obligations on Member parties, contrary to Article 3(2) of the DSU (of the WTO Agreement).[266] Moreover, the fact that the WTO dispute settlement system perpetuates the WTO law by a constant reference to its system's previous decisions, as observed by Pulkowsky, it has lead scholars to see the WTO as a strong 'self-contained' regime (Pulkowski 2005, pp. 10–11). However, as this author justly concludes, the WTO's effectiveness in becoming a strong 'self-contained regime' is impeded by its partial incompleteness since there are areas in the WTO law (such as treaty interpretation, burden of proof or rules that assist the panellists in administering the substantive provisions of the WTO law) that compel the WTO dispute settlement body to refer to 'rules and principles developed under international law'.[267] Some critics also see the WTO settlement body as a forum where countries complain before it purely for political purposes.[268] However, other authors consider that, with all strengths and weaknesses, the WTO settlement body should be analysed in the light of the role it plays in the contemporary international society (McRae 2004, p. 3). In the context of proliferation of international dispute settlement forums, the WTO settlement mechanism is thought to be a judicial body designed to interpret a specialised field: trade law. It exists among other specialised bodies and has a limited jurisdiction. Thus, given the specificity of the disputes brought before the WTO settlement body, and the challenges those disputes imply, much of the jurisprudence of other international dispute settlement forums are irrelevant for the WTO.[269] Looking from another angle, the fragmentation of the

[264]*Id.*

[265]*Id*, p. 88. The ILC notes that this difference in view derives from the fact that, while the public international law is based on state sovereignty, the WTO trade law derives its 'justification' from the theory of comparative advantage. From this perspective, the ILC proposes the 'self-contained' regime notion to be replaced with 'special regime'.

[266]*Id.*

[267]*Id*, p. 10.

[268]Kaufman (2011), p. 253. See also for the same argument Cho (2006).

[269]McRae (2004), p. 3. McRae argues that due to the procedures of the Appellate Body such as 'burden of proof', 'judicial economy' and 'completing the analysis', which were not based on procedural law development in other existing tribunals, there is no risk of overlapping jurisdiction of the WTO dispute settlement body and of other courts and tribunals.

WTO regime itself is thought likely to happen due to the loss of centrality of this system for international trading, as a result of proliferation of Regional Trade Agreements as *modus operandi* for trade liberalisation (Leal-Arcas 2010, p. 597). So the question that imposes in this regard is whether the proliferation of such Regional Trade Agreements complements the liberalisation of trade or is an obstacle for further multilateral trade liberalisation.[270] An argument expressed in the scholarship is that the WTO could become fragmented in the absence of the equilibrium between *multilateralism* and *regionalism*, established in 1940 under the GATT (Cho 2006, p. 39).

However, the ILC Study observes, in principle, that the notion of 'self-contained' regime is simply misleading since no special system (sub-system) or regime could fully be isolated from general international law.[271] Thus, an exclusion of general international law by special regimes 'could not be even conceptually possible', considering that even though states are entitled to establish 'self-contained' regimes that have priority over general rules, they 'cannot even as between themselves, provide for legal consequences of a breach of their mutual obligations which could authorize acts contrary to peremptory norms of general international law'.[272] A powerful statement in this regard was made recently by the ICJ in its *Jurisdictional Immunities* case (2012), outlining the primacy of customary international law.[273] Having to clarify an issue relating to state immunity, the ICJ held in this case: '[i]t is of course axiomatic that the material of customary international law is to be looked for primarily in the actual practice and *opinio juris* of States, even though multilateral conventions may have an important role to play in recording and defining rules deriving from custom, or indeed in developing them'.[274] Thus, the Court made clear in this case that 'any entitlement to immunity can be derived *only from customary international law, rather than the treaty*'.[275]

Furthermore, in a recent study on human rights law and its relation to general international law (GIL), Sheeran observes that, generally, the ICJ and other tribunals, including the ECtHR, admit that serious violations of international human rights law (IHRL) and international humanitarian law 'do not override state immunity' (Sheeran 2014, p. 90) and that the ECtHR even held in a series of cases that rules of human rights will be 'subservient to principles of GIL – such as immunity

[270]Leal-Arcas (2010), p. 597.

[271]ILC (2006), p. 82.

[272]*Id*, p. 81 (emphasis added). The ILC's observance based on the commentary on Article 55, relating to Draft Articles on State Responsibility (2001), p. 375, para 2. See on this point also Third Report on State Responsibility (1991), p. 26, paras 85–86. In particular, according to the Special Rapporteur, Arangio-Ruiz, the question which arises when speaking of so called 'self-contained' regimes, is 'whether the existence of remedies, sometimes more advanced- for which they make specific provision- affects to any degree the possibility for legal recourse by States parties to the measures provided for, or otherwise lawful, under general international law'.

[273]*Jurisdictional Immunities of the State (Germany v. Italy)*, Judgment of 3 February 2012, ICJ.

[274]*Id*, pp. 27–28, para 55.

[275]*Id*, p. 27, para 54 (emphasis added).

and jurisdiction'.[276] Relying on the ECtHR's practice, Sheeran concludes that the basic relationship of general international law (GIL) and international human rights law 'is conceived as one of *unity*'.[277] However, in Sheeran's view, this unity 'does not resolve inherent tension between GIL and IHRL' as this tension derives from 'distinct conceptual bases and origins, and different "object and purpose"' that these bodies of law have.[278] And such tension is reflected in the relation between *human rights rules* and *secondary rules of general international law*, which are part of the normative environment of the human rights law.[279] *Secondary rules* provided by general international law are, for example, those on the matter of 'jurisdiction' and 'state immunity', which according to Sheeran, operate as 'a constraint on the enjoyment of various human rights (e.g. right to a remedy, access to courts, implementing the prohibition against torture)'.[280]

Concerning the *European Convention of the Human Rights*, the ILC firmly admits that this Convention 'has not been conceived as a self-contained regime' in the sense that it would prevent the importation of general international law into its special context.[281] Moreover, the ILC makes clear that '[t]here was no *a priori* assumption that the rules of the Convention would override those of general law'.[282] For example, the ECtHR holds in the pair of cases *Behrami and Behrami v. France* and *Saramati v. France, Germany and Norway* (2007)[283] that the Court 'must also take into account relevant rules of international law when examining questions concerning jurisdiction and, consequently, determine State responsibility in conformity and harmony with *the governing principles of international law* of which [the European Convention on Human Rights] forms a part, although it must remain mindful of the Convention's special character as a human rights treaty'.[284]

Similarly to the ILC, Simma and Pulkowski suggest that the concept of 'self-contained regime' should not be used to circumscribe 'the hypostudy of a fully

[276]Sheeran (2014), p. 90 ('GIL'—general international law; 'IHRL'—international human rights law). The author refers, e.g., to the *Bankovic*, *Al Adsani*, *Fogarty*, *McElhinney* cases.

[277]*Id*, p. 82 (emphasis added).

[278]*Id*. According to Sheeran, a tension also exists within other international bodies of law.

[279]*Id*.

[280]*Id*. See, for example, *Neumeister v. Austria* (ECtHR), Series A, No. 17, 1975, at paras 28, 30, 31) mentioned by the ILC (2006) in its comments on (*lex specialis*) Article 55 of Report on Draft Articles on Responsibility of States for Internationally Wrongful Acts (2001). The ECtHR stated in *Neumeister* that *lex specialis* did not prevail over *lex generalis* in regard to that particular (human right) provision related to compensation. In the Court's words: 'the European Convention of Human Rights for compensation for unlawful arrest or detention did not prevail over the more general provision for compensation in article 50. In the Court's view, to have applied the *lex specialis* principle to article 5, para 5, would have led to "consequences incompatible with the aim and object of the Convention".'

[281]ILC (2006), p. 87.

[282]*Id*, p. 86.

[283]*Behrami and Behrami v. France* and *Saramati v. France, Germany and Norway* (App. Nos. 71412/01 and 78,166/01), ECHR, Decision on May 2007.

[284]*Id*, para 122 (emphasis added).

autonomous legal subsystem' (or 'closed legal circuit') and that even the Court of Justice of the European Union (CJEU) (which is seen, more than other regimes, as functioning in 'isolation') has asserted that principles of general international law are applicable residually within the context of the EU law (Simma and Pulkowski 2006, p. 483). Moreover, it is a widely shared view that specialised regimes appear in general to be more deferential to the ICJ on general international law matters than when dealing with rules relatively unique to their regimes.[285] However, exceptions from this deferential path appear to occur especially due to the *specific object and purpose* that each special regime claims. In fact, as correctly the ILC points out, the degree to which a regime is admitted as 'self-contained' is 'predominantly a *matter of interpreting* the treaties that form the regime'.[286] For instance, the European law's development into a 'self-contained regime' is thought to be due to the interpretative activity of the Court of Justice of the European Union (CJEU), not always performed with the full support of all Member States. Analogously in respect of the human rights law, such development into a 'self-contained regime' is thought to be due, for example, to the matters related to the treatment by human rights bodies of 'reservations' to the ECtHR's jurisdiction.[287] An illustration in human rights law is provided, for instance, by the *Belilos v. Switzerland* case (1988),[288] when the ECtHR concluded that the 'declaration' at issue was a 'reservation'; thus, the Court applied to the 'declaration' the rules relating to 'reservations', giving therefore no effect to the respective 'declaration'.[289] A similar illustration is provided in the *Loizidou v. Turkey* case (1995), where the ECtHR stated that the normal rules of reservations to treaties (thus under general international law) did not apply to human rights law.[290] On matters of 'jurisdiction' and 'state responsibility', such an illustration can be seen in the *Ilascu v. Moldova and Russia* case (2004),[291] where the ECtHR found that the actions of non-state actors (of Russia) in another territory can be attributed to a state, which is considered to have jurisdiction over such actors, thus having extraterritorial obligations under the European Court of Human Rights. In this case, the ECtHR applied the test of state control for attribution purposes differently from the 'effective control' test

---

[285]See discussion on this topic, e.g., Charney (1998a, b), Sheeran (2014).

[286]ILC (2006), p. 85 (emphasis added).

[287]*Id*, p. 84. See also on this point, e.g., Higgins (2007). According to Higgins, the opinions that human rights bodies or the Human Rights Committee depart from general rules in respect of 'reservations' are merely aberrations.

[288]*Belilos v. Switzerland,* Judgment of 29 April 1988, ECHR, Series A, Vol. 132. The ECtHR had to examine whether an 'interpretative declaration' constituted a 'reservation' in the meaning provided by the VCLT.

[289]*Id*, p. 33. See also the opinion of Charney (1998a, b) on this case and, also, in the *Loizidou* case (Loizidou v. Turkey), Preliminary Objections, Judgment of 23 March 1995, ECHR, Series A (1995) No. 310, p. 29, para 67. In brief, the ECtHR stated in *Loizidou* that the normal rules of reservations to treaties (thus under general international law) did not apply to human rights law.

[290]*Loizidou* (1995). See this case discussed in Chap. 5 of this book.

[291]*Ilascu v. Moldova and Russia* (App.No. 48787/99), ECHR, Judgment of 8 July, 2004.

established by the ICJ in the *Nicaragua* case (1986).[292] Similarly to the *Ilascu v. Moldova* case at the ECtHR, in the *Velasquez Rodriguez* case,[293] the Inter-American Court of Human Rights (IACtHR) held that a state is obliged to take measures and to control, regulate, investigate and prosecute actions by non-state actors that violate the human rights of those within the territory of that state.[294] It is noteworthy that the work of the Inter-American system is admitted to have a considerable influence on the work of domestic courts in the OAS Member States on matters of impunity and accountability (Tittemore 2005, p. 249). And indeed, the Inter-Amerian Court of Human Rights (IACtHR) has demonstrated a close relationship with the European Court of Human Rights (ECtHR),[295] and also with the African Court of Human Rights (ACHR).[296] The evidence shows that the IACtHR referred to the ECtHR in more than a half of all its decisions.[297] However, according to Charney's observation based on the analysis of the various specialised judicial bodies' approaches, such interpretative divergences from general international law and from the standards settled upon by the ICJ's jurisprudence are 'grounded upon the specific regimes under which the tribunal must operate, rather than upon a decision to reject the general international law pronounced by the ICJ'.[298] Similarly, Kamminga points out in respect of international human rights law that there are different types of obligations assumed by states for the protection

---

[292]*Id*, para 394. The ECtHR did not require in this case a high degree of control, thus not territorial or 'effective control', nor even 'overall control' to find Russia responsible. It finds that the actions of non-State actors (of Russia) in another territory can be attributed to a State, which is considered to have jurisdiction over such actors, having thus extraterritorial obligations under the ECHR.

[293]*Velasquez Rodriguez v. Honduras*, IACtHR, Judgment of 29 July 1989, Series C No. 4, 28 ILM 291.

[294]*Id*, paras 172–176.

[295]Blome (2010), p. 14. This relationship was confirmed by the former president of the Inter-American Commission, Paolo Carozza (Carozza 2009: 50th anniversary of the ECHR), in his statement:

> The historical influences have, not surprisingly, flowed primarily westwards from Europe across the Atlantic (. . .). For instance the Inter-American Commission . . . was consciously inspired by and the new defunct European Commission (. . .) Turning to the substantive law, the influence of Europe on the norms and jurisprudence of the Inter-American Human Rights System, are multiple. Same view is shared by Judge Trindade, or, also, Judge Tulkens, who stated that: "international human rights law in the twenty first century is a complex network of overlapping systems of law".

[296]African Court on Human and Peoples' Rights (AfCHPR) (available at: http://www.african-court.org/en/index.php/partners/2012-03-09-15-11-49/european-court-of-human-rights-and-inter-american-court-of-human-rights). The AfCHPR and IACtHR have now together a Memorandum of understanding and guide for their collaboration. The AfCHPR also collaborates with the ECtHR, having exchange of staff, information and general collaboration.

[297]Blome (2010), p. 14. The author observes that from a total of 213 decisions and judgments as of July 2010, the IACtHR showed 132 references to the European system of human rights. However, the IACtHR is searching its own path and aspires to equal participation in an emerging international human rights system.

[298]Charney (1998b), p. 142.

of human rights and that this special law, sometimes, adopts different approaches from the general application of various subject matters in international law (e.g., reservations, state responsibility, jurisdiction) because of its different scope and purpose.[299] Nevertheless, such a change, for example, in the understanding of the obligations of individuals for which 'state responsibility' extends within international human rights law sheds more light on the general understanding and application in special context of the obligations of state responsibility (their extent and nature).[300] According to Kamminga, by developing a range of interpretations, practices and principles on matters of general international law, directly or indirectly, international human rights law, however, influences other areas of international law (Kamminga 2008, pp. 253–254). Moreover, such developments should be perceived, as jusly admitted by Sheeran, as 'reactions to general international law's shortcomings in achieving the "object and purpose" of human rights' (Sheeran 2014, p. 94). And most importantly, such developments should be seen as *part of the changing structure of international law* and *not as 'deviations' from international law*.[301]

Despite the fact that 'special regimes' could be seen as 'self-contained' due to their own rules and procedures, the ILC's conclusion is that such regimes are not outside the framework of general international law.[302] It then appears doubtful that a complete isolation of an international regime can even be possible, as one commentator expresses, since such 'isolation' can receive legally binding force (validity): 'only by reference to valid and binding rules or principles outside of it'.[303] Furthermore, the lack of centralisation does not necessarily mean that different legal regimes have to conflict with one another or that they cannot deal with such conflicts.[304] For example, in a recent analysis of the practice of the ICJ, Ghandhi concludes that both the PCIJ and its successor, the ICJ, for its part, have played a crucial role in the development of the international protection of human rights, generally on issues that arose in the context of general international law and non-human-rights-specific treaties or provisions.[305] An interesting illustration of

---

[299]Kamminga (2008), p. 245. See Kamminga's analysis on 'state responsibility' at the ECtHR taken comparatively with 'state responsibility' notion analysed at the ICJ.

[300]*Id*, p. 252. Kamminga cites in this support, e.g., *LaGrand* (Germany v. United States of America), Merits, Judgment of 27 June, 2001, ICJ Reports 466.

[301]Sheeran (2014), p. 94. According to the author, there are three areas in which human rights law impacted positively general international law and its rules on states responsibility: development of positive obligations; the law of attribution; and reparations and remedies.

[302]Koskenniemi (2004), para 134. In brief, the ILC admits (at p. 85) the compliance, in general, of treaty bodies in human rights (such as the European and Inter-American Courts), and also in trade (WTO panels and the Appellate Body) with rules and principles of general international law (relating to, i.e., treaty interpretation, statehood, jurisdiction, immunity, as well as a wide variety of principles of procedural propriety).

[303]Khrebtukova (2008), p. 51.

[304]Fry (2007), p. 77.

[305]Ghandhi (2011), pp. 527–528. The author mentions the ICJ's contribution to international law of human rights on fields such as genocide, race discrimination, self-determination, immunities of experts, consular access, belligerent occupation, nuclear weapons, and diplomatic protection. See

the ICJ dealing with human rights issues is the recent *Case Concerning Ahmadou Sadio Diallo* (2010), where the Court stated that '[t]here is no doubt, moreover, that the prohibition of inhuman or degrading treatment is among the rules of general international law which are binding on States under all circumstances, even apart from any commitments'.[306] In this case, the ICJ appealed to the consistent jurisprudence of the ECtHR and IACtHR to support the interpretation of the provisions at issue of both the African Convention of Human Rights and African Charter.[307] This jurisprudence showed that there is no impediment to individuals to have *locus standi* or *jus standi* also before the World Court.[308]

Furthermore, according to Judge Higgins, *human rights* are now routinely addressed in the ICJ's judgments, and they are even at the centre of the work of the ICJ and not at its margin (Higgins 2007, p. 746). Just a few recent examples in this area can reveal a clear interaction between regimes at the ICJ, respectively between international human rights law and general law, as well as their impact on one another.[309] Such an example is the Advisory Opinion on the *Palestine Wall* case (2004), where the ICJ dealt with the nature of positive obligations under international human rights law and considered that Israel had obligations under the human rights instruments (the ICCPR, ICESCR and CRC) in relation to the occupied territories (Kamminga 2008). In this case, the ICJ took into account both branches of international law: human rights law and humanitarian law (Higgins 2007, p. 750). It held that the *International Covenant on Civil and Political Rights* (ICCPR) was 'applicable in respect of acts done by a State in the exercise of its jurisdiction outside its own territory',[310] and thus the wall must be immediately dismantled and Israel kept responsible for any damages to Palestinian property.[311] As pointed out in the scholarship, even if in *Palestine Wall* the ICJ treated one body of law as *lex specialis*, notably, international humanitarian law and human rights law as the predominant law in the case, it preferred to decline to treat *lex specialis* as a 'self-contained' regime and applied it in the broader context of *international*

---

for example the Advisory Opinion on the *Reservations to the Convention on the Prevention and Punishment of the Crime of Genocide*, Advisory Opinion, I.C.J., Advisory Opinion, 1951 I.C.J. 15), *Polish Upper Silesia* case *(Germany v. Poland)*, PCIJ, Rep. Series A No. 7, 1926.

306 *Case Concerning Ahmadou Sadio Diallo (Republic of Guinea v. Democratic Republic of Congo)*, Case 103, Judgment 30 November 2010, para 86.

307 *Id.*

308 Ghandhi (2011), p. 538. The author notes that the *Diallo* case was essentially a human rights case, and the first time in the history of the ICJ, the Court decided a case on the basis on an international human rights treaty, a regional human rights treaty, in addition to the relevant provision of the Vienna Convention on Consular Relations, also belonging to the domain of the international protection of human rights.

309 Also, it is to be reminded the PCIJ/ICJ's earliest practice in dealing with human rights issues, when there were no rooms in international instruments for human rights, as it will be illustrated inter alia in Chap. 4 of this book.

310 *Legal Consequences of the Construction of a wall in the Occupied Palestinian Territory*, Advisory Opinion of 9 July 2004, ICJ Reports 136, paras 107–113.

311 *Id.*

*law* as a whole.[312] This view was later adopted by the ICJ in the *Congo v. Uganda* case (2005), when it made clear that '[i]nternational human rights instruments are applicable in respect of acts done by a State in the exercise of its jurisdiction *outside its own territory*, particularly *in occupied territories*' (of the Democratic Republic of Congo).[313] Moreover, the Court stated in this case that Uganda could be kept responsible not only for its omissions in that region but also for any lack of vigilance in preventing violations (Higgins 2007, p. 750). That a state must have positive obligations, both *territorially* and *extraterritorially*, has been extended further by the ICJ in the recent *Genocide* case (2007).[314] Despite the fact that the ICJ firmly rejected in this case any test of control in terms of attribution to a state (Serbia) under the international law of state responsibility beyond the 'effective control' test,[315] it did decide that Serbia breached its positive obligation to prevent the genocide.[316] It can be assumed that these approaches point directly to the ICJ's consideration for the general *principle of legal unity* in its adjudicative process.

Unlike in regard to the human rights matter, the ICJ's jurisdictional relation with trade matter is much less, international trade disputes being hardly ever decided by the PCIJ and ICJ, though few economic and investment disputes were submitted to the ICJ (Petersmann 2006, p. 273). On the other hand, there is an increasing reference in the jurisprudence of human rights treaty bodies and trade bodies in the WTO to the ICJ's jurisprudence (Rosalyn Higgins 2007, p. 48). This aspect will be treated in great deal in the empirical part of this book from the perspective of treaty interpretation.

Although still rare in practice, there is also an interplay and checks and balance between human rights and trade in international law.[317] Arguably, as fundamental rights warrant in many ways support for freedom of economic players, or protection of these players from undue government intervention, human rights therefore are in interplay with the trade field.[318] An interplay exists also between trade field (the GATT/WTO) and other fields of international law, such as the Law of the Sea

[312]El Sheemy (2007), p. 5. See also *The Legality of the Threat of Use of Nuclear Weapons*, Advisory Opinion (1996), ICJ Reports 226.

[313]*Democratic Republic of the Congo v. Uganda*, Judgments of 19 December 2005, ICJ Reports 168, para 216 (emphasis added).

[314]*Application of the Convention on the Prevention and Punishment of the Crime of Genocide (Bosnia and Herzegovina v. Serbia and Montenegro)*, Judgment of 26 February 2007, ICJ Reports, para 430. The ICJ held that the Serbian Government was under a duty to 'employ all means reasonably available to them, so as to prevent genocide so far as possible'.

[315]Did not find Serbia having 'effective control' of the Bosnian-Serb paramilitary forces.

[316]See on this point Kamminga (2008), p. 249.

[317]Cottier et al. (2005), p. 5.

[318]*Id.* In this respect the authors mention the *Hertel v. Switzerland*, 59/1997/843/1049, ECtHR Judgment of 25 August 1998. This case explores the relation between unfair competition and the importance of free speech and freedom of information as a means to secure symmetry of market information, thus the functioning market economy.

Convention, which includes explicit reference to GATT rules,[319] and vice-versa, the LOS Convention rules may be relevant for the interpretation of various WTO exceptions.[320] Furthermore, the WTO rules are invoked occasionally and are applied, for example, by the Court of Justice of the European Union, North American Free Trade Agreement, European Free Trade Association, the Andean, Caribbean and Central American Courts of Justice, Permanent Review Court of the Mercosur, Economic Court of the Commonwealth of Independent States or various regional economic courts in Africa.[321]

In summary, the practice of courts and tribunals shows that there is nothing to stop any interaction between regimes to borrow from each other's decisions when they face difficulties in the decision-making process, although there are risks of incompatibility with the most relevant law for them (Fry 2007). Therefore, since there is no such hermetic regimes isolated from international law and none of the supposedly 'self-contained' regimes seems to materialise *in concreto*,[322] neither would the *fragmentation of international law* really occur or materialise *in concreto*.

## 2.4 Conclusions

The idea that proliferation of international judicial bodies does not pose a serious risk for fragmenting international law is best captured in Koskenniemi and Pavi's assertion that 'based on the information available at this time a serious problem does not appear to exist'[323] and that 'alternative forums complement the work of the ICJ and strengthen the system of international law, notwithstanding some loss of uniformity'.[324] However, as it could be drawn from this chapter's discussion, since the risks posed by the 'proliferation' phenomenon are perceived as such in theory and practice, and such risks constitute an argument supporting 'fragmentation', they cannot be ignored but further subjected to investigation. So since the multiplication of international judicial bodies appears to be an unstoppable and unavoidable phenomenon, implying risks for fragmentation of international law, questions

[319]This reference is to be found in: the Annex Relating To The Implementation Of Part XI of the Convention (UNCLOS), in Section 6 concerning Production Policy, which provides at '(b) The provisions of the General Agreement on Tariffs and Trade, its relevant codes and successor or superseding agreements shall apply with respect to activities in the Area'.

[320]Petersmann (2006), p. 273. The author notes that since 1990, an increasing number of new worldwide courts have been established, each having jurisdiction that overlap or interact with the WTO jurisdiction. However, he asserts that jurisdictional clashes among courts and tribunals and judicial challenges to the WTO jurisdiction have been avoided so far.

[321]*Id.*

[322]See ILC (2006), p. 79. The ILC citing Arangio-Ruiz, who concludes that there is no such hermetically regimes isolated from international law.

[323]Koskenniemi and Leino (2002), p. 575.

[324]*Id.*

may persist such as what types of 'fragmentation' could affect most severely the coherence and unity of international law? Is this fear for 'fragmentation' objectively justified? Or is 'fragmentation' just a powerful rhetoric, a matter of political interpretation/s?[325] If international law is really fragmenting, then what are the most important means through which fragmentation could be 'controlled' and therefore impeded? What is/are the regime/s most likely to contribute to fragmentation in international law? Also, at what levels, or on what matters/areas, is international law (more) susceptible of fragmentation, knowing, for example, that *treaty interpretation* at specialised regimes remains a key problem for the proponents of universalistic approach, namely, 'how far does specialty of the special treaty extent?'[326]

Yet answers to such questions are important as they can show the fate of *public international law* and international legal order. Answering it is important because upon an *international law* with coherency and integrity, which once a handful of enlightened men struggled to set up on a stone base (e.g., the League of Nations, the U.N. Charter) in reaction to wars and inhuman atrocities, depends primarily and ultimately a peaceful, healthy world community. Since many more questions could arise from the issue of 'proliferation' of international forums, and one of its major implications—'fragmentation of international law'—questions to which one such work could not fully respond, the present work will address only specific issues on this topic. Thus, the following chapters will attempt to answer the main question of this work: whether the practice of two specialised international forums, the ECtHR and WTO on treaty interpretation, presents similar features with the practice on treaty interpretation of the ICJ (since the ICJ is regarded as the guardian of international law), or these specialised adjudicative bodies differ fundamentally in respect of their approach to the general rules of treaty interpretation (codified in the 1969 VCLT), and what the implications of such findings are *vis-à-vis* the coherence and unity of international law. The conclusions provided in the empirical part of this book will then be able to confirm or refute the idea that 'fragmentation' of international law is occurring at these forums, and thus what the impact is of the specialised treaty interpretative practices of the ECtHR and WTO on international law. In order to respond to this question, a doctrinal discussion on *treaty interpretation* is first needed.

## References

Abi-Saab, G. (1998). Fragmentation or unification: Some concluding remarks. *New York University Journal of International Law and Politics, 31*, 919.

Arangio-Ruiz, G. (1991). *Third report on state responsibility*. United Nations, General Assembly.

Austin, J. (1995). In W. E. Rumble (Ed.), *The province of jurisprudence determined*. Cambridge, England: Cambridge University Press.

[325]See on this question Martineau (2009).

[326]Pulkowski (2005), p. 3 (emphasis added).

Basch, F. F. (2007). Doctrine of the Inter-American Court of Human Rights regarding States' duty to punish human rights violations and its dangers. *American University International Law Review, 23*, 195.

Bassiouni, M. C. (1996). International crimes: jus cogens and obligatio erga omnes. *Law & Contemporary Problems, 59*, 63.

Baudenbacher, C. (2003). Foreword: Globalization of the judiciary. *Texas International Law Journal, 38*, 397.

Benvenisti, E., & Downs, G. W. (2007). The empire's new clothes: Political economy and the fragmentation of international law. *Stanford Law Review, 60*, 595–631.

Blome, K. (2010). Wallflower or essential constituent? The Inter-American Court of Human Rights' role in an emerging International Judicial Human Rights System. In *SGIR 7th, Pan European international relations conference*.

Brierly, J. L. (1955). *The law of nations: An introduction to the international law of peace*. Oxford, England: Clarendon Press.

Brown, C. (2002). The proliferation of international courts and tribunals: Finding your way through the maze. *Melbourne Journal of International Law, 3*, 453.

Buergenthal, T. (2001). Proliferation of international courts and tribunals: Is it good or bad? *Leiden Journal of International Law, 14*(2), 267–275.

Carozza, P. (2009, January). *Fifty years of the European Court of Human Rights viewed by its fellows international courts, Strasbourg*. Retrieved from http://www.echr.coe.int/NR/rdonlyres/3B662702-FFDB-4187-AAC56B926725DF35/0/30012009PresidentCarozzaSeminar_eng_.pdf

Casanovas, O., & La Rosa, O. C. (2001). *Unity and pluralism in public international law* (Vol. 39). The Hague, The Netherlands: Martinus Nijhoff Publishers.

Charney, J. I. (1998a). The impact on the international legal system of the growth of international courts and tribunals. *New York University Journal of International Law and Politics, 31*, 697.

Charney, J. I. (1998b). *Is international law threatened by multiple international tribunals?* Dordrecht, The Netherlands: Martinus Nijhoff Publishers.

Charney, J. I., Bilder, R. B., Oxman, B. H., & Wald, P. M. (2002, March). The "horizontal" growth of international courts and tribunals: challenges or opportunities? In *Proceedings of the Annual Meeting* (pp. 369–380). Washington, DC: American Society of International Law.

Cho, S. (2006). Defragmenting world trade. *Northwestern Journal of International Law & Business, 27*, 39.

Ciobanu, D. (1991). *Introducere in Studiul Dreptului* [Introduction in the study of law]. Bucuresti: Ed. Hyperion XXI.

Cottier, T., Pauwelyn, J., & Bürgi, E. (2005). Linking trade regulation and human rights in international law: An overview. In T. Cottier, J. Pauwelyn, & E. Bürgi (Eds.), *Human rights and international trade* (p. 1). Oxford, England: Oxford University Press.

Crawford, J. (2014). *Chance, order, change: The course of international law, general course on public international law*. Leiden, The Netherlands: Brill.

Curran, V. G. (2001). Fear of formalism: Indications from the fascist period in France and Germany of judicial methodology's impact on substantive law. *Cornell International Law Journal, 35*, 101.

Detter, I. (1994). *The international legal order*. Aldershot, England: Dartmouth.

Dupuy, P. M. (1998). Danger of fragmentation or unification of the international legal system and the International Court of Justice. *New York University Journal of International Law and Politics, 31*, 791.

Dupuy, P. M. (2007). Unity of application of international law at the global level and the responsibility of judges. *European Journal of Legal Studies, 1*, 29.

Dworkin, R. (2013). A new philosophy for international law. *Philosophy & Public Affairs, 41*(1), 2–30.

Eikema Hommes, H. J. (1978). *Legal order and legal principles*. 1978 Working paper. Retrieved May 5, 2011, from http://biblio.juridicas.unam.mx/libros/1/468/5.pdf

El Sheemy, S. (2007). International law-making, problems of coherence and fragmentation, a summary of the Chatham House International Law discussion group meeting held on 23 March 2007, Chatham House. *Independent thinking on international affairs*. Retrieved from https://www.chathamhouse.org/sites/files/chathamhouse/public/Research/International%20Law/il230307.pdf

Finnis, J. (1992). Natural law theory. In R. P. George (Ed.), *Contemporary essays*. Oxford, England: Clarendon Press.

Fry, J. D. (2007). International human rights law in investment arbitration: Evidence of international law's unity. *Duke Journal of Comparative & International Law, 18*, 77.

Ghandhi, S. (2011). Human rights and the International Court of Justice: The Ahmadou Sadio Diallo case. *Human Rights Law Review, 11*(3), 527–555.

Guillaume, G. (2000, October 27). *The proliferation of international judicial bodies: The outlook for the international legal order*. Speech by his excellency Judge Gilbert Guillaume, President of the International Court of Justice, to the Sixth Committee of the General Assembly of the United Nations.

Han, S. W. D. (2006). Decentralized proliferation of international judicial bodies. *Journal of Transnational Law & Policy, 16*, 101.

Hart, H.L.A., Raz, J., & Bulloch, P.A. (1994). *The concept of law*. 2nd ed. with a Postcript. Oxford, England: Oxford University Press.

Higgins, R. (2007). Human rights in the International Court of Justice. *Leiden Journal of International Law, 20*(4), 745–751.

Hoof, G. J. (1983). *Rethinking the sources of international law*. Deventer, The Netherlands: Kluwer.

Hossain, K. (2005). Concept of Jus Cogens and the obligation under the UN charter. *Santa Clara Journal of International Law, 3*, i.

Jacobs, F. G. (2003). Judicial dialogue and the cross-fertilization of legal systems: The European Court of Justice. *Texas International Law Journal, 38*, 547.

Janis, M. W. (1999). *An introduction to international law*. Gaithersburg, MD: Aspen Publishers.

Janis, M. W. (2010). *America and the law of nations 1776–1939*. Oxford, England: Oxford University Press on Demand.

Kammerhofer, J. (2004). Uncertainty in the formal sources of international law: Customary international law and some of its problems. *European Journal of International Law, 15*(3), 523–553.

Kamminga, M. T. (June 1 2008). *Final Report on the impact of international human rights law on general international law*. Report of the 73d Conference of the International Law Association, pp. 663–685, 2008. SSRN: https://ssrn.com/abstract=1150664.

Kaufman, Z. D. (2011). The human element: The impact of regional trade agreements on the human rights and the rule of law: Comment. *University of Miami Inter-American Law Review, 42*, 253–443.

Kelsen, H. (1970). *Pure theory of law*. Translation from the 2d (Revised and Enlarged) German Edition by Max Knight.

Kelsen, I. (2003). *Principles of international law*. Clark, NJ: The Lawbook Exchange, Ltd. (Third Print 1959).

Khrebtukova, A. (2008). Call to freedom: Towards a philosophy of international law in an era of fragmentation. *Journal of International Law and International Relations, 4*, 51.

Kingsbury, B. (1998). Foreword: Is the proliferation of international courts and tribunals a systemic problem. *New York University Journal of International Law and Politics, 31*, 679.

Koskenniemi, M. (2004). *Study on the function and scope of the Lex Specialis Rule and the question of 'Self-Contained Regimes'*. Preliminary report by the Chairman of the Study Group submitted for consideration during the 2004 session of the International Law Commission.

Koskenniemi, M. (2007). The fate of public international law: Between technique and politics. *Modern Law Review, 70*(1), 1–30.

Koskenniemi, M., & Leino, P. (2002). Fragmentation of international law? Postmodern anxieties. *Leiden Journal of International Law, 15*(3), 553–579.

Leal-Arcas, R. (2010). Proliferation of regional trade agreements: Complementing or supplanting multilateralism. *Chicago Journal of International Law, 11*, 597.

Linton, S., & Tiba, F. K. (2009). The international judge in an age of multiple international courts and tribunals. *Chicago Journal of International Law, 9*(2), 407.

Martineau, A. C. (2009). The rhetoric of fragmentation: Fear and faith in international law. *Leiden Journal of International Law, 22*(1), 1–28.

McInerney-Lankford, S. (2012). Fragmentation of international law redux: The case of Strasbourg. *Oxford Journal of Legal Studies, 32*(3), 609–632.

McRae, D. (2004). What is the future of WTO dispute settlement? *Journal of International Economic Law, 7*(1), 3–21.

Michaels, R., & Paulwelyn, J. (2011). Conflict of norms or conflict of laws: Different techniques in the fragmentation of public international law. *Duke Journal of Comparative & International Law, 22*, 349.

Morgenthau, H. J. (1940). Positivism, functionalism, and international law. *American Journal of International Law, 34*(2), 260–284.

Morgenthau, H. J. (1948). *Politics among nations: The struggle for power and peace*. New York: Alfred A. Knopf. 51973.

Mosler, H. (1980). Supra-national judicial decisions and national courts. *Hastings International and Comparative Law Review, 4*, 425.

Nicolaidis, K., & Tong, J. L. (2003). Diversity or Cacophony-The continuing debate over new sources of international law. *Michigan Journal of International Law, 25*, 1349.

Oppenheim, L. F. (1912). *International law: A treatise* (Vol. I of 2). Longmans, Green, and Company.

Pauwelyn, J., & Salles, L. E. (2009). Forum shopping before international tribunals: (Real) concerns, (im)possible solutions. *Cornell International Law Journal, 42*, 77–118.

Payandeh, M. (2010). The concept of international law in the jurisprudence of HLA Hart. *European Journal of International Law, 21*(4), 967–995.

Petersmann, E. U. (2006). Justice as conflict resolution: Proliferation, fragmentation, and decentralization of dispute settlement in international trade. *University of Pennsylvania Journal of International Economic Law, 27*, 273.

Petsche, M. (2010). Jus Cogens as a vision of the international legal order. *Penn State International Law Review, 29*, 233.

Prost, M. (2012). *The concept of unity in public international law*. Oxford, England: Bloomsbury Publishing.

Prost, M., & Clark, P. K. (2006). Unity, diversity and the fragmentation of international law: How much does the multiplication of international organizations really matter? *Chinese Journal of International Law, 5*(2), 341–370.

Pulkowski, D. (2005). Narratives of fragmentation: International law between unity and multiplicity. *Paper presented at 'Agora' 2005 florence founding conference of the European Society of International Law (ESIL)*.

Rao, P. S. (2003). Multiple international judicial forums: A reflection of the growing strength of international law or its fragmentation. *Michigan Journal of International Law, 25*, 929.

Rayfuse, R. (2005). Future of compulsory dispute settlement under the law of the sea convention. *Victoria University of Wellington Law Review, 36*, 683.

Reed, L., & Jacovides, A. (2002). Great expectations: Where does the proliferation of international dispute resolution tribunals leave international law? In *Proceedings of the Annual Meeting (American Society of International Law)* (pp. 219–237). The American Society of International Law.

Romano, C. P. (1998). Proliferation of international judicial bodies: The pieces of the puzzle. *New York University Journal of International Law and Politics, 31*, 709.

Romano, C. P. (2001). The southern bluefin tuna dispute: Hints of a world to come ... like it or not. *Ocean Development & International Law, 32*(4), 313–348.

Romano, C. P. (2006). Shift from the consensual to the compulsory paradigm in international adjudication: Elements for a theory of consent. *New York University Journal of International Law and Politics, 39*, 791.

Romano, C. P. (2011). A taxonomy of international rule of law institutions. *Journal of International Dispute Settlement, 2*(1), 241–277.

Runersten, M., 2008. Defining 'Self-contained Regime'—A case study of the international covenant on civil and political rights.

Sands, P. (1998). Treaty, custom and the cross-fertilization of international law. *Yale Human Rights & Development Law Journal, 1*, 85.

Schermers, H. G., & Blokker, N. M. (2011). *International institutional law: Unity within diversity*. Leiden, The Netherlands: Martinus Nijhoff Publishers.

Schwelb, E. (1967). Some aspects of international jus cogens as formulated by the International Law Commission. *American Journal of International Law, 61*(4), 946–975.

Shaw, M. N. (2008). *International law*. Cambridge, England: Cambridge University Press.

Sheeran, S. (2014). The relationship of international human rights and general international law; hermeneutic constraint, or pushing the boundaries? In S. Sheeran & N. Rodley (Eds.), *Routledge handbook of international human rights law*. London: Routledge.

Simma, B. (1985). Self-contained regimes. *Netherlands Yearbook of International Law, 16*, 111–136.

Simma, B. (2009). Universality of international law from the perspective of a practitioner. *European Journal of International Law, 20*(2), 265–297.

Simma, B., & Pulkowski, D. (2006). Of planets and the universe: Self-contained regimes in international law. *European Journal of International Law, 17*, 483–529.

Slaughter, A. M., & Ratner, S. R. (1999). Appraising the methods of international law: A prospectus for readers. *American Journal of International Law, 93*, 291.

Spelliscy, S. (2001). Proliferation of international tribunals: A chink in the armor. *Columbia Journal of Transnational Law, 40*, 143.

Sweet, A. S. (2000). *Governing with judges: Constitutional politics in Europe*. Oxford, England: Oxford University Press.

Tate, C. N., & Vallinder, T. (1995). *The global expansion of judicial power*. New York: New York University Press.

Teitel, R., & Howse, R. (2008). Cross-judging: Tribunalization in a fragmented but interconnected global order. *New York University Journal of International Law and Politics, 41*, 959.

Tittemore, B. D. (2005). Ending impunity in the Americas: The role of the inter-american human rights system in advancing accountability for serious crimes under international law. *Southwestern Journal of Law and Trade in the Americas, 12*, 429.

Verdross, A. (1949). On the concept of international law. *American Journal of International Law, 43*, 435.

Verdross, A. (1966). Jus dispositivum and jus cogens in international law. *American Journal of International Law, 60*(1), 55–63.

Wellens, K. (2003). Fragmentation of international law and establishing an accountability regime for international organizations: The role of the judiciary in closing the gap. *Michigan Journal of International Law, 25*, 1159.

Wellens, K. C. (1994). Diversity in secondary rules and the unity of international law: Some reflections on current trends. *Netherlands Yearbook of International Law, 25*, 3–37.

## *Documents*

Charter, U. N. (26 June 1945). Charter of the United Nations.

International Law Commission, 2001. Draft articles on Responsibility of States for internationally wrongful acts. *Report of the International Law Commission on the Work of Its Fifty-third Session*.

International Law Commission, 2006. Fragmentation of international law: Difficulties arising from the diversification and expansion of international law. *Geneva: United Nations*.

# Chapter 3
# Treaty Interpretation

## 3.1 Introduction

The preceding chapter analysed the question of whether a proliferation of areas of law as well as of courts and other judicial bodies in international law is leading to fragmentation of international law. Because this question could be responded empirically by analysing the impact of 'proliferation' in specific areas or aspects of international law, the book will now turn to testing whether such 'fragmentation' can be witnessed in such a specific aspect of law. The chosen aspect of law must be one that is relevant to all specialised courts, and due to its centrality to international law and lawmaking, I follow the ILC's choice that the test bed should be the *methodology of treaty interpretation.*

Given the context of the last few decades characterised by an expansion of the regulatory ranges of international law, specialised and relatively autonomous rules, specialised legal institutions and spheres of legal practice,[1] 'interpretation' has gained significance. In particular, as the substantive fields covered by *treaties* multiply,[2] and the implementation of treaties depends on their 'interpretation', the importance of the doctrine of *treaty interpretation* continues to increase. Moreover, *treaty interpretation* matter attracts tremendous attention today since treaties occupy a central role in the international legal order; they are essential means of developing relations and peaceful cooperation among nations and are, certainly, the first and foremost, as also the persuasive, source of international law. Nevertheless, the subject of *treaty interpretation* is arguably one of the most difficult and controversial subjects. The interpretation of treaties has been and remains a constant activity of the courts and tribunals, and also of other international institutions, such as the most prominent among them—the International Law Commission

[1]ILC (2006), p. 6.

[2]There is a dramatic proliferation with respect to both bilateral and multilateral international treaties, purporting to govern broad subject matters.



L.E. Popa, *Patterns of Treaty Interpretation as Anti-Fragmentation Tools*,
DOI 10.1007/978-3-319-65488-1_3

(ILC), whose work culminated in the drafting of *Articles 31–33 of the 1969 Vienna Convention on the Law of Treaties* (VCLT), constituting the *general rule of interpretation*.[3] In the light of the ILC's findings, the formulation in Articles 31, 32 and 33 of the general rule and methodology of treaty interpretation provides, from one angle, a unifying framework for developments of international law, legal institutions and spheres of legal practice and, from another angle, a framework of analysing the possible fragmentation of international law.[4]

The current chapter thus sets out the *treaty interpretation doctrine*. The next section (Sect. 3.2) will analyse the concepts of *interpretation*, *legal reasoning* and *legal interpretation* in their doctrinal development. By relying on various scholarly insights, such analysis will constitute the theoretical framework for approaching the topic of *treaty interpretation* at two specialised courts, the ECtHR and WTO, in the subsequent chapters. Section 3.3 will outline first the treaty interpretation doctrine prior to the 1969 VCLT. This discussion is important since, in the following chapters (Chaps. 4–6), I will explore the evolution of legal interpretation at the international courts both prior to and after the adoption of the VCLT; thus, an understanding of the scholarly debates will enable the reader to better contextualise the treaty interpretative practice of the ECtHR and WTO. I will further provide in this section and the following (Sect. 3.4) an analysis of the debates related to the formulation of a 'general rule of interpretation'[5] as reflected in the ILC drafts on treaty interpretation and ultimately in the 1969 VCLT, as well as a doctrinal discussion on the treaty interpretation rules codified in Articles 31–33 of the VCLT. This analysis is equally important as it will constitute the theoretical foundation on which the subsequent chapters (Chaps. 4–6) will be developed. These chapters will focus on the empirical exploration of how both general and specialised international courts undertake treaty interpretation in practice, particularly on their techniques/methods and patterns of approaching the general rules of treaty interpretation. Since the following chapter (Chap. 4) will analyse case law from both the PCIJ and the ICJ that spans over 90 years of practice, the present chapter will enable the reader to recognise how the World Court developed its own doctrine of treaty interpretation and how later the ILC adopted specific rules on this subject, drawing from the practice of the World Court. The following chapter, therefore, will provide a helpful analysis of the PCIJ/ICJ's practice on treaty interpretation that will later be used as a benchmark against which to analyse comparatively the approaches of treaty interpretation of the two chosen specialised courts, the ECtHR and WTO, in Chaps. 5 and 6.

[3]ILC (2006), p. 6.

[4]*Id.*

[5]In the light of the varieties of approaches (schools of thought) related to treaty interpretation.

## 3.2 'Interpretation' and 'Treaty Interpretation' in the Scholarship

The question of how to approach *treaty interpretation* can hardly be answered without reference to basic key concepts such as *interpretation, legal reasoning* and *legal interpretation.* From the earliest times, a great number of philosophers were preoccupied with the concept of *interpretation* and its application to all human experience, including law (e.g., Gentili 1598, Grotius 1625, Pufendorf 1688, Vattel 1758). The notion of 'interpretation' has remained a central theme of debate in the legal field. The act of 'treaty interpretation' has also constituted a constant subject of interest and debate in the course of the development of international law due, in part, to the fact that after a treaty has entered into force, the application or putting into effect of a treaty presupposes a prior logical stage: its *interpretation* (Vitányi 1983, p. 41). By virtue of *treaty interpretation* activity, international courts and tribunals are required 'to give meaning to a treaty in the context of a particular case or fact pattern' in the scope of deciding 'whether or not a party is complying with the treaty'. (Pauwelyn and Elsig 2011). Therefore, while the text of a treaty is important in order for that text to become effective, it has to be first interpreted since, as succinctly put by Endicott, 'the law is indeterminate in virtue of any indeterminacy in the rules of the language' (Endicott 2001, p. 161). So interpretation of a text should be the process of coming with an answer to the question '[w]hat do you make of this?' requiring 'to make something of this'.[6]

Reflecting the constant scholarly preoccupation with *interpretation* in the legal field, the early modern scholars of international law observed that international agreements were vehicles for the development and attachment of international obligations.[7] Also, those scholars were able to perceive the need to create exogenous rules for international relations and norms separated by the will of the state's behaviour but consistent with the general trends of states' conduct.[8] Examining Grotius' theory of interpretation of treaties, Baderman, for instance, concludes that Grotius was optimistic in respect of the fact that, in all cases, *it is possible to discern the correct interpretation of any legal writing*, as also in respect of *the objective rules of interpretation that would make resolving disputes possible.*[9]

That the issues related to the act of interpretation of legal texts are major themes of reflection for the contemporary legal theorists, it becomes clear if recent scholarly contributions on the topic are further examined. This examination shows that given the difference of opinions in regard to the question of what 'interpretation' as

---

[6]Endicott (2001), p. 161.

[7]Bederman (2001), p. 22. According to Bederman, Grotius' intention was to refashion questions relating to the construction of agreements, especially agreements concerning the public domain in one single inquiry to provide a legal taxonomy that could form a *guide for the interpreter of a treaty.*

[8]*Id*, p. 23.

[9]*Id.*

a human act involves, a widespread debate over the nature of interpretation in the legal theoretical context could not be prevented. For example, Falk observes that the *inherent ambiguity* of international agreements makes 'law making' an inevitable aspect of the act of interpretation in international law (Falk 1967, p. 335). In his study on treaty interpretation, Falk formulates a definition of *interpretation*, starting with that found in the *Oxford English Dictionary* and extending it to the legal text.[10] He notes that the first definition of interpretation appears in words such as 'explanation; exposition',[11] while according to the dictionary's third definition, 'interpretation' is '[the] way in which a thing ought to be interpreted; proper explanation'.[12] Falk thus finds that there is a wavering between autonomy and objectivity of the interpretative process from the moment it starts, on one hand, and its normative instrumental function, on the other hand.[13] He observes, in principle, that in the act of interpretation there is an intimate interconnection between 'interpretation' and the central issues of power, justice and truth prevalent in society.[14] Importantly, as the author observes, is that there is a question that often arises and may properly be mentioned in this context, notably whether interpretation in legal reasoning can lead practitioners to 'one right answer' in respect of the legal issue at hand.[15] This question seems particularly important because there can be different 'right answers' for different interpreters.[16]

To avoid the possible conflict among interpretations, many other authors attempt thus to capture as comprehensively as possible the nature of *interpretation* as an act of reasoning and to extend it to interpretation of legal texts. Patterson, for instance, advocates the idea that 'interpretation' 'is a matter of being the master of a technique in whatever kind of interpretation is employed, be it of law or any other human practice' (Patterson 2005, p. 692). For Patterson, 'interpretation' emerges from the conception that *what counts as law may depend on a proper understanding of the role of interpretation in law*.[17] And this is so because in law, sometimes the specific language of a contract, for example, despite its degree of clarity, may simply do not 'settle the question of the parties' agreement', yielding therefore to other considerations.[18] Thus, interpretation is needed when understanding in law breaks down, serving 'to repair the fabric of understanding'.[19] Patterson makes it clear that 'understanding is not interpretation' but 'interpretation depends upon understanding'.[20] However, it is *interpretation* that makes a full

[10]Falk (1967), p. 324.

[11]*Id.*

[12]*Id.*

[13]*Id.*

[14]*Id*, p. 329.

[15]*Id.*

[16]*Id* (Falk quoting Finnis).

[17]Patterson (2005), p. 688.

[18]*Id*, p. 700.

[19]*Id*, p. 692.

[20]*Id.*

understanding of a law/norm possible.[21] For Patterson, interpretation becomes then 'a therapeutic, not a foundational activity'.[22] It can be inferred from his position that interpretation should lead not to change but, certainly, to preserve and clarify the law. Essentially, as the author correctly assumes, is that *interpretation* arises from *praxis*, meaning that interpretation depends upon an understanding already being in place, respectively upon the 'widespread agreement among legal practitioners with respect to most features of legal practice'.[23] Since *legal practice* becomes crucially important in the process of interpretation, Patterson assumes that what participants in legal practice have then in common makes possible the normativity and objectivity in law.[24]

In principle, Patterson sees that the need for interpretation arises when arguments conflict.[25] And by means of a proper *technique* for the legal interpretative activity, 'we can grasp the distinction between correct and incorrect action'.[26] The author further articulates that 'the nerve of the law is argument', where *the legal argument* is the technique used in the interpretation of law, as also the measure of the degree to which one has mastered the grammar of justification. So the legal argument is central to the practice of law.[27] Importantly, in explaining his views, Patterson starts with the idea that the fundamental form of expression in law is *assertion*, and the assertion is a claim according to which a given proposition is true as a matter of law.[28] But the nature of the argument is neither false nor true, so arguments are just tools for lawyers to show the truth or falsity of legal propositions.[29] Patterson further clarifies that the *normativity of law* consists in the distinction between *correct* and *incorrect* application of law, which is a matter of *the proper use of the nature of arguments*, as the context requires.[30] In brief, resolving the tension of the forms of argument is, in the author's view, what actually defines the activity of *legal interpretation*,[31] which has definitely an important role in preserving 'the common fabric of beliefs and dispositions that makes law possible'.[32]

Other authors bring to the fore various other elements/concepts in the attempt to define 'interpretation' as an act of 'legal reasoning' and applied it to legal texts. Also, Peczenik makes reference to and emphasises other factors in explaining the

[21]*Id*, p. 689.

[22]*Id*, p. 692.

[23]*Id*, p. 696.

[24]*Id*. See Patterson (2001) for a discussion on normativity in law.

[25]*Id*.

[26]*Id*, p. 692.

[27]*Id*, p. 693.

[28]*Id*.

[29]*Id*, pp. 693–694.

[30]*Id*. According to Patterson, a norm is defined as a linguistic formulation that performs a 'stimulative' function in a given context, a pattern of due behavior.

[31]*Id*, p. 697.

[32]*Id*, p. 709.

'legal interpretation' concept. He correctly admits that the act of interpretation has a special role to play in 'legal reasoning' because of the nature of law itself (Peczenik 1985, p. 291) and that, in the act of interpretation, all the steps of the 'legal reasoning' involve both application of social criteria and evaluative justification.[33] Therefore, according to Peczenik, some premises or inference rules, which a scholar or decision-maker may add to convert it to a logical deduction, consist in norms of 'legal reasoning' derived from other social areas than law, such as are those norms that may have social character or norms that express customary law or social morality, while other norms may even reflect the individual morality of the person who performs the act of legal reasoning. In consequence, some norms of legal reasoning may have more than one of these properties.[34]

In a more practical vein, Wroblewski proposes an 'operative interpretation' and a 'doctrinal interpretation' process in order to discover the 'true meaning' of the (interpreted) legal text (Wróblewski 1985, pp. 240–243). Making an in-depth analysis of the relation between *legal language* and *legal interpretation*, the author believes that, in the legal practice of the application of law, a 'norm formulation' requires interpretation *only where there is doubt* about its meaning, in a given context.[35] According to him, clarity is the lack of fuzziness, meaning that 'there are no consistency problems related to an applied legal norm'.[36] Wroblewski further explains that whether the norm formulation is accepted as such (clear text) or requires interpretation (seen as a case of fuzziness in text) depends on the *context* of its use.[37] Thus, for him, the same norm formulation may require interpretation in one context, whereas in others it does not, because the 'plain' or *prima facie* of the norm's meaning satisfies the needs of its use.[38] In other words, the context appears essentially determinative for any interpretative decision.[39]

Furthermore, Wroblewski uses the concept of *legal interpretation* in the widest sense when referring to any ascription of a normative meaning to a norm formulation and in a narrower sense when a norm formulation requires interpretation only where there is doubt about its meaning, 'interpretation' coming therefore as a clarifying act of the meaning of a doubtful legal norm formulation.[40] In this

[33]Peczenik (1985), p. 291.

[34]*Id.*

[35]Wróblewski (1985), pp. 240–243.

[36]*Id*, p. 150 (or, however, there are consistency problems in applying a norm, i.e., when the norm in question, understood as its *prima facie* meaning, contradicts other norms belonging to the legal system-conflict of norms that must be resolved or when fuzziness in the norm language is related to the rules governing the consistency of a legal system).

[37]*Id.* Wroblewski identifies the causes that generate doubts or fuzziness in the legal language of a norm on the basis of the type of contexts that influences the meaning of a norm (i.e., doubts or fuzziness due to the semantic features of the legal language, the features of the legal system, the functional context of the interpretation and application of law).

[38]*Id.*

[39]*Id*, p. 248.

[40]*Id.*

connection, the author distinguishes between the *operative* and the *doctrinal interpretation.*[41] He presents an interesting and practical method of interpretation—the *operative interpretation*—as an evaluative process applied to a concrete case of decision-making. Specifically, the author proposes that such interpretation be used 'to fix a doubtful meaning in a way sufficiently précis to lead to a decision in a concrete case', which should constitute 'the unique right answer to an interpretative doubt'.[42] Thus proceeding in this way the interpreter is able to reveal, by keeping account of the context of a given case, 'the true meaning of the interpreted text', rendering *the right interpretation.*[43] In search for the uniformity, certainty and predictability of the interpretative decision, Wroblewski ascribes an important role to *this operative interpretation*, instructing us that such interpretation removes the fuzziness of legal language for a given case, and if accepted, it can be applied to further (similar) cases.[44]

Equally valuable, the other type of interpretation described by Wroblewski is *doctrinal*. Its application implies essentially 'the systematization of valid law', as to 'construct an appropriate conceptual apparatus, and sometimes, to remove the doubts concerning norm formulation'.[45] Thus, the interpreter chooses one of the linguistic possibilities as the 'true meaning' of the text in question,[46] keeping in mind that 'certain features of the legal system are relevant for determining the meaning of interpreted rules'.[47] Wroblewski further clarifies that any interpretation concerns the legal language of a norm, and importantly, it is 'an interpretation of a norm related to other norms within a legal system'.[48] In other words, an interpreted legal rule/norm becomes part of a legal system, precisely because interpretation of such rule/norm relies on the rules of legal reasoning and takes into account other relevant rules/norms within a legal system (common standard justifications).[49] In this process of evaluation then, the application of *the rules of legal reasoning* becomes 'necessary for the justification of *interpretative decisions*'.[50] Noteworthy in this context is the importance that Wroblewski accredits to the active implication of the decision-maker (based on his/her legal culture) in the act of legal interpretation.[51] In sum, the decision is the result of both the chosen interpretative

---

[41] *Id*, p. 244.

[42] *Id.*

[43] *Id.*

[44] *Id*, pp. 245–246. The author notes (at p. 253) in this sense: 'There are arguments for treatening an interpretative decision as future-oriented, based on the axiology of formal justice and the role of precedent as a tool for safeguarding the decisional consistency in time'.

[45] *Id.*

[46] *Id.*

[47] *Id*, p. 254 (emphasis added).

[48] *Id.*

[49] *Id.*

[50] *Id.*

[51] *Id*, p. 248.

directions and the evaluation accepted by the decision-maker, so the process of interpretation could very well be seen as an 'individual norm transformation'.[52] Nevertheless, this 'norm transformation' cannot be viewed as leading to lawmaking.

In an interesting recent study with focus on how *the practice of interpretation* makes international law under the spell of international institutions' semantic authority, Venzke expands the understanding of *interpretation* in law. In principle, the author advocates the idea that the *practice of interpretation* accounts for semantic change and legal developments, which, however, develops international norms (Venzke 2012). Venzke justly admits that in the process of interpretation of a norm, *lawmaking* would be beyond permissible.[53] And without doubt, the interpreter would never be entirely free to perform an unconstrained reading of legal texts since by their legal nature concepts (legal texts/norms) come with a content already inherited from their past uses.[54] So in order to gain *authority* and *acceptance*, as well as to be successful, the interpretation of (legal) texts/concepts must relate to their past practices.[55] In other words, 'interpretation' of a legal text, as a constant battle between interpreters' objectivity and subjectivity (the plain meaning of the text and an unconstrained reading of the text), is, in Venzke's view, an act of legal reasoning in which interpreters have to justify in 'a context marked by legal concepts that have histories'.[56] Importantly, as Venzke admits, *the practice of interpretation* not only brings a norm into operation, but it is also responsible in part for revealing 'an account for why a norm should be'.[57] Focusing further on the role of *authority* in the practice of interpretation, Venzke believes that the analysis of authority has the significant advantage of 'illuminating the mixtures of *constraints* and *freedom* in interpretation'.[58] So while constrained by what the interpreter (authority) finds, notably by the text under interpretation and its meaning, *interpretation* involves at the same time a 'considerable degree of freedom' amounting to an exercise of authority.[59] It could be argued that Venzke's assertion resembles somehow Stone's view that a proper 'legal interpretation' depends on the legal authority in the international community. On the other hand, Stone's approach to treaty interpretation illustrates that the essence of legal interpretation is flawed by the absence of any adequate socio-ethical foundation for the assertion of legal authority in the international community (Stone 1953, pp. 367–368). Stone

[52]*Id*, p. 245 (emphasis added).

[53]Venzke (2012), p. 51.

[54]*Id*, pp. 48–50.

[55]*Id*.

[56]*Id*.

[57]*Id*, p. 7.

[58]*Id*, p. 64 (emphasis added).

[59]*Id*, p. 54. Venzke observes that a norm's meaning does not lie hidden in or behind the norm text itself but is a product of interpretation. While the author admits the text as 'the first and foremost authoritative reference point in legal argument', interpretations are, in his view, embedded in societal practice and past uses of the law.

concisely defines the act of 'treaty interpretation' as a dramatic conflict 'between the necessity of creative judicial choice, and the factors inhibiting conscious acceptance by international judges of the responsibility which such choice implies'.[60] Thus, an interesting open question in Stone's view is 'whether a tribunal will choose more wisely if it chooses in consciousness of its responsibility, rather than in the belief that it has no choice open'.[61]

However, what gives the interpreter the 'right' to be right is another important issue on which Fish, one of the most influential scholars writing on interpretation, focuses when asking *what makes an interpretation acceptable*. Fish takes what he calls *interpretative community* as generally determinative in shaping the interpretation of a text (Fish 1980, p. 342). He also considers that 'interpretation' accounts both for human understanding and for disagreements in understanding and correctly concludes that there are justified limits to what an interpreter can legitimately do with a legal text.[62] Disagreements cannot, according to Fish, be simply resolved by reference to the facts provided by the text because the text becomes an extension of the interpretative disagreements that divide interpreters.[63] Since the facts emerge only in the context of some points of view, disagreements are therefore ways by which the facts are settled.[64] For Fish, on the other hand, an interpreter is 'taught to think of himself as a transmitter of the best that had been thought and said by others' in a given field, so the interpreter becomes responsible for this transmission.[65] It results that an agreement, rather than being a proof of the stability of objects, is, in Fish's words, a '*testimony of an interpretative community* to constitute the object upon which its members can then agree'.[66]

To illustrate this claim, Fish uses interesting examples and discusses the interpretation of some literary texts. He justly assumes that if those examples of interpretation are 'ridiculous', for example, or perceived as such, it precisely represents the 'evidence that we are never without *canons of acceptability*'.[67]

---

[60]Stone (1953), pp. 367–368.

[61]*Id.*

[62]Fish (1980), p. 342. Fish observes that where there is no core of agreement in the text, there is, certainly, 'a core of agreement concerning the ways of producing the text', although one subject to change.

[63]*Id*, p. 340.

[64]*Id*, pp. 338–339. In the author's view, disagreements on the text depend on one's point of view, and some readers may choose to perversely substitute their own meanings for the meanings that texts obviously bear.

[65]*Id*, p. 355. Fish considers that the interpreter can stand charged of having substituted his own meanings for the meanings of which he is supposedly the guardian, or even found guilty of having interpreted.

[66]*Id*, p. 338.

[67]*Id*, p. 349 (emphasis added). Since these 'ridiculous' examples can be seen not as such under different conditions, it means that the canons of acceptability can change, not randomly but orderly, and to some extent they are predictable. Given this, Fish concludes that 'we are always right to rule out at least some readings'.

Thus, inasmuch as there can be two opposing interpretations (for some, the texts can be seen ridiculous, while for others the same texts are not ridiculous under different conditions), they cannot be both right. As Fish's important conclusion appears to be then, the words under interpretation will only have one meaning or the other 'in the light of an already assumed interpretation', and therefore 'no reading of a text, however outlandish it might appear, is inherently an impossible one'.[68]

In resonance with Fish's observation on 'disagreements' on a text, also Klabbers admits that the same text can lead to different conclusions as to its meaning (Klabbers 2010, p. 23). It can be so in Klabbers' view since interpreters may 'start from different premises, put on different spectacles and have different blind spots' and not because they use different interpretative techniques or have a different set of political values to endorse.[69] However, unlike other legal scholars, Klabbers seems not an adept of an 'interpretation' based on, and guided by, rules (though he does not deny that they have a role) because he believes that the act of interpretation depends much on the virtues of human personality.[70] Klabbers' interesting plea for a *virtuous interpretation* implies then a creative act of reasoning on the part of interpreters, relied on their personal virtues, knowledge, training and background.[71] He asserts that a proper *interpretation* cannot in principle be captured in rules, so a *virtuous interpretation*, clearly, differs from an interpretation based on rules.[72] The existence of rules of interpretation in Klabbers' view would only lead one to believe that the text under interpretation contains a hidden, 'perhaps a single, unitary meaning', which could be revealed if only 'the right tools to dig hard and deep enough' are employed.[73] Moreover, the rules of interpretation cannot prevent interpreters to approach differently the text from the perspective of their own cultural background. So when talking about *interpretation,* as admitted by Klabbers, the formation of an *interpretative community* (in the terms described by Fish) becomes essentially important. It requires the existence of an already *assumed interpretation* on the text and groups of people who share similar training, sensibilities, experiences, thus being able to know what other authoritative interpreters have held similar texts to mean.[74] In particular, Klabbers' view regarding the interpretation that should not be guided by rules does not appear widely shared in the scholarship. However, his views are definitively valuable as they contribute to expanding the understanding of the difficulties faced by interpreters in *the act of legal reasoning and interpretation*, generally, as well as the formation and the role of *interpretative communities* in *legal interpretation.*

[68] Fish (1980), p. 340. The author sees that, in this way, interpretation appears itself as remedying a deficiency in the interpretation that has come before it.

[69] Klabbers (2010), p. 23.

[70] *Id.*

[71] *Id.*

[72] *Id*, p. 25.

[73] *Id.*

[74] *Id.*

Finally, returning to Endicott, who provides, probably, even a more subtle response to the problems posed by *interpretation in law*, he argues, in principle, that an act of legal interpretation depends in general on what the situation allows (Endicott 2001, p. 161). Endicott treats *indeterminacy* as a feature of the application of the law to a particular case and *vagueness* as a feature of the law and expressions.[75] According to him, a legal expression is vague 'if there are borderline cases for its application'.[76] To the questions of how we can be following a rule when its requirements are indeterminate, or whether *legal interpretation* is the proper task of dealing with legal indeterminacy, Endicott answers that 'vagueness is not just a problem of indeterminacy in the application of the words that lawmakers use' since even if we leave behind the 'application' view of law in favour of the interpretive view, the problem still remains.[77] Endicott's argument in this respect is that *vagueness* in the authorities' linguistic formulations does not mean that any legal rights and duties are indeterminate since those formulations 'do not determine the law', but they 'become part of the preinterpretive material that an interpretation of the law must fit'.[78] And importantly, neither other (interpretive) resources of law, besides the meaning of words, eradicate indeterminacy because resources of the law are 'themselves typically vague'.[79] Given this, Endicott comes to the right and unassailable conclusion that 'there must be more to the requirements of the law than the mere application of the words'.[80] So since vagueness in law leads to legal indeterminacy,[81] *interpretation* of a vague statute has, in Endicott's view, a certain role, namely that it 'must at least *narrow down* the indeterminacies in its application'.[82] But it is not even so, as the author further clarifies, unless there is a clear notion of what indeterminacies are before and after the interpretative task is performed.[83] However, the author shares and supports the consensus among legal theorists that 'no legal question can be answered except by an interpretation'.[84] More conclusive in his view is that this consensus 'seems to stretch the notion of interpretation over instances of understanding that are not interpretive at all'.[85]

Thus, Endicott's claim that legal interpretation does not resolve all indeterminacies in law arises from his belief that vagueness or imprecision in law is not just a

[75]Endicott (2001), p. 20.

[76]*Id*, p. 30.

[77]*Id*, p. 162.

[78]*Id*, p. 160.

[79]*Id*, p. 165.

[80]*Id*, p. 163.

[81]*Id*, p. 31.

[82]*Id*, p. 181.

[83]*Id*. The author notes in this regard: 'Interpretive techniques make a difference to the requirements of the law, but it seems that we have no grounds for a general conclusion that they make the requirements of the law more precise.'

[84]*Id*, p. 12 (emphasis added).

[85]*Id*. See, e.g., Patterson's view discussed above.

problem of indeterminacy in the application of the words that lawmakers use.[86] Focusing on the place of *interpretation* in *legal reasoning*, the author justly concludes that indeterminacy in law is also due to vagueness in the considerations that are relevant to a *legal judgment*.[87] Specifically, *legal interpretation* has to do partly with the nature of the legal system and partly with the individual characteristics of an indefinite variety of legal problems.[88] So because 'legal interpretation' deals with legal *indeterminacy*, in Endicott's view a deeper interpretist claim has to be therefore considered.[89] The claim is that *interpretation* will not concern rules of interpretation that resolve indeterminacies, but an approach in the sense 'that the law itself is a holistic, constructive interpretation of the legal history of the community',[90] a view advocated similarly, as seen above, by other authors such as Patterson, Fish, Wroblewski, Venzke, Klabbers. Importantly, in the decision-making process, Endicott suggests caution for judges in making claims of 'determinacy'. He observes that *linguistic determinacy* should not mislead judges into thinking that this determinacy will even be possible to make a just decision in every case.[91] Moreover, he considers that a duty to decide is a reason for the interpreter to give a decision, but it 'is not a reason to conclude that the law requires one decision' or, in other words, that 'the law (or morality) requires a particular choice'.[92] Thus, keeping in mind the key notion presented by Endicott that *indeterminacy* is a feature of the law in general, it appears that the *context* plays a decisive role for an interpreter in providing a proper interpretation that gives effect to the law in question, an aspect underlined also, as it has been seen above, by authors such as Patterson and Wroblewski.

In addition, on the relation between *vagueness* and *interpretation*, Endicott sheds more light when distinguishing between *interpretation* and *understanding* and between *interpretation* and *invention*. Noteworthy here is his conclusion that 'the extent of the creativity of interpretation depends on what the situation allows',[93] so the 'context' is given a decisive role. The author's mere argument in respect of creative interpretation is that a judicial interpretation can be more or less inventive. He explains that every *legal interpretation* is, in fact, an invention. In the weak sense meaning, interpretation is 'a new answer to some legal question' (having in view inventions that are not applications of an existing rule), and in a strong sense, presumably interpretation creates 'a new answer to a legal question (where there is

[86]*Id*, p. 161.

[87]*Id*.

[88]*Id*, p. 30.

[89]*Id*.

[90]*Id*, pp. 161–162 (emphasis added).

[91]Endicott (2001), p. 29. The author suggests in this regard that 'if judges do not intent to do what a statute says to do, they should not take refuge in claims of indeterminacy or claim that they are interpreting the words of the statute' or in that the plain meaning of words compels a decision.

[92]*Id*.

[93]*Id*, p. 138.

no rule to apply, or in place of an existing rule)'.[94] Since the *legal interpretation* does not resolve or eliminate all indeterminacies in the application of legal rules,[95] in Endicott's understanding, *creativity* and *constraint* therefore complement each other in the process of legal interpretation.[96]

From the above discussion, several conclusions could be drawn in relation to the notion of *legal interpretation*, which will later be considered in analysing the practice of treaty interpretation at the ICJ, ECtHR and WTO (Chaps. 3–5). A first general conclusion is that although a degree of disagreement among various authors (discussed above) could be perceived in regard to what *legal interpretation* is, it is clear, nevertheless, that they admit, in general, the existence of an interplay between freedom and creativity of the interpreter on one side and constraints on the other side, which applies regardless of the particular context in which the interpreter applies the law. So in the process of interpreting a legal text (norm), an interpreter could never be entirely free to perform an unconstrained 'reading' of the text. It could be admitted that *interpretation* in law is, in essence, an inevitable and necessary aspect in applying a legal norm due, in principle, to an inherent *indeterminacy* (fuzziness, vagueness or ambiguity), which characterises in general the legal texts' formulation. And this is valid even in a situation where a text of a norm is admitted as being *clear* in a given context (i.e., of a case) since in order to declare its clarity, the norm is necessarily subjected to interpretation by the interpreter (determination/confirmation of the assumed clarity of the text).[97] So, in his/her duty to render a decision in any given case, which means giving full effect to the legal norm at issue, the interpreter/applier should be able to provide a unique, right answer to an interpretative doubt (only one meaning or the other) in the light of an already assumed interpretation (considering what other authoritative interpreters have found similar texts to mean, as suggested, generally, by the authors discussed above). In this attempt, the interpreter is necessarily required to keep account also of the *context* in which a specific legal norm is applied since the same norm requires more or less interpretation, thus depending on the particular conditions in which it is applied (context).

It could be concluded that in order to be legitimate, an interpretation of a legal norm/rule necessarily involves a combination of various factors. Accordingly, the interpreter should clearly act in responsibility of the choices he/she has in a given case, by providing a *holistic* approach to interpretation. It implies keeping account of the context (circumstances of a case) and, also, of other factors such as other

---

[94]*Id*, p. 180. To distinguish interpretation from invention, Endicott identifies two aspects: (1) 'When does an interpretation become so outrageous that it can be condemned as invention?' and (2) 'If a rule does not determine an action in a case, can a court be said to apply the rule at all? If not, then interpretation must simply be a subcategory of invention.'

[95]*Id*.

[96]*Id*, p. 160.

[97]See on this point Chap. 2 of this book, Ciobanu (1991); in this chapter De Vattel (1758), Endicott (2001). See also illustration of this aspect in case law analyses provided in the empirical part of this book.

norms within a legal system; legal practice (past practice as precedents); legal history of the community (*interpretative community*—the existence of an already *assumed interpretation* on a text, respectively, what authoritative interpreters have thought to be the meaning of similar texts); norms, other than those of legal nature that may reflect individual morality of the interpreter (personal characteristics, e.g. legal culture, training) or of social nature (social norms). Essentially, alongside *legal practice*, which remains fundamentally important in legal interpretation, various developed *techniques and rules of interpretation*, viewed as canons of acceptability, are considered necessary for performing the act of legal reasoning in interpretation. As it will be seen further in this chapter, such techniques and rules are crucially important since they facilitate finding the meaning of a legal norm and, consequently, its correct application to the circumstances of a (given) case. In consequence, the act of (legal) *interpretation* clearly becomes something more than the understanding of a legal norm/rule. It means clarifying or fixing a doubtful meaning of a legal norm/rule while revealing the indeterminacies that make that norm/rule unclear. So the act of legal interpretation should not become a norm transformation that leads to 'lawmaking'.

Finally, it could be stated that since the substantive fields covered by treaties continue to grow, and the proliferation of judicial bodies could lead to various interpretations in the process of applying the law,[98] the theory of *legal interpretation* constitutes an essential tool in the hand of the interpreter, enabling him/her to define and determine with better precision the legal norms. Moreover, from the perspective of expansion of new and highly specialised 'regimes', which, according to the International Law Commission, tend to claim relative autonomy from each other and from general international law, increasing the risks for fragmentation in international law, the process of *treaty interpretation* is perceived as central.[99] What unites all of these regimes is the fact that they claim binding force from the *law of treaties*, so interpreting treaties becomes paramount to solving any potential conflicts between these regimes.[100] As an essential tool in the application of treaties, *treaty interpretation* is thought to gain an important place in the contemporaneous international law by substantially settling the interpretative rules (canons) and accepted methodology through the formulation of *the 1969 Vienna Convention on the Law of Treaties* (Desierto 2010, p. 828). The following section (Sect. 3.3) thus focus on the development of *treaty interpretation* up to 1969 and then a further section will be dedicated to an analysis of the formulation of the general rule of interpretation as adopted and included in the 1969 VCLT (Sect. 3.4).

[98] ILC Report (2006), p. 614. According to the ILC, in applying international law, 'interpretation' is a prerequisite, i.e., in determining the relationships between two or more rules and principles that are both valid and applicable to a given situation.

[99] *Id.*

[100] *Id*, p. 11.

## 3.3 Treaty Interpretation: Doctrinal Development Prior to the 1969 Vienna Convention on the Law of Treaties

### *3.3.1 Early Views on Treaty Interpretation*

Etymologically, according to Constantinou, the word *treaty* dates back to the Latin word *tractus*, meaning treatment, handling, discussion and management or sometimes disagreement, but there was no Latin word with that origin to have the meaning of an (international) agreement (Constantinou 2005, p. 2).[101] The move to the term *treaty* in the sense of agreement to the sense of a *contract between states* is first recorded as *treete* in 1430.[102] According to the *Oxford English Dictionary*, *treaty* used as a technical term of international law is commonly employed from the end of the seventeenth century onwards.[103] In legal jargon, as codified in the preamble, as well as in Article 26 of the *1969 Vienna Convention on the Law of the Treaties*, a treaty comes under the fundamental principle *pacta sunt servanda* (agreements must be observed).[104] It is considered a Ciceronian[105] principle and has been adapted to modern treaty law.[106] The early views of treaty interpretation date back to Gentili's and Grotius' writings.[107] For Gentili,[108] who talked about treaties in the *De iure belli libri tres*, there is in every treaty a silent assumption, an understanding or mental reservation of a *clausula rebu sic stantibus* (things thus standing), which resulted from Gentili's doubt in the legal durability of treaties concluded with 'untrustworthy infidel rulers on scriptural qua moral grounds'.[109] It was later, in 1625, when Grotius published *De Jure Belli ac Pacis – On the Rights of War and Peace*, and it was considered ever since perhaps the most complete work on *treaties* and the first systematic treatment of international law.[110] The natural theory of law was the foundation upon which Grotius developed methods and rules

[101] Constantinou (2005), p. 2. The author finds a similar term for the Latin word *tractus* (treaty) as recorded *conventio*, from which the English word convention derives. According to the author, the term 'convention' 'is currently used as a synonym for treaty, especially when following long multilateral negotiations. *Conventio* has in addition the meaning of an assembly and is a word that literally translates *sumbasis*, an ancient Greek word for treaty. *Sumbainō* had the meaning of coming to an agreement but also of walking together, just like the Latin word *convenio*.'

[102] *Id.*

[103] *Id.*

[104] *Id.*

[105] *Id.* Constantinou citing Cicero (106–43 B.C.E.), who spoke extensively in *De officiis* (3.24) of ethical conduct, with no difference between agreements and promises (*pacta et promisa*).

[106] *Id.*

[107] *Id.*

[108] See Gentili (1933) for *De iure belli libri tres* (1612).

[109] *Id.* Constantinou citing Gentili: 'For although the impious oath of an infidel may be accepted, yet what trust can be put in an unbeliever.'

[110] Vitányi (1983), p. 45.

governing the interpretation of treaties.[111] Grotius' role in formulating explicit rules of treaty construction and principles that have had a great influence in the doctrinal development of *treaty law* and *canons of treaty interpretation* is incontestable.[112] His treaty interpretation theory has even more value, according to Scott, since Grotius was a learned advocate and was accustomed to regard even theoretical questions from the practical point of view (Scott 1935, pp. xiii and 8787; 1925). Since Grotius' work on this theme has remained of pivotal significance until the present day, several references on Grotius' rules of interpretation will be further analysed.

A direct reading of the text entitled *Of Interpretation*[113] reveals Grotius' preoccupation with a system of intelligible, objective and universal rules of treaty interpretation. His belief is that promises (agreements/conventions) could not be constructed in any way the parties desire, 'according to their fancy and thus render treaty obligations illusory',[114] so that 'some certain rule must be agreed upon' as to know the parties' obligations.[115] In the quest to achieve the *correct interpretation*, Grotius places the problem of *intent* at the core of his theory of interpretation of treaties. While advancing the idea that 'the proper rule of interpretation is to gather the *intention* of the parties pledged from the most probable signs', Grotius proposes two kinds of interpretation: '*words* and *conjectures*, which may be considered either separately, or together'.[116] He suggests further that 'words are to be understood in their ordinary sense' only 'if other implications are lacking' and only where no other 'conjunctures' exist to the contrary.[117] However, Grotius makes clear that 'words are not to be taken strictly in their original or grammatical sense, but in their common acceptation, for it is the arbitrary will of custom, which directs the laws and rules of speech'.[118] As it will be seen later in this chapter, this rule will find expression in the later formulation of Article 31, paragraph 1, of the 1969 VCLT (the 'ordinary meaning' rule).

---

[111]*Id.*

[112]*Id.*

[113]Grotius (2005), II, p. 848. It should be reminded that there are several authoritative English translations of Grotius' seminal work, corresponding to the various editions of the *De Jure Belli ac Pacis*. Here, a majority of references are made to the most recent English translation (2005) made by Richard Tuck, corresponding to the 1720 Jean Barbeyrac's edition. In addition to this text, there is also the Francis W. Kelsey translation (Grotius 1925), not utilised here, which was drawn from the second, vastly revised version by Grotius of *The Rights of War and Peace* in 1646, near the conclusion of the Thirty Years' War. See, e.g., Gordon (1995), noting that Grotius made nearly a thousand corrections to the first edition. In several instances, I have chosen to cite the 1814 translation by A. C. Campbell, republished in 1901 as part of the Universal Classics Library. This was a translation of the first, 1625, edition of the book. So references in this section will be made to Tuck's (Grotius, *De Jure*. . .1720) and, also, to Campbell's (Grotius, *De Jure*...1625) translation, Book II, Chapter XVI.

[114]*Id.*

[115]*Id.*

[116]Grotius (1901) (emphasis added).

[117]*Id.*

[118]*Id.*

In addition, Grotius suggests recourse to 'conjectures whenever words and sentences in a treaty are doubtful or ambiguous, or words produce manifest obscurity or have several meanings, as also, when several parts in the treaty provision seem to clash with one another, and therefore need to be reconciled'.[119] Thus, Grotius considers the use of both *words* and *conjectures* from those words as equally important in establishing the *intention* element. Indeed, he suggests resort to 'conjectures' as a source of interpretation of treaties, 'especially where a clause taken in its literal meaning would lead to consequences foreign or even repugnant to the intention of a treaty'.[120] This principle will find embodiment in the VCLT's 'rule of interpretation', particularly in Article 32 providing for the 'supplementary means' of interpretation.

Another source of interpretation, and thus of ascertaining the intention of the parties that can be drawn from Grotius' theory, is 'from the circumstances and connection of the words with others'.[121] In this sense, Grotius proposes to pay attention to a 'meaning of an expression from the circumstances of its being used by the same person, express the same intention on other similar occasions, and from its relation to what goes before, and what follows the place, where it stands'.[122] This source of interpretation could be related to the rule of 'context' that will find formulation in the text of Article 31(2) of the VCLT. Furthermore, Grotius mentions 'circumstances of place' as signs (conjectures) by which the intent of law can be traced. Among such circumstances, 'the reason of the law' (the 'motive', 'scope', not to be confounded with the intent of law) is described by Grotius as 'the principal and the most weighty' of all 'conjectures',[123] which will be, as well, reflected in the 'general rule of interpretation' codified in the 1969 VCLT, particularly in Article 31, paragraph 1.

In addition, Grotius speaks about the way of interpreting a treaty by 'conjectures' outside of the meaning of the words in which the promise is expressed, either by extending or restricting the meaning of the words.[124] These interpretative indications or guidelines appear to be perpetuated and perceived as principles of international law that relate to both *extensive* and *restrictive interpretation*. Grotius suggests, for example, an extended or broad interpretation by 'conjectures', which, however, ought to be taken with 'caution' and be 'extremely certain', when in an obligation words are allowed a wide meaning that is not of much use.[125] Or when

---

[119]Grotius (2005), p. 863.

[120]Grotius (1901).

[121]Grotius (2005), p. 866.

[122]*Id.*

[123]*Id.*

[124]*Id*, p. 871.

[125]*Id.* Grotius observes that '... conjecture that enlarge the obligation is not rashly to be admitted, but with a great deal more caution ... where words are allowed a large signification ... for here we look for a conjecture, which the words of the promise do not directly imply, and therefore this conjecture ought to be extremely certain, to form an obligation from it'.

the words are ambiguous, 'then they must be taken in a largest sense ... and an indefinite expression shall be understood universally'.[126] Also, a restrictive interpretation, or in Grotius' words 'the interpretation that restrains the import of the words promising', is suggested to be applied, for example, when there is an 'original defect in the will of the speaker',[127] or when the 'will of the speaker' is not evident due to 'some accident falling out inconsistent with his design'.[128] These approaches appear, in addition, to have had an influence in the development of the rules that later form Article 32 of the VCLT, providing for the 'supplementary means' of interpretation.

In sum, Grotius is widely admitted as bringing into light the most valuable study on the art of treaty interpretation (Vitányi 1983). According to Vitanyi's observation, Grotius' idea that interpretation should seek to discover the *intention of the parties* and not to clarify the meaning of the text independently of those intentions has produced a strong impact and influence ever since the development of the doctrine of treaty interpretation.[129]

Further, the scholar who expanded Grotius' theory on treaties and his canons of interpretation was Samuel Pufendorf, in his writing *On the Law of Nature and Nations* (Pufendorf 1934, v. 12.1). Pufendorf brings some additional precepts on the matter of treaty construction and also a gloss on Grotius' canons of interpretation.[130] While admitting Grotius' 'textual conjectures', Pufendorf appears more concerned with obscure phrasing and words in construction of treaties. In his chapter devoted to treaty interpretation, *On Interpretation*, Pufendorf focuses on this aspect, stating that 'when words, if taken in their plain and simple meaning will produce an absurd or even no effect, [then] some exception must be made from their more generally accepted sense, that they may not lead to nothingness or absurdity'.[131] This approach may very well be reflected in the formulation of the *effectiveness principle* as part of the later *Drafts Articles on Treaty Interpretation*. Pufendorf's further

[126]*Id*, p. 870.

[127]*Id*, p. 875. An original defect according to Grotius derives 'either from the absurdity which would otherwise evidently follow, or upon failure of the reason which alone did fully and efficaciously move the will, or from a defect in the matter'.

[128]*Id.*

[129]*Id.*

[130]Bederman (2001), p. 28. The author notes that both Grotius' and Pufendorf's use of textual conjectures form the essence of basic, grammatical canons:

(1) the plain meanings of words should be used unless they lead to absurd results;
(2) technical words should be given their technical meanings; and
(3) a correct interpretation of doubtful words and phrases might be made in relation to the use of the terms or expressions in the same, or related, documents.

[131]Pufendorf (1934), v. 12.8.

suggestion in regard to obscurity in the treaty's construction is that '[a] great light is cast upon the interpretation of obscure phrasings and words if they are compared with others which have some affinity with them; with those passages, for instance, where the same writer discusses a similar subject, or with their antecedents and consequences'.[132] Such an approach may be seen reflected in the later text of Article 31, particularly in paragraph 2, related to the context of the treaty, and paragraph 3 (c) of the VCLT, regarding the resort of the interpreter to 'any relevant rules of international law applicable in the relation between the parties'.

It is worth noting that Pufendorf, similarly to Grotius, considers the 'reason for the law'[133] as the principal and the strongest source in the interpretation of treaty.[134] This concept is to be later reflected in the draft articles on treaty interpretation, in particular in what will become Article 31(1) of the VCLT related to the 'object and purpose' elements of a treaty, which will be discussed further in this chapter. Pufendorf outlines this rule as follows: 'it is the greatest aid to this end, if it be established that the will of the lawgiver was moved by some reason as the single cause, which is not less true in pacts than in laws. So in this case the old saying holds good: "*When the reason for the law ceases the law itself ceases.*"'[135] In principle, many authors share the view that Pufendorf endorsed the 'natural meaning' doctrine of Grotius, adding contributions to it (McDougal et al. 1994, p. 217).

Most of the rules on the construction of treaties promoted by Grotius were adopted further by Emmerich de Vattel.[136] Influenced by Grotius' views, Vattel shares the conception that the rules of treaty interpretation were 'founded on reason, and authorised by the law of nature'.[137] In the legal scholarship, Vattel has been best remembered for the 'golden rule' (McDougal et al. 1994, p. 10) of his theory on treaty interpretation, according to which it 'is not permissible to interpret what has no need of interpretation' (*in claris non fit interpretatio*)—the first of Vattel's general maxim of interpretation (De Vattel 1758, p. 263). This canon of interpretation is perceived as being reflected later in the 'textualist' approach of treaty interpretation, however without any structure or schematic of analysis.[138] Yet, despite his unfortunate influential doctrine that *a clear meaning need not be interpreted*,[139] Vattel held that if proportionate evidence was adduced to prove that a contrary meaning was intended by participants, it should be adopted.[140]

---

[132]*Id*, passage v. 12.9.

[133]*Id*, passage v. 12.10 (or 'that cause and concern which moved the lawgiver to have the law passed').

[134]*Id*.

[135]*Id* (emphasis added).

[136]Bederman (2001), p. 37.

[137]*Id*, p. 36.

[138]*Id*, p. 37.

[139]McDougal et al. (1994), pp. 216–217.

[140]De Vattel (1758), p. 271. Vattel makes clear in this regard that '[i]n the interpretation of treaties, compacts, and promises, we ought not to deviate from the common use of the language, unless we have very strong reasons for it'.

It could therefore be admitted that to establish if a norm is clear, it necessarily must be subjected to interpretation.[141]

In his chapter entitled *On the Interpretation of Treaties*, Vattel explains that in concessions, conventions, treaties and in all contracts, as well as in law, it is impossible to predict and point out all the particular cases/situations that may arise. Therefore, the true interpretation would still consist in 'making, in all the particular cases that present themselves, a just application of what has been decreed in a general manner'.[142] Thus, like Grotius, also Vattel suggests that interpretation of treaties *ought* to be made according to certain rules, and this is one of Vattel's general maxims of interpretation.[143] Vattel is convinced that *if certain obligatory rules will not be followed* as to determine the sense in which the expressions are to be taken, more precisely, to discover what the contracting parties have agreed upon ('not only what one of the parties intended to promise, but also what the other must reasonably and candidly have supposed to be promised to him'), *treaties will be only empty words.*[144] Essentially, Vattel assumes, moreover, that since *the intention*, sufficiently known, furnishes the true matter of the treaty/convention, and thus parties' obligations became clear, then '[a] violation of the treaty is rather a deviation from the intention which it sufficiently manifests, than from the terms in which it is worded: *for the terms are nothing without the intention by which they must be dictated*'.[145] However, for Vattel, the most important clue in discovering *the intention of the parties* and, thus, the true meaning of a treaty's terms is 'the reason of the law' (or of the treaty), notably 'the motive which led to the making of it, and the object in contemplation at the time'.[146] Generally, Vattel admits that for a proper interpretation of treaties, all the rules he provides ought to be combined together. Importantly, he considers that the interpretation must be made in such a manner as to accord with all the rules, as well as to adjust them properly to the case in question.[147] In respect of the weight attached to the rules in a given case, Vattel indicates that 'when these rules appear to clash, *they reciprocally counterbalance and limit each other, according to their strength and importance, and according as they more particularly belong to the case in question*'.[148] In short, Vattel advocates the importance of establishing rules of interpretation founded on reason, authorised by the law of nature, capable of diffusing light over what is obscure, or ascertaining

[141]See Ciobanu (1991).

[142]De Vattel (1758), p. 262.

[143]*Id*, para 268.

[144]*Id*.

[145]*Id*, para 274 (emphasis added).

[146]*Id*, para 287.

[147]*Id*, para 322.

[148]*Id* (emphasis added).

what is uncertain or doubtful.[149] Like Grotius, also Vattel laid at the foundation of his treaty interpretation theory the element of *good faith* in treaties, considering it an intrinsic element in interpreting treaties. He essentially claims in this regard that 'as good faith ought to preside in conventions, they are always interpreted on the supposition that it actually did preside in them'.[150] It is also a principle that will later find expression in the (text) formulation of Article 31(1) of the VCLT, which requires, *inter alia*, that a treaty must be interpreted in *good faith*.

In addition, by according full importance to treaty clauses, Vattel is thought in the scholarship as anticipating *the principle of effectiveness in the interpretation* of treaties (Orakhelashvili 2008, p. 302). In this respect, according to Vattel's general rules, '[t]he interpretation which will make a treaty null and inefficient, cannot be admitted'.[151] It implies, in Vattel's words, that '[t]he terms of a treaty ought to be interpreted in such a manner as that it may have its effect, and not to prove vain and nugatory'.[152] The concept according to which 'whenever we meet with any obscurity in it, we are to consider what probably were the ideas of those who drew up the deed and to interpret it accordingly'[153] constitutes 'the general rule for all interpretations' proposed by Vattel. Noteworthy is that this rule remains at the core of his system of rules of treaty interpretation,[154] certainly influencing the later codification of the general rule of interpretation, particularly the rule of 'supplementary means' stated in Article 32 of the VCLT.

Later, in the nineteenth and early twentieth centuries, the conception of the necessity of fixed rules to guide treaty interpretation as a precondition for establishing treaty relations was also present (Phillimore 1856, p. 70). For example, Robert Phillimore was one of the scholars who adhered to the necessity of fixed rules of interpretation of treaties.[155] In his view, since rules are demanded by the necessities of international society, fixed rules of interpretation are needed to discover the textual meaning of treaties/conventions, generally written in imperfect language.[156] Phillimore commences his *Interpretation of Treaties* with an emphasis

---

[149] *Id*, p. 262. Among Vattel's principles of treaty interpretation (maxims) are: 'if he who could and ought to have explained himself has not done it, it is to his own detriment'; 'neither of the contracting parties has a right to interpret the treaty according to his own fancy'; 'what is sufficiently declared, is to be taken for true'; 'we ought to attend rather to the words of the persons promising'; 'the interpretation ought to be made according to certain rules'; 'the faith of treaties lays an obligation to follow these rules'.

[150] *Id*, para 280 (emphasis added).

[151] *Id*, para 283.

[152] *Id* (emphasis added).

[153] *Id*, para 207.

[154] *Id*.

[155] Orakhelashvili (2008), p. 303.

[156] Phillimore (1856), p. 70. As Phillimore, also W. E. Hall adopted the approach of established rules for treaty interpretation in his work: *A Treaties in International Law* (1895). He pronounced for treaty interpretation to be undertaken on the basis of predetermined rules. See also Sir Eric Beckett (1950).

on the 'good faith' element necessary for a treaty's conclusion. He states that 'all international treaties are covenants *bonae fidei*, and are, therefore, to be equitable and not technically constructed'.[157] However, in Phillimore's view since all laws and all treaties' language are constructed in general terms, there may be doubts and ambiguity in their terms or clauses. Therefore, for Phillimore, '*imperfection of language* as an instrument of expressing intention must occasionally, if there were no other reasons, *render interpretation necessary*'.[158] As shown in the preceding section, such a view was greatly influential with many contemporary legal theorists. Phillimore memorably captures the *act of interpretation* as 'the life of the dead letter' and 'a meaning governed by settled rules and fixed principles, originally deduced from right reason and rational equity, and subsequently formed into law'.[159] He regards many of such rules and principles as maxims of interpretation.[160]

Furthermore, Phillimore's position about the 'principal rule' that should govern the treaty interpretative process is that the interpreter must 'follow the ordinary and usual acceptation, the plain and obvious meaning of the language employed . . . If the meaning be evident, and the conclusion not absurd, you have no right to look beyond or leave beneath it, to alter or add to it by conjecture'.[161] He assumes that doing so, it would mean 'to remove all certainty from human transactions'.[162] As it will be seen in the following sections of this chapter, this approach/rule will be refined through the various ILC's drafts on the rules of treaty interpretation and reflected in the rules referring to 'supplementary means of interpretation', then codified in Article 32 of the VCLT. Phillimore focuses also on those situations of *uncertainty* or *impropriety* in the language of treaties that give rise to doubts, or ambiguity, which therefore justify 'interpretation' of such treaties.[163] In this respect, he proposes resort to specific rules (sources) of interpretation to deduce the intention of the parties.[164] Like his predecessors, Phillimore also discusses and expands the concepts of *extensive* and *restrictive interpretations*, thus contributing to the crystallisation of the basic principles of interpretation such as the *good faith* and *effectiveness principles*. He states in this regard, for example, that in case of ambiguity due to 'impropriety of the words', the interpretation (by narrowing or restricting the meaning of the words) depends of the context, thus 'entirely on question, whether these words relate to the whole of the foregoing paragraph, or to a

[157] *Id*, p. 89.

[158] *Id* (emphasis added).

[159] *Id*.

[160] *Id*.

[161] *Id*, p. 97.

[162] *Id*.

[163] *Id*.

[164] *Id*, pp. 98–99.

part of it'.[165] This approach can be recognised also in the later formulation of the VCLT rules of interpretation, particularly Article 31(1) relating to the elements of *good faith* and *context*, which must necessarily be taken into account in the interpretation of a treaty provision, together with the text and the object and purpose of that treaty. It can be admitted then that, by expanding the theories already existent at that time, Phillimore's (own) theory of treaty interpretation has greatly contributed to the further development of canons of interpretation.[166] Nevertheless, the later stages in the evolution of the treaty interpretation doctrine are marked by reluctance concerning the relevance of fixed rules of interpretation, as also of the textualist approach.[167] This reluctance has roots mainly in the classic controversies on treaty interpretation, in principle on the relation between the 'textualist' and 'subjective' approaches (methods) or, in other words, between the language used by the parties and their intentions (Jacobs 1969, p. 319).

Summing up, the ideas of Grotius, Vattel, Pufendorf and Phillimore relating to notions such as 'ordinary meaning', 'context', 'intention', 'special meaning', 'preparatory work' and 'surrounding circumstances' are thought to be transmitted over time, introduced into the field of international law and applied (Merkouris 2010a, p. 5). According to Merkouris, these concepts have been tested and applied by relevant arbitral tribunals, leading to an ever-increasing corpus of international jurisprudence on treaty interpretation, which culminated in *the general acceptance of certain customary principles of interpretation, and their reflection in the later Articles 31–33 of the VCLT on treaty interpretation.*[168] It can be deduced that legal theorists have been continuously preoccupied with the necessity for fixed rules to guide treaty interpretation as a precondition for establishing treaty relations, from the earliest times. Yet the most significant legacy on this matter is thought to be left by theorists such as Grotius and Vattel. As it will be seen in the next sections,

[165] *Id*, pp. 102–105. General maxims such as 'good faith clings to the spirit, and fraud to the letter of the convention' or 'that no one is supposed to intend what is absurd' are intended by Phillimore to guide an interpreter, especially, when adopting an extensive interpretation and, respectively, a restrictive interpretation. For example, in a case not foreseen or provided by the treaty, an interpretation must be conducted, according to Phillimore (at p. 109), 'as nearly as possible in accordance with what the party would have done if the circumstance which has now happened had been foreseen'.

[166] For the value of the rules proposed by Phillimore and their influence upon the doctrinal development of canons of interpretation, it is worth noting here some of his rules, as for example: 'interpretation in the context of the whole treaty'; 'the rule of considering the ground or reason (ratio legis) in which the treaty originated, and the object of those who were parties to it'; 'the rule of instituting a comparison between the treaty in dispute and other treaties (prior, posterior or contemporary, upon the same subject and between the same parties to that treaty)'; 'when a provision or clause in a treaty is capable of two significations, it should be understood in that one which will allow it to operate, rather than in that which will deny to it effect'; or 'when the same provision or sentence expressed two meanings, it should be adopted that on which most conduces to carry into effect the end and object of the Convention.'

[167] Orakhelashvili (2008), p. 302.

[168] Merkouris (2010a), p. 5.

whereas most of the rules that Grotius advocated in the construction and interpretation of treaties were adopted by the 'intent school' of treaty interpretation, Vattel's rules on treaty interpretation mostly influenced the 'textualist school'. Furthermore, Grotius and Vattel's elaborated theory on interpretation of treaties (formulation of intelligible rules and principles of treaty construction and interpretation), as well as the theories of their followers, had a strong impact on the later developments of the ILC on the *treaty interpretation* 'question' and codification of a 'general rule of interpretation' in the *1969 Vienna Convention on the Law of Treaties*. In this context, it has to be reminded the major role that the World Court's doctrine and practice of treaty interpretation played in the ILC's adoption of specific rules on treaty interpretation. Thus, the next section will analyse the formulation of the relevant rules in the 1969 VCLT and the methods/approaches of treaty interpretation proposed by different doctrinal 'schools' of thought, which found reflection in the VCLT's *general rule of interpretation*.

## *3.3.2 Formulation of the Rules of Treaty Interpretation in the ILC Drafts and Subsequently in the Text of Articles 31, 32 and 33 of the VCLT: Reference to Methods of Treaty Interpretation—Scholarship Review*

In considering that the International Law Commission (ILC) had a seminal role in the preparation of the VCLT, it is necessary to analyse further the work of the ILC and its role in the formulation of the *general rule of interpretation* as later incorporated in Articles 31–33 of the VCLT. This doctrinal analysis will provide a basis for examination in the next chapters, through empirical research, of the responses of the PCIJ/ICJ and two specialised courts, the ECtHR and WTO, concerning the application of the unitary system of treaty interpretation rules embodied in Articles 31, 32, 33 of the VCLT.

### 3.3.2.1 Principles of Interpretation as Reflected in the Various Approaches to Treaty Interpretation

By the middle of the twentieth century, the *customary international law of treaties* had grown to a fairly comprehensive body of rules (Zemanek 2009). Consequently, the necessity for bringing to order rules of law governing treaties found expression at the International Law Commission's first session, in 1949, which placed it among the topics suitable for codification.[169] At its 11th session, in 1959, the Commission

[169]Zemanek (2009).

envisaged its work on the law of treaties as taking the form of 'a code of general character' rather than one or more international conventions (ILC 2007, p. 143). Then, at its 13th session, in 1961, the Commission worked towards the change from a mere expository statement of the law of treaties to the preparation of draft articles with the scope to form the basis for an international law convention.[170] Further, the Commission proceeded with the first reading of the draft articles and submitted the provisionally adopted draft articles to governments for comments from 1962 to 1964 and then completed the draft articles at its 16th session, in 1964.[171] Thus, the *Third Report on the Law of Treaties*, in 1964, covers, among other topics related to the law of treaties, the *interpretation of treaties* and the corresponding draft articles.[172]

For the consideration of the Commission, the Special Rapporteur had prepared four draft articles dealing generally with the interpretation of treaties.[173] They were Articles 70–73, which took their inspiration from the *1956 Resolution of the Institute of International Law* and from Fitzmaurice's formulation of the 'major principles' of interpretation in an article on the law and procedure of the International Court, published in 1957.[174] Nevertheless, the roots of these principles date back further in time when a clear formulation of the approaches to treaty interpretation was already expressed in Articles of the Draft Convention on the Law of Treaties prepared in 1935 as part of the *Harvard Research in International Law*.[175] However, the principles of treaty interpretation had constantly been a controversial topic, which culminated in considerable criticism of the articles embodied further in the Drafts of the Convention formulated by the International Law Commission.[176]

##### 3.3.2.1.1 Towards a General Agreement as to the Principle Governing the Process of Interpretation

Noteworthy is the fact that in the formulation by the ILC of the draft articles, four approaches to treaty interpretation classified as doctrinal 'schools' of thought are reflected: (1) *the subjective approach* (intentional school), (2) *the textual approach* (textualist school), (3) *the teleological approach* (teleological or purposive school),

---

[170] ILC (2007), p. 143. To orient the work towards the preparation of draft articles serving as a basis for an international convention, the International Law Commission appointed the last Special Rapporteur, Sir Humphrey Waldock, in 1961.

[171] *Id*, p. 113.

[172] *Id.*

[173] *Id*, p. 55.

[174] *Id.* See Fitzmaurice's formulation of the 'major principles' of interpretation in Fitzmaurice (1957).

[175] Jacobs (1969), p. 322.

[176] *Id*, p. 318.

(4) *the New Haven School* ('shared expectations' school). As stated in the scholarship, these 'schools' of thought have emerged from judicial practice, mainly that of the World Court, as also of specialised courts and tribunals (Orakhelashvili 2008, p. 305). Although each school has its own approach to interpretation of treaty texts, it is widely admitted that they could not provide a definitive answer to the question of what the interpretative treaty process outcome should be.[177] Some aspects related to the principles of treaty interpretation reflected in the most relevant instruments that need further discussion for a better understanding of these principles' evolution in light of the various approaches to treaty interpretation, ultimately reflected in the formulation of the *general rule of interpretation* of the *1969 Vienna Convention on the Law of Treaties.*

*The 1935 Draft of the Harvard Research in International Law*

As the nucleus of the ILC's further *Draft of the Convention on the Law of Treaties*, the goal of Article 19 in the *1935 Draft of the Harvard Research in International Law*[178] was to discover and effectuate the purpose of a treaty: '[a] treaty is to be interpreted in the light of the general purpose which it is intended to serve' (Harvard Research 1957, p. 938). Providing a clear teleological (or purposive) approach, for which the 'purpose' of the treaty is at the core, Article 19 was intended not to apply automatically the 'canons' to any and every treaty text. On the contrary, this article intended to give considered attention to a number of *factors* that might reasonably be regarded as likely to yield reliable evidence of what the purpose of the treaty was and also how it could be best effectuated under the prevailing circumstances (Jacobs 1969, p. 318). Thus, Article 19 (a) set forth the factors indicating the general purpose (object and purpose) of a treaty.[179] The most important factors to be considered in connection with the general purpose that the treaty is intended to serve were the historical background of a treaty, the subsequent conduct of the parties, the circumstances surrounding the adoption and interpretation of the treaty and the *travaux preparatoire.*[180]

Noteworthy is that the authors of the *Harvard Draft Convention on the Law of the Treaties* considered that *interpretation* was a matter not of occasional but of the most frequent occurrence, which was almost necessarily involved in the

[177]Orakhelashvili (2008), p. 305.

[178]Articles 19(a) of the Harvard Draft provided a more teleological approach:

> A treaty is to be interpreted in the light of the general purpose which it is intended to serve. The historical background of the treaty, *travaux preparatoire*, the circumstances of the parties at the time the treaty was entered into, the change in these circumstances sought to be effected, the subsequent conduct of the parties in applying the provisions of the treaty, and the conditions prevailing at the time interpretation is being made, are to be considered in connection with the general purpose which the treaty is intended to serve.

[179]Zhang (1933).

[180]Jacobs (1969), p. 318.

'application' of treaties, including the 'construction' of them (Zhang 1933). They also considered that it would seem both desirable and important for there to exist a measure of general agreement as to the principle governing the process of interpretation.[181]

*The Resolution Adopted by the Institute of International Law in 1956*

The Resolution adopted by the *Institute of International Law* (IIL) in 1956 is also important in the process of formulation of the rules of interpretation. This Resolution formulated two articles 'in somehow cautious language', containing a small number of basic principles of treaty interpretation. Those two articles were influential in the further drafting of Articles 70 and 71 in the ILC's *Third Report on the Law of Treaties*,[182] later reflected in the 'general rule of treaty interpretation', formulated in the ILC's final draft. Unlike the *1935 Draft of the Convention on the Law of Treaties* (Harvard Research), the articles formulated in 1956 by the *Institute of International Law* placed primary emphasis on the text, apparently giving considerable discretion to the court on the use of other means of interpretation.[183]

The Resolution of IIL provides in Article 1(1) that '[t]he agreement of the parties having been embodied in the text of the treaty, it is necessary to take the natural and ordinary meaning of the terms of the text as the basis of interpretation. The terms of the provisions of the treaty should be interpreted in the context as a whole, in accordance with good faith and in the light of the principles of international law.'[184] And Article 1(2) provides that '[h]owever, if it is established that the terms employed should be understood in another sense, the natural and ordinary meaning of those terms is set aside'.[185] Further, the Resolution states in Article 2(1) that '[i]n case of a dispute brought before an international tribunal, it will be for the tribunal, taking into account the provision of article 1 to determine whether and to what extent other means of interpretation should be employed'.[186] By not specifying any criteria for the admissibility of extrinsic sources, the criteria of ambiguity or obscurity of the text, the second paragraph of Article 2 simply enumerates the other means of interpretation: '(a) consultation of *travaux preparatoire*; (b) the practice followed in the actual application of the treaty; (c) the consideration of the object of the treaty'.[187]

[181] Zhang (1933).

[182] Jacobs (1969), p. 322.

[183] *Id*, p. 332.

[184] Harvard Research (1957).

[185] *Id*.

[186] *Id*.

[187] Jacobs (1969), p. 322.

*The Draft Articles of the Third Report on the Law of Treaties*

The principles of treaty interpretation contained in both Articles 1 and 2 of the Institute of International Law mentioned above were further reflected in Draft Articles 70 (General rules)[188] and 71 (Application of the general rules)[189] of the *Third Report on the Law of Treaties.* These articles, together with the following Article 72 (Effectiveness interpretation of the terms—*ut res magis valeat quam pereat*),[190] Article 73 (Effect of a later customary rule or a later agreement or

[188]ILC (1964) **Article 70**: 'General rules' provided:

1. The terms of a treaty shall be interpreted in good faith in accordance with the natural and ordinary meaning to be given to each term-

a) in its context in the treaty and in the context of the treaty as a whole; and
b) in the context of the rules of international law in force at the time of the conclusion of the treaty.

2. If the natural and ordinary meaning of a term leads to an interpretation which is manifestly absurd or unreasonable in the context of the treaty as a whole, or if the meaning of a term is not clear owing to its ambiguity or obscurity, the term shall be interpreted by reference to-

a) its context and the objects and purposes of the treaty; and
b) the other means of interpretation mentioned in article 71, paragraph 2.

3. Notwithstanding paragraph 1, a meaning other than its natural and ordinary meaning may be given to a term if it is established conclusively that the parties employed the term in the treaty with that special meaning.

[189]*Id.* **Article 71**: 'Application of the general rules' provided:

1. In the application of article 70 the context of the treaty as a whole shall be understood as comprising in addition to the treaty (including its preamble)—Taking shape in any agreement arrived at between the parties as a condition of the conclusion of the treaty or as a basis for its interpretation; any instrument or document annexed to the treaty; any other instrument related to, and drawn up in connection with the conclusion of the treaty.
2. Reference may be made to other evidence or indications of the intentions of the parties and, in particular, to the preparatory work of the treaty, the circumstances surrounding its conclusion and the subsequent practice of parties in relation to the treaty, for the purpose of:

(a) confirming the meaning of a term resulting from the application of paragraph 1 of article 70;
(b) determining the meaning of a term in the application of paragraph 2 of that article;
(c) establishing the special meaning of a term in the application of paragraph 3 of that article

[190]**Article 72**—Effective interpretation of the terms (*ut res magis valeat quam pereat*):

In the application of articles 70 and 71 a term of a treaty shall be so interpreted as to give it the fullest weight and effect consistent — (a) with its natural and ordinary meaning and that of the other terms of the treaty; and (b) with the objects and purposes of the treaty.

interpretation of a treaty),[191] Article 74 (Treaties drawn up in two or more languages), Article 75 (Interpretation of treaties having two or more texts or versions), reflect the major principles formulated by Fitzmaurice and provide for general rules of interpretation of treaties.[192] As there was some reluctance among the international community for the need to include treaty interpretation in the Commission's work, according to Van Damme's recent study on this matter, the ILC affirmed *the necessity* to codify certain principles of treaty interpretation in international law.[193] This goal was taking shape through the formulation of the provisions of Article 70, in which the Commission had given a certain primacy to the text of the treaty without excluding the possibility to resort to other means of interpretation, provided in a more explicative language.[194]

The 'textualist' approach to interpretation takes the 'ordinary meaning of the words' as dominant and advocates for 'what did the parties say in this case' (Fitzmaurice 1951, p. 1). This rule is thought to confer primacy of the text of the treaty while admitting extrinsic sources to be used *only* in case the text is ambiguous or leads to absurd results.[195] As admitted in the scolarship, Vattel's first general maxim, stating that it *is not allowable to interpret what has no need of interpretation* (De Vattel 1758, para 268) had greatly influenced the 'textualist' approach. However, according to Lauterpacht, it is most unlikely that Vattel regarded this 'first general principle' from his armoury of rules of interpretation as being of a decisive practical importance (Lauterpacht 1949, p. 52). And this appears as true since, as shown above in the analysis of Vattel's 'plain meaning' rule among the other rules of interpretation, Vattel made clear that if proportionate evidence was adduced to prove that a contrary meaning was intended by participants, it should be adopted (De Vattel 1758, p. 271). By stating that 'words are to be understood in their ordinary sense' and adding 'if other implications are lacking', Vattel seemed to imply that the alleged clear treaty term/text should be subjected to interpretation.

Another exponent of the textualist approach who advocated fixed rules of interpretation with the purpose of discovering the meaning of a treaty text is thought

[191] **Article 73**—Effect of a later customary rule or of a later agreement on interpretation of a treaty:

> The interpretation at any time of the terms of a treaty under articles 70 and 71 shall take account of — (a) the emergence of any later rule of customary international law affecting the subject-matter of the treaty and binding upon all the parties; (b) any later agreement between all the parties to the treaty and relating to its subject-matter; (c) any subsequent practice in relation to the treaty evidencing the consent of all the parties to an extension.

[192] Waldock (1964).

[193] Van Damme (2009), p. 42. According to Van Damme, the Commission's decision to codify was based on the relevance of principles such as 'good faith' interpretation for the effectiveness of the principle of *pacta sunt servanda*, the need to interpret other draft articles and the function of principles of interpretation in drafting treaties.

[194] Waldock (1964).

[195] Fitzmaurice (1951), p. 1.

to be Phillimore.[196] In principle, Phillimore's argument that the parties' expressed intention in the text of treaties must be taken as true, and thus not undermined, shows a mixed intentionalist and textualist views on treaty interpretation.[197] Later, the firm expression of the ILC in its comments on the draft articles on the law of treaties, that the (treaty) *text* constitutes the starting point in establishing the meaning of its terms, and not an *ab initio* investigation of the intention of the parties, was not free of criticism.[198] For example, by viewing the emphasis on the 'ordinary meaning' rule in treaty interpretation as a non-functional perspective, renowned international law professor McDougal, a critic of the restrictive nature of the textualist approach, states that '[t]he great defect, and tragedy, in the International Law Commission's final recommendations about the interpretation of treaties is in their insistent emphasis upon an impossible, conformity-imposing textuality' (McDougal 1967, p. 992). McDougal's important claim is that the textualist approach relies on artificial, hierarchical distinctions between primary and secondary sources of interpretation (Jacobs 1969, pp. 325–326). However, the divergence on the primacy of one or another approach to interpretation is better explained in the words of another renowned international law scholar, Stone: '[t]he primacy of the canons sanctifying the parties' intention was denied as well as asserted' and also '[t]he primacy of the "objective" expression (or "plain meaning") was asserted and denied with a vehemence no less great' (Stone 1953, p. 345).

In contrast with the textualist approach to interpretation, the 'intention' or 'subjective' approach is also reflected in the debate over the formulation of the draft articles towards a *general rule of treaty interpretation*. The subjective approach was called the 'intention of the parties', 'founding fathers' school' or the 'intentions school' (Fitzmaurice 1951, p. 1). It seeks to investigate the 'real will', the *real intention* of the parties, relying on the text (ordinary meaning of the

---

[196]Oppenheim (1921), p. 555. Oppenheim, citing and analysing Phillimore's rules of interpretation, observes that such rules 'recommended themselves on account of their suitability'. According to Oppenheim, Phillimore's mixed intentionalist and textualist views on interpretation are reflected in the following rules:

> 'all the treaties must be interpreted in their literal sense; the terms used in the treaty must be interpreted in their usual meaning of everyday language, that they are not expressly used in a certain technical meaning or that another meaning is not apparent from the context; the whole of the treaty must be taken in consideration, if the meaning is doubtful, and not only the wording of the treaty, but also its purpose; in case of discrepancy between the clear meaning of a stipulation and the intention of one party as declared upon negotiations, which preceded the signing of a treaty, the decision must depend on the merits of the case; if two meanings of a stipulation are admissible according to the text of a treaty, such meaning should prevail'.

Oppenheim concludes that the essence of treaty interpretation is a matter, in the first instance, of consent between the contracting parties.

[197]*Id.*

[198]ILC (1964). The ILC admits that the principle of natural and ordinary meaning of the terms is at the core of the textualist approach and is to be determined not in the abstract but by reference to the context in which the terms occur.

terms) of the treaty (Jacobs 1969, p. 318). As mentioned earlier in this chapter, the idea that the interpretation should aim to discover the intention of the parties, and not to clarify the meaning of the text independently of such intention, originates in Grotius' theory on treaty interpretation (Vitányi 1983). Thus, identifying the *true intention* of the parties became, in Grotius' view, the object of all interpretation and the key to opening the door to the meaning of all treaties.[199] As it can be seen, this idea has exercised considerable influence on the development of the treaty interpretation doctrine.[200] Most strongly, the subjective approach was advocated in the twentieth century by Lauterpacht, during the 'intentions' school debate on treaty interpretation, starting in the 1930s.[201] The so-called principle of the 'intent school' formulated by Lauterpacht provides that in the absence of any indication of the actual intention of the parties to a treaty, the tribunal has the task of filling the gap in conformity with the fundamental requirements of international law and justice.[202]

On the contrary, the view advanced by the textualist school on treaty interpretation is different in the sense that the intentions or presumed intentions of the framers cannot be invoked to fill the gaps or import into the treaty something that was not there.[203] In this regard, G. G. Fitzmaurice claims that 'an obscurity in the text is usually itself a reflection of obscurity or deficiency in the intentions of the parties',[204] and thus an attempt to ascertain the usually lacking intentions, actually, will not lead to any useful result.[205] Conversely, while not contesting the fact that the absence of a relevant common intention is not confined only to treaties, Lauterpacht explains that the decision in interpreting an agreement or treaty must be given by reference to the *implied intentions* of the parties because the actual subject matter of the dispute could not possibly be present in the minds of the parties at the time of the conclusion of the agreement/treaty (Lauterpacht 1949, p. 52). Based on his observance of the interpretation of treaties by international courts and tribunals, Lauterpacht's view is that a treaty could be far from giving expression to any common intention. So a treaty could, actually, register absence of any common intention or even contain provisions that are mutually inconsistent.[206] As the author suggests, in such situations, there is a requirement of creative work of interpretation that it must be reduced to some coherent meaning.[207] Also, the act of the very choice of any single rule or a combination of them is the result of a

[199]Vitányi (1983).

[200]*Id*, p. 49.

[201]Jacobs (1969), p. 320. The author mentions Lauterpacht's proposals to the Institute of International Law in 1950, which laid particular stress on recourse to *travaux preparatoire* in ascertaining the intentions of the parties.

[202]*Id*, p. 321.

[203]Fitzmaurice (1951), p. 7.

[204]*Id*.

[205]*Id*, p. 5.

[206]Lauterpacht (1949), p. 52.

[207]*Id*.

judgment arrived at, independently of any rules of construction, by judging in consideration of the *good faith principle*.[208] The ILC embodies in Article 70 principles of common sense and good faith, which derive directly from the rule of *pacta sunt servanda* and were repeatedly affirmed by the World Court in its practice on treaty interpretation.[209] Moreover, the Commission puts the *good faith* element at the core of interpretation of treaties, which reflects in Article 70 (and in the later Article 31(1) of the VCLT) *the principle of effective interpretation* (Engelen 2004, p. 69).

Regarding the resort to means of interpretation other than the ordinary meaning of the words, the ILC admits, basing on the ICJ's practice, that such recourse is usually required in case of textual ambiguity or obscurity.[210] In this regard, Article 70 (2) ensured resort to some other means of interpretation.[211] It can be admitted then that the ILC reconciled in Articles 70(2) and 71(1) and (2) the 'textualist', 'teleological' and 'intent' approaches to interpretation. As suggested by the ILC, the general principle that applies in the situations occurring under Article 70, paragraph 2, is that interpretation must be performed in the context of the treaty as a whole and, certainly, in the light of its object and purpose.[212] With regard to paragraph 3 of Article 70, the ILC comments that the practice of the World Court has evidenced the admission of an exception to the 'natural and ordinary meaning' rule in cases where it was established conclusively that the parties employed a particular term with a special meaning.[213] Further, the Commission suggests in respect of Article 71, paragraph 2, that the meaning of the terms is to be established by any relevant evidence or indications of the intention of the parties in using the terms ('in particular, to the preparatory work of the treaty, the circumstances surrounding its conclusion and the subsequent practice of parties in relation to the treaty').[214] It also points out that the *travaux preparatoire* are not authentic means of interpretation but simply evidence to be pondered against any other relevant evidence of the intention of the parties.[215]

---

[208]*Id*, p. 53.

[209]Waldock (1964), p. 56.

[210]Engelen (2004), pp. 56–57. For example, the ICJ held in *The Admission of a State to the United Nations* case: 'The Court considers it necessary to say that the first duty of a tribunal which is called upon to interpret and apply the provisions of a treaty, is to endeavor to give effect to them in their natural and ordinary meaning in the context in which they occur. If the relevant words in their natural and ordinary meaning make sense in their context that is an end of the matter.' It added: 'The Court considers that the text is sufficiently clear; consequently, it does not feel that it should deviate from the consistent practice of the Permanent Court of International Justice, according to which there is no occasion to resort to preparatory work if the text of a Convention is sufficiently clear in itself.'

[211]ILC (1964).

[212]*Id*, p. 48.

[213]*Id*.

[214]*Id*.

[215]*Id*.

Relying on the PCIJ/ICJ's practice, the ILC proposes further in Articles 74 and 75[216] of the *Third Report on the Law of Treaties* rules for interpreting 'treaties drawn up in two or more languages' and 'treaties having two or more texts or versions'. These two articles embodied rules dealing with situations of interpretation of plurality of the authentic treaty texts, in which both or all the texts authoritatively state the terms of the agreement between the parties.[217] According to the ILC's commentary on these provisions, the first rule or principle that can be drawn up from Article 74, paragraph 1, is the equality of the languages and the equal authenticity of the texts in the absence of any provision to the contrary.[218] Then paragraph 2 of the same article reveals the rule of interpretation covering the situation of a treaty's version that is not adopted or 'authenticated' as a text, but it is prescribed by the treaty or accepted by the parties as authentic for the purpose of interpretation.[219] It also provides for the possible situation when a treaty is concluded with an organisation, in which, by means of its organs, it may prescribe that

---

[216] *Id*, p. 62.

**Article 74** 'Treaties drawn up in two or more languages', provided:

1. When the text of a treaty has been authenticated in accordance with the provisions of article 7 in two or more languages, the text is authoritative in each language, except in so far as a different rule may be agreed upon by the parties.
2. A version drawn up in a language other than one in which the text of a treaty was authenticated shall also be authoritative, and considered as an authentic text if:

   a) the parties so agree; or
   b) the established rules of an international organisation so provide.

**Article 75** 'Interpretation of treaties having two or more texts or versions' provided:

1. The expression of the terms of a treaty is of equal authority in each authentic text, subject to the provisions of the present article. The terms are to be presumed to be intended to have the same meaning in each text and their interpretation is governed by article 70-73.
2. When a comparison between two or more authentic texts discloses a difference in the expression of a term and resulting ambiguity or obscurity as to the meaning of the terms is not removed by the application of articles 70-73, the rules contained in paragraphs 3-5 apply, unless the treaty itself provides that, in the event of divergence, a particular text or method of interpretation is to prevail.
3. If in each of two or more authentic texts a term is capable of being given more than one meaning compatible with the objects and purposes of the treaty, a meaning which is common to both or all the texts is to be adopted.
4. If in one authentic text the natural and ordinary meaning of a term is clear and compatible with the objects and purposes of the treaty, whereas in another it is uncertain owing to the obscurity of the term, the meaning of the term in the former text is to be adopted.
5. If the application of the foregoing rules leaves the meaning of a term, as expressed in the authentic text or texts, ambiguous or obscure, reference may be made to the text or version which is not authentic in so far as it throw light on the intentions of the parties with respect to the term in question.

[217] *Id*.

[218] *Id*.

[219] *Id*, pp. 61–62.

texts will be prepared in other official languages of the organisation and be authentic.[220]

Further, Article 75, paragraphs 1 and 2, puts into light as rule or principle of interpretation the unity of the treaty and of each of its terms (honouring the 'context of the whole treaty' rule), along with the equal authority of each authentic text of the plurilingual treaty.[221] The ILC makes clear that the means/rules of interpretation governing plurilingual form of the treaty, including the situation where two or more authentic texts disclose a difference in the expression of a term, are those normal means/rules 'of resolving an ambiguity or obscurity on the basis of the objects and purposes of the treaty, *travaux preparatoire*, the surroundings circumstances, subsequent practice, etc', established in Articles 70–73.[222] However, where there is a possibility of more than one meaning in each of the authentic texts compatible with the objects and purposes of the treaty, paragraph 3 of Article 75 instructs to adopt a meaning that is common to both or all the texts.[223] As it can be observed, the teleological approach of interpretation appears as clearly adopted and underlined in paragraph 3 of Article 75. It is also present in the next paragraph (4), combined with the textualist approach, when the drafters indicated that in the case in which the ordinary meaning of a term is in one authentic text clear and compatible with the objects and purposes of the treaty and in another text the term is uncertain, 'the meaning of the term in the former text is to be adopted'.[224] In addition, the last paragraph, 5, of Article 75 reveals a subjective (intent) approach to interpretation, when it proposes for the rule of admission of non-authentic texts, versions or translations as subsidiary evidence to be used in the 'last resort to throw light on the intentions of the parties with respect to the term in question', of course after the other means of interpretation prescribed by the foregoing rules (including the rules in Articles 70–73) leave the meaning of the text still obscure or ambiguous.[225] It can be concluded that the ILC reconciled also in Articles 74 and 75 the 'textualist', 'teleological' and 'intent' approaches of interpretation.

###### 3.3.2.1.2 Resort to Secondary Sources as Reflected in the Various Approaches to Interpretation

In respect of the resort to 'supplementary means' of interpretation, although none of the four schools categorically reject recourse to them, particularly to the *travaux*

[220]*Id.*

[221]*Id.*

[222]*Id.*

[223]*Id*, p. 64.

[224]Article 75, para 4, see *supra* note 216.

[225]ILC (1964), p. 65.

*preparatoire*, they disagree about the circumstances that justify such recourse.[226] The 'textualist' position is that the interpreter may consult other sources than the treaty itself such as the *travaux preparatoire, only to confirm the meaning derived from the text when it is obscure* and then only to shed light on the text but not on the intentions of the parties apart from the text (Ris 1991, pp. 114–115). G. G. Fitzmaurice, who, as it was mentioned earlier, represents the textualist approach, considers that while the *travaux preparatoire* contain only the statement of intentions of the parties, the 'subsequent practice' instead shows, moreover, the putting into operation of that intention, which helps in ensuring the confirmation of the meaning of the terms under interpretation.[227]

For the 'intention' approach to interpretation instead (subjective method), in the process of ascertaining the intention of the parties, the interpreter is justified to resort to supplementary sources such as the *travaux preparatoire, even when the text of the treaty appears to be clear, unambiguous.*[228] The *travaux preparatoire* appear thus for the 'intention' school almost a priority over the actual text of the treaty (Fitzmaurice 2013). Unlike the 'textualist' approach, the 'intent' approach admits that no disputed text is ever completely clear. And even in a case of an apparently clear text, it is seldom so clear that reference to the records will not make it clearer still and that the very notion of clarity is, actually, a subjective one.[229] Conversely, according to G. G. Fitzmaurice, 'teleologists' 'bypass' the idea of intention and see the text construed in the light of the known or presumed 'objects' of the treaty as it is declared within it, or to be inferred from other means of interpretation, such as the circumstances of its making, or from its subsequent history and proceedings.[230] Unlike the subjective and textualist approaches (doctrines), the 'teleological' approach does not strictly distinguish between primary and secondary sources of interpretation.[231]

The later drafting of Article 27 (in the 1966 *Draft Articles on the Law of Treaties*), providing for the 'general rule of interpretation', and of Article 28, providing for the 'supplementary means of interpretation', establishes a clear hierarchy in favour of the ordinary meaning of the words, thus primacy for the textualist approach.[232] The essential difference between these articles (Articles 27 and 28)

[226] Fitzmaurice (1951), p. 7. G.G. Fitzmaurice specifies that the object of interpretation consists in determining the meaning of the text, which speaks for itself, rather than the intention of the parties, because '[a] common intention may not even exist or be very obscure, and if it does not exist, there will be no dispute' and that the conclusion of the treaty itself must be presumed to express the real intention of the framers of the treaty.

[227] *Id*, p. 2.

[228] *Id.*

[229] *Id.*

[230] *Id.*

[231] *Id.*

[232] Jacobs (1969), p. 326.

and those originally drafted (Articles 70 and 71) was that the 'subsequent practice' became admitted *as principal means of interpretation*.[233] Contrary to the traditional approaches to interpretation, the 'subsequent practice' was admitted (in former Article 71, para 2) as evidence of the original intention of the parties, not only in throwing light on the intention but also as supplementary means of interpretation.[234]

Further and related to these arguments should be mentioned Lauterpacht's conception that when the common intention is not found, full effect has to be given in the terms of the agreement to the *object of the treaty* for which it was concluded.[235] This idea is reflected in the 'principle of effectiveness' to which Lauterpacht gave full consideration. He explains that 'it is seldom that the unavoidable choice is between requiring a total frustration of the apparent purpose of the treaty and endowing it with full measure of effectiveness in disregards of the intentions of the parties'.[236] Although the ICJ in its practice of treaty interpretation (pre-1969) had often employed the *principle of effectiveness*, the ILC excluded it from its literal codification in the VCLT.[237] However, this principle finds reflection within the general rule of interpretation, particularly in Article 31 of the VCLT. As it was drawn up initially and proposed in a separate article (entitled 'Effective interpretation of the terms (*ut res magis valeat quam pereat*))'[238] by G. G. Fitzmaurice among the six fundamental principles of interpretation, the effectiveness principle instructs the interpreter as follows:

> Treaties are to be interpreted with reference to their declared or apparent objects and purposes; and particular provisions are to be interpreted so as to give them their fullest weight and effect consistent with the normal sense of the words and with other parts of the text, and in such a way that a reason and a meaning can be attributed to every part of the text.[239]

[233]*Id*, p. 327.

[234]*Id*, pp. 327–328. And this is, as appreciated by G. Jacobs, 'the most striking innovation in the interpretative provisions of the Convention' and the most significant modification of the textual approach as the main characteristic of the second Draft Convention.

*Id*, p. 321.

[235]*Id*.

[236]Lauterpacht (1949), p. 73. As observed by Lauterpacht, 'the intention of the parties expressed or implied – is the law'. He implies that whatever considerations of effectiveness or otherwise that tend to transform 'the ascertainable intention of the parties into a factor of secondary importance' are detrimental to the true purpose of a treaty.

[237]Van Damme (2009).

[238]See the principle of effectivness as formulated in Draft Article 72, in the ILC's Third Draft on the Law of Treaties (1964), p. 55, *supra* note 190.

[239]Besides the principle of effectivness, as part of the general rules of interpretation (provided in Articles 70–75), the (general) principles regarding *interpretation of treaties* proposed by G. G. Fitzmaurice were clearly defined as follows:

I. *Principle of actuality* (or *textuality*).Treaties are to be interpreted primarily as they stand, and on the basis of their actual texts.

Noticeable is that the principle of effectiveness played an essential role for *the New Haven* school of interpretation.[240] The essence of the New Haven approach to interpretation consists in contextualism, the *context* being relevant to the expectation of the parties and to the determination of *how world community policies enter the interpretative process*.[241] Towards this purpose, the interpreter should inquire into all indices of the expectations of the parties (Ris 1991, p. 116). The particular characteristic of the New Haven School is that it removes the text as the principal object of the interpretative process and 'redefines the intentions of the parties to an agreement into their "shared expectation"' (Hernandez 2014, p. 343). Thus, the New Haven School's emphasis is on ascertaining the 'subjective, common agreement of the parties, which in turn is understood against a common (objective) "standard of justice"'.[242]

In detailing this aspect, Gardiner explains that there are treaties that need development or further elaboration in their lifetime, which suppose collaboration of the parties in their implementation, as well as there are treaties that do not require such collaboration (Gardiner 2008, p. 65). The author differentiates between a

---

II. *Principle of the natural and ordinary meaning*. Subject to principle IV below, when applicable, particular words and phrases are to be given their normal, natural, and unstrained meaning in the context in which they occur. This meaning can only be displaced by direct evidence that the terms used are to be understood in another sense than the natural and ordinary one, or if such an interpretation would lead to an unreasonable or absurd result. Only if the language employed is fundamentally obscure or ambiguous may recourse be had to extraneous means of interpretation, such as consideration of the surrounding circumstances, or *travaux preparatoire*.

III. *Principle of integration*. Treaties are to be interpreted as a whole, and particular parts, chapters or sections also as a whole.

IV. *Principle of effectiveness*. Treaties are to be interpreted with reference to their declared or apparent objects and purposes; and particular provisions are to be interpreted so as to give them their fullest weight and effect consistent with the normal sense of the words and with other parts of the text, and in such a way that a reason and a meaning can be attributed to every part of the text.

V. *Principle of subsequent practice*. In interpreting a text, recourse to the subsequent conduct and practice of the parties in relation to the treaty is permissible, and may be desirable, as affording the best and most reliable evidence, derived from how the treaty has been interpreted in practice, as to what its correct interpretation is.

VI. *Principle of contemporaneity*. The terms of a treaty must be interpreted according to the meaning which they possessed, or which would have been attributed to them, and in the light of current linguistic usage, at the time when the treaty was originally concluded.

[240]Falk (1967), pp. 334–335.

[241]*Id*. Falk mentions the influence of McDougal, Lasswell and Miller's theory on interpretation of international agreements in the relevant provisions of the final Draft Articles of Treaties of the ILC. According to Falk, for these authors the primary aim of a process of interpretation is to discover the 'shared expectations' that the parties to the relevant agreement succeeded in understanding each other to have over it.

[242]Hernandez (2014), p. 343.

treaty concluded by two states that may simply contain a deal done between them and treaties that require 'a kind of interpretation that may well need to take account of community values', such as those reflected in human rights treaties, or reflecting values of a community of states (at universal or regional scale) that can be seen in the object and purpose of each of such treaties.[243] According to Gardiner, when referring to values accepted by the parties, the New Haven School has in sight those values accepted as relevant, which are 'explicitly and implicitly agreed values' by the parties within the framework of international law and not demanded by some 'nebulous community values'.[244]

Interestingly, in the supporters' vision of the New Haven approach, such as McDougal, Lasswell and Miller, the 'principle of projecting genuine expectation' has been expressed under the rubric of 'effectiveness' and 'restrictive interpretation' (McDougal et al. 1994, p. 156). The authors claim that this principle has been most influential in past decisions of the World Court, as the widely accepted interpretative standard in the traditional repertoire.[245] This principle has been named in various ways in practice, for example the principle of 'major purposes' or of 'extensive interpretation' (which goes back to Grotius, Vattel and Pufendorf).[246] Also, it was considered a version of the principle according to which '[a] treaty is to be interpreted in the light of the general purpose which it is intended to serve', as seen expressed in the Draft Convention of the ILC, in 1935, part of the *Harvard Research in International Law*.[247] Both the 'teleological' and 'New Haven' schools leave the use of the *travaux preparatoire* to the discretion of the decision-maker interpreter.[248] But, unlike the textualist and teleological schools, for the New Haven School, a treaty (text) and its *travaux preparatoire* are equally valid sources of interpretation.[249]

In the light of the above discussion, it could be stated that the process of the formulation of a general rule of treaty interpretation emerged from a long doctrinal debate, characterised by a continued controversy over the principles of treaty interpretation advanced by the approaches/schools of thought of interpretation. As G. G. Fitzmaurice observes, the reason for this controversy is to be found in the fact that each doctrinal approach to interpretation has tended to confer primacy on one particular rule/element of interpretation, if not to the exclusion, certainly to the subordination of the others (Fitzmaurice 1951). Yet, according to Jacobs, the necessity to answer the question of which school has monopoly over the interpretative outcome persists as the jurisprudence of international tribunals could not

[243] Gardiner (2008), p. 66.
[244] *Id.*
[245] *Id.*
[246] *Id.*
[247] Harvard Research (1957), p. 938.
[248] *Id.*
[249] *Id.*

pronounce specifically upon which approach to interpretation it relies most (Jacobs 1969, p. 318). The answer instead is brought to light by the rules of interpretation, which are rules that settle the difference of views, as also the content of rules (Orakhelashvili 2008, p. 304).

#### 3.3.2.2 The International Law Commission's Final Draft on Treaty Interpretation

If the previous section took into account a general context of the development of principles of treaty interpretation that led to the formulation of the 'general rule of interpretation' of treaties, the next section is going to look in some detail at the formulation of the final draft articles on treaty interpretation for a better picture of how these articles subsequently appear codified in the 1969 VCLT's 'general rule of interpretation' (Articles 31–33). There will be a focus on a doctrinal discussion mainly from the perspective of the ILC. This analysis provides a basis for understanding the application by the PCIJ/ICJ, ECtHR and WTO of the general rules of treaty interpretation in their practices, both prior to and after the adoption of the 1969 VCLT. Before proceeding to examine further the process of formulation of the rules/principles of treaty interpretation and their final embodiment in the articles providing for the 'general rule of interpretation', a definition of *treaty* is needed. According to the final ILC draft articles on the law of treaties, Article 2(1)(a) provides that 'a "treaty" is an international agreement concluded between States in written form and governed by international law, whether embodied in a single instrument, or in two or more related instruments and whatever its particular designation'.[250]

It is important to note here that, in the final draft of the articles on treaty interpretation, at the 18th session in 1966,[251] the ILC made clear that the basic approach to treaty interpretation proposed by Waldock was adopted virtually without change in the structure and substance of the articles (Engelen 2004, p. 72). A large majority supported the textualist approach and endorsed the proposition that extraneous evidence or indications of the intention of the parties that can be found, for example, in the preparatory work of the treaty, or in the circumstances of its conclusion, only have a subsidiary role to play in the process of treaty interpretation.[252]

The corresponding provision of Article 70, discussed above, in the new (final) Draft of 1966 is Article 27, which set forth the 'general rule of interpretation'. As it was expressed in the Commentary on the original draft prepared by Waldock,

[250]ILC (1966), p. 187.

[251]Koskenniemi (2006), p. 143.

[252]Engelen (2004), p. 72.

Article 27 became an almost *verbatim* expression of Article 70.[253] It is worth mentioning that by entitling Article 27—'General rule of interpretation'—in the singular and underlining the connection between paragraphs 1 and 2, and then between paragraph 2 and 3, the Commission is thought to indicate that the application of the means of interpretation in this article would constitute *a single combined operation*; *a single closely-integrated rule*.[254] Admitted as the key of any treaty interpretative process, this aspect is reflected in ILC's following statement:

> All the various elements, as they were present in any given case, would be thrown into the crucible and their interaction would give the legally relevant interpretation.[255]

As the final draft of the ILC can show, Article 27 provided that the 'ordinary meaning' should be given to each term 'in the context of the treaty and in the light of its object and purpose'.[256] Also, in the ILC's commentaries, it is pointed out that the term 'context' in paragraph 2 (of Article 27) is designed to link all the elements of interpretation mentioned therein to the word 'context' in paragraph 1 and to incorporate them in the provision contained in that paragraph.[257] In the same vein, the opening phrase of paragraph 3—'[t]here shall be taken into account together with the *context*'—is construed as to incorporate in paragraph 1 the elements of interpretation set forth in paragraph 3 of Article 27.[258] Arguably, one of the most important aspects outlined by the ILC, based on the comments submitted by governments, is that Article 27 read as a whole cannot lay down a legal hierarchy of norms for interpretation of treaties but that these norms are only arranged in some order regarding considerations of logic.[259] However, the ILC admits that the

---

[253]ILC (1966), p. 228.

**Article 27** of the Draft Article (1966) stated:

1. A treaty shall be interpreted in good faith in accordance with the ordinary meaning to be given to the terms of the treaty in their context and in the light of its object and purpose;
2. The context for the purpose of the interpretation of a treaty shall comprise, in addition to the text, including its preamble and annexes (a) Any agreement relating to the treaty which was made between all the parties connection with the conclusion of the treaty; (b) Any instrument which was made by one or more parties in connection with the conclusion of the treaty and accepted by the other parties as an instrument related to the treaty.
3. There shall be taken into account, together with the context: (a) Any subsequent agreement between the parties regarding the interpretation of the treaty; (b) Any subsequent practice in the application of the treaty which establishes the understanding of the parties regarding its interpretation; (c) Any relevant rules of international law applicable in the relations between the parties;
4. A special meaning shall be given to a term if it is established that the parties so intended.

[254]*Id*, p. 220 (emphasis added).

[255]*Id*, pp. 219–220.

[256]*Id*.

[257]*Id*, p. 204.

[258]*Id* (emphasis added).

[259]*Id*.

wording of Article 27 conveys the idea that the text of the treaty is presumed to be the authentic expression of the intention of the parties, the starting point of interpretation in the elucidation of the text, similar in structure and substance to Article 70 (in the previous draft articles).[260] In paragraph 3 of Article 27, the Commission considers it necessary to add three 'elements', all deemed 'extrinsic to the text' and of an 'obligatory character', which 'shall be taken into account, together with the context' in interpretation (McDougal 1967, p. 995).

It is noteworthy that, aside from the ILC, many authors provided comments on the draft articles more or less supporting the ILC's views on the matter. For example, according to McDougal, similarly to Article 70 of the original draft articles, Article 27 (1) lays down three separate principles of interpretation: (1) interpretation should be made in good faith, which flows from the *pacta sunt servanda* principle; (2) the parties are presumed to have that intention, which appears from the ordinary meaning of the terms used by them; and (3) the ordinary meaning of the terms is to be asserted, not in the abstract but in the context of the treaty and in the light of its object and purpose.[261] By comparing Article 27 with the first draft article (its corresponding Article 70), Jacobs admits that the 'object and purpose' of the treaty were only admitted in Article 70 as, what were later called, 'supplementary means of interpretation'.[262]

Further, according to the ILC commentaries, as an authentic element of interpretation and objective evidence of the understanding of the parties, 'any subsequent agreement between the parties' and 'subsequent practice' are required to be taken into account, together with the context (paragraph 3 (a) and (b) of Article 27).[263] The Commission acknowledges that in the final draft, respectively in Article 27, paragraph 3 (a and b), it adopts the text that speaks of a practice that 'establishes the understanding of all the parties', but the word 'all' is omitted 'merely to avoid any possible misconception that every party must individually have engaged in the practice when it suffices that it should have accepted the practice'.[264] Further rule contained in paragraph 4 of Article 27 is, in essence, similar to the previous draft of Article 70, paragraph 3, and is similarly linked to the rule contained in paragraph 1 of the same article through the word 'special' related to a meaning of a term that the parties agreed to give.[265] However, the formulation of Article 27 on treaty interpretation in the final draft of the Commission is not free of criticism. For example, McDougal argues that in the explicit rejection of a quest for the 'intention

[260] *Id.*

[261] *Id.*

[262] Jacobs (1969), p. 334. See for comparison with Article 70, which provided in paragraph 2 (a) that 'If the natural and ordinary meaning of a term leads to an interpretation which is manifestly absurd or unreasonable in the context of the treaty as a whole . . . shall be interpreted by reference to —a) its context and the objects and purposes of the treaty'.

[263] ILC (1966), pp. 221–222. These means of interpretation were part of Article 73 of the Draft Articles of the Third Report on the Law of Treaties (1964).

[264] *Id.*

[265] *Id.*

of the parties as a subjective element distinct from the text', the ILC implicitly adopts a 'basic approach' that merely demands the designation of interpretation to a text (McDougal 1967, p. 992). As it has been argued above, this 'basic approach' clearly imposes a hierarchy among the means of treaty interpretation that supposes, in McDougal's words, 'an impossible, conformity-imposing textuality'.[266] Moreover, by bringing into light the distinction between 'canons' and 'general rules' of interpretation, McDougal argues that whereas the 'so-called canons' are not 'automatic' in their application but depend upon discretion, in contrast 'the general rules' of interpretation appear as 'obligatory' and presumably 'automatic', including within it the promotion of the good faith interpretation of treaties.[267]

The ILC provides further in Article 28 of the final draft for recourse to the 'supplementary means of interpretation', including preparatory work, to be permissible when the text of a treaty leaves the meaning ambiguous or obscure or leads to a result that is manifestly absurd or unreasonable.[268] According to the commentary on the (final) Draft Articles, the fact that Article 28 admits recourse to the supplementary means for the purpose of 'confirming' the meaning resulting from the application of Article 27 establishes a general link between the two articles and ensures *the unity* of the act of interpretation.[269] Importantly, the Commission establishes that Article 28 does not draw a rigid boundary between the 'supplementary means' of interpretation and the means of interpretation contained in Article 27.[270] Yet McDougal sees the construction of these two articles differently. He asserts that the Commission's insistence upon the 'primacy of the text' is still maintained in Article 28 as it authorises 'a minimum recourse to preparatory work, and other features of the process of the agreement prior to its culmination in the sacred words of commitment'.[271]

The following Article 29,[272] which corresponds to Articles 74–75 of the *Third Report on the Law of Treaties*, was proposed by the ILC to deal with the languages

---

[266] McDougal (1967), p. 992.

[267] *Id.* McDougal concludes that the 'ordinary meaning' expression itself is an invincible term of textuality.

[268] ILC (1966), p. 204.

**Article 28** stated:

> Recourse may be had to supplementary means of interpretation, including the preparatory work of the treaty and the circumstances of its conclusion, in order to confirm the meaning resulting from the application of article 27, or to determine the meaning when the interpretation according to Article 27: (a) Leaves the meaning ambiguous or obscure; or (b) Leads to a result which is, manifestly absurd or unreasonable.

[269] *Id*, p. 220.

[270] *Id.*

[271] McDougal (1967), p. 995.

[272] ILC (1966) **Article 29**: 'Interpretation of treaties in two or more languages', stated:

1. When a treaty has been authenticated in two or more languages, the text is equally authoritative in each language, unless the treaty provides or the parties agree that, in case of divergence, a particular text shall prevail.

in which treaties were considered usually written (in two or more languages) and their role in the interpretation of treaties. Although a comparison of more authentic texts is introduced in the interpretation of the treaty as a new element, the ILC concludes that it supposes not a different system of interpretation but an interpretation of the texts by the normal means of interpretation.[273] The provision in paragraph 1 of Article 29 establishes that treaties, sometimes, provide expressly that only certain texts of a treaty drafted in two or more languages are to be authoritative.[274] So the paragraph provides that in case of divergence between the texts, a specific text is to prevail. The first important principle in the interpretation of plurilingual treaties, reflected in Article 29, is, according to the ILC, the equality of texts (that each of the versions may have the status of authentic text of the treaty), or one of more of them may be merely an 'efficient' or the 'master' text.[275] Further, paragraph 2 of this provision prescribes for the case of a version of the treaty that is not 'authenticated', but it is nevertheless provided by the treaty or accepted by the parties as authentic for the purpose of interpretation.[276] Another principle reflected in Article 29, and underlined by the ILC as fundamentally important, is the unity of the treaty and of its terms, which are intended to have the same meaning in each text.[277] It means that despite the fact that the treaty is drawn in plurilingual expressions, it remains 'a single treaty with a single set of terms of interpretation of which is governed by the rules set out in article 27 and 28'.[278] Finally, in paragraph 3 of Article 29, the drafters provide for the presumption of equality of the meaning of each authentic text, except from the cases where the parties have agreed upon the priority of a particular text, when in case of a divergence between authentic texts, a meaning that so far as possible reconciles the different texts is to be adopted.[279] Notice should be made here that the drafters did not make any reference in Article 29, like in the corresponding Article 75 (above discussed), to the teleological method when a comparison of the texts discloses a difference of

2. A version of the treaty in a language other than one of those in which the text was authenticated shall be considered an authentic text only if the treaty so provides or the parties so agree.

3. The terms of the treaty are presumed to have the same meaning in each authentic text, except in the case mentioned in paragraph 1, when a comparison of the texts discloses a difference of meaning which the application of articles 27 and 28 does not remove, a meaning which as far as possible reconciles the texts shall be adopted.

[273]*Id*, p. 224, paras 6–7. According to the ILC, 'the first rule for the interpreter is to look for the meaning intended by the parties to be attached to the terms by applying the standard for the interpretation of treaties'.

[274]*Id*, para 2.

[275]*Id*, para 1.

[276]*Id*, para 2.

[277]*Id*.

[278]*Id*, p. 225, para 7. The ILC stated that 'The unity of the treaty and of each of its terms is of fundamental importance in the interpretation of plurilingual treaties . . .'.

[279]*Id*, para 8.

meaning. However, as it will be seen below in the later (corresponding) Article 33 of the VCLT, the drafters will revise this aspect, specifically indicating a teleological perspective of interpretation. As observed by Gardiner, despite the fact that the draft of Article 29 was originally handled by the ILC drafters 'separately from the rest of the section on interpretation' (*the general rule* and *the supplementary means of interpretation* as were set out initially together), this provision was always considered part of the general rule of interpretation and of no less importance (Gardiner 2008, p. 355).

Significantly is that there are to be recognised two important stages of approaching the 'general rule of interpretation' as set forth in Article 27 and Article 28 of the final Draft (1966). As observed by Merrills, the first stage *is to enumerate factors to determine the ordinary meaning of the treaty terms in question*; and the second stage *is to confirm an interpretation arrived at by applying the ordinary meaning, or to confirm an interpretation when the ordinary meaning leaves the meaning ambiguous or obscure* (Merrills 1968, p. 81). The next section will show that these stages will also be reflected in the 'general rule of interpretation' set forth in Articles 31 and 32 of the 1969 VCLT.

## 3.4 The 'General Rule of Interpretation' as Codified in Articles 31–33 of the 1969 VCLT: Scholarship Review

One of the results of the development that the VCLT brought to light was the rule of interpretation in Article 31, which establishes, *inter alia*, the 'object and purpose' of a treaty and the 'context' as guidelines for interpretation (Zemanek 2009). These are considered in the scholarship to be the rules of interpretation that the teleological approach stresses as essential in determining the intention of the parties, which militate against a special emphasis on a literal narrow construction of the text of a treaty.[280]

### *3.4.1 Article 31 of the VCLT*

As codified in the VCLT, Article 31 provides for the 'General rule of interpretation':

1. A treaty shall be interpreted in good faith in accordance with the ordinary meaning to be given to the terms of the treaty in their context and in the light of its object and purpose.

[280] *Id.* In the Judgment on the Arbitral Award of 31 July 1989, the International Court of Justice held that '... [a]rticles 31 and 32 of the Vienna Convention on the Law of Treaties may in many respects be considered as a codification of existing customary international law ...' (I.C.J. Reports 1991, pp. 69–70, para 48).

2. The context for the purpose of the interpretation of a treaty shall comprise, in addition to the text, including its preamble and annexes:

   (a) any agreement relating to the treaty which was made between all the parties in connection with the conclusion of the treaty;
   (b) any instrument which was made by one or more parties in connection with the conclusion of the treaty and accepted by the other parties as an instrument related to the treaty.

3. There shall be taken into account, together with the context

   (a) any subsequent agreement between the parties regarding the interpretation of the treaty or the application of its provisions
   (b) any subsequent practice in the application of the treaty which establishes the agreement of the parties regarding its interpretation;
   (c) any relevant rules of international law applicable in the relations between the parties.

4. A special meaning shall be given to a term if it is established that the parties so intended (VCLT 1969).

Nevertheless, far from being a closed topic once codified, the VCLT's 'general rule of interpretation' constitutes an ongoing debate over its strengths and weaknesses. For example, in Jacobs' observation, an interesting similarity as between the 'resolution' on treaty interpretation of the Institute of International Law (discussed above) and Article 31(1) of the VCLT appears to show an attempt to reconcile the three opposing approaches (methods) of treaty interpretation: *textualist*, *subjective* and *teleological*.[281] In regard to the *New Haven approach*, Gardiner explains that the main difference between the 1969 VCLT and the New Haven School is that the VCLT gives more concrete indications as to the boundaries of the interpretation process and differentiates to some extent between primary and secondary rules of interpretation (Gardiner 2009). In any case, the shared expectations of the parties to a treaty (as specific characteristic of the New Haven approach to interpretation) must be that the treaty will be interpreted according to the VCLT rules.[282]

In support of the ILC's suggestion for a single rule of interpretation, for example, Villiger's opinion is that the structure of Article 31, as a 'General Rule', does leave no doubt that all its component elements, as well as the supplementary means of interpretation in Article 32, lead to this end: *a general rule of interpretation*.[283] He explains that Article 31 provides in its title for a 'general rule of interpretation' because paragraph 1 states in *general terms* that 'a treaty shall be interpreted ... in accordance with ... and in the light of ...' and, further, according to paragraph 2, 'the context shall comprise ...', and to paragraph 3: 'there shall be taken into account together with the context ...'.[284] Thus, Villiger admits that the various

---

[281]VCLT (1969).

[282]Gardiner (2009).

[283]Villiger (2009), p. 434. According to Villiger, in its final draft articles on treaty interpretation with regard to Article 27, the ILC makes it clear that the 'general rule' in the actual Article 31 functions as a single process of application in which all means will be considered in one.

[284]*Id.*

means of interpretation mentioned in Article 31 are all of equal value, giving the interpreter the perspective of viewing *the treaty as a whole*, and so there is no hierarchy among them, and none is of an inferior character.[285] As the same author observes, the 'ordinary meaning' of the terms can only be assessed in the *context*, which involves the entire article at issue and the remainder of the treaty, its text, preamble and annexes, as also the other means mentioned in paragraphs 2 and 3 of Article 31.[286] In addition, the notion of 'good faith' is thought to be at the core of the 'General Rule' and requires the parties to act honestly, fairly and reasonably and to refrain from taking unfair advantage; thus, the notion has a normative quality.[287] Or, in the words of Bjorge, 'good faith acts as a guarantor of expectations legitimately held by one of the parties to the treaty', so treaties must be interpreted 'in conformity with loyalty and reciprocal confidence' (Bjorge 2014, p.191). 'Good faith' implies the consideration of the 'object and purpose' of a treaty, and it is important in establishing the 'subsequent practice', as also in determining the need to resort to the 'supplementary means' of interpretation provided by Article 32.[288]

A similar opinion regarding Article 31 is expressed by French, who observes that this provision is in fact, in its entirety, the 'general rule of interpretation', not just Article 31 paragraph 1, as is sometimes presumed (French 2006, p. 301). So this article, seen as a whole, demands the *holistic* and comprehensive approach to be taken by interpreters when applying it.[289] The fact that the reference to the 'context' in paragraph 1 confirms the relativity of the 'ordinary meaning' rule as governing rule is best reflected in one particular statement of the ILC's commentaries in the final Draft, already mentioned above:

> The application of the means of interpretation in the article would be a single combined operation. All the various elements, as they were present in any given case, would be thrown into the crucible and their interactions would give the legally relevant interpretation.[290]

In regard to the limitations of Article 31(1), for example, McDougal claims that 'a concern for a text alone, apart from the circumstances of its conclusion can afford no criteria for ascribing a meaning to the text' (McDougal et al. 1994, p. 438). However, McDougal admits that the reference to the terms 'context' and 'object and purpose' in Article 31(1) remedies, at least, the 'blindness and arbitrariness' of the 'ordinary meaning' context (McDougal 1967, p. 993). Also, Buffa observes that by initially prescribing a preference for textualism in the phrase 'ordinary meaning given to the terms' within Article 31, which directs the interpreter to begin looking

[285] *Id*, pp. 434–436. Villiger admits that the starting point in interpretation is 'ordinary meaning' but then on equal level follows consideration of the 'context', 'object and purpose' and 'any relevant rules of international law'.

[286] *Id*.

[287] *Id*.

[288] *Id*. In respect of paragraph 3(a) and (b), Villiger observes that it differs from paragraph 2 as 'any subsequent agreement' and 'any subsequent practice' by definition originate after the conclusion of the treaty; however, they are to be equally considered to be the subject matter of the treaty itself.

[289] French (2006), p. 301.

[290] ILC (1966), pp. 219–220 (emphasis added).

at the words as they are commonly understood in the text, without taking other sources into account, in practice, this article can give an advantage to skilful lawyers (Buffa 2010, p. 604). For example, the words of Article 31 can usually assign ambiguity to apparently straightforward phrases when a state asserts a particular construction as to gain an advantage in international relations.[291] In assisting with a strict reading of the text, Buffa's view is that paragraphs 2 and 3 of Article 31 come to list specific documents that the interpreter may take into account in order to deduce the 'meaning to be given to the terms of the treaty in their context and in the light of its object and purpose'.[292]

Further, Article 31(3)(c), which provides for taking into account, together with the context, 'any relevant rules of international law applicable in the relations between the parties', is the provision that has generated most-heated debate, and various views have been advanced in the scholarship in respect of its content. More recently, for example, Merkouris' view is that the terms of this provision, by being vague, offer little assistance in determining its exact content.[293] The author claims that this provision is, in essence, the point of convergence between 'norm' and 'system'. He admits, however, that not all elements pertinent to the principle of 'systemic integration' that this article promotes are explicitly mentioned in Article 31(3)(c), such as 'inter-temporal law'; the notion of 'parties', the rules as covering not only general principles and customary international law but also conventional rules; or the notion of 'equity' as a guide for the interpreter to opt for an extensive interpretation to avoid a conflict of norms and not cause 'unwarranted harm to parties'.[294]

Also, according to McLachlan, Article 31(3)(c) does not specify what to do about overlapping treaty obligations and whether the other applicable international law needs to be in force at the conclusion of the treaty, or otherwise (McLachlan 2005, p. 268). However, in McLachlan's observation, the task of this provision is one of 'operationalizing',[295] having also the purpose of reducing fragmentation and promoting coherence in international law.[296] And importantly, Article 31(3)(c) has the task to reinstate the central role of customary or general international law in the interpretation of treaties, locate the other relevant conventional international law in the process and also shed new light on the position of treaties in the progressive

[291]Buffa (2010), p. 604.

[292]*Id.*

[293]Merkouris (2010b), pp. 17–19. The author takes each of the terms of the provision into analysis. He observes, for example, that 'the rules' create confusion for an interpreter, who should bear in mind not only the principles but also all the relevant rules, be they treaty or customary nature, also the term 'general' that could link to regional custom to which the drafters could not contemplate, or the term 'parties' that could identify either a party to an agreement (or legal transaction), i.e., a treaty, or a party to a legal dispute.

[294]*Id*, p. 34. The author refers to 'equity' (advocated by Vattel) in reference to things that 'tend to the common advantage' of the contracting parties or 'useful and salutary to human society'.

[295]McLachlan (2005), p. 268.

[296]*Id.*

development of international law (inter-temporality).[297] In the same vein, Pauwelyn and Elsig admit that the use of generic terms in treaties is, in general, the reason that international courts such as the ICJ, ECtHR, WTO are forced to adopt an evolutionary rather than an original interpretation[298] under Article 31(3)(c). An evolutionary interpretation implies interpreting treaties in the broader context of other treaties and general international law and in the light of international law's new developments.[299] By resorting to such an approach, the courts attempt to reconcile different treaties and read them from the perspective of a coherent system (systemic integration).[300] The belief in the suitability of Article 31(3)(c) for dealing with the issue of 'fragmentation of international law' receives keen attention in academic writings, precisely for its design to 'take into account, together with the context', *general international law* in the act of treaty interpretation (McLachlan 2005, p. 268).

Because Article 31(3)(c) has been criticised as being unclear in its substantive and temporal scope, as well in its normative force,[301] the ILC Study's focus on this provision revives its importance among the other means of interpretation. In essence, the Study is admitted as bringing Article 31(3)(c) to the fore, suggesting that it introduces an autonomous method of interpretation, called 'systemic integration' (Tzevelekos 2009, p. 624). According to Pauwelyn and Elsig, the term 'systemic' (in reference to 'integration') signifies an outward looking and links to general international law (including the VCLT), other treaties and tribunals, as well as to academic writings.[302] By providing for the taking into account together with the context of 'any relevant rules of international law applicable in the relations between the parties', the ILC concludes that Article 31(3)(c) is 'a reasonable or even necessary aspect of the practice of legal reasoning'.[303] Therefore, this

[297] *Id.*

[298] Based on treaty terms as drafted at the time of its conclusion.

[299] Pauwelyn and Elsig (2013), pp. 460–462. The authors define 'evolutionary' as 'meaning at the time the dispute is decided (dynamic, evolves with new developments); addresses problem of treaty rigidity'.

[300] *Id.* According to the authors, the WTO, for example, by using broad, unspecified terms such as 'exhaustible natural resources', 'public morals', 'essential security interests' (in GATT Articles XX, XXI), indicates that the drafters of the WTO Agreements intended these terms to evolve with society and international law, foreseeing an evolutionary interpretation to be approached. The authors see this approach as both logical and necessary also in respect of interpreting the ECHR by the ECtHR. I.e., in the *Tyrer* case, the ECtHR recalled that 'the Convention is a living instrument which ... must be interpreted in the light of the present day conditions ... the Court cannot but be influenced by the development and commonly accepted standards in the penal policy of the member States of the Council of Europe in this field'. See also on 'evolutionary interpretation' subject: Bjorge (2014).

[301] ILC (2006), p. 213.

[302] Pauwelyn and Elsig (2013), p. 460.

[303] ILC (2006), p. 213 (emphasis added). In the words of the ILC Study Group (at p. 413, para 18): 'Systemic integration governs all treaty interpretation, the other relevant aspects of which are set out in the other paragraphs of Articles 31 and 32 VCLT. These paragraphs describe a process of legal reasoning, in which particular elements will have greater or less relevance depending upon the nature of the treaty provisions in the context of interpretation.'

provision is thought to serve in the elucidation of the questions related to the alleged fragmentation of international law.[304]

One of the basic ideas that support the *systemic integration* concept is that all treaty provisions set up rights and obligations that exist alongside rights and obligations established by other treaty provisions and rules of customary international law.[305] The ILC Study observes that there is both the practice and doctrine that attest to the application of the 'systemic integration' principle under Article 31 (3)(c), providing for *customary law*, *general principles of law* and *general treaty provisions* as 'the interpretative background for specific treaty provisions'.[306] Also, the Study mentions in this regard that customary law and general principles of law, which Article 31(3)(c) refers to as 'relevant rules of international law', by their very nature, are often applied alongside particular treaties.[307] Moreover, the ILC Study supports the idea that if in their treaty relations states can specifically exclude one, more or, in theory, all rules of general international law (other than those of *jus cogens*), however, they cannot contract out of the system of international law.[308] This aspect is illustrated by the ILC Study, for example, by reference to human rights adjudicative bodies, the ECtHR and IACtHR. When interpreting their relevant treaties, these specialised courts take into account the rules of international law of 'state responsibility', 'immunity', 'jurisdiction' and 'the general principles of law recognized by civilized nations'.[309] In this respect, the words of a former member of the ECtHR and the President of the IACtHR, are conclusive when admitting that 'the systems in cause are an integral part of the international general law and conventional law. This signifies the idea that fragmentation of international law is not pertinent for the international systems of human rights protection.'[310] In fact, it suggests what the ILC highlights further in its Study Report that '[t]o make or defend a claim of "speciality" is only possible in "general" terms', so fragmentation of the substance of international law 'does not pose any very serious danger to legal practice' (ILC 2006, p. 114).

Although the ILC admits with some exceptions that special law has priority over general law,[311] in practice, Article 31(3)(c) appears to prescribe in effect that

---

[304]*Id*, p. 213.

[305]*Id*, p. 206.

[306]*Id*, p. 211.

[307]*Id*, p. 223.

[308]*Id*, p. 93. See in this regard the ILC citing the *Georges Pinson* case *(France v. United Mexican States)*, Award of 13 April 1928, UNRIAA, vol V, p. 422, in which the Permanent Court of Arbitration held that: 'Every international convention must be deemed tacitly to refer to general principles of international law for all the questions which it does not itself resolve in express terms and in a different way'.

[309]*Id*, p. 96.

[310]*Id* (the ILC citing Lucius Caflisch and Cancado Trinidade's Study on European and American conventions on human rights).

[311]*Id*, pp. 411–414, paras 237–251. The ILC concludes that *jus cogens* is expressly non-derogable and that customary international law and general principles of law are of particular relevance to the

general rules (e.g., on interpretation, sovereignty, statehood, jurisdiction, immunity) always have precedence over rules of special regimes (e.g., human rights law, trade law, criminal law). For example, the ICJ adopted this position in the recent *Jurisdictional Immunities Case* (2012)[312] or in an earlier case, *Arrest Warrants* (2002),[313] where the ICJ made an authoritative statement in respect of the customary law on the question of immunity.[314] Though the decision in the *Arrest Warrants* case was criticised,[315] the ICJ provided in this case an important point of integration with regard to 'immunity *rationae personae*' and 'state immunity' when it admitted beyond doubt that immunity *rationae personae* applies to heads of state under *customary international law*, and it also applies to a broader range of state officials (Webb 2013, pp. 73–76).

However, skeptical in respect of the function of Article 31(3)(c), Klabbers claims that this provision does not advocate communication between the various sub-systems (sub-regimes). The author is of the opinion that this article is often used by sub-regimes, such as the European Community law or the WTO trade law, to some extent in justifying 'the building of a fence' around them as they consider themselves no longer part of international law (Klabbers 2010, p. 33). Thus, because Article 31(3)(c) is used by such regimes to protect and safeguard their own 'system', the principle of 'systemic integration', which this provision prescribes, is, in Klabbers' view, 'bound to remain toothless'.[316] At best and on its own, Article 31(3)(c) is admitted by the author as only suggesting that sub-regimes be interpreted against the background of general international law.[317]

Despite that under the principle of systemic integration provided by Article 31 (3)(c) normative conflicts are suitable for harmonisation,[318] it is widely admitted, including by the ILC, that sometimes special regimes do not take this position. Conflicting interpretations of general law may appear, for example, when two different institutions deal with analogous facts and interpret the law differently,

---

interpretation of a treaty under Article 31(3)(c) in certain situations, which are 'when the treaty rule is unclear or open textured; the terms used in the treaty has a recognized meaning in customary international law or under general principles of law; the treaty is silent on the applicable law'.

[312] *Jurisdictional Immunities of the State (Germany v. Italy)*, ICJ, Judgment of 3 February 2012, p. 27, para 54. The Court held that 'any entitlement to immunity can be derived only from customary international law, rather than the treaty'.

[313] *Arrest Warrants Case (Democratic Republic of Congo v. Belgium)*, ICJ Reports 3, 2002, 41 ILM 536, para 58.

[314] Webb (2013), p. 72. The author states that the Court actually provided a functional justification for an expansion of the categories of persons enjoying immunity *rationae personae*.

[315] See, e.g., El Sheemy (2007). The author observes that many writers have disagreed on the desirability of lawmaking on the basis of functional necessity in *Arrest Warrants* as many were astonished by the ICJ taking this position because there was no apparent legal foundation for rules on which the case was decided.

[316] Klabbers (2010), p. 35.

[317] *Id*, p. 34.

[318] ILC (2006), p. 27. The ILC admits that 'systemic integration' provides in general an acceptable outcome for normative conflict.

as the *Tadic* case (1999) at the ICTY can show, by comparing it with the *Nicaragua* case (1986) at the ICJ in respect of the 'effective control' test[319] or the *Al Adsani* case (2001) at the ECtHR,[320] which relates to a conflict between the peremptory norm of international law on the prohibition of torture and the rules on state immunity.[321] The majority of the judges in *Al Adsani* accepted[322] that the rules of sovereign immunity overrode a *jus cogens* rule,[323] despite initially admitting that the rule on the *prohibition of torture* is a rule of *jus cogens*, hierarchically higher than any other rule of international law.[324] So despite the ECtHR stating that '[t]he Convention should so far as possible be interpreted in harmony with other rules of international law of which it forms part, including those relating the grant of State immunity',[325] it proved itself unable to give effect under Article 31(3)(c) to the ECHR's provisions at issue. As expressed by the ILC, the ECtHR made use of Article 31(3)(c) in *Al Adsani* so as 'to set aside the rules of the European Convention' (ILC 2006, p. 221). Also, at the WTO regime, a limited use of 'harmonization' under Article 31(3)(c) can be illustrated in the *EC-Biotechnical Products* case (2006).[326] Although the Panel stated in this case that the *precautionary principle* might have been established as a general principle of international law, and thus it would be relevant to the case under Article 31(3)(c), it decided that the 'legal status of the precautionary principle remains unsettled'.[327] Similarly to the position taken by the Appellate Body (also the Panel) in the *Beef Hormones* case (1998),[328] the Panel in the *EC-Biotechnical Products* case (2006) decided that it needed 'not take

---

[319] See reference to this case in Chap. 2 of this book.

[320] *Case of Al Adsani v. the United Kingdom*, Application no. 35763/97, ECHR, Judgment of 21 November 2001. In principle, the issue concerned whether a state enjoyed immunity from civil suit in the courts of another state where acts of torture are alleged.

[321] *Id.*

[322] *Id.* See Joint dissenting opinion of Judges Rozakis and Caflisch joined by Judge Wildhaber, Costa, Cabral Barreto and Vajic, pp. 31–35. According to these judges, in the situation of 'a conflict between a *jus cogens* rule and any other rule of international law, the former prevails', and therefore 'State immunity, deriving from both customary and conventional international law, have never been considered by the international community as rules with a hierarchically higher status'.

[323] *Id*, paras 59–60. The ECtHR relied its finding on a number of international instruments/authorities, which demonstrates that the *prohibition of torture* has gradually been crystallised as a *jus cogens* rule. Also, the statutes of both the ad hoc tribunals for the Former Yugoslavia and Rwanda, as well as the statute of the International Criminal Court give a definition of this crime.

[324] *Id.*

[325] *Id*, paras 55–56.

[326] *European Communities – Measures Affecting the Approval and Marketing of Biotech Products*, 7 February 2006, WT/DS291-293/INTERIM.

[327] *Id*, p. 300, para 7.70.

[328] *European Communities-Measures Concerning Meat and Meat Products (Hormones)*, 13 February 1998, WT/DS26/AB/R, WT/DS48/AB/R, p. 47, para 123. For the Appellate Body, it was 'less than clear' in this case that the precautionary principle has been accepted as general or customary international law. However, the Body held: 'the principle does not by itself, and without a clear distinction to that effect, relieve a panel from the duty of applying the normal (i.e. customary international law) principles of treaty interpretation in reading the provision of the SPS Agreement'.

a position on whether or not the precautionary principle is a recognized principle of general or customary international law'.[329] Also, norm conflict can occur at the new (specialised) International Criminal Court (ICC), for instance in the recent *Bashir* case (2010),[330] on the issue of immunity of a head of state (Al Bashir, President of Sudan). Subject to strong debate within the academic community is the misapplication by the Pre Trial Chamber I in this case on the standard of proof required by Article 58(1) of the Statute of this Court for the crime of 'genocide'.[331] The Pre Trial Chamber I imposed a higher threshold of proof (beyond a reasonable doubt) in establishing *dolus specialis* (specific intent) only on evidence[332] necessary to hold accountable the head of the state for the crime of 'genocide'.[333]

Commenting on Article 31(3)(c), Sands observes that this provision has the potential to construct a general international law by reconciling norms arising in treaty and customs across different subject matter areas of law (Sands 1998, p. 87). Importantly, as Sands observes, is that Article 31(3)(c) emphasizes 'both the *unity of international law* and the sense in which *rules* should not be considered in isolation of general international law'.[334] In a more recent study on Article 31(3)(c) of the VCLT, and especially on the ILC Study's undertaking of this article, authors Sands and Commission admit that this provision 'was not meant as a "panacea in reducing fragmentation", but rather a call upon lawyers to interpret treaties so as *to ensure consistency with their normative environment, the integration into the process of legal reasoning – including reasoning by courts and tribunals of a sense of meaningfulness*' (Sands and Commission 2010, p. 56). Thus, what is most interesting about Article 31(3)(c) is that it is the only provision in international law that has the facility to integrate all the various sources of international law (French 2006, p. 300).

---

[329] *Id.*

[330] *Prosecutor v. Omar Hassan Ahmad Al Bashir*, Judgment on the appeal of the Prosecutor against the Decision on the Prosecution's Application for Warrant of Arrest against Omar Hassan Ahmad Al Bashir (ICC-02/05-01/09, P.T.C.I.), Appeals Chamber, 3 February 2010. In the appeal, the prosecution is asked not to establish that there are 'reasonable grounds to believe', as required by Article 58(1) of the statute, but to establish the genocidal intent 'beyond reasonable doubt', however, without indicating how to apply the standard of proof, given the particular nature of the evidence provided.

[331] See on this aspect, e.g., Jacobs (2010).

[332] *Prosecutor v. Omar Hassan Ahmad Al Bashir* (2009), pp. 53–54, paras 150–151 ('the only reasonable [one] available on the evidence').

[333] Jacobs (2010). The author considers that this is nothing but a multiplication of standards of proof that leads to unnecessary semantic debates on such vague notions as 'reasonableness' and serves to prolong the proceedings. See the analogy with the *Genocide* case (2007), where the ICJ established a high threshold for the finding of control of non-state actors by a state for the purpose of attribution to the state of the acts of those non-actors. The ICJ found in *Genocide* that Serbia did not have 'effective control' over the Bosnia-Serb paramilitary forces accused of purported acts of genocide, but it found, however, a breach of Serbia's *duty to prevent genocide*.

[334] Sands (1998), p. 95 (emphasis added).

Finally, the last paragraph (4) of Article 31 refers to the '*special meaning* to be given to a term if it is established that the parties so intended'. It is of note that the provision is admitted as not indicating *per se* a burden of proof for the party intending to show a special meaning.[335] According to Engelen, the 'special meaning' term within Article 31(4) deals with a minor point of limited application and not in the sense suggested by some scholars (e.g., Bernhardt) that this provision could reverse the whole systematic order of Articles 31 and 32 of the VCLT. Such an admission would have been inconceivable for the ILC to give priority to the intention of the parties as a subjective element distinct from the text (Engelen 2004, p. 165).

### 3.4.2 Article 32 of the VCLT

Article 32 provides for 'supplementary means' to be used in the interpretation of treaties, such that:

> Recourse may be had to supplementary means of interpretation, including the preparatory work of the treaty and the circumstances of its conclusion, in order to confirm the meaning resulting from the application of article 31, or to determine the meaning when the interpretation according to article 31:
>
> (a) leaves the meaning ambiguous or obscure;
> (b) or leads to a result which is manifestly absurd or unreasonable (VCLT 1969).

Contrary to what is widely believed that the VCLT has embedded prejudice against the use of drafting history and that, however, it is placed on an inferior position in rapport to Article 31, the VCLT drafters were not hostile to drafting history. On the contrary, according to a recent analysis of the draft history of Articles 31 and 32 of the VCLT, Mortenson concludes that the VCLT drafters 'meant for treaty interpretation to asses drafting history for what is worth in each case: no more, but certainly no less', and that the drafters did not promote in these articles a rigid hierarchy of sources of interpretation (Mortenson 2013, pp. 781 and 788). It follows that the customary nature of Article 31 can also be extended to Article 32.[336]

The reading of Article 32 of the VCLT provides that in order to deduce the parties' intention, an interpreter can very well take into account 'supplementary means of interpretation, including the preparatory work of the treaty and circumstances of its conclusion' (VCLT 1969). This provision, however, is not free of criticism, many showing hostility to history as a source of meaning for the terms of treaties (Mortenson 2013, p. 780). As observed by Mortenson, it is this hostility that triggered the widely shared idea that 'when an interpreter thinks a text is fairly clear

[335] Villiger (2009). Villiger observes that the 'special meaning' is often to be found in the technical or historical context of specialised treaties.

[336] *Id*, pp. 436–437.

and produces results that are not manifestly unreasonable or absurd, she ought to give that prima facie reading reclusive effect over anything the travaux might suggest to the contrary'.[337] The 'preparatory work', often referred as *travaux preparatoire*, or simply *travaux*, is thought to play 'a more important role in the actual practice of treaty interpretation, than the dominant theoretical understanding of the VCLT would suggest' (Mortenson 2013, p. 784). In addition, the 'circumstances of its conclusion' expression in Article 32 clearly allows for the examination of the historical background against which the treaty was negotiated (Buffa 2010, p. 604). These 'supplementary means', according to Buffa, refer to those sources that shed light on the parties' intention, and they are often thought to be brought into the interpretative process due to a particular term admitted as ambiguous in a given circumstance.[338] However, this conception is not what the drafters of the VCLT really intended in regard to the use of 'supplementary means'. In this respect, Mortenson concludes that 'the drafters repeatedly reiterated that *any serious effort to understand a treaty should rely on a careful and textually grounded resort to travaux*, without embarrassment or apology. They themselves leaned heavily on *travaux* when debating any legal question that turned on the meaning of an existing treaty. *And each time a handful of genuinely anti-travaux delegates attempted to restrict the use of drafting history to cases where the text was ambiguous or absurd, those efforts were roundly rejected.*'[339] It implies that in the quest to find the real meaning of a treaty text (drafters' intention), interpreters should rely on drafting history in addition to other tools (provided by Article 31), not only in 'every plausibly contestable case' but also 'in some cases even to override what had initially seemed like its clear import'.[340] Moreover, the historical evidence (relating to the course of discussions, negotiations and compromises that resulted in the treaty text) is expected to *automatically* be consulted in any seriously contested case[341] and, indeed, in cases where an interpreter is required to apply the intended meaning of treaty terms, if it is established by the parties that those terms have that (intended) meaning.[342] Thus far for being disfavoured, as correctly observed by Mortenson, *travaux* were intended by the VCLT drafters 'to be an *integral* component of interpretation'.[343] And the *travaux* ('preparatory work') of a treaty includes, as noted by Villiger, all documents and materials relevant to that treaty, provided by parties during the treaty's preparation for its conclusion,

[337]Mortenson (2013), p. 780.

[338]Buffa (2010), p. 604.

[339]Mortenson (2013), p. 781 (emphasis added).

[340]*Id*, p. 821.

[341]*Id*.

[342]*Id*, p. 788.

[343]*Id*, p. 821 (emphasis added).

some of them being included but not listed in Article 32.[344] However, according to Gardiner, the conditions stated in Article 32 provide a 'loose framework from which elements relevant to the particular case need to be selected', so those conditions are not 'so restrictive as they may appear' (Gardiner 2008, p. 50).

It can be summed up that Article 31 appears as a compromise of three schools of treaty interpretation: *the textualist school*, which the primary goal is to ascertain the meaning from the *text*; *the subjective school*, by contrast states that the *intention* of the parties must be the primary and the only goal of interpretation; and *the teleological school*, which must first focus on the *object and purpose* of the treaty and ascertain the intention of the parties from it. However, despite this compromise combining all three approaches, the textualist component is perceived as dominant (Jonas and Saunders 2010, p. 578). Yet, while Article 31 contains three elements and uses mandatory language, this provision does not shed any light on how much weight each element deserves (Waibel 2011, p. 573). By contrast, the language of Article 32 suggests that recourse to the supplementary means is at the interpreter's discretion.[345] An important, additional assumption is that the language of Articles 31 and 32 does not appear to be designed as exhaustive in the enumeration of the factors that may be taken into account in the interpretation of a treaty (Merrills 1968, p. 57). And that the Vienna Convention rules of interpretation need to be considered only as the starting point for treaty interpretation (Gardiner 2008). However, it has not been unnoticed by various scholars that the ILC 'wisely refrained' from attempting to codify these discretionary aids to interpretation, by admitting that 'the interpretation of documents is to some extent *an art, not an exact science*'.[346]

### 3.4.3 Article 33 of VCLT

As part of the formulation of the 'general rule of interpretation' in the VCLT, Article 33 of the VCLT refers to *interpretation of treaties authenticated in two or more languages*, its paragraphs 1, 2, 3, remaining *verbatim* as in Article 29 of the final draft (commented earlier in Sect. 3.3.2.2), with the exception of paragraph 4. Thus, Article 33 of the VCLT provides:

[344]Villiger (2009), p. 436. The author enumerates some of the supplementary means, included but not listed in Article 32., e.g: *travaux preparatoire* of the earlier version of the treaty, interpretative declaration made by treaty parties which does not qualify as a reservation; documents not strictly labeled as *travaux preparatoire*, the rational techniques of interpretation, such *as per a contrario, contra proferentem, expresio unius est exclusio alterius, lex posterior derogat legi priori, lex specialis*, etc.

[345]Waibel (2011), p. 573.

[346]See, e.g., Merrills (1968) (emphasis added). Also, for a similar opinion, see Van Damme (2009), pp. 605–648; Merkouris (2010a, b).

1. When a treaty has been authenticated in two or more languages, the text is equally authentic in each language, unless the treaty provides or the parties agree that in case of divergence, a particular text shall prevail.
2. A version of the treaty in a language other than one or two in which the text was authenticated shall be considered an authentic text only if the treaty so provides or the parties so agree.
3. The terms of the treaty are presumed to have the same meaning in each authentic text.
4. Except where a particular text prevails in accordance with paragraph 1, when a comparison of the authentic texts discloses a difference of meaning which the application of articles 31 and 32 does not remove, the meaning which best reconciles the texts, having regard to the object and purpose of the treaty, shall be adopted.

An interesting move away from the textualist approach as governing interpretation (Article 31 (1)) to a teleological approach is witnessed in Article 33 of the VCLT. Specifically, paragraph 4 of Article 33 differs from the previous version of the provision (Article 29 (3)) in regard to the meaning of the language version that has to be chosen of the equality of all authentic texts, 'which best reconciles the texts, *having regard to the object and purpose* of the treaty'. As observed by Villiger, while in Article 31 the teleological interpretation is only one means among other means of interpretation that can be chosen, by contrast, in Article 33 (4), the teleological interpretation is specifically and explicitly adopted (Villiger 2009, pp. 459–460). Villiger sees in the renewed paragraph 4 of Article 33 a 'teleological test hailing back to the 1935 Harvard Draft', asking 'which meaning serves the treaty's purpose best'.[347] Also, the teleological approach can be clearly seen embodied in Article 75 (of the 1964 ILC's Third Draft), prior to the formulation of Article 29 (of the 1966 final Draft Articles), providing for the rules relating to interpretation of treaties authenticated in two or more languages.[348]

Since the VCLT drafters considered that it was *one single treaty* but drafted in different languages, their preoccupation was to state clearly in one provision which texts were authoritative, given the possible alternative that the terms set out in different languages were different *versions* (Gardiner 2008, p. 357). Relying on the history of the preparatory work of Article 33, Gardiner observes that the text of this provision acknowledges in the first paragraph the equal authority of the treaty text in each language in which it has been authenticated while giving 'an interpretative slant by particularizing the exception so that it is "in the case of divergence" that a particular text is to prevail where this is agreed in the treaty or otherwise agreed by the parties'.[349] According to the author, in the second paragraph, with the term 'version' specified therein, drafters included 'the new entrant in the collectivity of languages of a particular treaty'.[350] It refers to a treaty that 'was not one in which the treaty was originally authenticated', and it is to be considered authentic if so

[347] Villiger (2009), pp. 459–460.

[348] See the comparison between Articles 74–75 and Article 29 regarding the teleological approach, *supra* note 216.

[349] Gardiner (2008), p. 357.

[350] *Id.*

provided in the treaty or if the parties so agreed.[351] And only when a version of a treaty text became admitted by the interpreter as authentic text under paragraph 2 of Article 33 that the text is further regarded for the purpose of paragraphs (3) and (4) of that article.[352]

Under paragraph 3 of Article 33, the terms of the treaty must be presumed to have the same meaning in each authentic texts. An interpreter must examine that all the authenticated texts convey the same meaning (Linderfalk 2007, p. 356). However, if a difference in meaning is discovered, then the situation will change as the texts should then be subjected to reconciliation.[353] The term referring to 'reconciling' in paragraph 4 of Article 33 (admitted as more problematic than other terms in the provision) suggests in its context, according to Gardiner, 'a contrast between the case where one language is specified as prevailing and the situation where two or more equally authentic but differing statements of the same propositions have to be brought into harmony or made compatible' (Gardiner 2008, p. 360). When two authenticated texts in a multi-language treaty reveal a clear difference in meaning, several available methods are to be identified in respect of 'reconciliation'. According to Linderfalk, the interpreter should first investigate whether the difference in meaning cannot be removed through the application of Articles 31 and 32 of the VCLT (Linderfalk 2007, p. 359). Second, if the first method is insufficient, the interpreter should establish whether the treaty provides, or the parties agree, that in case of divergence, a particular text prevails. Third, if this second method, too, is insufficient, then the meaning that best reconciles the texts, having the object and purpose of the treaty, must be adopted.[354] By adopting the meaning 'which having regard to the object and purpose of the treaty best reconciles the [authenticated] texts', the interpreter always has multiple texts to consider, but the interpreter's selection is limited to the meaning already given and not to other possible meanings.[355] It is therefore the interpreter's duty to set side by side a number of alternative meanings and to choose that one 'which best reconciles the [authenticated] texts' so as to decide the outcome of the entire 'reconciliation' process.[356] As observed by Linderfalk, all texts that can be reconciled by applying Article 33(4) of the VCLT cannot be reconciled by applying Article 31(1) of the VCLT.[357]

---

[351] *Id.*

[352] *Id.*

[353] Linderfalk (2007), p. 356.

[354] *Id*, p. 359.

[355] *Id*, p. 363.

[356] *Id.*

[357] *Id.*

### 3.4.4 Summary Articles 31–33 of VCLT

In summarising the above discussion on the Vienna rules of interpretation, it can be recognised that the struggle of the drafters to formulate a *general rule of treaty interpretation* culminated with an attempt to reconcile in Articles 31, 32, 33 of the VCLT all three approaches to interpretation: textualist, subjective and teleological.[358] However, despite the fact that the ILC drew sufficiently clear views in respect of the rules of interpretation, and these rules found codification in the VCLT, their nature as legal rules, or mere logical rules of reasoning, as well as their practical applicability in various contexts, has generated a perennial controversy. In this sense, some additional scholarly views will better put into perspective these general rules of treaty interpretation.

For instance, Abi-Saab talks about the VCLT rules of interpretation as *secondary rules of international law* (which do not dictate any particular result as primary rules do), 'principles' or 'guidelines', which guide states and adjudicators in performing the act of interpretation (Abi-Saab 2010, p. 105). As to the weight attributed to the various 'principles' of interpretation, Abi-Saab correctly admits that it depends on the specificity of the subject matter of forums.[359] In his view, the use of the VCLT rules of interpretation 'is but a first step that does not tell the whole story' and that they are 'a toolkit used by all international fora', however in different ways, yielding varied results.[360] Thus, this variety in results is a matter mainly of 'judicial policy'—a function that is particular to each forum's environment.[361] In a similar vein, Linderfalk sees the regime laid down in the Vienna Convention, Articles 31–33, as an 'open-textured' system of rules, which admittedly 'still allows the political judgment of each individual applier to play a part' (Linderfalk 2007, pp. 273–274). For the author, Articles 31–33 of the Vienna Convention can best be described as 'a system of rules' that enable appliers to use specific interpretative (data) information while instructing them *how they should argue to arrive at a conclusion about the meaning of the interpreted provision*.[362]

On the other hand, Klabbers, mentioned earlier in this chapter, focuses on the idea that 'interpretation cannot be subjected to rules, let alone legal rules' since the interpretation process depends much on personal characteristics of the interpreter (of his/her moral activity and obligations as a moral actor).[363] He even advances the

[358]Despite each approach tried to impose the principle governing the process of interpretation.

[359]Abi-Saab (2010), p. 105.

[360]*Id*, p. 106.

[361]*Id*. The author gives a great deal to the specificity of the subject matter of forums, which 'may affect the relative weight attributed to the various principles of interpretation'.

[362]Linderfalk (2007), pp. 273–274.

[363]Klabbers (2010), p. 29. As the author notes, interpretation depends of interpretative community as well (and can come to radically different conclusions of one and the same text, and can do so by relying also on rules of interpretation).

argument that these rules 'may not be of customary law nature', perhaps not even of legal nature.[364] If they were proper rules of law, as Klabbers assumes, the breach of these rules could certainly be claimed as a wrongful act (like in the case of *torture*, *use of force*, etc).[365] But since an interpreter is not free to give whatever meaning he wants to a text, Klabbers admits, nevertheless, that *rules on how to give meaning to words* should then, certainly, exist.[366] However, in his view, even if all sub-systems use the same interpretative devices, respectively the VCLT rules, it does not guarantee the unity of various sub-systems, existing in connection and communicating with each other.[367] Klabbers believes that there can be unity in the method of interpretation of various sub-systems, but this unity appears only as 'a mere simulation of unity' (human rights rules will be given a human rights interpretation, trade rules a trade interpretation, etc), notably without any agreement as to what is to be achieved by applying that methodology.[368] He justly concludes that even if the VCLT rules of interpretation 'do not fit the regular patterns of rules', these rules are, nevertheless, 'immensely valuable' as *methodological devices which tell interpreters how to read legal instruments*.[369] And most importantly is that these rules 'are of great importance when it comes to guaranteeing *the unity of international law*' and '*the very relevance of international law*'.[370] Klabbers, therefore, correctly sees it as necessary that some guidelines on how to read treaties should exist and, essentially, that without such devices things in international law 'could easily derail'.[371]

The prevalent view in the academic debate is that the Vienna rules of interpretation are neither rules nor principles in the classic sense of a *rule* to explain or provide the reason for it (Merkouris 2010a, p. 11). Since the drafters of the VCLT ensured that the articles on interpretation leave enough freedom to interpret them in a flexible way and adapt them to each particular case,[372] these rules must be seen as 'principles of logic and good sense', having a creative function (Van Damme 2009). They guide the interpreter in finding or clarifying, as also confirming, the meaning of the treaty language. Moreover, a consensus among scholars as to the customary origin and nature of the VCLT rules of interpretation could be perceived since these rules apply even to those states that are not parties to this Convention (Klabbers 2010, p. 23). However, since the VCLT principles of interpretation leave some issues incompletely resolved, as observed by Gardiner, to employ and apply them is a skill of evaluating the materials and shaping interpretative arguments (Gardiner

---

[364]*Id.*

[365]*Id.*

[366]*Id*, p. 23.

[367]*Id.*

[368]*Id*, p. 33.

[369]*Id*, p. 31.

[370]*Id*, pp. 30–31 (emphasis added).

[371]*Id.*

[372]Merkouris (2010a), p. 11. See also on this point, e.g., Van Damme (2009).

2008). Gardiner's important suggestion here is that these rules cannot be actually understood as 'simple precepts that can be applied to produce a scientifically verifiable result'.[373] Then the essential point in respect of the act of treaty interpretation, as succinctly captured by Toufayan, is that *interpretation*, 'far from being the accounting of raw interpretative data or the prioritization of certain interpretative means over others', is 'in reality *a holistic construct*'.[374] This aspect was acknowledged as such, in particular, by the New Haven School[375] and the ILC.[376] Therefore, as correctly concluded by Fitzmaurice and Merkouris in a recent analysis on Vienna rules, *Articles 31–33 must be understood as a general rule of interpretation that prescribes* for a *single logical operation, where its components connect and complement each other in a holistic exercise* (Fitzmaurice and Merkouris 2010, p. 187). And *this exercise must be directed as to render the treaty provisions legally effective, which implies approaching a harmonious and coherent interpretation in the light of the treaty as a whole.*[377] Such interpretation that gives meaning to every element of the text of the treaty/agreement was acknowledged by the ILC in its *Third Report on the Law of Treaties* (1964) as a reflection of the 'Principle of Including All Strategic Acts', which is, actually, as described by Gardiner, 'a principle underlying the Vienna rules'.[378]

## 3.5 Conclusions

Making an analogy with a physical science experiment when reflecting upon the interpretation of treaties, Jean-François Lévesque shows that as 'even the most limpid of glasses produces an effect of diffraction, an optical phenomenon of slight deviation of the luminous rays', so *a 'text' is no perfect clear* (Lévesque 2006, p. 53). Since treaties are based on *language conventions*, as Lévesque underlines, it implies that they 'constitute more than a perfectly clear intermediary from the signifier to the signified'.[379] And this fact gives the text of treaties an iterative nature, which 'precludes any quest for the explicit and exclusive intentions of the transmitter of the norm'.[380] Then once again, as Lévesque explains, 'becoming subject of the law when the treaty is cast off, the State parties are submitted to the

---

373 Gardiner (2008).

374 Toufayan (2005), p. 19 (emphasis added).

375 As pointed earlier in Sect. 3.3.2.1.1 of this chapter, the New Haven School leaves the use of the *travaux preparatoire* to the discretion of the decision-maker interpreter, but for this school a treaty and its *travaux preparatoire* are equally valid sources of interpretation. See above: Harvard Research in International Law (1957), p. 938.

376 See the ILC (1966), pp. 219–220.

377 *Id.*

378 Gardiner (2008), p. 67 (emphasis added).

379 Lévesque (2006), p. 53.

380 *Id.*

filter of interpretation for which the *Vienna Convention on the Law of the Treaties* provides a pertinent *holistic frame*'.[381] Thus, despite the iterative nature of the 'signifier' (the text of a treaty), its property is to repeat itself in different situations, every change diffracting its first meaning.[382] The point made by Levesque nicely and concisely illustrates what this chapter attempted to show.

Summing up, the words of the ILC that 'interpretation is an art' and the question that naturally followed—'is there any rule for practising that art?'—formulated by the Chairman to the ILC at its 16th session,[383] reveal the concern and uncertainty that have governed the *treaty interpretation* topic. This aspect is reflected in the further questions that were expressed at the 1964 ILC session, such as 'what precisely is a technical rule', 'was it or was not mandatory', 'was there or was there not a rule under which the terms of a treaty must be construed in the etymological sense or having regard to the context of a treaty' or 'was there or was there not a rule that in deciding between two possible interpretations of a treaty, the preparatory work, the object of the treaty and the practice of the parties concerned must be taken into account?'[384] Also, the topic of treaty interpretation continues to preoccupy legal scholars and practitioners today. As Julian Arato points out, questions still await to be answered such as 'how should the rules be applied to this particular treaty', 'how should the rules be weighed against one another' or 'what if they appear to lead to contradictory results?'(Arato 2010, p. 103).

Lévesque considers that even if the VCLT codified 'the general rule of interpretation' and its complementary means in Articles 31 and 32, 'blurriness remains on the privileged methods of the different actors – notably the ICJ to execute the text' (Lévesque 2006, p. 53). There is the perception expressed in the scholarship that principles of treaty interpretation are neither rules nor principles in the classic sense of a rule to explain or provide the reason for it but rules that have a creative function (Van Damme 2009). Scholars simply underline the interpretation of the rule, not the rule itself; thus, Vienna rules are 'principles of logic and good sense' that guide the interpreter in finding and justifying the meaning of the treaty language.[385] Importantly, it was widely admitted that *the drafters of the VCLT ensured that the articles on interpretation leave enough freedom of interpretation and flexibility to adapt to each particular case, or regime, as well as to the changes that the evolution of the international community generates* (Merkouris 2010a, b, p. 11). Whether this is so, it will be further examined in the next chapter, in the light of the World Court's *practice on treaty interpretation*, and in the subsequent chapters, in the special context of the ECtHR and the WTO specialised adjudicative bodies.

[381] *Id.*

[382] *Id.*

[383] See ILC's Summary records of the sixteenth session (1964), 1:23; the comment of the Chairman-member of the International Law Commission.

[384] *Id.*

[385] Van Damme (2009).

## References


Abi-Saab, G. (2010). The Appellate Body and treaty interpretation. In *Treaty interpretation and the Vienna Convention on the Law of Treaties: 30 years on* (pp. 97–110). Leiden, The Netherlands: Brill.

Arato, J. (2010). Two perspectives on the rules of treaty interpretation: A review of Richard Gardiner, treaty interpretation. *New York University Journal of International Law and Politics, 43*(2).

Beckett, E. (1950). Comments by Sir E. Beckett. *Annuaire de L'institut de Droit International, 43*, 435.

Bederman, D. J. (2001). Grotius and his followers on treaty construction. *Journal of the History of International Law, 3*(1), 18–37.

Bjorge, E. (2014). *The evolutionary interpreation of treaties*. Oxford: Oxford University Press.

Buffa, D. G. (2010). Proposed remedy for the dilemma of innumerable futures: Ukraine, Russia, and NATO Membership. *Brooklyn Journal of International Law, 35*, 593.

Ciobanu, D. (1991). *Introducere in Studiul Dreptului* [Introduction in the study of law]. Bucuresti: Ed. Hyperion XXI.

Constantinou, C. M. (2005). *Treaty. New York New Dictionary of the history of ideas* (Vol. 6). Charles Scribner Publisher. http://works.bepress.com/costas_constantinou/24/.

Desierto, D. A. (2010). Necessity and supplementary means of interpretation of non-precluded measures in bilateral investment treaties. *University of Pennsylvania Journal of International Law, 31*, 827.

De Vattel, E. (1758). *The law of nations or the principles of natural law*. Washington, DC: Carnegie Institution of Washington.

El Sheemy, S. (2007). *International law-making: Problems of coherence andfragmentation-A summary of the Chatham house international law discussion group meeting held on 23 March 2007*. Chatham House. In *Independent thinking on international affairs*. Available at: https://www.chathamhouse.org/sites/files/chathamhouse/public/Research/International%20Law/il230307.pdf

Endicott, T. A. (2001). *Vagueness in law*. Oxford, England: Oxford University Press.

Engelen, F. A. (2004). *Interpretation of tax treaties under international law* (Vol. 7). Amsterdam: IBFD.

Falk, R. A. (1967). On treaty interpretation and the New Haven approach: Achievements and prospects. *Virginia Journal of International Law, 8*, 323.

Fish, S. E. (1980). *Is there a text in this class?: The authority of interpretive communities*. Cambridge, MA: Harvard University Press.

Fitzmaurice, G. G. (1951). Law and procedure of the International Court of Justice: Treaty interpretation and certain other treaty points. *British Year Book of International Law, 28*, 1.

Fitzmaurice, G. G. (1957). Law and procedure of the International Court of Justice 1951-4: Treaty interpretation and other treaty points. *British Year Book of International Law, 33*, 203.

Fitzmaurice, M. (2013). Interpretation of human rights treaties. In D. Shelton (Ed.), *The Oxford handbook of international human rights law* (pp. 739–772). Oxford University Press. www.oxfordhanbooks.com. https://doi.org/10.1093/law/970199640133.003.0032.

Fitzmaurice, M., & Merkouris, P. (2010). Canons of treaty interpretation: Selected case studies from the World Trade Organization and the North American Free Trade Agreement. In *Treaty interpretation and the Vienna Convention on the Law of Treaties: 30 years on* (pp. 153–238). Leiden, The Netherlands: Brill.

French, D. (2006). Treaty interpretation and the incorporation of extraneous legal rules. *International and Comparative Law Quarterly, 55*(2), 281–314.

Gardiner, R. K. (2008). *Treaty interpretation*. NewYork: Oxford University Press.

Gardiner, R. K. (2009, March 4). Beyond the Vienna rules. *Opinio Juris Blog*. Retrieved August 31, 2011, from http://opiniojuris.org/2009/03/04/beyond-the-vienna-rules/

Gentili, A. (1933). *De iure belli libri tres*. Oxford, England: Clarendon Press. (1612, No. 16).

Gordon, E. (1995). Book review. *American Journal of International Law, 89*, 461–463.

Grotius, H. (1901). *The rights of war and peace* (A. C. Campbell, AM, Trans. Rev., p. 293). Washington, DC: M. Walter Dunne Publisher.
Grotius, H. (1925). *De Jure Belli ac Pacis Libri Tres. Vol. 2: The classics of international law* (J. B. Scott, Ed. & F. W. Kelsey, Trans.). Oxford, England: Clarendon Press.
Grotius, H. (2005). *De Jure Belli ac Pacis* [The rights of war and peace] (Jean Barbeyrac, Ed.). Amsterdam. (1724)
Hernandez, J. G. (2014). Interpretation. In J. Kammerhofer & J. d'Aspremont (Eds.), *International legal positivism in a post-modern world*. Cambridge, England: Cambridge University Press.
Jacobs, D. (2010). The Al Bashir appeals Chamber Judgment on genocide: A critical appraisal in law and in context. *Hague Justice Portal*. Retrieved from http://www.haguejusticeportal.net/index.php?id=10761
Jacobs, F. G. (1969). Varieties of approach to treaty interpretation: with special reference to the Draft Convention on the law of treaties before the Vienna Diplomatic Conference. *International and Comparative Law Quarterly, 18*, 318.
Jonas, D. S., & Saunders, T. N. (2010). Object and purpose of a treaty: Three interpretive methods. *Vanderbilt Journal of Transnational Law, 43*, 565.
Klabbers, J. (2010). Virtuous interpretation. In *Treaty interpretation and the Vienna Convention on the Law of Treaties: 30 years on* (pp. 15–38). Leiden, The Netherlands: Brill.
Koskenniemi, M. (2006). *From apology to utopia: The structure of international legal argument*. Cambridge, England: Cambridge University Press.
Lauterpacht, H. (1949). Restrictive interpretation and the principle of effectiveness in the interpretation of treaties. *British Year Book of International Law, 26*, 48.
Lévesque, J. F. (2006). Traites de Verre: Reflexions sur l'Interpretation. *Revue quebecoise de droit international, 19*, 53.
Linderfalk, U. (2007). *On the interpretation of treaties: The modern international law as expressed in the 1969 Vienna Convention on the law of treaties* (Vol. 83). Springer Science & Business Media.
McDougal, M. S. (1967). The international law commission's draft articles upon interpretation: Textuality redivivus. *American Journal of International Law, 61(4)*, 992–1000.
McDougal, M. S., Lasswell, H. D., & James Clifford Miller, J. C. (1994). *The interpretation of international agreements and world public order*. Leiden, The Netherlands: Martinus Nijhoff Publishers.
McLachlan, C. (2005). The principle of systemic integration and article 31 (3)(c) of the Vienna Convention. *International and Comparative Law Quarterly, 54*(2), 279–320.
Merkouris, P. (2010a). Introduction: Interpretation is a science, is an art, is a science. In M. Fitzmaurice, O. A. Elias, & P. Merkouris (Eds.), *Treaty interpretation and the Vienna Convention on the Law of Treaties: 30 years on* (Vol. 1). Leiden, The Netherlands: Brill.
Merkouris, P. (2010b, January). *Article 31(3)(c) of the VCLT and the principle of systemic integration*. Study submitted for the degree of Ph.D., Queen Mary University of London School of Law.
Merrills, J. G. (1968). Two approaches to treaty interpretation. *Australian Year Book of International Law, 4*, 55.
Mortenson, J. D. (2013). Is the Vienna Convention hostile to drafting history? *American Journal of International Law, 107*, 780.
Oppenheim, L. F. (1921). *International law: A treatise*. R.F. Roxburgh, (Ed) (1923), London: Longmans, Green & Co, 2:2.
Orakhelashvili, A. (2008). *The interpretation of acts and rules in public international law*. Oxford University Press.
Patterson, D. (2001). Normativity and objectivity in law. *William & Mary Law Review, 43*, 325.
Patterson, D. (2005). Interpretation in law. *San Diego Law Review, 42*, 685.
Pauwelyn, J., & Elsig, M. (2011). *The politics of treaty interpretation: Variations and explanations across international tribunals*. https://ssrn.com/abstract=1938618 or https://doi.org/10.2139/ssrn.1938618.
Pauwelyn, J., & Elsig, M. (2013). *Interdisciplinary perspectives on international law and international relations: The state of the art* (L. J. Dunoff & A. M. Pollack, Eds.). Cambridge, England: Cambridge University Press.

Peczenik, A. (1985). Moral and ontological justification of legal reasoning. *Law and Philosophy, 4* (2), 289–309.
Phillimore, R. (1856). Commentaries upon international law. *Law Library Journal, 88*, i.
Pufendorf, S. (1934). *De jure naturae et gentium libri octo* (C. H. Oldfather & W. A. Oldfather, Trans., Vol. 2). Oxford, England: Clarendon Press.
Ris, M. (1991). Treaty interpretation and ICJ recourse to Travaux Préparatoires: Towards a proposed amendment of Articles 31 and 32 of the Vienna Convention on the Law of Treaties. *Boston College International and Comparative Law Review, 14*, 111.
Sands, P. (1998). Treaty, custom and the cross-fertilization of international law. *Yale Human Rights & Development Law Journal, 1*, 85.
Sands, P., & Commission, J. (2010). Treaty, custom and time: Interpretation/application? In *Treaty interpretation and the Vienna Convention on the Law of Treaties: 30 years on* (pp. 39–58). Leiden, The Netherlands: Brill.
Scott, J. B. (1925). Grotius' De Jure Belli ac Pacis Libri Tres: The work of a lawyer, stateman and theologian. *American Journal of International Law, 19*, 461.
Scott, J. B. (1935). *Hugo Grotius De Jure Belli Ac Pacis Libri Tres*. Washington, DC: Carnegie Endowment for International Peace.
Stone, J. (1953). Fictional elements in treaty interpretation-A study in the international judicial process. *Sydney Law Review, 1*, 344.
Toufayan, M. (2005). *Human rights treaty interpretation: A postmodern account of its claim to "speciality"*. NYU Centre for Human Rights and Global Justice Working Paper.
Tzevelekos, V. P. (2009). Use of Article 31 (3)(C) of the VCLT in the case law of the ECtHR: An effective anti-fragmentation tool or a selective loophole for the reinforcement of human rights teleology-between evolution and systemic integration. *Michigan Journal of International Law, 31*, 621.
Van Damme, I. (2009). *Treaty interpretation by the WTO Appellate Body*. Oxford, England: Oxford University Press.
Venzke, I. (2012). *How interpretation makes international law: On semantic change and normative twists*. Oxford, England: Oxford University Press.
Villiger, M. E. (2009). *Commentary on the 1969 Vienna Convention on the Law of Treaties*. Leiden, The Netherlands: Brill.
Vitányi, B. (1983). Treaty interpretation in the legal theory of Grotius and its influence on modern doctrine. *Netherlands Yearbook of International Law, 14*, 41–67.
Waibel, M. (2011). Demystifying the art of interpretation. *European Journal of International Law, 22*(2), 571–588.
Webb, P. (2013). *International judicial integration and fragmentation*. Oxford, England: Oxford University Press.
Wróblewski, J. (1985). Legal language and legal interpretation. *Law and Philosophy, 4*(2), 239–255.
Zemanek, K. (2009). Vienna Convention on the Law of Treaties. *United Nations Audiovisual Library of International Law*. Retrieved from http://untreaty.un.org/cod/avl/pdf/ha/vclt/vclt-e.pdf
Zhang, Y. (1933). *The interpretation of treaties by judicial tribunals* (No. 389). New York: Columbia University Press.

## *Documents*

Harvard Research in International Law, 1957. "Draft Convention of the Law of Treaties (1935)", 29 American Journal of International Law (Supp), p. 938.
International Law Commission, 2006. Fragmentation of international law: Difficulties arising from the diversification and expansion of international law. *Geneva: United Nations.*

International Law Commission. (1966). Draft articles on the law of treaties with commentaries. In *Yearbook of the International Law Commission* (Vol. 2).

*Summary records* of the *sixteenth session*. 11 May-24 July 1964, vol. I, UN. UN Doc A/CN.4/SER A/1964.

The Work of International Law Commission. (2007). *Office of legal affairs* (7th ed.p. 1). New York: United Nations.

Vienna Convention on the Law of Treaties, opened for signature May 23, 1969, 1155 UNTS 331, available at http://untreaty.un.org/ilc/texts/instruments/english/conventions/1_1_1969.pdf.

Waldock, H., 1964. Third Report on the Law of Treaties, by Sir Humphrey Waldock, Special Rapporteur. *Yearbook of the International Law Commission*, 2.

# Chapter 4
# PCIJ/ICJ Practice on Treaty Interpretation

## 4.1 Introduction

The discussion related to *interpretation* and *the evolution of the general rules of interpretation* and *their codification* in *the 1969 Vienna Convention on the Law of Treaties* provided in the previous chapter attempted to shed light on some of the theoretical and conceptual difficulties accompanying *treaty interpretation*. Indirectly, these conceptual difficulties relate to the issue of fragmentation in international law. In this chapter, I move the more doctrinal discussion of treaty interpretation provided in the previous chapter towards a more empirical investigation, respectively, to the analysis of *treaty interpretation at the International Court of Justice* (ICJ). The analysis of treaty interpretation at the World Court, as the ICJ is commonly referred, is important for at least two reasons. First, it can show whether there is a consistent approach at the World Court towards interpretations of treaties both prior to and after the 1969 VCLT's adoption. Thus, in analysing the treaty interpretation approaches of the PCIJ/ICJ over the last 90 years, it is impossible to ignore the adoption in 1969 of the VCLT's rules. This practice is analytically differentiated between the two periods: before and after the adoption of the VCLT. Taking the 1969 VCLT's adoption as historical reference point for the analysis of the rules of treaty interpretation as *customary* would, arguably, allow me to capture the trend of the World Court's treaty interpretation practice, respectively, whether there is a *coherent approach towards treaty interpretation at this Court.* Second, since the World Court is admitted as the most important among the other international courts in developing principles and methods of treaty interpretation, the analysis of treaty interpretation at this Court allows me to decipher *the methods and patterns of interpretation* (application of the customary rules of treaty interpretation) it uses. These methods and patterns of interpretation will be further verified at the specialised courts, the ECtHR and WTO, taking into analysis their practices on treaty interpretation (Chaps. 5 and 6).



L.E. Popa, *Patterns of Treaty Interpretation as Anti-Fragmentation Tools*,
DOI 10.1007/978-3-319-65488-1_4

However, if one admits that *the 1969 Vienna Convention on the Law of Treaties* purports to eliminate some of the conceptual difficulties related to treaty interpretation, and therefore contributes to diminishing the possibility of fragmentation, then it is necessary to evaluate its impact. More specifically, it is necessary to evaluate comparatively whether the ICJ and the two specialised international courts, the ECtHR and the WTO, approach treaty interpretation (general rules and methods) differently prior to and after the adoption of the VCLT. Any patterns of treaty interpretation observable in the ICJ general regime could be significant for the existence of such patterns (similar tendencies) more widely in specialised regimes, and it could therefore be evidence for homogeneous preferences, in terms of resort to the general rules of treaty interpretation, of such different international (specialised) regimes. Conversely, if those two specialised courts approach differently the general rules of treaty interpretation, then what particular implications do such approaches have for international law? Therefore, the present and following chapters would attempt to answer this question.

The chapter is divided into three parts. The first part (Sect. 4.2) addresses two points: (1) a very brief historical background of the World Court and (2) a rationale for the case selection and case analysis undertaken in this chapter, as also references to methodology. The second part (Sect. 4.3) focuses on the analysis of the PCIJ/ICJ's practice (case law) on treaty interpretation prior to the 1969 VCLT's adoption in order to assess the matter of consistency in the application by the PCIJ/ICJ of the general rules of treaty interpretation. The third part (Sect. 4.4) is devoted to treaty interpretation cases adjudicated by the ICJ in the period following the adoption of the 1969 VCLT. The purpose of this analysis is to discover whether there is variance in the approaches of the World Court towards the customary rules of interpretation in both pre and post VCLT's adoption periods. This analysis is needed because *consistency* in treaty interpretation has, arguably, not only a historical dimension but also an internal one, which is reflected in the coherence between the declared interpretative approaches and those actually followed by the World Court in each particular case. In other words, *what the ICJ says it does, and what it actually does in any given case is important in identifying the existence of coherence in the treaty interpretative approaches adopted by this Court.* This type of coherence could be additionally inferred from the analysis of whether the ICJ, in its quest to solve the issues of interpretation asked of it, gives preference to one rule or another or gives equal value to all the (general) rules of interpretation, irrespective of the difficulties encountered in interpreting the text of treaties (insufficient clarity, ambiguity, inconclusiveness, vagueness, silence in the language of the treaty). Thus, to determine whether the ICJ's approach to treaty interpretation changed in this regard with the adoption of the VCLT, or whether it remained constant, helps in responding to the question of a more general concern related to the *fragmentation/unity of general international law*.

## 4.2 Background and Case Selection

### *4.2.1 Historical Background*

The two Hague Peace Conference in 1908 and 1918 constituted the inspiration for the creation of the Central American Court of Justice and for the Permanent Court of International Justice (PCIJ) within the framework of the new international system set up after the end of the First World War.[1] The PCIJ was brought into being through and by the League of Nations, but it was not part of it.[2] It was set up as a court to be competent not only to hear and determine any dispute of an international character submitted to it by the parties to the dispute but also to give an advisory opinion upon any dispute or question referred to it by the Council or by the Assembly of the League of Nations.[3] In 1920, the Statute of the PCIJ was adopted, and, unlike arbitral tribunals, the PCIJ was constituted as a permanently judicial forum tantamount to the PCA (Permanent Court of Arbitration).[4] The Statute of the PCIJ, specifically listing the sources of law, was to be applied in deciding contentious cases and in giving advisory opinions, without prejudice to the power of the Court to decide a case *ex bono* if the parties so agreed.[5] The PCIJ entered upon its duty on 15 February 1922 as a groundbreaking institution that had to build its own reputation (Spiermann 2007, p. 116). In principle, the PCIJ was accessible to all states for the judicial settlement of their international disputes, and they were able to declare in advance that for certain classes of legal disputes they recognised the Court's jurisdiction as compulsory, in relation to other states accepting the same obligation.[6] A related point to consider is that most of the cases decided by the PCIJ in the 1920s had concerned *treaty interpretation*.[7] A good number of the PCIJ's decisions laid bare the close relationship between treaty interpretation and general international law.[8] In addition, the PCIJ rendered judgments in some serious international disputes, many of them consequences of the First World War.[9] To give a statistic view of the PCIJ's rulings, between 1922 and 1940, the PCIJ dealt with 29 contentious cases between states and delivered 27 advisory opinions[10];

---

[1]International Court of Justice (available at: http://www.icjcij.org/court/index.php?p1=1&p2=1).

[2]*Id.*

[3]*Id.*

[4]*Id.*

[5]*Id.*

[6]*Id.*

[7]Spiermann (2007), p. 122.

[8]*Id.*

[9]International Court of Justice, *supra* note 1. See, e.g., the *S.S. Wimbledon* case (PCIJ, Ser. A, No. 1, 1923).

[10]*Id.* In addition, several hundred treaties, conventions and declarations conferred jurisdiction upon the PCIJ over specified classes of disputes.

some will be discussed in this chapter from the perspective of treaty interpretation application.

The PCIJ demonstrated its value as a representative judicial international body of the international community and of the major legal systems of the world.[11] This Court proved to build an effective judicial mechanism, often clarifying previously unclear areas of international law, while developing a constant practice, continuity and consistency in its decisions.[12] Also, the PCIJ brought a greater contribution to international law like no other international tribunal ever before,[13] giving the fact that it functioned in addition to the Court of Arbitration and also to the special Tribunals of Arbitration to which states have always freedom to submit their disputes for settlement (Houchins 2002, p. 463). However, the outbreak of the war in September 1939 had serious consequences for the PCIJ, which had already experienced for some years a period of diminished activity.[14] Due to an increase in tensions on the international arena, during the Second World War, the PCIJ declined its activity.[15] From 1937 until the PCIJ ceased to exist, being replaced by the ICJ in 1946, only seven contentious cases and no advisory requests were submitted to the Court (Scott et al. 1996, p. 1). The PCIJ lasted only 20 years, and its activity ended at the onset of Second World War.[16] A new court was to be conceived in 1946 as a substitute 'for the vicissitudes of war and the reign of brutal force', and it was predicted that 'the judicial process will have a central place in the plans of the United Nations for the settlement of international disputes by peaceful means' (Gross 1971, p. 256). So, after the Second World War, the Committee of the Permanent Court at the San Francisco Conference decided to create a new Court, which has been a continuation of the old Court.[17] Its Statute is virtually the same; the jurisdiction under instruments referring to the old Court has been transferred to the new Court, as also the jurisprudence is a continuation of the old Court.[18] The Statute of the new Court provides for the creation of a standing, permanent international tribunal in which states have confidence, especially for the fact that

[11]*Id.*

[12]*Id.*

[13]*Id.*

[14]*Id.*

[15]*Id.*

[16]*Id.*

[17]Charter of the United Nations (1945) Article 92 of the UN Charter (Chapter XIV) provides: 'The International Court of Justice shall be the principal judicial organ of the United Nations. It shall function in accordance with the annexed Statute, which is based upon the Statute of the Permanent Court of International Justice and forms an integral part of the present Charter.'

[18]International Court of Justice, *supra* note 1. The ICJ exercises the advisory form of jurisdiction, and only states may be parties to contentious proceedings. The Court's authority in cases between states is given by the states concerned. It is thought that of all international judicial bodies, the ICJ is probably the one that still adheres most closely to the consensual paradigm.

it clearly maintains the independence of the judges once appointed.[19] The sources of law with which the Court deals are reflected in Article 38 of its Statute, and the power of the Court to decide disputes is defined in its Statute—as contentious jurisdiction. In addition, the ICJ exercises the advisory form of jurisdiction (Romano 2006, p. 818).

The ICJ is generally considered in the scholarship as a forum where sovereignty is still treasured, and where the limits imposed by the principle of consent are the strongest, probably because the ICJ's jurisdiction *ratione materiae* is the widest possible, supposing any dispute between sovereign states on any matter of international law (Scott et al. 1996, p. 1). Only states may be parties to contentious proceedings, and the Court's authority in cases between states is given by the states concerned (Merrills 2005, p. 127). It is thought that of all international judicial bodies, the ICJ is probably the one that still adheres most closely to the consensual paradigm (Romano 2006, p. 818). However, the 'compulsory jurisdiction' of the Court is a controversial matter. Some scholars expressed concern and skepticism at the reliance of the states on compulsory jurisdiction that would fuel its increasing docket (Llamzon 2007, pp. 818–819). Such authors rely on the ground that, in the last few decades, the overwhelming majority of the Court's case docket has been initiated by unilateral invocation by the applicant states of 'compulsory jurisdiction'.[20] For example, despite the fact that sovereign states have consented to its jurisdiction and are able to litigate before the Court (ICJ Statute, Articles 34–36),[21] only a minority is willing to accept the jurisdiction of the Court *ex ante* as it is proved by the evidence that 'only one out of seven cases put on the ICJ docket in sixty years of existence has been submitted by way of agreement between the parties' (Romano 2006, p. 818). The ICJ currently reports 268 treaties (among thousands worldwide in number), both bilateral and multilateral, containing clauses granting jurisdiction to the Court in contentious proceedings.[22] However, a state could avoid compulsory jurisdiction by not filing a declaration (Posner and De Figueiredo 2004, p. 7).

An interesting point in support of the ICJ's weaknesses is shared by those scholars who consider that the ICJ has rigid procedure and that the enforceability of its decisions decreases, as sometimes the Security Council must take measure to enforce the ICJ's judgments (Irwin 1997, p. 759). Examples of decisions of the ICJ,

---

[19]Gross (1971), p. 256. The author notes that 'the experience of the 25 years is otherwise, in the sense that the Court did not become a substitute for the reign of brutal force, although the Court enabled to adjudicate some tension disputes. Neither this Court has occupied a "central" place in the procedures for the settlement disputes.'

[20]Llamzon (2007), pp. 818–819.

[21]Henkin et al. (1999), p. 665. In conformity with Articles 34–36 of the ICJ's Statute, states can provide such consent in various ways, i.e., by agreements with respect to a particular dispute, through a clause in a treaty by the states parties agreeing to submit disputes arising under the treaty to the ICJ or by making a declaration under so-called optional clause, prospectively recognising the Court's jurisdiction.

[22]Romano (2006), p. 818.

such as in the *Corfu Channel* (1949), the *Iranian Hostages* (1980) or the *Nicaragua* (1986) cases, illustrate that not always do states comply with the ICJ's judgments.[23] Given the present context of the world politics, the conception that there is the time for the ICJ to contemplate a doctrine of judicial restraint, as there are cases of compulsory jurisdiction where states appear unlikely to respect the ICJ's judgments, has gained space in the scholarship debate (Janis 1987, p. 144). An achievement in this direction is seen in a large number of treaties providing for the reference of disputes to the Court, and the number of states with declarations of some kind under the 'optional clause'[24] is slowly rising in the recent years.[25] In addition, for the reason that several disputes have been settled following reference of the matter to the Court without requiring a decision, some scholars see the effectiveness of the ICJ with moderate optimism as this Court has been used by states in a variety of ways (Scott et al. 1996). For example, it is evidenced in a number of cases that the ICJ has been used by states to gain judicial settlement as an element in the international bargaining process, culminated with the states reaching a solution without prior judgment.[26]

By analysing the long trajectory of the ICJ, one can observe that its activity appears to be influenced by the socio-economic and political changes that have occurred in the international community. For example, after the Second World War, the ICJ had an increased activity, while the decade of the 1960s brought very few cases before the ICJ, and then again an increase in its activity was marked in the early 1970s and mid-1980s.[27] Further, the ICJ decreased its activity due to the intensification of the tension in the international relations between nations during the Cold War; the proliferation of new states, mostly former colonies; and the fact that the Court was dominated by western state judges.[28] Since the end of the Cold War, the cases before the ICJ approximated the number marked before the Court at each of the two World Wars.[29] However, despite the fact that the ICJ has been criticised for its limited effectiveness and many failures, this Court is thought to still

[23]Irwin (1997), p. 759.

[24]Henckaerts (1993), reviewing Renata Szafarz's book on the compulsory jurisdiction of the International Court of Justice (Renata Szafarz served as rapporteur of a Working Group set up by the Polish Branch of the International Law Association to draft a Polish declaration accepting the compulsory jurisdiction of the ICJ).

[25]Merrills (2005), p. 167. An example of a treaty clause providing for submission of disputes to the ICJ at the request of states parties, known as a *compromissory clause*, is Article IX of the *Genocide Convention on the Prevention and Punishment of the Crime of Genocide* (adopted by Resolution 260 (III) A of the UN General Assembly on 9 December 1948, entry into force: 12 January 1951), which provides: 'Disputes between the Contracting Parties relating to the interpretation, application or fulfillment of the present Convention, including those relating to the responsibility of a State for genocide or for any other acts enumerated in article III, shall be submitted to the International Court of Justice at the request of any of the parties to the dispute'.

[26]Scott et al. (1996).

[27]*Id.*

[28]*Id.*

[29]*Id.*

play the most important role in the international judicial system for matters falling outside the jurisdiction of specialised courts and tribunals (LU 2004). While critics point out to political considerations as influencing the ICJ's decisions,[30] defenders of the ICJ sustain in principle that this Court 'plays the leading role in legitimating the [international legal] system by resolving its disputes in a principled manner' (Posner and De Figueiredo 2004, p. 7). In addition, *the ICJ is thought as a leading Court with a vast experience in matter of treaty interpretation* (considering the PCIJ practice, too), and that *it has mostly contributed to the development and clarification of the rules and principles of international law* (Lauterpacht 1982, p. 282). From the proliferation of judicial settlement forum perspective, the ICJ is known as always coexisting with other third-party dispute settlement forums (ILC 2006, pp. 14 and 16). Nevertheless, on matters of international law, the ICJ's opinions (regardless of their formally non binding character) are considered greatly influential with other judicial international bodies, national courts, governments, and scholars (Weisburd 2009, p. 6).

### 4.2.2 *Scope of the Analysis and Methodology*

During its long existence, the PCIJ/ICJ has dealt with many cases of treaty interpretation.[31] However, given the space limitations of the book, it is both impossible and unnecessary to provide an analysis of all those cases. Therefore, to illustrate the treaty interpretation issues proposed to be discussed in this chapter, particularly the interpretative techniques adopted by the ICJ, I selected several ICJ cases decided prior to, and post, the VCLT's adoption, covering all the interpretative methods that this Court usually applies. The cases are relevant from the treaty interpretation perspective and aim to identify the existence of *patterns of treaty interpretation* in both periods: pre and post the adoption of the VCLT. In this scope, the cases attempt to cover both *express* and *implied* (indirect) techniques/ways in which the ICJ has usually resorted to the customary rules of treaty interpretation prior and after the adoption of the 1969 VCLT. On one side, the implied or indirect techniques/ways of interpretation include the ICJ's *suggestion* to apply the customary rules of interpretation (both pre and post the VCLT's adoption periods) and, on the other side, the resort to the Vienna rules of interpretation (thus after the adoption of the VCLT) *without a technical ascription of these rules*. The ICJ case law analysis is provided here and used further to illustrate in the next two chapters

[30]See, e.g., Irwin (1997), p. 759; Scott et al. (1996), p. 1. According to Irwin, one of ICJ's limits is that the ICJ has a rigid procedure and that the enforceability of its decisions decreases as sometimes the Security Council must take measure to enforce the ICJ's judgments. See also Llamzon (2007), pp. 818–819. Llamzon observes that, in the last few decades, the overwhelming majority of the Court's case docket has been initiated by unilateral invocation by the applicant states of 'compulsory jurisdiction'.

[31]International Court of Justice, *supra* note 1. From 22 May 1947 to 16 September 2013, had been entered 153 cases in the General List of the ICJ (contentious cases and advisory opinions).

how the ICJ's practice on treaty interpretation may influence the treaty interpretative process of the ECtHR and WTO (panels and the Appellate Body) under the same body of general rules and principles of treaty interpretation (as reflected in the VCLT methodology), or, conversely, may not do so.

One interesting aspect of the PCIJ/ICJ practice in matters related to treaty interpretation, observed by some commentators but not theoreticised as such, is arguably, from the beginning of the World Court's existence, what I could term as 'overbuilding'.[32] It means that even if a conclusion of a case apparently could be obtained by the Court after applying one method/rule of interpretation, the Court does not stop the interpretation, but it continues with the application of other methods/rules, which eventually lead to the same conclusions. Thus, the cases selected here provide clear approaches of treaty interpretation that could shed light on the *interpretative patterns* used by the ICJ, while they also can be sufficient to illustrate all the issues related to treaty interpretation that this chapter attempts to respond to the suggestion of 'overbuilding'.

Overall, the cases are analysed in this author's view and aim to show how the Court develops its process of building/overbuilding the case of interpretation by successive steps and whether each of the steps enhances the conclusions reached by the Court after applying the method/rule it expressly (or implicitly) declared. Thus, even if a conclusion of a case could apparently be obtained after applying the declared method/s, the question of *how* the Court adopts, in addition, other methods, rules and principles of interpretation when dealing with various difficulties of treaty text construction (such as *insufficiently clear*, *ambiguous*, *inconclusive, vague language of the text* or *silent, not providing for the circumstances of the case*) or when apparently there are no difficulties in interpretation (the text is admitted by the Court as being *clear*) will be in depth examined, together with the conditions under which the Court ponders each of the interpretative tools. In this attempt, I will proceed to analyse each of the selected cases (both prior to and post the 1969 VCLT's adoption periods) so as to reveal *what the ICJ declares it does*, and *what it actually does*, considering that not always does this Court expressly spell out what methods, rules or principles it relies upon in addition to the declared means of interpretation (method/s, rule/s, principle/s).

Furthermore, the case analyses attempt to evidence the *customary* character of the rules of treaty interpretation by providing an insight into how these rules have been adopted by the PCIJ/ICJ, developed in its practice and perpetuated to become *custom*, as reflected in Articles 31–33 of the VCLT. The cases will be treated in detail in order to show the general tendency of the World Court to resort *holistically* and in *patterns* to the general rules/methods of treaty interpretation (always the Court adopting in a given case more rules and methods of interpretation than it actually declares, or than are necessary to solve the case, both to determine and to confirm the meaning of the treaty terms in question), as also the issue of *consistency*

[32]'Overbuilding'—is the present author's suggestion for explaining the Court's pattern (tendency/preference) in building its case of interpretation.

of this Court's approaches to treaty interpretation (pre and post the VCLT). This examination will constitute the framework of analysing comparatively (in Chaps. 4 and 5) whether the ECtHR's and WTO's treaty interpretative techniques based on the general rules of interpretation diverge fundamentally from those used by the ICJ or, conversely, whether both these specialised courts apply techniques of interpretation similarly to the ICJ and what the relevance of this aspect is *vis-à-vis* the unity of international law.

## 4.3 Pre-VCLT Treaty Interpretation at the PCIJ/ICJ: Scholarship and Case Analysis

In order to illustrate the issues raised in this chapter, several ICJ cases selected from the period that preceded the adoption of the VCLT, which are relevant from the treaty interpretation perspective, will be taken into analysis in this part. While organised on questions/topics that focus on the method, rule or principle on which the Court appears to rely (or to emphasise) more in a particular case, the case analyses aim, in general, to reveal gradually and in detail the other methods, rules and principles that the Court actually adopts in this 'overbuilding' interpretation. The case analyses attempt to cover various situations/difficulties that the PCIJ/ICJ encounters when interpreting the text of treaties (e.g., insufficiently clear, ambiguous, dubious, inconclusive, vague/silent text), relying on methods, rules and principles of interpretation. Some cases will be analysed in brief, pointing out the Court's emphasis on a method, rule or principle of interpretation while succinctly revealing the other means of interpretation that the Court adopts. Other cases will reveal in greater detail a whole picture of all the interpretative means applied by the Court in a single combined, logical interpretative act, so the analyses will be more extensive. Thus, in this part, the following cases will be analysed to build up a picture of *how* the Court approached treaty interpretation in the pre-VCLT period:

– *Wimbledon (Britain, France, Italy, Japan v. Germany)* (1923)[33];

– *The Conditions of Admission of a State to Membership in the United Nations (Article 4 of the Charter)* (Advisory Opinion) (1948)[34];

– *The Interpretation of Peace Treaties with Bulgaria, Hungary and Romania* (Advisory Opinion) (1950)[35];

---

[33] *Case of S.S. Wimbledon,* PCIJ, Ser. A., No. 1, 1923, p. 6.

[34] *Condition of admission of a state to membership in the United Nations (Article 4 of the Charter),* ICJ, Advisory Opinion of May 28th, 1948.

[35] *Interpretation of Peace Treaties with Bulgaria, Hungary and Romania* (second phase), Advisory Opinion of July 18th, 1950.

– *Haya de la Torre* (*Colombia v. Peru*) (1951)[36];
– *Exchange of Greek and Turkish Population (Greece v. Turkey*) (1925)[37];
– *Ambatielos (Greece v. United Kingdom)* (1952)[38];
– *Acquisition of Polish Nationality* (Advisory Opinion) (1923)[39];
– *The Constitution of the Maritime Safety Committee of the Inter-governmental Maritime, Consultative Organization* (Advisory Opinion) (1960).[40]

### *4.3.1 The Predominance of the Textualist Approach: But Not the Sole Approach*

In spite of recommendations of the schools of thought, each suggesting a certain method of interpretation,[41] it appears to have been always difficult for the PCIJ/ICJ to use one single approach of interpretation in determining the outcome of a case. Therefore, as the case analyses in this chapter show, the Court almost never stops at the employment of a single method/rule (i.e., the textualist, based on the 'plain or ordinary meaning' rule), even after it has expressly declared it to be so, and proceeds with another method/rule or more methods/rules in combination. The Court tends to employ more methods/rules in an effort to show that all of those methods/rules point in the same direction indicated by the first (declared) method/rule. By using some of the leading cases of the PCIJ/ICJ related to treaty interpretation (pre-VCLT), I attempt to explore in this part *how* the World Court approaches the issue of interpretation in the light of the methods and rules proposed by the various schools of thought. In addition, the case analysis in this part attempts to answer the question of whether the ICJ generally shows preference for a particular method/rule, governing the interpretative process.

#### 4.3.1.1 Textualist Approach?

The ICJ often declares that its method of interpretation will be to honour the 'ordinary' or 'plain' meaning of the treaty text. This declared approach suggests

[36]*Haya de la Torre Case*, Judgment of June 13th, 1951: ICJ Reports 1951.
[37]*Exchange of Greek and Turkish Population (Lausanne Convention VI, January 30th, 1923, Article 2)*, Advisory Opinion, PCIJ, Series B, No 10, 1925.
[38]*Ambatielos Case (Greece v. United Kingdom)*, ICJ, Preliminary objections, Judgment of July 1st, 1952.
[39]*Question Concerning the Acquisition of Polish Nationality*, Advisory Opinion of 15 September 1923, Series B, PCIJ, No. 7.
[40]*Constitution of the Maritime Safety Committee of the Inter-governmental Maritime, Consultative Organization*, Advisory Opinion of 8 June, ICJ, 1960.
[41]See Chap. 3 of this book.

that the text indeed has one ordinary mean and that by using such an approach, the meaning of the text can be identified without recourse to any other methods/rules. However, as the case analyses will show, the Court implicitly or explicitly and also irrespective of the treaty text construction (e.g., clear, insufficiently clear, ambiguous, doubtful, silent) adopts, in addition, other rules of interpretation such as the 'context', 'good faith', 'object and purpose', 'subsequent practice', 'supplementary means' so as to ascertain and confirm the result reached on the 'ordinary meaning' rule while emphasising/weightening more or less one rule or another.

The analyses on cases will also show that the process of application of these general rules of interpretation is not performed by the World Court in a mechanical way, or as a mathematical formula. Such application could not be possible since this initial selectivity of the rules/principles implies in itself balancing and attachment of heavier normative weight to some of the rules/principles, rather than to others. Thus, the Court, as interpreter, appears overall to balance *ex ante* various principles and to choose what requires its attention on those specific circumstances of the case. It also appears to emphasise some aspects/circumstances, while others do not in the same case, applying accordingly those rules and principles it considers necessary to adopt in order to give effect to the norm/law at issue and justify on this basis its approach to interpretation. In addition to this aspect, the cases analysed in this part can illustrate the ICJ's general tendency to apply a *holistic* judgment, taking also into consideration international law principles relevant to the interpretative process. A prime example is the ***Wimbledon* (1923)** case,[42] in which the World Court approached a much broader interpretation than the textualist it declared, having to interpret a text of a treaty that allegedly presents no difficulties in interpretation (*clear* text).

The issue of interpretation before the Court in *Wimbledon* concerned the request of four nations' governments (Britain, France, Italy, Japan), in 1921, to establish whether the refusal by the German authorities of an English steamship, called 'S.S. Wimbledon', having on board ammunition and artillery stores consigned to the Polish Naval Base at Danzig, to pass through the Kiel Canal was in violation of Article 380 of the Treaty of Versailles.[43] The German authorities based their refusal to allow passage upon neutrality Orders issued by Germany in connection with the Russian–Polish war, Orders by which cargoes of this kind destined for Poland and Russia were prohibited.[44] The provision under interpretation in this case was Article 380 of the 1919 Treaty of Versailles, which created a new international regime for the Kiel Canal, providing that 'The Kiel Canal and its approaches shall be maintained free and open to the vessels of commerce and of war of all nations at peace with Germany on terms of entire equality'.[45] Thus, under this new regime, the Kiel Canal was equally open to all vessels, without making any distinction

[42]*Wimbledon* (1923), p. 6, *supra* note 33.

[43]*Id*, p. 20 (titled 'Ports, Waterways and Railways').

[44]*Id*.

[45]*Id*, p. 21.

between war vessels and vessels of commerce, but on one condition, namely, that these vessels must belong to nations at peace with Germany.[46] Germany argued that by allowing free passage to 'Wimbledon', it would imperil its neutrality.[47]

The Court considers the 'text' of Article 380 to be 'categorical and gives rise to no doubt', suggesting the application of the 'plain meaning' rule of interpretation of the terms in their context.[48] Based on this rule, the Court determines that the Kiel Canal is not an internal and national navigable waterway, but it has an international status 'intended to provide under the treaty guarantee easier access to the Baltic for the benefit of all nations of the world'.[49] However, in order to evidence more the real intention of the drafters, the Court suggests further resort to the 'context' rule and provides an interpretation of Article 380 in the context of the Treaty as a whole. The context, as the Court itself admits, furnishes more light on the meaning of Article 380 already deduced from 'the spirit and letter'.[50] In this regard, the Court concludes that '[t]he intention of the authors of the Treaty of Versailles to facilitate access to the Baltic by establishing an international regime, and consequently to keep the canal open at all times to foreign vessels of every kind, appears with still greater force from a comparison of the wording of Article 380 with that of the other provisions to be found in Part XII'.[51] As it can be observed, the Court approaches this case in a much broader way than the textualist interpretation it declared. For instance, in determining whether the use of the great international waterway is free (in time of war and peace, for all kinds of vessels, of war or commerce), and not incompatible with the neutrality of the riparian sovereign, the Court resorts in addition to 'any relevant rules of international law' found in international agreements or treaties (e.g., with regard to the Suez Canal, and Panama Canals, or the Convention of Constantinople of 9 October 1888, the Treaty between Great Britain and the United States of 18 November 1901).[52] This approach is reflected in what

---

[46] *Id*, p. 22.

[47] *Id*, p. 29. Thus, Germany argued that the general grant of a right of passage to vessels of all nationalities through the Kiel Canal cannot deprive Germany's exercise of its rights as a neutral power in time of war to allow the passage through the Canal of contraband destined for one of the belligerents.

[48] *Id*, p. 8. Albeit recognising that the Kiel Canal was constructed as an internal waterway of the German state, the Court considers that 'the Treaty has taken care not to assimilate it to the other internal navigable waterways of the German Empire' and 'a special section has been created at the end of Part XII, dealing with ports, water-ways and railways, and in this special section rules exclusively designed for the Kiel Canal have been inserted'.

[49] *Id*, p. 23.

[50] *Id*, p. 24.

[51] *Id*, p. 23. Also, the 'context' is revealed by the Court when stating that the rules provided by Part XII for the Kiel Channel 'differ on more than one point from those to which other internal navigable waterways of the Empire are subjected by Article 321 to 327'.

[52] *Id*, p. 26 (and closed to the vessel of war and commerce of nations not at peace with Germany).

later becomes Article 31(3)(c) of the VCLT (resort to 'any relevant rules of international law').

Furthermore, from the Court's reference to the intention of the drafters of the Treaty to have the channel regime treated differently than that of an internal waterway (as claimed by Germany), it could be inferred as a possible reliance of the Court on the *travaux preparatoire* of the Treaty of Versailles and hence on the 'intention' (subjective) method.[53] The Court gives, however, a vague indication in this regard, stating that '[t]he Kiel Canal . . . was until 1919 an internal waterway . . . and the treaty has taken care not to assimilate it to the other navigable waterways of the German Empire'.[54] To better clarify and also confirm the intention of the drafters, the Court appears to extend even more this approach by implicitly adopting a teleological reading of Article 380, thus in the light of the 'object and purpose' of the Treaty of Versailles. It appears to rely on this method when referring, for example, to the drafters' contemplation of the possibility of Germany being at war, case in which the Kiel Canal would have been closed to the vessels of war or commerce of nations not at peace with Germany.[55] Moreover, by adopting a *per a contrario* technique of argumentation in further clarifying the meaning of Article 380, the Court appears to rely on the interpretative principle of effectiveness. It states accordingly that the provisions relating to the Kiel Canal in the Treaty of Versailles are 'self-contained' and that 'if they had to be supplemented and interpreted by the aid of those referring to the inland navigable waterways of Germany in the previous Sections of Part XII', as Germany argued, 'they would lose their "*raison d'être*"'.[56] The Court implies that it cannot interpret a treaty text by revising it, adding something that it was not there.

*Wimbledon* proved to be the first contentious case in a general series of cases where the PCIJ was demanded to interpret various provisions from the treaties concluded under the Versailles 'system' treaties, in order to solve various international conflicts between the states in the *League of the Nations*. One could argue that the adopted approach by the Court in this case favours the 'plain meaning' rule of interpretation and could be understood as the Court's intent to emphasise the importance of the Treaty of Versailles as a *pacta sunt servanda* written agreement. The emphasis on the 'text' indicates the idea that the text of the treaty is presumed to be the authentic expression of the common intention of the contracting parties. Thus, being a matter of consent between the parties, and concluded on their 'free will', which is at the core of defining the extent of the parties' rights and obligations, the Treaty is suggested to be taken by the parties as it stands. Thus, the Court concludes that Germany is bound by the contractual obligations assumed under the Treaty it entered into at Versailles on 28 June 1919[57] and that no sovereignty

---

[53] *Id*, p. 24.

[54] *Id*.

[55] *Id*, p. 23.

[56] *Id*, p. 24.

[57] *Id*, p. 14.

principle could be invoked above and against the will of the states, as expressed in the Treaty.[58] However, the fact that the majority of the Court gave primacy to the 'plain meaning' rule was not seen by some judges as reasonable and acceptable. For example, in a dissenting opinion, judges Anzilotti and Hubert argued that the terms of the treaty 'have no value except in so far as they express an idea which leads to contradictory or impossible consequences or which, in the circumstances must be regarded as going beyond the intention of the parties'.[59] The judges considered then the rule on which the Court based its approach as a 'purely grammatical interpretation', which in their view would work as 'a threat' to 'every contract, and more especially of international treaties' that 'must stop at this point'.[60]

Nevertheless, it could be deduced from the above analysis that the 'plain meaning' rule of interpretation, which will later find reflection in Article 31(1) of the VCLT, is here only the starting point, the base and guide of the Court for launching into a deeper interpretive analysis. Thus, the Court, actually, could not reduce its reasoning to a simple 'grammatical interpretation' of the text article in question by ignoring the circumstances of the conclusion of the Treaty under the Versailles 'system' of Treaties and, most importantly, its object and purpose. Moreover, the Court shows in this case a preference to be progressive, giving prevalence to treaties, instead of being more attached to older and established notions such as 'state sovereignty'.[61] It performs in *Wimbledon* a normative judgment, going to the nature of the Treaty of Versailles, interpreting the provision at issue *holistically*, in the light of the text, context, 'object and purpose', 'any relevant rules of international law', the 'good faith' and effectiveness principles, and also taking into account other provisions and the historical context of the Treaty as a whole.

#### 4.3.1.2 Textualist or Holistic Approach?

When the ICJ confronts with a text of the treaty that it admits as being *clear* or *sufficiently clear*, the use of more rules and methods of interpretation than necessary may suggest the Court's sensitivity towards legitimacy issues and preference for rational deliberations that have the potential to enhance their legitimacy. It follows that this 'overbuilding' interpretation in a given case could be attributed either to some sort of uncertainty that the Court may have with respect to the efficiency of the method chosen initially to reach a conclusion or to convincing the losing party in the dispute that any rational interpreter would reach the same and single conclusion as result of interpretation, or both of these reasons. It appears that the

[58] *Id*, p. 25.

[59] *Id*. Dissenting Opinion by Judges Anzilotti and Huber, p. 36.

[60] *Id*, p. 19.

[61] In this sense the Court was faithful to such progressive body of treaties as those concluded under the Versailles system, which acknowledged the dissolution of three empires, allowed for the principle of self-determination, and also the creation of several new nation states.

judges engaged in the interpretation of a treaty text need to *converge on a single (holistic) interpretation*, which should include all interpretive methods. However, despite the usual and strong emphasis on the textualist method, the Court appears, in general, not to give preference in reliance on this method, or treat one rule superior over another, even when the text, at prima facie reading, is found *clear* or *sufficiently clear* and the textualist method would suffice to solve the issue of interpretation, as the next example will show, but rather the Court approaches these methods *holistically*, all combined in a unitary, logical act of interpretation. Therefore, when employing the 'plain' and 'ordinary' meaning rule, the Court approaches the terms of the provision at issue not in a strictly grammatical sense, but in their context, and only as a starting point in commencing the act of interpretation. According to Koskenniemi, the 'plain' meaning rule is actually 'not a rule of interpretation at all' as it only '*assumes what has to be proved*; that the expression has a certain meaning instead of another one'.[62] In his view, the result is that the interpretative method of the 'plain meaning' must not look to assign a specific meaning to individual words of the text of the treaty.[63] The ***First Admissions* (1948)**[64] case, for example, is considered in the scholarship to be a leading example of the application of the textualist method of interpretation in a situation where the Court finds the text of the Convention at issue *sufficiently clear* in itself as to warrant a rejection of other means of treaty interpretation. However, the Court does not limit itself to the text as to give effect to the 'natural', 'normal' or 'ordinary' meaning of the words in their context, but it adopts in addition other rules of interpretation in order to shed more light on the meaning of the terms at issue.

The Court was asked in this case to pronounce whether a state called upon to cast a vote on the admission of another state into the UN, in virtue of Article 4 of the UN Charter, could make its consent to the admission dependent on conditions other than those not expressly provided by Article 4(1) of the UN Charter. Notably, whether a state, while recognising that the conditions set forth in Article 4 were fulfilled by the state seeking admission, could subject its affirmative vote to the additional condition that other states be admitted to membership in the UN with the state seeking admission.[65] The issue of interpretation concerns Article 4(1) of the UN Charter regarding the membership criteria for states to join the UN, which stipulates that 'Membership in the United Nations is open to all other peace-loving States which accept the obligations contained in the present Charter and, in the judgment of the Organization, and able and willing to carry out these obligations'.[66]

By adopting the 'natural' meaning rule, the Court declares that the conditions provided by Article 4(1) constitute an exhaustive list and that they 'are not merely stated by way of guidance or example'.[67] The Court insists that the text of this

---

[62]Koskenniemi (2004), pp. 333–334 (emphasis added).

[63]*Id.*

[64]*First Admissions Case* (1948), *supra* note 34.

[65]*Id*, p. 5.

[66]*Id.*

[67]*Id*, p. 9.

provision is *sufficiently clear* and that 'beside it fixes the conditions of admission, it also determines the reason for which the admission can be refused'.[68] It concludes in this regard that '[m]embership in the United Nations is open to all *peace-loving* States ...'.[69] In supporting this result, the Court applies an interpretation of both English and French texts of Article 4(1) and finds that they have the same meaning.[70] This approach will be later adopted in Article 33 of the VCLT as a rule of interpretation of treaties authenticated in two or more languages.

Nevertheless, the Court's interpretation develops beyond that afforded by the 'ordinary' meaning rule declared; it is supplemented with an implicit resort to the interpretative principle of effectiveness. Accordingly, the Court asserts that the conditions enumerated in Article 4(1) could not 'represent only an indispensable minimum, in the sense that political considerations could be superimposed upon them, and prevent admission of an applicant which fulfils them'.[71] Such an interpretation, as the Court admits, would confer indefinite and unlimited power of discretion upon members of the UN to impose new conditions, so if the drafters wanted it, 'they would undoubtedly have adopted a different wording'.[72]

In addition, the teleological method appears to be adopted implicitly when the Court assumes that the object and purpose of the drafters of the UN Charter were to state clearly in the terms of Article 4, which are the conditions of admission of new states to membership in the UN, and that these conditions provided by the Charter 'clearly constitutes a legal regulation of the question of the admission of new States'.[73] Judging from the teleological perspective given by the object and purpose of the Charter, the Court looks to reaffirm a normative proposition envisaged by the Charter, notably, that of preserving world peace and encouraging the peaceful resolution of states' conflicts. Therefore, by giving full effect to this objective, the Court makes an explicit assertion that it is desirable for states to become members of the UN. Admitting the criteria provided by Article 4(1) as designed to coexist in accordance with the spirit of principles and obligations enshrined in the UN Charter, the Court approaches a *holistic* interpretation of this provision, in the context of the Charter as a whole.[74] To shed more light on the meaning of Article 4 (1), the Court takes this provision in connection with Rule 60 of the Provisional Rules of Procedure of the Security Council, which lays down the power of the

[68] *Id.*

[69] *Id* (emphasis added).

[70] *Id.*

[71] *Id*, pp. 9–10.

[72] *Id*, p. 10.

[73] *Id.*

[74] *Id.* However, the Court concludes that a State could only be subjected to a limited set of conditions in order to be admitted to the UN, and such limitation is explicitly provided by the Charter.

Security Council to decide and recommend an applicant state for membership.[75] Accordingly, the Court finds that Article 4 of the Charter 'does not forbid taking into account of *any factor* which it is possible *reasonably* and *in good faith* to connect with the conditions laid down in that Article', which are to (1) be a state, (2) be peace loving, (3) accept the obligations of the Charter, (4) be able to carry out these obligations, (5) be willing to do so.[76]

It is worth observing that the words 'the spirit' and 'the terms' convey the intent of the Court to underline the idea that the terms of Article 4 are clear so they cannot give birth to multiple interpretations, which certainly would contravene the scope and purpose of the Charter's drafters. It could be implied, however, that despite expressly stating that 'there is no occasion to resort to preparatory work if the text of a convention is sufficiently clear in itself',[77] the Court's viewpoint appears based also on evidence of the intention of the Charter's drafters (and doctrine), thus not simply on a literal interpretation of the terms in the context of their use. Nevertheless, the judges in the joint dissenting opinion did not see that Article 4 was clear enough for the Court to provide a simple and unambiguous answer to the question posed, relying thus only on the text as the Court itself expressly declared that it would do.[78] Therefore, these judges suggested that the Court must have applied the rules generally recognised in relation to the interpretation of treaties,[79] implying a clear and express reliance on such rules. They stated in this regard that '[i]t is a rule of interpretation which was well recognized and constantly applied by the PCIJ that a treaty provision should be read in its *entirety*'.[80] But, in reality, as the case analysis above can show, the Court adopted this approach implicitly so by suggesting only the rules/methods it actually relies upon in addition. The textualist approach (implying the 'ordinary meaning' rule of the terms in their context) constitutes only the starting point in interpretation, as actually acknowledged by the Court itself in the case at hand, when stating that it 'must in the *first* place consider the text of that Article'.[81] Why the Court declared the 'plain meaning' rule as governing the interpretation could be because of its intent to underline, as seen, for example, in *S.S. Wimbledon*, the importance of the *good faith* principle, which flows directly from the *pacta sunt servanda* principle on which treaties are supposed to rely. The main idea behind this emphasis seems to be that a treaty text must

---

[75] *Id.* Rule 60 provides: 'The Security Council shall decide whether in its judgment the applicant is a peace loving State and is able and willing to carry out the obligations contained in the Charter, and accordingly whether to recommend the applicant State for membership.'

[76] *Id*, pp. 9–10 (emphasis added).

[77] *Id*, p. 10.

[78] *Id.* See Joint dissenting opinion of Judge Basdevant, Winiarski, McNair and Read, p. 86.

[79] *Id.*

[80] *Id* (emphasis added). The disagreement between judges in the present case was therefore not on the principle but on the application of principle to the case. They argued that 'when confronted with a rule or principle of law ... no restriction on it can be presumed, unless it has been clearly established, and ... in case of doubt it is the rule or principle of law which must prevail'.

[81] *Id*, p. 10 (emphasis added).

be interpreted as it stands, without reference to extraneous means. It implies an interpretation based on what actually the text says, and not on what might say, as the (treaty) text is presumed to be the expression of the common intention of the parties, a meeting of their will. As it was shown in the previous chapter, the 'good faith' principle constitutes the foundation on which the general rule of interpretation is later formulated in the VCLT's text of Article 31(1).

In sum, the Court proceeds in the *First Admissions* case beyond the declared approach, relying in addition to the text on other rules of interpretation. Though the Court's approach appears not consistent in totality with its declared approach, it, nevertheless, proves to be consistent with its own practice by adopting *holistically* other means of interpretation: when it feels *to confirm* the result obtained on a textualist approach, as it was the situation in the case at hand, or when the result obtained on the 'ordinary meaning' of the term leads to an ambiguous meaning of that specific term. The judgment of the *First Admissions* case is considered in the scholarship as influencing the drafters of the VCLT in adopting the general rule of treaty interpretation, following the textualist canons that will be reflected in the text of Article 31(1) of the VCLT.[82]

#### 4.3.1.3 Restrictive, Textualist Approach?

Generally, by highly articulating the 'plain' or 'ordinary' meaning rule, the ICJ seems to intend to convey the idea that a treaty is a *pacta sunt servanda* written agreement, concluded by states in good faith and on their free will, which gives the agreement the force to be binding upon all parties to it. Accordingly, the Court tends to prefer declaring the 'plain' or 'ordinary' meaning rule as the prevalent rule in interpretation, even if the Court is not necessarily convinced that this approach would suffice to reach a single pertinent interpretation of the issue before it. However, the ICJ's practice records circumstances when it took an excessive attachment to the letter of the text, and therefore not conforming itself with its traditional attitudes and its developed practice (established precedents) to rely, in addition, on other methods and rules of interpretation. In this respect, Endicott's recommendation that judges should take a modest attitude when making a claim of determinacy appears to be highly instructive here (Endicott 2000, p. 29). Endicott's view is that judges 'should not take refuge in claims that the plain meaning of words compels a decision', as they also 'should not take refuge in claims of indeterminacy or claim that they are interpreting the words of the statute'.[83] For Endicott, therefore, it appears decisively important to give account, generally, to the role of the principle of effectiveness in interpreting a legal text when pointing out that

> The possibility that a rule does not answer a dispute, and that a good interpretation of the law would not make something of the rule that would decide the case, is never a reason for a

[82]See e.g. ILC's Draft Articles on the Law of Treaties with commentaries (1966), pp. 187 and 204.

[83]Endicott (2000), p. 29.

> court to abandon its attempt to give effect to the law, or its responsibility for the wise development of the law.[84]

Similarly, but putting emphasis on the role of the *intention* element alongside the *principle of effectiveness* in determining the meaning of a treaty text (provision) and giving effect to it, Lauterpacht observes that the practice of the PCIJ had demonstrated that

> alongside the fundamental principle of interpretation, namely, that effect is to be given to the intention of the parties, full use can be made of another hardly less important principle, namely that the treaty must remain effective rather than ineffective. *Res magis valeat quam pereat.* It is a major principle, in the light of which the intention of the parties must always be interpreted, even to the extent of disregarding the letter of the instrument and of reading into it something which, on the face of it, it does not contain.[85]

Comparing with the other cases discussed in this chapter, and generally with other treaty interpretation cases of the ICJ's practice, the next example will show a situation when the Court took rather a narrower view of its judicial function in dealing with indeterminacy in the language of a treaty text. It shows the situation when the identity of a canon of interpretation, namely *ut res magis valeat quam pereat*, is far from being wholly agreed by the judges in the case. As perceived by Stone, such an attitude appears to question the role of the principles of interpretation that an international court must have 'as a check on caprice and subjectivity'.[86] The analysis of the ***Interpretation of the Peace Treaties with Bulgaria, Hungary and Romania* (1950)**[87] case will show the Court's reliance on other methods and rules of interpretation in addition to the textualist method, which is based on the 'plain', 'natural' or 'ordinary' meaning rule, highly emphasised by the Court. The resort to other methods and rules of interpretation is done by the Court despite the *clearness* in the construction of the treaty text it declares to deal with.[88] However, this case is perceived in the scholarship as one of the rare examples of the World Court's taking a narrower view of its function as interpreter, in disregard of the general legal principle of effectiveness.[89]

In the first phase of the case,[90] the Allied and Associated Powers, parties to the 1946 Treaty of Peace, had charged Bulgaria, Hungary and Romania with violations

---

[84] *Id*, p. 183.

[85] Lauterpacht (1982), pp. 69–70.

[86] Stone (1953), p. 345. Stone states in this regard that by no means it is always clear 'whether it means that the principles of interpretation (a) do in fact give objectivity to the Court's conclusions, or (b) merely free the Court from the suspicion of deciding cases on subjective or arbitrary grounds'.

[87] *Interpretation of Peace Treaties with Bulgaria, Hungary and Romania* (1950), *supra* note 35.

[88] *Id*, p. 12.

[89] McDougal and Gardner (1951), p. 266. See also a similar restrictive ICJ approach to interpretation (after the VCLT's adoption) in: *Land, Island and Maritime Frontier Dispute* ((El Salvador/Honduras: Nicaragua intervening) [1992] ICJ Reports 351, Separate Opinion of Torres Bernardez, p. 719, para 35)—pointed out in Gardiner (2008), p. 18.

[90] In the first phase of this case, the Court was asked to give an advisory opinion in principal on whether diplomatic exchanges between Bulgaria, Hungary and Romania, on the one hand, and certain Allied and Associated Powers signatory to the Treaty of Peace, on the other hand, disclosed the existence of disputes subject to the Treaty provisions.

of the provisions of the articles dealing with human rights and fundamental freedoms,[91] which these countries rejected. The ICJ had given an Advisory Opinion in which it declared that all the three countries were bound to carry out the provisions of the Peace Treaties for the settlement of disputes, and in particular their obligation to appoint their own Commissioners, which these countries refused to follow. In the second phase (the present case),[92] the Court was asked to pronounce whether one party failed to appoint a representative to a Treaty Commissions, pursuant to the provisions of the Peace Treaties with Bulgaria, Hungary and Romania (Articles 36, 40 and 38)[93] for the settlement of disputes concerning the interpretation or execution of these Treaties, the Secretary-General has then the power to appoint the third member of the Commission upon the request of the other party to a dispute, according to the provisions of the respective Treaties.[94]

Thus, the issue at stake here is whether the provision empowering the Secretary-General to appoint the third member of the Commission applies to the situation in which *one of the parties refuses to appoint its own representative to the Commission.*[95] Since the word 'third' in the expression 'third member' within the articles at

[91](Under Article 2 of the Treaty with Bulgaria and Hungary and Article 3 of the Treaty with Romania). Article 2 of the Treaty with Bulgaria (to which correspond *mutatis mutandi* Article 2, paragraph 1, of the Treaty with Hungary and Article 3, paragraph 1, of the Treaty with Romania) provides:

> Bulgaria shall take all measures necessary to secure to all persons under Bulgarian jurisdiction, without distinction as to race, sex, language or religion, the enjoyment of human rights and of fundamental freedom, including freedom of expression, of press and publications, of religious worship, of political opinion and of public meeting.

[92]*Interpretation of Peace Treaties with Bulgaria, Hungary and Romania* (1950).

[93]*Id*, pp. 7–8. Article 36 of the Treaty with Bulgaria (to which correspond mutatis mutandis Article 40 of the Treaty with Hungary and Article 38 of the Treaty with Romania) provides:

> 1. Except where another procedure is specifically provided under any article of the present Treaty, any dispute concerning the interpretation or execution of the Treaty, which is not settled by direct diplomatic negotiations, shall be referred to the Three Heads of Mission acting under Article 35, except that in this case the Heads of Mission will not be restricted by the time- limit provided in that Article. Any such dispute not resolved by them within a period of two months shall, unless the parties to the dispute mutually agree upon another means of settlement, be referred at the request of either party to the dispute to a Commission composed of one representative of each party and a third member selected by mutual agreement of the two parties from nationals of a third country. Should the two parties fail to agree within a period of one month upon the appointment of the third member, the Secretary-general of the United Nations may be requested by either party to make the appointment.
> 2. The decision of the majority of the members of the Commission shall be the decision of the Commission, and shall be accepted by the parties as definitive and binding.

[94]*Id*. This request was formulated in Question III of the General Assembly (in the first phase for an advisory opinion) of 22 October 1949.

[95]*Id*, p. 13. In sum, the Court acknowledges that the governments of Bulgaria, Hungary and Romania denied from the beginning the very existence of a dispute and refused to take part in the disputes' clauses of the Treaties and also to appoint a representative to a Treaty Commission, disregarding the Court's Advisory Opinion.

issue was susceptible of rising doubts, as it is also used in reference to selection 'by mutual agreement of the two parties from nationals of a *third* country', the Court makes an express use of the textualist method. It establishes that according to the 'natural' and 'ordinary' meaning of the terms of the Treaties of Peace, the 'third member' term *could not be admitted* (a) as 'simply to distinguish the neutral member from the two Commissioners appointed by the parties without implying that the third member can be appointed only when the two nationals Commissioners have already been appointed . . .' and (b) also that 'the failure of the parties to select the third member by mutual agreement, within the stipulated period, satisfies the condition required for the appointment of the third member by the Secretary-General'.[96] To clarify further this view, the Court reads the meaning of the 'third member' term in the 'context' and finds that 'it was intended that the appointment of both the national Commissioners should precede that of the third member'.[97] Relying on the 'text', the Court asserts further that '[i]n the absence of any express provision to the contrary there is no reason to suppose that the parties wished to depart from it'.[98] Consequently, by providing a contextualist reading, the Court does not admit that the literal sense of the text completely excludes the appointment of the 'third member' by the Secretary-General in the situation of the failure of the parties, within the stipulated period, to select 'the third member'.[99] Nevertheless, the Secretary-General can only appoints this 'third member' *solely by mutual agreement of the parties* as the Court assures that this 'clearly results from the sequence of the events contemplated by the article'.[100] The Court clarifies that the power of the Secretary-General to appoint a third member is derived 'solely from the agreement of the parties as expressed in the dispute clause of the Treaties'[101] and that such a clause, by its very nature, 'must be strictly construed and can be applied only in the case expressly provided therein'.[102]

In addition, relying on the textualist method, the Court clarifies that the Treaties at issue provide exclusively for 'the *failure* of the parties to agree upon the selection of a third member and *by no means the much more serious case of a complete refusal of co-operation by one of them, taking the form of refusing to appoint its own Commissioner*',[103] as is the situation at hand, when the three countries categorically refused to give due course to the procedure in the dispute clauses of the Treaties. Thus, reasoning on 'the ordinary meaning of the terms in their context' rule, the Court concludes that by appointing a third member by the Secretary-

[96] *Id*, p. 10.
[97] *Id.*
[98] *Id.*
[99] *Id.*
[100] *Id* (emphasis added).
[101] *Id.*
[102] *Id.*
[103] *Id* (emphasis added).

General, 'instead of bringing about the constitution of a three member Commission such as the Treaties provide for, would result only in the constitution of a two-members Commission', which would not have 'the same degree of moral authority', a condition, as the Court itself admits, not provided by the Treaties.[104] The Court asserts further that it cannot justify itself in attributing to the provisions for the settlement of disputes in the Peace Treaties a meaning that 'would be contrary to their *letter* and *spirit*'.[105] Given this, the Court reiterates that it is its duty to interpret the Treaties and not to revise them.[106] In essence, the Court's viewpoint is that by interpreting a treaty, it cannot by any means add something that is not therein, exceeding its judicial function. As the Court holds, the *refusal* of Bulgaria, Hungary and Romania to appoint their own Commissioners made the constitution of Commission contemplated by the Treaties impossible, depriving the appointment of the third member by the Secretary-General of every purpose.[107] And the principle *ut res magis valeat quam pereat*, often referred to as the rule of effectiveness, 'cannot justify the Court in attributing to the provisions for the settlement of disputes in the Peace Treaties a meaning which . . . would be contrary to their letter and spirit'.[108]

Unlike the majority opinion in the instant case, in Judge Read's (dissenting) opinion, the Dispute Articles at issue (within the Treaties of Peace) should have been interpreted in a manner that would not deprive them of all effectiveness.[109] Based on a rich body of the PCIJ case law, Judge Read states in essence that 'the treaty must be read as whole, and that its meaning is not to be determined merely upon particular phrases which, if detached from the context, may be interpreted in more than one sense'.[110] Admitting that there is 'a gap or lacuna' in the Dispute Articles at issue, and that the Court in this case confronts with two possible constructions, 'neither of which are based upon inferences drawn from the expression actually used in the text',[111] Judge Read concludes that an interpretation leading to a negative answer to the question of the establishment of a Treaty Commission 'would deprive the Treaties of Peace of a great part of their value, and that it would conflict with their general purposes and objects'.[112]

[104] *Id*, p. 11.

[105] *Id*, p. 12.

[106] *Id*.

[107] *Id*, pp. 11–12.

[108] *Id*, p. 12.

[109] *Id*. Dissenting opinion of Judge Read, p. 23.

[110] *Id*.

[111] *Id*, pp. 23–25. Judge Read admits that all the three countries denied all the charges justification of the conduct complained of and finds in arguing such situation that 'international practice has treated those provisions as conferring rights or privileges upon the parties to the dispute which they would refrain from exercising at their peril– the peril of being confronted with an arbitral decision by a tribunal on which they had no representatives'.

[112] *Id*.

Therefore, by de facto completely disregarding the general legal principle of effectiveness from its decision to assert the constitution of a Commission when confronting with such a clear refusal of those three countries to appoint the representatives to the Treaty Commission, it appears rather a restrictive interpretation adopted by the Court. However, in justifying its position, the Court finds the constitution of the Commission asked for by the Secretary-General as being contrary to the 'object and purpose' of the respective Treaties. So given the importance of the matter at stake, notably the grave violations of human rights and fundamental freedoms, one can admit, on the other hand, that the Court could not overlook the object and purpose of the Treaties of Peace (teleological approach). The Court assumes that since these Treaties were concluded in 'good faith', they must be respected by all the signatory parties. In its view, the refusal of the three countries to appoint their representatives to the Treaty Commissions as provided by the Treaties at issue clearly involves *international responsibility so these countries must respect the Treaties as they stand.*[113] Thus, one could not deny, however, that the Court grounds its reasoning on moral considerations and respect for the basic principles of international law, despite its rejection to sanction the constitution of a commission when confronting with an absolute refusal on the part of all the three countries in question. The Court's viewpoint (the justification for its interpretation) appears to be simply that Bulgaria, Hungary and Romania *must co-operate* in examining the grave charges related to their violations of the 'letter and spirit' of the Treaties of Peace which they ratified, so these countries must assume the responsibility *to appoint their representatives to the Treaty Commissions as provided by those Treaties.*

In addition, to justify the outcome reached, the Court appears to resort to the relevant international law practice in looking for any rules related to the constitution of a commission, an approach that, admittedly, reflects in the later text formulation of Article 31(3)(c) of the VCLT. Relying on this approach, the Court finds that the arbitration practice indicates that 'whereas the draftsmen of arbitration conventions have very often taken care to provide for the consequences of the inability of the parties to agree on the appointment of a third party member, they have apart from exceptional cases, refrained from anticipating *a refusal by a party to appoint its own commissioner*'.[114] Thus, since the governments of the three countries (Bulgaria, Hungary and Romania) in the case at hand did not show a direct interest in appointing a representative to a Treaty Commission, and observing their Treaties' obligations, the Court concludes that this fact does not justify the Court in 'exceeding its judicial function on the pretext of remedying a default for the occurrence of which the Treaties have made no provision'.[115] However, in Judge Reads' view, and as it is generally perceived in the scholarship, the Court in this case should have adopted a broad liberal interpretation, more in accordance with the traditional attitudes of the Court and its established precedents in matter of

[113] *Id*, p. 11.

[114] *Id*, p. 12 (emphasis added).

[115] *Id*, p. 13.

treaty interpretation than some of the language in the majority opinion (McDougal and Gardner 1951, p. 266).

In sum, the Court strongly relied in the present case on the textualist method, rather adopting a restrictive interpretation (taking an excessive attachment to the letter of the text) of the provisions at issue than a progressive/evolutive interpretation so as to give effect to the law, or its responsibility for the wise development of the law. Thus, by not giving effect to the treaty provisions at issue, the Court ended up by choosing a narrower view of its judicial function, the treaty remaining rather ineffective than effective on the issue of interpretation, contrasting with its own established treaty interpretative precedents.[116]

#### 4.3.1.4 Different Approach on Textual Silence?

Even if apparently a case could be solved by relying on the method/rule of interpretation that the Court explicitly or implicitly adopts, in the course of interpretation the Court usually adopts in a flexible manner other methods/rules in addition, if considered necessary to reinforce the method/rule it declared or suggested as sufficient to decide upon that case. And the Court usually does so irrespective of whether the terms of the treaty at issue are declared to be clear, presenting no difficulties in interpretation, sufficiently clear, inconclusive, ambiguous, vague or silent in respect of the circumstances of the case. This propensity for employing more rules and methods than (eventually) necessary may very well define and explain the *interpretation* process—an act of understanding, clarifying and expressing the meaning of an authoritative legal text and its embodied value—as applied to the circumstances of the (given) case. However, it is worth mentioning that '[w]hen a treaty provision fairly admits of two constructions, one restricting, and the other enlarging rights which may be claimed under it, the more liberal interpretation is to be preferred'.[117] The ***Haya de la Torre*** **(1951)**[118] case constitutes an illustration of a situation *of textual silence* in treaty provisions, which does not provide for the circumstances of the case, and the Court suggests other rules of interpretation in addition to the 'ordinary meaning' (the basis of interpretation). The analysis of this case attempts to show whether the Court approaches differently the rules and methods of treaty interpretation when dealing with a *textual silence*.

As the civil war broke out on 3 October 1948 in Peru, a prominent Peruvian civil leader, Víctor Raúl Haya de la Torre, took safe haven at the Columbian Embassy of

---

[116]A view that can accord with, and to effectuate, the larger general purpose which the parties desired that these Treaties to serve. See on this point McDougal and Gardner (1951), also the Dissent Opinion of M. Azeveda in this case (p. 33) in which Azeveda points out that 'conventions will often be shown to be useless if, by excessive attachment to the letter of the texts and by resorting to vague penalties especially when it is known that there is an intention to evade the agreements, the defects attributed to the undertakings are allowed to prevail'.

[117]See *Nielsen v. Johnson*, 279 U.S. 41, 51, 2, 1929.

[118]*Haya de la Torre Case* (1951), *supra* note 36.

Lima, and he was subsequently granted asylum by the Columbian government.[119] The Peruvian government contested the asylum as improperly granted under Articles 1(1) and 2(2) of the 1928 Havana Convention on Asylum.[120] The Court was asked in this case to establish in what manner the asylum should be terminated and whether the Government of Colombia was bound to return la Torre to the Peruvian authorities. Adopting a textualist approach on the issue of surrender (Articles 1 and 2 of the Havana Convention), the ICJ finds in this case that the Convention does not give a complete answer to the question in which manner asylum shall be terminated, in a variety of different situations.[121] However, the Court finds also, based on the 'ordinary meaning of the terms in their context' rule, that, according to Article 2(2) of the Convention, asylum can be clearly granted only 'for the period of time strictly indispensable for the person who has sought asylum to ensure in some other way his safety'.[122] Similarly, in interpreting Article 1 of the Havana Convention, the Court finds that this article is also clear as to the requirements that the 'persons accused of, or condemned for common crimes shall be surrendered to the territorial authorities'[123]; however, it clearly does not contain any similar provision in regard to 'political offenders'.[124]

The Court actually adopts a broader interpretation than the one based on the textualist method declared. It further relies on the effectiveness principle and concludes accordingly that 'this silence cannot be interpreted as imposing an obligation to surrender the refugee in case the asylum was granted to him contrary to the provisions of Article 2 of the Convention', because '[s]uch an interpretation would be repugnant to the spirit which animated that Convention'.[125] Then supporting this approach with the teleological perspective given by the 'object

---

[119]See *Asylum Case (Colombia v. Peru)*, ICJ, Judgment of November 20th, 1950. This case originated from circumstances related to the 1948 civil war in Peru. As the war broke out on 3 October 1948, a prominent Peruvian civil leader, Víctor Raúl Haya de la Torre, head of the American People's Revolutionary Alliance, fearing for his life, took safe haven in the Columbian Embassy of Lima and was subsequently granted asylum by the Columbian Ambassador and by the Columbian government. The Peruvian government refused to grant him safe passage out of Peru.

[120]*Haya de la Torre Case* (1951). Article 1 of the 1928 Havana Convention on Asylum provides:

> It is not permissible for states to grant asylum in legations, warships, military camps, or military aircraft, to persons accused of or condemned for common crimes, or to deserters from the army or navy. Persons accused of or condemned for common crimes taking refuge in any of the places mentioned in the preceding paragraph, shall be surrendered upon request of the local government. Should said persons take refuge in foreign territory, surrender shall be brought about through extradition, but only in such cases and in the form established by the respective treaties and conventions or by the constitutional laws of the country of refuge.

[121]*Id*, p. 14.

[122]*Id.*

[123]*Id*, p. 13.

[124]*Id.*

[125]*Id.*

and purpose' of the Convention, the Court holds that it cannot infer from the silence of the text the fact that there is any obligation to surrender a person to whom asylum was accorded in an *irregular* way.[126] The Court assumes that this would mean to 'disregard both the role of these extra-legal factors in the development of asylum in Latin America, and the *spirit* of the Havana Convention itself'.[127] Thus, adopting in addition a contextualist and teleological approach, the Court interprets the provisions in the broader context of the Havana Convention (taken as a whole), its object and purpose, and the practice of asylum.[128]

It could be implied from the Court's argument that at the core of the right to grant asylum stands a fundamental principle of international law, namely the *territorial sovereignty* of states from which it derives the competence of according asylum.[129] Therefore, according to the Court's finding, a state has no obligation under *customary law* to extradite.[130] It also appears that the unanimous decision of the Court could be considered an important aspect in appreciating the agreement of the judges on the principles at stake that stood as the foundation of the right of asylum under international law, given the practice of violence that many states promoted. By grounding their judgments on human rights considerations, and advocating the warrant for preservation of life against violence to it, the judges promoted in this case a progressive thinking on the asylum matter. Thus, leaving the final resolution of the conflict to the 'convenience' and 'political expediency' of the parties,[131] it could, however, be considered a reasonable attitude of the Court based on respect for *fundamental human rights principles* of international law, which stood at the foundation of the Latin American tradition in regard to *asylum*, and thus of the Havana Convention, 'a tradition in accordance with which political refugees should not be surrendered'.[132]

As it could be observed, the Court in *Haya de la Torre* gives preference to a more liberal interpretation than a restrictive one on a treaty provision that does not provide for the circumstances of the case. Unlike in the *Interpretation of the Peace Treaties* case discussed above, the Court interprets the Convention in the case at hand in the manner to give full effect to the provision at issue and not restricting it to the greatest possible. The Court argues that if it had intended to abandon that tradition, which does not indicate that any exception should be made when asylum has been irregularly granted, an express provision to that effect would

[126] *Id.* The Court concludes that the Government of Peru had not proven that the acts of Mr. Haya de la Torre constituted 'common crimes' (emphasis added).

[127] *Id*, p. 14 (emphasis added).

[128] *Id.*

[129] *Id.*

[130] *Id.*

[131] *Id*, p. 16. The Court assumes that the parties 'will be able to find a practical and satisfactory solution by seeking guidance from those considerations of courtesy and good neighbourliness which, in matters of asylum, have always held a prominent place in the relations between the Latin-American republics'.

[132] *Id.*

have been needed, and 'the Havana Convention contains no such provision'.[133] However, unlike in the *Interpretation of the Peace Treaties* case analysed above, in confirming the original intention of the drafters, the Court appears to rely additionally in the *Haya de la Torre* case on the rule of 'supplementary means' of interpretation. It finds on this rule that '[t]he *silence* of the Convention in regard to asylum irregularly granted – was *intended* to leave the adjustment of the consequences of this situation to decisions inspired by considerations of convenience or of simple political expediency'.[134] By not choosing to resort expressly and explicitly to the *travaux preparatoires*, as such a difficulty in treaty text construction would require, the Court's intention appears here to underline the importance of the Havana Convention as a written agreement concluded in *good faith*, presumed to be intended to have a definite force and effect that is binding upon all the signatory parties.

In sum, the ICJ appears to adopt in *Haya de la Torre* a *holistic* interpretation, which allows it to be faithful to both the text of the treaty and the drafters, thus consistent with the treaty interpretation canons and principles (relating to text, context, good faith, object and purpose, 'supplementary means', as reflected in the later text formulation of Articles 31(1) and 32 of the VCLT), while promoting a creative, progressive (evolutive) interpretation when it established the international law practice (customary law) as relevant when the text of the treaty is silent with respect to the circumstances of the case (an approach that could be seen consistent with the rules later codified in Article 31(3)(c) of the VCLT).

#### 4.3.1.5 Reliance on the 'Ordinary Meaning' and/or 'Travaux Preparatoire' Rules?

The *holistic* character that the ICJ confers in general to treaty interpretation appears to be reflected not only in giving effect to all the terms of the treaty at issue (text, context, object and purpose, *travaux*) but also in this Court's tendency to give equal interpretative value to all the rules of interpretation employed in a given case, even if the Court allows for a different weight to these rules, depending on the circumstances of that case. For example, the frequent resort of the ICJ to the *travaux preparatoire*, either explicitly or implicitly, as a means used either to determine or only to confirm the intention of the parties (or altogether), could indicate both the importance and the equal value that the Court ascribes to this rule in relation to the other rules of interpretation in reaching a final result (interpretation).

Like *Wimbledon*, also the ***Exchange of Greek and Turkish Population* (1925)**[135] case is considered in the scholarship among the first batch of cases where the Court adopted the principle of the 'natural meaning', according to

[133] *Id*, p. 16.

[134] *Id* (emphasis added).

[135] *Exchange of Greek and Turkish Population* (1925), *supra* note 37.

which terms are to be given their normal, natural and unstrained meaning in the context in which they occur (Villiger 2009, p. 436). Nevertheless, it is also a case in which the Court referred expressly to the *travaux* as supplementary means needed in interpretation, despite declaring the use of this means only in so far as the Court considered it absolutely necessary in the course of its judgment. The question before the Court in this case was related to the interpretation of the meaning of Article 2 of the Convention on the Exchange of Greek and Turkish populations signed at Lausanne on 30 January 1923, according to which 'established' persons would be exempted from the exchange of populations between Turkey and Greece. In particular, the Court was asked to elucidate what conditions the persons described in Article 2, under the name of 'inhabitants of Constantinople', must fulfil so as to be considered 'established' under the terms of the Convention and, hence exempted from compulsory exchange.

The Court declares in this case that it will rely on the 'ordinary meaning' of the term 'established', not 'in the abstract' but only to determine the meaning and the scope of that word as used in Article 2 of the Convention of Lausanne.[136] So the term *established* within this article prohibits the exchange of 'a) The Greek inhabitants of Constantinople: b) The Muslim inhabitants of Western Thrace ... who were already *established* before the 30th of October, 1918 within the areas under the Prefecture of the City of Constantinople, as defined by the law of 1918',[137] who would thus be able to remain in Turkey. However, the Court proceeds to clarify first the meaning and scope of the word *établissement* according to its etymology as the text was written in French.[138] It finds that the term *é tablissement* corresponds to the verb *etablir*, which in the current practice of the French language means 'residence and stability, i.e., an intention to continue the residence in a particular place for an extended period'.[139] Further, according to the Court, the term 'established' describes 'a portion of Greek inhabitants of Constantinople', respectively those inhabitants who on 30 October 1918 were already

[136]*Id*, p. 17.

Article 1 of the Convention, reflecting the principles of emigration in questions provides:

> As from May 1st, 1923, there shall take place a compulsory exchange of Turkish nationals of the Greek Orthodox religion established in Turkish territory, and of Greek nationals of the Moslem religion established in Greek territory ...

The word 'established' appears in this provision, and it is related to the scope and meaning of the word used in

Article 2, which provides:

> The following persons shall not be included in the exchange provided for in Article 1: a) The Greek inhabitants of Constantinople. b) The Moslem inhabitants of Western Thrace. All Greeks who already established before the 30th October, 1918, within the areas under the Prefecture of the City of *Constantinople, as defined by the law of 1912, shall be considered as Greek inhabitants of Constantinople.*

[137]*Id.*

[138]*Id*, p. 18.

[139]*Id.*

*residing* at Constantinople with the intention of remaining there for an extended period of time.[140] Thus, the Court admits, relying on the textualist method ('ordinary meaning of the terms in their context' rule) that the necessary condition to constitute 'establishment' is that the residence of the inhabitants of Constantinople must be of a 'lasting nature and must have been so at the time in question'.[141] So their residence 'must be regarded as established'.[142]

To better elucidate the meaning of the term 'established', the Court relies further on the 'context rule', used both at the level of the provision at issue and the Convention as a whole. So the 'context' is revealed when the Court states that the word 'established', taken in conjunction with the reference *to date* and *place* indicated in Article 1 of the Convention,[143] clearly distinguishes 'parts both of the Greek population of Constantinople and of the Moslem population of Western Thrace'.[144] And also, the Court considers it justifiable to further ascertain the meaning of the word 'established' in the context of the Convention as a whole, for example, by connecting Article 2 to Article 3 of the Convention, which contains the definition of an 'immigrant', as well as to Article 10, which expressly refers to persons 'who have left the territory of the High Contracting Parties ...'.[145] In this way, the Court makes a comparison and thus a distinction between what means an 'immigrant' and an 'established' person.

Based in addition on the subjective method, the Court assumes that the intention of the authors of the Convention of Lausanne was hardly likely to refer to the term 'established' by means of a reference to national legislation, as Turkey claimed.[146] To reinforce this result, the Court suggests, in addition, reading Article 2 in the light of the object and purpose of the Convention. It finds on this approach (teleological) that such a reference to Turkish and Greek legislation, as Turkey claimed in respect of the mentioned provision, would have negative consequences for the population of Constantinople, which would be 'divided and carried out' in a different manner in Turkey, as well in Greece, a fact that 'would not be in accordance with the *spirit* of the Convention'.[147] Thus, the Court clearly reasons in consideration of the object and purpose of the Convention when it admits that this Convention's spirit is 'the intention of which is undoubtedly to ensure, by means of the application of identical and reciprocal measures in the territory of the two States, that the same treatment is accorded to the Greek and Turkish populations'.[148]

---

[140] *Id*, p. 19.

[141] *Id*, p. 23.

[142] *Id*.

[143] *Id*. See for Article 1 of the Convention on the Exchange of Greek and Turkish, *supra* note 136.

[144] *Id*, p. 20.

[145] *Id*, p. 25.

[146] *Id*. Turkey Government based its arguments on sovereign rights, that municipal courts should decide, respectively, 'whether a person is established or not within the meaning of Article 2'.

[147] *Id* (emphasis added).

[148] *Id*, p. 21.

Further, to confirm the intention of the drafters, the Court makes an express use of the preparatory work of the Convention of Lausanne of 30 January 1923. It heavily relies on the *travaux* during the judgment,[149] despite declaring that '[t]he Court is however of the opinion that there is no need to refer to *preparatoire* of the Convention'[150] but that it 'will only refer to it in so far as they consider it absolutely necessary to do so in the course of the following juridical examination of the question'.[151] Accordingly, the Court finds that the discussion that took place before the Treaty's adoption, notably in the Mixed Commission and the League of Nations' Council, 'played a very important part' in drafting the Convention.[152] Thus, by relying on the evidence supported by the *travaux preparatoire*, the Court establishes that the original intention of the drafters of the Convention in respect of Article 2 at issue may very well contemplate 'a mere situation of fact, sufficiently defined by the Convention itself without any reference to national legislation'.[153] Arguably, by insisting on the *travaux preparatoires* in this case, the Court wishes to confirm its result arrived at, based on the interpretation of the 'text', and to clarify to the parties in the dispute that the provision in question of the Convention of Lausanne constitutes the authentic expression of the drafters' intention. And as an international written agreement, this Convention is legally binding upon the signatory states parties; thus, its scope and object cannot be undermined.[154] To better support this position, and thus the general principle of international law on which it relies, the Court invokes the *Wimbledon* case. Specifically, the Court reiterates in the case at hand that since states have the right of entering into international engagements based on the state sovereignty principle, it could be implied that '*the obligations* of the contracting States are *absolutely equal and reciprocal*'.[155] The Court concludes in consequence that it is impossible to admit that 'a convention which create obligations of this kind, construed according to its natural meaning, infringes the sovereign rights of the High Contracting Parties'.[156] Therefore, the Court interprets Article 2 in accordance with the spirit of the Convention,

[149] *Id*, p. 16.

[150] *Id*, p. 17.

[151] *Id.*

[152] *Id.*

[153] *Id*, p. 19. Later, the Court again refers to the preparatory work of the Convention in clarifying the criterion (date and place) after which inhabitants of Constantinople would be considered 'established'. It states that to consider the date of 18 October 1912 to Greek inhabitants of Constantinople who establish themselves there between that and 30 October 1918 (which was a subject of long discussion at the Lausanne), would deprive Article 2 of a great part of value.

[154] The Turkish Government claimed that the term 'established' must be interpreted as understood in its national law, for an international agreement could not infringe the sovereign rights of the High Contracting Parties, nor could it permit the abrogation of a municipal law in a specific provision to the contrary.

[155] *Exchange of Greek and Turkish Population* (1925), p. 21 (emphasis added).

[156] *Id.*

giving protection to Greek *inhabitants of Constantinople* as 'established' persons to be exempted from compulsory exchange, and not reading in the provision something that it was not there. Clearly, by this approach, the Court gives in this case full effect and value to all the terms of the Convention of Lausanne.

In sum, although it could be well perceived how the Court reiterates in the present case the primacy of the textualist interpretation, as, for example, when concluding that '[e]verything therefore seems to indicate that in regard to this point, the Convention is self-contained and that the Mixed Commission in order to decide what constitutes an established inhabitant must rely on the natural meaning of the words',[157] the Court engages altogether the textualist, subjective and teleological methods. It heavily relies on the preparatory work that is supported by all these methods of interpretation (to confirm and/or to determine), which are reflected in what will later become Articles 31(1), (2), and 32 of the VCLT.

#### 4.3.1.6 Explicit Reliance on the 'Travaux Preparatoire' and 'Any Instrument Related to the Treaty' Rules

The ILC stresses that the specified categories of documents (preparatory work) should not be regarded as mere evidence to which recourse may be had for the purpose of resolving an *ambiguity* or *obscurity, but as part of a context* in the scope of arriving at the 'natural' and 'ordinary' meaning of the terms of a treaty.[158] It appears as a clear suggestion of the ILC for a *holistic* approach to interpretation that an interpreter should adopt when interpreting a treaty provision. The case-law analyses in this chapter can show in this regard that the ICJ tends to rely in a given case on more rules of interpretation than it expressly declares. The Court does so not only when it deals with *insufficiently clear, ambiguous, doubtful, vague* or *silent* text but also when the text is declared by the Court to be *clear* or *sufficiently clear*, and this perhaps in order to show that all the rules or methods allow for that interpretative outcome realised initially on the 'natural and ordinary meaning of the terms in the context of their use', an approach I presented above as 'overbuilding'. Such a holistic approach, which is adopted by the ICJ as a path in its interpretative practice, dispels, actually, the belief that interpretation is an issue only when the text is 'ambiguous, insufficiently clear, dubious, obscure or silent', a rule regarded in the scholarship as *in claris non fit interpretatio* (when a rule is clearly intelligible, there is no need of proposing a (usually extensive) interpretation).[159]

Although many authors declare in respect of the authority of a legal text that there is no need for interpretation when that legal text is *clear*, it constitutes in reality, as described by Ciobanu, a *contradictio in subiecto* since for establishing

[157] *Id*, p. 19.

[158] Waldock (1964), p. 48 (emphasis added).

[159] Often is cited Vattel (unjustly) in the scholarship in regard to this rule.

whether a legal norm is clear, that norm must necessarily be subjected to interpretation (Ciobanu 1991, p. 91). And this is so because the scope of interpretation is always the identification of the parties' will (intention), which, however, could have been expressed in a treaty text more or less clear or correct.[160] The form in which the will of the parties is materialised (expressed in writing in the published norm) is thought to be, actually, a matter of legal technique, in general, and also of legislative technique, in particular.[161] So in other words, as it was pointed out in Chap. 2 of this book, a legal text/norm, because it 'is indeterminate in virtue of any indeterminacy in the rules of the language', should be necessarily interpreted in order to become effective (Endicott 2000, p. 161). The ***Ambatielos Case* (1952)**[162] is chosen here to illustrate these points. This case is considered in the scholarship to be a situation of apparent judicial indecision, where the ICJ inexplicably resorted to the *travaux preparatoire*,[163] after it declared the text of the Declaration annexed to the 1926 Treaty as being *clear* and that there was no reason to resort to the preparatory work. In the stage of the Preliminary Objections, the case concerned the claim made by Greece on behalf of one of its nationals, the shipowner Ambatielos, who incurred substantial loss in consequence of a commercial contract concluded in 1919 with the United Kingdom government to buy steamships. Greece asked the Court to declare that the claim against the United Kingdom must, in accordance with the terms of the Treaties concluded in 1886 and 1926 between Greece and the United Kingdom, should be submitted to arbitration.[164] Since the United Kingdom contested that the Declaration of 16 July 1926 was not part of the Treaty of Commerce between the United Kingdom and Greece on which Greece based its request (Article 29),[165] the main question for the Court was to determine whether the 1926 Declaration, signed at the same time as the Treaty of 1926, formed part of this Treaty.[166]

Based on a textual reading (ordinary meaning of the terms in their context) of Article 29 of the Treaty of 1926,[167] the Court establishes first that any dispute as to

[160]Ciobanu (1991), p. 91.

[161]*Id.*

[162]*Ambatielos* (1952), *supra* note 38.

[163]Ris (1991), p. 129.

[164]*Ambatielos* (1952) On the other hand, the Government of the United Kingdom contended that the Court lacked jurisdiction to decide on that question.

[165]*Id*, p. 20.

[166]*Id*, p. 24. The United Kingdom contested that the provisions of that Declaration were not provisions of that Treaty within the meaning of Article 29. And both parties agreed on the question that 'the Declaration was signed separately from the Treaty proper, thought by the same signature and on the same day'.

[167]Article 29 of the Treaty of Commerce between the United Kingdom and Greece provides:

> The two Contracting Parties agree in principle that any dispute that may arise between them as to the proper interpretation or application of any of the provisions of the present Treaty shall, at the request of either Party, be referred to arbitration.

the interpretation or application of any of the provisions of the Treaty of 1926 is referable by either party to the present Court. The Court specifies that '[t]he court of arbitration to which disputes shall be referred shall be the Permanent Court of International Justice at the Hague, unless in any particular case the two contracting Parties agree otherwise'.[168] In proceeding further to determine the intention of the drafters, the Court relies on the subjective ('intentions') method of interpretation. It implies a resort to any instrument related to the conclusion of the treaty (a rule that will later form part of Article 31, paragraph (2), (b), of the VCLT) and also to supplementary means of interpretation (as set forth in the later formulation of Article 32 of the VCLT), such as the *travaux preparatoire* of the Treaty of 1926. The Court finds, as instruments related to the Treaty of 1926, that after the exchange of ratification, the Government of the United Kingdom issued 'Treaty Series No. 2 (1927), a single document entitled Treaty of Commerce and Navigation between the United Kingdom and Greece and accompanying Declaration, and presented it to the Parliament'.[169] In addition, the Court infers from cogent evidence that Greece treated the Declaration as part of the Treaty of 1926.[170] Also, the Court finds that it is the instrument of ratification exchanged between the United Kingdom and Greece, which clarifies that 'this instrument made no distinction between Treaty on one hand, and the Customs Schedule – which is indisputable a part of the Treaty, and the Declaration annexed to the Treaty, on the other'.[171]

Since the United Kingdom refers to the negotiations history of the Declaration and supports its argument by stating that, according to this Declaration, Greece could rely claims against the United Kingdom on the Treaty of 1886, only if it had formulated them before it signed the 1926 Declaration,[172] the Court feels it necessary to confirm the result it reached by consulting the *travaux preparatoire*. Reviewing the (*travaux*) records and negotiations of the Declaration, the Court finds that the parties had deleted the term 'anterior' from a Greek draft, which originally provided for 'anterior claims eventually deriving from the Anglo-Greek

---

The court of arbitration to which disputes shall be referred shall be the Permanent Court of International Justice at The Hague, unless in any particular case the two Contracting Parties agree otherwise.

[168] *Ambatielos* (1952), pp. 18–19.

[169] *Id*, p. 42.

[170] *Id.*

[171] *Id.*

[172] *Id.* The United Kingdom claimed that 'before Declaration being signed and that Greek Government did not formulate any legal claim in respect of M. Ambatielos until 1933, not indeed any legal claim under the Treaty of 1886 until 1939'.

Commercial Treaty of 1886'.[173] But this draft was not accepted, and both parties adopted the text of the Declaration as it appears now, omitting the word 'anterior'.[174] Thus, the Court does not support the view of the United Kingdom and concludes that there is not any reference in the Declaration as to the 'date' of formulation of the claims.[175]

However, the Court returns on the textual interpretation of the Declaration after reviewing the *travaux preparatoire*, stating that '[i]n any case where as here, the text to be interpreted is clear, there is no occasion to resort to preparatory work'.[176] Arguably, it could be said that irrespective of its resort to the *travaux preparatoire*, the Court seems to be fully aware of the clarity of the Declaration text, but feels to use anyway all the extraneous sources it considered necessary to prove this clarity, and to ensure the soundness of its first conclusion.[177] The Court supports its initial interpretation by applying in addition the effectiveness principle and finds accordingly that '[i]f the United Kingdom Government's interpretations were accepted, claims based on the Treaty of 1886, but brought after the conclusion of the Treaty of 1926, would be left without solution'.[178] The Court adds, reasoning in addition in consideration of the object and purpose of the Declaration, that if the Court would accept it, the result obtained would be 'contrary to the language of the Declaration and to the continuous will of both Parties to submit all differences to arbitration of one kind of another'.[179]

In sum, by emphasising the textualist interpretation like in other cases discussed above, the Court wishes in *Ambatielos* to convey that the terms of a treaty (in this case declaration), in so far as they are the expression of the free will of the states, are intended to have fullest value and effect, consistent with the other parts (elements) of the treaty. Thus, the Declaration binds all signatory parties by virtue of the *pacta sunt servanda* principle. Despite the (apparent) judicial indecision in respect of resort to the 'supplementary means' (on which the Court actually relies), the ICJ does not deviate in *Ambatielos* from the interpretative pattern it used in its past adjudicative practice. It therefore applies a *holistic* interpretation in accordance with the customary rules and principles of treaty interpretation, which later will find codification in Article 31 paragraph (1), (2) (b), and Article 32 of the VCLT.

[173] *Id.*

[174] *Id.*

[175] *Id.*

[176] *Id*, p. 45.

[177] *Id*, p. 24.

[178] *Id*, p. 42. The phrase used in the Declaration is 'claims based on the provisions of the Anglo-Greek Commercial Treaty of 1886'.

[179] *Id.*

#### 4.3.1.7 Reliance Not Only on Rules but Also on Principles: An Emphasis on the 'Object and Purpose' Rule; 'Good Faith' and 'Ut Res Magis Valeat Quam Pereat' Principles

According to the teleological school of interpretation, an interpreter sees the text construed in the light of the known or presumed 'objects' of the treaty as they are declared within it, or to be inferred from other means of interpretation such as the circumstances of the treaty's making, or from its subsequent history and proceedings (Fitzmaurice 1951, p. 1). However, in the act of interpretation, irrespective of the emphasis on a rule/method or another, the Court appears, generally, motivated by a normative judgment that implies taking into consideration general principles of international law, such as *effectiveness* and *good faith*. The *principle of effectiveness*, which has been seen employed by the PCIJ/ICJ in treaty interpretation cases, is thought to be applicable only when the intention of the parties is *ambiguous* or *doubtful*.[180] However, according to G. G. Fitzmaurice, this principle's position within the doctrine of treaty interpretation remains unclear, especially as to whether it enjoys priority over other principles of interpretation (Fitzmaurice 1951, p. 9). It is noteworthy that the principle of effectiveness stands at the foundation of the rule of interpretation codified in Article 31(1) of the VCLT, according to which *an interpreter must give full meaning and effect to all the terms of the treaty*. In essence, as explained by Fitzmaurice and Merkouris, the principle of effectiveness—*ut res magis valeat quam pereat*—supposes that treaties must be 'interpreted with reference to their declared or apparent object and purpose, and particular provisions are to be interpreted as to give fullest effect consistent with the normal sense of the words and with other parts of the text, in such a way that a reason and meaning are to be attributed to every part of the text (Fitzmaurice and Merkouris 2010, p. 155). Also, there is the *good faith principle* of international law by virtue of which the PCIJ/ICJ has used to interpret treaties. As widely admitted in the scholarship, under the good faith principle, parties are not allowed to evade their obligations stipulated in the treaty they signed, so this principle prohibits the abuse of the rights therein (Villiger 2011, p. 110). Therefore, *good faith* requires the parties to a treaty to act honestly, fairly and reasonably and to refrain from taking advantages.[181]

The following example, the ***Acquisition of Polish Nationality* (1923)**[182] case, shows that, despite the Court (PCIJ) considering the text of the treaty *clear enough* and emphasising on the text, it, nevertheless, gave a great deal to the 'object and purpose', principles of effectiveness and good faith, supporting the approach by resort to 'supplementary means' of interpretation. The issue of interpretation in the *Acquisition of Polish Nationality* case concerns Article 4(1) of the Treaty of 28 June

[180] See the effectiveness principle applied in, e.g., *Condition of Admission Case* (1948), p. 73, discussed above, as also other cases analysed in this chapter.

[181] Villiger (2011), p. 110.

[182] *Acquisition of Polish Nationality* (1923), *supra* note 39.

1919 between the Principal Allied and Associated Powers and Poland (hereafter the Peace Treaty). The question before the ICJ was whether this article granted *ipso facto* Polish nationality to German nationals and, therefore, whether the Polish Government's refusal to grant automatically Polish citizenship to such nationals, and the double request of it imposed for German children born in Polish territory, contravened the Treaty in question.

The Court proceeds with treaty interpretation in this case by admitting the clause within Article 4(1) of the Polish Treaty of Minorities as leaving 'little to be desired in the nature of clearness', so the Treaty must be accepted as it stands for the purpose of applying it.[183] The Court approaches first the 'plain' or 'ordinary' meaning of the terms of the provision in their context. Relying on this rule, the Court considers that the Treaty clearly takes the date of birth of those persons as a basis, finding 'an intentional synchronism between their *birth and habitual residence* of their parents'.[184] To determine that the words of Article 4(1) admit and declare clearly that it refers to 'residence of the parents at the time of the birth of the child and at this time only',[185] the Court finds it sufficiently conclusive in the 'context' of the provision that at 'the date of birth, the parents should have been habitually resident, that is to say should have been established in a permanent manner, with the intention of remaining'.[186]

The Court relies on the subjective (intentionalist) method when assuming that Poland acted in *good faith* at the time of concluding the Polish Treaty of Minorities and the Treaty of Peace on the same day, both being connected.[187] In addition, by admitting that the parties concluded the Peace Treaty in *good faith*, and relying on the effectiveness principle, the Court holds that by imposing an additional condition for the acquisition of Polish nationality (for the persons of German origin to be born in the territories ceded to Poland of parents habitually residing there, both on the day of the coming into force of the Treaty of 10 January 1920 and on the day of the birth of the individual),[188] thus not provided in the Peace Treaty, it would mean not to interpret the Treaty but to reconstruct it, which in the view of the Court is not permissible.[189]

The view put further by the Court admits a teleological perspective in regard to the meaning of Article 4(1), in the light of the 'object and purpose' of both the

---

[183]*Id*. Article 4 of the Polish Treaty of Minorities provides:

> Poland admits and declares to be Polish nationals ipso facto and without requirement of any formality persons of German, Austrian, Hungarian, or Russian nationality who were born in the said territory of parents habitually resident there even if at the date of the coming into force of the present treaty they are not themselves habitually resident there.

[184]*Id*, p. 18.

[185]*Id*, pp. 12–13.

[186]*Id*, p. 21.

[187]*Id*, p. 14.

[188]*Id*, p. 18.

[189]*Id*.

Minorities Treaty and the Treaty of Peace, which Poland signed in the same day. For example, the Court goes to the Preamble of the Minorities Treaty, where Poland declares that it desires 'to conform her institutions to the principles of liberty and justice, and to give a sure guarantee to the *inhabitants* of the territory over which she has assumed sovereignty'.[190] The Court concludes on this basis that the term 'minority' includes inhabitants who differ from the population of territory incorporated in Poland, notably inhabitants of non-Polish origin.[191] It confirms this result by relying additionally on the 'context' rule and finds, pursuant to Article 2 of the Minorities Treaty, that these minorities enjoy the protection of life and liberty as *inhabitants*, 'without distinction of birth, nationality, language, race or religion'.[192] So in a further attempt to establish the original intention of the drafters of the Polish Treaty of Minorities, the Court interprets Article 4 in the context of the Treaties at issue, relating this provision to other relevant provisions within the Treaties.[193] Essentially, the Court finds that the drafters' general intention of these Peace and Minorities Treaties, which were interrelated, was to ensure the protection of the minorities by 'preventing these States from refusing their nationality, on racial, religious or linguistic grounds, to certain categories of persons in spite of the link which effectively attached them to the territory allocated to one or other of these Sates'.[194] It could be assumed that the ICJ wishes to convey in this case the importance of the protection of minorities because of World War I, when states had their territories considerably enlarged and their populations did not have a clear defined political status.[195]

To shed more light on the intention of the drafters in respect of the scope of Article 4(1), the Court implies reliance on the particular historical circumstances that surrounded the Minorities Treaties and Polish Treaty's conclusion (as supplementary means of interpretation: 'any instrument related to the treaty'). The Court refers in this sense to 'any Treaty of annexation hitherto concluded'[196] and to the intention of the Principal Allied and Associated Powers: 'to create a sure guarantee in favour of these persons'.[197] Thus, the approach of the Court suggests the importance it attributes to the matter of protecting the (human) rights of the minorities at a time when, after World War I, there was no room for the recognition of the rights of minorities in either instrument. It also suggests the importance of the

[190] *Id*, pp. 14–15.

[191] *Id*, p. 15.

[192] *Id*.

[193] *Id*, p. 18. See, i.e., the discussion of the Court in respect of Article 12 of the Minorities Treaties relating to the League of Nations' competence to protect minorities.

[194] *Id*.

[195] *Id*. The Court interpreted the protection of the minorities Treaty as extended to persons who were not of Polish nationality for the reason that 'it here were not the case, the value and sphere of application of the Treaty would be greatly diminished'.

[196] *Id*, p. 20.

[197] *Id*, p. 17.

*League of Nations* as guarantor of the principles laid down in the Peace Treaties and Minorities Treaty.[198] According to the scholarship, the PCIJ dealt with human rights dimension in several cases (as in this), making a memorable contribution to the problem of minority rights.[199]

In sum, despite an emphasis on the text, the Court attaches in the *Acquisition of Polish Nationality* case a great deal to the object and purpose of the treaties at issue, supported by other rules (context of the treaty, supplementary means) and principles of interpretation (in particular, the effectiveness and good faith principles), which later will find embodiment in Articles 31(1), (2), and 32 of the VCLT.

#### 4.3.1.8 Emphasis on the 'Context' Rule

As it can be shown by the case analyses presented in this chapter, in the process of 'overbuilding' of interpretation, the Court tends to emphasise sometimes more, sometimes less one rule or another, depending on the circumstances of the case. According to Linderfalk, an interpreter must reason in consideration of the grammatical construction of the phrase, guided by the morphological and syntactic rules taken not in isolation but as lexicon that must be assumed (Linderfalk 2007, p. 110). It implies that the ordinary and natural meaning of particular words in a treaty provision is given by the grammatical structure of that provision. Therefore, the words in a provision obtain their meaning from the *context* in which they are used and only if the words therein are reading as a whole and not in isolation by recourse to its usual or common meaning. The role and importance of the *context* in conferring the proper meaning to the terms of treaty provisions under interpretation could be clearly inferred from the following ILC's comment in its Third Report on the law of treaties:

> In most instances interpretation involves giving a meaning to a text – not just any meaning which appeals to the interpreter, to be sure, but a meaning which, in the light of the text under consideration and of all the concomitant circumstances of the particular case at hand,

---

[198] See a similar line of argument relating to the protection of the human rights of minorities, in, e.g., *Settlers of German Origin in Poland, Advisory Opinion*, 1923 P.C.I.J. (ser. B) No. 6 (Sept. 10), p. 25. The Court held in this case: 'The effect of the enforcement of the law of July 14th, 1920, would be to eradicate what had previously been done, so far as de-"Germanisation" would result from requiring the settlers in question to abandon their homes. But, although such a measure may be comprehensible, it is precisely what the Minorities Treaty was intended to prevent. The intention of this Treaty was no doubt to eliminate a dangerous source of oppression, recrimination and dispute, to prevent racial and religious hatreds from having free play and to protect the situations established upon its conclusion, by placing existing minorities under the impartial protection of the League of Nations.'

[199] Ghandhi (2011), p. 528. See earlier cases involving a human rights dimension, e.g., *Rights of Minorities in Upper Silesia (Minority Schools)* (1928), PCIJ, Series A 15; *Treatment of Polish Nationals and Other Persons of Polish Origin or Speech in the Danzing Territory* (1932) PCIJ, Series A/B 44; *Minority Schools in Albania* (1935) PCIJ, Series A/B 64.

> appears in his considered judgment to be one which is logical, reasonable, and most likely to accord with and to effectuate the larger general purpose which the parties desired the treaty to serve.[200]

The next case, ***IMCO* (1960)**,[201] illustrates a strong reliance and emphasis of the Court on the *context* rule in dealing with an *insufficient clear* text of a treaty. The question before the Court in the *IMCO* case was whether the Maritime Safety Committee of the Inter-Governmental Maritime Consultative Organization (IMCO), elected on 15 January 1959, had been constituted in accordance with the Convention for the Establishment of the Organization.[202] The Court is called to interpret Article 28(a) of the Convention for the Establishment of the Inter-Governmental Maritime Consultative Organization and to appreciate whether in not electing Liberia and Panama to the IMCO, among the 'eight largest ship owning nations', the Assembly complied with that provision.[203] Liberia and Panama were among the first 'eight countries listed on the registered tonnage table' but failed on election.

It can be observed that unlike in other past cases, where the Court commenced its interpretation with emphasis on the 'ordinary meaning' rule, in the present case it begins by suggesting an approach in accord with the 'ordinary meaning of the *terms in their context*',[204] clearly stressing the 'context' in which the terms are going to be interpreted. According to the textualist/contextualist suggested interpretation, the Court finds that the word 'elected' in Article 28(a) applies to all Members of the Committee and refers to a 'notion of choice which was said to imply an individual judgment on each member to be elected and a free appraisal as to the qualifications of that member'.[205] Further, from the 'ordinary meaning of the terms in their context', the Court implies that the term 'elected' applies to 'both the election of the eight largest ship-owning nations and that of the remainder of six'.[206]

Since the Court observes that it is not clear from the words of Article 28(a) if the 'eight largest ship-owning nations' should necessarily qualify to have 'an important interest in maritime safety', it focuses on the relationship between these two propositions.[207] Relying on the 'context' rule, the Court concludes that any nation

---

[200]See Third Report on the law of treaties, ILC (1964), p. 53.

[201]*Constitution of the Maritime Safety Committee of the Inter-governmental Maritime, Consultative Organization, (IMCO), supra* note 40.

[202]*Id*, pp. 5–7.

[203]*Id*, p. 8. The provision of Article 28(a) provides that the 14 members of the Committee shall be elected by the Assembly from the members, governments of those nations having an important interest in maritime safety, of which not less than eight shall be the largest ship-owning nations.

[204]*Id* (emphasis added).

[205]*Id*.

[206]*Id*.

[207]*Id*, p. 13.

that is one of the 'largest ship-owning nations' is therefore qualified as possessing 'an important interest in maritime safety'.[208] The Court makes the distinction between 'the eight largest ship-owning nations', in referring to 'the largest gross registered tonnage', and the other nations with an important interest in maritime safety, such as those interested in the supply of large number of crews, etc., which make a contribution to the field of maritime safety. Articulating further the role of the 'context' in interpreting the terms of the provision at issue, the Court explains that 'the meaning of the word 'elected' in the Article cannot be determined in isolation by recourse to its usual or common meaning and attaching that meaning to the word where used in the Article'.[209] In other words, the Court explains that the meaning of the word 'elected' is given by the *context* in which it is used and assumes that 'if the word connotes a wide choice, it must be construed accordingly, just as it must be given a restrictive meaning if the context in which it is used so requires'.[210] Moreover, the Court highlights the 'context' also using a similar deductive reasoning for the words 'shall be' in relation to the election of the 'eight largest ship-owning nations to the Committee', which 'on their face, are mandatory'.[211] Thus, by relying on the 'context' rule, reinforced by the principle of effectiveness, the Court demonstrates that if the words 'of which no less than eight shall be the largest ship-owning nations' within Article 28(a) would involve a mandatory designation, there would certainly be an evident contrast between such a designation and 'a free choice'.[212]

It is only later that the Court specifically explains the connotation of an 'ordinary meaning' reading, stating that the terms of Article 28(a) 'must be read in their natural and ordinary meaning, in the sense which *they would normally have in their context*'.[213] In addition, the Court interprets the provision at issue in relation to other articles in the 'context' of the whole Convention, such as Article 60, which throws some light on the condition of 'tonnage', required for 'the eight largest ship-owning nations'.[214] The 'context' is further emphasised when the Court states that it would permit the Assembly to choose 'the eight largest ship-owning nations', not on an 'uncontrolled by any objective test of any kind' but only on the criteria provided within the meaning given by the context of these words. However, the Court extends and supports this approach by looking at a number of international treaties dealing with safety and working conditions on sea that could be of rele-

[208] *Id.*

[209] *Id.*

[210] *Id.*

[211] *Id.*

[212] *Id.*

[213] *Id* (emphasis added).

[214] *Id*, p. 21.

vance in better ascertaining the meaning of the terms in question,[215] a type of approach seen embodied in what later became Article 31 (3)(c) of the VCLT. Moreover, the Court resorts to the rule of interpretation which provides for interpreting texts authenticated in two or more languages, concluding, for example in respect of the words 'to own' and 'to posses' in Article 28 (a), that both English and French versions are equally authentic.[216] This approach will find later codification in Article 33 of the VCLT.

Somehow with caution, the Court suggests further recourse to other methods of interpretation, admitting that '[i]t is only if, when this is done, the words of the Article are ambiguous in any way that resort need be had to other methods of construction'.[217] Thus, based on the 'subjective' method, which implies and supports resort to 'supplementary means' of interpretation, the Court confirms the expression 'no less than eight shall be the largest ship-owning nations' as having a mandatory sense, which 'precisely carry out the intention of the framers of the Convention'.[218] The Court bases on the drafters' debate (various preparatory drafts documents)[219] of the Convention of the same United Maritime Consultative Council of the United Nations that confirms the principle on which Article 28(a) of the Convention relies.[220] Additionally, the Court puts the above expression into a teleological perspective and relates it to 'the general purpose of the Convention and the special functions of the Maritime Safety Committee',[221] relying therefore on the 'object and purpose' rule.

It could be concluded that the manner of approaching the methods, rules and principles of interpretation as a single logical combined operation reveals the Court's intention in the *IMCO* case to give each of these interpretative tools the weight and value required by the circumstances, counterbalancing them, regardless of its prevalent emphasis on the 'context' rule. The Court, actually, performs in this case a *holistic* approach, in accordance with the customary rules of interpretation later to be adopted in Articles 31(1), (2), (3)(c); 32; and 33 of the VCLT.

The following part now moves to an analysis of treaty interpretation post-VCLT in order to explore further the *patterns* of interpretation in the ICJ's approach.

---

[215] *Id.* This approach could be reflected in the later formulation of Article 31(3)(c) VCLT. According to the scholarship, there is an extensive jurisprudence predating the VCLT that makes reference to 'the relevant rules of international law' as interpretative means. See discussing this aspect, e.g., Merkouris (2010a).

[216] *Id*, p. 21.

[217] *Id.*

[218] *Id.*

[219] *Id*, p. 21.

[220] Namely, that whichever were the largest ship-owing nations that each possessed an important interest in maritime safety was accepted as axiomatic.

[221] *Id*, p. 24.

## 4.4 Post-VCLT Treaty Interpretation at the ICJ: Case Analysis and Scholarship

The case analyses provided in the previous part (Sect. 4.3) of this chapter can evidence that the ICJ's practice has been consistent with its predecessor, the PCIJ, revealing an already existing pattern in the process of application of the methods and rules of treaty interpretation. Thus, the purpose of the case analyses provided in this part (Sect. 4.4) is to identify the existence of consistency in the ICJ's approaches of the general (customary) rules (the Vienna rules) and methods of treaty interpretation, in the period that followed the adoption of the 1969 VCLT. The analyses also attempt to show whether this Court has articulated preference for one method, or rule of interpretation over another in the process of 'overbuilding' the case of interpretation. To this end, some of the most relevant cases of the ICJ's practice on treaty interpretation in the period that followed the VCLT's adoption will be further examined.

The case analyses are arranged in this part similarly to those in the preceding part, respectively on questions/topics which attempt to cover the means of interpretation that the ICJ usually applies, either explicitly or implicitly, in solving various treaty interpretative difficulties (e.g., on apparently clear/insufficiently clear, ambiguous/equivocal, dubious, vague or silent language of treaty text), as well as on the Court's emphasis on one means or another. Thus, in this part, the following cases will be reviewed for the manner in which the Court approached the task of treaty interpretation:

- *Kasikili/Sedudu Island (Botswana v. Namibia)* (1999)[222];
- *Case Concerning Military and Paramilitary Activities in and Against Nicaragua (Nicaragua v. United States of America)* (1986)[223];
- *The Border and Transborder Armed Actions (Nicaragua v. Honduras)* (1988)[224];
- *The Application of the Interim Accord of 13 September 1995* (*The Former Yugoslavia Republic of Macedonia v. Greece*) (2011)[225];
- *Case Concerning Oil Platforms (Islamic Republic of Iran v. United States of America*) (1996)[226];

---

[222]*Kasikili/Sedudu Island (Botswana v. Namibia)*, I.C.J. Judgment of 13 December, 1999, p. 18.

[223]*Case concerning military and paramilitary activities in and against Nicaragua (Nicaragua v. United States of America)*, Merits, I.C.J., 27 June 1986.

[224]*Border and Transborder Armed Actions (Nicaragua v. Honduras)*, Jurisdiction of the Court and admissibility of the Application, I.C.J., Judgment of 20 December, 1988.

[225]*Application of the Interim Accord of 13 September 1995 (The Former Yugoslavia Republic of Macedonia v. Greece)*, Judgment of 5 December 2011.

[226]*Case Concerning Oil Platforms (Islamic Republic of Iran v. United States of America)*, Preliminary Objection, I.C.J., 12 December 1996, I.C.J. Summary 1996/4 Order of 12 December 1996.

– *Case Concerning the Territorial Dispute (Libyan Arab Jamahirya v. Chad)* (1994).[227]

### *4.4.1 Reliance on the VCLT Rules*

The *1969 Vienna Convention on the Law of Treaties* provides for a number of factors to be resorted to in the treaty interpretation process. Although the Vienna Convention embraced the concept of the 'plain and natural' meaning of treaty provisions as the basic rule for interpretation, the ICJ has showed flexibility in administering all the VCLT rules of interpretation, however combining them in a single logical act. The problematic question in this process appears to be when the method of 'plain meaning' does not warrant a straightforward result (Orakhelashvili 2008, p. 338). In such a situation, it becomes essential to determine the conditions of resorting to extra-textual factors as are the 'object and purpose' of the treaty, 'context' of the whole treaty, 'relevant rules of general international law', 'subsequent practice', as well as principles of international law.[228] If these methods fail to provide a pertinent interpretation, the use of the 'supplementary means' of interpretation can be justified.[229] A comparison between the post-VCLT cases analysed in this part and the pre-VCLT cases analysed in the previous part of this chapter can clearly reveal a similarity in the *patterns of treaty interpretation* used by the ICJ, as also a *consistency* of the interpretative approaches adopted by this Court in those two periods. Similarly to the pre-VCLT period, the case analyses provided below show, moreover, that the ICJ's application of the customary rules of interpretation in the post-VCLT period has not been performed in a mechanical way. Thus, one can accept the idea that a mechanical application of the *codified rules* in the VCLT is refuted by the initial selectivity of rules of interpretation and principles. As a process of legal reasoning, this selectivity implies, therefore, pondering the value of each of the interpretative means in accordance with the particular circumstances of a given case.

#### 4.4.1.1 VCLT as Embodiment of Custom?

It is important to note that the *customary* status of the rules codified in the VCLT can be reflected not only in a consistent application by the ICJ of the rules of interpretation in the period that preceded the adoption of the Vienna rules but also

[227] *Case concerning the territorial dispute (Libyan Arab Jamahirya v. Chad)*, I.C.J., Judgment of 3 February 1994.

[228] Orakhelashvili (2008), p. 338.

[229] *Id.*

by those cases after the adoption of these rules, where the ICJ expressly admitted to interpret treaties that predate the VCLT and even if the states in disputes were not parties to the VCLT. In Article 4, the 1969 VCLT provides in essence that '... the Convention applies only to treaties which are concluded by States after the entry into force of the present Convention with regard to such States'.[230]

According to Linderfalk, the VCLT does not define the term 'ordinary meaning', and neither does it qualify the word 'ordinary'.[231] Also, the 'ordinary meaning' expression supports a non-specific definition, and it is determined not by everyday language but by everyday language and technical language as a single whole.[232] This point and the ones mentioned above (Sects. 4.4.1 and 4.4.1.1) could be reflected in the approach taken by the Court in the ***Kasikili/Sedudu Island* (1999)** case,[233] when it encountered the difficulty of determining *ambiguous* treaty terms. This is also a case where the Court admitted that it 'has already had the occasion in the past to hold that *customary international law* found expression in Article 31 of the Vienna Convention'.[234] The ICJ was asked in *Kasikili/Sedudu Island* by Botswana and Namibia to give its opinion based on the 1890 Treaty between the former colonial powers, Germany and the United Kingdom, on the boundary to be drawn in the River Chobe between Namibia and Botswana, now independent states, respectively to pronounce on the legal status of Kasikili and Sedudu Island. The issue of interpretation was related to Article III (para 2) of the Anglo-German Treaty of 1 July 1890, specifically to determination by the Court of the meaning of the terms 'main channel' of the River Chobe so as to establish the sphere of influence of the contracting parties in relation to it.[235]

---

[230]See *1969 Vienna Convention on the Law of the Treaties* (entered into force in Jan. 1980), United Nations, Treaty Series, vol 1155, p. 331. Article 1 of the VCLT provides that 'The present Convention applies to treaties between States'.

[231]Linderfalk (2007) (emphasis added).

[232]*Id.*

[233]*Kasikili/Sedudu Island* (1999), *supra* note 222.

[234]*Id*, p. 18 (emphasis added). See a similar ICJ holding in Sovereignty over *Pulau Ligitan* and *Pulau Sipadan (Indonesia v. Malayesia)*, (2002) ICJ Reports, pp. 23–23, para 37. This case is a also an illustratiion of the ICJ's application of the VCLT rules of interpretation even if the parties involved in litigation were not parties to the VCLT. See other such cases, e.g., *Legal Consequences of the Construction of a Wall in the Occupied Palestinian Territory*, Advisory Opinion of 9 July 2004, ICJ Reports; *Case Concerning Legality of Use of Force (Serbia and Montenegro v. United Kingdom)* (Preliminary Objections) [2004], ICJ Reports; *Oil Platforms* case discussed further in this chapter.

[235]Article III of the 1890 Treaty provides:

> In Southwest Africa the sphere in which the exercise of influence is reserved to Germany is bounded: 1) To the south by a line commencing at the mouth of Orange river, and ascending the north bank of that river to the point of its intersection by the 30th degree of east longitude; 2) To the east by a line commencing at the above-named point, and following the 20th degree of east latitude; it runs eastward along that parallel to the point of its intersection by the 22nd parallel of south latitude; it runs eastward along that parallel to the point of its intersection by the 21st degree of east longitude; thence it follows that

The Court expressly states at the beginning of interpretation in this case that to elucidate the meaning of Article III of the 1890 Treaty, it would adhere to the rules of interpretation set forth in the *1969 Vienna Convention on the Law of Treaties*. The *Kasikili/Sedudu* case is an example of a clear applicability of Article 31 of the VCLT, a reflection of the *customary* status of this provision as 'neither Botswana nor Namibia are parties to the Vienna Convention on the Law of Treaties of 23 May 1969'[236] and the treaty to be interpreted (the Anglo-German Treaty of 1 July 1890) even predates the VCLT. The difficulty for the Court consists in determining the meaning of the term 'main channel' of the River Chobe as it is not clearly identified in the provision of Article III, paragraph 2, of the 1890 Treaty.[237] Like in many cases before it, the Court emphasises in the case at hand the textualist approach by stating that '[i]nterpretation must be based above all upon the text of the treaty'.[238] Relying on a rich body of cases, where it already had the occasion 'to hold that customary international law found expression in Article 31 of the Vienna Convention', the Court makes a sound statement acknowledging the *customary* character of the rules contained in Article 31.

Since the Treaty in question is not a proper boundary treaty, but a treaty delimiting spheres of influence, the Court considers next how and to what extent the 'object and purpose' of the Treaty might shed light on the meaning of the term 'main channel'.[239] The suggested resort to the 'object and purpose' rule can be deduced, for example, from the Court's statement that it does not consider that 'navigation was the sole objective of the provisions of Article III, paragraph 2, of the Treaty'.[240] On the teleological approach, the Court finds that the contracting parties opted for the expression 'centre of the main channel', with the aim 'to secure for themselves freedom of navigation on the river and delimit as precisely as possible their respective spheres of influence'.[241] In addition, the Court looks for 'any relevant rules of international law', though it does not technically refer to Article 31(3)(c) of the VCLT, and admits that it 'will revert to the issue – in dispute between the parties'—and hence to the rules of international law, since they permit the Court 'to entertain Namibia's alternative argument founded on the doctrine of prescription'.[242] Thus, in trying to determine the meaning of the term 'main

degree northward to the point of its intersection by the 18th parallel of south latitude; it runs eastward along that parallel till it reaches the river Chobe, and descends the centre of the *main channel* of that river to its junction with the Zambezi, where it terminates (emphasis added).

[236]*Kasikili/Sedudu Island* (1999), p. 18.

[237]*Id*, pp. 19–20.

[238]*Id*.

[239]*Id*, p. 33.

[240]*Id*.

[241]*Id*.

[242]*Id*, p. 18.

channel', the Court refers to 'the most commonly used criteria in international law and practice, to which the parties have referred'.[243] Specifically, the Court looks at the international law documents/instruments indicated by the parties in the Special Agreement such as *Charter of the United Nations*, *Charter of the Organization of African Unity* (OAU), Resolution AHG/Res 16(1) adopted in Cairo on 21 July 1964 under OAU and others.

As it can be seen, despite the fact that the Court declares that the interpretation must be made above all upon the text of the treaty, it actually looks beyond it, the text being just the starting point of commencing the act of interpretation. The Court enhances furthermore the textualist approach with the subjective one by searching for the intention of the parties on the basis of any 'subsequent practice in the application of the treaty which establishes the agreement of the parties regarding its interpretation'—'a means of interpretation well-established in the jurisprudence of international tribunals' as the Court itself points out.[244] So expressly relying on the 'subsequent practice' rule reflected in Article 31, paragraph 3(b), of the VCLT,[245] the Court finds no events to constitute 'subsequent practice in the application of the treaty [of 1890] which establishes the agreement of the parties . . .'.[246]

To better clarify and confirm the intention of the drafters of the 1890 Treaty, the Court expressly relies further on the 'supplementary means' rule, although it does not refer technically to 'Article 32 of the VCLT' when employing this rule. It recalls that when an interpretation based on Article 31 leads to a meaning that is ambiguous, obscure or unreasonable, '[a]s a supplementary measure recourse may be had to means of interpretation such as the preparatory work of the treaty'.[247] On this rule basis then, the Court concludes that it 'is moreover clear from the *travaux preparatoire* of the Treaty that there was an expectation of navigation on the Chobe by both contracting parties, and a common intention to exploit this possibility'.[248] In addition, during the course of the judgment, confronting both authentic texts (in two languages), the Court decides that, in accordance with the customary rule provided by Article 33, paragraph 3, of the VCLT ('the terms of the treaty are presumed to have the same meaning in each authentic text'), the words 'centre of

---

[243] *Id*, p. 22.

[244] *Id*, p. 61.

[245] *Id*, p. 46.

[246] *Id*, p. 61.

[247] *Id*, p. 46. The Court invokes the *Libyan Arab Jamahiriya/Chad* case (1994). See a similar approach adopted by the ICJ in the recent case *Maritime Delimitation in the Indian Ocean (Somalia v. Kenya)* Preliminary Objections, Judgment of 2 February 2017. This case is an interesting illustration of the manner in which the ICJ declared expressly that it looked first to establish the intention of the Parties to the treaty in question, showing an emphasis on the *intention* element rather than on the text as the Court usually did in many other cases before it.

[248] *Id*, p. 60. In his Separate Opinion (at p. 102), Judge Oda suggests that, rather than a laborious analysis by virtue of the plain meaning rule dedicated to the word 'Thalweg', which was just simply a translation of the English term 'centre', as the Judgment itself admits, the Court could have considered the historical background, past practices and a scientific expert as sufficiently determinative of the boundary, without having any bearing on the provisions of the VCLT.

the main channel' in Article III, paragraph 2, of the 1890 Treaty, have the same meaning as the words *Thalweg des Hauptlaufes*.[249]

It can be concluded that the *Kasikili/Sedudu* case demonstrates that the ICJ strongly holds onto its traditional language of interpretation when choosing to follow the path already taken in the past, as the Court itself admits. It performs an interpretation on the basis of customary rules provided by Articles 31, 32 and 33 of the VCLT.[250]

#### 4.4.1.2 Emphasis on the 'Object and Purpose' Rule

According to Merkouris, to issue a single interpretation for each case, to consider factors and circumstances, to appreciate and weigh each of their values or insufficiency through the application of the principles of interpretation, while a scientific process, is, nevertheless and undeniably, a work of art.[251] It is widely admitted, however, that courts and tribunals often chose to interpret a provision of a treaty by reference not only to an aspect of itself such as text, context, object and purpose, but also to an extrinsic source such as other treaties or customary law (under Article 31(3)(c) VCLT), in order to shed light on unclear, ambiguous, dubious or obscure treaty provisions.[252] However, explicitly or implicitly applied, this resort to extrinsic sources strengthens the idea that the VCLT's 'general rule of interpretation' of treaties appears as vital tool in maintaining the coherence of international law. Further example of the ICJ's treaty interpretative practice, the ***Nicaragua* (1986)** case,[253] illustrates a situation where the Court proved that it handled masterfully the art of treaty interpretation. It concluded in this case that *customary international law* remains applicable to the case while performing an interpretation on the treaty in question (concluded by states before the entry into force of the VCLT) in accordance with the standard of interpretation mandated by Article 31 of the VCLT. The analysis of the ICJ's interpretative approach in this case can show flexibility in this Court's use of the rules of treaty interpretation. It conveys the idea that there is not one rule/method of interpretation superior to another and that the Court is not compelled to commence the interpretation following one specific rule/method or use specific rules/methods and exclude others just because in similar difficulties of treaty text interpretation (such as *insufficient clarity* or *ambiguity* in certain treaty provisions in this case), it used those specific rules/methods and in that order.

In the first phase of the *Nicaragua* (1984) case related to the establishment of the jurisdiction of the Court and admissibility of the application, Nicaragua instituted proceedings against the United States alleging unlawful military and paramilitary

[249] *Id*, p. 21.

[250] See a similar approach, e.g., in the *Libyan Arab Jamahirya/Chad* and *Oil Platforms* cases discussed further in this chapter.

[251] Merkouris (2010b), p. 9.

[252] See Merkouris' analysis of 'Article 31(3)(c) of the VCLT' in Merkouris (2010a), p. 41.

[253] *Case concerning military and paramilitary activities in and against Nicaragua* (Merits) (1986), *supra* note 223.

acts by the US in Nicaragua.[254] While the United States contested the jurisdiction of the Court relying on a reservation that the Court's jurisdiction would not apply to certain disputes arising under multilateral treaties (in this case the UN Charter), Nicaragua responded that its claim was based on rules of customary international law. The Court found that it had jurisdiction and concluded that the claims in Nicaragua's Application constituted a dispute as to the interpretation of several articles (Articles 19, 14, 17, 21) of the Treaty of Friendship, Commerce and Navigation (FCN) between the parties signed at Managua on 27 January 1956.[255] In the second phase of the *Nicaragua* (1986) case,[256] the judgment on the merits, the Court proceeded to analyse the United States' breach of duty not to deprive the 1956 FCN Treaty of its object and purpose.[257]

It can be observed that, in the course of the judgment, the Court's reference directly to the elements of the treaty, notably the 'object and purpose', signifies its choice to interpret the 1956 FCN Treaty teleologically, consistently with the rules provided by Article 31(1) of the VCLT.[258] A reliance on the teleological approach can be clearly illustrated, for example, when the Court proceeds to determine the nature of the actions of the United States complained of by Nicaragua as breaches of the 1956 FCN Treaty, respectively whether such actions can be regarded as "measures ... necessary to protect its essential security interests ... since Article XXI of the Treaty provides that 'the present Treaty shall not preclude the application of 'such measures'".[259] By relating to the object and purpose of the 1956 Treaty, the Court admits that '[t]he question thus arises whether Article XXI similarly affords a defence to a claim under customary international law based on allegation of conduct depriving the Treaty of its *object and purpose* if such conduct can be shown to be 'measures ... necessary to protect' essential security interests'.[260] The Court adds that 'an act cannot be said to be one calculated to deprive a treaty of its *object and purpose*, or to impede its due performance, if the possibility of that act has been foreseen in the treaty itself, and it has been expressly agreed that the treaty 'shall not preclude' the act ...'.[261]

In so far as the Court looks at the US military activities in Nicaragua, it concludes by virtue of a teleological interpretation that 'there are certain activities of the United States which are such as to undermine the whole *spirit* of bilateral

---

[254] *Case concerning military and paramilitary activities in and against Nicaragua (Nicaragua v. United States of America)*, Jurisdiction of the Court and Admissibility of the Application, I.C.J. Judgment of 26 November, 1984, p. 7. (Nicaragua claimed that a violation of the United Nations Charter is equally a violation of Articles 20 and 21 of the Organization of American States Charter).

[255] *Nicaragua* (1984), p. 37.

[256] *Nicaragua* (1986).

[257] *Id.*

[258] *Id.*

[259] *Id*, p. 126.

[260] *Id* (emphasis added).

[261] *Id* (emphasis added).

agreement directed to sponsoring friendship between the two States parties to it'.[262] Specifically, the Court refers to the Preamble of the 1956 FCN Treaty, stating that the direct attack on ports, oil, installations, etc.; the mining of Nicaraguan ports; as well any action less calculated, such as to serve the purpose of 'threatening the bonds of peace and friendship traditionally existing between the Parties, stated in Preamble of the Treaty' could hardly be imagined.[263] Therefore, the Court decides that the United States acted in breach of its obligations under Article XIX of the 1956 FCN Treaty, which provides in the first place that '[b]etween the territories of the two Parties there shall be freedom of commerce and navigation'.[264]

In addition, the Court approaches the provisions at issue in the 'context' of the treaty as a whole. It acknowledges that certain other articles of the treaty 'were ... regarded as reflecting, or as crystallising, received or at least emergent rules of customary international law'.[265] For example, the 'context' is clearly displayed by the Court when it proceeds to ascertain the scope of Article XXI, paragraphs 1 (c) and 1(d), stating that this article 'is covered by the provision in Article XXIV that any dispute about the 'interpretation or application' of the Treaty lies within the Court's jurisdiction'.[266] The Court focuses further on the terms 'measures' and 'essential interests' (to which the 1956 Treaty refers in Article XXI), in their 'context' so as to question whether the 'measures' taken by the US were 'necessary to fulfil the obligations of a Party for the maintenance or restoration of international peace and security'.[267] Thus, implying an interpretation based on the rule of 'ordinary meaning of the terms in their context', the Court establishes that 'measures' under the Treaty involves an obligation under international law that the state in question has a commitment of which 'any evasion constitutes a breach'.[268]

To better clarify that the term 'measures' encompasses a wide category of measures necessary to protect the 'essential security' of a party, the Court considers necessary to expand its approach by resort to extrinsic sources such as 'any relevant rules of international law', implying an application of Article 31(3)(c) of the VCLT. Pursuant to this approach, the Court consults international instruments such as the UN Charter (Article 26) or the Inter-American Treaty of Assistance

---

[262] *Id*, p. 128 (emphasis added).

[263] *Id*.

[264] *Id*, p. 137. Article XIX, para 1, of the 1956 FCN, provides:

> Between the territories of the two Parties there shall be freedom of commerce and navigation'... and continues at para 3): 'Vessels of either Party shall have liberty, on equal terms with vessels of other Party and on equal terms with vessels of any third country, to come with their cargoes to all ports, places and waters of such other Party open to foreign commerce and navigation...

[265] *Id*, p. 95.

[266] *Id*.

[267] *Id*, p. 106.

[268] *Id*.

(Articles 3 and 20).[269] As the Court needs further confirmation of the result reached on the above methods, it supplements that result by looking for 'any subsequent agreement between the parties regarding the "interpretation of the treaty or the application of its provision"', under Article 31(3)(a) of the VCLT, an approach consistent with the subjective method (intention).[270] Consequently, the Court finds, for example, that the embargo on trade with Nicaragua in 1985 'constitutes a measure in contradiction with Article XIX of the FCN Treaty, and in a breach of its object and purpose'.[271]

Being confronted with a case of violations of such magnitude, as well as with serious findings of fundamental human rights violations, the majority of the Court's judges in *Nicaragua* were motivated to perform a normative and moral judgment, supported by the adoption of customary rules of interpretation embodied in Article 31 of the VCLT. As Moore concisely remarked about the *Nicaragua* case, 'the dedicated judges believed they saw an opportunity to curtail some of the increasing violence sweeping the world and to uphold the rule of law'.[272] This case clearly illustrates what Somarajah expressed in this regard: 'the FCN treaties came to be used in ways quite unintended by the powerful state which secured the treaty'.[273] However, according to Boyle, the Court failed in *Nicaragua* 'to hold the United States fully responsible for the violations of the law and customs of warfare committed by the contras forces in Nicaragua',[274] deciding 'out of an excess of caution for the perfectly sound reason of better preserving its institutional integrity from unjustified attack'.[275]

In sum, despite an emphasis on the 'object and purpose' rule, which makes interpretation look mainly based on the teleological approach, the Court reasons in *Nicaragua* equally in consideration of other rules of interpretation (pursuant to Article 31 of the VCLT), applying them *holistically* and giving full effect to all the terms of the Treaty at issue. It appears obviously to be pointing out the gravity of the US's acts of violence deemed to undermine the object and purpose of the bilateral

---

[269] *Id*, pp. 106–107. The Court refers, i.e., to 'decisions of the Security Council taken as basis of Chapter VII of the UN Charter, decisions taken by the Organ of Consultation of the Inter American-System'.

[270] *Id*, p. 27.

[271] *Id*, p. 132.

[272] According to the ILC, general international law consists in *general customary law* and *general principles of law*.

[273] Sornarajah (2010), p. 181 ('FCN'—Treaties of friendship, commerce, and navigation).

[274] Boyle (1987), p. 86.

[275] *Id*. According to Boyle, the Court 'carefully premised this result on finding that it had insufficient evidence to reach a definitive conclusion on such a delicate matter' and 'apparently decided to avoid adjudicating the politically charged issue of whether United States government officials are personally responsible for any degree of complicity in the commission of international crimes by contra forces against the civilian population in Nicaragua'. The reason for doing so, as concluded by the author, was that 'the Court realized full well that its ruling in favor of Nicaragua would be subjected to an enormous amount of hostile criticism from one source that has traditionally served as its foremost proponent - The United States Government'.

agreement (between the US and Nicaragua), which thus compelled the Court to decide in favour of Nicaragua. In addition, the Court appears to make clear its position about human rights abuses, in principle that they cannot be invoked to justify the US armed intervention.[276] In this regard, as the Court itself admits, it finds in the *Nicaragua* case an opportunity to emphasise that the *basic principles of international law* must be respected, among which are, certainly, *human rights*.[277]

#### 4.4.1.3 Reliance on the 'Context of the Treaty' and 'Good Faith' Rules

As observed by Koskenniemi, Article 31(1) of the VCLT seems to take the objective position of interpretation, namely 'what counts in the text, and in the context – together with good faith – shall be decisive'.[278] Importantly, the practice of international courts and tribunals has shown that when an interpreter has to interpret a provision using 'the text' of the treaty, one of the standards on which the applier relies in the interpretative process is that 'if a state produces an utterance taking the form of a treaty provision, then the provision should be drawn up so that in the *context* there will be no instance of a logical tautology'.[279] The ***Border and Transborder Armed Actions* (1988)**[280] case illustrates this situation and how the Court resolved *ambiguity* in a treaty text by expressly adopting the customary rules of interpretation set forth in the VCLT's general rule of interpretation. It stressed the contextualist approach under 31(2) of the VCLT, which provides for a reading of the provision in the 'context of the treaty' taken as a whole, however, relying in addition on other Vienna rules of interpretation. In this case, Nicaragua asked the Court to declare that it had jurisdiction to decide the dispute and to hold Honduras responsible under international law for Honduras' activities of conducting armed bands, from Honduras on the border between Honduras and Nicaragua and in Nicaragua's territory. The issue of interpretation concerned the 1948 American Treaty on Pacific Settlement (the Pact of Bogota), Article XXXI, by which the jurisdiction of the Court is conferred as compulsory *ipso facto*, without the necessity of any special agreement, in all disputes between the parties.[281]

The Court suggests first that it would proceed with the 'ordinary meaning' rule of interpretation. It focuses on elucidating the meaning of both Articles XXXI[282]

---

[276] *Nicaragua* (1986), p. 167. Equally worthy is that the Court found the U.S. responsible under general principles of humanitarian law.

[277] Moore (1987), p. 152.

[278] Koskenniemi (2006), p. 292.

[279] Linderfalk (2007), p. 110 (emphasis added).

[280] *Border and Transborder Armed Actions* (1988), *supra* note 224.

[281] *Id*, p. 10.

[282] Article XXXI provides:

> In conformity with Article 36, paragraph 2, of the Statute of the International Court of Justice, the High Contracting Parties declare that they recognize, in relation to any other

and XXXII[283] of the Bogota Pact, whether or not they should be read as conferring jurisdiction upon the Court under the circumstances of the case.[284] Honduras contested the Court's jurisdiction to decide upon the dispute, conditioning it to be supplemented under Article XXXI of the Pact, by a declaration of acceptance made subsequently by the state party to the Pact, under Article 36 (2) of the Court's Statute.[285] As Honduras claimed, the Court could only be seized if, according to Article XXXII, there had been a prior recourse to conciliation and lack of agreement, which Honduras stated was not the case.[286] The Court finds on the 'plain' or 'ordinary' meaning basis that the term 'question' within the expression '*le droit de porter la question devant la Cour*' might be thought to refer to the 'question' provided by Article XXXI of the Bogota Pact.[287] Implying, in addition, resort to Article 33 of the VCLT (which provides for the interpretation of treaties authenticated in two or more languages), the Court finds that 'the text uses the term "question" in a way that leaves room for uncertainty, rather than the French word "*differend* (dispute)", used in Article XXXI which would have been perfectly clear'.[288]

Although the Court reaches a firm logical conclusion by proceeding first with the 'ordinary meaning' rule of interpretation of the terms of the provisions at issue, pursuant to Article 31(1) of the VCLT, it still feels the need to shed more light on and confirm it by applying the contextualist approach, thus looking at other relevant articles (e.g., Articles VII, LV) in the 'context' of the Bogota Pact, pursuant to

---

American State, the jurisdiction of the Court as compulsory *ipso facto*, without the necessity of any special agreement so long as the present Treaty is in force, in all disputes of a judicial nature that arise among them concerning:

a) The interpretation of a treaty;
b) Any question of international law;
c) The existence of any fact which, if established, would constitute the breach of an international obligation;
d) The nature or extent of the reparation to be made for the breach of an international obligation.

[283] *Border and Transborder Armed Actions* (1988). Article XXXII of the Bogota Pact provides:

When the conciliation procedure previously established in the present Treaty or any agreement of the parties does not lead to a solution, and the said parties have not agreed upon an arbitral procedure, either of them shall be entitled to have recourse to the International Court of Justice in the manner prescribed in Article 40 of the Statute thereof. The Court shall have compulsory jurisdiction in accordance with Article 36, paragraph 1, of the said Statute.

[284] *Id*, p. 25.

[285] *Id*, pp. 14–16.

[286] *Id*, p. 23.

[287] *Id*, p. 24.

[288] *Id*, p. 20. Moreover, the Spanish, English and Portuguese versions speak in general terms of an entitlement to have recourse to the Court and do not justify the conclusion that there is a link between Article XXXI and Article XXXII of the Bogota Pact.

Article 31(2) of the VCLT. As a result, the Court finds that it would have jurisdiction to settle a dispute according to the provisions of Article XXXI of the Pact in cases covered by that article, regardless of whether there had been previous recourse to conciliation in conformity with Article XXXII (the interpretation suggested by Nicaragua).[289] Based on the contextualist approach, the Court concludes that both Articles XXXI and XXXII confer jurisdiction to the Court, but in distinct ways.[290] Moreover, the Court confirms this finding by additionally looking to the 'subsequent practice' of the parties in relation to the interpretation of Article XXXI, suggesting an approach pursuant to Article 31(3)(b) of the VCLT.[291]

Having reached these conclusions, the Court moves next to strenghten them, shedding more light on intention of the parties. It finds further confirmation of the reading of Article XXXI in the *travaux preparatoire*,[292] which is a means supported by the textualist method as a confirmatory tool but also *travaux preparatoire* is supported by the subjective and teleological methods as both determinative and confirmatory tools. Relying on the *travaux*, the Court concludes that it is 'quite clear from the Pact that the *purpose of the drafters* was to reinforce their mutual commitments with regard to judicial settlement'.[293] However, by referring to the *travaux preparatoire*, the Court suggests 'caution', instructing that 'not all the stages of the drafting of the texts of the Bogota Conference were subject to detailed records'[294]; thus, the drafts of Article XXXI could not be taken as absolutely confirmatory and decisive. It might be implied that by suggesting 'caution' in administering the preparatory work, the Court could contemplate an important principle of interpretation, according to which an interpreter is not allowed to add something in the treaty that it is not there.

Furthermore, the Court's interpretation moves towards the object and purpose of the Bogota Pact (adopting the teleological method), in accordance with Article 31 (1) of the VCLT, although not technically referring to this interpretative provision. By refuting Honduras' interpretation, according to which the commitment 'set forth in Article XXXI, would in fact, be emptied of all content, if for any reason, the dispute were not subjected to prior conciliation', the Court concludes that it would be 'clearly contrary to both the object and purpose of the Pact' and that by this purpose the American states intended to 'reinforce their mutual commitments with regard to judicial settlement'.[295] In addition, the Court reasons by virtue of the 'good faith' principle, recalling it as 'one of the basic principles governing the creation and performance of legal obligations', which by itself imposes obligation

[289]*Id*, p. 23.

[290]*Id*, p. 25.

[291]*Id*, p. 22.

[292]*Id*, p. 24.

[293]*Id*.

[294]*Id*.

[295]*Id*.

to respect the treaty.[296] The Court reiterates this way, that the *normative value of peace* protected by 'international obligations' is of a higher value than that invoked by Honduras. Therefore, the Court appears to have considered that 'the use of force'[297] supersedes any other evaluative judgment in the case.

In sum, the Court shows in *Border and Transborder Armed Actions* that all the rules adopted in this case lead together to one unambiguous result, actually complementing each other. By admitting an interpretation of the provisions at issue which points towards the rules embodied in Articles 31, 32 and 33 of the VCLT, the Court performs a *holistic* interpretation, however, stressing more in this case the 'context of the treaty' and 'good faith' interpretative rules.

#### 4.4.1.4 Clear Holistic Approach and Emphasis on the 'Ut Res Magis Valeat Quam Pereat' Principle

According to Lauterpacht, no principle of effectiveness can properly be employed to give efficacy to agreements if they were not intended to produce such results.[298] In this sense, Article 31 of the VCLT prescribes an 'integration approach' under which the application of the various elements of interpretation, as set out in the article, *is a single combined operation*.[299] This conception can be well reflected, for example, in the recent case of the ***Application of the Interim Accord of 13 September 1995* (2011)**.[300] The Court in this case expressly declared its intention to perform a *holistic interpretation* of the Interim Accord on *sufficiently clear* text, in accordance with Article 31 of the VCLT's 'general rule of interpretation'. Supported by a rich body of precedents, the Court follows here the traditional patterns of interpreting treaties used in its long practice on this matter.

On 7 June 1991, the Assembly of the Socialist Republic of Macedonia enacted a constitutional amendment, changing the name 'Socialist Republic of Macedonia' to the 'Republic of Macedonia'. The main issue before the Court was whether Greece's objection to the admission of the Former Yugoslav Republic of Macedonia, on the basis of its adopted constitutional name of 'Republic of Macedonia',[301]

---

[296]*Id*, p. 40.

[297]The concept of the 'use of force' is provided by Article 52 of the 1969 VCLT, according to which a treaty is void if its conclusion has been procured by the threat or use of force in violation of the principles of international law embodied in the Charter of the United Nations. Also, Article 2 (4) of the United Nations Charter provides:

> All members shall refrain in their international relations from the threat or use of force against the territorial integrity or political independence of any state, or in any other measure inconsistent with the purposes of the United Nations.

[298]Lauterpacht (1949), p. 73.

[299]Engelen (2004), p. 175.

[300]*Application of the Interim Accord of 13 September 1995* (2011), *supra* note 225. Macedonia requests the Court to make a declaration to this effect and to order Greece to 'take all necessary steps to comply with its obligations under Article 11, paragraph 1, of the Interim Accord'.

[301]*Id*.

for membership in NATO or any other international, multilateral or regional organisation or institution of which the Respondent was a member, violated the Respondent's legal obligation under Article 11 of the Interim Accord, notably, not to object to the application by, or the membership of, Macedonia (the Applicant) in such organisations and institutions of which Greece (the Respondent) has been a member.[302] One of the main objectives underpinning this Accord was to stabilise the relations between the parties pending on the resolution of the name change. The Court proceeds to establish first on the textualist method whether it has jurisdiction in the case under Article 21(2) of the *Interim Accord*, which sets out any 'difference or dispute' as to the 'interpretation or implementation' of this Accord.[303] Greece's argument was that the final resolution over the *name difference*, as any dispute relating to this issue (the only reason upon which Greece objected to Mecedonia's admission to NATO), was within the competence of the Security Council and not of the Court.[304]

In trying to clarify the meaning of the word 'difference' within Article 21(2) and Article 5(1), the Court relies in the present case on the 'plain meaning' of the term in the context of the *Interim Accord*.[305] It finds on this rule that the term 'difference' refers to the *difference* over the *name* and not to *disputes* regarding Greece's obligations under Article 11(1) of the *Interim Accord*.[306] Applying the subjective method, and reasoning on the effectiveness principle basis in looking to determine the drafters' intention, the Court asserts that if the drafters had intended to entrust to the Court only limited jurisdiction, they could have expressly excluded the subject matter provided in Article 11 (1) of the *Interim Accord* from the grant of jurisdiction in Article 21(2) of the same *Accord*.[307]

---

[302]The Interim Accord concluded between the parties on 13 September 1995 provided for the establishment of diplomatic relations between them and addressing other related issues.

Article 11, paragraph 1, of the Interim Accord provides:

> 'Upon entry into force of this Interim Accord, the Party of the First Part agrees not to object to the application by or the membership of the Party of the Second Part in international, multilateral and regional organizations and institutions of which the Party of the First Part is a member; however, the Party of the First Part reserves the right to object to any membership referred to above if and to the extent the Party of the Second Part is to be referred to in such organization or institution differently than in paragraph 2 of United Nations Security Council resolution 817 (1993).' A note here: the Interim Accord refers to the Applicant as 'Party of the Second Part' and to the Respondent as 'Party of the First Part' so as to avoid using any contentious name.

[303]With the exception of the 'difference' referred to in Article 5, paragraph 1, of the Interim Accord, which reads as follows: 'The Parties agree to continue negotiations under the auspices of the Secretary-General of the United Nations pursuant to Security Council resolution 845 (1993) with a view to reaching agreement on the *difference* described in that resolution and in Security Council resolution 817 (1993).'

[304]*Application of the Interim Accord of 13 September 1995* (2011), pp. 16–17.

[305]*Id*, p. 18.

[306]*Id.*

[307]*Id.*

After establishing that it has jurisdiction, the Court proceeds with the merits of the case.[308] It tries to determine whether Greece failed to comply with the obligation not to object to the admission of Macedonia, particularly, in NATO, at the Bucharest Summit, and whether such act fell within the exception contained in the second clause of Article 11, paragraph 1, of the *Interim Accord*.[309] In doing so, the Court expressly states that Articles 31 and 32 of the VCLT are applicable to interpreting Article 11(1) of the *Interim Accord*. The Court recalls the applicable customary rules to this case, namely 'the ordinary meaning to be given to the terms of the treaty in their context and in light of its object and purpose'.[310] Focusing first on the ordinary meaning of the terms in their context, in the phrases 'to the extent' and 'to be referred to … differently than in paragraph 2 of Security Council resolution 817 (1993)', within the second clause of Article 11(1),[311] the Court finds, for example, that the parties formulated the second clause of Article 11, using the passive voice. It states that 'if and to the extent the [Applicant] *is to be referred to* …, differently than in paragraph 2 of Resolution 817',[312] it would be 'difficult to reconcile with the Respondent's view that the clause covers not only how the organisation is to refer to the Applicant but also the way that the Applicant is to refer to itself'.[313]

To make clear and more comprehensible the meaning of the terms of the provision at issue, the Court underlines next the 'context' of the whole treaty (the Interim Accord), in which the wording of the second clause of Article 11(1), above mentioned, needs to be interpreted in relation to other provisions.[314] For example, the Court finds that '[t]he Court, considering that Parties did not intend Article 22 to render meaningless the first clause of Article 11, paragraph 1, is therefore unable to accept the broad interpretation originally advanced by the Respondent'.[315] Thus, in light of the 'context', as well as of the 'object and purpose' of the *Interim Accord* (contextualist and teleological approach), the Court concludes that Greece's objection to Macedonia's admission to membership in an organisation using its constitutional name cannot be upheld, so that no constraint should be imposed on the Applicant's consistent practice of calling itself by its constitutional name, by mere implication in Article 11(1).[316] Yet in a further step, the Court tests this result by an

[308] *Id*, p. 16.
[309] *Id*, p. 30.
[310] *Id*.
[311] *Id*, p. 37.
[312] *Id*, p. 38.
[313] *Id*.
[314] *Id*.
[315] *Id*.
[316] *Id*.

express resort to 'the subsequent practice of the Parties in the application of Article 11, paragraph 1, of the *Interim Accord*, under Article 31, paragraph 3(b), of the 1969 Vienna Convention'[317] and, thus, to the subjective method. It finds, for example, that between the conclusion of the *Interim Accord* and the *Bucharest Summit*, Macedonia joined at least 15 international organisations, as also in dealings with NATO, when it referred continuously to itself by its constitutional name.[318] Although the Court declared at the outset of interpretation that it would interpret the *Interim Accord* also in accordance with Article 32 of the VCLT (resort to 'supplementary means'), it 'considers that it is not necessary to address this additional evidence'.[319]

In comparison with other cases discussed above, in the case at hand the Court makes a more explicit justification of why it does not need to resort to supplementary means of evidence. It states that the extensive evidence introduced by the parties, related to the *travaux préparatoires* of the *Interim Accord* and of *Resolution 817*, 'does not bear directly on the question whether the Interim Accord permits the Respondent to object to the Applicant's admission to or membership in an organisation based on the Applicant's self-reference by its constitutional name'.[320] Thus, the Court implies that the text at issue is *sufficiently clear* as to not require supplementary evidence from the *travaux preparatoire* to clarify this question and that its task is to give full effect to the provision at issue and not to construct it (by finding something that is not therein). The Court finds enough evidence obtained on the rules of Article 31 of the VCLT to conclude that the *Interim Accord* does not entitle the Respondent to object to the Applicant's admission to NATO.[321] It stresses in addition that although Article 5(1) of the *Interim Accord* contains no express requirement that the parties negotiate in *good faith*, such an obligation, as the Court admits, is implicit under this provision according to the 1969 Vienna Convention's 'general rule of interpretation'.[322]

In sum, the Court performs in the *Application of the Interim Accord of 13 September 1995* case a clear *holistic* interpretation, giving meaning and full effect to all the terms of the treaty (the Interim Accord), under Article 31 paragraphs (1) (2) (3) (b) of the VCLT, and the effectiveness principle.

---

[317]*Id*, p. 35.

[318]*Id*, p. 36. The Applicant was admitted under the provisional designation prescribed by paragraph 2 of resolution 817 and has been referred to in the organisation by that name.

[319]*Id*. According to Greece's interpretation, 'duties' under a prior treaty would take precedence over obligations in the Interim Accord (referring to its right under Article 10 of the North Atlantic Treaty), a view which the Court admitted as unacceptable.

[320]*Id*.

[321]*Id*.

[322]*Id*, p. 44.

#### 4.4.1.5 Clear Holistic Approach and Emphasis on the 'Object and Purpose' and 'Context of the Treaty' Rules

In the above case law analyses, the Court's pattern has already been identified and shown, namely reading the terms of a treaty provision, in addition to the 'context' of their immediate use, also in the light of the 'object and purpose', as well as in the 'context of the whole treaty' (*holistic interpretation*). This approach could be seen as a *sine qua non* condition required by Article 31(1)(2) VCLT for interpreting a treaty properly (the standard of interpretation). According to Jonas and Sanders, the *object and purpose* should be understood as an objective concept, referring to the *goals* of the treaty's drafters, which, certainly, are reflected in the text of the treaty.[323] Consequently, the 'text' of a treaty (its provisions) can only be properly understood when it is interpreted in light of the 'object and purpose' of that treaty.[324] And similarly, the *context*, as succinctly put by Villiger, is simply necessary because treaty terms are not drafted in isolation, and thus their meaning can only be determined by considering the *entire text of the treaty*.[325] The ***Case Concerning Oil Platforms* (1996)**[326] shows a situation where the Court dealt with *ambiguous* text(s), susceptible of raising *doubts*, and it gave meaning and effect to all the terms of the treaty, pursuant to Article 31 of the VCLT. However, in consonance with its own (already) developed path of interpretation of treaties, and by virtue of judicial discretion, the Court chose in this case to adopt, in addition to the rules expressly stated as applicable to the case, other rules of interpretation that it considered necessary to both determine and confirm the result reached on the previous rules basis. The Court showed a clear emphasis on the 'object and purpose' and 'context of the treaty' rules and followed a rather different order in applying the rules of treaty interpretation than it followed in other cases when dealing with *ambiguity* in the text of treaties.

The *Oil Platforms* case was brought as a result of the destruction of three Iranian offshore oil platforms and multiple United States Navy warships during the Iran–Iraq War. Specifically, the issue of interpretation was whether the Court may ascertain the violations of the 1955 Treaty of Amity, Economic Relations and Consular Rights between Iran and United States, pleaded by Iran as falling within the provisions of this Treaty, and whether the Court had jurisdiction *rationae*

---

[323] Jonas and Saunders (2010), p. 581.

[324] *Id.* The authors address in this connection Article 19, paragraph (c), of the VCLT, referring to the importance of the 'object and purpose' as a test to preserve treaty rule coherence. Article 19 provides:

> A state may, when signing, ratifying, accepting, approving or acceding to a treaty, formulate a reservation, unless: ...c)... the reservation is incompatible with the object and purpose of the treaty.

[325] Villiger (2009), p. 110. See in this regard one of the most recent cases decided at the ICJ: *Maritime Delimitation in the Indian Ocean (Somalia v. Kenya)* (2017), *supra* note 247. In this case the Court made an express statement that when interpreting a treaty provision which does not provide clarity (insufficient clear text), the Court must look to ascertain first the *intention* of the Parties in respect of that provision *in the context of the treaty as a whole.*

[326] *Oil Platforms* (1996), *supra* note 226.

*materiae* pursuant to Article XXI(2) of the 1955 Treaty.[327] The US admitted that it destroyed Iran's platforms in question, but it argued that it did so in self-defence against previous acts of aggression committed (against the US) by Iran. Iran claimed that the Treaty prohibited the use of force in self-defence. Since Iran's claims raised issues relating to the 'use of force', falling within the ambit of the 1955 Treaty, the Court had to determine whether the Treaty of 1955 could apply to question concerning the 'use of force', a claim that the United States contested. The US also contested the Court's jurisdiction to entertain Iran's submission.[328]

Although the Court observes in this case that the Treaty of Amity contains no provision expressly excluding certain matters from the Court's jurisdiction, it admits that matters relating to the 'use of force' are not per se excluded from the Court's reading of the Treaty of 1955.[329] In determining the meaning of the relevant Treaty's provisions, the Court expressly declares Article 31 of the VCLT to be customary international law applicable to the case.[330] It recalls that 'a treaty must be interpreted in good faith in accordance with the ordinary meaning to be given to its terms in their context and in the light of its object and purpose'.[331] Then the Court adds that '[u]nder Article 32, recourse may be had to supplementary means of interpretation such as the preparatory work and the circumstances in which the treaty concluded'.[332]

Further, to establish whether the issue before the Court is 'as to the interpretation or application' of the Treaty according to Article XXI(2) of the Treaty of 1955, the Court proceeds to interpret the relevant provisions in the context of the Treaty as a whole. In respect of Article I of the Amity Treaty (the basis in establishing the Court's jurisdiction on the issue before it), which provides that: 'There shall be firm and enduring peace and sincere friendship between the two contracting states', Iran contends, on the one hand, that, read in the context of the whole Treaty and reinforced by the circumstances of the Treaty's conclusion, Article I actually imposes obligations on the contracting parties, 'obliging them to maintain long-lasting peaceful and friendly relations'.[333] On the other hand, the US considers that Iran 'reads far too much into Article I', which 'contains no standards' but only a 'statement of aspiration'.[334] Given the difficulty in interpreting Article I of the 1955 Treaty, particularly since a 'plain' meaning of the terms in the context of this provision could not provide a straightforward result, the Court considers that it must

[327] *Id*, p. 12.

[328] *Id*, p. 11.

[329] *Id*, p. 13.

[330] *Id*. Although the United States has not ratified the VCLT, it has declared that the VCLT is 'generally recognized as the authoritative guide to current treaty law and practice' (see for this opinion, e.g., Roger Alford: Treaty Interpretation, at opiniojuris.org/2006/10/19treaty-interpretation-101/).

[331] *Id*, p. 23.

[332] *Id*, p. 24.

[333] *Id*, p. 14.

[334] *Id*.

be read in the broader 'context' of the Treaty, thus in relation to other provisions. Moreover, the Court observes that such a general formulation of Article I 'cannot be interpreted in isolation from the 'object and purpose' of the Treaty in which it is inserted',[335] suggesting an application of the teleological method. In this respect, the Court considers that the meaning of Article I must have regard to the Preamble of the 1955 Treaty, which provides for 'encouraging [of] mutually beneficial trade and investments and closer economic intercourse generally', as well as 'regulating consular relations' between the two states.[336]

To achieve clarity in the meaning of Article I in relation to the object and purpose of the Treaty of 1955, the Court looks at the nature of other 'friendship, commercial and navigation' treaties (FCN), in particular at some concluded after the Second World War. It finds on this approach that 'the object and purpose of the Treaty of 1955 was not to regulate peaceful and friendly relations between the two States in a *general* sense, incorporating all of provisions of international law concerning the relations the Court found in other treaties, but that Article I must be regarded as fixing an objective, in the light of which the other Treaty provisions are to be interpreted and applied'.[337] The Court concludes therefore that the interpretation of Article I is meant to throw light on the meaning of the other Treaty provisions.[338] In strengthening this interpretation the Court relies on a similar conclusion to that reached in the *Nicaragua* (1986) case on the merits. The Court interpreted in *Nicaragua* an identical clause included in the Treaty of Friendship, Commerce and Navigation between the United States and Nicaragua on 21 January 1956, finding that '*the object and purpose is the effective implementation of friendship in the specific fields provided for in the Treaty, not friendship in a vague general sense*'.[339] Therefore, the Court admits that 'there is no reason to vary the conclusions arrived at in the 1986.'[340] Moreover, to test this result, the Court apparently considers as the *travaux preparatoire* ('supplementary means' under Article 32 VCLT) the documents produced by the parties in support of their respective position concerning the meaning to be given to Article I.[341] It holds in this regard, for example, that if Article I 'had the scope that Iran gives it, the Parties would have been led to point out its importance during the negotiations on the process of ratification. However, the Court does not have before it any Iranian document in support of this argument.'[342]

In respect of the resort to the extraneous means of interpretation ('supplementary means' under Article 32 VCLT), the Court's wording is criticised in some of the separate opinions of this case. For instance, in Judge Rigaux's opinion, the

---

[335] *Id*, p. 14.

[336] *Id*, p. 13.

[337] *Id*, p. 15.

[338] *Id*, p. 16.

[339] *Id* (emphasis added). The Court cites *Nicaragua* (1986), p. 137, para 273.

[340] *Id*, p. 15.

[341] *Id*.

[342] *Id*.

interpretation given by the Court to Article I, in the light of the documents submitted by the parties, 'contains considerations not referred to in the methods of interpretation provided by the Vienna Convention on the Law of Treaties of 23 May 1969', and also these documents provide 'no information as to the circumstances in which the instrument was drafted and adopted'.[343] Judge Rigaux refers to this particular aspect as a failure of the Court to interpret.[344]

In trying to determine with better precision the meaning of Article I, thus the real (authentic) intention of the drafters in its respect, the Court resorts to the subjective method of interpretation, looking in addition for 'any subsequent practice', pursuant to Article 31(3)(b) of the VCLT. It finds according to this rule that 'an established body of interpretation already exists' and that '[t]he practice followed by the Parties in regard to the application of the Treaty does not lead to any different conclusions'.[345] In brief, the Court relies on the context of the treaty; its Preamble; the 'subsequent practice'; other Treaties of Friendship, as well as its own precedents, specifically on the *Nicaragua* case. On this combined approaches, which imply the adoption of the textualist, contextualist, teleological and subjective methods, the Court finds that the terms of Article I of the 1955 Treaty would rather 'stress the intention of the two States that peace and friendship to constitute the precondition for a harmonious development of their commercial, financial and consular relations', a development that warrants the objective of 'that peace and that friendship'.[346]

The *context of the Treaty* as *a whole* is even more clearly revealed when the Court holds that it 'considers that the objective of peace and friendship proclaimed in Article I of the Treaty of 1955 is such as to throw light on the interpretation of the other Treaty provisions, and in particular of Article IV and X. Article I is thus not without legal significance for such an interpretation, but cannot, taken in isolation, be the basis for the jurisdiction of the Court.'[347] Therefore, the Court looks to establish further whether the actions of the US complained of by Iran had the potential to affect 'freedom of commerce' as guaranteed by Article X, paragraph 1, of the 1955 Treaty, which provides for freedom of commerce and navigation between the territories of the High Contracting Parties.[348] A similar holistic approach of interpretation is given by the Court to this article, which is,

---

[343] *Id.* See Separate Opinion of Judge Rigaux (at p. 65, para 29). Also in the Dissenting Opinion of Vice President Schwebel, 'these papers may properly be weighed by the Court not as *travaux preparatoire* but as part of the circumstances of the conclusion of the Treaty of Friendship, Commerce and Navigation'.

[344] *Id.*

[345] *Id*, p. 16. In particular, the Court finds that 'The United States has never relied upon that Article I in proceedings involving Iran and, more particularly, did not invoke that text in the case concerning United States Diplomatic and Consular Staff in Tehran. Neither did Iran rely on that Article, for example in the proceedings before the Court in the case concerning the Aerial Incident of 3 July 1988.'

[346] *Id*, pp. 13–15.

[347] *Id*, p. 16.

[348] Article X, paragraph 1, provides:

however, of value here only in illustrating the express use in this case of other rules of interpretation, in addition to the above. For example, the Court stresses the 'plain' or 'ordinary meaning' of the term 'commerce' in the text of Article X, which is tested by resort to the Oxford English Dictionary. In this regard, the Court finds that the term *commerce* 'is not restricted in ordinary usage to the mere act of purchase and sale', but it has the significance of 'the whole of the transactions, arrangements, etc, therein involved'[349] and that it 'has a broader meaning than the mere reference to purchase and sale', whether it is taken in 'the ordinary sense or in its legal meaning at the domestic or international level'.[350] Therefore, as the Court concludes, the notion of 'freedom of commerce' has a broader meaning which presupposes the prohibition of any act that impedes 'that freedom'.[351]

In determining the nature of the Treaty at issue, the Court suggests in addition the use of the principle of interpreting treaties authenticated in two or more languages, pursuant to Article 33, paragraph 1, of the VCLT. The Court finds in accordance with this rule that 'in the original English version, the actual title of the Treaty of 1955- contrary to that of most similar treaties concluded by the United States at that time, such as the Treaty of 1956 between the United States and Nicaragua – refers, besides "Amity" and "Consular Rights", not to "Commerce" but, more broadly, to "Economic Relations"'.[352] Then, stressing again the rule of 'context' of the treaty, the Court holds that the conclusions reached as to Article X, paragraph 1, 'are confirmed by the nature of the Treaty of which this provision forms a part'.[353] Finally, bringing all the arguments to the table and outlining the role of the context of the Treaty as a *whole*, the Court concludes that 'the spirit and intent set out in Article I animate and give meaning to the *entire* Treaty and must, in case of doubt, incline the Court to the construction *which seems more in consonance with its overall objective of achieving friendly relations over the entire range of activities covered by the Treaty*'.[354]

In sum, the Court in *Oil Platforms* renders a clear *holistic* approach, abiding by the standard of interpretation provided by Article 31 of the VCLT. It takes into account other customary rules of treaty interpretation as reflected in Articles 31, 32, 33 of the VCLT, stressing, however, the 'object and purpose', as also the 'context of the treaty as a whole' rules of interpretation.

---

Between the territories of the High Contracting Parties there shall be freedom of commerce and navigation.

[349] *Id*, p. 16.
[350] *Id*, p. 19.
[351] *Id*, p. 35.
[352] *Id*, p. 20.
[353] *Id*, p. 21.
[354] *Id*.

#### 4.4.1.6 Reliance on the 'Supplementary Means' and Emphasis on the 'Ordinary Meaning' Rule

It is admitted in the scholarship that a decision influenced by reference to preparatory work under Article 32 of the VCLT may result in a decision closer to the parties' intention than a literal application of Article 31 of the VCLT (Merrills 1968, p. 61). Thus, having both *confirmatory* and *determinative* function, according to Fitzmaurice and Merkouris, Article 32 of the VCLT 'is what completes the system of interpretation, ensures that the judge can always arrive at *one interpretative result* and closes the door to any *non liquet* scenarios' (Fitzmaurice and Merkouris 2010, 185). However, Gardiner explains that it is precisely the principle, according to which 'there is only one correct interpretation of a treaty', that actually leads whoever is interpreting the treaty to consider that 'there can only be one set of preparatory work' as admissible.[355] He also admits that preparatory work extends to materials that can be characterised as 'illuminating a common understanding' of the negotiators to a treaty.[356] The case analyses in this chapter can show that the ICJ does not always spell out when or why it needs to resort to the supplementary means of interpretation. Nevertheless, the frequent resort of the ICJ to the supplementary means (especially the *travaux preparatoire*) when it feels necessary to determine and/or to confirm the intention of the parties, whether it is expressly stated or only implied (suggested), could indicate the importance in value and role that the ICJ assigns to this rule in reaching a final result.

The ***Territorial Dispute* (1994)**[357] case illustrates a situation when the Court expressly declared that it would apply an interpretation of the treaty at issue in accord with customary international law set forth in Article 31 of the VCLT. The case is interesting, however, for the manner in which the Court made an implicit use of the 'supplementary means' of interpretation (*travaux preparatoire* and circumstances of the treaty's conclusion) on a *sufficiently clear* (treaty) text. In particular, the Court resorted to the *travaux preparatoire*, after stating that interpretation 'must be based above all upon the text of the treaty'[358] and that it had no difficulty in ascertaining the terms of the Treaty so that it was not necessary to refer to the *travaux preparatoire*.[359] The question of interpretation before the Court in this case

---

[355] Gardiner (2008), p. 104.

[356] *Id*, p. 100.

[357] *Territorial dispute* (1994), *supra* note 227.

[358] *Id*, p. 22.

[359] *Id*, p. 20. As in other cases before the adoption of the VCLT, also similar approaches could be observable in the ICJ's practice after the adoption of the VCLT, i.e., in *LaGrand* (Germany v. United States of America), Judgment, I.C.J. Reports 2001, p. 466, at paras 41–43. The Court held in *LaGrand*: 'Given the conclusions reached by the Court above in interpreting the text of Article 41 of the Statute in the light of the object and purpose, it does not consider it necessary to resort to the preparatory work in order to determine the meaning of that Article.' However, the Court explicitly resorted in the course of the *LaGrand*'s judgment to the preparatory work of the provision at issue (Article 41 of the Statute of the Court), finding that 'it is clear that none of the

was the territorial dispute between the Republic of Chad and Libya Arab Jamahirya.[360] The Court had to decide upon the limits of their respective territories under Article 3 of the 1955 Treaty of Friendship and Good Neighbourliness, the basis of interpretation, which provided for 'the frontiers between the territories of Tunisia, Algeria, French West Africa and French Equatorial Africa on the one hand, and the territory of Libya on the other' to be determined 'from the international instruments in force on the date of the constitution of the United Kingdom of Libya as listed in the attached Exchange of Letters'.[361]

The Court expressly declares in *Territorial Dispute* that it will follow an approach in accord with the customary rules as reflected in Article 31 of the VCLT.[362] Based on the textualist method, the Court recalls that interpretation 'must be based above all upon the text of the treaty'[363] and admits that it has no difficulty in ascertaining its terms. However, the Court expressly admits afterwards that 'as a supplementary measure recourse may be had to means of interpretation such as the preparatory work of the treaty and circumstances of its conclusion'.[364] In the course of the judgment, the Court refers again to the *travaux preparatoire*, conveying this time that it does not merely rely on it. It states cautiously that 'it is not necessary to refer to the *travaux preparatoire* to elucidate the context of the 1955 Treaty, but as in previous cases, it finds it possible by reference to the *travaux preparatoire* to confirm its reading of the text, namely that the Treaty constitutes an agreement between the parties, which, *inter alia*, defines the frontiers'.[365] Nevertheless, the Court chooses to consult the relevant historical background, such as the negotiations of the 1955 Treaty, a number of conventional instruments reflecting

---

sources of interpretation referred in the relevant Articles of the Vienna Convention on the Law of Treaties, including the preparatory work, contradict the conclusions drawn from the terms of Article 41 read in their context and in the light of the object and purpose of the Statute'.

[360] *Id*, p. 9. The application had been drawn up pursuant to Article 2 of the Framework Agreement [Accord-Cadre] on the Peaceful Settlement of the Territorial Dispute between the Great Socialist People's Libyan Arab Jamahirya and the Republic of Chad on 31 August 1989 as basis for the Court's jurisdiction, and subsidiary on Article 8 of the Franco-Libyan Treaty of Friendship and Good Neighbourliness of August 1955.

Article 2 (a) of the Accord Cadre provides:

> In the absence of a political settlement of their territorial dispute, the two parties undertake:
> a) to submit the dispute to the International Court of Justice.

[361] *Id*, pp. 12–13. Article 3 of the 1955 Treaty provides:

> The two High Contracting Parties recognize that the frontiers between the territories of Tunisia, Algeria, French West Africa and French Equatorial Africa on the one hand, and the territory of Libya on the other, are those that result from the international instruments in force on the date of the constitution of the United Kingdom of Libya as listed in the attached Exchange of Letters.

[362] *Id*, p. 20.

[363] *Id*.

[364] *Id*.

[365] *Id*, p. 27.

that history, diplomatic exchanges, contemporary conventional maps and archival records, and relies on the observance that the parties had recognised the 1955 Treaty.[366]

It could be observed that the Court approaches an interpretation clearly in consideration of the 'good faith' principle, highly emphasised here. It asserts that parties manifested their intention to recognise cumulatively the frontiers between them in the instruments referred to in Annex I of the 1955 Treaty.[367] To test this result, the Court relies on the principle of effectiveness, which it describes as 'one of the fundamental principles of interpretation of treaties, consistently upheld by international jurisprudence'.[368] It finds accordingly that 'no relevant frontier was to be left undefined and no instrument listed in Annex I was superfluous' and that '[a]ny other construction would be contrary to the actual terms of Article 3'.[369]

Mention should be made that the Court only apparently relies in this case (like in the other cases already discussed in this chapter) on the 'ordinary meaning' of the terms used in their context—as the rule governing the interpretation.[370] On one hand, the Court reiterates the clarity of Article 3 of the Treaty and the effect resulting from it, stating that this provision 'clearly conveys the intention of the parties to reach a definitive settlement of the question of their common intention'.[371] And on the other hand, the Court admits that it needs to extend its reading of the treaty provision at issue in the 'light of its object and purpose'.[372] It remains conclusive for the Court by expressly stating that the 'object and purpose' of the Treaty is recalled to 'confirm the interpretation of the Treaty' as it naturally leads to defining the territory of Libya and, thus, of its boundaries.[373] Moreover, the Court also stresses the 'context' rule, stating that '[t]he conclusions which the Court has reached are reinforced by an examination of the *context* of the Treaty',[374] an approach that qualifies the interpretation as *holistic*.

---

[366] *Id.*

[367] *Id*, p. 25.

[368] *Id.*

[369] *Id.*

[370] *Id.*

[371] *Id.*

[372] *Id.*

[373] *Id*, p. 26. See similarity between the interpretative approaches adopted by the ICJ in the *Case Concerning the Territorial Dispute* and the recent case *Maritime Delimitation in the Black Sea (Romania v. Ukraina)*, ICJ, Judgment of 3 February 2009.

[374] *Id* (emphasis added). See similarity with the approach adopted by the ICJ in the recent *Maritime Delimitation in the Indian Ocean (Somalia v. Kenya)* (2017), *supra* note 247. In this case the Court's emphasis was on the context of the treaty (treaty as a whole) as determinative for other elements of the treaty. For example, the Court stated that: '[i]t is, however, difficult to understand that paragraph without a prior analysis of the text of the MOU as a whole, which provides the context in which any particular paragraph should be interpreted and gives insight into the object and purpose of the MOU.'

The basic point of this case which the Court appears to convey is that treaties that delineate borders are considered to be *permanent* (unless a new treaty changes the borders), the essential aspect in defining a state territory and securing peace.[375] Thus, by putting emphasis on the text (interpretation 'must be based above all upon the text of the treaty'), the Court underlines, like in other cases, that the treaty must be presumed as having a definite force and effect in its letter and spirit by virtue of the parties' consent to it. Despite constantly asserting the clarity of the text of the Treaty provision at issue in *Territorial Dispute*, the Court feels the need to confirm the interpretative outcome obtained initially on the basis of the 'ordinary meaning' by resort to the context of the whole Treaty, its object and purpose, pursuant to Article 31(1) and (2) of the VCLT, clearly supported by the 'supplementary means' of interpretation, as provided by Article 32 of the VCLT. The Court follows this way the patterns it has used in previous cases of interpreting treaties when dealing with a *clear* or *sufficiently clear* text of treaties, both prior to and after the 1969 VCLT's adoption.

## 4.5 Conclusions

Based on the above PCIJ/ICJ case law analyses, several conclusions could be drawn. First, without exception, the interpretations given by the Court to the treaties are amply supported with the aid of the established rules of interpretation (e.g., the ordinary meaning of the words, context, object and purpose, *travaux*). However, the impression that there is a normative judgment and balancing that the Court makes with respect to international law principles, in addition to the rules of interpretation in most of the cases, could not be avoided. The firm grounding on rules of interpretation in the judgments issued by the Court appears to be made somehow ex post facto the normative deliberation, fact that, nevertheless, enhances the legitimacy and authority of the Court's interpretations.

Further, the case analyses in this chapter can clearly show that the ICJ appears to employ more than one rule and method of interpretation after declaring that rule (method) as governing the case (almost without exception the 'ordinary meaning' supported by the textualist method), in an effort to determine and confirm the meaning of the provision under interpretation. Thus, the Court builds its case of interpretation in successive steps, every step further enhancing the conclusions

[375] E.g., *Interpretation of Article 3, para 2, of the Treaty of Lausanne*, PCIJ, Advisory Opinion of 21 November 1925, Series B, No. 12, dealing with a provision of the Treaty of Lausanne: 'It is . . . natural that any article designed to fix a frontier should if possible, be interpreted that the result of the application of its provisions in their entirety should be the establishment of a precise, complete and definitive frontier'; *The Temple of Preah Vihear Case* (*Cambodia v. Thailand*), Merits, ICJ Reports, 1962, where the Court held that it based its decision upholding the 'map line' on the fact that 'both Parties, by their conduct recognized the line and thereby in effect agreed to regard it as being the frontier line'; or *Sovereignty over Certain Frontier Land*, ICJ Reports 1959, pp. 221–222.

reached upon the application of the method/rule it expressly (or implicitly) declared that it would use. Moreover, the ICJ performs this approach to interpretation not only when it encounters an *insufficiently clear*, *ambiguous*, *doubtful*, *vague or silent treaty text* but also when the text is found and declared by the Court as being *clear*, with no difficulty of interpretation. The Court does so, perhaps, in order to show that all the rules or methods allow for the interpretative outcome realised initially, an approach described by this author as 'overbuilding'. Nevertheless, such use of more rules and methods of interpretation than eventually necessary (either expressly declared or only implied) may suggest the Court's sensitivity towards legitimacy issues, a preference for rational deliberations that have the potential to enhance its interpretative legitimacy. Thus, the rules of interpretation appear as logical deductive means used in rational deliberation, which serve the purpose of enhancing the legitimacy of the interpreter, here the ICJ.[376]

However, the analyses can also show that the process of application of rules of interpretation could not be performed in a mechanical way as the syllogism can appear when one reads the draft of a judicial decision of the Court. For example, there is no guarantee that if I follow a rule of interpretation and undoubtedly arrive at the conclusion x, I would arrive at the same conclusion and solely at this conclusion if I follow another rule of interpretation, in the absence of similar premises. There is no possibility to arrive at similar conclusions when applying a syllogism unless the premises are similar or identical. In other words, to arrive at an identical conclusion in both cases (by using different rules), there is a need for a *holistic* judgment of the case and of the international law principles involved in the interpretation process, in addition to the application of the rules of treaty interpretation. Such a holistic approach implies a selectivity of the Court of international law rules and principles of interpretation, depending of the circumstances deducted to adjudication, and an emphasis on some but not on others in the same case while performing the act of interpretation. From the legal interpreter perspective, it appears that in order to be selective, one needs to balance *ex ante* various rules/principles and to choose what requires its attention on that specific issue/case. It could be stated that the internal coherence and the logic and elegancy of a judgment rendered by the ICJ would not be possible without this sort of initial 'seeing the wood for the trees', which puts the issues into larger perspective, *holistically*. So even if after this initial selectivity of rules/principles of international law one can accept the idea that a mechanical application of the rules/principles of treaty interpretation is possible, it could not be so since this initial selectivity itself implies balancing and attachment of heavier normative weight to some of the rules/principles rather than to others, depending on the circumstances of the case before the Court. It might be argued that, on the one hand, this 'overbuilding' interpretation that the Court performs could be attributed in many situations to some sort of uncertainty that it may have with respect to the efficiency of the method/rule chosen to reach a conclusion. Or, in other situations, this 'overbuilding' realised by the

[376]See on this aspect, e.g., Hagle (1990).

adoption of more methods and rules of interpretation than is sometimes necessary is dictated by a desire to convince the losing party in the dispute that any rational interpreter would reach the same and single conclusion (interpretation). Thus, in this latter case, the Court justifies that all methods of interpretation lead to one conclusion. It appears, generally, that the Court never loses sight of its active judicial role in solving disputes between states and seems guided by the idea that its decisions aim both to solve the problems that appear in international relations between states (violations of treaties) in conformity with international law norms and principles, as also to prevent future disputes from arising by creating precedents that could be used as models of treaty interpretation. On the other hand, this 'overbuilding' in interpretation may have a complementary, if not different, explanation. Thus, based on the conclusions of the cases analysed in this chapter, it can also be observed that in the majority of cases, the Court emphasises the 'plain' or 'ordinary' meaning (of the terms in the context of their use) rule to convey the importance of the principle of respect for treaties in international law. For the Court, there seems always to be an important presumption in the interpretative process: that a treaty is an international written agreement, concluded by states on *consent* and in *good faith*, by virtue of the *pacta sunt servanda* principle, which implies that the treaty must be respected by all parties to it, so it must stand as it is. And the Court, almost without exception, conveys that the 'plain' or 'ordinary' meaning rule governs the interpretation (the textualist method), even if it is not necessarily convinced that this approach would suffice to reach a single pertinent interpretation of the issue brought before it.

However, even if the 1969 Vienna Convention embraced the concept of 'plain and natural' meaning as the basis of interpretation, and admitted the prevailing recognition and long-standing development of this principle in the ICJ's practice, with rare exceptions,[377] the Court in practice appears to show flexibility in considering this rule in different situations. As it could be deduced from the case analyses above, the Court approaches the terms of the provision at issue not in a strictly grammatical sense when it employs their 'plain' and 'ordinary' meaning rule but in their context and usually as a starting point, more as a guide in commencing the process of interpretation. And at times, the Court does not follow that order, notably to begin the interpretation with the rule of 'plain' and 'ordinary' meaning of the terms in their context. As the case analyses can evidence, the *holistic* character that the ICJ imprints (as a path) to interpretation is reflected not only in the ICJ's tendency to resort to all the rules and methods needed in order to ascertain and confirm a result but also in its tendency to give to all of these means an equal interpretative value, before rendering the final decision. For example, the frequent resort to the *travaux preparatoire* when the Court adopts it to determine and/or

[377] See e.g. the case discussed in this chapter: *Interpretation of Peace Treaties with Bulgaria, Hungary and Romania* (1950). This case is perceived in the scholarship as one of the rare examples of the World Court's taking a narrower, restrictive view of interpretation (textualist method as prevalent in this case).

confirm the intention of the parties, even when only implied (suggested), could indicate the importance in value and role accorded by the Court to this rule in reaching a final result. In other words, despite the usual emphasis on the textualist method, the Court appears actually to give no preference to rely (mainly) on this method or treat a rule superior to another. So even if a meaning of a treaty provision could be found out upon one method (i.e., textualist), the ICJ rather tends to employ in each given case more rules in combination, harmoniously, in a *single unitary* and *logical act of interpretation*. This Court's tendency is therefore to treat the rules as equally valid sources of interpretation, each rule having its own value, weight and strength in determining and confirming the meaning of a treaty provision; thus, each matters in rendering the final decision. In addition, as the case analysis in this chapter has shown, the Court appears always motivated by a normative judgment and also mindful to take into consideration (other) *general principles of international law*.

Another conclusion based on the case analyses relates to the *consistency* of the ICJ's interpretative practice with the previous practice of its predecessor, the PCIJ. This consistency is reflected in the ICJ's application of the same (customary) rules and principles of interpretation, independently of their later codification in the 1969 VCLT. The *customary* character of the rules of interpretation embodied in Articles 31, 32, 33 of the VCLT can therefore be explained by their long and consistent application by the ICJ. In addition, as some of the case analyses in this chapter can show (post-VCLT period), the *customary* nature of the rules codified in the VCLT is also reflected in the ICJ's application of these rules to treaties ratified long before the VCLT's entry into force, despite the non-retroactivity of this Convention (Article 4). Similarly, this customary nature is reflected in the application of the VCLT rules to disputes involving states which are not parties to the Vienna Convention on the Law of Treaties.[378]

Finally, from the 'fragmentation' perspective, it could be concluded on the basis of the case analyses in this chapter that the general rules and principles of treaty interpretation have been overall applied by the PCIJ/ICJ with consistency both prior to and after the 1969 VCLT's adoption so that *coherence* in this Court's interpretative approaches can be observed. Moreover, the ICJ shows consistency in its use of the general principles of international law both prior to and after the VCLT's adoption, an approach reflected in Article 31(3)(c) of the VCLT (systemic integration). The Court has often chosen to interpret a provision of a treaty at issue by

[378]E.g., *Kasikili/Sedudu Island* (1999), discussed in this chapter. Article 4 of the VCLT provides for 'Non-retroactivity' of the Convention, namely that it applies only to treaties that are concluded by states after the entry into force of the present Convention with regard to such states. See also the recent case at the ICJ: *Maritime Delimitation in the Indian Ocean (Somalia v. Kenya)* (2017), *supra* note 247. In this case the Court held that the customary international law of treaties were applicable to the dispute even if neither Somalia nor Kenya were party to the Vienna Convention. This case is important since the Court clearly and expressly admits that the treaty interpretation act must be a *unitary, single combined operation*. It confirms this approach by placing on the same footing the various elements enumerated in the four paragraphs of Article 31 of the VCLT, also admitting the rules provided by Article 32 of the VCLT as equally important interpretative devices in reaching the final interpretation/decision.

reference to an extrinsic source (implicitly or explicitly) such as other treaties, in addition to other rules of interpretation, so as to shed light, especially, on obscure and/or dubious treaty provisions or only on individual terms within a (treaty) provision. This conclusion strengthens the idea that the general methodology of treaty interpretation, and in particular Article 31(3)(c), appears as an important tool of maintaining the *coherence* and *unity* of international law. And the ICJ's practice on treaty interpretation responds overall affirmatively in this respect, the Court approaching holistically the treaties it interprets. Thus, regardless of whether the Court employs the treaty interpretative means in an express or only suggested way (implying the situation when the Court is cautious in following a rule, stating that it would not follow it, but later in the judgment chooses to apply it anyway), overall its approaches to interpretation (prior to and after the VCLT's adoption) show consistency with the canons of treaty interpretation that this Court has successfully applied and developed mostly since its inception.

Whether judges from newer international courts and tribunals adopt different patterns than those established by the ICJ in applying *the customary rules and principles of treaty interpretation* on the same types of difficulties in interpreting the text of treaties (e.g., insufficient clear, equivocal or doubtful, ambiguous, vague or obscure, silent) constitutes the object of inquiry in the next chapters (Chaps. 5 and 6). Thus these chapters, which focus on the practice of treaty interpretation at the ECtHR and WTO, will attempt to identify and evidence whether there are homogeneous preferences of these specialised courts in terms of approaching the same (VCLT) body of general rules and methods of treaty interpretation (possible patterns of interpretation similar to those used by the ICJ) and to assess what the implications of such findings are *vis-a-vis* international law.

## References


Boyle, F. A. (1987). Determining US responsibility for contra operations under international law. *American Journal of International Law, 81*(1), 86–93.

Ciobanu, D. (1991). *Introducere in studiul dreptului* [Introduction in the study of law]. Bucuresti: Ed. Hyperion XXI.

Endicott, T. A. (2000). *Vagueness in law*. Oxford, England: Oxford University Press.

Engelen, F. A. (2004). *Interpretation of tax treaties under international law* (Vol. 7). Amsterdam: IBFD.

Fitzmaurice, G. G. (1951). Law and procedure of the International Court of Justice: Treaty interpretation and certain other treaty points. *British Year Book of International Law, 28*, 1.

Fitzmaurice, M., & Merkouris, P. (2010). Canons of treaty interpretation: Selected case studies from the World Trade Organization and the North American Free Trade Agreement. In *Treaty interpretation and the Vienna Convention on the Law of Treaties: 30 years on* (pp. 153–238). Leiden, The Netherlands: Brill.

Forowicz, M. (2010). *The reception of international law in the European Court of Human Rights*. New Yrok: Oxford University Press.

Gardiner, R. K. (2008). *Treaty interpretation*. New Yrok: Oxford University Press.

Ghandhi, S. (2011). Human rights and the International Court of Justice: The Ahmadou Sadio Diallo case. *Human Rights Law Review, 11*(3), 527–555.

Gross, L. (1971). The International Court of Justice: Consideration of requirements for enhancing its role in the international legal order. *American Journal of International Law, 65*(2), 253–326.
Hagle, T. M. (1990). So many cases, so little time: Judges as decision makers. In *American politics in the heartland*. Dubuque, IA: Kendall Hunt.
Henckaerts, J. M. (1993). The compulsory jurisdiction of the International Court of Justice, by Renata Szafarz. Dordrecht, The Netherlands: Martinus Nijhoff Publishers, 1993. *George Washington Journal of International Law and Economics, 27*, 265–573.
Henkin, L., Neuman, G. L., Orentlicher, D. F., & Leebron, D. W. (1999). *Human rights*. New York: Foundation Press.
Houchins, D. L. (2002). Extending the application of the ICJ's July 8, 1996, advisory opinion to environment-altering weapons in general: What is the role of international environmental law in warfare. *Journal of Land, Resources, & Environmental Law, 22*, 463.
Irwin, J. C. (1997). Alternative role for the International Court of Justice: Applied to Cameroon v. Nigeria. *Denver Journal of International Law and Policy, 26*, 759.
Janis, M. W. (1987). Somber reflections on the compulsory jurisdiction of the international court. *American Journal of International Law, 81*(1), 144–146.
Jonas, D. S., & Saunders, T. N. (2010). Object and purpose of a treaty: Three interpretive methods. *Vanderbilt Journal of Transnational Law, 43*, 565.
Koskenniemi, M. (2004). *Study on the function and scope of the Lex Specialis Rule and the question of 'Self-Contained Regimes'*. Preliminary report by the Chairman of the Study Group submitted for consideration during the 2004 session of the International Law Commission (unpublished, on file with the author).
Koskenniemi, M. (2006). *From apology to utopia: The structure of international legal argument*. Cambridge, England: Cambridge University Press.
Lauterpacht, H. (1949). Restrictive interpretation and the principle of effectiveness in the interpretation of treaties. *British Year Book of International Law, 26*, 48.
Lauterpacht, H. (1982). *The development of international law by the international court*. Cambridge, England: Cambridge University Press.
Linderfalk, U. (2007). *On the interpretation of treaties: The modern international law as expressed in the 1969 Vienna Convention on the law of treaties* (Vol. 83). Springer Science & Business Media.
Llamzon, A. P. (2007). Jurisdiction and compliance in recent decisions of the International Court of Justice. *European Journal of International Law, 18*(5), 815–852.
Lu, B. (2004). Reform of the international court of justice—A jurisdictional perspective. *In Perspectives, Overseas Young Chinese Forum, 5*(2).
McDougal, M. S., & Gardner, R. N. (1951). The Veto and the Charter: An interpretation for survival. *Yale Law Journal, 60*(2), 258–292.
McInerney-Lankford, S. (2012). Fragmentation of international law redux: The case of Strasbourg. *Oxford Journal of Legal Studies, 32*(3), 609–632.
Merkouris, P. (2010a). *Article 31 (3)(c) of the VCLT and the principle of systemic integration*. Doctoral dissertation.
Merkouris, P. (2010b). Introduction: Interpretation is a science, is an art, is a science. In M. Fitzmaurice, O. A. Elias, & P. Merkouris (Eds.), *Treaty interpretation and the Vienna Convention on the Law of Treaties: 30 years on* (pp. 1–14). Leiden, The Netherlands: Brill.
Merrills, J. G. (1968). Two approaches to treaty interpretation. *Australian Year Book of International Law, 4*, 55.
Merrills, J. G. (2005). *International dispute settlement*. Cambridge, England: Cambridge University Press.
Moore, J. N. (1987). The Nicaragua case and the deterioration of world order. *American Journal of International Law, 81*(1), 151–159.
Orakhelashvili, A. (2008). *The interpretation of acts and rules in public international law*. Oxford University Press.
Posner, E. A., & De Figueiredo, M. (2004). Is the International Court of Justice biased? *University of Chicago Law & Economics, Olin Working Paper*, 234.

Ris, M. (1991). Treaty interpretation and ICJ recourse to Travaux Préparatoires: Towards a proposed amendment of Articles 31 and 32 of the Vienna Convention on the Law of Treaties. *Boston College International and Comparative Law Review, 14*, 111.

Romano, C. P. (2006). Shift from the consensual to the compulsory paradigm in international adjudication: Elements for a theory of consent. *New York University Journal of International Law and Politics, 39*, 791.

Scott, G. L., Bothwell, H. M., & Pennell, J. (1996). Recent activity before the International Court of Justice: Trend or cycle. *ILSA Journal of International & Comparative Law, 3*, 1.

Sornarajah, M. (2010). *The international law on foreign investment*. Cambridge, England: Cambridge University Press.

Spiermann, O. (2007). Judge Max Huber at the permanent court of international justice. *European Journal of International Law, 18*(1), 115–133.

Stone, J. (1953). Fictional elements in treaty interpretation-A study in the international judicial process. *Sydney Law Review, 1*, 344.

Van Damme, I. (2009). *Treaty interpretation by the WTO Appellate Body*. Oxford, England: Oxford University Press.

Villiger, M. E. (2009). *Commentary on the 1969 Vienna Convention on the Law of Treaties*. Leiden, The Netherlands: Brill.

Villiger, M. E. (2011). The rules on Interpretation-Misgivings, Misunderstandings, Miscarriage? The "Crucible" intended by the International Law Commission. In E. Cannizzaro (Ed.), *The law of treties beyond the Vienna Convention*. Oxford University Press.

Weisburd, A. M. (2009). International Court of Justice and the concept of state practice. *University of Pennsylvania Journal of International Law, 31*, 295.

## Documents

Charter, U. N. (26 June 1945). Charter of the United Nations.

International Law Commission. (1966). Draft articles on the law of treaties with commentaries. In *Yearbook of the International Law Commission* (Vol. 2).

International Law Commission, 2006. Fragmentation of international law: Difficulties arising from the diversification and expansion of international law. *Geneva: United Nations.*

Waldock, H., 1964. Third Report on the Law of Treaties by Sir Humphrey Waldock, Special Rapporteur. *Yearbook of the International Law Commission, 2.*

# Chapter 5
# Treaty Interpretation at the European Court of Human Rights

## 5.1 Introduction

This chapter examines the treaty interpretation practice at the European Court of Human Rights.[1] The selection of the European Court of Human Rights (hereafter ECtHR or Strasbourg Court) as a testing case for the uniform development of customary rules and principles of treaty interpretation is not random as several of its characteristics allow for a thorough test of the conclusion drawn in respect of the ICJ's interpretative practice. The Strasbourg Court is admitted to be by far the most active of the specialised courts, working in a very dynamic area of international law that has witnessed many developments over the years.[2] The dynamism of the human rights field and of the Strasbourg Court is reflected in the number of judgments it issued, which is higher than all of the other standing international tribunals.[3] Unlike the breadth of the jurisdictional remit of the International Court of Justice (World Court), which examines legal disputes between states (albeit such disputes may involve injury to individuals), the Strasbourg Court is called to adjudicate (dominantly) on matters arising between states and individuals. Thus, individuals are at the heart of human rights protection offered by *the European Convention on Human Rights* (hereafter ECHR, European Convention or Convention), the treaty that forms the basis of the ECtHR's jurisdiction. In spite of the characteristics that radically differentiate the treaties which the Strasbourg Court and the World Court are called to interpret, I propose to test in this chapter whether

[1]The ECtHR is a permanent, full-time court with compulsory jurisdiction over all member states to which aggrieved individuals enjoy direct access, and its judgments are binding in all the Council of Europe member states (including Russia, Turkey), and all European Union member States (see Protocol No. 11 to the Convention for the Protection of Human Rights and Fundamental Freedoms, Restructuring the Control Machinery Established Thereby, ETS No. 155).

[2]Mowbray (2005).

[3]Voeten (2010). Based on statistics, the author found that the ECtHR has issued more than 10,000 judgments over the period of 50 years.



L.E. Popa, *Patterns of Treaty Interpretation as Anti-Fragmentation Tools*,
DOI 10.1007/978-3-319-65488-1_5

the methods, customary rules and principles of treaty interpretation used and developed by the PCIJ/ICJ are applied similarly in the specialised context of human rights.

The chapter is divided into two main parts. The first part (Sect. 5.2) offers an overview of scholarly discussions about the ECtHR's emergence as a specialised court and the concept of 'human rigths', as well as an overview of the main and specific characteristics of treaty interpretation at the ECtHR. The chapter continues in the second part (Sect. 5.3) with various questions/themes related to issues of treaty interpretation at this court, which cover both pre- and post-VCLT periods (Sects. 5.3.2 and 5.3.3). By analysing several ECtHR judgments, which in my view are key decisions of this Court on treaty interpretation issues, in comparison with decisions of the ICJ on treaty interpretation, I offer an empirical analysis that adds to the scholarly debate related to the ECtHR's specific interpretative ethos. The case law analysis provided in the second part revolves mainly around the question of whether the customary rules of treaty interpretation (reflected in Articles 31, 32 and 33 of the VCLT) are assimilated by the ECtHR as the standards of interpretation and whether these rules are applied consistently (prior to, and after, the adoption of the 1969 VCLT), in patterns similar to those used by the ICJ when dealing with analogous difficulties in interpreting treaty text (e.g., insufficiently clear, ambiguous, doubtful, vague or silent language of the text with regard to the circumstances of the case).

Treaty interpretation matter attracts tremendous attention today due to the proliferation of treaties,[4] but especially due to the perceived relation between the proliferation of (specialised) international judicial bodies (often admitted to interpret their treaties—*lex specialis*—independently of general international law), and its related problem of fragmentation in international law. Therefore, the analysis in this chapter seeks to provide an answer to the question of whether the practice of the ECtHR on treaty interpretation, as the most dynamic in the human rights field, could be a tool for unification of an alleged fragmented landscape of international law or, conversely, it contributes to the 'fragmentation' of international law.

## 5.2 Human Rights Background and Specific Characteristics of Human Rights Treaties

The notion of human rights dates back to what an earlier language of European philosophers had called 'natural law' and 'natural right(s)' (Heard 1997). According to Heard, who examines 'human rights' in a historical and philosophical perspective, the concept of *human rights* is a product of a philosophical debate that has raged for over 2,000 years within European societies and their colonial descendants.[5] Heard asserts that the search for moral standards of political organisations

[4]See on this point Pauwelyn and Elsig (2011).

[5]Heard (1997).

and binding rules of/for moral human behaviour has preoccupied many scholars from the earliest times.[6] In the twentieth century, philosophical writers and many authors who have written on this topic became unsatisfied with the notion of 'rights' while asserting that what is right or good is simply a reflection of what a particular society or ruling elite feels is right or good at any given time.[7]

In spite of this philosophical skepticism with rights, international law after the Second World War was developed as to incorporate individuals and individuals' rights under its protective umbrella. When examining the causes of what prompted these changes in international law, Lauterpacht explains that 'in the sphere of international duties there has been an enhanced realisation of the fact that the direct subjection of the individual to the rule of law is an essential condition of strengthening the ethical basis of international law and of its effectiveness in a period of history in which the destructive potentialities of science and the power of the machinery of the state threaten the very existence of civilised life' (Lauterpacht 1950, p. 61). Lautherpacht's enlightened view was that 'fundamental human rights are rights superior to the law of the sovereign State' and that '[t]he recognition of inalienable human rights and the recognition of the individual as a subject of international law are synonymous'.[8] Thus, it was a historical moment in 1948, when the United Nations General Assembly adopted the *Universal Declaration of Human Rights*,[9] in which it emphasised that 'recognition of the inherent dignity and of the equal and inalienable rights of all members of the human family is the foundation of freedom, justice and peace in the world'.[10] The General Assembly acknowledged that the adoption of the declaration was a reaction to the atrocities that had occurred in the Second World War. And today, it is recognised that human rights are not some abstract, inchoate 'good'[11] but defined claims listed in international instruments and, especially, in the *1948 Universal Declaration* and in the major covenants and conventions.[12]

In 1950, only 2 years after the adoption of the *Universal Declaration*, the *European Convention for the Protection of Human Rights and Fundamental Freedoms* was adopted, entering into force as soon as in 1953. This Convention mandates the Strasbourg Court (European Court of Human Rights) to adjudicate

[6]*Id.*

[7]*Id.*

[8]Lauterpacht (1950), p. 61.

[9]*Universal Declaration of Human Rights* (1948).

[10]*Id.*

[11]Henkin et al. (1999), p. 3 (see Preamble of the Universal Declaration of Human Rights).

[12]*The International Covenant on Civil and Political Rights* (ICCPR) is as a multilateral treaty adopted by the United Nations General Assembly on 16 December 1966, in force from 23 March 1976, and also *The International Covenant on Economic, Social and Cultural Rights* (CESCR), which opened for signature on December 19, 1966 in New York, and came into force on January 3, 1976.

claims related to its violation by the signatory states.[13] The European Court of Human Rights was established by the *1950 European Convention for the Protection of Human Rights and Fundamental Freedoms* (ECHR) but started to function only in 1959.[14] In time, and especially since the end of the Cold War, the Court became so successful and 'popular' that it began to be overwhelmed by the sheer number of applications, and it had to change its own procedural rules in order to advert repetitive applications and to better address systemic violations of the Convention rights by the state members of the Convention (Greer 2006). Nowadays, it is admitted that the *European Convention on Human Rights* introduced the most advanced and effective human rights treaty system (Henkin et al. 1999, p. 3). Certainly, the Western European countries, which were the first signatories of the ECHR, could not play a human rights 'card' in their dealings with foreign nations, without guaranteeing an adequate protection of those rights for their own citizens,[15] and this may explain the success story that became the *European Convention on Human Rights*. As a typical multilateral treaty, the ECHR serves as a kind of regional quasi-constitution, which delimits an increasingly integrated public order and seeks to protect certain values within a very specific geographical, cultural, political and economic European environment (Tzevelekos 2009, p. 627).

For more than four decades, two bodies supervised compliance by the High Contracting Parties with the European Convention: *the European Commission of Human Rights* and *the European Court of Human Rights* (Henkin et al. 1999, p. 550). It was in November 1998 when the European Commission and European Court of Human Rights were replaced by a single full-time court (Bermann et al. 2002, p. 208). Under the ECHR system, applications against Signatory Parties for human rights violations can be brought before the Court either by the States Parties or by individuals.[16] Since its inception, the Convention's supervisory bodies have addressed a tremendous range of issues traditionally considered to be matters of domestic jurisdiction and produced an extensive body of substantive human rights jurisprudence (Henkin et al. 1999, p. 551). It is through the practice of the ECtHR that the nature of the European Convention has been defined as a human rights instrument that 'creates over and above a network of mutual, bilateral undertakings, objective obligations which, in the words of the Preamble, benefit from a "collective enforcement"'.[17]

---

[13]*The European Convention on Human Rights - Convention for Protection of Human Rights and Fundamental Freedoms* (1950).

[14]See European Court of Human Rights (online at *PICT*).

[15]Henkin et al. (1999), p. 3.

[16]Bermann et al. (2002), p. 208. According to the authors, most members of the Council of Europe, including all EU member states have incorporated the Convention into their domestic legal systems. Parties to the Convention agree to accept and be bound by the judgments of the Court.

[17]See e.g. *Case of Mamatkulov and Askarov v. Turkey*, (Applications no. 46827/99 and 46951/99), Judgment of 4 February 2005, Strasbourg), para 100; *Ireland v. the United Kingdom* (18 January 1978, Series A no. 25), para 154.

The European Convention was not the only comprehensive regional human rights treaty adopted after the war. In addition to the two 1966 international covenants (*International Covenant on Civil and Political Rights* and *International Covenant on Economic, Social and Cultural Rights*), in 1978, the *American Convention on Human Rights* entered into force. This *American Convention* was accompanied by a central adjudicatory system, most strongly proclaiming, as one commentator expressed,[18] *the universal character of human rights*, 'recognizing that the essential rights of man are not derived from one's being a national of a certain state, but are based upon attributes of human personality, and that they therefore justify international protection'.[19] As Dworkin claims, human rights must not be taken in the abstract since '[i]ndividual rights are political trumps held by individuals. Individuals have rights when, for some reason, a collective goal is not sufficient justification for denying them what they wish, as individuals, to have or to do, or not a sufficient justification for imposing some loss or injury upon them . . . it does not suppose that rights have some special metaphysical character' (Dworkin 1978, p. xi). Furthermore, in 1981, the *African Charter on Human and Peoples' Rights* was adopted, and more recently, in 2004 and 2007 were adopted the *Arab Charter of Human Rights*, respectively the *ASEAN Charter of Human Rights.*[20]

What all these human rights treaties have in common is that they recognise rights which arise from the very nature of man and are inherited from this condition.[21] These rights exist independently of the will or volition of the parties, in a similar way in which human dignity exists.[22] In fact, as Carozza observes, *human dignity* serves as the single most widely recognised and invoked foundation for human rights and is *admitted as a widespread denominator in the judicial evaluation about the meaning and scope of a specific right.*[23] Since the concept of morality and the idea that morality is not conventional but natural has entered more powerfully on the scene of international relations governed by international law, according to Carozza, the gap between 'universal' and 'particular' becomes the heart of the problem of *human dignity* and judicial interpretation.[24] However, Carozza justly admits that the general principles involved in the interpretation and adjudication of

[18]See Shelton (2002), p. 304.

[19]See Preamble of the *American Convention of Human Rights* (Adopted at the Inter-American Specialized Conference on Human Rights, San Jose, Costa Rica, 22 November 1960).

[20]African Charter on Human Rights and Peoples' Rights was adopted at Nairobi in 1981, and entered into force in 1987; Arab Charter was adopted by the Council of the League of Arab States on 22 May 2004, entered into force in March 2008; and the ASEAN Charter as a constitution for the Association of Southeast Asian Nations adopted on 13 November 2007.

[21]Fitzmaurice (2013). In this respect, M. Fitzmaurice cites the ICJ Advisory Opinion in *Reservations to the Genocide Convention* (1951) where the Court refers for the first time to 'non-reciprocal' or 'unilateral international humanitarian obligations' included in the Genocide Convention.

[22]*Id.*

[23]Carozza (2008), pp. 931–932.

[24]*Id.*

human rights, such as 'equality', 'justice', 'peace', 'democracy', 'freedom' or 'common good', are foundational aspirations that have a multiplicity of possible values and implications that may diverge in the context.[25] Given this characteristic, human rights have undetermined meanings that make them susceptible to substantial manipulation, and therefore they require *interpretation*.[26] So in essence, *interpretation* becomes a process of seeking '*to persuade the relevant interpretative community to adopt a particular meaning of a standard protected under an international human rights treaty*' (Tobin 2010, p. 13).

In addition to the interpretation problems posed by human rights as foundational aspirations, there are also specific interpretative difficulties that derive from the very specificity of human rights treaties. For example, in a recent comprehensive analysis of interpretation of human rights treaties, Malgosia Fitzmaurice discusses the specificity of human rights treaties as derived from their 'constitutional', 'non reciprocal' nature and specific subject matter. According to the author, one common and important feature that renders the interpretation of human rights treaties *special* in comparison with the interpretation of other treaties is given by their 'so called "constitutional" nature', particularly, by the '*non reciprocal*' nature of the rights and obligations enshrined in the human rights treaties (Fitzmaurice 2013). This 'non reciprocal nature' is influencing the 'object and purpose' of human rights treaties, and it becomes determinative in the adoption by human rights' tribunals of an often strong teleological approach to interpretation.[27] In Fitzmaurice's view, the 'object and purpose' also influences the emphasis that the human rights *fora* put on the effectiveness principle and on the development of the so-called *pro-homine*, or *ad personam* approach.[28] Another common feature underlined by Fitzmaurice relates to the *subject matter* of the human rights treaties. Such *subject matter* appears to have 'a fundamental impact well beyond that found in relation to most, if not all, other treaties', and it confers a *pro homine* character to interpretation.[29] These characteristics, which distinguish human rights treaties from other types of treaties, certainly imprint a peculiar character on the interpretation of human rights treaties.

Given these specific traits of human rights treaties, it is not surprising that the interpretation of the *European Convention* by the ECtHR has raised scholarly debates. One such debate is related, for instance, to the scope and the principles that should govern interpretation. Arato, for example, states that the ECHR as a whole and its provisions individually are susceptible of evolution under certain conditions.[30] However, as observed by Mahoney, 'the open-textured language and the structure of the Convention *leaves the [ECtHR] significant opportunities for*

[25] *Id.*

[26] *Id.*

[27] *Id.*

[28] *Id.* M. Fitzmaurice notes that it is generally admitted that 'human rights instruments require a more expansive attitude toward their interpretation than has been applied when interpreting of other types of international law treaties'.

[29] *Id.*

[30] Arato (2011), p. 11 (emphasis added).

*choice in interpretation*; and in exercising that choice, particularly when faced with changed circumstances and attitudes in society, the [ECtHR] makes new law' (Mahoney 1998, p. 2). However, it does not mean that the rights enshrined in human rights treaties could be interpreted in whatever manner. Several principles are provided in this regard by the recent scholarship analysing the interpretation of the *European Convention of Human Rights* by the Strasbourg Court.

For example, accordingly to Letsas, who focuses on the interpretative ethos of the ECtHR, it is nowhere written in the European Convention that the ECtHR should interpret the Convention in a strict way (Letsas 2010a, p. 267). A number of factors, such as changes in beliefs and progress in many areas of human knowledge, are, usually, thought to affect the meaning we feel inclined to attribute to human rights concepts.[31] Notwithstanding, as Letsas rightly points out, it would be within the judge's responsibility to adjust the meaning of the ECHR provisions to such contemporary changes and circumstances while respecting the intention of the European Convention's drafters.[32] Thus, even if the Convention's human rights provisions appear to be drafted in abstract, general terms, the drafters in 1950 are thought to have had, nevertheless, a 'concrete intention about which situations in their view human rights cover'.[33] It follows that the most important limit in discovering the true nature and content of people's rights is established by the human rights Court's interpretation.[34] This process implies the ECtHR's obligation to reason in *good faith*, which in Letsas' view, is akin to seeking 'to discover the principles that underline and justify human rights and apply them to the case at hand' while striving 'to justify its decisions according to a scheme of principles that represent an intelligible and coherent vision of justice'.[35] And essentially important in this regard, as the same author underlines, it becomes the fact that the ECtHR must be *consistent* with itself in applying the Convention's rights. It implies that the Court, simply, '*cannot rely on one principle to decide a case and then offend that very same principle to decide the next case*'.[36] It is worth adding that an important aspect of the interpretation of the European Convention's human rights relates to certain provisions therein, such as Articles 17 and 18,[37] which provide for a

[31]Letsas (2010a), p. 267.

[32]*Id.*

[33]*Id*, p. 268.

[34]Letsas (2012), p. 23.

[35]*Id.*

[36]*Id* (emphasis added).

[37]Article 17 of the ECHR provides for Prohibition of abuse of rights:

> Nothing in this Convention may be interpreted as implying for any State, group or person any rights to engage in any activity or perform any act aimed at the destruction of any of the rights and freedoms set forth therein or at their limitation to a greater extent than is provided for the Convention.

Article 18 provides for Limitation on use of restrictions on rights:

> The restrictions permitted under this Convention to the said rights and freedoms shall not be applied for any purpose other than those for which they have been prescribed.

*pro homine* framework of interpretation.[38] These provisions require, in principle, that rights restrictions be interpreted narrowly against the state.[39] And this is due to the essential rights of man that are derived not from one's being a national of a certain state but purely from the person's attribute of being a *human being*.[40]

Finally, it is widely admitted in the legal scholarship that the ECHR evolves especially by means of interpretation of its provisions by the Strasbourg Court and that through its own case law, this Court has made the Convention a 'living instrument' (Letsas 2010a, b). The European Court developed its own labels for interpretative techniques in order to give meaning to the Convention's provisions, such as 'living instrument', 'practical and effective rights', 'dynamic' or 'evolutive interpretation', 'margin of appreciation', 'common values' or 'commonly accepted standards', etc.[41] In regard to these interpretative techniques, usually called *doctrines*, Letsas provides a detailed analysis that aims to map out ECtHR's interpretative ethos and, in general, interpretation of human rights treaties. He observes that what all of these techniques/methods or doctrines, specific to the ECtHR's treaty interpretation have in common, is the rejection of the idea that 'the Convention's rights must be interpreted in the light of what their meaning was back in the 1950s' (Letsas 2007, p. 59). Letsas strongly and justly believes that the interpretation of the ECHR's provisions should be creative rather than strict and not isolated from the evolution of law (Letsas 2010a, b, p. 267). And this idea clearly conforms to the abstract belief of the drafters in the *moral objectivity* and *universality of human rights* since the drafters, according to Letsas, intended 'to protect the fundamental rights that people are entitled to' rather than 'to protect those rights that they were fifty years ago'.[42] It results that the existence of the ECHR as a 'living instrument' implies an absolutely necessary *evolutive interpretation* of human rights since this evolutive interpretation is essential for the ECtHR's *legitimacy* (Letsas 2012, pp. 23–24). This evolutive character of the interpretation of the European Convention involves a constant work for the Strasbourg Court to adjust, modify and reshape the scope and meaning of the Convention's rights 'in the light of the body of principles' that this Court uses.[43]

That the Convention is a 'living instrument' that must be interpreted in *the present-day conditions* is a feature observed by Letsas as existing at the core of the ECtHR's practice of human rights interpretation, even from this Court's inception.[44] And precisely, this *evolutive interpretation* adopted by the ECtHR should be

---

[38]Fitzmaurice (2013). The author also refers to Article 29 of the American Convention of Human Rights (providing for 'Restrictions Regarding Interpretation'), and Article 60 and 61 of the African Charter (providing for 'Applicable Principles').

[39]*Id.*

[40]See Preamble of the *American Convention of Human Rights*, as also Preamble of the *African Charter on Human Rights and Peoples' Rights*.

[41]Letsas (2012), p. 3. See also on this aspect Fitzmaurice (2013).

[42]Letsas (2010b), p. 268 (emphasis added).

[43]Letsas (2012), pp. 23–24.

[44]*Id*, p. 2.

understood as the *moral reading* of the Convention's rights.[45] Thus, in respect of the ECtHR's *treaty interpretation*, Letsas' main argument is that 'treaty interpretation is fundamentally neither about the meaning of the words nor about the intention of states parties'.[46] It is in essence 'an inherently evaluative exercise in seeking to determine how fact-independent moral values normatively constrain the pursuit of states joint projects'.[47] As argued in the scholarship, this characteristic of the European Convention as a contract by which sovereign states agree to limitations upon their sovereignty justifies the Convention's role of guaranteeing the protection of human rights, which must be interpreted in a dynamic, evolutive manner so as to allow its development with time (the Convention's lawmaking character) (Harris et al. 2014, p. 8). What justifies the European Convention as an instrument of public order is that, by its interpretation and application, *the Convention imposes objective obligations upon the contracting states for the protection of human rights in Europe*, which evolve in the direction of becoming Europe's constitutional bill of rights.[48] Therefore, it may be true that the *special characteristics* of human rights and obligations justify the application of approaches that differ from those of traditional international law, as some scholars believe (Fitzmaurice 2013). In this regard, the ILC Study Group observes that 'it has become a practice of human rights bodies to adopt readings of human rights conventions that look for their *effect utile* to an extent perhaps wider than regular treaties' (ILC 2006, p. 216, para 428).

However, what is essentially important in respect of the interpretation of human rights, as Fitzmaurice observes, is the fact the human rights tribunals assert with frequency that their interpretative methods are consistent with the Vienna Convention's customary rules of interpretation (Fitzmaurice 2013). Nevertheless, it has also been observed that, despite this general compliance with the VCLT rules, the human rights *fora* adopted sometimes interpretative positions that are hard to reconcile with human rights treaty provisions before them (ILC 2006, p. 216, para 428). Such positions, which are described by Fitzmaurice as 'at least expanding on traditional methods of interpretation, if not as introducing interpretative techniques outside the VCLT provisions',[49] could, certainly, lead some scholars to consider the human rights regimes (including the ECHR) as 'self-contained', promoting judicial activism. However, there is a perceived move

[45]*Id*, p. 3.

[46]*Id.*

[47]*Id.* In Letsas' view 'interpretation' used by the ECtHR means any general normative proposition which the Court has systematically endorsed in its case law, in relation to either the nature of treaty interpretation or the nature of human rights treaty interpretation.

[48]Harris et al. (2014), p. 8.

[49]In Fitzmaurice (2013), the author explains that such positions are possible due to two reasons: one is because the VCLT rules of interpretation are themselves far from being clear and fluid in their relationship to each other, and the other is because the concept of human rights and the treaty formulations of the rights are frequently general, vague, and subjective.

today towards a uniform methodology of interpreting human rights treaties by human rights tribunals.[50] And this move is regarded as the human rights tribunals' *compliance with the VCLT rules of interpretation*, which according to Fitzmaurice, develops 'possibly, in a rather expansive, but nevertheless legitimate manner'.[51] Therefore, on this aspect, we witness an emerging consensus among international scholars.[52]

In sum, given the particularities of human life, or human personality (e.g., dignity, liberty, equality, justice), the fact that they require protection under human rights standards, and that these human rights can come into conflict as they constantly evolve, to determine the extent of human rights protected by the European Convention can often prove to be a difficult task.

## 5.3 Case Law Analysis and Scholarship

### *5.3.1 Scope of the Analysis and Methodology*

This chapter examines some of the alleged difficulties in interpreting human rights provisions under the *European Convention of Human Rights and Fundamental Freedoms*. It examines these difficulties from an empirical perspective, providing analyses of the cases which, in my view, express the ECtHR ethos on treaty interpretation, and from a theoretical perspective, which links the analysis of cases with views expressed in the academic literature on the topic of *interpretation of human rights treaties*. The main goal of this chapter is to show how the ECtHR makes use of the customary rules and methods of treaty interpretation and applies them to its human rights specialised context, and also whether the ECtHR's process of interpretation of the *European Convention of Human Rights* (ECHR) is influenced by the techniques and general methods of treaty interpretation greatly developed by the ICJ. A secondary goal is to determine how the ECtHR applies its own specific doctrines of interpretation along with the general (customary) rules of treaty interpretation; how they interplay. In this purpose, the case analyses provided below will attempt to respond to the following specific questions: whether in interpreting the European Convention's provisions the ECtHR resorts to the same canons of treaty interpretation as does the ICJ, using common interpretative patterns in dealing with similar difficulties in interpreting the text of treaties (e.g., insufficiently clear, ambiguous, dubious, vague, silent); whether the customary rules of interpretation embodied in the 1969 VCLT are applied by the ECtHR simultaneously and in combination with its own special interpretative techniques, often called 'doctrines' or, conversely, whether the ECtHR gives preference to its

[50] *Id.*

[51] *Id.*

[52] *Id.*

own techniques/doctrines of interpretation. In addition, the ECtHR case law analyses will attempt to determine whether there is *continuity* and *consistency* (coherence) in the practice of the ECtHR on the application of the customary rules of treaty interpretation, considering both pre and post the 1969 VCLT periods. The *consistency* (coherence) in the ECtHR's interpretative approaches is crucially important in assessing whether the practice of the ECtHR on treaty interpretation could contribute to the fragmentation of international law (is 'part' of the 'fragmentation' problem) or, conversely, could be a tool for unification of international law (is 'part' of the solution to 'fragmentation').

Although all the cases in which the ECtHR has resorted to the general rules of interpretation reflected in the VCLT could be discussed, a selection of cases is necessary, and it must be made on the basis of their value in demonstrating the interpretative issues proposed to be examined in this chapter. In making the case selection, as mentioned in this book's introduction, I followed Yin's theory related to the scope and meaning of a 'case study', according to which 'the case study, like experiment, does not represent a "sample", and in doing a case study [the] goal will be to expand and generalise theories (analytic generalisation) and not to enumerate frequencies (statistical generalisation)'.[53] Thus, the analyses of the selected case law I provided in this chapter contribute to expanding and generalising the existent theory of application by the ECtHR (and by other specialised human rights adjudicative bodies) of the VCLT's universally accepted methodology of interpretation, together with the 'rules' of interpretation (autonomous doctrines) that the Strasbourg Court itself created. According to this methodological rationale, each of the cases selected below illustrates a different aspect of treaty interpretation performed by the ECtHR (relating to the type of difficulties it encounters in the construction of the text of the Convention's provisions) and attempts to answer how the relational theories play out in the context of the practice of treaty interpretation of this Court.

The case analyses in the following sections and their subsections are mainly organised around several questions/topics. They focus on the emphasis put by the ECtHR on a method, rule or principle of interpretation in a given case while revealing the other methods/rules and principles that this Court adopts gradually (explicitly or implicitly) in solving various treaty interpretative difficulties (e.g., apparently clear or insufficiently clear text, ambiguous/dubious text, vague language of the text or silent text – not providing for the circumstances of the case). Some of the cases selected by necessity require more extensive analysis than others in order to show the tendency of this Court to approach broadly the treaty interpretation process, while other cases, however, will be analysed more succinctly and on the basis of their value in demonstrating the interpretative issues that this chapter deals with in addition.

[53]See Yin (2003), p. 11 (emphasis added) (According to Yin the *explanatory case study* deals with 'how' or 'why' questions).

### 5.3.2 *Pre-VCLT Interpretative Approaches*

The reception by the ECtHR of international law and, in particular, the customary rules of treaty interpretation has not been generally contested in the scholarship. From the viewpoint of the 1964 ILC Report on the Law of Treaties, the international tribunals' jurisprudence furnished examples of all the different approaches to interpretation: textualist, subjective, teleological. However, none of these were viewed as being exclusively the correct one, and their use in any particular case was seen, to some extent, to be a matter of choice and appreciation.[54] Nevertheless, in reference to the human rights tribunals' approach to interpretation, M. Fitzmaurice observes that human rights *fora* developed a methodology of interpretation prior to the VCLT, which broadly recognised the particular importance of the teleological method of interpretation (Fitzmaurice 2013).

The case analyses provided in this part (Sect. 5.3.2) show that, even from the beginning of its practice of interpretation, the Strasbourg Court has tended to lean towards the reception and recognition of customary rules of treaty interpretation. Moreover, despite the difference in the characteristics of the treaties interpreted by the ECtHR and ICJ, these courts' approaches to customary rules of interpretation (both explicit, by expressly stating so, and implicit, by suggesting or applying a rule without a technical description appended to it) appear to display *common patterns* prior to the 1969 VCLT's adoption. The case analysis starts with the question whether there were any rules of interpretation at the ECtHR before the VCLT's adoption.

#### 5.3.2.1 Reliance on Rules of Interpretation?

The pre-VCLT ***Case of Lawless v. Ireland* (1961)**,[55] the first Strasbourg Court's judgment involving the interpretation of human rights, epitomises the 'ordinary meaning' rule—the starting point of interpretation – as is taken equally by the ICJ in a majority of its treaty interpretation cases and as is taken by the ECtHR in the majority of cases analysed in this chapter. The *Lawless* case shows reliance on the three primary dimensions of the 'ordinary meaning' of the treaty terms in their 'context' and according to the 'object and purpose' of the treaty. The Court provided in this case a *holistic* interpretation, despite highlighting the text (textualist method) of the Convention's provision at issue as being *clear* and *unequivocal*. *Lawless* is also one of the earliest uses by the ECtHR's organs of

---

[54]ILC (1964), p. 4.

[55]*Case of Lawless v. Ireland* (No. 3), (Application no. 332/57), Judgment (Merits), Strasbourg, 1 July 1961. *Lawless* was the first lawsuit taken by a private citizen against a state, and brought into operation the provisions of the Convention by inaugurating the precedent for individuals to appear for the first time as party before the ECtHR.

the doctrine of 'margin of appreciation'.[56] It is related to Mr. Lawless, a member of the banned organisation the Irish Republican Army (IRA), who was held without trial (internment). Mr. Lawless complained that this internment amounted to a breach of Article 5 (the right to liberty and security of person),[57] Article 6 (the right to fair trial), Article 7 (no punishment without law) and Article 15 (measures of derogation from the Convention's obligations in time of emergencies by the High Contracting Parties)[58] of the ECHR by Ireland. The Court had to determine whether or not the facts of the case disclosed that the Irish Government failed in its obligations under the Convention (fact contended by the Irish Government), respectively whether the Irish Government derogated from Article 5 in order to permit detention without charge or trial, as the applicant was detained between 13 July and 11 December 1957.

The Court's starting point in interpreting the Convention's provisions at issue is the 'plain and natural meaning of the terms in their context'.[59] This approach is

---

[56]See e.g. O'Boyle (1998), p. 715. The author mentions *Greece v. United Kingdom*, App. No. 176/56, 2 Yearbook European Commission on Human Rights 174 (1959), as the first case when the ECtHR used the doctrine of 'margin of appreciation'. See also the application of 'margin of appreciation' along with customary rules of interpretation (an approach based on the 'ordinary meaning' of the terms in their 'context', and according to the 'object and purpose') in *Case 'relating to certain aspects of the laws on the use of languages in education in Belgium' v. Belgium*, (Application no 1474/62; 1677/62; 1691/62; 1769/63; 1994/63; 2126/64), Judgment, Strasbourg, 9 February, 1967.

[57]Article 5 (art. 5) of the Convention reads as follows:

> (1) Everyone has the right to liberty and security of person. No one shall be deprived of his liberty save in the following cases and in accordance with a procedure prescribed by law:
> (a) the lawful detention of a person after conviction by a competent court;
> (b) the lawful arrest or detention of a person for non-compliance with the lawful order of a court or in order to secure the fulfillment of any obligation prescribed by law;
> (c) the lawful arrest or detention of a person effected for the purpose of bringing him before the competent legal authority on reasonable suspicion of having committed an offence or when it is reasonably considered necessary to prevent his committing an offence or fleeing after having done so;
> (d) the detention of a minor by lawful order for the purpose of educational supervision of his lawful detention for the purpose of bringing him before the competent legal authority;
> (e) the lawful detention of persons for the prevention of the spreading of infectious diseases, of persons of unsound mind, alcoholics or drug addicts or vagrants;
> (f) the lawful arrest or detention of a person to prevent his effecting an unauthorised entry into the country or of a person against whom action is being taken with a view to deportation or extradition.
> (2) Everyone who is arrested shall be informed promptly, in a language which he understands, of the reasons for his arrest and of any charge against him.
> (3) Everyone arrested or detained in accordance with the provisions of paragraph 1 (c) of this Article (art. 5-1-c) shall be brought promptly before a judge or other officer authorised by law to exercise judicial power and shall be entitled to trial within a reasonable time or to release pending trial. Release may be conditioned by guarantees to appear for trial.

[58]Article 15 of the ECHR provides for measures of derogation from Convention's obligations in time of emergencies by the High Contracting parties.

[59]*Lawless* (No. 3) (1961).

disclosed in certain phrases of the Court's judgment, as, for example, in respect of Article 5, which provides for the right to liberty and security aimed to protect the right of a person not to be arbitrarily deprived of his/her liberty. The Court states that 'the *plain and natural meaning of the wording* of both paragraph 1(c) and 3 of Article 5 . . . entails *clearly* the obligation to bring everyone arrested or detained in any circumstances provided by these provisions before a judge'.[60] Thus, the Court ascertains that it deals with a *clear* and *unequivocal* text.

Additionally, the Court expressly employs the 'context' of the provision from which the meaning of the words is extracted, finding that Article 5(1) (c) on detention has to be construed in conjunction with Article 5(3) on entitlement of 'everyone' to trial within a reasonable time, 'with which it forms a whole'.[61] The reference to the rule of 'context' as a customary rule was similarly confirmed by the ICJ, for example in the *IMCO* (1960) case.[62] As it was shown in the preceding chapter, the ICJ had to interpret in *IMCO* a sufficiently clear provision of a multilateral treaty, and it disclosed the proper connection between two important phrases (clauses) of the provision, relying on the 'context' rule. It stressed that '[t] he words of Article 28(a) must be read in their natural and ordinary meaning, in the sense which they would normally have in their *context*'.[63]

By stressing the 'natural and customary meaning of the words'[64] in *Lawless*, the ECtHR recognises this first principle of treaty interpretation. Accordingly, the Court finds that the provision leaves little room for exceptions to the right to trial. However, despite ensuring the clarity of the text of Article 5, the Court feels the need to confirm this result by adopting a teleological approach, in the light of this provision's own scope and purpose. It finds on the 'object and purpose' rule that 'the text of Article 5, paragraphs 1 (c) and 3 . . . is sufficiently clear in itself and means'.[65] Also, the Court interprets the provisions of Article 5 in the light of the object and purpose and context of the Convention taken as a whole, finding that 'the meaning thus arrived at by grammatical analysis is fully in harmony with the purpose of the Convention which is to protect the freedom and security of the individual against arbitrary detention or arrest'.[66] It concludes that there is no legal foundation for detention without trial. Here, the ECtHR appears to provide a strong signal statement for those states that seek to circumvent the protections afforded by the Convention.

---

[60] *Id* (emphasis added).

[61] *Id*, para 14.

[62] *Constitution of the Maritime Safety Committee of the Inter-governmental Maritime Consultative Organization (IMCO)*, Advisory Opinion of 8 June 1960, I.C.J. Rep. 1960, 15, p. 160 (see this case analysed in Chap. 4 of this book).

[63] *Id*. The ICJ added: 'One context at which the Court looks, is, of course, the other parts of the treaty. That is, it reads the treaty, and particular articles thereof, as a *whole*' (emphasis added).

[64] *Lawless* (No. 3) (1961), para 14.

[65] *Id.*

[66] *Id.*

Furthermore, in an endorsement of prevalent customary rules of treaty interpretation, the ECtHR holds that since the terms of Article 5 appear sufficiently clear, 'in accordance with a well established rule concerning the interpretation of international treaties, it is not permissible to resort to preparatory work when the meaning of the clauses to be construed is clear and unequivocal'.[67] Again, this approach appears to resemble the one adopted in the *IMCO* case, for example, when the ICJ held that only if the words of the provision at issue were ambiguous in any way would resort to other methods of construction be needed.[68] However, it is at this point when the ECtHR appears to diverge from the 'well established rule' it recalls, by seeking confirmation of the result from the preparatory work of Article 5 of the Convention. In doing so, the Court relies on the subjective method, cautiously admitting, however, that 'even reference to the preparatory work can reveal no ground for questioning the Commission's interpretation of Article 5'[69] and that this article 'leaves no room for doubt about the intention of the authors of the Convention…'.[70] Yet, despite a cautious, inconclusive language, the ECtHR appears to utilise the *travaux preparatoire* of Article 5 as a confirmatory test, just as the ICJ did on some similar occasions, when it, too, had found the text at issue to be *sufficiently clear*, or even *clear*, presenting no difficulties in interpretation. Such an example is the *Ambatielos* (1952) case, where despite having specifically declared that '[i]n any case where as here, the text to be interpreted *is clear*, there is no occasion to resort to preparatory work'; the ICJ did so in order to confirm the intention of the drafters of the provision in question.[71]

Reliance on the preparatory work (*travaux*) is clearly revealed further, when the ECtHR, by using another customary rule of interpretation that later will find codification in Article 33 of the VCLT (interpretation of treaties authenticated in two or more languages), finds that the English version of Article 5 was in line with the French version of it.[72] The Court states: 'that proposal was based on a text introduced in the United Nations by a group of States which included not only the United Kingdom but also France; that the United Nations text was prepared in a number of languages … particularly in that of Article 5, paragraph 1 (c) (art. 5-1-c), during the preparatory work at the Council of Europe were intended to bring it into line with the French text'.[73] Even more, the clear reliance of the *travaux* is evidenced when the Court concludes that 'the English version cannot therefore be regarded as the dominant text; that on the contrary, all the evidence goes to show that the changes made in the English version, particularly in that of

[67] *Id*, para 11.

[68] *IMCO* (1960).

[69] *Lawless* (No. 3) (1961), para 11.

[70] *Id*, para 12.

[71] See Chap. 4 of this book for the analysis of the *Ambatielos* Case (*Greece v. United Kingdom*), ICJ, Preliminary objections, Judgment of July 1st, 1952, p. 24 (emphasis added).

[72] *Lawless* (No. 3) (1961), para 11.

[73] *Id*.

Article 5, paragraph 1 (c) (art. 5-1-c), during the preparatory work at the Council of Europe were intended to bring it into line with the French text, which, apart from a few drafting alterations of no importance to the present case, was essentially the same as that finally adopted for Article 5 (art. 5) of the Convention'.[74]

Ultimately then, despite assurances that the 'plain' and 'natural' meaning of Articles 5(1)(c) and 5(3) follows 'from the precise words used and from the impression created by their context',[75] the ECtHR seeks to test the result by virtue of the effectiveness principle. It finds on this principle basis that 'the construction placed by the [domestic] Court on the aforementioned provisions were not correct, anyone suspected of harboring an intent to commit an offence could be arrested and detained for an unlimited period on the strength ... whereas such an assumption, with all its implications of arbitrary power, would lead to conclusions repugnant to the fundamental principles of the Convention'.[76] Important to mention in this connection is the Strasbourg Court's heavy reliance on the doctrine of the 'margin of appreciation' in this case as an autonomous means of interpretation developed by this Court.[77] This doctrine is revealed, for example, when the Court determines whether there is a 'public emergency threatening the life of the nation', holding that the Contracting States would have a certain margin of appreciation.[78]

Like the ICJ on numerous occasions when it emphasised the textualist interpretation, also the ECtHR in *Lawless* appears to stress more this approach,[79] conveying that the text of the Convention is presumed to be the expression of the authentic intention of the parties so it must be taken as it stands.[80] In other words, an interpretation of the Convention provisions is not permitted to add something that it is not there. The ECtHR's emphasis on the text appears to be justified as the Court upholds the notion of human protections in the face of serious internal state

[74]*Id.*

[75]*Id*, para 14.

[76]*Id.*

[77]See O'Boyle (1998), p. 715, for comments on this aspect.

[78]*Id*, paras 28–30. See also on this point the Individual Opinion of Judge Maridakis in the *Lawless* case.

[79]*Id*, para 14. The Court's emphasis on the textualist method can clearly be observed when it repeatedly indicates the plain and ordinary meaning of the terms of Article 5, as, for example, '... paragraph 3 (art. 5-3) stipulates categorically that "everyone arrested or detained in accordance with the provisions of paragraph 1 (c) of this Article (art. 5-1-c) shall be brought promptly before a judge ..." and "shall be entitled to trial within a reasonable time"'; 'whereas it plainly entails the obligation to bring everyone arrested or detained in any of the circumstances contemplated by the provisions of paragraph 1 (c) (art. 5-1-c) before a judge for the purpose of examining the question of deprivation of liberty or for the purpose of deciding on the merits'; 'whereas such is the plain and natural meaning of the wording of both paragraph 1 (c) and paragraph 3 of Article 5 (art. 5-1-c, art. 5-3)...'.

[80]See a similar approach of interpretation in *Case relating to certain aspects of the laws on the use of languages in education in Belgium v. Belgium*, (Merits), Appl. No. 1474/62; 1677/62; 1691/62; 1769/63, 1994/63; 2126/64, Judgment of 23 July, 1968.

problems[81] (a position similarly adopted by the ICJ on occasions), which, of course, is exactly what the Convention was set up to protect. Therefore, despite highlighting the text (textualist method), the ECtHR provides in *Lawless* a *holistic* approach to interpretation, equally valuing and applying other rules and principles of treaty interpretation (context, object and purpose, *travaux preparatoire*, 'interpretation of treaties authenticated in two or more languages', good faith and effectiveness principles), which will later find reflection in the texts of Articles 31, 32 and 33 of the VCLT.

#### 5.3.2.2 Reliance on Customary Rules, Principles and the Convention's 'Special Character'

It has been pointed out in the scholarship that a restrictive interpretation is hardly admissible in the context of the European Convention (Tobin 2010, p. 13). However, according to Tobin, since the meaning of a particular right enshrined in the Convention is usually surrounded by uncertainty, there is a need to persuade states and the broader interpretative community to adopt a particular meaning of that right.[82] Tobin considers that the achievement of *a* meaning of a right, which is designed to persuade *an interpretative community*, requires a certain interpretative methodology that will enhance the persuasiveness of the interpretation provided.[83] While the traditional techniques of interpretation (general rules of treaty interpretation) are admitted by the Strasbourg Court and proved to be necessary in interpreting the Convention' rights, however, they proved also to be insufficient in delivering the meaning of a human right.[84]

The scholarship admits that in some cases prior to the adoption of the 1969 VCLT, the ECtHR has shown flexibility in employing what it deemed were the customary rules of interpretation and other principles or guidelines.[85] The analysis of the ***Case of Wemhoff v. Germany* (1968)**[86] will illustrate this aspect, the ECtHR having to interpret an *unclear*, *ambiguous* text. Indeed, it is an early case where the ECtHR showed clearly openness towards understanding the human rights principles as public standards of morality that override other considerations related to state interests that could contradict human rights. *Wemhoff* is used here to show how the Court relies on the customary rules and principles of treaty interpretation in a broader manner (holistically) while underlining the Convention's 'special

[81]E.g. *Exchange of Greek and Turkish Population* (*Lausanne Convention VI, January 30th, 1923, Article 2*), Advisory Opinion, PCIJ, Series B, No. 10, 1925; *Question Concerning the Acquisition of Polish Nationality*, Advisory Opinion of 15 September 1923, Series B, PCIJ, No. 7. ( see Chap. 4 for analysis of these cases).

[82]Tobin (2010), p. 13.

[83]*Id*, p. 14.

[84]*Id.*

[85]See e.g. Orakhelashvili (2003), p. 534.

[86]*Case of Wemhoff v. Germany*, (Application of 2122/64), ECtHR, Judgment of 27 June 1968.

character'. At issue in this case was Article 5(3) and the definition of the notion of the 'reasonable time' to trial in the entitlement to trial, notably whether this entitlement to trial was 'within a reasonable time or to release pending trial', in the case of Mr. Wemhoff, who was arrested under suspicion of being involved in offences of breach of trust.[87] Wemhoff requested the Court to decide whether or not the facts reveal any violation by the Federal Republic of Germany of its obligations under Articles 5(3) and 6(1) of the Convention.

In interpreting Article 5(3), the ECtHR expressly refers to the rule of 'ordinary' or 'plain' meaning of the terms in their context, recalling that '[t]o understand the precise scope of the provision in question, it must be set in its context'.[88] But the key aspect here is that 'a purely grammatical interpretation would leave the judicial authorities with a choice between two obligations, that of conducting the proceedings until judgment within a reasonable time or that of releasing the accused pending trial necessary against certain guarantees'.[89] Since States Parties could not be left with such a choice, the Court is compelled to consult the preparatory work, which is in conformity with the approach of both the rules formulated later in the VCLT and the ICJ's interpretative practice, especially when dealing with *ambiguous* treaty texts. Reliance on the *travaux preparatoire* of Article 5(3) and in addition on the effectiveness principle leads the ECtHR to confirm the intention of the drafters. The Court states that '[i]t is inconceivable that they should have intended to permit their judicial authorities, at the price of release of the accused, to protract proceedings beyond a reasonable time. This would, moreover, be flatly contrary to the provision in Article 6 (1)'[90]—thus suggesting that the 'reasonable time' was that period until the trial.

Further, since the Court here is confronted with the difficulty of choosing between 'two versions of a treaty which are equally authentic but not exactly the same',[91] it expressly employs the customary rule that deals with it, namely 'interpretation of treaties authenticated in two or more languages' (later codified in Article 33 of the VCLT). The Court recalls that it must follow established international law precedents and interpret these versions 'in a way that will reconcile them

[87] Article 5(3) of the Convention provides:

> Everyone arrested or detained in accordance with the provisions of paragraph 1 of this article shall be brought promptly before a judge or other officer authorized by law to exercise judicial power and shall be entitled to trial within a reasonable time or to release pending trial. Release may be conditioned by guarantees to appear for trial.

Article 6(1) provides:

> in the determining of civil rights and obligations or any criminal charge against him, everyone is entitled to a fair and public hearing within a reasonable time by an independent and impartial tribunal established by the law.

[88] *Wemhoff* (1968), para 5.

[89] *Id*, para 4.

[90] *Id*. The Court mentions that Article 6(1) poses questions of interpretation similar to those raised in Article 5(3), in particular, regarding the term 'time'.

[91] *Id*.

as far as possible'.[92] A similar rationale for this rule's application could be observed in the ICJ's past decisions, for instance, in the *Mavrommatis* (1924) case, where the ICJ had encountered similar difficulties in ascertaining the meaning of certain general treaty terms. The ICJ held that 'when two versions possessing equal authority exist one of which appears to have a wider bearing than the other, it [the Court] is bound to adopt the more limited interpretation which can be made to harmonise with both versions and which, as far as it goes, is doubtless in accordance with the common intention of the Parties'.[93]

What is worth noting in this case is the ECtHR's emphasis on the 'special character' of the Convention and on the fact that the Convention is a 'law-making treaty'.[94] The Court's active role in providing a dynamic, evolutive interpretation of the Convention is clearly revealed when stressing the necessity 'to seek the interpretation that is most appropriate in order *to realize the aim and achieve the object of the treaty, not that which would restrict to the greatest possible degree* the obligations undertaken by the Parties'.[95] This approach shows clearly the consistency of the ECtHR with the 'object and purpose' of the Convention, that of giving priority to an effective protection of individual freedoms over state sovereignty. In addition to the teleological method, highly emphasised, the Court adopts in *Wemhoff* the textualist and subjective methods, clearly relying on the customary rules and principles of interpretation, which later will find formulation in the text of Articles 31, 32, and 33 of the VCLT.

## *5.3.3 Post-VCLT Interpretative Approaches*

### 5.3.3.1 Broader Implications of International Law

Although the reception of general international law and, in particular, of the Vienna rules by the ECtHR is not contested, opinions in the scholarship are divided on the extent of this reception. Some of such opinions are more flexible than are others about the role of the Vienna rules in interpreting the European Convention of Human Rights. For example, while admitting that the ECtHR rarely makes a specific reference to incorporation of general international law into the Convention's context, Charney admits, nonetheless, that this Court has made clear that it would take into account especially general principles of law in treaty interpretation (Charney 1998, p. 210). In this respect, the ECtHR itself acknowledges in the *Golder* (1975) case that the Legal Committee of the Consultative Assembly of

---

[92]*Id.*

[93]*Mavrommatis Palestine Concessions Case* (*Greece v. Britain*), Judgment of 30 August, PCIJ, Ser A, No. 2, 1924, p. 19. (the terms in Article 11 (which in the original versions contrasted) of the Mandate of Palestine: a) public ownership or control of the natural resources of the country or of the public works, services and utilities).

[94]*Wemhoff* (1968), para 8.

[95]*Id* (emphasis added).

the Council of Europe foresaw, in August 1950, that 'the Commission and the Court must necessarily apply such principles in the execution of their duties and thus considered it to be "unnecessary" to insert a specific clause to this effect in the Convention'.[96] Interestingly, as observed by Gardiner, the ECtHR in *Golder* firmly 'espoused use of the Vienna rules well before the ICJ gave its full endorsement'.[97] Moreover, as shown earlier in the discussion on 'self-contained' regimes (in - Chap. 2), the ILC Study's findings show that the ECtHR itself has made it clear that 'the Convention rights should be read in harmony with that general law and without an *a priori* assumption that Convention rights would be overriding' (ILC 2006, p. 86).

According to Tzevelekos, the ECtHR has a significant number of interpretative tools at its disposal (Tzevelekos 2009, p. 627). And one of these tools is given by Article 31(3)(c) of the VCLT, which allows this Court 'to enjoy wide discretion in the choices it often has to make regarding the dilemma between unconditional integration into the international legal order and its (regional) human rights specialty'.[98] Although Article 31(3)(c) of the VCLT represents the codification of just one tool of the larger interpretation process, the ILC introduced it as an autonomous method of interpretation, called 'systemic integration', which allows for the interpretation of international legal instruments in the light of 'any relevant rules of international law' (ILC 2006, p. 223). As the ILC points out, the application of Article 31(3)(c) concerns the possibility and extent of recourse to rules of the same level of generality and binding force as the treaty to be interpreted.[99] Generally, in respect of human rights regimes, as observed by Fitzmaurice in her recent study on the topic, Article 31(3)(c) stands as a basis for the human rights interpretative methodology. Moreover, this provision has even played an important role in the development by the human rights *fora* of a distinctive *pro homine* human rights approach to interpretation, as the *Golder* case (discussed below) can evidence (Fitzmaurice 2013).

However, as it was underlined in Chap. 3 of this book, Article 31(3)(c) of the VCLT is a provision that continues to generate controversy.[100] For example, Klabbers, who although is more skeptical than others towards the idea that 'interpretation' can meaningfully be subjected to rules of interpretation, admits that, at best and on its own, Article 31(3)(c) 'can only suggest that the sub-regimes be interpreted against the background of general international law' (Klabbers 2010, p. 33). Recently, in her analysis of the practice of the ECtHR, Forowicz instead is

---

[96]See *Case of Golder v. United Kingdom* (Application no. 4451/70, ECtHR, Judgment of 21 February, 1975), discussed below.

[97]Gardiner (2008), p. 17. The author mentions in this regard the *Arbitral Award of 31 July 1989 (Guinea-Bissau v. Senegal)* Judgment, [1991] ICJ Reports 53.

[98]Tzevelekos (2009), p. 627.

[99]*Id.* Generally, this Article refers to sources external to the treaty which may include other treaties, customary rules or general principles of law relevant in its interpretation.

[100]See Chap. 3 of this book on this aspect.

confident that this provision confirms that resort to 'relevant rules of international law' appears to operate in the ECtHR's practice as a clear means for projecting human rights law into the broader system of international law. And in this respect, Article 31(3)(c) is the most influential provision concerning the reception of international law at the ECtHR (Forowicz 2010, p. 58). Similarly, McInerney-Lankford observes that by means of this provision, in some cases treaties were invoked by the ECtHR to fill gaps where it could not provide the necessary protection or such protection appeared to the Court not explicitly provided (i.e., child rights provisions).[101] In the author's view, this resort of the ECtHR to other treaties constitutes an anti-fragmentation of international law tool and is due to an overriding concern of this Court with enhancing human rights protection that, clearly, it does not constitute a departure from international law, as some authors tend to believe.[102]

Also, in a more recent analysis concerning *lex specialis/lex generalis*, Sheeran's observation that 'any new rule is made taking into account other existing rules' (Sheeran 2014, p. 92) has implications upon both understanding the relationship between general international law and *lex specialis* and the problem of fragmentation in international law. Based on the mentioned assumption, the author concludes that the principle of 'systemic integration', as reflected in the VCLT, is based on a 'formal unity' of the legal system and also on a hierarchical relationship of rules of general international law over international human rights law.[103] Thus, because human rights law relies on the foundation of general international law, and a *unitary relationship* between the two bodies of law exists, this relationship is justly admitted as one that cannot be 'characterized by fragmentation'.[104] Some of the case analyses in this chapter can show that the ECtHR has resorted to the customary rule reflected in Article 31(3)(c) VCLT in order to find effective clarification of the principles on which human rights practice is based. As with the ICJ,[105] the ECtHR has also shown reliance on this customary rule to overcome discrepancies in human

[101]McInerney-Lankford (2012), p. 617. See, e.g., a recent case on this matter: *Raban v. Romania* (Application no. 25437/08), Judgment Strasbourg, 26 October 2010. The ECtHR made an explicit resort in this case (para 28) to Article 31(3) (c) of the VCLT: 'The Convention cannot be interpreted in a vacuum, but, in accordance with Article 31 § 3 (c) of the Vienna Convention on the Law of Treaties (1969), account is to be taken of any relevant rules of international law applicable to the Contracting Parties (*Streletz, Kessler and Krenz v. Germany* [GC], nos. 34044/96, 35532/97 and 44801/98, § 90, ECHR 2001-II).'

[102]*Id.*

[103]Sheeran (2014), p. 92.

[104]*Id*, p. 82.

[105]The most relevant example is *Legal Consequences for States of the Continued Presence of South Africa in Namibia*, (Advisory Opinion, 1971, I.C.J., 16, 31), where the ICJ held that 'an international instrument has to be interpreted and applied within the framework of the entire legal system prevailing at the time of its interpretation'.

rights protection, both prior to and after the adoption of the VCLT. In addition, a search on the ECHR website (HUDOC) shows the reliance of the Strasbourg Court on Article 31(3)(c) with even greater frequency in the last few years.[106] Consequently, the European Court of Human Rights appears itself to be a tool for promoting and extending the application of general international law, as well as diversifying this use by applying it to its special law. This resort, although just one interpretative means among others, strongly demonstrates that the ECtHR is relating the Convention's human rights provisions to general international law.[107] An illustrative example in this sense is the ***Case of "Vagrancy" v. Belgium* (1972)**,[108] in which the ECtHR applied the principle of 'systemic integration', later to be reflected in Article 31(3)(c) of the VCLT, before the VCLT entered into force in 1980. The case related to three Belgian nationals kept in detention for the suppression of vagrancy and begging.[109] The applicants complained of arbitrary detention and ill treatment while in detention such as punishments, confinement without privileges, hindrance of correspondence, violation of liberty of conscience and religion, etc. The issue of interpretation was whether internal Belgian law allowed

---

[106]Resort of the ECtHR to Article 31(3) (c) VCLT could be seen in recent cases, e.g., in: *Case of Oleynikov v. Russia*, Appl. No. 36703104, Judgment, Strasbourg, 14 March, 2013, at para 56; *Case of Nada v. Switzerland*, Appl. No. 10593108, Strasbourg, 12 September, 2012, para 169; *Case of Hirsi Jamaa and others v. Italy*, App. no. 27765/09, Judgment, Strasbourg, 23 February, 2012, at para 70; *Case of Cudak v. Lithuania*(GC), Appl. No. 15869/02, Judgment, 23 March, 2010, at para 56; *Fabris v. France*, Judgment (Merits), Appl. No. 16574108, Strasbourg, 7 February, 2013; *Case of Raban v. Romania*, (Application no. 25437/08), Judgment Strasbourg, 26 October 2010, at para 28; *Manoilescu and Dobrescu v. Romania and Russia*, Appl. no. 60861/00, Strasbourg, 3 March, 2005, at para 70, *Case of Al-Adsani v. The United Kingdom*, Appl. no. 35763/97, Judgment Strasbourg, 21 November 2001, para 55; *Case of Selmouni v. France*, Appl. no. 25803/940), Judgment, Strasbourg, 28 July 1999, para 95. There are more other cases in which the ECtHR resorts *indirectly* (not technically to the Vienna rules) to Article 31(3) (c) of the VCLT, such as is the *Case of Al-Skeini and others v. United Kingdom* (Application no. 55721/07), Judgment, Strasbourg, 7 July 2011.

[107]See on this discussion, e.g., Yearbook of International Law Commission (Summary Records on the sixteen session, A/CN.4/SER.1 A/1964, p. 116), in which Verdross claims the relation of human rights law to international law. Verdross admits that 'the treaty is created by States, the human rights derived from the treaty itself'. He added that 'it was unnecessary to say that treaties could act on individuals through the State, because that was the normal process' and because 'individuals could posse international rights or obligations and were consequently subject of international law'.

[108]*Cases of De Wilde, Ooms and Verssyp ('Vagrancy') v. Belgium* (Article 50), (Merits), (Application no. 2832/66;2835/66; 2899/66), ECtHR, Judgment of 10 March 1972, paras 1, 10 and 12. The three persons were in detention for the suppression of vagrancy and begging, by decisions on 19 April 1966, 21 December 1965 and respective 4 November 1965.

[109]*Id.*

the state to make full reparation to the applicants as required under Article 50 of the Convention.[110]

Having analysed the text of Article 50 of the Convention relying implicitly on the *travaux preparatoire*, the rule of 'ordinary meaning' to be given to the terms in their context,[111] in light of the 'object and purpose' of the treaty and the treaty as a whole, as well as on the principle of effectiveness,[112] the Court extends its interpretation with resort to 'any relevant international law rules' found in relevant international law instruments/documents. Employing this customary rule, later to be reflected in the text of Article 31(3)(c) of the VCLT (systemic integration), the ECtHR attempts to establish the general principle that justifies the *raison d'être* of Article 50. It finds that Article 50 of the ECHR originates 'in certain clauses which appear in treaties of a classical type – such as Article 10 of the *German Swiss Treaty on Arbitration and Conciliation*, 1921, and Article 32 of the Geneva *General Act of the Pacific Settlement of International Disputes*, 1928, and have no connection with the rule of exhaustion of domestic remedies'.[113] Hence, the Court chooses to analyse the impact of such clauses found generally in other relevant treaties and to assess if that was similarly the intended impact of Article 50.

The Court complements this approach by relying in addition on its autonomous means of interpretation. However indirectly, the Court stresses the 'special character' of the Convention (which is reflected in its 'object and purpose') when considering that 'the total length of the procedure instituted by the Convention would scarcely be in keeping with the idea of the effective protection of Human Rights if the victim, after exhausting in vain the domestic remedies before complaining at Strasbourg of a violation of his rights, were obliged to do so a second time

---

[110] *Id*, para 18. Article 50 of the Convention provides:

> If the Court finds that a decision or a measure taken by a legal authority or any other authority of a High Contracting Party is completely or partially in conflict with the obligations arising from the present Convention, and if the internal law of the said Party allows only partial reparation to be made for the consequences of this decision or measure, the decision of the Court shall, if necessary, afford just satisfaction to the injured party.

[111] *Id*, para 16. These rules, as well as the resort to the textualist/contextualist and subjective methods of interpretation are revealed in the following Court's statement: 'If the draftsmen of the Convention had meant to make the admissibility of claims for "just satisfaction" subordinate to the prior exercise of domestic remedies they would have taken care to specify this in Article 50 (art. 50) as they did in Article 26 (art. 26), combined with Article 27 (3) (art. 27-3), in respect of petitions addressed to the Commission. In the absence of such an explicit indication of their intention, the Court cannot take the view that Article 50 (art. 50) enunciates in substance the same rule as Article 26 (art. 26).'

[112] *Id*. The effectiveness principle and the 'object and purpose' rule, which implies the application of the teleological method of interpretation are clearly evidenced when the Court holds that 'if the victim, after exhausting in vain the domestic remedies before complaining at Strasbourg of a violation of his rights, were obliged to do so a second time before being able to obtain from the Court just satisfaction, the total length of the procedure instituted by the Convention would scarcely be in keeping with the idea of the effective protection of Human Rights. Such a requirement would lead to a situation incompatible with the aim and object of the Convention.'

[113] *Id*.

before being able to obtain from the Court just satisfaction'.[114] By stating that such an interpretation would 'lead to a situation incompatible with the aims of the Convention', the Court appears to reason on the effectiveness principle basis. In addition, the Court employs the 'margin of appreciation' doctrine when pondering whether the supervision of the detained applicant's correspondence during his detention amounted to a violation of Article 8 of the Convention. It holds in this regard that the Belgian authorities 'did not transgress the limits of the power of appreciation which Article 8(2) of the Convention leaves to the Contracting State'.[115]

In sum, the ECtHR adopts in the *Vagrancy* case a *holistic* approach to interpretation. It clearly uses a language that attests to a reliance not only on the three dimensions of the 'ordinary meaning' of the terms in their 'context' and in light of the 'object and purpose' of the treaty but also on the context of the treaty as a whole, the *travaux preparatoire* and 'relevant international law rules'—an approach reflected in what later became Article 31(1), (2), (3)(c) and Article 32 of the VCLT'.

#### 5.3.3.2 Reliance on the Vienna Convention's Formulation and/or Autonomous Rules?

According to the Icelandic Human Rights Centre, the human rights courts have expressly stated that the rules of interpretation embodied in the VCLT provide the relevant law principles for interpreting treaties.[116] However, the Centre's research concludes that these rules do not resolve all the problems of human rights interpretation.[117] Other interpretative means were developed by human rights bodies, which directly derived from the special nature of human rights treaties. Among such means are 'living instrument', 'practical and effective rights', 'autonomous

---

[114]*Id*, para 16.

[115]*Id*, para 93. See for more detail on the 'margin of appreciation' doctrine, George Letsas' 'The interpretation of the European Convention of Human Rights' (2007), p. 89. The author notes that certain clauses in the ECHR (Arts. 8–11) and other international human rights documents provide for state authorities' interference with the exercise of a right in pursuit of legitimate aims (i.e. national security, public safety, economic well-being, prevention of crime etc). Regarded as clauses of 'accommodation' or 'limitation', Letsas observes that these clauses 'leave states a "power" or "margin" of appreciation to interfere with those Convention freedoms', but this interference is 'impermissible if the conditions set out in the second paragraph of arts 8-11 are met'.

[116]See e.g. Icelandic Human Rights centre, Interpretation of Human Rights Treaties (available on line at: http://www.humanrights.is/).

[117]*Id*. In particular, the study mentions *Soering v. United Kingdom* (161 EctHR, ser. A, 7 July 1989, para 87, p. 7). In this case the ECtHR held that 'the principles for interpretation of human rights treaties upon which have been relied the European and Inter-American Court of Human Rights do not differ substantially from the methods of treaty interpretation, which are available under general international law, especially if it is assumed that the VCLT is not a complete codification of the customary international law on treaties, including its norms on treaty interpretation'.

concepts', 'margin of appreciation', 'evolutive' or 'dynamic interpretation', etc.[118] Fitzmaurice observes that the ECtHR, in particular, has been involved in the development of the concept of the Convention as a 'living instrument' (present-day standard), which mostly contributed to the doctrine of 'evolutive interpretation' (interpretation in the light of international law's developments).[119] As mentioned earlier in this chapter, the 'living instrument' concept postulates that the Convention must be interpreted in the light of present-day conditions.[120] According to Letsas, the *present-day standard* that the Court takes into consideration when interpreting the Convention' rights 'must somehow be *common or shared* amongst contracting states' (Letsas 2012, p. 2). In this respect, the author makes clear that the Court 'will not assign decisive importance to what the respondent state (be it its authorities or public opinion) considers to be an acceptable standard in the case at hand'.[121]

Furthermore, the Strasbourg Court's *evolutive interpretation* concept directly relates to other two doctrines: *autonomous concepts* and *margin of appreciation*.[122] Less clearly defined by the ECtHR in its case law is admitted to be the substantive concept of 'margin of appreciation',[123] naturally seen as a constraint on the doctrine of evolutive interpretation.[124] For Letsas, for example, the margin of appreciation concept epitomises 'the relation between fundamental freedoms and collective goals, under an ideal theory of political morality'.[125] So in the process of ascertaining and balancing individual rights and national interests, the doctrine of 'margin of appreciation' plays an important role in assisting the Court in the application of the *evolutive interpretation*.[126] Certainly, the Strasbourg Court would update the Convention when it interprets its provisions based on an evolutive interpretation.[127] However, in this complex act of moral reading of the Convention,

---

[118]Fitzmaurice (2013). M. Fitzmaurice mentions the ECtHR's contribution to the development of concepts such as the 'proportionality', 'margin of appreciation' concepts, 'common values' or 'commonly accepted standards', which allows this Court to interpret the ECHR provisions as common European values and in the context of other instruments of international law (under Article 31(3)(c) of the VCLT) binding or non-binding.

[119]*Id.*

[120]*Id.*

[121]Letsas (2012), p. 2.

[122]*Id*, p. 5.

[123]Letsas (2007), p. 84. See more on the ECtHR's practice on the 'margin of appreciation' doctrine, e.g., in Henkin et al. (1999), pp. 561–575, discussing in particular the *Handyside v. United Kingdom* case, European Court of Human Rights, 1976; Macdonald (1993); or in the *Buckley v. United Kingdom* case, European Court of Human Rights, 1996.

[124]Letsas (2012), p. 7 (emphasis added).

[125]*Id*, p. 84.

[126]*Id.* According to Letsas, the ECtHR has specified that, for a number of rights to have an autonomous meaning (e.g., criminal charge, civil rights and obligations, association, victim, lawful detention, etc), they must be interpreted 'in the context of the Convention and not on the basis of their meaning in domestic law'.

[127]*Id.*

there is, however, as Letsas observes, the 'common ground' or '*consensus* amongst contracting states' that is to consider *as the ultimate limit of how far this evolutive interpretation can go.*[128] Other authors, such as Bakircioglu, see the 'margin of appreciation' doctrine as analogous to the concept of judicial discretion.[129] He observes that this doctrine relies, in principle, on the idea that 'each society is entitled to certain latitude in balancing individual rights and national interests, as well as in resolving conflicts that emerge as result of diverse moral convictions'.[130]

Importantly, in explaining the interpretation of human rights, Letsas strongly advocates the idea that the *moral reading* of the Convention, which the ECtHR should perform, requires a 'process of moral discovery', not in the sense of 'expanding or inflating the scope of the ECHR rights as a living instrument' but rather *discovering what these human rights always meant to protect* (Letsas 2012, p. 14). Thus, most significantly is that 'the *moral reading* of the Convention is *essential* to the Court's overall *legitimacy* and its only possible ground'.[131] Arguably, it could be admitted then that the specific concepts developed by the ECtHR in its efforts to interpret human rights would appear to some authors as an indication of a 'self-contained' regime interpretative ethos. And it could be so, moreover, as even the degree of reception of the VCLT by the ECtHR is contested by those authors. However, as observed by Fitzmaurice, the practice of the ECtHR can evidence the reception of the VCLT rules of interpretation, and even more, there is a consensus among scholars in respect of the human rights tribunals' compliance with Vienna rules.[132] Also, Forowicz confirms that the VCLT became an integral part of international law's receptive process in the Strasbourg's case law (Forowicz 2010, p. 23).

As other examples below will demonstrate, the ECtHR has approached the Vienna Convention's general rules in a flexible manner, using in parallel its own concepts (doctrines) of interpretation, such as 'living instrument', 'margin of appreciation', 'law-making character', 'dynamic' or 'evolutive interpretation', 'practical and effective rights', 'special character'. Given this, the question that naturally arises is whether such autonomous concepts, developed by the ECtHR as guidelines for the interpretation of the Convention, would, of themselves, be sufficient to warrant the interpretation of the human rights provisions enshrined therein. The case analyses provided so far and those that will follow in this chapter answer that question by suggesting that the Strasbourg Court has basically been guided in interpreting the European Convention by the customary principles of interpretation of general

[128] *Id* (emphasis added).

[129] Bakircioglu (2007), p. 711. 'Judicial discretion', in the author's view, is when 'a judge, in line with certain constraints prescribed by legislation, precedent or custom, could decide a case within a range of possible solution'.

[130] *Id.* Bakircioglu states that this doctrine being designed as to provide flexibility in solving conflicts emerging from diverse social, political, cultural and legal traditions of the Contracting States within the European context.

[131] Letsas (2012), p. 14.

[132] *Id.*

international law. For example, the ECtHR shows generally a dependency on the textualist interpretation so as to 'grasp' the prima facie meaning of the (treaty) text in question, by starting the interpretative process with it, just as the ICJ usually does. However, as the case analyses will also show, the autonomous concepts and the general rules and principles of treaty interpretation coexist and work symbiotically. In this context, the general rules/principles of interpretation appear as constantly playing an important role in shaping the ECtHR's own specific approach to treaty interpretation. Moreover, the application with consistency of the general rules of treaty interpretation by the ECtHR appears, in general, as contributing to the formation and crystallisation of these rules as 'customary'.

Furthermore, even if a direct reference to the ICJ's practice on treaty interpretation is scarcely found in the ECtHR's practice, and an express reference to the VCLT rules is not always provided expressly in a technical sense (after the VCLT's adoption), nevertheless, it appears that the ECtHR has used to employ these rules in patterns similar to those used by the ICJ. Further case analyses can also show that the ECtHR, usually, employs more methods and customary rules of interpretation in a given case. And the Court does so (either expressly or tacitly) irrespective of the difficulty of the text interpreted (whether the text is, e.g., insufficiently clear, doubtful, ambiguous, vague or silent) and irrespective of whether the treaty text is declared clear by the Court, with no difficulty of interpretation, in an attempt to ascertain and confirm a certain interpretative result. As it has already been seen in the above case law analyses, the Court deploys these methods and rules gradually ('overbuilding'), similarly to the ICJ, by combining them in one unitary, logical interpretative act. Thus, whether the principles and rules of interpretation reflected in Articles 31–33 of the VCLT contemplate a 'balancing' of values that enable human rights interpretation, and whether the Strasbourg Court's application of such rules to its *lex specialis*' interpretation (the ECHR) would constitute a means for keeping the coherence and unity of international law are the main queries that remain to be answered further by relying on case law analysis.

##### 5.3.3.2.1 Clear Holistic Approach and Emphasis on the 'Object and Purpose' and 'Living Instrument' Rules

It could be admitted that the ECtHR has developed an elaborate system that keeps track of the ICJ's case law in respect of applying the general methods, rules and principles of treaty interpretation, as the analysis of the ***Case of Golder v. United Kingdom*** **(1975)**[133] can illustrate. This case is known in the scholarship as laying the foundation for the specific interpretative methods used by the ECtHR, which were not fully advanced until the VCLT entered into force (1980).[134] In all, *Golder*

[133] *Case of Golder v. United Kingdom*, (Application no. 4451/70), ECtHR, Judgment of 21 February, 1975.

[134] Letsas (2012), p. 4 (*Golder* is used in dozens of application at the ECtHR).

is considered the most important ECtHR case from the perspective of treaty interpretation at this Court. It contains the first and highly comprehensive application of the VCLT's 'general rule of interpretation' to interpreting the Convention's human rights, described as a *unitary, single combined operation.*[135] The interpretative approach adopted in this case endorses the absolute equality of all the elements of Article 31(1)[136] when dealing with *silence* in the text of the Convention provision (not providing for the circumstances of the case). *Golder* also promotes an evolutive interpretation (under Article 31(3)(c) VCLT) while marking in addition a clear usage of its own autonomous techniques of interpretation, such as the Convention (ECHR) as a 'living instrument', interpreted in the light of the present-day conditions. Convicted of robbery, Mr. Golder, while a serving prisoner, petitioned for permission to consult a solicitor in order to bring a civil action for libel against a prison officer, but this was denied. The main issue of interpretation concerns whether Article 6(1) of the Convention[137] guarantees the applicant's right to have a fair trial in legal proceedings that are already pending or whether it secures to *everyone* a right to have any claim relating to his civil rights and obligations brought before a court or tribunal.[138] To elucidate the meaning of Article 6(1) and fit it to the facts of the case, the Court expressly declares that 'it is prepared to consider ... that it should be guided by Articles 31 to 33 of the Vienna Convention ...', albeit the VCLT was not yet in force.[139] The Court recalls that 'Articles 31 to 33 enunciate in essence generally accepted principles of international law to which the Court has already referred on occasion'.[140]

In applying the customary rules of interpretation, the Court appears to adopt in *Golder* techniques of interpretation that resemble those developed and used by the

---

[135] *Id.*

[136] See also Fitzmaurice (2013) for the approach of interpretation in *Golder*.

[137] Article 6 (1) provides:

> In the determination of his civil rights and obligations or of any criminal charge against him, everyone is entitled to a fair and public hearing within a reasonable time by an independent and impartial tribunal established by law. Judgment shall be pronounced publicly but the press and public may be excluded from all or part of the trial in the interests of morals, public order or national security in a democratic society, where the interests of juveniles or the protection of the private life of the parties so require, or to the extent strictly necessary in the opinion of the court in special circumstances where publicity would prejudice the interests of justice.

[138] *Golder* (1975), p. 4. The applicant complained of interference with his right to a fair and public determination of his civil rights and obligations under Article 6 of the Convention but faced the difficulty that, without legal help, he had been unable to initiate a proceeding to which his fair trial right could attach. Despite this difficulty his application succeeded.

[139] *Id*, para 29. The Court specifically recalled that 'for the interpretation of the European Convention account is to be taken of those Articles subject, where appropriate, to "any relevant rules of the organization" – the Council of Europe – within which it has adopted (Article 5 of the Vienna Convention)'.

[140] *Id*, para 4. For example, the Court invokes *Lawless* (No. 3) (1961), see *supra* note 55; *Delcourt* (Delcourt v. Belgium) judgment of 17 January 1970, Series A no. 11; *Wemhoff* (1968), see *supra* note 86.

ICJ and provides a *holistic* approach. In justifying the adopted interpretative position, the Strasbourg Court proceeds to examine the article at issue in a relatively lengthy analysis, in the light of the means of interpretation provided by the VCLT. For example, it analyses Article 6(1) by resorting to the rules set forth in *Articles 31–33 of the VCLT* in an interpretative action consisting of several steps. First, the Court seems to consider a textualist approach under Article 31(1) of the VCLT. Based on dictionary definitions, the Court analyses the ordinary meaning of the terms such as 'civil claims', 'reasonable time', 'independent and impartial tribunal' within Article 6(1).[141] It concludes that the article does not necessarily refer to procedures pending on a court's docket but extends to situations similar to that of *Golder*, where there is no case submitted to a Court.[142] In addition, the Court expressly provides an interpretation under Article 33 VCLT when it compares both the French and English versions of the terms in Article 6(1) so as to identify if they have the same meaning in each authentic text. The Court concludes in this regard that 'the clearest indications are to be found in the French text, first sentence'.[143]

Second, the Court adopts a contextualist approach when it rejects the contextual or mutually supporting reading of Articles 6(1), 5(4) and 13 of the Convention, also proposed by the British Government.[144] It finds in this regard the Commission's interpretation as being more persuasive,[145] thus drawing sharp distinctions between the scope and coverage of the respective articles.[146] Relying on the 'context' rule (which is supported, in principle, by the subjective method), the Court concludes that 'the three provisions do not operate in the same field', as, for example, 'Article 13 speaks of an effective remedy before a national authority ... which may not be a "tribunal" or "court" within the meaning of Article 6 para. 1, and 5 para. 4'.[147]

Third, the Court states that it would apply Article 31(2) of the VCLT to justify its further recourse to the Preamble of the European Convention in deciphering the context of the Convention.[148] So the Court honours, here, the teleological method of interpretation (based on the 'object and purpose' rule), which is applied expressly along with the textualist/subjective methods. Similar to the Commission, the Court emphasises that the Preamble's reference to the rule of law was more than a 'merely... rhetorical reference', devoid of relevance for those interpreting the Convention,[149] but that it was an important expression that elucidates the meaning

---

[141] *Id*, para 29.

[142] *Id.*

[143] *Id*, para 32.

[144] *Id*, para 17.

[145] *Id.*

[146] *Id.*

[147] *Id*, para 33. The Court invokes *Neumeister's* judgment of 27 June 1968, Series A no. 8, p. 43, para 23; *Matznetter* judgment of 10 November 1969, Series A no. 10, p. 35, para 13; De *Wilde, Ooms and Versyp*, *supra* note 108.

[148] *Id*, para 34.

[149] *Id.*

of Article 6(1).[150] Then the ECtHR expressly states that, in Article 31(2) of the Vienna Convention, the Preamble to a treaty forms an integral part of the context.[151]

Fourth, in elucidating the meaning of Article 6, the Court goes on to look to the 'relevant rules of international law applicable in the relations between the parties', pursuant to Article 31(3) (c) of the VCLT.[152] Accordingly, the Court finds that there is a principle of international law that forbids the denial of justice. So a civil claim must be capable of being submitted to a judge, and it is among those rules that form 'general principles of law' and especially 'general principles of law recognized by civilised nations' set forth in Article 38 para 1(c) of the Statute of the International Court of Justice.[153] Such an approach could be found in the ICJ's case law, for example in the *Fisheries Case* (1951), where the ICJ dealt with a similar difficulty in interpreting a treaty text; the text not providing for the situation of the case. In this case, the ICJ held that '[i]t does not at all follow that, in the *absence of rules having the technically precise character* ... the delimitation undertaken by the Norwegian Government in 1935 is not subject to certain principles which make it possible to judge as to its validity under international law'.[154] Similarly, the rule reflected in Article 31(3)(c) of the VCLT was clearly drawn in the *Legal consequences for states of the continued presence of South Africa in Namibia* (1971)

[150] *Id.*

[151] Id.

[152] *Id*, para 35. See, for a similar (evolutive interpretation) approach based on Article 31(3)(c) of the VCLT, the *Case* of *Selmouni v. France 9* (Application no. 25803/940), Judgment, Strasbourg, 28 July 1999. Since the ECtHR found in *Selmouni* the right under Article 3 not to be subjected to torture or degrading treatment or punishment being formulated in general terms, as also Article 6 of the Convention providing in part for the right for everyone to a hearing within a reasonable time by a tribunal, the Court had to look at external sources, and take also into consideration the evolution of international law. In doing so, the Court looked for a more concrete meaning of the term 'torture' to reiterate its absolute prohibition (Article 3); for there may be special circumstances which absolve the applicant from the obligation to exhaust the domestic remedies (Article 6). See also similarity with *Case of Al-Adsani v. The United Kingdom* (Application no. 35763/97), Judgment Strasbourg, 21 November 2001. The ECtHR reiterated in this case (at p. 17, para 55) that:

> the Convention has to be interpreted in the light of the rules set out in the Vienna Convention on the Law of Treaties of 23 May 1969, and that Article 31 § 3 (c) of that treaty indicates that account is to be taken of any relevant rules of international law applicable in the relations between the parties'.

However, by failing to consider 'torture' *Al-Adsani* as an act of sovereignty of State, accepting it as *jus cogens*, peremptory norm, and that a state must exercise their rights in accordance with their specific obligations under international law, the ECtHR acted in the detriment of an evolutionist interpretation, in the light of the object and purpose of the Convention, and the Convention as a "living instrument".

[153] *Id.* The ECtHR adds that it makes no sense 'that Article 6 para 1 ... should describe in detail the procedural guarantees afforded to parties in a pending lawsuit' and that read in its context provides for the inclusion under its umbrella 'rights' not specifically enumerated, such as the right to access counsel in order to formulate a civil complaint, a principle of international law invoked in the case of *Golder*.

[154] *Fisheries Case* (*United Kingdom v. Norway*), Judgment of 18 December, ICJ, 1951, para 132 (emphasis added).

case, where the ICJ stated that 'an international instrument has to be interpreted and applied within the framework of the entire legal system prevailing at the time of interpretation'.[155]

Arguably, the key point of the Court's interpretation in *Golder* is the way it describes the process of treaty interpretation as a 'unity, a single combined operation'.[156] This view is clearly reflected in what the Court adds further in respect of the rules provided by Article 31 of the VCLT, notably, that it is 'closely integrated, places on the same footing the various elements enumerated in the four paragraphs of the Article'.[157] Finally, despite expressly stating that it reaches the conclusion without needing to resort to the 'supplementary means of interpretation' rule,[158] the Court goes without saying that it looks to the drafts of the Convention. It could be so, moreover, as the Court itself declares that it is 'prepared to consider' that 'it should be guided by [Articles 31 *to* 33] of the Vienna Convention',[159] which implies resort also to Article 32, thus to all the respective articles.

As it could be observed, the Court in *Golder* appears to show a stronger emphasis and reliance on the rules of 'context' (the Convention as a whole) and 'object and purpose', as well as on 'any relevant rules of international law applicable in relation between the parties' (under Article 31(3)(c) VCLT), than on the *travaux preparatoire*. Such an approach could imply the rejection of a backward-looking approach epitomised by resort to the *travaux* (especially in the case of vagueness, obscurity or silence in treaty text), and hence the ECtHR's focus on the 'special character' of the Convention, and the Convention as a 'living instrument', which must be interpreted in present-day conditions. By focusing also on the lawmaking character of the Convention, the Court makes it clear, however, that its interpretation would not lead to 'an extensive interpretation forcing new obligations on the Contracting States'.[160] In addition, the Court resorts expressly to the principle of effectiveness, concluding that it 'would be inconceivable, in the opinion of the Court, that Article 6 para. 1 should describe in detail the procedural guarantees afforded to parties in a pending lawsuit and should not first protect that which alone makes it in fact possible to benefit from such guarantees, that is, access to a court'.[161] An interpretation based on the effectiveness principle has often been applied by the ICJ for similar interpretative difficulties (as seen in *Golder*—a *silent* text), as, for instance, in the *Haya de la Torre* (1951) case. As pointed out in Chap. 4, there was no express provision in *Haya de la Torre* with regard to the circumstances of the case

[155] *Legal consequences for states of the continued presence of South Africa in Namibia (South West Africa)*, Advisory Opinion, ICJ, 1971, p. 32, para 53. The ICJ added that the interpretation of an instrument governing the institution of mandate (instituted in 1919) 'cannot remain unaffected by the subsequent development of law, through the Charter of the United Nations and by way of customary law'.

[156] *Golder* (1975), para 30.

[157] *Id* (emphasis added).

[158] *Id.*

[159] *Id*, para 29 (emphasis added).

[160] *Id*, para 36.

[161] *Id*, para 35.

(termination of asylum). The ICJ reasoned that the refusal to grant asylum was contrary to the treaty provisions since '[s]uch an interpretation would be repugnant to the spirit which animated that Convention in conformity with the Latin-American tradition in regard to asylum, a tradition in accordance with which political refugees should not be surrendered'.[162]

Summing up, the Court in *Golder*, although stressing an indubitable emphasis on the teleological approach to interpretation (object and purpose), which directly supports the 'living instrument' doctrine, supplies these means with a clear textualist and subjective approaches. By placing on the same footing the various interpretative rules enumerated in Articles 31, 32 and 33 of the VCLT, the Court performs, in this case, similarly to the ICJ when confronting with a *silence* in a treaty text construction, a *holistic* interpretation of the provision at issue. In essence, the Court makes an express application of the rules stated in Article 31 (1), (2), (3) and Article 33 and an implicit application of Article 32 of the VCLT, underlining the universally accepted methodology of interpretation.[163] By virtue of this approach, the Strasbourg Court conveys in *Golder*, on the one hand, the importance it attaches to the Convention (ECHR) both as a *pacta sunt servanda* written agreement and as a 'living instrument' that must be interpreted in the light of the present-day conditions. And on the other hand, it projects the Convention within the broader system of international law by means of Article 31(3)(c) of the VCLT. *Golder* has been subsequently invoked by the ECtHR in many further cases, where it applied a similar treaty interpretative approach, as some of the examples below can show.

#### 5.3.3.2.2 Reliance on the 'Travaux Preparatoire' and 'Margin of Appreciation' Rules

While in the majority of the cases already analysed in this chapter the ECtHR shows an implicit resort to the *travaux preparatoires*, apparently not attaching a decisive importance to it in confirming or/and determining the meaning of a Convention's

---

[162] *Haya de la Torre*, Judgment of 13 June, I.C.J. Reports 1951, p. 14. See Chap. 4 of this book for this case analysis.

[163] See *Tyrer v. the United Kingdom* (Application nr. 5856/72), Judgment, Strasbourg, 25 April, 1978, for a comparison with the *Golder* case regarding the application of the customary rules of interpretation performed by the ECtHR. One could notice that in *Tyrer*, which is decided after *Golder*, the ECtHR approached an interpretation, however, in a different manner, by not (expressly) explaining and justifying the application of the VCLT's general rules of interpretation, although the Court resorted to these rules. The reason for such a tactic in *Tyrer* could be due both to the confidence of the Court in a direct applicability of the VCLT rules of interpretation without explanation, as they already were established in *Golder*, and to its intention to emphasise more in this case the *evolutionist interpretation* it promoted regarding the Human Rights Convention, expressly stating (at p. 15, para 38) that '[t]he Court must also recall that the Convention is a living instrument which, as the Commission rightly stressed, must be interpreted in the light of present-day conditions...'.

provision, the following case illustrates analytically a situation of a clear and express usage of the *travaux preparatoire*.[164] However, the case analyses I provided in the previous sections, and also in Chap. 4, can show that, unlike the ICJ, the ECtHR has generally a stronger tendency to interpret the Convention without necessarily relying on the *travaux preparatoire* to confirm a result obtained on the basis of Article 31 of the VCLT, or at least not expressly stating that it would adopt this 'supplementary means'. Unlike the ICJ, the ECtHR has shown more often discretion, reluctance or unpredictability in resort to such extraneous sources of interpretation. This interpretative ethos appears to be fair as the ECtHR's primary aim is to interpret the Convention in a manner that renders its rights practical and effective, which, clearly, involves *an evolutive, dynamic interpretation* of the rights, thus keeping account of the evolution and developments of law.[165]

Having to interpret *a sufficiently clear* text, as the ECtHR suggested was its task in the ***Case of Witold Litwa v. Poland* (2000)**,[166] the Court chose to resort to the *travaux preparatoire* in addition to other rules, including the 'margin of appreciation' autonomous doctrine. This case shows an explicit receptive attitude towards the application of the Vienna Convention's customary rules set forth in Articles 31 and 32 by reiterating their importance in interpreting the Convention's human rights. Similar to *Golder*, the Court recalls in *Witold* that the general rule contained in Article 31 of the VCLT 'places on the same footing the various elements enumerated in the four paragraphs of that Article',[167] confirming the order of interpretation that an interpreter must follow. The case also illustrates a strong emphasis of the Court on the 'margin of appreciation' doctrine in pondering whether the measure taken by the national authorities interfered with fundamental freedoms of the individual, violating the applicant's rights. Important to mention in this relation is that when the Strasbourg Court has used in general the 'margin of appreciation' concept, as observed by Letsas, 'it was to make a very general and simple point about the limitability *or non-absoluteness of the Convention rights*'[168] that is reflected in the 'inherent tension between individual freedoms and collective goals'.[169]

---

[164] See for a similar reliance on the *travaux preparatoire* that supports a textualist approach, examples of the ICJ's practice, e.g., *Aegean Sea Continental Shelf (Greece v. Turk.)*, 1978 I.C. J., p. 3; *Border and Transborder Armed Actions (Nicar. v. Hond.)*, 1988 I.C.J., 69 (Jurisdiction of the Court and Admissibility of the Application), reprinted in 28 I.L.M. 338 (1989).

[165] See for this point, e.g., Fitzmaurice (2013).

[166] *Case of Witold Litwa v. Poland* (Application no. 26629/95), Strasbourg, Judgment of 4 April, 2000.

[167] *Id*, para 58.

[168] Letsas (2007), pp. 85–86 (emphasis added).

[169] *Id*. In order to find out the limits of the Convention rights, as Letsas notes, the Court has used the proportionality principle (by far the most important and most demanding criterion) in order to ascertain whether the limitation of a right was permissible under the Convention.

The *Witold* case relates to the deprivation of liberty of an almost blind man, Mr. Witold, who was mistakenly described as being drunk and who was taken by the police to a sobering-up detention centre where he was detained for 6 h and 30 min. The ECHR had to determine whether this measure constituted a deprivation of liberty and violated the applicant's rights under the scope of Article 5(1)(e) of the Convention. In order to consider whether the applicant's detention falls within any of the permitted grounds of deprivation of liberty listed in Article 5(1),[170] the Court proceeds by establishing the meaning of the term 'alcoholics' within paragraph (e) of this provision. In doing so, the Court makes it clear that it 'will be guided by Articles 31 to 33 of the Vienna Convention of 23 May 1969 on the Law of Treaties, as it has repeatedly been in other cases where an interpretation of the Convention was required'.[171]

Relying on *Golder*, the Court provides an explicit approach of interpretation, recalling that '[t]he sequence in which those elements are listed in Article 31 of the Vienna Convention regulates, however, the order which the process of interpretation of the treaty should follow'.[172] Then the ECtHR Court acknowledges, just as the ICJ has usually done in its interpretative practice,[173] that the interpretation process 'must start from ascertaining the ordinary meaning of the terms of a treaty –

---

[170] Article 5 (1) of the Convention provides:

1. Everyone has the right to liberty and security of person. No one shall be deprived of his liberty save in the following cases and in accordance with a procedure prescribed by law:

(a) the lawful detention of a person after conviction by a competent court;
(b) the lawful arrest or detention of a person for non-compliance with the lawful order of a court or in order to secure the fulfilment of any obligation prescribed by law;
(c) the lawful arrest or detention of a person effected for the purpose of bringing him before the competent legal authority on reasonable suspicion of having committed an offence or when it is reasonably considered necessary to prevent his committing an offence or fleeing after having done so;
(d) the detention of a minor by lawful order for the purpose of educational supervision or his lawful detention for the purpose of bringing him before the competent legal authority;
(e) the lawful detention of persons for the prevention of the spreading of infectious diseases, of persons of unsound mind, alcoholics or drug addicts or vagrants;
(f) the lawful arrest or detention of a person to prevent his effecting an unauthorised entry into the country or of a person against whom action is being taken with a view to deportation or extradition.

[171] *Witold* (2000), *supra* note 166, para 57 (emphasis added). The Court invokes *Johnston and Others v. Ireland* judgment of 18 December 1986, Series A no. 112, p. 24, § 51 et seq., and *Lithgow and Others v. the United Kingdom*, Judgment of 8 July 1986, Series A no. 102, pp. 47–48, § 114 in fine, and p. 49, § 117.

[172] *Id*, para 59.

[173] *Competence of the General Assembly for the Admission of a State to the United Nations*, (Second Admissions Case) (1950), I.C.J. Reports, p. 8; *Case concerning the territorial dispute (Libyan Arab Jamahirya v. Chad)*, Judgment of 3 February 1994, p. 20.

in their context and in the light of its object and purpose, as laid down in Article 31(1)'.[174] However, to confirm the result obtained on the basis of the ordinary meaning,[175] context,[176] and object and purpose,[177] the ECtHR explicitly resorts to the Convention's preparatory work. The *travaux* reveals in the commentary on the preliminary draft Convention that the term 'alcoholics' is recorded and that 'the text of the relevant Article covered the right of the Signatory States to take measures to combat vagrancy and 'drunkenness' (*l'alcoolisme* in French)',[178] as also that '[i]t is further recorded that the Committee of Experts had no doubt that this could be agreed "since such restrictions were justified by the requirements of public morality and order"'.[179] At the same time, the Court relies additionally on Article 33 of the VCLT in elucidating the meaning of the term 'd'un alcoolique' in the French text of the Convention.

Thus, there is no doubt that in the process of ascertaining the true meaning of the terms of the Convention's provision at issue, the ECtHR is consistent with the general rule laid down in Article 31 of the VCLT as 'a unity and a single combined operation'.[180] However, a weak aspect in the Court's approach appears to come from the meaning of the term 'alcoholism' that the Court assesses within paragraph 1(e) of Article 5, which refers to 'the lawful detention of ... alcoholics'. So to clarify the term 'alcoholism' and ponder whether the measure taken by the national authorities may or may not amount to a violation of the applicant's rights, the Court relies in addition on the 'margin of appreciation' doctrine. When deciding that the applicant's detention falls within the ambit of Article 5(1)(e) of the Convention,[181] the Court appears to give a wider 'margin of appreciation' to the respondent state than is necessary.[182] And this, in spite of admitting that Article 5(1)(e) cannot be interpreted as permitting the detention of an individual merely because of his alcohol intake and despite the Court showing doubt for the government's ability to justify the applicant's detention under this sub-paragraph.[183]

One could admit that in elucidating the meaning of the term *alcoholism*, the Court adopted at one point a limited interpretation of the term 'alcoholics' within

---

[174]*Witold* (2000), para 59.

[175]*Id*, para 51.

[176]*Id*. The Court admits that the term 'alcoholics' within Article 5 § 1 of the Convention 'is found in a context that includes a reference to several other categories of individuals, that is, persons spreading infectious diseases, persons of unsound mind, drug addicts and vagrants'.

[177]*Id*, para 61.

[178]*Id*, para 63.

[179]*Id*.

[180]*Id*, para 53.

[181]*Id*, para 64.

[182]*Id*, para 62. The Court states that 'in the text of Article 5 there is nothing to suggest that this provision prevents that measure from being applied by the State to an individual abusing alcohol, in order to limit the harm caused by alcohol to himself and the public, or to prevent dangerous behaviour after drinking'.

[183]*Id*, para 77.

Article 5(1)(e) on the basis of the rule of 'plain and ordinary meaning of the terms in their context'.[184] Pursuant to this rule of interpretation, the Court's rationale was that the word 'alcoholics' in its common usage denotes 'persons who are addicted to alcohol'.[185] Thus the Court interpreted the meaning of the term 'alcoholics' indicating that the object and purpose of Article 5 para 1 (e) cannot be understood as only allowing the detention of 'alcoholics' in the limited sense of persons in a clinical state of 'alcoholism'. However, it is only when the Court refers further to *the 'object and purpose' of the Convention*, which sheds light on the importance of physical freedom, when the Court clarifies and admits, actually, that the exceptions set forth in Article 5(1) 'cannot be given an extensive interpretation'.[186] Then the emphasis of the Court moves clearly to the effectiveness of the procedural rights and safeguards. It focuses on the prevention of arbitrary deprivation of liberty, stressing that '[t]he detention of an individual is such a serious measure that it is only justified where other, less severe measures have been considered and found to be insufficient to safeguard the individual or public interest which might require that the person concerned be detained'.[187]

In sum, in spite of some inconsistencies in approaching the 'ordinary meaning' rule (as for the term 'alcoholism'), the Court ends up providing in *Witold* a *holistic* interpretation that leads to realising the aim and achieving the object and purpose of the Convention (by giving full effect to the provision at issue), clearly relying on the VCLT methodology of interpretation. It shows the Court's understanding of the Convention as a 'living instrument', which is meant, as Letsas clearly and succinctly captured, '*to protect whatever human rights people in fact have, and not what human rights domestic authorities or public opinion think people have*' (Letsas 2012, p. 23). Therefore, there is clear support in this case for Farowicz's opinion that the ECtHR has adopted Article 32 of the VCLT with flexibility and discretion when it felt that it would contribute to the resolution of a case, generally, using the *travaux preparatoire* as a working hypothesis (Forowicz 2010, p. 68).

#### 5.3.3.3 VCLT as Embodiment of Custom

Some authors express more skeptical views in regard to the application of the VCLT's rules and support the idea that these rules are not proper for the interpretation of human rights instruments. For example, Scheinin explains that the VCLT is a general treaty applicable in any treaty relationship between states, but it contains many hidden assumptions that are not justified with respect to human rights (Scheinin 2009, p. 27). Scheinin observes that the VCLT's 'general rule of interpretation' is insufficient and inadequate for capturing the operation of human

[184]*Id*, see for a discussion in this light the Concurring opinion of Judge Bonello in this case.

[185]*Id*, para 51.

[186]*Id*, para 59. The Court relies on the *Vagrancy* (1972), see *supra* note 108, and the *Winterwerp v. the Netherlands*, Judgment of 24 October 1979, Series A no. 33, pp. 16–17, § 37.

[187]*Id*, para 78.

rights treaties, which are more than just treaties between states as they have 'an embryonic form of a global constitution'.[188] A question that necessarily arises in relation to treaty interpretation applied by the ECtHR is then how it can be determined what the 'object and purpose' of a specific human rights treaty is, considering that Article 31 of the VCLT 'is not at all clear about this question, especially in regards to how much weight should be given to its contained elements to determine the object and purpose within the preamble of a treaty this article refers to' (Letsas 2010a, b, p. 14). This question is important, especially because, as observed by McDougal, the terms of Article 31(1) are vague and imprecisely formulated,[189] so an interpretation of the Convention's human rights relying on such general rules becomes even more difficult. According to Letsas, the appropriateness of different interpretative methods that the ECtHR adopts 'depends on the nature of the treaty in question and the moral value in play' (Letsas 2012, p. 18). Given this, the term 'purpose' within Article 31(1) of the VCLT 'simply means normative "point" or "value"', and by means of Article 31(1), 'interpretation must be relative to the point or value of that which is interpreted'.[190]

In spite of the existent criticism as to the Vienna rules' applicability in special contexts (e.g., human rights), it is widely admitted in the scholarship that an *interpretative community* has developed and accepted practices in respect of the use and application of the VCLT's interpretative principles, which constrains a decision-maker to interpret human rights not outside of their limits (Tobin 2010, p. 15). As Tobin observes, since it is necessary to have an interpretative outcome with a persuasive force within an interpretative community, this outcome must be constructed 'in the light of the principles that have been agreed upon by that community to guide the interpretative exercise'.[191] The essential aspect in this sense is that states, which are the central actors in the interpretative community, have accepted the VCLT principles of interpretation.[192]

Based on the case analyses provided in this chapter, one can admit that, even when in certain situations after the adoption of the VCLT the ECtHR has not expressly declared resort to the rules of interpretation set forth in Articles 31–33 of the VCLT, the Court has chosen a language of interpretation that proved to point towards their application. The ECtHR has shown adherence to the same traditional techniques of interpretation (customary rules and principles) utilised by the ICJ. Moreover, the Strasbourg Court has applied these techniques consistently, both prior to and after the VCLT' adoption, in a fashion similar to that established by the PCIJ/ICJ, as a basis of operation for the interpretation of the Convention's human

---

[188] Scheinin (2009), p. 27.

[189] McDougal (1967), p. 998. The author considers also that these rules are 'so impossible of effective application that a sophisticated decision-maker can easily escape their putative limits'.

[190] Letsas (2012), p. 14. Letsas explains this aspect by using the term 'truism' as 'something should be interpreted as it should be interpreted, or an interpreter's got to do what an interpreter's got to do'.

[191] Tobin (2010), p. 19.

[192] *Id.*

rights. Indeed, this human rights Court has proceeded with this approach in a flexible way, adapting the traditional interpretative techniques to its special context, as other examples below will demonstrate, using in parallel its own conceptual means (doctrines) of interpretation such as 'living instrument', 'margin of appreciation', 'special character', 'law-making character', 'evolutive interpretation'. In addition, the case analyses in this chapter illustrate how the ECtHR adopts a 'holistic' approach of interpretation, combining in a single act the methods, customary rules and principles of treaty interpretation, similarly to the ICJ.

One of the recent cases, ***Catan and Others v. Moldova and Russia* (2012)**,[193] supports the argument that the ECtHR appeals to the customary rules of interpretation reflected in Articles 31–33 of the VCLT and performs a holistic approach, although without appending to these rules an express technical description (referenced as VCLT rules) as it did, for example, in *Golder*. Additionally, the Court relies on its autonomous doctrines of 'living instrument', 'margin of appreciation' and 'special character'. *Catan* is also a repetition of the jurisdictional issues raised in the previous ECHR case of *Ilascu and Others v. Moldova and Russia* (2004)[194] as to the extent of responsibility for each state in securing the human rights of those in the area of the Moldavian Republic of Transdniestria (MRT).[195] In elucidating the 'state responsibility' issue in this case (under Article 1 of the Convention), the ECtHR looked to an impressive body of its own precedents, as also to general international law, notably to the International Law Commission's Draft Articles on the Responsibility of States for Internationally Wrongful Acts ('Draft Articles'), adopted in August 2001, and to the relevant ICJ's precedents.[196] The case concerned a number of children and parents from the Moldovan community in Transdniestria who complained about actions taken by the authorities of the Moldavian Republic of Transdniestria, in 2002 and 2004, to enforce decisions forbidding the use of the Latin alphabet in schools, requiring that all schools must adopt an 'MRT' approved curriculum and the Cyrillic script.[197] The applicants complained that they had been discriminated against on the grounds of their ethnicity and language and required to study in an artificial language.[198] They

[193] *Case of Catan and Others v. Moldova and Russia* (Applications nos. 43370/04, 8252/05 and 18454/06), Judgment Strasbourg, 19 October 2012. See also, e.g., the recent *Case of M. and others v. Italy and Bulgaria*, (Appl. no. 40020/03, Judgment, Strasbourg, 31 July, 2012, para 146)—where the ECtHR similarly adopted an express holistic approach (text, context, object and purpose, context of the whole treaty, pursuant to Article 31(1) and (2) of the VCLT).

[194] *Ilascu and others v Moldova and Russia* (GC), App. No. 48787/99, Judgment, 8 July 2004; Cyprus v. Turkey, App. 25781/94, 10 May 2001, ECtHR, p. 25.

[195] *Catan and Others* (2012), paras 74–75.

[196] *Id.* The ECtHR relies on the ICJ cases such as *Legal consequences for States of the continued presence of South Africa in Namibia, notwithstanding Security Council resolution 276* (1970); the *Case Concerning the Application of the Convention on the Prevention and Punishment of Genocide* (2007), in which the ICJ invoked the *Military and Paramilitary Activities in and against Nicaragua* (1986) case.

[197] *Catan and Others* (2012).

[198] (Which was not of use and also unrecognised outside Transdniestria). According to Article 12 of the MRT 'Constitution', the official languages within the MRT are 'Moldavian', Russian and

complained that the measures taken by the 'MRT' against them, such as the forcible closure of their schools, harassment and intimidation because of their choice to pursue education at the Moldovan/Romanian language schools, violated their rights under the European Convention, respectively Article 2 Protocol 1—the right to education; Article 8—the right to respect for private and family life; Article 14—the right to enjoy freely, without discrimination, the rights and freedoms set forth in the Convention.

In order to find out whether the applicants came within the jurisdiction of the Russian Federation for the purpose of Article 1 of the Convention,[199] as the Russian Federation contested such jurisdiction, the ECtHR acknowledges in *Catan* approaches of interpretation of Article 1 that it adopted in deciding previous cases of extraterritorial jurisdiction.[200] The Court applies here the exception to the principle that jurisdiction under Article 1 is limited to a state's own territory.[201] The approach in this case, however, aims to elucidate more clearly than in other cases the distinction between 'jurisdiction' and 'attribution' of the respondent state.[202] Thus, suffice to mention in regard to the interpretation of Article 1 that the Court relies on *Banković, Al-Skeini,*[203] *Ilascu and Ivantoc and Others* in finding

Ukrainian. Article 6 of the 'MRT Law on languages', which was adopted on 8 September 1992, states that, for all purposes, 'Moldavian' must be written with the Cyrillic alphabet. The 'law' provides further that use of the Latin alphabet may amount to an offence.

[199] Article 1 of the ECHR provides:

> The High Contracting Parties shall secure to everyone within their jurisdiction the rights and freedoms defined in Section I of [the] Convention.

[200] *Catan and Others* (2012), paras 102–107—for the Court's arguments related to the exceptional circumstances capable of giving rise to the exercise of jurisdiction by a Contracting State outside its own territorial boundaries. The Court relies on its relevant past decisions such as *Case of Loizidou v. Turkey* (Preliminary Objections), Application no. 15318/89, Judgment of 23 March, 1995; *Case of Al-Skeini and others v. United Kingdom* (Application no. 55721/07), Judgment, Strasbourg, 7 July 2011; *Bankovic v. Belgium and Others*, Application no. 52207/99, The European Court of Human Rights, sitting as a Grand Chamber (Admissibility), 24 October and 12 December 2001; *Ilascu and others v. Moldova and Russia* (GC), App. No. 48787/99, Judgment, 8 July 2004; *Cyprus v. Turkey*, App. 25781/94, 10 May 2001, ECtHR; *Ivatoc and Others v. Moldova and Russia*, no. 23687, 15 November, 2011.

[201] *Id*, para 106. The exception which the Court underlines occurs when, as a consequence of lawful or unlawful military action, and when a Contracting State exercises effective control of an area outside that national territory, whether this control 'is to be exercised directly, through the Contracting State's own armed forces, or through a subordinate local administration'.

[202] See for comparison with cases such as *Bankovic, Ilascu, Loizidou.*

[203] See *Al-Skeini and Others* (2011), *supra* note 200. The ECtHR strongly relied in *Al-Skeini* on the approach it adopted in *Ilaşcu and Others* (2004) in respect of Articles 1 and 2 of the Convention. Also the Court relied in *Al-Skeini* on a rich body of case law such as: *Soering v. the United Kingdom*, 7 July 1989, § 86, Series A no. 161; *Banković and Others v. Belgium and Others* [GC] (dec.), no. 52207/99, § 66, ECHR 2001-XII; *Güleç v. Turkey*, 27 July 1998, § 81, Reports of Judgments and Decisions 1998-IV; *Ergi v. Turkey*, 28 July 1998, §§ 79 and 82, Reports 1998-IV; *Ahmet Özkan and Others v. Turkey*, no. 21689/93, §§ 85–90, 309–320, and 326–330, 6 April 2004; *Isayeva v. Russia*, no. 57950/00, §§ 180 and 210, 24 February 2005; *Kanlibaş v.Turkey, no. 32444/96*, §§ 39–51, 8 December 2005; as also on the ICJ practice such as *The Legal Consequences of the*

that 'individuals detained in Transdniestria fell within Moldova's jurisdiction because Moldova was the territorial State, even though it did not have effective control over the Transdniestrian region' and that 'Moldova's obligation under Article 1 to "secure to everyone within their jurisdiction the [Convention] rights and freedoms", was, however, limited in the circumstances to a positive obligation to take the diplomatic, economic, judicial or other measures that were both in its power to take and in accordance with international law'.[204] In addition, the Court strengthens the interpretation of Article 1 of the Convention by implicitly applying the customary rules of interpretation reflected in Article 33 of the VCLT ('interpretation of treaties authenticated in two or more languages'). It finds that 'as provided by this Article, the engagement undertaken by a Contracting State is confined to "securing" ("reconnaître" in the French text) the listed rights and freedoms to persons within its own "jurisdiction"'.[205]

To determine further the alleged violation of Article 2 of Protocol No. 1 of the Convention, which provides for 'the right of parents to ensure such education and teaching in conformity with their own religious and philosophical convictions',[206] the Court suggests the application of the customary rule of interpretation of reading the provision as a *whole* (in the light of the ordinary meaning of the terms in their context, object and purpose, and context of the whole treaty), pursuant to Article 31 (1)(2) of the VCLT. In particular, the Court notes neighbouring rights such as those proclaiming the right to freedom of thought, conscience and religion.[207] Supported

*Construction of a Wall in the Occupied Palestinian Territory,* Advisory Opinion (9 July 2004) (para 102); *Armed Activities on the Territory of the Congo (Democratic Republic of Congo (DRC) v. Uganda)*, ICJ, 19 December 2005.

[204]*Catan and Others* (2012), para 109. See also, e.g., the recent *Al-Skeini* case for a similar argument. The Court intended in *Al-Skeini* to clarify that the provisions of the Convention did not apply in *abstracto*, or in '*vacuum*', but in accord with logic, the spirit and purpose of the Convention, as also with international law. Unlike in *Bankovic*, the ECtHR performed in *Al-Skeini* a normative and moral judgment when holding (at p. 27) that '[i]t was inconceivable that the drafters of the Convention should have considered that the prospective responsibilities of States should be confined to violations perpetrated on their own territory' and (at p. 56) that 'one principle which emerged from the case law of the ICJ inter alia', in accordance to which 'once situation was qualified as an occupation within the meaning of international humanitarian law, there was a strong presumption of "jurisdiction" for the purpose of the application of human rights...'.

[205]*Id*, para 103. The ECtHR invokes in this *regard Soering v. the United Kingdom*, 7 July 1989, § 86, Series A no. 161; *Banković and Others v. Belgium and Others* [GC] (dec.), no. 52207/99, § 66, ECHR 2001-XII).

[206]Article 2 of Protocol No. 1 to the ECHR provides:

> No person shall be denied the right to education. In the exercise of any functions which it assumes in relation to education and to teaching, the State shall respect the right of parents to ensure such education and teaching in conformity with their own religious and philosophical convictions.

[207]*Catan and Others* (2012), para 136. The Court relies on its own precedents such as *Kjeldsen, Busk Madsen and Pedersen v. Denmark*, judgment of 7 December 1976, Series A no. 23, § 52; *Folgerø and Others v. Norway* [GC], no. 15472/02, § 84, ECHR 2007-III; *Lautsi and Others*

by its own (relevant) past decisions, the ECtHR adopts a *holistic* approach in interpreting Article 2 of Protocol No. 1 of the Convention while recalling the Convention's special character. It stresses: 'the Court must have regard to the fact that its context is a treaty for the effective protection of individual human rights and that *the Convention must be read as a whole, and interpreted in such a way as to promote internal consistency and harmony between its various provisions* ... The two sentences of Article 2 of Protocol No. 1 must be read not only in the light of each other but also, in particular, of Article 8, 9 and 10 of the Convention which proclaim the right of every one, including parents and children, 'to respect for his private and family life', to 'freedom of thought, conscience and religion' and to 'freedom ... to receive and impart information and ideas".[208] A similar holistic approach can be seen in many cases of the PCIJ/ICJ's practice; one of this could be the *Competence of the International Labour Organisation* case (1922), where the PCIJ declared that the treaty concerned must be read in its entirety, emphasising that 'the context is the final test' in providing the meaning of its provisions.[209]

Furthermore, the ECtHR expressly states that it also must take into account 'any relevant rules and principles of international law applicable in relations between the Contracting Parties and *the Convention should so far as possible be interpreted in harmony with other rules of international law of which it forms part*',[210] an approach consistent with Article 31(3)(c) of the VCLT. By taking into account 'the relevant rules of international law', the Court has to ascertain whether international law contains a general rule that could be determined with reference to the

*v. Italy* [GC], no. 30814/06, § 60, ECHR 2011 (extracts); *Cyprus v. Turkey* [GC], no. 25781/94, § 278, ECHR 2001-IV.

[208] *Id* (emphasis added). The Court invokes: *Stec and Others v. the United Kingdom* (dec.) [GC], nos. 65731/01 and 65900/01, § 48, ECHR 2005-X; *Austin and Others v. the United Kingdom* [GC], nos. 39692/09, 40713/09 and 41008/09, § 54, 15 March 2012.

[209] *Competence of the International Labour Organization in regard to International Regulation of the Conditions of Labour of Persons Employed in Agriculture*, Advisory Opinion, CIJ, Ser. B, No. 2&3, 1922, para 24. A similar contextualist approach could also be illustrated in the ICJ's practice, e.g., in: *Competence of General Assembly for the Admission of a State to the United Nation* (1950), *supra* note 173. The ICJ held in this case: 'It is a cardinal principle of interpretation that words must be interpreted in the sense which they would normally have in their context, unless such an interpretation would had to something unreasonable or absurd.' Also, a holistic approach is clear illustrated in the *Ambatielos Case* (*Greece v. the United Kingdom*), Merits: Obligation to Arbitrate, ICJ, Rep. 10, Judgment of May 19, 1953—where in the purpose to determine the obligation of the United Kingdom to accept arbitration, the ICJ considered the words 'claims ... based on the provisions of the ... Treaty of 1886 "within the Declaration of 1926, *insufficiently clear as to not be read in the context of the whole Treaty* of 1886..."' (emphasis added).

[210] *Catan and Others* (2012), para 136 (emphasis added). In supporting this approach, the Court relies on its relevant past decisions *in Al-Adsani v. the United Kingdom* [GC], no. 35763/97, § 55, ECHR 2001-XI; *Demir and Baykara v. Turkey* [GC], no. 34503/97, § 67, ECHR 2008; *Saadi v. the United Kingdom* [GC], no. 13229/03, § 62, ECHR 2008; *Rantsev v. Cyprus and Russia*, no. 25965/04, §§ 273–274, ECHR 2010 (extracts).

particular facts of the case at hand, respectively to the 'right of education' under Article 2 of Protocol No. 1 of the Convention,[211] which admittedly is drafted in general terms. Relevant rules, according to the ECtHR's findings here, are those found in the *Universal Declaration of Human Rights*; the *Convention Against Discrimination in Education*; the *International Covenant on Economic, Social and Cultural Rights*; the *International Convention on the Elimination of All Forms of Racial Discrimination*; and the *Convention on the Rights of the Child*.[212] Rather than explicitly insisting on the 'living instrument' doctrine as in other cases, in *Catan*, the Court merely appears to base its interpretation on international law when it examines any violation of the complainants' rights under Article 2 of Protocol 1 of the Convention. So the resort to general rules of international law appears here as a test that the Court applies to determine where the *right to education* is to be found in various international treaties. The Court appears to do so as to make it clear that the interpretation of this Convention's provision is also in harmony with different standards relating to this right.

The 'object and purpose' rule of interpretation is also clearly in evidence with the Court's emphasis on the Convention as an instrument for the 'protection of individual human beings', which 'requires that its provisions be interpreted and applied so as to make its safeguards practical and effective'.[213] Thus, the Court provides in *Catan* an approach in accordance with Article 31, paragraphs 1, 2 and 3 (c), of the VCLT in respect of Article 2 of Protocol No. 1, but it appears to attach less emphasis to the literal, 'natural' or 'ordinary meaning' rule in this case, unlike in other cases when it started with, and clearly emphasised, this rule.[214] The ECtHR indicates the application of the 'natural' or 'ordinary meaning' rule after employing the rules of 'context', 'relevant rules of international law' and 'object and purpose'. It relies this approach on its own past decision in the *Belgian Linguistic* Case (No. 2),[215] making use of the rule of 'ordinary meaning of the terms in their context'

[211]See a similar approach taken by the ECtHR, e.g., in the recent *Al-Skeini* case (see *supra* note 200, para 129). In this case the ECtHR took into account 'the relevant rules of international law' pursuant to Article 31(3)(c) VCLT. The Court did so as to find whether international law contains a general rule that could apply to the exercise of jurisdiction by a Contracting State outside its own territorial boundaries, and if such a rule existed, whether it could be determined with reference to the particular facts of the case in question under Article 1 of the Convention. Consequently, by relying on the relevant ICJ practice related to the application of human rights, the ECtHR found, for example, 'one principle which emerged from the case law of the ICJ inter alia', in accordance to which 'once situation was qualified as an occupation within the meaning of international humanitarian law, there was a strong presumption of "jurisdiction" for the purpose of the application of human rights...'.

[212]*Catan and Others* (2012), para 136.

[213]*Id*. The Court supports the teleological approach relying on its case law, e.g., *Soering v. the United Kingdom*, 7 July 1989, § 87, Series A no. 161; and *Artico v. Italy*, 13 May 1980, § 33, Series A no. 37.

[214]*Id*, paras 105–106.

[215]It relies this approach on its own past decision in the *Belgian Linguistic Case* (No. 2), and making use of the rule of "ordinary meaning of the terms in their context", the Court finds in the

and finds that '[b]y binding themselves, in the first sentence of Article 2 of Protocol No. 1, not to "deny the right to education", the Contracting States guarantee to anyone within their jurisdiction a right of access to educational institutions existing at a given time'.[216] Keeping account of the result obtained on the other rules of interpretation already employed, the Court clarifies further that 'this right of access constitutes only a part of the right to education set out in the first sentence. For the right to be effective, it is further necessary that, *inter alia*, the individual who is the beneficiary should have the possibility of drawing profit from the education received, that is to say, the right to obtain, in conformity with the rules in force in each State, and in one form or another, official recognition of the studies which he has completed'.[217] Then by adopting again the contextualist approach and concluding that '[t]he right set out in the second sentence of the Article is an adjunct of the fundamental right to education set out in the first sentence'[218] and that '[t]he second sentence aims at safeguarding the possibility of pluralism in education which possibility is essential for the preservation of the "democratic society" as conceived by the Convention',[219] the Court appears to confirm the meaning of Article 2 of Protocol No. 1 it ascertained on the previous rules.

In addition, the Court employs the 'margin of appreciation' doctrine and specifies on this basis that '[a]lthough the final decision as to the observance of the Convention's requirements rests with the Court, the Contracting States enjoy a certain margin of appreciation in this sphere'.[220] In this regard, the Court finds, for example, that 'in spite of its importance, the right to education is not absolute, but may be subject to limitations', and that 'a limitation will only be compatible with Article 2 of Protocol No. 1 if there is a reasonable relationship of proportionality between the means employed and the aim sought to be achieved'.[221] The Court concludes that there is no evidence before it to suggest that the measures taken by the 'MRT' authorities in respect of the schools involved[222] pursued a legitimate aim.[223] Summing up, the *Catan* case shows an instance where the Strasbourg Court

---

present case that: "[b]y binding themselves, in the first sentence of Article 2 of Protocol No. 1, not to "deny the right to education", the Contracting States guarantee to anyone within their jurisdiction a right of access to educational institutions existing at a given time.

[216] *Catan and Others* (2012), para 137.

[217] *Id.*

[218] *Id.*

[219] *Id*, para 136.

[220] *Id*, para 140.

[221] *Id.*

[222] *Id*, para 143 (schools where children were forced to be sent by the measures imposed by the 'MRT', 'where they would face the disadvantage of pursuing their entire secondary education in a combination of language and alphabet which they consider artificial and which is unrecognised anywhere else in the world, using teaching materials produced in Soviet times or, alternatively, subjecting their children to long journeys and/or substandard facilities, harassment and intimidation').

[223] *Id.*

interprets the Convention's provisions by virtue of the VCLT general rules of interpretation, confirming their customary character. The Court relies in addition on 'living instrument', 'special character' and 'margin of appreciation' as autonomous techniques (doctrines) of interpretation, making the Convention's safeguards practical and effective.[224]

#### 5.3.3.4 Consistency in Approaching VCLT Customary Rules?

An important argument put forward by McLachlan is that the VCLT general rules of interpretation are one of the means by which the international legal system as a whole gives form and meaning to individual rules (McLachlan 2005). Nevertheless, the process of treaty interpretation, as described by Tobin, 'is very much an active process of constructing *a* meaning rather than finding *the* meaning which lies latent with the text' (Tobin 2010, p. 5). Tobin shares the widely accepted idea that the '[m] eaning is not present in the expression itself'.[225] He admits that *the VCLT rules of interpretation are instrumental means for revealing the normative concept*, and also *for making the interpreter conscious of his own normative concept.*[226] This tension between the potential of the rules of interpretation and the realisation of this potential is clearly captured by Fitzmaurice when claiming that while the VCLT rules can be seen as rigid and inflexible, they are also perceived to be 'so flexible that it is almost impossible to arrive at an "illegal" interpretation' when applying them (Fitzmaurice 2013). As observed by Fitzmaurice and Merkouris, Articles 31 and 32 were actually conceived as a complete system, 'which does not allow its function to result in multiple "permissible" interpretations'.[227]

Other illustrations of cases that will be further analysed from the perspective of the ECtHR's approach to general rules and methods of treaty interpretation could raise the question of deviation from the standard of interpretation mandated by the VCLT, notably whether these rules/methods really serve in ascertaining the meaning of human rights provisions. Such an example is the ***Bankovic v. Belgium and Others*** **(2001)** case,[228] where the ECtHR was tasked with interpreting the notion of 'jurisdiction' within Article 1 of the Convention

[224]See a similar approach, e.g., in *Case of Lautsi and others v. Italy*, Application nr. 30814/06, Judgment, Strasbourg, 18 March 2011. In this case the Court proved fidelity to the customary rules (provided a holistic interpretation, although not using a technical description by directly referring to the VCLT) while applying its own developed rules in addition.

[225]Tobin (2010), p. 5.

[226]*Id*, p. 15.

[227]Fitzmaurice and Merkouris (2010), p. 185 (emphasis added).

[228]*Bankovic v. Belgium and Others*, Application no. 52207/99, The European Court of Human Rights, sitting as a Grand Chamber (Admissibility), 24 October and 12 December 2001.

(ECHR), which provides for the obligation of the High Contracting Parties 'to secure to everyone within their jurisdiction the rights and freedoms defined in Section I of [the] Convention'.[229] Since the language of this provision is thought to be *vaguely* formulated (in general terms), the approaches to interpretation adopted by the ECtHR in its respect have proved not always to be consistent.

One can observe in *Bankovic* patterns of application of the customary rules of interpretation that resemble those used by the ICJ.[230] However, the decision in this case is disappointing because the ECtHR chooses here a restrictive interpretation of Article 1 of the Convention (unlike the approach adopted in *Catan, Loizidou, Ilascu, Al-Skeini*, or other cases), basing its approach more on the 'ordinary meaning' and *travaux preparatoire* rules. The Court appears to deviate from the requirement of the fundamental rule of interpretation mandated by Article 31, paragraphs 1 and 2, of the VCLT, notably to give full meaning and effect to all the terms of the treaty at issue, thus to provide a holistic interpretation. This basic rule requires the interpreter to give meaning and effect, indeed, to the 'object and purpose' of the Convention and to its context, taking the Convention (treaty) as a whole. The Court appears to be acting in *Bankovic* in a way that is inconsistent with its own previous case law on similar interpretative issues, notably the case of *Loizidou* (1995), where the Court emphasised a teleological interpretation on the 'jurisdiction' matter within Article 1 of the Convention. The Court found in *Loizidou* that 'the responsibility of a Contracting Party may also arise when as a consequence of military action – whether lawful or unlawful – it exercises effective control of an area outside its national territory'.[231] It also made clear that the object and purpose of the Convention 'consists in the obligation to secure outside the national territory – the rights and freedoms set out in the Convention'.[232]

*Bankovic* relates to six citizens of the Federal Republic of Yugoslavia (FRY), who were victims or relatives of victims of those killed in the 1999 NATO air strikes against Yugoslavia that targeted a Radio Station. They alleged violations of Article 2 (Rights to Life), Article 10 (Freedom of Expression) and Article 13 (Right to an Effective Remedy) of the ECHR against all the European NATO member states who were parties to the Convention for their role in that action. Since FRY was outside of the territory of all NATO state respondents, the issue of interpretation raised before the ECtHR was whether the scope of the territorial jurisdiction of the ECHR extended beyond the territories of its members states, thus concerning the interpretation of Article 1 of the Convention.

---

[229]Article 1 of the Convention reads as follows:

> The High Contracting Parties shall secure to everyone within their jurisdiction the rights and freedoms defined in Section I of [the] Convention.

[230]In the *Libyan Arab Jamhirya/Chad and Kasikili/Sedudu* cases (discussed in Chap. 4 of this book) the Court resolved the ambiguities in the text of the treaties at issue by adopting in addition the teleological method, and providing a holistic interpretation.

[231]*Case* of *Loizidou v. Turkey* (Preliminary Objection), Application no. 15318/89, Judgment of 23 March, 1995, para 62.

[232]*Id.*

After referring to the rules of 'ordinary meaning', 'context', 'object and purpose', the Court expressly declares that it will resort to 'any subsequent practice' rule,[233] pursuant to Article 31(3)(b) of the VCLT.[234] On the 'subsequent practice' rule basis, the Court finds that '[a]lthough there have been a number of military missions involving Contracting States acting extra-territorially since their ratification of the Convention (*inter alia*, in the Gulf, in Bosnia and Herzegovina and in the FRY), no State has indicated a belief that its extra-territorial actions involved an exercise of jurisdiction within the meaning of Article 1 of the Convention'.[235] However, the Court in *Bankovic* goes further and expressly recalls that the principles underlying the Convention must be interpreted in the context of 'any relevant rules of international law when examining questions of jurisdiction and, consequently, determine State responsibility in conformity with the governing principles of international law' (under Article 31(3)(c) VCLT).[236] It finds in this respect, for example, that 'from the standpoint of public international law, the jurisdictional competence of a State is primarily territorial'[237] and that 'no State has indicated a belief that its extra-territorial actions involved an exercise of jurisdiction within the meaning of Article 1 of the Convention by making a derogation pursuant to Article 15 of the Convention'.[238] At this point, the Court makes an express choice for extraneous sources of interpretation. It reiterates that the *travaux préparatoires* can also be consulted with a view to confirming any meaning, which was what the Court alluded as being its role in this case.[239] Nevertheless, it appears that the Court mainly relies on the *travaux preparatoire* despite stressing the 'ordinary meaning'

[233]The 'subsequent practice' rule was confirmed by the ICJ, for example, in the following cases: *Corfu Channel, (United Kingdom of Great Britain and Northern Ireland v. Albania)* (Merits), Judgment of April 9th, 1949, ICJ, Rap. 4, 18, p. 25. Or in its earlier practice, e.g., in *Arbitral Award Made by the King of Spain on 23 December 1906*, Judgment, I.C.J. Reports 1960, pp. 206–207; *Temple of Preah Vihear*, Merits, Judgment, I.C.J. Reports 1962, pp. 33–35; *Certain Expenses of the United Nations* (Article 17, Paragraph 2, of the Charter), Advisory Opinion, I.C.J. Reports 1962, pp. 157, 160–161, and 172–175. Also, the Court has had occasion to apply this rule several times recently, e.g., *in Arbitral Award of 31 July 1989 (Guinea-Bissau v. Senegal)*, Judgment, I.C.J. Reports 1991, pp. 69–70, para 48; *Land, Island and Maritime Frontier Dispute (El Salvador/Honduras: Nicaragua intervening)*, Judgment, I.C.J Reports 1992, pp. 582–586, paras. 373–380, and p. 586, para 380; *Territorial Dispute (Libyan Arab Jamahirya v. Chad)*, Judgment, I.C.J. Reports 1994, pp. 21–22, para 41; *Maritime Delimitation and Territorial Questions between Qatar and Bahrain (Qatar v. Bahrain)*, Jurisdiction and Admissibility, Judgment, I.C.J. Reports 1995, p. 18, para 33.

[234]*Bankovic* (2001). The Court invokes *Loizidou* (preliminary objections).

[235]*Id*, para 62.

[236]*Id*, para 57.

[237]*Id*, para 59. The Court relies on international law sources such as: Mann (1964, 1984); Bernhardt (1997), pp. 55–59; Meng (1987); Jennings and Watts (1992), para 137; Dupuy (1998), p. 61; Brownlie (1998), pp. 287–301 and 312–314.

[238]*Id*, para 62.

[239]*Id*, paras 65–58.

reading of Article 1, which was said to strengthen the assumption that 'Article 1 of the Convention must be considered to reflect this ordinary and essentially territorial notion of jurisdiction'.[240] The Court holds that the extracts from the *travaux pré paratoires*, which confirm that the words 'all persons residing within their territories' were replaced by a reference to persons 'within their jurisdiction',[241] constitute 'a clear indication of the intended meaning of Article 1 of the Convention which cannot be ignored'.[242]

It is to be observed, however, that by failing to adopt in addition a teleological interpretation, thus giving meaning and effect to all the terms of the Convention under Article 31(1) of the VCLT (text, context, object and purpose), the Court complies rather with a restrictive than a dynamic interpretation, which it has usually promoted in its treaty interpretative practice. Despite stressing that the *travaux preparatoire* must not be considered 'solely' and 'decisive' in finding the meaning of Article 1, the Court actually ends up by expressly supporting its reasoning on the basis of the *travaux preparatoire*, thus taking it to be decisive.[243] The Court strengthens its result by suggesting resort to the effectiveness principle, asserting that '[h]ad the drafters of the Convention wished to ensure jurisdiction as extensive as that advocated by the applicants, they could have adopted a text the same as or similar to the contemporaneous Article 1 of the four Geneva Conventions of 1949'.[244] Thus, the Court appears to over-rely in *Bankovic* on the *travaux preparatoire*, adopting a restrictive interpretation, despite recalling the Convention as 'a living instrument to be interpreted in light of present day conditions', which the Court itself admitted as being 'firmly rooted in the Court's case-law',[245] and this also despite the fact that the Court stressed its obligation to take into consideration the 'special character' of the Convention: 'as a constitutional instrument of European public order for the protection of individual human beings ... to ensure the observance of the engagements undertaken by the Contracting Parties'.[246]

In conclusion, the ECtHR's interpretative approach in *Bankovic* appears to be not entirely consistent with the approach it expressly declared initially. The Court appears to have decided in principle on the arguments stemming from the 'ordinary meaning' of the terms and the *travaux preparatoire*, providing a restrictive interpretation, not precisely in harmony with the 'object and purpose' of the

[240] *Id*, para 61.

[241] *Id*, para 63 ('with a view to expanding the Convention's application to others who may not reside, in a legal sense, but who are, nevertheless, on the territory of the Contracting States').

[242] *Id*, para 65.

[243] *Id*, para 63.

[244] *Id*, para 75. Article 1 of each of these Conventions ('the Geneva Conventions 1949') requires the Contracting Parties to undertake 'to respect and to ensure respect for the present Convention in all circumstances'.

[245] *Id*, para 64.

[246] *Id*, para 80.

Convention, the Convention taken as a whole (under the basic rule mandated by Article 31(1)(2) VCLT), as well as with the 'special character' and 'living instrument' doctrines that it itself admitted as relevant to the present case. It fails in this way to give prevalence to fundamental human rights considerations, as reflected in the provisions at issue.[247]

#### 5.3.3.5 Interplay of Lex Specialis/Lex Generalis? Reliance on the Convention's 'Law-Making Character'

Another argument towards understanding the nature of human rights interpretation is made by Toufayan, who claims that the so-called specialty of human rights treaties is well reflected in the provisions of the VCLT on treaty interpretation, even if these rules do not contemplate a 'balancing' of values that is often needed to enable a human right interpretation (Toufayan 2005, p. 6). According to the author, the text and rules of interpretation are like the materials used by an interpreter only in helping him to construct the meaning of the text.[248] However, it must be recalled in this connection the ILC Study Report's clarification that the 1969 Vienna Convention 'does not purport to be an exhaustive statement of interpretative techniques – there is no mention, for example, of *lex specialis* or *lex posterior*' (ILC 2006, p. 215, para 427).

As observed by Mowbray, since the European Convention of Human Rights is a multilateral treaty, its interpretation must be governed by the principles of interpretation codified in the VCLT (Mowbray 2005, pp. 58–59). He admits that despite the fact that Articles 31–33 of the VCLT are seldom cited in judgments of the ECtHR, these rules seem to be a constant source of inspiration for this Court.[249] In her recent study, Fitzmaurice admits that since the VCLT rules of interpretation were ultimately drafted in a flexible way, allowing varying constructions, generally the human rights *fora*'s decision-making can develop within the framework of the VCLT's general methodology of interpretation.[250] Thus, in respect of its interpretative practice the Strasbourg Court is thought to confirm the reception of the VCLT customary rules of interpretation into its special context and also that the Court has given consideration to general international rules and

[247]The applicants filled the application, invoking Article 2 (the right to life), Article 10 (freedom of expression) and Article 13 (the right to an effective remedy) of the Convention.

[248]Toufayan (2005), pp. 22–23.

[249]Mowbray (2005), pp. 58–59.

[250]*Id.*

principles when it has had the occasion.[251] Moreover, as observed by Kamminga, the customary rules of interpretation of treaties have shaped the way of approaching treaty interpretation by the ECtHR.[252] Importantly, the principle of dynamic interpretation (*the Convention is a living instrument which must be interpreted in the light of present-day conditions*)[253] is thought to be reflected to a considerable extent in Article 31(3)(b) of the VCLT (Kamminga 2008, p. 9). As shown in Chap. 3 of this book, this provision provides for the rule of taking into account, together with the context, *any subsequent practice in the application of the treaty that establishes the agreement of the parties regarding its interpretation.* Actually, the approach taken by the *human rights fora* in respect of Article 31(3)(b), together with Article 31(3)(c) of the VCLT, may constitute, as observed by Fitzmaurice, 'the most important aspect of their common ground in relation to interpretation' (Fitzmaurice 2013).

The ***Case of Loizidou v. Turkey* (1995)**[254] marks an explicit reconciliation between the ECtHR's own doctrines of interpretation such as 'living instrument' and 'special character' and the VCLT rules of interpretation. Notably, the Court here emphasizes that the Convention's 'special character' is epitomized by the doctrine of the 'living instrument', which requires an interpretation of its provisions in the light of present-day conditions. The Court also makes it clear that the Convention has a 'law-making character' and that its focus is to seek that interpretation of the Convention's provisions which is most appropriate in order to realise the aim and achieve the object of the Convention and not to restrict to the greatest possible degree the obligations undertaken by the parties to it. However, certain methodological aspects in *Loizidou* regarding the ECtHR's interpretative approach (the patterns of approaching the customary rules: ordinary meaning, context, object and purpose, subsequent practice, supplementary means, as also principles of good faith and effectiveness) could find common ground with the ICJ on a similar difficulty in the construction of a treaty text, as is when a text is drawn in *insufficient clear* terms. The background to the case is the arrest of the complainant, Mrs. Loizidou, a Cypriot national, in the area of Northern Cyprus occupied illegally by Turkey, as well as the denial to her of access to her property situated there. In order to examine whether the applicant's complaints were admissible on the ground that they fall within the 'jurisdiction' of the

---

[251] Fitzmaurice (2013). See, for example, in this respect *Al-Adsani v. United Kingdom*, Judgment of 21 November 2001, ECHR 2001-XI, p. 79. In *Al-Adsani*, the ECtHR relied on Article 31(3)(c) VCLT to find whether the rules of state immunity might conflict with the right of access of court under Article 6(1) of the ECHR, and decided by majority to give effect to state immunity.

[252] Kamminga (2008), p. 9. Kamminga gives as example the emphasis put by the Court on the object and purpose of a treaty (under Article 31(1) of the VCLT) in *Wemhoff*.

[253] *Tyrer v. the United Kingdom, supra* note 163, para 31. This case is important for the reason that the ECtHR fully admitted and explicitly declared the 'living instrument' doctrine. It held: 'The Court also recall that the Convention is a living instrument which as the Commission rightly stressed, must be interpreted in the light of present day conditions.'

[254] *Loizidou* (1995).

respondent government (Turkey), the Court had to determine whether Turkey's presence in Northern Cyprus constituted an exercise of 'jurisdiction' under Articles 1,[255] 25 and 46 of the Convention regarding whether states (here Turkey) could impose limitations on their acceptance of the Court's jurisdiction to hear cases.[256]

To determine whether the matters complained of by the applicant fell within the 'jurisdiction' of Turkey (which Turkey contested), under Article 1 of the Convention, even though they occurred outside its national territory,[257] the Court proceeds by invoking its own relevant jurisprudence. Unlike in *Bankovic*, which was thus decided after *Loizidou*, the Court in *Loizidou* adopts a wide and dynamic (evolutive) interpretation to the terms of Article 1. It recalls that 'the concept of "jurisdiction" under this provision is not restricted to the national territory of the High Contracting Parties'.[258] Thus, the Court's focus appears to be on the 'object and purpose' of the Convention (set forth in the Preamble), that of achieving greater unity in the maintenance and further realisation of human rights,[259] and also on the special character of the Convention as a 'living instrument' that must 'be interpreted in the present day conditions'.[260]

---

[255]For Article 1 of the Convention, see *supra* note 229.

[256]The provisions at issue in this case were Article 25 and Article 46 of the Convention regarding the unconditional acceptance of the Court's jurisdiction which the parties to this Convention may make.

Article 25 of the Convention provides:

1. The Commission may receive petitions addressed to the Secretary General of the Council of Europe from any person, non-governmental organisation or group of individuals claiming to be the victim of a violation by one of the High Contracting Parties of the rights set forth in [the] Convention, provided that the High Contracting Parties receive such petitions. Those of the High Contracting Parties who have made such a declaration undertake not to hinder in any way the effective exercise of this right.
2. Such declarations may be made for a specific period.

Article 46 provides:

1. Any of the High Contracting Parties may at any time declare that it recognises as compulsory ipso facto and without special agreement the jurisdiction of the Court in all matters concerning the interpretation and application of the Convention.
2. The declarations referred to above may be made unconditionally or on condition of reciprocity on the part of several or certain other High Contracting Parties or for a specified period.
3. These declarations shall be deposited with the Secretary General of the Council of Europe who shall transmit copies thereof to the High Contracting Parties.

[257]*Loizidou* (1995), para 61.

[258]*Id.*

[259]*Id*, para 77. According to the scholarship the Strasbourg organs have been consistently willing to interpret the Convention as a 'living instrument', creating the possibility that obligations can be understood in a manner not necessarily foreseen by the drafters.

[260]*Id*, para 71.

The Court clearly distinguishes in *Loizidou* the special character of the Convention from international treaties of the classic kind.[261] For example, when refuting the Turkish Government's argument that restrictions attaching to declarations (within Article 25 and Article 46) 'must have been envisaged by the drafters of the Convention in the light of practice under Article 36 of the Statute of the International Court of Justice',[262] the ECtHR underlines the *law-making character* of the Convention and the Convention's role as a human rights guarantee that must be interpreted as to permit its development in time. Also, the Court makes clear that it must seek that interpretation that is most appropriate in order to realise the aim and achieve the object of the Convention. It explains in this regard that 'unlike the Convention institutions, the role of the International Court is not exclusively limited to direct supervisory functions in respect of a lawmaking treaty such as the Convention'.[263] Moreover, the ECtHR asserts that 'the long-established practice of the International Court of Justice in accepting restrictions on the jurisdiction of the Court under Article 36 of the Statute affords no assistance ... because of the substantial differences between the two systems'.[264]

In further attempting to establish the real meaning of the terms of Articles 25 and 46 of the Convention (which are concerned with the unconditional acceptance of the Strasbourg Court's jurisdiction that the parties to this Convention may make), the Court also relies on the Vienna rules of treaty interpretation. It expressly declares the application of the VCLT methodology of interpretation, stating that '[t]o determine whether the Contracting Parties may impose restrictions on their acceptance of the competence of the Commission and Court under Article 25 and 46, the Court will seek to ascertain the *ordinary meaning* to be given to the terms of these provisions in their *context* and in the light of their *object and purpose*. It shall also take into account, together with the context, *any subsequent practice* in the application of the treaty which establishes the agreement of the parties regarding its interpretation.'[265] The Court appears to choose, in addition, to resort to the *travaux preparatoire* as to shed more light on, and to confirm, the intention of the Convention's drafters in respect of the provisions at issue, pursuant to Article 32 of the VCLT. However, the Court does not adopt this approach in express terms (resort to the *travaux*), as it does in respect of the other rules employed under Article 31 of the VCLT. Further, to better explain the special character of the Convention, the Court relies in addition on the 'subsequent practice' rule, under Article 31(3)(b) of the VCLT, finding that '[s]uch a fundamental difference in the role and purpose of the

[261]*Id*, para 78.

[262]*Id*, para 82. The Government of Turkey submitted that 'the drafting history of the Convention reveals that Article 36 of the Statute served as a model for Article 46 . . .of the Convention'.

[263]*Id*, para 84. The Court invokes *Ireland v. the United Kingdom*, Application no. 5310/71, Judgment of 18 January 1978, Series A no. 25, p. 90, para 239.

[264]*Id*.

[265]*Id*, paras 73 and 89 (emphasis added).

respective tribunals, coupled with the existence of a practice of unconditional acceptance under Articles 25 and 46 … provides a compelling basis for distinguishing Convention practice from that of the International Court'.[266]

Since the ECtHR arrives at an extraterritorial application of the Convention under Article 1 of the Convention in *Loizidou*, although this is later impacted by *Bankovic* but confirmed in other cases recently, such as *Al-Skeini* (2011)[267] or *Catan* (discussed above), it could be seen as a possible instance of deviation from international law as it implies the substantive issue of 'state responsibility' on which the ICJ greatly developed jurisprudence. However, in this regard, it has been observed in the scholarship that:

> If the European Court was truly adopting an interpretation of the law on state responsibility at odds with that of the pre-eminent international Court, the ICJ, it would presumably have had the courtesy of saying so, as the ICTY itself did in *Tadic*. Yet, not a peep on this matter has even been heard from the European Court. Moreover, when *Loizidou* was delivered, not a single author (and one might add, not even the ICJ President) thought that the European Court was initiating a conflict of jurisprudence with the ICJ.[268]

Under the exception to the principle of territoriality, as the Court applies in *Loizidou*, the jurisdiction of a Contracting State may extend (pursuant to Article 1 of the Convention) to acts of its authorities that produce effects outside its own territory.[269] Therefore, when making the extraterritorial application of the Convention in *Loizidou* (under Article 1), the ECtHR seems to be careful in rebutting the 'jurisdiction' reservations. The Court's argument laid down in this regard is that the Convention has a 'standard-setting character' and is not like any ordinary treaty concluded by two states,[270] so the Convention imposes 'objective obligations' upon the Contracting States for the protection of human rights. In sum, though the Court highly relies on, and emphasises in *Loizidou*, its own doctrines of interpreting the Convention (e.g., the Convention's 'law-making character', 'living instrument'), it complements these autonomous means of interpretation with the Vienna rules of

[266]*Id*, para 85.

[267]See *Al-Skeini*, *supra* note 200.

[268]Milanovic (2011), p. 50. Similar reservations in respect of the fragmentation of the international law *vis-a-vis* 'state responsibility' provoked by ECtHR in *Loizidou* could be inferred also from other authors' comments on ECtHR's contribution to state responsibility doctrine such as De Frouville (2010), p. 269, who argued that 'contrary to what was suggested by James Crawford, the "*Loizidou* judgment of the European Court of Human Rights are not on the same level as the *Nicaragua* judgment", since *Loizidou*, unlike ICJ's *Nicaragua*, dealt with a definition of a "de facto" organ of state'.

[269]The recent case *Fabris v. France* (Judgment (Merits), Appl. No. 16574108, Strasbourg, 7 February, 2013), reaffirms the constitutional force of the Court's judgments and the Court's jurisdiction to verify whether a State Party has complied with the obligations imposed on it by one of the Court's judgments, as *Loizidou* brought full recognition of the Court as 'Europe's Constitutional Court', whose task could not be endangered by States Parties exercising their right of reservation.

[270]See e.g. Wilde (2005), p. 117—discussing the special character of the ECHR and the European Convention of Human Rights as a 'living instrument'.

interpretation, which are fully applied and adapted to the *lex specialis*' context (the ECHR).

#### 5.3.3.6 Complementarity of Practice and Reliance on the ICJ's Methods/Techniques of Interpretation and 'Living Instrument'

An interesting view on the Strasbourg Court's jurisprudence comes from the perspective of a human rights practitioner, formerly Vice-President of the ECtHR, Judge Rozakis, who has identified two major jurisprudential trends that serve the concept of 'living instrument'. According to Rozakis, one such trend is given by the 'wide interpretation of the rights and freedoms contained in the Convention, favouring the individual *vis-a-vis* the respondent State', while the other by the 'restrictive interpretation of the Convention's clauses to the State's benefit, thereby limiting the rights and freedoms provided for by the Convention' (Rozakis 2005, p. 5).

When the ECtHR deals with human rights provisions that are drawn in generic terms (sometimes they do provide vaguely or not provide at all for a specific circumstance), it appears to show flexibility in its reception of international law into its conceptual framework (McInerney-Lankford 2012, p. 621). Such a situation would involve, in Forowicz's words, an *evolutive and dynamic interpretation*, which allows 'contemporary realities to be taken into account and a departure from the circumstances which prevailed at the time of the drafting of the Convention' (Forowicz 2010, p. 11). According to Pegorier, this 'evolutive', 'dynamic' interpretation finds reflection in the *living instrument* doctrine, which is a principle that, 'in permitting an extension of interpretative parameters, encourages active protection of human rigths' (Pegorier 2013, p. 29). In realising this approach, Fitzmaurice observes that the ECtHR has frequently looked for interpretative guidance at Article 31(3)(c) of the VCLT (Fitzmaurice 2013). The ECtHR has expressly stated this approach in some of the cases, as, for example, in the *Demir and Baykara* case (2008), where it reiterated that it has always taken account 'of evolving norms of national and international law in its interpretation of Convention provisions'.[271] However, as it was shown earlier in Chap. 3 of this book, some exceptions to this approach can be evidenced in cases such as *Al-Adsani* (2001). Here the use of Article 31(3)(c) did not lead the Strasbourg Court to provide an interpretation of the (Convention) provision at issue in a broader context of international law, an approach that could, arguably, be admitted as a deviation from international law. Thus, despite initially admitting that the rule on the

[271] *Demir and Baykara*, *supra* note 210, para 68. See on this point, e.g., Fitzmaurice (2013), mentioning the *Golder* and *Demir and Baykara* cases, as fundamentally in illustrating the ECtHR's general approach to interpretation. For example, the ECtHR held in the recent *Demir and Baykara* case (2008) that '[i] has never considered the provisions of the Convention as the sole framework of reference for the interpretation of the rights and freedoms enshrined therein', and it 'can and must take into account elements of international law other than the Convention'.

'prohibition of torture' is a *jus cogens* rule and that '[t]he Convention should so far as possible be interpreted in harmony with other rules of international law of which it forms part . . .', the Strasbourg Court decided that the rules of sovereign immunity overrode a *jus cogens* rule.[272] The Court justified its approach by asserting in *Al-Adsani* that 'international law could be used only to assist in interpreting lacunae or ambiguities in a statute, and when the terms of a statute were clear, the statute had to prevail over international law'.[273]

Moreover, the ECtHR also resorts on occasion to the ICJ's practice on treaty interpretation. But even if an express reference of the ECtHR to the ICJ's precedents is not frequently made, when it does occur, it is nevertheless an indication that the 'cross-fertilization' phenomenon (which implies using precedents of other international courts and tribunals, borrowing and changing views between them), actually, is taking place at the ECtHR. However, a clear reliance on the VCLT's and ICJ's practice on treaty interpretation appears to occur when the Court deals with certain difficulties of interpreting the Convention's human rights provisions, such as when the text is *silent* in respect of a specific circumstance in a given case (i.e., 'interim measures of protection'). Further analysis of the ***Case of Mamatkulov and Askarov v. Turkey* (2005)**[274] illustrates a wide approach adopted by the ECtHR that serves the interpretation of the *Convention* as a *living instrument*. It implies a reliance on the Vienna rules and ICJ's interpretative practice as a basis for interpreting a provision of the Convention which is *silent* in regard to the circumstances of this case. Often invoked by the ECtHR in its decisions, this case is, in Judge Rozakis's view, an illustration of the ECtHR's relationship with international law, which marks a change in this Court's approach to international law's developments taken in previous judgments (Rozakis 2005). As the analysis of this case shows further, the ECtHR chose a flexible and dynamic interpretation of the provisions of the Convention at issue in the light of the law of treaties, international law precedents and general principles of international law of which the Convention (European Convention of Human Rights and Fundamental Freedoms) forms a part.[275] The Court also took into account the special nature of the Convention as an instrument for the human rights protection, applying its own developed doctrines.

In the case of *Mamatkulov and Askarov*, the applicants were opposition party members in Uzbekistan charged with political offences, who asked Turkey for political asylum as their lives were at risk. Since Turkey failed to comply with the interim measures indicated by the ECtHR under Rule 39 of the Rules of Court,[276] the applicants' extradition by Turkey thus proved a real obstacle to the effective

---

[272]See *Case of Al-Adsani*, *supra* note 251, para 55.

[273]*Id.* The ECtHR seemed not to give prevalence to that number of legal authorities which affirmed that 'the prohibition of torture has attained the status of a peremptory norm or *jus cogens*'.

[274]*Case of Mamatkulov and Askarov v. Turkey*, Applications no. 46827/99 and 46951/99, Strasbourg, Judgment of 4 February 2005.

[275]The Court invokes the *Al-Adsani* case.

[276]Judgment of 6 February 2003.

presentation of their application to the Court. The issue of interpretation was therefore whether Turkey was in breach of its undertaking under Article 34 of the Convention not to hinder the applicants in the exercise of their right of individual application.[277]

While there is no specific provision in the Convention concerning the domain in which Rule 39 of the ECtHR applies, the Court has to determine whether in the absence of an express clause in the Convention (*silence* in the text) it could derive the power to order binding *interim measures* from Article 34 of the Convention taken alone or in conjunction with Rule 39.[278] In so doing, the Court suggests first the application of the teleological method. It looks to the object and purpose of the Convention while pointing out its special character: 'as a treaty for the collective enforcement of human rights and fundamental freedoms', which 'creates, over and above a network of mutual, bilateral undertakings, objective obligations which, in the words of the Preamble, benefit from a "collective enforcement"'.[279] Moreover, the Court underlines the Convention as a 'living instrument' and, thus, the evolutive (dynamic) approach which it must take in interpreting the Convention provisions. It states that 'as an instrument for the protection of individual human beings', the Convention requires that 'its provisions be interpreted and applied so as to make its safeguards practical and effective, as part of the system of individual applications'.[280] Relying further on the 'object and purpose' rule (teleological method), the Court finds that any interpretation of the rights and freedoms guaranteed has to be consistent with 'the general spirit of the Convention, an instrument designed to maintain and promote the ideals and values of a democratic society'.[281]

The Court suggests, in addition, the application of the 'context of the treaty' rule, referring to the human rights that are usually of concern for *interim measures*,

---

[277] *Mamatkulov and Askarov* (2005), para 99. Article 34 of the Convention provides:

> The Court may receive applications from any person, non-governmental organisation or group of individuals claiming to be the victim of a violation by one of the High Contracting Parties of the rights set forth in the Convention or the Protocols thereto. The High Contracting Parties undertake not to hinder in any way the effective exercise of this right.

[278] Rule 39 of the Rules of the ECtHR provides:

> 1. The Chamber or, where appropriate, its President may, at the request of a party or of any other person concerned, or of its own motion, indicate to the parties any interim measure which it considers should be adopted in the interests of the parties or of the proper conduct of the proceedings before it.
> 2. Notice of these measures shall be given to the Committee of Ministers.
> 3. The Chamber may request information from the parties on any matter connected with the implementation of any interim measure it has indicated.

[279] *Mamatkulov and Askarov* (2005), para 100.

[280] *Id*, para 101.

[281] *Id* (emphasis added). The Court invokes *Loizidou*, see *supra* note 254; *Soering v. the United Kingdom*, Judgment of 7 July 1989, Series A no. 161, and, mutatis mutandis, *Klass and Others v. Germany*, Judgment of 6 September 1978, Series A no. 28, p. 18, § 34.

notably the right to life (Article 2), freedom from torture (Article 3) and, exceptionally, the right to respect for private and family life (Article 8).[282] Interpretation in the light of other VCLT rules such as 'any relevant rules of international law' applicable in the relations between the parties is also invoked by the Court.[283] Referencing its approach in the *Golder* case, the Court reconciles the special character of the Convention with international law. Accordingly, the Court finds that it must determine 'the responsibility of the States in accordance with *the principles of international law governing this sphere*, while taking into account the special nature of the Convention as an instrument of human rights protection'.[284] To strengthen this interpretation, the Court invokes the *Al-Adsani* case, recalling that the Convention must be interpreted 'so far as possible consistently with the other principles of international law of which it forms a part'.[285] It is true that until one point, the ECtHR in *Al-Adsani* reasoned in consideration of the principle of 'systemic integration'. But, as it was seen, the Court proved itself 'unable' in the end to give effect under Article 31(3)(c) to the provision at issue, which makes this case an illustration of fragmentation of international law rules under this article.[286] Thus, by adopting an approach in compliance with the requirements of Article 31(3)(c) of the VCLT, the Court finds in *Mamatkulov and Askarov*, for example, that the Human Rights Committee considers that the failure to comply with 'interim measures' is a breach of a state's treaty obligations under the two 1966 covenants.[287] To reinforce this argument, the Court looks in addition for 'practice' regarding the 'interim measures' in the views of other international bodies such as the IACHR and ICJ. The ECtHR makes in this connection a specific reference to Article 31(1) of the VCLT, notably to the need for interpreting Article 34 of the Convention (ECHR) in consideration of the 'good faith' and in accordance with the principle of effectiveness.[288] Recognising the ICJ's stance on 'interim measures' as binding, the ECtHR expressly states that it will refer to the approach adopted by the ICJ in the *LaGrand* case (2001).[289] *LaGrand*'s reasoning was based on the teleological approach adopted previously in the *Application of the*

---

[282]*Id*, para 103.

[283]*Id*, para 111. The Court also finds that the United Nations Committee against Torture has considered the issue of a State Party's failure to comply with interim measures on a number of occasions.

[284]*Id*.

[285]*Id*. See *Al-Adsani*, *supra* note 251.

[286]*Id*, para 55. See Chap. 3 for comments on *Al-Adsani* from the perspective of 'systemic integration'.

[287]*Id*, para 114.

[288]*Id*, para 123.

[289]*Id*, para 117. *LaGrand* (*Germany v. the United States of America*), ICJ, Judgment of 27 June 2001. In this regard the ECtHR also invokes *Avena and other Mexican nationals* (*Mexico v. the United States of America*), ICJ, 31 March 2004, and in *Nicaragua v. the United States of America*, ICJ, 27 June 1986, p. 136, para 271. In *Nicaragua* the ICJ held: 'The question thus arises whether Article XXI similarly affords a defence to a claim under customary international law based on

*Convention on the Prevention and Punishment of the Crime of Genocide* (1993) case, where the ICJ held that Article 41 of the Statute of the ICJ 'has as its object to preserve the respective rights of the parties pending the decision of the Court, and presupposes that irreparable prejudice should not be caused to rights which are the subject of dispute in judicial proceedings'.[290]

Thus, the ECtHR expressly resorts in *Mamatkulov and Askarov* to the effectiveness principle, finding accordingly that if a respondent state fails to comply with 'interim measures', it will undermine the effectiveness of the right of individual application guaranteed by Article 34, as also the state's formal undertaking in Article 1 to protect the rights and freedoms set forth in the Convention.[291] Then, the ECtHR recalls that a similar approach was adopted by the ICJ in *LaGrand* on the effectiveness principle basis and found that '[t]he contention that provisional measures indicated under Article 41 might not be binding would be contrary to the object and purpose of that Article'.[292] Stressing the teleological method, it appears that the ECtHR's main focus in *Mamatkulov and Askarov* is on the 'object and purpose' of the Convention, which, nevertheless, points towards a dynamic or evolutive interpretation that the Court intends to adopt.

As it can be seen, in its effort to give full meaning and effect to the provision at issue (Article 34 of the Convention), as also to the Convention as a 'living instrument', the Court's resort to the 'object and purpose' rule is indubitably supported by the rules of 'text'/'context', the 'good faith' and effectiveness principles, as also by 'any relevant rules of international law'—an approach consistent with Article 31, paragraphs 1, 2 and 3(c), of the VCLT. The original intention of the Convention's drafters in respect of the meaning of Article 34 of the Convention is furthermore suggested by the Court to be investigated and confirmed on the 'supplementary means' basis. Consulting the *travaux preparatoire*, the Court finds that 'although the Convention right to individual application was *originally intended* as an optional part of the system of protection, it has over the years become of high importance and is now a key component of the machinery for protecting the rights and freedoms set forth in the Convention'.[293] Therefore, the

---

allegation of conduct depriving the Treaty of its object and purpose if such conduct can be shown to be "measures . . . necessary to protect" essential security interests.'

[290] *Id*, para 47. The ECtHR invokes the Order of 13 September 1993 in *Application of the Convention on the Prevention and Punishment of the Crime of Genocide (Bosnia and Herzegovina v. Yugoslavia)*, ICJ, 1993. Also, the ECtHR notes that, measures designed to avoid aggravating or extending disputes have frequently been indicated in the ICJ's practice with the purpose of being implemented, such as in: *Nuclear Tests (Australia v. France)*, Interim Protection, Order of 22 June 19 73, ICJ Reports 1973, p. 106; *Nuclear Tests (New Zealand v. France)*, Interim Protection, Order of 22 June 1973, I.C.J. Reports 1973, p. 142; *Frontier Dispute*, Provisional Measures, Order of 10 January 1986, I.C.J. Reports 1986, p. 11, para 32, point 1 A; *Land and Maritime Boundary between Cameroon and Nigeria, Provisional Measures*, Order of 15 March 1996, I.C.J. Reports 1996-II), pp. 22–23, para 41, and p. 24, para 49 (1).

[291] *Id*, para 124.

[292] *Id*, para 117.

[293] *Id*, para 122 (emphasis added).

ECtHR's concern appears to be here to clarify that indications of 'interim measures' given by this Court permit the assurance that the protection afforded to the applicant is effective.[294] Driven by the effectiveness principle in support of this view, additionally relying on the Vienna rules of interpretation and relevant ICJ's treaty interpretative experience and practice, the ECtHR renders in *Mamatkulov and Askarov* a *holistic* and *dynamic (evolutive)* interpretation. It considers of 'crucial importance that the Convention is interpreted and applied in a manner which renders its rights practical and effective, not theoretical and illusory', as the Convention 'is a *living instrument* which must be interpreted in the light of present-day conditions',[295] thus by keeping account of contemporary realities.

#### 5.3.3.7 Deviance from Customary Rules of Interpretation?

It is the notion of *human dignity* that makes human rights treaties have a unique character, compared with most other international agreements, since these rights proclaim solemn treatment to the inhabitants of participating states (Mowbray 2005, p. 60). In the process of interpreting the European Convention, it is worth recalling that a judge's duty is to provide '*the best understanding of the moral values* that underline the human rights' therein.[296] However, human rights judges should not be constrained by what is most states' understanding of the moral values of human rights.[297] As Fitzmaurice points out, the ECtHR has clearly conveyed the notion that 'the first and foremost responsibility for safeguarding human rights rests within national authorities and courts' since they know better their countries' context of social needs, so they clearly have a 'margin of appreciation' in adopting national measures (Fitzmaurice 2013). However, the purpose of human rights *fora* (and certainly the ECtHR) is, according to Letsas, to protect the autonomy of individuals against the majoritarian will of their state, giving effect to individuals' rights and freedoms rather than to the state's will (Letsas 2010a, b, p. 272). From this perspective, the ECtHR has made clear that 'the states' margin of appreciation is never unlimited' (Fitzmaurice 2013).

Generally, in respect of the human rights tribunals, Fitzmaurice reiterates that the primary aim of these regimes is *the effective application of human rights*

[294] *Id*, para 125.

[295] *Id*, para 121 (emphasis added). The Court based here on *Tyrer*, see *supra* note 163, and *Christine Goodwin v. the United Kingdom* [GC], no. 28957/95, § 74, ECHR 2002-VI. Although the ECtHR admits in *Mamatkulov and Askarov* that the ICJ and the other international bodies operate under different treaty provisions to those of the Court itself (ECtHR), it concludes that those bodies 'have confirmed in their reasoning in recent decisions that the preservation of the asserted rights of the parties in the face of the risk of irreparable damage represents an essential objective of interim measures in international law'.

[296] Letsas (2012), p. 19 (emphasis added).

[297] *Id*.

*treaties* (*effect utile*). It involves a clear reliance on the effectiveness principle, which the author admits as being 'inherent in the VCLT reference to the "object and purpose" of treaties', an approach highly regarded by the human rights *fora*.[298] So this overarching approach of the *object and purpose* of human rights treaties is, as one commentator simply puts it, precisely the protection of the rights of individuals (Mechlem 2009, p. 912). It results that the way of reading the drafters' original intentions of the human rights treaties constitutes, as expressed by Letsas, 'the result of, rather than an alternative to, a theory about the object and purpose of the treaty' (Letsas 2007, p. 72).

The next case will display an analysis of a doubtful approach adopted by the ECtHR, which, despite reasoning in consideration of the VCLT rules and ICJ's practice to elucidate the meaning of an *ambiguous* text provision, ends up by providing rather a restrictive interpretation of the Convention's clauses, limiting the rights and freedoms of the individual, to the benefit of the state. The ***Case of Stoll v. Switzerland* (2007)**[299] shows an instance where the ECtHR approaches the issue of interpretation in a way that is inconsistent with both its own practice and the standard of interpretation established by Article 31 (1), (2) of the VCLT, thus deviating from it. This case analysis is provided here, however, as to show how the ECtHR, having to interpret an *ambiguous* provision, makes use of the VCLT customary rules of interpretation and of the relevant ICJ's practice, and also to show how, if the patterns of interpretation initially adopted had been exactly followed (general rules and methods of treaty interpretation, compliant with its own established interpretative approach and practice), the ECtHR would have given in this case full effect to the Convention's provision at issue. As the five judges succinctly expressed in their Dissenting Opinion, the decision in this case is a 'dangerous and unjustified departure from the Court's well established case-law concerning the nature and vital importance of freedom of expression in democratic societies'.[300] These judges also affirmed that the ECtHR has

[298] Fitzmaurice (2013).

[299] *Case of Stoll v. Switzerland*, Application no. 69698/01, Strasbourg [GC], Judgment of 10 December 2007.

[300] *Id.* See Dissenting opinion of Judge Zabrebelsky joined by judges Lorenzen, Fura-Sandstrom, Jaeger and Popovic, relying on a rich body of the Court (ECtHR) case law: *Handyside v. the United Kingdom*, 7 December 1976, § 48, Series A no. 24; *The Sunday Times v. the United Kingdom* (no. 1), 26 April 1979, § 59, Series A no. 30; *Lingens v. Austria*, 8 July 1986, §§ 39–41, Series A no. 103; *Observer and Guardian v. the United Kingdom*, 26 November 1991, § 59, Series A no. 216; *Hertel v. Switzerland*, 25 August 1998, § 46, Reports of Judgments and Decisions 1998-VI; and *Steel and Morris v. the United Kingdom*, No. 68416/01, § 87, ECHR 2005-II. The dissenting judges concluded (at para 105) that 'the criterion for assessing whether interference is necessary in a democratic society must be whether it corresponds to a "pressing social need"', that 'the authorities have only a limited margin of appreciation' in this sphere and that '[t]he most careful scrutiny on the part of the Court is called for when, as in the present case, the measures taken ... by the national authority are capable of discouraging the participation of the press in debates over matters of legitimate public concern'.

consistently held that 'freedom must be construed broadly and that any restrictions must, by contrast, be applied restrictively'.[301]

The case is related to a journalist, Mr. Stoll, who obtained a copy of a 'strategic document', classified as 'confidential' (drawn up by the Swiss Ambassador to the United States), which concerned the possible strategies with regard to the compensation due to Holocaust victims for unclaimed assets deposited in Swiss banks, and he published two articles accompanied by extracts from the document. The Court had to determine whether the impugned measures taken by the national authorities, notably the penalty imposed on the applicant,[302] had been designed to prevent the 'disclosure of information received in confidence' and were aimed at protecting 'national security' and 'public safety', as also whether the measures 'interfered' with the exercise of his freedom of expression under Article 10 of the Convention.

The Court's focus in this case is on clarifying the meaning of the phrase 'the disclosure of information received in confidence' within Article 10(2) of the Convention,[303] admitted by the Court as being 'apt to give rise to confusion'.[304] Since the French and English versions of this provision, while equally authentic, are found not in complete harmony,[305] the Court considers it necessary to apply Article 33 of the VCLT, expressly admitting it to reflect 'international customary law in relation to the interpretation of treaties authenticated in two or more languages'.[306] On this basis rule, the Court finds that it cannot accept either the French version of Article 10(2) of the Convention, which refers in general terms to measures necessary '*pour empêcher la divulgation d'informations confidentielles*', or the English version, which refers too restrictively to measures necessary 'for preventing the disclosure of information received in *confidence*', by not encompassing 'third parties, including working in the media'.[307] So to shed more light on the meaning

---

[301] *Id.*

[302] Mr. Stoll was sentenced to a fine of 800 Swiss francs (520 euros) for publishing 'official confidential deliberations' within the meaning of Article 293 of the Criminal Code.

[303] Article 10 of the Convention provides:

1. Everyone has the right to freedom of expression. This right shall include freedom to hold opinions and to receive and impart information and ideas without interference by public authority and regardless of frontiers. This Article shall not prevent States from requiring the licensing of broadcasting, television or cinema enterprises.
2. The exercise of these freedoms, since it carries with it duties and responsibilities, may be subject to such formalities, conditions, restrictions or penalties as are prescribed by law and are necessary in a democratic society, in the interests of national security, territorial integrity or public safety, for the prevention of disorder or crime, for the protection of health or morals, for the protection of the reputation or rights of others, for preventing the disclosure of information received in confidence, or for maintaining the authority and impartiality of the judiciary.

[304] *Stoll* (2007), para 57.

[305] *Id*, para 59.

[306] *Id.*

[307] *Id.*

of Article 10(2), the ECtHR looks for relevant ICJ practice. It invokes the *LaGrand* case,[308] where the ICJ, too, having to solve a similar difficulty in interpreting the text of a treaty (*ambiguity*), utilised Article 33 of the VCLT, particularly its paragraph 4. The ICJ held that '[i]n the absence of agreement between the parties in this respect, it is appropriate to refer to paragraph 4 of Article 33 of the Vienna Convention on the Law of Treaties'.[309] Referencing its own previous (relevant) case law in addition, the ECtHR establishes that 'when a comparison of the authentic texts discloses a difference of meaning, which the application of Articles 31 and 32 does not remove, the meaning which best reconciles the texts, having regard to the *object and purpose* of the treaty, is to be adopted'.[310] The ECtHR seems to look further for any confirmatory indication in the *travaux preparatioire* of the common intention of the drafters as to Article 10 of the Convention. It finds that 'in the light of paragraph 3 of Article 33 of the Vienna Convention, and in the absence of any indication to the contrary in the drafting history of Article 10, the Court considers it appropriate to adopt an interpretation of the phrase "preventing the disclosure of information received in confidence" that could encompass confidential information disclosed *either by a person subject to a duty of confidence or by a third party and, in particular, as in the present case, by a journalist*'.[311]

Furthermore, to remove the differences from the authentic texts' meaning within Article 10(2), the Court suggests reading this provision in the light of the 'object and purpose' of the Convention (notably, *the interest of any democratic society in guaranteeing freedom of the press*) while applying the 'margin of appreciation' doctrine/technique of interpretation: here viewed as the limited 'margin of appreciation' left to states when information of public interest was at stake. At one point, the Court expressly admits that '[w]here freedom of the "press" is at stake, the authorities have only a limited margin of appreciation to decide whether a "pressing social need" exists'.[312] However, one could observe that despite taking into account what was not disputed, notably that the applicant's conviction (by national authority) amounted to 'interference' with the exercise of his freedom of expression, the Court's approach takes suddenly a different course. The Court disappointingly appears to have deliberately missed further in its judgment an important step regarding the interpretation of Article 10(2) in the light of the 'object and purpose' of the Convention and its 'context', thus taking the Convention as a whole, also in disregard of the effectiveness principle. Actually, the Court simply denies its initial interpretation (of Article 10 (2)) provided in consideration of the 'object and

[308] *Id. LaGrand (Germany v. the United States of America)*, Judgment of 27 June 2001, I.C.J. Reports 2001, p. 101.

[309] *Id*, para 101.

[310] *Id*, para 60 (emphasis added). The Court invokes its own precedents, e.g., *Sunday Times v. the United Kingdom* (no. 1), 26 April 1979, § 48, Series A no. 30; *James and Others v. the United Kingdom*, 21 February 1986, § 42, Series A no. 98).

[311] *Id*, para 61 (emphasis added).

[312] *Id*, para 105.

purpose' and 'context of the whole treaty' customary rules of interpretation. In other words, the Court *in Stoll* does not seem to give full meaning and effect to all the terms of the treaty under the VCLT's standard of treaty interpretation, despite initially providing a proper (holistic) interpretation in this respect, respectively an evolutive, dynamic interpretation that clearly pointed towards making the Convention's safeguards practical and effective.[313] Seen from this angle then, the Court's finding of no violation of the right to freedom of expression under Article 10 of the Convention, and its improper justification of the 'interference' with the 'right of free expression',[314] clearly contrasts with the perspective given by the 'living instrument' doctrine, notably, that the Convention should be interpreted in the light of present-day conditions. And this is moreover so since the Strasbourg Court itself advocates the 'living instrument' doctrine in the present case, which is, as the Court puts it, 'well established in the Court's case-law'.[315]

In sum, unlike in *LaGrand* invoked here by the Strasbourg Court, where the ICJ took into consideration the meaning that best reconciled the texts having regard to the *object and purpose* of the treaty (under Article 33 (4) of the VCLT),[316] the ECtHR in *Stoll* does not relate Article 10 to the 'object and purpose' of the Convention stated in its Preamble. It should be reminded here that, in conformity with Article 31(2) of the VCLT, the Preamble of the Convention forms *an integral part of the context*,[317] and therefore it constitutes an important prerequisite under the basic rule of treaty interpretation, which the ECtHR did not consider ultimately in *Stoll*. In addition, an interpretation that gives too wide a margin of appreciation to the will of the state would clearly contrast with the perspective given by the 'living instrument' doctrine, which this Court has adopted and is well established in its case law,[318] notably that the Convention must be interpreted in the light of contemporary realities.[319] So despite using patterns of treaty interpretation that resemble those of the ICJ and references to the relevant ICJ precedent, as also its own precedents, the ECtHR shows ultimately in *Stoll* an inconsistency with the VCLT's standard of

---

[313] *Id*, para 63.

[314] *Id*. See Dissenting Opinion of this case. The dissenting judges argued that the fact that the journalist focused his remarks on the ambassador, who did not complain as a result, should not be relevant for the Court's perspective.

[315] *Id*, para 104. The Court states (at para 105) that: 'Where freedom of the "press" is at stake, the authorities have only a limited margin of appreciation to decide whether a "pressing social need" exists.' The Court based on its own precedent such as *Tyrer*, see *supra* note 163; *Airey v. Ireland*, 9 October 1979, § 26, Series A no. 32; *Vo v. France* [GC], no. 53924/00, § 82, ECHR 2004-VIII; *Mamatkulov and Askarov*, see *supra* note 274.

[316] *LaGrand*, *supra* note 308, para 102. The ICJ found in this case that '[t]he object and purpose of the Statute is to enable the Court to fulfil the functions provided for therein . . .'.

[317] Article 31 paragraph 2, of the VCLT provides:

> The *context* for the purpose of interpretation of a treaty shall comprise in addition to the text, including its preamble and annexes ....

[318] *Stoll* (2007), para 104.

[319] *Id*.

interpretation (provided by Article 31 of the VCLT) and also with its own past decisions. This aspect leads the ECtHR to not ensure in this case the realisation of the human rights and fundamental freedoms at issue, precisely in the light of the 'living instrument' doctrine. However, as in *Bankovic*, such an approach that deviates from the VCLT standard of treaty interpretation and from the ECtHR's own practice does not seem to be at all the result of a technical mistake or a misinterpretation by the judges of the Vienna rules or of the special character of the Convention. Rather, such approaches appear as a matter of policy that the Strasbourg Court sometimes adopts.

## 5.4 Conclusions

Based on the case law analysis provided in this chapter, several conclusions could be drawn. First, the methods of approaching the customary rules of interpretation by the ECtHR, prior to, and after the adoption of the VCLT, do not appear to differ in principle. Even if the ECtHR has built its own flexible techniques of interpreting the Convention, it has resorted to the same methodological foundation given by the customary rules and principles of interpretation of public international law. However, the teleological approach has distinguished itself as a central method in the treaty interpretative process at the ECtHR, an approach adopted by the ICJ in many cases, but, arguably, not of the same resonance. Furthermore, the autonomous or specific concept doctrines (techniques) of interpretation that the ECtHR operates with, such as the 'margin of appreciation', 'living instrument', 'special character', 'law-making character', 'evolutive interpretation', 'dynamic interpretation', do not appear to blur or impede the application of the customary rules in the interpretation of the Convention provisions. There could be a temptation to conclude that these autonomous concepts draw an absolute dividing line from the general rules and principles of treaty interpretation. However, the case law analysis presented in this chapter can demonstrate that they coexist and clearly work symbiotically. It also can be concluded that the methods of application of customary rules do appear to play an important role in shaping the ECtHR's own approach to treaty interpretation (i.e., the rule of 'object and purpose' supports, and finds reflection, in the 'living instrument' doctrine).[320] Overall, the case law analyses presented in this chapter can show that the ECtHR has adopted all general (customary) rules and methods of treaty interpretation in patterns similar to those used by the ICJ, either explicitly (by stating them expressly) or implicitly (by suggesting/applying them without a technical description). The ECtHR proceeds in this manner by employing gradually in any given case more of these means than it initially declared as necessary for interpretation (an approach I described as 'overbuiding'), irrespective of the types

[320]Kamminga (2008).

of difficulties encountered in interpreting the text of the Convention provisions (e.g., insufficiently clear, ambiguous, doubtful, vague or silent language of the text).

Another similarity between the ECtHR and the ICJ may be reflected in these courts' patterns to approach *holistically* the treaties before them, in an attempt to give full effect and meaning to all the terms of the treaty provisions at issue, independently of these courts' emphasis on one rule or another. However, as it was pointed out in the introductory part of this chapter, the special characteristics of the European Convention of Human Rights imprint a peculiar character on its human rights interpretation, making it distinctive in relation to the interpretation of other types of treaties (e.g., treaties interpreted by the ICJ, WTO, ITLOS). As the case analyses in this chapter can evidence, the ECtHR's approach to interpretation is, in principle, teleological (purposive) due to the nature of human rights enshrined in the Convention and the type of values they serve. The analyses also evidence that this human rights' specific nature is clearly determinative of the ECtHR's performance, in general, of a dynamic, evolutive interpretation of the Convention, rather than a more restrictive one that tends only 'to protect those rights that they fifty years ago, believed individuals are morally entitled to'.[321] The case analyses here can show that this evolutive or dynamic interpretation finds reflection in the 'living instrument' doctrine, a principle that encourages active protection of the human rights embodied in the Convention.[322]

In addition, by relying on the customary rules (the VCLT general rules) of interpretation, and overall applying them with consistency and in the same patterns both prior to and after the adoption of the VCLT, the ECtHR's approaches appear to enhance the formation of these rules as *customary*. It could be said that the ECtHR's practice of application of the customary rules and methods of treaty interpretation contributes to expanding the understanding of the universal applicability of the general methodology of treaty interpretation provided by Articles 31–33 of the VCLT. Thus, contrary to those views that often see the ECtHR promoting a 'self-contained regime', detached from international law, the case law analysis provided here shows that this institution, generally, aims to improve the quality of its decisions by relying on the universally admitted methodology of treaty interpretation, functioning therefore within the framework of general international law. However, some instances provided in this chapter, such as those illustrated by *Bankovic*, *Stoll* and, in a certain respect, *Witold*, show the contrary.[323] These cases can demonstrate, at least, that the ECtHR does not always go in one direction. It shows instead that the *Strasbourg Court* can be unpredictable on certain matters of human rights interpretation (taking different views on the same issue as a matter of policy, i.e., under Article 1 of the Convention).[324] Such examples can illustrate

[321]Letsas (2010a, b), p. 268.

[322]See Pegorier (2013).

[323]See *Bankovic*, *Stoll*, *Witold* discussed in this chapter, or also *Al-Adsani* (mentioned succinctly).

[324]I.e. on the issue of 'jurisdiction' under Article 1 of the Convention in, e.g., *Loizidou*, *Bankovic*, *Catan*.

what Judge Rozakis described as 'restrictive interpretations of the Convention's clauses to the State's benefit' (by allowing states too wide a 'margin of appreciation'), clearly 'limiting the rights and freedoms provided for by the Convention'.[325] Seen from this angle, these interpretations certainly contrast with the perspective given by the 'living instrument' doctrine (the Convention should be interpreted in the light of present-day conditions), which is 'well established in the Court's case-law'.[326] Although rarely, cases such as *Bankovic* and *Stoll* can show that a certain degree of deviation from the standard (basic rule) of interpretation under Article 31(1)(2) of the VCLT occurs in the practice of the ECtHR. In the light of the requirements of this rule, an interpretation should be performed in the manner to give full meaning and effect to all the terms of the treaty at issue, thus in addition to the 'ordinary meaning of the terms in their context', also to the 'object and purpose' and the 'context' of the Convention as a whole. Since Vienna rules appear to be of the essence in revealing with more precision the moral value of the Convention's human rights, and not optional means of interpretation, these rules must be applied in a way that would not restrict those rights to the greatest degree possible, as the Court did, for example, in the above-mentioned cases.[327]

However, such cases cannot prove that the ECtHR goes in the other direction, that of deviation from the VCLT's general rule of interpretation, as overall such examples do not appear to form a path in the ECtHR's interpretive practice, not occurring with frequency. And this is so because the tendency of the ECtHR is that after delivering a case that deviates from the standard of treaty interpretation (i.e., on matter of 'jurisdiction'), the Court has shown in general willingness to improve such an approach by 'returning' to a path that is more in line with that standard and with its own previously adopted approaches.[328] Moreover, such different deviating approaches, as those seen in *Bankovic*, *Stoll* or *Al-Adsani*, can evidentiate that they are not a result of a technical mistake or a misinterpretation of the Vienna rules by the judges at the Strasbourg Court, or of the special character of the Convention, but rather such approaches are influenced by other considerations that reflect a policy that this Court chooses to adopt sometimes. Therefore, such deviations cannot link

[325] See Rozakis (2005), p. 5.

[326] See the case of *Stoll* (2007), para 104.

[327] In *Bankovic*, *Stoll*, *Witold* (in certain degree), or *Al-Adsani* (also in disregarding the fundamental principle of effectiveness which flows from the requirements of Article 31 of the VCLT).

[328] See, e.g., the recent cases at the ECtHR: *Catan*, *Al-Skeini*, or the older case of *Loizidou* (comparing with the *Bankovic* case) concerning the issue of 'jurisdiction' under Article 1 of the ECHR, where the Court applied the exception to the principle that jurisdiction under Article 1 is limited to a State's own territory. For example, in *Al-Skeini* (2011) the ECtHR performed a normative and moral judgment of interpreting Article 1 of the Convention in accord with its own evolutive interpretation path. The ECtHR held (at para 128) that '[i]t was inconceivable that the drafters of the Convention should have considered that the prospective responsibilities of States should be confined to violations perpetrated on their own territory'. The Court had repeatedly regarded to the Convention's special character as an instrument for human rights protection, citing in this support its own precedents (e.g., *Al-Skeini and Others, Ilaşcu and Others; Güleç; Ahmet Özkan and Others; Isayeva; Kanlibaş*).

closely enough to a fragmentation that affects substantially general international law, moreover, since overall the ECtHR proves to approach with consistency the interpretation of the Convention (considering both pre- and post-VCLT periods), providing a uniform development of jurisprudence.

Another observation based on the case law analyses concerns the relationship of the ECtHR with international law from the perspective of 'systemic integration'. However rare, the citations of 'external case law' of other international courts,[329] or even the infrequent resort to Article 31(3)(c) of the VCLT, could, nevertheless, constitute by their mere existence evidence that the ECtHR is part of the international legal system. So even if only several ECtHR cases appear to provide examples of a straightforward application of other international judicial bodies' case law, especially of the ICJ,[330] it nevertheless indicates that a dialogue between the courts is actually taking place at the ECtHR, and thus the ECtHR does not function independently of general international law and the legal system.[331] Also, by means of Article 31(3)(c) of the VCLT, the ECtHR appears to clarify human rights principles, or fills gaps where the Convention's provisions do not provide enough for the circumstances of the given case, or the necessary protection of human rights.[332] Moreover, even when the ECtHR shows reluctance to resort in express terms to the VCLT's rules of interpretation (after the VCLT's adoption), some case analyses in this chapter show that this Court, nevertheless, relies on these rules implicitly.[333] In addition, the fact that the ECtHR has generally shown

[329] Sparse in citing other international courts, the ECtHR has proved, however, to be influenced by other international courts, e.g., the IACHR, ICJ, ECJ, ICTY. See illustration of this aspect, e.g., in *Case of Mamatkulov and Askarov* (2005), *Case of Stoll* (2007), *Case of Catan* (2012) discussed in this chapter. For 'cross-fertilization' discussion, see, e.g., Sands (1998); Kamminga (2008), observing that 'the borrowing process is of course facilitated by the fact that an increasing number of ICJ judges and members are themselves former members of international human rights bodies'.

[330] The ECtHR has referred to the ICJ case law mostly for rules on treaty interpretation, but also for other matters of international law such as temporal jurisdiction *in Blečić v. Croatia*, App. no. 59532/00, Judgment of 8 Mar. 2006, para 47.

[331] See Voeten (2010), pp. 19–24. The author claims that 'the analysis of ECtHR citations reveals that while the court is reluctant to formally acknowledge the influence of other courts, external case-law does play a role in its deliberations'. An interesting statistical finding of Voeten reveals that from 7319 ECtHR judgments, made before October 2006, 29 cases or 4% of cases cited one or more decisions of foreign constitutional courts or international courts, which shows that the ECtHR is not a 'self-contained' regime and does not tend to adjudicate exclusively in its own separate way. Also Voeten found that there were 46 cases (at the ECtHR) in which one or more separate opinions referenced an external decision. This finding is all the more remarkable given that only 17% of all cases were accompanied by a separate opinion.

[332] See in this regard, e.g., cases of *Mamatkulov and Askarov*, or *Catan* discussed in this chapter; the opinion of the ILC (2006); McInerney-Lankford (2012).

[333] See illustration of this aspect, e.g., in the *Catan* case, discussed in this chapter, or the situation when the ECtHR invokes other cases in which it applied the Vienna rules of treaty interpretation, such as *Golder*—a landmark decision, often cited by the ECtHR in cases without needing further to provide in those cases a similar express or detailed description/explanation of the application of the Vienna rules.

preference to rely on its own past decisions, creating its own pattern of adjudication, cannot confirm the proposition that this Court promotes a 'self-contained' regime, naturally, because many of the cases invoked by the Strasbourg Court already relied on the VCLT's general rule of interpretation (e.g., *Golder*, *Mamatkulov*, *Witold* analysed in this chapter).

However, certain aspects concerning the interpretative process have developed differently (in analogous situations relating to the structure of the treaty text or other interpretative difficulties) at the Strasbourg Court, in comparison with the ICJ. For example, relying on the case law analysed in this chapter, it could be observed that, unlike the ICJ, which generally has given a great deal of attention to the *travaux preparatoires* (although not always expressly) for all types of treaty interpretative difficulties, the ECtHR rarely appears to show an express need to rely on this supplementary means of interpretation. Rather, the ECtHR, more than the ICJ, has shown in general a greater discretion, reluctance and unpredictability in administering these means, using an inconclusive language in their respect. So this attitude is manifested generally in not providing an indication or explanation of why the Court resorted to 'supplementary means' if it did or, otherwise, why it had not been necessary to resort to them if the Court said so. As the case analyses can show, instead the ECtHR has usually based its interpretative legal act on the object and purpose of the Convention, orienting itself towards the effective realisation (application in practice) of the Convention's rights (*effect utile*). As it has been shown, the protection of the rights of individuals by the ECtHR is reflected in an 'overarching' emphasis on the 'object and purpose' of the Convention, which can be properly achieved on the basis of an evolutive interpretation of the Convention's provisions, thus keeping account of evolving norms of national/international law.[334] Alternatively, in Letsas' words, '[w]e cannot know whether (and the extent to which) drafters' intention are relevant unless we settle first on the *object and purpose* of the treaty'.[335] Thus, to perform this evolutive and dynamic interpretation, generally, the ECtHR has engaged the 'special character' and 'living instrument' doctrines as highly relevant, supposing the interpretation of the Convention's human rights in the light of the present-day standards. The picture that emerges then is that the Vienna rules of interpretation have their own defined place and role in interpreting the Convention's human rights, even if the specific context of the human rights regime requires an adaptation of these customary rules of interpretation. In principle, Articles 31–33 of the VCLT come, basically, to assist and serve the sophisticated process of 'constructing' the meaning of the human rights provisions. Thus, the VCLT rules appear to contemplate a balancing of values that, actually, enable human rights interpretation, necessarily facilitating the complex act of a *moral reading of the Convention*.

---

[334]See Letsas (2010a, b, 2012). According to Letsas, the *evolutive interpretation* of the ECHR is 'understood as the moral reading of the Convention'.

[335]See Letsas (2007), p. 72 (emphasis added).

Therefore, from the perspective of the ECtHR's intrinsically evaluative task in identifying the special character of human rights' moral value,[336] the analysis in this chapter can show that this Court has, in general, expressed clarity and openness towards understanding of the human rights principles as public standards of morality, which override other considerations related to state intentions and interests that could contradict human rights. However, despite the differences between the nature of the treaties to be interpreted by the ECtHR and the ICJ, there is a common ground between the two, and this is given by the normative judgment that both courts as interpreters show, overall, that they consider first. Yet this aspect, the recognition by the Strasbourg Court of the VCLT's universal methodology of treaty interpretation, and its application in patterns similar to those used by the ICJ, as well as this specialised Court's use of the ICJ's precedents, constitutes important devices that work in favour of the unity of international law, hence against its fragmentation.

## References

Arato, J. (2011). *The constitutional transformation of international organizations through treaty interpretation: The ECtHR's use of VCLT 31(3)(c).* Working Paper. http://papers.ssrn.com/sol3/papers.cfm?abstract_id=1951547.

Bakircioglu, O. (2007). Application of the margin of appreciation doctrine in freedom of expression and public morality cases. *German Law Journal, 8*, 711.

Bermann, G. A., Goebel, R. J., Davey, W. J., & Fox, E. M. (2002). *Cases and materials on European Union law*. St. Paul, MN: West Group.

Bernhardt, R. (1997). *Encyclopedia of public international law* (Vol. 3). Amsterdam: North Holland Publishing Company.

Brownlie, I. (1998). Principles of international law. In *See also convention on international liability for damage caused by space objects (adopted 29 November 1971, entered into force 1 September 1972), Article IV* (p. 458).

Carozza, P. G. (2008). Human dignity and judicial interpretation of human rights: A reply. *European Journal of International Law, 19*(5), 931–944.

Charney, J. I. (1998). *Is international law threatened by multiple international tribunals?* Dordrecht, The Netherlands: Martinus Nijhoff Publishers.

De Frouville, O. (2010). Attribution of conduct to the state: Private individuals. In *The law of international responsibility* (pp. 257–280). Oxford, England: Oxford University Press.

Dupuy, P. M. (1998). *Droit international public*. Paris: Dalloz.

Dworkin, R. (1978). *Taking rights seriously* (Vol. 136). Cambridge, MA: Harvard University Press.

Fitzmaurice, M. (2013). Interpretation of human rights treaties. In D. Shelton (Ed.), *The Oxford handbook of international human rights law* (pp. 739–772). Oxford University Press. www.oxfordhanbooks.com. https://doi.org/10.1093/law/970199640133.003.0032.

Fitzmaurice, M., & Merkouris, P. (2010). Canons of treaty interpretation: Selected case studies from the World Trade Organization and the North American Free Trade Agreement. In *Treaty interpretation and the Vienna Convention on the Law of Treaties: 30 years on* (pp. 153–238). Leiden, The Netherlands: Brill.

[336]See on this aspect e.g. Letsas (2007, 2010a, b, 2012), Fitzmaurice (2013), Heard (1997), Carozza (2008), Shelton (2002).

Forowicz, M. (2010). *The reception of international law in the European Court of Human Rights*. New York: Oxford University Press.

Gardiner, R. K. (2008). *Treaty interpretation*. New York: Oxford University Press.

Greer, S. (2006). *The European Convention on Human Rights: Achievements, problems and prospects*. Cambridge, England: Cambridge University Press.

Harris, J. D., O'Boyle, M., Bates, P. E., & Buckley, M. (2014). *Law of the European convention on human rights*. Oxford, England: Oxford University Press.

Heard, A. (1997). *Human rights: Chimeras in sheep's clothing*. Simon Fraser University. http://www.sfu.ca/-aheard/intro.html.

Henkin, L., Neuman, G. L., Orentlicher, D. F., & Leebron, D. W. (1999). *Human rights*. New York: Foundation Press.

Jennings, R., & Watts, A. (1992). *Oppenheim's international law (Vol. 1): Peace* (9th ed.). Longman Higher Education, Longman Group UK Ltd.

Kamminga, M. T. (June 1 2008). *Final Report on the impact of international human rights law on general international law*. Report of the 73d Conference of the International Law Association, pp. 663–685, 2008. SSRN: https://ssrn.com/abstract=1150664.

Klabbers, J. (2010). Virtuous interpretation. In *Treaty interpretation and the Vienna Convention on the Law of Treaties: 30 years on* (pp. 15–38). Leiden, The Netherlands: Brill.

Lauterpacht, H. (1950). *International law and human rights*. New York: F. A. Praeger.

Letsas, G. (2007). *A theory of interpretation of the European Convention on Human Rights*. Oxford, England: Oxford University Press.

Letsas, G. (2010a). Intentionalism and interpretation of human rights. In M. Fitzmaurice, O. A. Elias, & P. Merkouris (Eds.), *Treaty interpretation and the Vienna Convention on the Law of Treaties: 30 years on* (Vol. 1, pp. 257–272). Leiden, The Netherlands: Brill.

Letsas, G. (2010b). Strasbourg's interpretive ethic: Lessons for the international lawyer. *European Journal of International Law, 21*(3), 509–541.

Letsas, G. (2012). *The ECHR as a living instrument: Its meaning and its legitimacy*. https://papers.ssrn.com/sol3/papers.cfm?abstract_id=2021836.

Macdonald, R. S. J. (1993). The margin of appreciation. In R. S. J. Macdonald, F. Matscher, & H. Petzold (Eds.), *The European system for the protection of human rights*. Martinus Nijhoff.

Mahoney, P. (1998). The doctrine of the margin of appreciation under the European Convention of Human Rights: Its legitimacy in theory and application in practice. *Human Rights Law Journal, 19*(1), 3.

Mann, F. A. (1964). The doctrine of jurisdiction in international law. *Rec des Cours, 111*, 1.

Mann, F. A. (1984). The doctrine of jurisdiction in international law, twenty years later. *Rec des Cours, 1*, 9.

McDougal, M. S. (1967). The International Law Commission's draft articles upon interpretation: Textuality redivivus. *American Journal of International Law, 61*(4), 992–1000.

McInerney-Lankford, S. (2012). Fragmentation of international law redux: The case of Strasbourg. *Oxford Journal of Legal Studies, 32*(3), 609–632.

McLachlan, C. (2005). The principle of systemic integration and article 31 (3)(c) of the Vienna Convention. *International and Comparative Law Quarterly, 54*(2), 279–320.

Mechlem, K. (2009). Treaty bodies and the interpretation of human rights. *Vanderbilt Journal of Transnational Law, 42*, 905.

Meng, W. (1987). Extraterritorial effects of administrative, judicial and legislative acts. *Encyclopedia of Public International Law, Instalment, 10*(1987), 155.

Milanovic, M. (2011). *Extraterritorial application of human rights treaties: Law, principles, and policy*. Oxford, England: Oxford University Press.

Mowbray, A. (2005). The creativity of the European Court of Human Rights. *Human Rights Law Review, 5*(1), 57–79.

O'Boyle, M. (1998). The margin of appreciation and derogation under Article 15: Ritual incantation or principle? *Human Rights Law Journal, 19*, 23–29.

Orakhelashvili, A. (2003). Restrictive interpretation of human rights treaties in the recent jurisprudence of the European Court of Human Rights. *European Journal of International Law, 14* (3), 529–568.

Pauwelyn, J., & Elsig, M. (2011). *The politics of treaty interpretation: Variations and explanations across international tribunals.* https://ssrn.com/abstract=1938618 or https://doi.org/10.2139/ssrn.1938618.

Pegorier, C. (2013). *Ethnic cleansing: A legal qualification.* New York: Routledge.

Rozakis, C. L. (2005). European judge as Comparatist. *Tulane Law Review, 80*, 257.

Sands, P. (1998). Treaty, custom and the cross-fertilization of international law. *Yale Human Rights and Development Law Journal, 1*, 85.

Scheinin, M. (2009). Impact on the law of treaties. In M. T. Kamminga & M. Scheinin (Eds.), *The impact of human rights law on general international law* (p. 33). Oxford: OUP.

Sheeran, S. (2014). The relationship of international human rights and general international law; hermeneutic constraint, or pushing the boundaries? In S. Sheeran & N. Rodley (Eds.), *Routledge handbook of international human rights law.* London: Routledge.

Shelton, D. (2002). Hierarchy of norms and human rights: Of trumps and winners. *Saskatchewan Law Review, 65*, 301.

Tobin, J. W. (2010). Seeking to persuade: A constructive approach to human rights treaty interpretation. *Harvard Human Rights Journal, 23*, 1–50.

Toufayan, M. (2005). *Human rights treaty interpretation: A postmodern account of its claim to "speciality"*. NYU Centre for Human Rights and Global Justice Working Paper.

Tzevelekos, V. P. (2009). Use of Article 31 (3)(C) of the VCLT in the case law of the ECtHR: An effective anti-fragmentation tool or a selective loophole for the reinforcement of human rights teleology-between evolution and systemic integration. *Michigan Journal of International Law, 31*, 621.

Voeten, E. (2010). Borrowing and nonborrowing among international courts. *The Journal of Legal Studies, 39*(2), 547–576.

Wilde, R. (2005). The 'legal space' or 'espace juridique'of the European Convention on Human Rights: Is it relevant to extraterritorial state action? *European Human Rights Law Review, 10*, 115–124.

Yin, R. (2003). *Case study research: Design and method* (3rd ed.). London: Sage.

## *Documents*

Assembly, U.G., 1948. Universal declaration of human rights. *UN General Assembly.*

International Law Commission, 2006. Fragmentation of international law: Difficulties arising from the diversification and expansion of international law. Geneva*: United Nations.*

The European Convention on Human Rights - Convention for Protection of Human Rights and Fundamental Freedoms (1950), available at: http://conventions.coe.int/Treaty/en/Treaties/Html/005.htm

The European Court of Human Rights, available on line at Projects on International Courts and Tribunals., http://www.pict-pcti.org/courts/ECHR.html

Waldock, H., 1964. Third Report on the Law of Treaties by Sir Humphrey Waldock, Special Rapporteur. *Yearbook of the International Law Commission, 2.*

# Chapter 6
# Treaty Interpretation at the World Trade Organization

## 6.1 Introduction

The preceding chapter has provided an analysis of the ways in which the most productive international adjudicative (specialised) regime, the ECtHR, applies the customary rules of treaty interpretation in comparison with the PCIJ/ICJ. The present chapter proposes to extend that analysis to a different specialised international regime by examining the practice on treaty interpretation of the dispute settlement mechanism at the World Trade Organisation (WTO). Since the WTO regulates trade and economic matters susceptible to broad contestations, and has produced a more extensive jurisprudence than almost any other international judicial body in the world,[1] an analysis of the practice of the WTO from the treaty interpretation perspective allows for a specific answer to the more general question of whether the application of *lex generalis* by an international specialised adjudicative body into its special context could contribute to the fragmentation of international law. Recognised in the scholarship as one of the most active and effective international dispute settlement mechanism in the world today,[2] the WTO has also developed one of the most dynamic treaty interpretative practices in the history of international dispute settlement.[3] Nevertheless, like in the case of the ECtHR, there is an increasing number of scholars who criticise the WTO system and perceive it as an international 'self-contained' economic regime,[4] endowed with a uniqueness of agreements, special rules of adjudication and special

[1]Jackson (1998), p. 830. The World Trade Organization (WTO) is an international organisation of 159 members that deals with the rules of trade between nations.

[2]Panitchpakdi (2006), p. 8.

[3]Van Damme (2010), p. 641.

[4]See Chap. 2 of this book—for a discussion on 'self- contained' regime, in, e.g., Simma and Pulkowski (2006).



L.E. Popa, *Patterns of Treaty Interpretation as Anti-Fragmentation Tools*,
DOI 10.1007/978-3-319-65488-1_6

adjudicative bodies that promote rather a creative or innovative interpretation.[5] As this perception has led to considerable controversy, and the matter of treaty interpretation at the WTO constitutes an ongoing debate, the goal of this chapter is to add to this debate with empirical research. More specifically, the chapter examines whether the WTO dispute settlement bodies (panels and the Appellate Body) apply the general (customary) rules of interpretation of public international law similarly to the ICJ. Although there are differences in the nature of the treaties the ICJ and WTO are called to interpret, certain characteristics at the WTO regime also allow for a thorough test of the conclusion drawn in respect of the ICJ's interpretative practice. Basically, that the WTO dispute settlement regime applies the *canons of treaty interpretation in patterns* resembling those developed and applied by the ICJ when confronted with similar treaty interpretative difficulties (e.g., insufficiently clear, ambiguous, obscure, vague language or silence in the text of treaty provisions) would imply that this international specialised body could not function in isolation, independently of (general) international law and the legal system. If this is the case, then the scholarly view of the WTO law qualified as a 'self-contained' economic regime would find little empirical support. Moreover, the identification of a *continuity* and *consistency* in the GATT's/WTO's application of customary rules of interpretation of treaties (prior to and post the 1969 VCLT), as well as the WTO's use of the ICJ's precedents, allows to assert that the WTO's practice on treaty interpretation is unlikely to be part of the 'fragmentation' problem.

The chapter is divided into two parts: the first (Sect. 6.2) provides a brief explanation of the background of the GATT/WTO system, and the second (Sect. 6.3) is devoted to the investigation of several cases decided by the GATT/WTO prior to (Sect. 6.3.3) and after (Sect. 6.3.4) the adoption of the 1969 VCLT. The cases will be analysed in the context of a number of theoretical questions derived from the existing doctrinal controversy regarding treaty interpretation at the WTO dispute settlement regime, and they will be used to illustrate the theoretical points discussed in the chapter. The focus of this analysis will be on the approaches of treaty interpretation performed by the GATT's/WTO's adjudicative bodies (panels and the Appellate Body), while the ICJ's practice on treaty interpretation is taken as the comparator.

## 6.2 GATT/WTO Treaty Interpretation Background

Immediately after the Second World War, the victorious nations considered the United Nations as the international tool through which more established institutions could eradicate the economic causes of war (Merrills 2005, p. 205). Institutions

[5]See for this argument, e.g., McRae (2004), Kelly (2002), Kuyper (1994), Trachtman (1999), Beckford (2008).

such as the *International Monetary Fund*, *International Trade Organization* (ITO), *the World Bank* and *the General Agreement on Tariffs and Trade* (GATT) were created with the purpose of providing the framework for international economic relations.[6] These were supplemented by numerous subsequent instruments and organisations, including regional arrangements set up for particular purposes.[7] Built on the foundations of the ITO, *the General Agreement on Tariffs and Trade* (GATT) was created in 1947 as an organisation for establishing and enforcing through dispute settlement procedures the international trade rules.[8] The hope when establishing the GATT was to prevent another global conflict (Jennings 2004, p. 2). Through five rounds of multilateral negotiations and dispute settlement, the GATT succeeded to lower barriers to free trade and tariff barriers substantially.[9] In 1994, the GATT expanded and added 12 side agreements.[10] Almost 50 years later, the Eighth Round of negotiations under the GATT, known as the *Uruguay Round*, culminated in the establishment of the *World Trade Organization (WTO) in 1995*. The WTO system, which incorporated the GATT and other 'covered agreements' in 1995, came thus into force to serve the interests of the international community by resolving disputes relating to international trade.[11] Accordingly, the *Marrakesh Agreement* establishing in 1995 the WTO (a multilateral treaty) is now an arena where major trade disputes are resolved.[12] In principle, the WTO is an organisation for liberalising trade and (through the Dispute Settlement Body (DSB)) a forum to negotiate and settle trade disputes.[13]

The WTO's main goal is to keep trade on course, to help the production of goods and services, as well as to help exporters and importers to conduct their business while allowing governments to achieve social and environmental objectives.[14] Through the Marrakesh Agreements, treaties and associated legal instruments included in Annexes 1, 2 and 3 to this Agreement, the WTO functions as 'a single treaty instrument, creating rights and obligations under international law' (Jennings 2004, p. 2). Thus, the GATT still functions since the substance of its provisions was incorporated in and forms part of an annex to the WTO Agreement (Jackson 2006,

---

[6]Merrills (2005), p. 205.

[7]*Id.*

[8]*Id.* According to Merrills, when the GATT becomes a permanent system, with organs and decision making powers, it gave power to more than 200 multilateral trade agreements.

[9]Jennings (2004), p. 2.

[10]*Id.*

[11]*Id*, p. 6.

[12]Bermann et al. (2002), p. 1073. According to the authors the WTO was assigned with three functions: First, the WTO oversees the operation of the WTO agreements on international trade (these include GATT and 12 related agreements on trade in goods, GATS and TRIPS). Second, the WTO serves as a forum for trade negotiations. Third, the WTO administers a dispute settlement system which plays a very significant role in EU-US relations.

[13]The WTO guide website (available at https://www.wto.org/, last visited April, 2017).

[14]*Id.*

p. 87). The power to take decisions on all matters under any of the multilateral trade agreements is conferred to the highest authority: *the Ministerial Conference* composed of representatives of all WTO members.[15] As subsidiary bodies, *the General Council*, which concludes its day-to-day work on behalf of the Ministerial Conference, convenes in two particular forms: as *the Dispute Settlement Body*, which oversees the dispute settlement procedures, and as *the Trade Policy Review Body*, which conducts regular reviews of the trade policies of individual WTO members.[16] It is to be noted that only state parties that accepted the jurisdiction of the WTO may bring disputes to the WTO settlement body, and the disputes are only related to the implementation by states of the WTO Agreements.[17]

Since trade relations have been expected to be marked by conflicting interests, and such conflicts arose, a dispute settlement mechanism was designed to resolve disputes over the meaning of particular WTO rules and to determine in the context of each dispute whether the (WTO) rules have been violated.[18] The mechanism of dispute resolution involves an ad hoc Panel that makes a recommendation on the GATT/WTO compatibility of the national measure.[19] Since 1995, the parties to the GATT/WTO Agreements may appeal the Panels' decisions to the WTO Appellate Body, which constitutes an important innovation introduced in the WTO system, as compared with the GATT 1947 (Jackson 2006, p. 87). The Appellate Body was established by the WTO *Dispute Settlement Body* (DSB) as a standing tribunal, assigned to deal with questions of law (Gardiner 2008, p. 116). The WTO Dispute Settlement Body automatically adopts the Appellate Body's decisions, unless rejected by a consensus of the WTO members.[20] Thus, in order to be given effect, interpretations (of the WTO agreements and associated instruments) performed by the Appellate Body must be adopted by the Ministerial Conference and the General Council of the WTO (Gardiner 2008, p. 116). However, the interpretations of the WTO Ministerial Conference and the General Council are meant to be in accord with the Vienna Convention's general rule of interpretation.[21]

Further, a set of rules and procedures was constituted for the dispute settlement system, called the *Dispute Settlement Understanding* (DSU),[22] which to a large degree is considered the result of the evolution of rules, procedures and practices developed over almost half a century under the General Agreement on Tariffs and

---

[15]*Id.* See the Structure of WTO.

[16]*Id.*

[17]*Id.*

[18]Bermann et al. (2002), p. 1073.

[19]WTO guide website: the Structure of WTO, *supra* note 13.

[20]*Id.* See WTO Analytical Index.

[21]Gardiner (2008), p. 117.

[22]Contained in Annex 2 of the WTO Agreement.

Trade (GATT) 1947.[23] For example, Article 4 of the DSU requires that states engage in consultation before requesting a panel, and Article 5 sets forth alternative forms of dispute settlement such as good offices, conciliation and mediation.[24] In addition, Article XXII of the GATT/WTO provides for an 'adequate opportunity for consultation' that each contracting party may have at its disposal when another contracting party raises 'any matter affecting the operation of this Agreement' or 'in respect of any matter for which it has not been possible to find a satisfactory solution through consultation under paragraph 1' of this Article.[25]

The *interpretation* of the GATT/WTO Agreements by *Panels* and *the Appellate Body* is one of the general roles of the DSU that gives these bodies the power to adjudicate disputes between WTO members, by virtue of Article 3.2 of DSU. The scope of this article is 'to preserve the rights and obligations of Members under the covered Agreements, and *to clarify the existing provisions of those agreements in accordance with the customary rules of interpretation of public international law.* Recommendations and Rulings of the DSB cannot add to or diminish the rights and obligations provided in the covered agreements.'[26] In addition, other provisions also refer to the *interpretation* of the GATT/WTO Agreement, as, for example, Article 17.6 (ii) of the Anti-Dumping Agreement, which implicitly recognises that panels may develop legal interpretations. This article adds how to interpret the Anti-Dumping Agreement when 'a relevant provision of the Agreement admits of more than one permissible interpretation'.[27] Also, the 'exclusive authority' within Article IX (2) of the WTO Agreement refers to the possibility of adopting 'authoritative' interpretations, which are of general validity for all WTO members.[28] These

---

[23]WTO guide website, *supra* note 13.

[24]*Id.*

[25]Article XXII of the General Agreement on Tariffs and Trade (GATT 1947).

[26](Emphasis added) Article 3.2 of the D.S.U. provides in full:

> The dispute settlement system of the WTO is a central element in providing security and predictability to the multilateral trading system. The Members recognize that it serves to preserve the rights and obligations of Members under the covered agreements, and to clarify the existing provisions of those agreements in accordance with customary rules of interpretation of public international law. Recommendations and rulings of the DSB cannot add to or diminish the rights and obligations provided in the covered agreements.

[27]Article 17.6 (ii) of the Anti-Dumping Agreement (Committee on Anti-Dumping Practices) provides:

> the panel shall interpret the relevant provisions of the Agreement in accordance with customary rules of interpretation of public international law. Where the panel finds that a relevant provision of the Agreement admits of more than one permissible interpretation, the panel shall find the authorities' measure to be in conformity with the Agreement if it rests upon one of those permissible interpretations.

[28]See WTO guide website, *supra* note 13.

Article IX (Decision Making) of the Marrakesh Agreement Establishing the World Trade Organization provides:

> The Ministerial Conference and the General Council shall have the exclusive authority to adopt interpretations of this Agreement and of the Multilateral Trade Agreements. In the

'authoritative' interpretations are unlike interpretations performed by panels and the Appellate Body that are applicable only to the parties and to the subject matter of a specific dispute.[29]

In the process of resolving conflict interests of trade relations, the act of *interpretation* of the WTO Agreement's rights and obligations is a sine qua non condition. As admitted in the scholarship, the interpretation of the WTO Agreements is of crucial importance since the WTO dispute resolution often involves interpretation when the parties disagree about the meaning of specific provisions in the relevant treaty (Trachtman 1999, p. 340). Such disagreements are generally thought to arise because the meaning of the rights and obligations contained in the WTO Agreement is not always evident and because these rights and obligations are 'often drafted in general terms so as to be of a general applicability and to cover a multitude of individual cases, not all of which can be specifically regulated'.[30] Moreover, *interpretation* is considered necessary since there 'is no independent ground on which to fix the meaning of the rules' containing in the WTO law (Smith 2010, p. 5).

## 6.3 Case Law Analysis and Scholarship

### *6.3.1 Scope of the Analysis*

In this part of the chapter, several important cases at the GATT/WTO concerning treaty interpretation, prior to and after the establishment of the WTO in 1995, and also prior to and after the adoption of the 1969 VCLT, are analysed. Thus, the *adoption of the VCLT* and the *adoption of the Marrakesh Agreements* in 1995 (the WTO) are treated in this analysis as variables. The case law analyses seek to answer the theoretical question of whether the WTO adjudicative bodies (panels and the Appellate Body), in interpreting the GATT/WTO covered agreements, apply with consistency the customary rules of interpretation as reflected in the 1969 VCLT's universal methodology of treaty interpretation, or, conversely, by making use of their discretionary power, these bodies promote an innovative interpretation. If a continuity and consistency (coherence) in the GATT/WTO adjudicative bodies' approaches to customary rules of treaty interpretation is identified, as well as

case of an interpretation of a Multilateral Trade Agreement in Annex 1, they shall exercise their authority on the basis of a recommendation by the Council overseeing the functioning of that Agreement. The decision to adopt an interpretation shall be taken by a three-fourths majority of the Members. This paragraph shall not be used in a manner that would undermine the amendment provisions in Article (X).

[29] *Id.*

[30] *Id* ('Chapter 1: Introduction of the WTO Dispute Settlement System', *Dispute Settlement System Training Module*).

a similarity between the GATT/WTO and the ICJ in respect of the use of the methods, customary rules and principles of treaty interpretation (*similar interpretative patterns*), then it could be asserted that the WTO dispute settlement body's practice on treaty interpretation is unlikely to be part of the 'fragmentation' problem. More specifically, based on a comparative case law analysis, this chapter proposes to identify those instances where GATT/WTO panels and the Appellate Body apply canons of treaty interpretation similarly to the ICJ when dealing with similar difficulties of interpretation related to the construction of the treaty texts (e.g., insufficiently clear, inconclusive, ambiguous, obscure, vague or silent language of the text which does not provide for the circumstances of the given case). Therefore, the analysis provided here assesses the strengths and weaknesses of the WTO's application of the traditional canons of interpretation of treaties and offers an answer to the question of whether this specialised adjudicative body's practice on treaty interpretation is likely or not to contribute to 'fragmentation' in international law.

The cases presented here are not exhaustive, and so several observations about the cases' selection may be appropriate. With respect to the WTO's practice, there are obviously more cases concerning treaty interpretation than those discussed in this chapter, in which panels or the Appellate Body make direct reference to the PCIJ/ICJ jurisprudence or reference to Articles 31–33 of the VCLT.[31] However,

[31]See, e.g., Panel Report, *United States Antidumping Act of 1916, Complaint by the European Communities* (US—1916 Act (EC), WT/DS136/R (circulated March 31, 2000, adopted 26 September 2000, upheld by Appellate Body Report WT/DS136/AB/R, WT/DS162/AB/R, DSR 2000:X, 4593), para 6.53 and FN 329. This case illustrates the Panel's approach in weighting and assessing divergent municipal courts' jurisprudence when determining that a question related to municipal law was in line with the reasoning of the PCIJ in the *Brazilian Loans* case; Panel Report, United States – *Anti-Dumping Duty on Dynamic Random Access Memory Semiconductors (DRAMS) of One Megabit or Above from Korea, (US – DRAMS)*, WT/DS99/R, adopted 19 March 1999, DSR 1999:II; 1999 WL 38403 (W.T.O.), paras 4.113–15—for reference to Vienna Convention art 31–32 when interpreting a treaty, and especially FN 65 and the reference to ICJ's case *Admission of a State to the United Nations (Second Admissions Case)* [1950], ICJ Rep., at p. 8)—for an indication of justification of the interpretative approach taken by the Panel in the case; Panel Report, *United States – Countervailing Duties on Certain Corrosion-Resistant Carbon Steel Flat Products from Germany, (US – Carbon Steel)* WT/DS213/R and Corr. 1, 3 July 2002, as modified by Appellate Body Report WT/DS213/AB/R, DSR 2002:IX, 3833, 2002 WL 1438051 (W.T.O.) at para 6.5, and especially FN 187—for specific reference to ICJ practice: the *Conditions of Admission of a State to the United Nations (Second Admissions Case)*, [1950], ICJ Rep., in establishing the first duty of an international court, respectively of the WTO panels, when engaging in treaty interpretation; Appellate Body Report in *United States-Final Countervailing Duty to determination with respect to certain softwood from Canada* (*US – Softwood Lumber IV*, AB-2003-6, January 2004), WT/DS257/AB/R, adopted 17 February 2004, DSR 2004:II, 571 at para 59 and FN 49 and 50—for direct reference to VCLT Art. 33, to the ILC interpretation (preparatory work) on VCLT, and on ICJ's *Case Concerning Elettronica Sicula S.p.A. (ELSI) (United States v. Italy)*, Merits. 1989, ICJ Reports, para 132; Panel Report in *Canada Term of Patent Protection, (Canada – Patent Term)*, WT/DS170/R, circulated 5 May 2000, adopted 12 October 2000, upheld by Appellate Body Report WT/DS170/AB/R, DSR 2000:XI, 5121 (2000 WL 631059 (W.T.O.), para 6.49—for reference to ICJ practice in determining the principle

those selected are sufficient to demonstrate the theoretical points that, in interpreting the WTO Agreement, the GATT/WTO panels and the Appellate Body rely on the customary rules of interpretation as reflected in the VCLT and, also, on the PCIJ/ICJ's practice on treaty interpretation. Illustrating in principle how the GATT/WTO adjudicative bodies approach the general (customary) rules of treaty interpretation, the case selection here suffices to evidence the resemblance between the techniques adopted by the GATT/WTO adjudicative bodies and those adopted by the ICJ when applying the general rules of treaty interpretation; the coherence between the approaches adopted by the GATT/WTO, considering both pre and post the VCLT's adoption periods; and the implications of these aspects *vis-à-vis* the international law's unity. A mention should be made, however, that the major (post-1995) cases in which *the WTO established that the VCLT rules of treaty interpretation had attained the status of customary international law* (e.g., in *Gasoline*,[32] *India*[33]) are significantly cited or referred to in other decisions (and documents) of the WTO panels or the Appellate Body. For example, the *Gasoline* case (discussed in depth in this chapter), although it deals not only with matters related to treaty interpretation but also with other matters, is cited or referred in over 100 WTO documents. Thus, if we consider that by the end of 2014 there have been brought approximately 488 disputes since the WTO's inception,[34] those over 100 documents making reference to *Gasoline* indicate that this case has a tremendous impact on the subsequent WTO panels and the Appellate Body's practice, in particular on the practice of treaty interpretation. And such an impact is also valid for some other cases discussed in this chapter.[35]

---

of effective interpretation; Panel Report in *European Communities – Measures Affecting Trade in Large Civil Aircraft (EC and certain member States – Large Civil Aircraft)*, WT/DS316/R (30 June 2010), at p. 379 (FN 2331)/2010 WL 2671492 (June 30, 2011), at p. 367—for references to International Arbitration cases (*Island of Palmas Arbitration, 2 R. of Int'l Arb. Awards* (1928) 829, 845, *The Grisbadarna Case, 11 R. Int'l Arb. Awards* 155 (1909), and *The North Atlantic Coast Fisheries Case, 11 R. Int'l Arb. Awards 167* (1910)), and to ICJ cases (*The Fisheries Case, (United Kingdom v Norway)*, ICJ Reports 1951, p. 116; The *Minquiers and Ecrehos* case, ICJ Reports 1953, p. 47; and the *Aegean Sea Continental Shelf* Case, ICJ Reports 1978, p. 3)—when establishing the applicable doctrine of inter-temporal application of international law (reflected in Article 31(3)(c) VCLT).

[32] *United States – Standards for Reformulated and Conventional Gasoline*, WT/DS 2/AB, 29 April, 1996.

[33] *India – Patent Protection for Pharmaceutical and Agricultural Chemical Products*, WT/DS50/AB/R, adopted 16 January 1998.

[34] See WTO Chronological list of disputes cases, available online at: http://www.wto.org (last visited February 2017).

[35] E.g. *US – Shrimp/Turtle* (1998), *Japan – Alcoholic Beverages II* (1996), discussed further in this chapter.

### 6.3.2 Methodology

The GATT/WTO cases selected in this chapter are analysed in depth and in the context of the relevant views expressed in the scholarship, derived from the existing doctrinal controversy regarding treaty interpretation at the WTO dispute settlement regime. The case analyses are organised around questions/themes with focus on the emphasis of the GATT/WTO adjudicative bodies (panels and the Appellate Body) on a method, rule or principle of interpretation, while revealing the whole picture of the interpretative approach that these bodies adopt in each particular case discussed. These case analyses attempt to uncover whether the GATT/WTO adjudicative bodies approach the traditional cannons of interpretation in patterns which resemble those of the ICJ by resorting to more methods/rules than necessary ('overbuilding') in any given case, either expressly or implicitly, and whether these bodies assign more weight to, or preference of one method/rule or principle over another.[36] Some of the cases selected will be analysed necessarily more extensively than others so as to show the tendency of the WTO adjudicative bodies to approach broadly the treaty interpretative act (holistically).[37] Other cases, however, will be analysed more succinctly on the basis of their value in demonstrating the particular interpretative issues that this chapter deals with. The case analyses serve ultimately in examining whether, through its approach of interpretation based on both general rules of interpretation and specific (autonomous) interpretative rules for clarifying the GATT/WTO Agreements, the WTO promotes a 'self-contained' regime, respectively what the implications of this investigation's findings are for the unity of international law. To this purpose, first, the following section (Sect. 6.3.3) will examine what rules of interpretation the GATT's Panel relied on prior to the adoption of the 1969 VCLT.

### 6.3.3 Reliance on Customary Rules and/or Autonomous Techniques of Interpretation Before the DSU?

Scholarly opinions are divided on the issue of treaty interpretation at the GATT/WTO, with perspectives being dependent upon a particular scholar's view on the relationship between international law and trade law. For the present purposes, for example, Lennard's opinion on the GATT's practice is of particular significance. Explaining the historical divergence between international trade law and international law, Lennard observes that prior to the WTO, the interpretation of the GATT by panels was 'not one of the most illustrative examples of practice' that referred to the principles of public international law at the time of the Vienna Convention

[36]By virtue of judicial discretion to, e.g., ordinary meaning, context, good faith, object and purpose, intention, etc.

[37]As the Court with no exception employs more than a method/rule in a case.

Conference, since 'international trade and public international law disciplines have had different ways of evolution and culture in many aspects' (Lennard 2002, pp. 86–87). And for this reason international trade was seen as 'an alien, inhospitable, and often an uninteresting and peripheral landscape to most international lawyers, as compared with the international law of the sea, of war, or environment or of human rights'.[38] However, Lennard concludes that 'the increasingly sophisticated WTO consideration of treaty interpretation issues is a sign of convergence between these worlds, and perhaps one day it could be cemented by the ICJ drawing upon WTO jurisprudence and economic thinking in its decisions'. [39] The following section (Sect. 6.3.3.1) thus will analyse this issue by focusing on a case analysis of the GATT, prior to the adoption of the WTO (1995) and prior to the VCLT's adoption in 1969, respectively, with regard to the Panel's use of the tools of treaty interpretation.

#### 6.3.3.1 Rules of Interpretation Before the DSU

One could be tempted to assume that panels did not use a clear approach in respect of the application of the *customary rules of interpretation* (as developed especially by the ICJ) in the early GATT period, and prior to the adoption of the Vienna Convention, since these rules apparently were not clearly expressed or identified as such by the GATT's panels. This aspect leads us to question on what rules of interpretation panels based their decisions when there was no interpretative guidance (later to be reflected in Article 3.2 of the DSU) as to clarify the GATT's provisions. However, the following cases adjudicated under the GATT prior to the adoption of the VCLT, and prior to the WTO's creation in 1995, can clearly show the panels' reliance on (customary) rules of treaty interpretation. Also, certain similarities as between the decisions of the ICJ and panels can be observed in respect of the ways/techniques of approaching the methods and general rules of treaty interpretation. As the following case analysis and others provided in the next sections illustrate, prior to the adoption of the VCLT, and also prior to the WTO's adoption, the GATT's panels, similarly to the ICJ, shows a tendency to rely, either directly or indirectly, upon more rules of interpretation they usually declared as necessary to solve the case at hand. For example, despite declaring the 'ordinary meaning' of the terms in their 'context' as relevant or even decisive, panels engage in the adoption of a broad interpretation, using in combination more rules such as the 'object and purpose', 'context' of the whole treaty, 'relevant rules of international law', 'subsequent practice', 'preparatory work', 'circumstances of the conclusion the treaty', 'interpretation of treaties authenticated in two or more languages', depending on the circumstances of the case. And similarly to the ICJ, the panels

[38]Lennard (2002), pp. 86-87.

[39]*Id* (emphasis added).

tend to proceed in this way even when they declare the text of a treaty provision as being *clear*, or *sufficiently clear*, presenting no interpretative difficulties. The case ***Italy – Agricultural Machinery*** **(United Kingdom v. Italy) (1958)**[40] is an illustration of how the Panel's approach involves an application of other relevant rules of interpretation on an apparently *clear* text, in addition to the 'ordinary meaning' of the terms in the 'context' of their use which points directly to the customary rules of treaty interpretation, later to be codified in Articles 31, 32 and 33 of the VCLT (e.g., 'object and purpose', '*travaux preparatoire*', 'interpretation of treaties in two or more languages'). The Panel in this case was requested to examine whether Italian law,[41] in granting special credit facilities for farmers to purchase domestic agricultural machinery, was inconsistent with Article III: 4 of the GATT, which provides for equal treatment of imported products and like domestic products.[42] The Panel's starting point in this case is to elucidate the 'slight difference of wording' between the two official versions of Article III: 4, which could raise a problem of interpretation.[43]

By consulting both French and English versions of the treaty (GATT), the Panel finds that the French text, submitted to the Italian Parliament for approval, stated that the imported products '*ne seront pas soumis à un traitement moins favorable*', whereas the English text stated that 'the imported product shall be accorded treatment no less favourable'.[44] The Panel admits the English text to be clear, which provides for 'any favourable treatment granted to domestic products would have to be granted to like imported products'.[45] By focusing on the differences of the meaning of both versions, particularly applied to the terms 'like products' and 'affecting', the Panel suggests a textualist approach, based on the 'ordinary mean-

[40] *Italian discrimination against imported agricultural machinery*, report adopted on 23 October 1958, L/833-7S/60. The Italian Law No. 949 of July 1952 provides special credit facilities to some categories of farmers or farmer's cooperatives for the purchase of agricultural machinery produced in Italy.

[41] Law No. 949 of July 1952.

[42] Whether the Italian Law was inconsistent with Article III:4 of the GATT which provides:

> The products of the territory of any contracting party imported into the territory of any other contracting party shall be accorded treatment no less favourable than that accorded to like products of national origin in respect of all laws, regulations and requirements affecting their internal sale, offering for sale, purchase, transportation, distribution or use. The provisions of this paragraph shall not prevent the application of differential internal transportation charges which are based exclusively on the economic operation of the means of transport and not on the nationality of the product.

[43] *Italy-Agricultural Machinery* (1958), *supra* note 40, para 11.

[44] *Id.*

[45] *Id.*

ing of the terms in their context'.[46] The 'contextualist' approach, which implies taking into account the context of provision and of the treaty as a whole, is also revealed, for example, when the Panel connects the scope of Article III.1 of the GATT,[47] mainly designed to prevent the contracting party from using internal taxes and other regulatory measures, to the provisions contained in paragraph 8(b), as one of this article's clauses.[48]

Although the Panel does not make any specific reference to the rules applied as customary rules, methods or principles of treaty interpretation, the language of the report clearly shows a reliance on such means. However, the Panel's approach appears to accentuate more the textualist method by pointing out that '[i]t was *clear* from the English *text* that any favourable treatment granted to domestic products would have to be granted to like imported products ...'.[49] The Panel seems to convey here the idea that the text is, basically, the manifested will of the contracting parties, hence their manifested common intention. Though the Panel places principal emphasis on the textualist method, it actually appears to take equally into account other methods of interpretation such as teleological and subjective when trying to identify the intention of the drafters in respect of Article III: 4, as it will be shown further.

In the Panel's further (suggested) resort to the *travaux preparatoire* (which supports all methods of interpretation: textualist, teleological, subjective/intentionalist), this rule appears to have both confirmatory and determinative roles. It is evident, for example, when the Panel finds that 'the drafters of Article III 4 *intended* to cover in paragraph 4 not only the laws of regulations which directly governed the conditions of sale or purchase ... but also any laws or regulations which might adversely modify the conditions of competition between the domestic and imported products on the internal market'.[50] Thus, the Panel expressly takes into account the 'intention' element, clearly adopting a subjective method in addition to the textualist, moreover, when it reiterates that the 'intention of the

---

[46] *Id.*

[47] Article III*: National Treatment on Internal Taxation and Regulation:

> 1. The contracting parties recognize that internal taxes and other internal charges, and laws, regulations and requirements affecting the internal sale, offering for sale, purchase, transportation, distribution or use of products, and internal quantitative regulations requiring the mixture, processing or use of products in specified amounts or proportions, should not be applied to imported or domestic products so as to afford protection to domestic production. *The scope of this Article is mainly designed to prevent the contracting party of using internal taxes and other regulatory measures 'as to afford protection to domestic production', to undermine negotiated tariff concession.

[48] *Italy-Agricultural Machinery* (1958), para 13. Article III: 8(b) provided

> The provisions of this Article shall not prevent the payment of subsidies exclusively to domestic producers, including payments to domestic producers derived from the proceeds of internal taxes or charges applied consistently with the provisions of this Article and subsidies effected through governmental purchases of domestic products.

[49] *Id* (emphasis added).

[50] *Id* (emphasis added).

drafters of the Agreement' 'was clearly to treat the imported products in the same way as the like domestic products. Otherwise indirect protection could be given'.[51]

In dealing with the principle of 'competitive conditions', which flows directly from the first paragraph of Article III of the GATT concerning the national treatment's obligations towards internal taxation and regulation, the Panel also appears to be highly reliant in this case on the 'object and purpose' rule (teleological method), and equally on the principle of effectiveness. For example, the Panel concludes that the text of Article III: 4, when read in its 'context' and in the light of the 'object and purpose' of the GATT, cannot be interpreted in the sense 'to limit the right of a contracting party to adopt measures which appeared to it necessary to foster its economic development or to protect a domestic industry, provided that such measures were permitted by the terms of GATT, as it was not the intention of the drafters'.[52] The effectiveness principle, according to which an interpreter must give full effect to all the terms of the treaty (the text, context, object and purpose, context of the whole treaty), has often been applied by the PCIJ/ICJ in its practice on treaty interpretation when dealing with any type of construction of the treaty text, even when the text was declared by the Court as *sufficiently clear* or *clear* (as is declared in the case at hand). A similar approach and reasoning could be seen, for example, in the earlier practice of the ICJ, in the *Exchange of Greek and Turkish Population* (1923) case, where the ICJ underlined the principle of effectiveness as 'a principle which is self-evident'.[53]

It appears that the Panel applies in *Italy-Agricultural Machinery* a *holistic* approach on a text declared *clear*, in a manner that could resemble those approaches taken by the ICJ on many similar situations (relating to the construction of the text of treaties) before the adoption of the VCLT. For example, *in the Conditions of Admission of a State to Membership in the United Nations (Article 4 of the Charter)* (1948) case, the ICJ wanted to clarify the meaning of the text of Article 4 of the Charter, in accordance with 'the spirit' and 'the terms' of it, despite the Court declaring the provision as being *clear*.[54] By adopting such a holistic approach (text, context, object and purpose, context of the treaty), the ICJ recalled a rule of interpretation well recognised in its jurisprudence, according to which *a treaty provision should be read in its entirety*.[55] Thus despite an emphasis on the textualist method and apparently basing its interpretation on this method, a tactic the ICJ has ussually adopted irrespective of the interpretative difficulties encountered on the text of treaties, the Panel in *Italy – Agricultural Machinery* equally promotes the

[51] *Id*, para 11.

[52] *Id*, para 16.

[53] *Exchange of Greek and Turkish Population* (*Lausanne Convention VI, January 30th, 1923, Article* 2), Advisory opinion, PCIJ, Series B, No. 10, 1925, p. 20. (See the analysis of this case in Chap. 4 of this book).

[54] *The Conditions of Admission of a State to Membership in the United Nations (Article 4 of the Charter)*, ICJ, May 28th, 1948, p. 62. See the analysis of this case in Chap. 4 of this book.

[55] *Id.* See Joint dissenting opinion of Judge Basdevant, Winiarski, McNair and Read, at p. 86.

teleological and subjective methods. It provides a *holistic* interpretation of the provision at issue, in the light of the GATT as a *whole*.

The following section (Sect. 6.3.4) will examine cases of the GATT/WTO's practice on treaty interpretation after the adoption of the DSU in 1995 (thus after the adoption of the 1969 VCLT), comparatively with cases prior to the DSU's adoption.

### 6.3.4 The VCLT as an Embodiment of Custom?

From the perspective of the compatibility of the VCLT rules of interpretation with the WTO Agreements, for some authors, supplementing the obligations of the WTO trade regime with rules of public international law remains a controversial matter. For example, Kelly considers that without the designation by Article 3.2 of the DSU of the customary rules of treaty interpretation, the WTO adjudicative bodies would be required to develop their own rules of interpretation on a case-by-case basis (Kelly 2002, p. 365). More critical from the perspective of what lies behind the interpretative results found by using the VCLT methodology in the WTO trade-specific context, Smith observes that while many current scholars think that the wording of Article 3.2 is deemed to lay down the legitimate interpretation formula, in fact this article 'misses the deeper significance of the ways in which the language of the rules both shapes and constrains interpretation' (Smith 2010, p. 3). In Smith's view, the language of Article 3.2, in which the rules of interpretation are expressed, does not have any autonomous power in its own right. Instead, as the author claims, the article is only the 'container for the transmission of messages' from the trade negotiators to those who are going to interpret the rules about the way the members felt international trade should be regulated in the WTO.[56] Smith explains that the language of the WTO rules has its own dynamic character, and by applying the toolbox of the VCLT (provided in Article 3.2) for interpretation of the WTO provisions in any way just to fit their meaning would only keep the WTO rules unconnected with, and 'outside', of their own language.[57] Although Smith expresses the idea that international trade law has its own 'interpretative culture', its own way of speaking, she admits that the WTO has many roots in public international law.[58] In this regard, she observes that the Appellate Body has frequently discussed and applied other customary rules of international law by resort to Article 31(3)(c) VCLT, and, however, this Body sometimes uses the notion of this provision for other norms binding on the parties.[59]

---

[56]Smith (2010), p. 5.

[57]*Id.* Based on the WTO practice, Smith observes that the language of the VCLT rules of interpretation pushes the panel and Appellate Body to see, for example, certain understandings of the "ordinary meaning" and "context" of the Agreement on Agriculture's rules as correct.

[58]*Id.*

[59]*Id*, p. 11.

From a different angle, McRae observes that this method/process of the panels and Appellate Body of looking beyond the specific rules the WTO adopted to interpret its covered agreements appears basically more akin to that used by a common law court when ascertaining the content of the common law (McRae 2004, p. 8). Specifically, with reference to the applicability of the VCLT rules of interpretation in the WTO specialised context as being problematic because some WTO members (including the United States) are not parties to VCLT, Gray and Cameron conclude that since those VCLT rules reflect customary international law, they should be binding on all WTO members.[60] Similarly, Lennard asserts that the term 'parties' in Article 31 of the VCLT applies to 'the parties to the WTO Agreement generally, not the parties to a dispute or some other subset of these whose relationships are being examined' and that such an interpretation may result from a careful reading of Article 31(3)(c) of the VCLT (Lennard 2002, p. 43). Along this line of thought, Van Damme argues that the ILC actually intended to articulate in the VCLT's 'general rule of interpretation' 'a set of principles applying generally in different contexts, and with possible different outcomes' (Van Damme 2010, p. 641). She attempts to explain the principles of interpretation as provided by the VCLT through the prism of their 'creative function', in the sense that these rules 'help answer why a rule is to be given one meaning and not another' (Van Damme 2009, p. 34). The author further explains that the WTO Appellate Body has tried to justify its interpretations on the basis of the VCLT's general rule of interpretation without treating it 'as a rigid, binding structure of rules', yet she admits that exceptions exist and their justifications have sometimes been excessive.[61] Van Damme' s view in this regard is that the Appellate Body, nevertheless, has generally approached treaty interpretation as a matter governed by principles, not rules.[62]

Clearly, as the following case analyses will show, a development in the technical language of the customary rules of interpretation adopted by the GATT/WTO adjudicative bodies in their decisions is to be perceived after the adoption of the 1969 VCLT. This aspect points towards the confirmation of the applicability and persistence/perpetuation in time of the same rules of treaty interpretation in the practice of the GATT/WTO and also towards these rules' nature as *customary*. However, the relevance of this development in the technical language of treaty interpretation is only one aspect that the case analyses in the present author's view will show further. In principle, the following section will reveal the clear reliance of the WTO panels and the Appellate Body on the VCLT's rules of interpretation, in the period that followed the adoption of the *Vienna Convention*, in ways similar to those adopted by the ICJ, but more vigorously in an express and explicative manner

[60]Cameron and Gray (2001), p. 275. The authors note that this uncertainty was resolved by the Appellate Body in the *Japan – Taxes* case, when ruled that 'the VCLT represent a codification of customary international law and is therefore binding on all States.' See also Mitchell (2007), p. 807—for a similar conclusion based WTO's practice on treaty interpretation.

[61]Van Damme (2009), p. 34.

[62]*Id.*

after 1995, when Vienna rules found reflection in Article 3.2 of the DSU (the established WTO interpretative guideline).

Besides the persistence/perpetuation of the customary rules and methods, the issue of *consistency* in the interpretative approaches adopted by the GATT's/WTO's adjudicative bodies, and the *reference by these bodies to the ICJ's precedents*, will be examined further in this chapter by using case law. The WTO cases will be analysed comparatively with cases of the ICJ's practice on treaty interpretation. The identification of a *coherence* in the approaches to treaty interpretation (in both pre- and post-VCLT periods) adopted by the GATT/WTO (adjudicative bodies) is important in assessing the impact that this specialised international body's practice has upon the *coherence* and *unity* of international law. To this purpose, the next three cases will be analysed comparatively on the same provision (Article XX of the GATT/WTO) in Sect. 6.3.4.1: a comparative approach between the Appellate Body (Sect. 6.3.4.1.1) and the Panel (Panel prior to the WTO's adoption) (Sect. 6.3.4.1.2), and Sect. 6.3.5.1, an approach by the Appellate Body.

#### 6.3.4.1 Comparative Approaches Between the Appellate Body and Panel (Prior to the WTO) on the Same Provision: Article XX (g)

During the past two decades, one of the areas in which the DSU interpretative ethos came to be vividly contested was in relation to Article XX of the WTO Agreement.[63] This provision is entitled 'General Exceptions' and lays down a number of specific instances in which WTO members may be exempted from GATT rules.[64] The reason why Article XX is not free from controversy (particularly *vis-à-vis* its interpretation) is thought to be because this article connects the WTO general regime, based on free trade principles, with other important areas of international law, based on principles of environmental law, public morals and state sovereignty. Thus, since such principles are sometimes in conflict, they need to be reconciled.[65]

Although far from being exhaustive, the case analyses presented below support the argument that the WTO adjudicative bodies, generally, use patterns of reasoning similar to the ICJ when approaching methods and customary rules of interpretation in order to solve treaty interpretation difficulties (e.g., insufficient clarity, ambiguity, vagueness, obscurity in the text of treaty provisions). Moreover, just as the ICJ does, also the WTO has generally shown a tendency to value all the methods

---

[63]McInerney (2009), p. 154. Article XIV of the GATS which contains similar provisions as Article XX of the GATT sets out a "two tier analysis" for justifying a measure.

[64]See WTO guide website, *supra* note 13. (WTO rules and environmental policies: GATT exceptions).

[65]*Id.*

and customary rules of interpretation, either admitting them explicitly or implicitly or showing an emphasis on one or another. As the following case analyses can further illustrate, the overall attitude of the WTO adjudicative bodies to treaty interpretation is that 'interpretation must give meaning and effect to all the terms of a treaty' under the basic rule provided by Article 31(1)(2) of the VCLT. By appending to each interpretative rule or principle its own role, weight and place, generally, and giving a *holistic* character to interpretation, the WTO adjudicative bodies can reach the level of objectivity required for an interpretation to be in conformity with the VCLT standard of interpretation and, certainly, with Article 3.2 of the DSU, which demands such an approach.

Since a detailed analysis of case law, especially in respect of Article XX of the GATT/WTO, is beyond the scope of this book, I will provide (in the next three sections) an analysis of only three important decisions,[66] necessary for understanding the articulation of the WTO's interpretation rules/doctrines and the VCLT rules in the controversial field covered by this provision.

#### 6.3.4.1.1 The Appellate Body's Approach

In the light of the above considerations, the ***Gasoline (United States v. Brasil/ Venesuela) (1996)*** case[67] illustrates an interesting and flexible interpretation of Article XX (g) of the GATT/WTO, a provision considered by the Appellate Body in this case to be *ambiguous*. Here, the Appellate Body approaches holistically the customary rules of interpretation reflected in Articles 31 and 32 of the VCLT,

---

[66]See, e.g., the *Gasoline*; *Shrimp/Tuna; US – Canadian Tuna* cases. As a statistic of such cases: under the GATT (1948–1994), six panel proceedings involving an examination of environmental measures or human health-related measures under GATT Article 20 (XX) were completed. Of the six reports, three were not adopted. In 1995, the WTO's dispute settlement procedure took over from GATT. Since then, three such proceedings have been completed. Adopted, pre-WTO, GATT panel reports (on Article XX): *United States – Taxes on Automobiles*, ruling not adopted, circulated on 11 October 1994. Case brought by EU; *United States – Restrictions on Imports of Tuna, "son of tuna-dolphin"*, ruling not adopted, circulated on 16 June 1994. Case brought by EU'. *United States – Restrictions on Imports of Tuna, the "tuna-dolphin"* case, ruling not adopted, circulated on 3 September 1991. Case brought by Mexico; *Thailand – Restrictions on the Importation of and Internal Taxes on Cigarettes*, ruling adopted on 7 November 1990. Case brought by US; *Canada – Measures Affecting Exports of Unprocessed Herring and Salmon*, ruling adopted on 22 March 1988. Case brought by US; *United States – Prohibition of Imports of Tuna and Tuna Products from Canada*, ruling adopted on 22 February 1982, case brought by Canada. After 1995: *European Communities – Measures Asbestos and Products Containing Asbestos* (Complainant: Canada), WT/DS135/R, 12 March, 2001, *United States – Import Prohibition of Certain Shrimp and Affecting Shrimp*, WT/DS58/AB/R, 12 October, 1998; and *United States – Standards for Reformulated and Conventional Gasoline*, WT/DS 2/AB, 29 April, 1996.

[67]*Gasoline* (1996), *supra* note 32. The dispute was related to the implementation by the United States of its domestic legislation known as Clean Air Act of 1990, and in addition to the regulation enacted by the United States-Environmental Protection Agency, pursuant to that Act, to control toxic and other pollution caused by the combustion of gasoline manufactured in or imported into the United States. The regulation is referred to Part 80 of Title 40 of the Code of Federal Regulations, and known as the 'Gasoline Rule'.

stressing the practical value of each of the rule employed in the complex process of interpretation. As it will be seen, the Appellate Body's approach in this case appears to develop down the paths used by the ICJ in various similar situations (*ambiguity* in treaty text), showing compliance with the VCLT universally accepted methodology of interpretation. The main issue of interpretation before the Appellate Body in the *Gasoline* case was to establish whether the United States' measure to apply stricter rules for imported gasoline than it did for domestically produced gasoline was discriminatory and in favour of domestic refineries, as Venezuela and Brazil claimed, and whether this measure was justified under the GATT 1995, Article XX (g), which provides an exemption from other GATT obligations for measures relating to conservation of exhaustible natural resources.[68]

The Appellate Body finds first in *Gasoline* that the Panel 'overlooked a fundamental rule of treaty interpretation' in the application of Article XX (g) to the baseline established rules, notably the rule embodied in Article 31(1) of the VCLT, according to which '[a] treaty shall be interpreted in good faith in accordance with the ordinary meaning to be given to the terms of the treaty in their context and in the light of its object and purpose'.[69] It underlines next that this general rule of interpretation 'forms part of the "customary rules of interpretation of public international law" which the Appellate Body has been directed, by Article 3.2 of the DSU, to clarify the GATT's provisions and other "covered agreements"'.[70] The intention of the Appellate Body to adopt the textualist, subjective and teleological methods is displayed when it expressly states that, according to the 'basic international law rule of treaty interpretation', 'the terms of a treaty are to be given their ordinary meaning, in context, so as to effectuate its object and purpose, is applicable here, too'.[71]

For a textualist illustration, it suffices to mention here the Appellate Body's reliance on the 'ordinary meaning of the terms in their context' rule applied to the term 'measures' within Article XX, used both in the chapeau and in paragraph (g) of Article XX, or when the Appellate Body finds that Article XX uses different terms in respect of different categories such as 'necessary'—in paragraphs (a), (b) and (d); 'relating to'—in paragraphs (c), (e) and (g); or 'in pursuance of'—in paragraph (h), etc.[72] Notable is the Appellate Body's recalling further that the 'general rule of interpretation has attained the status of a rule of customary or general international

---

[68]Article XX of the GATT provides:

> Subject to the requirement that such measures are not applied in a manner which would constitute a means of arbitrary or unjustifiable discrimination between countries where the same conditions prevail, or a disguised restriction on international trade, nothing in this Agreement shall be construed to prevent the adoption or enforcement by any contracting party of measures: paragraph (g) relating to the conservation of exhaustible natural resources if such measures are made effective in conjunction with restrictions on domestic production or consumption.

[69]*Gasoline* (1996), pp. 16–17.

[70]*Id.*

[71]*Id*, p. 16.

[72]*Id*, p. 13.

law'.[73] The Body supports this statement by making direct reference, among other international tribunals' practice (such as of the ECtHR or IACHR),[74] to the ICJ's practice, for example, invoking the *Territorial Dispute* case (1994), as the most illustrative in confirming the rule prescribed by Article 31(1) of the VCLT as 'customary international law'.[75]

Furthermore, by admitting that the Panel failed to take adequate account of the words actually used by Article XX (of the GATT) in its several paragraphs, the Appellate Body looks to read the terms of this provision in their 'context' and in the light of the treaty's 'object and purpose'.[76] It appears not without relevance that, even by making only a vague reference further to the drafting history of Article XX, the Appellate Body describes it actually as 'a valuable one',[77] implying a possible use of and reliance on *the travaux preparatoire* in confirmation of the intention of the drafters, in addition to the 'object and purpose' of the introductory clauses of Article XX.[78]

One could observe that the approach adopted by the Appellate Body in *Gasoline* appears overall to be consistent with its expressly declared approach, however, stressing less or more some aspects of it. Although the Appellate Body clearly relies upon the basic principles of treaty interpretation, it appears to lay at various times more emphasis on the 'object and purpose' rule in interpreting Article XX and its 'general exceptions'. A clear emphasis on this rule is pointed out, for example, when the Appellate Body concludes that the expression of Article XX(g), 'relating to the conservation of exhaustible natural resources', needs 'to be read in context and in such a manner as to give effect to the purposes and objects of the General Agreement'.[79] Yet, whatever the emphasis on one method (or rule of interpretation) or another, the Appellate Body's overall approach in this case does not appear to diminish the goal of the 'basic rule of interpretation'. The Body adopts a clear *holistic* interpretation, placing the terms of the treaty on the same footing.

In addition, without formally stating it, the Appellate Body resorts to the (unwritten/uncodified in the VCLT) effectiveness principle, often applied by the Body so as to ensure the legal effect of the provision at issue. It reveals in this context that '[o]ne of the corollaries of the "general rule of interpretation in the *Vienna Convention*" is that the "interpretation must give meaning and effect to all

[73] *Id*, p. 17 (emphasis added).

[74] *Id.*

[75] *Id*, p. 23. See *Territorial Dispute Case (Libyan Arab Jamahiriya v. Chad)* (1994) I.C.J. Reports, p. 20.

[76] *Id.*

[77] *Id*, p. 22.

[78] *Id.*

[79] *Gasoline* (1996), p. 18. The Appellate Body invokes *Canada – Measures Affecting Exports of Unprocessed Herring and Salmon*, BISD 35S/98, para 4.6; adopted 22 March, 1988, cited in Panel Report, para 6.39. This customary rule of interpretation of treaties can also be illustrated in ICJ's practice, in cases such as *Competence of the ILO to Regulate the Personal Work of the Employer*, PCIJ, Series B, No. 13, 1926, pp. 6–18; *International Status of South Africa*, ICJ, Reports, 1962, p. 128, para 336.

the terms, of a treaty"'.[80] For example, admitting that Article XX's chapeau 'is not without ambiguity', the Appellate Body concludes that the phrase 'relating to the conservation of exhaustible natural resources' may not be read so expansively as seriously to subvert the purpose and object of Article III: 4[81] and '[n]or may Article III: 4 be given so broad a reach effectively to emasculate Article XX (g) and the policies and interests it embodies'.[82] This interpretative reasoning appears to comply fully with the principle reflected in Article 3.2 of the DSU, in brief, that an interpretation should not mean to reconstruct a treaty.[83] Then the Appellate Body expands this reasoning again by means of the effectiveness principle, adding that '[an] interpreter is not free to adopt a reading that would result in reducing whole clauses or paragraphs of a treaty to redundancy or inutility'.[84] The Body supports this approach by express reference to the ICJ's relevant practice, particularly to the *Corfu Channel* (1949)[85] and *Territorial Dispute* (1994)[86] cases, where the ICJ, by relying on the PCIJ's relevant precedents, confirmed the effectiveness principle. For example, the ICJ in *Corfu Channel* (1949) applied the effectiveness principle and concluded that 'it cannot be supposed that the Parties while drafting these clauses in the same form, intended to give them opposite meaning ...', and therefore 'it would indeed be incompatible with the generally accepted rules of interpretation to admit that a provision of this sort occurring in a special agreement should be devoid of purpose or effect'.[87]

---

[80]*Id*, p. 22.

[81]*Id.*

[82]*Id*, p. 17. The approach of interpretation involves 'the national treatment principle' (special principle) reflected in Article III of the GATT (providing for equally treatment for domestic and imported products), with which the 'Gasoline Rule' is claimed by Venezuela and Brazil as inconsistent.

Article III (National Treatment on Internal Taxation and Regulation), paragraph 4, in the main part, provides that:

> The products of the territory of any contracting party imported into the territory of any other contracting party shall be accorded treatment no less favourable than that accorded to like products of national origin in respect of all laws, regulations and requirements affecting their internal sale, offering for sale, purchase, transportation, distribution or use ...

[83]See Article 3.2 of DSU, *supra* note 26.

[84]*Gasoline* (1996), p. 32.

[85]*Id.* The Appellate Body invokes the *Corfu Channel Case* (1949), I.C.J. Reports, p. 26, ICJ. The ICJ in *Corfu Channel* invoked the *Free Zones* case (*Free Zones of Upper Savoy and District of Gex (Fr. v. Switz.)*, 1929 P.C.I.J. (ser. A) No. 22 (Order of Aug. 19), pp. 13–24), and it found that: 'in case of doubt, the clauses of a special agreement by which a dispute is referred to the Court must, if it does not involve doing violence to their terms, be construed in a manner enabling the clauses themselves to have appropriate effects.' Also, the effectiveness principles is illustrated earlier in the PCIJ practice, such as in *Competence of the Int'l Labour Org. to Regulate, Incidentally, the Personal Work of the Employer*, Advisory Opinion, 1926 P.C.I.J. (ser. B) No. 13 (July 23), p. 19. The PCIJ held in this case: 'the Court, in determining the nature and scope of a measure, must look to its practical effect rather than to the predominant motive that may be conjectured to have inspired it.'

[86]*Territorial Dispute Case (Libyan Arab Jamahiriya v. Chad)* (1994), *supra* note 75, p. 23. See the analysis of this case in Chap. 4 for similarities of the effectiveness principle's application.

[87]*Corfu Channel Case* (1949), see *supra* note 85, p. 26.

It can be stated that the *holistic* approach of interpretation adopted by the Appellate Body in *Gasoline* strengthens the idea that the dispute settlement process at the WTO tends to appeal to the general international law rules and principles in carifying the meaning of the the WTO Agreement's provisions. This approach confirms the statement made by the Appellate Body in this case that the WTO's specialised bodies cannot read the General Agreement 'in clinical isolation from public international law',[88] an aspect that attests to the linkage between *lex specialis* (WTO Agreement) and *lex generalis*, reflected, however, in Article 3.2 of the DSU (providing for the interpretation of the WTO Agreement according to *the customary rules of interpretation of public international law*).

##### 6.3.4.1.2 The Panel's Approach Prior to the WTO's Specific Adoption of the Customary Rules of Treaty Interpretation in Article 3.2 DSU

The following example will show what rules of interpretation the Panel used in interpreting Article XX (g) of the GATT before the adoption of the WTO (and after the adoption of the VCLT), when there was no specific interpretative guideline, as also in what ways the Panel's approach differs from approaches taken by the Appellate Body (hence after the WTO's adoption) on the same matter. In the ***US – Canadian Tuna (Canada v. US)*** **(1982)**[89] case, the Panel shows flexibility in applying the customary rules of interpretation, apparently not giving them the order established and developed mainly by practice, that of starting with 'the ordinary meaning of the terms in the context of their use'. Instead, the Panel chooses to rely first on the 'context of the treaty as a whole' rule, following by the 'subsequent practice', 'context' and 'ordinary meaning of the terms', 'object and purpose' rules, however combining them in one single interpretative act. Thus, the Panel resorts in this case to the customary rules of treaty interpretation, confirming their status as *customary* law and their procedural applicability to the interpretation of the provisions of the *General Agreement on Tariffs and Trade* (GATT 1947). The issue of interpretation for the Panel in this case was whether the United States' import prohibition on tuna and tuna products from Canada was contrary to the provisions of Article XI of the GATT 1947, which prohibited import restrictions other than duties, taxes or other charges, etc., on any product of the territory of any other

[88] *Gasoline* (1996), p. 17.

[89] *United States – Prohibition of imports of tuna and tuna products from Canada*, Report of the Panel adopted on 22 February 1982 (L/5198-29S/91). The dispute arose as result of the Canada seizure of 19 U.S. tuna boats caught fishing inside Canada's 200-mile fisheries zone. The disagreement between Canada and the United States appeared related to jurisdiction over Pacific fisheries.

contracting party.[90] The import prohibition was invoked by the United States as a measure related to the conservation of exhaustible natural resources, under Article XX (g) of the GATT 1947.[91]

The Panel begins its interpretation in *US – Canadian Tuna*, as it itself admits, in accordance with the GATT's prevailing practice. It suggests first resort to the 'context of the treaty' (GATT 1947) as a whole, finding on this rule that the United States' measure will be analysed 'in the light of relevant GATT provisions'; however, 'the dispute was part of a wider disagreement mainly related to fisheries and that the trade aspect constituted a part of a broader complex'.[92] Then the Panel suggests resort to 'any subsequent agreement' between the parties regarding the interpretation of the treaty (GATT) or 'any subsequent practice' regarding the application of the treaty that could establish the agreement of the parties regarding its interpretation.[93] Relying on these rules, codified in Article 31 (3) (a) and (b) VCLT, the Panel finds, for example, that 'an interim arrangement on albacore tuna fisheries between Canada and United States was reached', and furthermore, 'subsequent negotiations between the parties resulted in the establishment of the Treaty on Pacific Coast Albacore Tuna Vessels and Port Privileges'.[94]

The 'context' rule is indeed revealed at the level of provision when the Panel proceeds to determine the legal basis of the United States' prohibition on the import of tuna and tuna products from Canada. The Panel examines Article XI: 1 in the context of the exceptions listed in its paragraph 2.[95] By showing at the same time the difference in language between Article XI: 2(a) and (b) and Article XI: 2(c),[96]

---

[90]Article XI:1 of the GATT provides:

> No prohibitions or restrictions other than duties, taxes or other charges, whether made effective through quotas, import or export licences or other measures, shall be instituted or maintained by any contracting party on the importation of any product of the territory of any other contracting party or on the exportation or sale for export of any product destined for the territory of any other contracting party.

[91]See for Preamble of Article XX of the GATT (1947) (General exceptions), *supra* note 66. Article XX(g):

> relating to the conservation of exhaustible natural resources if such measures are made effective in conjunction with restrictions on domestic production or consumption.

[92]*US – Canadian Tuna* (1982), *supra* note 89, para 4.1.

[93]*Id.*

[94]*Id.*

[95]*Id*, para 4.4.

[96]*Id*, para 4.6. Article XI: 2 provides:

> The provisions of paragraph 1 of this Article shall not extend to the following:
>
> (a) Export prohibitions or restrictions temporarily applied to prevent or relieve critical shortages of foodstuffs or other products essential to the exporting contracting party;
> (b) Import and export prohibitions or restrictions necessary to the application of standards or regulations for the classification, grading or marketing of commodities in international trade;
> (c) Import restrictions on any agricultural or fisheries product, imported in any form,* necessary to the enforcement of governmental measures which operate: … Any contracting

the Panel ensures that an interpretation based on the 'ordinary meaning' rule is inseparable from the context.[97] Accordingly, the Panel finds that 'the provisions of Article XI: 2 (c) could not justify the application of an import prohibition'.[98] Such an approach that enables an interpreter to give effect to the terms of a treaty in their natural and ordinary meaning, underlying the 'context' in which they occur, is a customary rule frequently highlighted by the ICJ (as seen in Chap. 4 of this book) from its early practice, more strongly, as for example, in the *Second Admission Case* (1950)[99] or the *IMCO Case* (1960).[100]

Furthermore, by pointing out the Preamble of Article XX,[101] the Panel suggests resort to the 'object and purpose' of this provision and, thus, an adoption of a teleological approach of interpretation[102], reflected in Article 31 (1) VCLT. This approach implies relating paragraph (g) of Article XX, an exemption from other GATT obligations for measures related to conservation, to *the chapeau* (Preamble) of Article XX. The *chapeau* provides in essence that measures cannot be applied in a manner that would constitute a means of arbitrary or unjustifiable discrimination between countries where the same conditions prevail or be a disguised restriction on international trade.[103] Thus, based on the rules of 'text' (textualist method), 'object and purpose' rule (teleological method), context of the treaty as a whole, as well as on the rules of 'subsequent practice'/'subsequent agreement' between the parties (which support the subjective method), the Panel concludes that the United States'

party applying restrictions on the importation of any product pursuant to subparagraph (c) of this paragraph shall give public notice of the total quantity or value of the product permitted to be imported during a specified future period and of any change in such quantity or value...

[97] *Id.*

[98] *Id*, para 4.6. The Panel found that the ban applied to the catch of species (e.g. albacore and skipjack) whose domestic production the United States had not been limited, and that it was maintained when restrictions on the catch were no longer maintained (e.g. Pacific yellowfin tuna in 1980).

[99] *Competence of the General Assembly for the Admission of a State to the United Nations (Second Admissions Case)* (1950), I.C.J. Reports, p. 8. The ICJ acknowledged that: 'the first duty of a tribunal which is called upon to interpret and apply the provisions of a treaty, is to endeavour to give effect to them in their natural and ordinary meaning and in the context in which they occur.'

[100] *Constitution of the Maritime Safety Committee of the Inter-Governmental Maritime Organization*, ICJ, Advisory Opinion of 8 June, 1960, p. 12. The ICJ highly emphasised the textualist-contextualist approach in this case. It concluded that the terms of the provision 'must be read in their natural and ordinary meaning, in the sense which they would normally have in their context' and that 'the meaning of the word "elected" in the Article cannot be determined in isolation by recourse to its usual or common meaning and attaching that meaning to the word where used in the Article'.

[101] *US – Canadian Tuna* (1982), para 4.8.

[102] *Id.*

[103] See for Article XX of the GATT, *supra* note 68.

prohibition on imports of all tuna and tuna products from Canada could not constitute a measure of a type listed in Article XX.[104]

From a *prima facie* inspection of this GATT Panel's report, it could be observed that while the Panel apparently neglects an express reference to each of the Vienna (customary) rules of treaty interpretation employed, it nevertheless approaches an interpretation in harmony with such rules, giving effect to all the terms of the treaty (GATT 1947) provision at issue. Apparently, the Panel does not follow the traditional interpretation by starting with the 'ordinary meaning' rule, as seen, for example, in the previous case. Only later in the report does the Panel imply that its argument is based on the 'plain' or 'ordinary' meaning of the terms in their context rule of interpretation, by explaining in footnote 4 (of the report) the difference between the meanings of certain terms within the context of Article XI:2 such as 'prohibitions or restrictions'.[105]

As it could also be observed, the Panel does not make any express reference to the 'object and purpose' of the GATT. However, the resort to the 'object and purpose' rule could only be deduced from the Panel's alluding to the United States' action: prohibition of imports of tuna and tuna products from Canada, as not having complied with the objectives set forth in the Preamble of the GATT 1947. Or, in the Panel's words, the United States' measure 'should not be considered to be a disguised restrictive on international trade', supposing that this measure had been taken by the United States 'as a trade measures and publicly announced as such.'[106] Noticeable here is the Preamble of the GATT 1947, which provides in favour of *the reduction of barriers to trade and to the elimination of discriminatory treatment in international commerce.*[107] Furthermore, the Panel does not make any reference or indication from which it could be inferred that the preparatory work (*travaux preparatoire*) of the General Agreement was used in order to possibly confirm the intention of the drafters. Instead, based on the rules already employed and not losing sight of the GATT's Preamble, the Panel finds sufficient evidence to conclude that the US measure was not consistent with the provisions of Article XI and indeed, the US did not provide sufficient evidence to demonstrate that its measure complied with Article XX and, notably, with sub-paragraph (g) of this article.[108] In sum, it could be admitted that, though the Panel does not approach the customary rules of interpretation precisely following the established (traditional) order, it, nevertheless, performs an interpretation in accordance with these rules and with its own prevailing practice, combining all the rules, *holistically*, in one single unitary

[104]*US – Canadian Tuna* (1982), para 4.13. In fact, as the Panel noted, 'the United States prohibition of imports of all tuna and tuna from Canada had been imposed in response to Canadian arrest of United States vessels fishing albacore tuna'.

[105]*Id.*

[106]*Id*, para 4.8.

[107]See Preamble of the GATT 1947.

[108]*US – Canadian Tuna* (1982), para 4.15.

and logical operation. The Panel's approach in *US – Canadian Tuna* is therefore fully in accordance with the customary rules of interpretation that point directly to the rules codified in Articles 31(1), (2) and (3) (a) (b) of the VCLT.

The next section (Sect. 6.3.5) will provide an analysis of the GATT/WTO approach to interpretation *in a broader context of international law*. The case presented is an illustration of how the Appellate Body, in interpreting Article XX of the WTO Agreement, expressly relies in addition to the VCLT rules, also on the ICJ's practice and interpretative techniques (e.g. 'evolutive interpretation', in Sect. 6.3.5.1).

### 6.3.5 The Complementarity of Practice and Reliance on ICJ Techniques

In the ILC's view, while the law applicable within the WTO does not exclude the emergence of a specific 'WTO ethos' in the interpretation of its Agreements, this law reconciles two positions: one of the positions 'holds the WTO as part of international law, operating within the general system of international law rules and principles',[109] and a second position focuses 'on the provisions in the DSU that requires the panels and the Appellate Body neither add nor diminish the obligations under the covered treaties'.[110] In responding to the question of how international law interacts with the WTO system, for example, Jackson, by embracing the ILC's view, answers that the WTO system is not a 'hermetically sealed regime', despite some scholars wrongly claiming it to be.[111] Also, Gray and Cameron, relying on the GATT/WTO jurisprudence, conclude that 'the careful linkages which have been made between the specialised system of rules in the WTO and general principles of international law have aided the growth in credibility' (Cameron and Gray 2001, p. 298). What is important to retain along this line of arguments is that the basic principles of international law, including those underlying the GATT/WTO law, have been observed to remain the same (Pauwelyn 2003, p. 33). Based on the case analyses in this chapter, the demonstrable relationship between the practice of the WTO on treaty interpretation and that of the ICJ suggests that the WTO does not function in isolation, independently of international law, and hence it does not promote a 'self-contained regime'. The WTO dispute settlement's practice seems to be strongly influenced by the ICJ's long experience on treaty interpretation and,

[109]ILC (2006), p. 90. The justification is based on the presumption that the States adopted the Marrakesh agreements in accordance with, and under the rules and principles of international law.

[110]*Id*. This position, according to the ILC, accepts an even wider use of international customary law and other treaties by considering them incorporated in the WTO, either explicitly (in article 3 (2) DSU, or implicitly by reference to the context in which the WTO agreements were made.

[111]Jackson (1998), p. 829. The author adds other examples such as: 'the right of a government to hire a private counsel of its own choosing', which has been influenced by general international law.

generally, on international law. In addition, the relationship between the WTO trade regime and international law is evidenced by those situations when the WTO adjudicative bodies choose to resort to 'any relevant rules of international law' pursuant to Article 31(3)(c) of the VCLT, although this is, admittedly, not so frequent. Such resort appears to be performed similarly to the ICJ, especially when it had to interpret *doubtful*, *ambiguous*, *vague* language of the treaty texts or *silent* with regard to the circumstances of the case in question. As the case analyses presented in Chap. 4 can show, to find the real intention of the drafters beyond such treaty language (text), the ICJ had to find out, for instance, how in comparable treaties or other instruments of international law similar terms were expressed with words not found in the treaty at issue. However, rarely occurring, as admitted in the scholarship, there are situations when the WTO regime deviates from substantive international law (general and customary), showing a limited use of Article 31(3)(c), thus in dissonance with the perspective offered by the 'systemic integration' of this provision, as the *EC – Biotechnical Products* (2006) and *Beef Hormones* (1998) cases can evidence.[112] In any event, as it is generally thought, such deviations, if they become frequent, could have a negative impact upon the unity of international law.[113]

#### 6.3.5.1 Reliance on the 'Relevant Rules of International Law' and 'Evolutionary Interpretation'

In comparison with the ICJ, the GATT/WTO regime appears, in general, to promote more of a dynamic or evolutive interpretation, predominantly in the light of the 'object and purpose' of the WTO Agreement, rather than an interpretation relied upon the GATT's/WTO's negotiating history. The ***US – Shrimp/Turtle (India, Pakistan, Thailand v. US)* (1998)**[114] case illustrates an approach based on the VCLT's rules of interpretation, particularly on the 'relevant rules of international law' and the principle of 'evolutionary interpretation' applied to interpret environmental concerns under Article XX (g) of the GATT/WTO, a provision admitted as being written in *equivocal* terms. Since the *US – Shrimp/Turtle*'s decision, as this case is known, is one of WTO's most contentious decisions that provoked criticism and debate in the academic scholarship, some of these views will be briefly discussed before proceeding with the case analysis. Among the critics of this decision, Kelly, for example, raises notable objections to the interpretative approach adopted by the WTO in the *US – Shrimp/Turtle* case, which could be seen justified if one can look at the decision in this case from only one

[112] See for this discussion Chap. 3 of this book. In these cases the Appellate Body refused to take the *precautionary principle* in general international law and treat it as *customary* under Article 31 (3)(3) VCLT.

[113] Sheeran (2014), p. 90.

[114] *United States – import prohibition of certain shrimp and shrimp products*, WT/DS58/AB/R, 12 October, 1998.

angle. Kelly considers that the *US – Shrimp/Turtle* case raised several concerns about how the Appellate Body made use of its authority to expand the substantive rights of economically powerful nations at the expense of less-developed countries, promoting judicial activism.[115] He explains that by upholding the environmental exception invoked by the US, it can affect the interests of developing countries and permit wealthy nations with large markets to impose unilaterally their preferred environmental policies'[116] and that in addition, such exception has the potential to reduce the bargaining power in subsequent negotiations of those states, primarily of developing countries that have lost market access.[117] However, according to McInerney, the above argument is weakened by the later upholding of exclusionary measures adopted by developing countries, which shows that the ruling in question goes both ways. So the argument that the dispute resolutions of both the Panel and the Appellate Body, having overstepped their powers in adopting an activist stance, is not necessarily a treaty interpretation issue (McInerney 2009, p. 199). McInerney argues that, actually, by its decision in *Shrimp/Turtle*, the Appellate Body was constructing a framework for members who in the future will intend to adopt environmental measures using Article XX of the GATT/WTO as justification.[118] Also, the same author observes that recent decisions have shown that the chapeau of Article XX will not be violated where the discrimination is 'justified by the same protective rationale as the measure itself'.[119] In fact, as observed by McInerney, such an approach rewards nations that genuinely seek to protect a fundamental value, such as public health; enact legislation; or take other actions for that purpose. Thus Articles XX and XIV of the GATT 'are not the tool of only developed nations but lie ripe for all WTO Members to utilise'.[120] In the same vein, under the so-called lie test of Article XX's chapeau, Marceau explains that members invoking non-trade concerns need to demonstrate that the environmental, health or religious measures in no way impose disguised restrictions on trade and that the WTO

[115]See Kelly (2002)—for a critique of the 'evolutionary interpretation' approach in this case. Also, Kelly argues that the WTO Appellate Body's reference to the ICJ's *Namibia* case is misplaced, since the concept of 'evolutionary' was much narrow defined.

[116]See also Kelly (2005), p. 459.

[117]Kelly (2008).

[118]McInerney (2009), p. 199. McInerney observes that Panels and the Appellate Body focus on whether the resulting discrimination is reasonable related to the goals behind the measure.

[119]*Id*, p. 199. McInerney gives as example *Brasil-Measures Affecting Imports of Retracted Tyres*, 146, WT/DS332/AB/R, December 3, 2009—suggesting that a demonstration of an import ban's material contribution towards its stated objective would be sufficient to determine its necessity. Also, *United States Gambling and Betting Services*, 1, WT/DS285/AB/R, April 7, 2005, and *Korea-Measures Affecting Imports of Fresh Chilled and Frozen Beef*, 174, WT/DS161/AB/R;WT/DS169.AB/R, December 11, 2000—these cases constitute the background upon which the Appellate Body based its decision in *Brasil-Tyres*.

[120]*Id*, p. 200. Or, in the author words, 'if a trade distorting measure flies too close to the chapeau's sun, its supposed wings will burn of necessity'.

jurisprudence had established a balance between trade and environment (Marceau 2006, p. 30).

From the perspective of the application of the rules of interpretation, the *US – Shrimp/Turtle* case constitutes in the present author's opinion a clear illustration of a balanced and holistic application of the customary international law rules (of treaty interpretation), which reveals the *linkage between the WTO provisions and international law*. However, unlike in other cases, some discussed above,[121] where the Panel proved to be more pro trade and less inclined towards considering principles of environmental law, in *US – Shrimp*, as also in *Gasoline*, the Appellate Body approaches a 'dynamic' or 'evolutionary interpretation', similarly to that taken by the ICJ in various circumstances of treaty interpretation.[122] In *US – Shrimp/Turtle*, the Appellate Body had to determine whether the United States' measure of prohibition on certain shrimp and shrimp products imposed on exporting countries[123] constituted a ban for any country not meeting certain policy conditions under Section 609, respectively, to use the approved Turtle Excluder Devices (TED), and thus an unjustifiable discrimination between countries when the same conditions prevail, contrary to the scope of measures under Article XX of the GATT 1994.[124]

The Appellate Body admits first that in interpreting Article XX at issue, the Panel did not follow all the steps in applying the 'customary rules of interpretation of public international law', as Article 3.2 of the DSU requires, and it reverses the

[121]See, e.g., *US – Canadian Tuna* (1982), *supra* note 89.

[122]See the recent case concerning the *Dispute Regarding Navigational and Related Rights (Costa Rica v. Nicaragua)*, ICJ, Judgment of 13 July 2009, paras 66–67. This case shows how the ICJ adopted a clear *dynamic/evolutive* treaty interpretation approach with regard to navigational and related rights on the river San Juan. The Court gave an evolutionary dimension to treaty interpretation, when interpreted the term 'commerce' in the 1858 treaty concluded between the two parties to the dispute. It held that 'where the parties have used generic terms in a treaty, the parties necessarily having been aware that the meaning of the terms was likely to evolve over time, and where the treaty has been entered into for a very long period or is "of continuing duration", the parties must be presumed, as a general rule, to have intended those terms to have an evolving meaning'.

[123]*US – Shrimp/Turtle* (1998), para 2, *supra* note 114. See also the first phase of this case: *United States – import prohibition of certain shrimp and shrimp products*, WT/DS58/R, 15 May 1998. The Department of State determined in the first phase that all shipments of shrimp and shrimp products into the United States must be accompanied by a declaration attesting that the shrimp or shrimp product in question has been harvested 'either under conditions that do not adversely affect sea turtles ... or in waters subject to the jurisdiction of a nation currently certified pursuant to Section 609'. The restriction was imposed by the USA by Section 609 of Public Law 101-162 and associated regulations and judicial rulings, measure necessary 'to protect human, animal or plant life or health'.

[124](Specifically under Article XX of the GATT 1994) Article XX paragraphs: '(b) (necessary to protect human, animal or plant life or health'; and '(g) relating to the conservation of exhaustible natural resources if such measures are made effective in conjunction with restrictions on domestic production or consumption.'

Panel's 'chapeau down' approach.[125] It further proceeds with the textualist-contextualist method, following the established rule, according to which 'a treaty interpreter must begin with, and focus upon, the text of the particular provision to be interpreted'.[126] Specifically, the Appellate Body reiterates that 'the rules call for an examination of the ordinary meaning of the words of a treaty, read in their context, and in the light of the object and purpose of the treaty involved'.[127] A similar approach could be observed in the ICJ's case law, such as in the *Case Concerning Oil Platforms*, when the Court relied on the existing pattern of judicial reasoning, particularly, in situations dealing with *ambiguous* or *inconclusive* treaty provision (as is admitted to be Article XX of the GATT/WTO).[128]

Relying on the 'ordinary meaning' rule, the Appellate Body examines whether the terms 'exhaustible' and 'renewable' in relation to natural resources are mutually exclusive.[129] It further applies a teleological approach, reiterating the role of the 'object and purpose' rule in interpretation. It stresses in this regard that '[i]t is the words constituting that provision, read in their context, that the *object and purpose* of the states parties to the treaty *must first be sought*'.[130] What is different in this case compared to the two GATT/WTO cases discussed above is that the adjudicative body establishes the intention of the drafters in regard to Article XX (g) on the basis on an express approach of this provision in the light of the 'relevant rules of international law', pursuant to Article 31(3)(c) of the VCLT. The Appellate Body clearly explains that its task in this case 'is to interpret the language of the chapeau, seeking interpretative guidance, as appropriate, from the *general principles of international law*'.[131] It finds using this approach, for example, that 'the modern international conventions and declarations make frequent reference to natural resources as embracing both living and non-living resources'.[132]

[125] *US – Shrimp/Turtle* (1998), para 114.

[126] *Id.*

[127] *Id.*

[128] *Case Concerning Oil Platforms (Islamic Republic of Iran v. United States of America)*, Preliminary Objection, ICJ, 12 December, 1996, p. 13. The ICJ recalled in this case that 'a treaty must be interpreted in good faith in accordance with the ordinary meaning to be given to its terms in their context and in the light of its object and purpose.' The Treaty of 1955 contained no provision which expressly excluded certain matters from the jurisdiction (the treaty language being equivocal or inconclusive), however, the Court found that either this aspect 'does not restrict its jurisdiction in the present case.' It gave a great account to the object and purpose and context of the Treaty (see Chap. 4 of this book).

[129] *US – Shrimp/Turtle* (1998), para 115.

[130] *Id*, para 114 (emphasis added).

[131] *Id*, para 158 (emphasis added).

[132] *Id*, para 130. The Appellate Body interprets the requirements of Article XX(g) in the light of certain conventions and agreements between the contracting parties such as: 1982 UNCLOS, The Convention on Biological Diversity Resolution on Assistance to Developing Countries, in conjunction with the Convention on the Conservation of Migratory Species of Wild Animals.

Since the language of Article XX and its exceptions (in particular, the concerned paragraph (g)) is admitted by the Appellate Body as being *equivocal/ambiguous*, susceptible of raising different interpretations, the Body adopts an extended approach in order to fully elucidate the meaning of this provision. In so far as it can be ascertained that the Appellate Body stresses the 'ordinary meaning' rule of interpretation by using expressions such as '[t]extually, Article XX (g) is not limited to the conservation of "mineral" or "non-living" natural resources'[133] or '[t]he precise language of the chapeau…',[134] its main focus appears to be on the 'object and purpose' of both the provision in question (Article XX) and of the WTO Agreement. However, the fact that the Appellate Body feels in this case to lay strong emphasis on the text, despite stressing the 'object and purpose' as determinative in finding the real meaning of the provision at issue, it could be due to its intention to reiterate that the WTO Agreement is a *written* treaty/agreement, so the parties that are bound by its provisions must 'perform' this treaty in good faith and not undermine it. The idea behind the text emphasis appears to be similar to that conveyed by the ICJ in the majority of its treaty interpretation cases, namely, that the *pacta sunt servanda* and *bona fide* principles stand at the basis of every treaty's conclusion. As it will be seen later in the judgment of *US – Shrimp/Turtle*, the Appellate Body addresses the issue of 'good faith' (*bona fide*) in express terms.

By considering that Article XX is not limited to the conservation of 'mineral' or 'non-living' natural resources, the Appellate Body highlights the object and purpose set forth in the Preamble of the WTO Agreement, which 'explicitly acknowledges' the objective of *sustainable development*.[135] Thus on the teleological method basis, the Appellate Body makes it clear that '[w]here the meaning imparted by the text itself is equivocal or inconclusive, or when confirmation of the correctness of the reading of the text itself is desired', it is proper 'to take into account, as part of the context of the chapeau, the specific language of the preamble of the WTO Agreement'.[136] With this approach in mind, the Appellate Body appears to move towards an 'evolutionary interpretation' as to shed more light on certain ambiguous terms within the chapeau of Article XX and its paragraph (g).[137] In so doing, the Body states that it is its duty as treaty interpreter to read the words of Article XX (g): 'exhaustible natural resources', which actually were crafted more than 50 years ago, 'in the light of contemporary concerns of the community of nations about the protection and conservation of the environment'.[138] More conclusive in choosing to take a dynamic interpretation is the Appellate Body's view

[133]*Id*, para 112.

[134]*Id*, para 150.

[135]*Id*, para 115.

[136]*Id*, para 155.

[137]*Id*. The Appellate Body found that 'While Article XX was not modified in the Uruguay Round, the preamble attached to the WTO Agreement shows that the signatories to that Agreement were, in 1994, fully aware of the importance and legitimacy of environmental protection as a goal of national and international policy.'

[138]*Id*.

that 'the generic term "natural resources" in Article XX (g) is not "static" in its content or reference but rather "by definition, evolutionary"'.[139]

Arguably, the Appellate Body in this case appears to proceed similarly to the ICJ in various situations, by explicitly adapting the object and purpose of the treaty at issue to the actual conditions and law developments. It itself supports its finding by referring to the approach taken by the ICJ in the *Namibia (Legal Consequences)* (1971) case. In this case, the ICJ explained that where concepts embodied in a treaty are, 'by definition, evolutionary', their 'interpretation cannot remain unaffected by the subsequent development of law ... Moreover, an international instrument has to be interpreted and applied within the framework of the entire legal system prevailing at the time of the interpretation'.[140] In addition, the Appellate Body invokes the *Aegean Sea Continental Shelf Case* (1978), where a similar approach was taken by the ICJ in clarifying the terms 'territorial status'. The ICJ found that it was a 'generic expression which comprises within its meaning various legal conditions and relations of territory, and thus it follows *the evolution of international law*'.[141]

One could find that even in some earlier cases, the ICJ adopted a similar interpretative approach that could show a possible importation by the WTO adjudicative bodies of the principle of 'evolutionary interpretation' in their trade adjudicative practice. For example, in the *Fisheries Case* (1951), the ICJ conveyed the view that the acts should be judged in the light of the law contemporaneous with their creation and that this law must be in accordance with changes in international law.[142] Or, in a more recent example, the *Case Concerning the Gabčíkovo-Nagymaros Project* (1997), the ICJ took into account the new standards of the law regarding the protection of the international environment that had developed during the period from the conclusion of the bilateral treaty in 1977 to the moment of its revision. The Court concluded that 'in order to evaluate the environmental risk, current standards must be taken into consideration'.[143]

---

[139] *Id*, para 30.

[140] *Id*. For example, the Appellate Body invokes here *Legal Consequences for States of the Continued Presence of South African Namibia, (South West Africa) notwithstanding SC Resolution* 276, Advisory Opinion of 21 June 1971, ICJ, p. 31, para 53, and the *Aegean Sea Continental Shelf Case* (*Greece v. Tur*key), 1978, ICJ, Rep., p. 3.

[141] See *Aegean Sea Continental Shelf Case*, *supra* note 140, p. 34 (emphasis added). The ICJ pointed out in this regard that: 'the concept embodied in Article 22 of the Covenant—the strenuous conditions of the modern world and the well-being and development of the people concerned - were not static, but were by definition evolutionary.'

[142] *Fisheries Case (United Kingdom v. Norway)*, Judgment of December 18th, ICJ Reports, 1951, p. 21. Also, the ICJ adopted a dynamic interpretation in *Rights of Nationals of the United States of America in Morocco (France v. United States of America)*, Judgment of 27 August 1952, ICJ Reports, p. 189. The Court concluded that: 'the system of delimitation in 1935, a system characterised by the use of straight lines, does not therefore infringe the general law, it is an adaptation rendered necessary by local conditions.'

[143] *Gabčíkovo-Nagymaros Project* (*Hungary/Slovakia*), Judgment of 25 September 1997, ICJ Reports, p. 78, para 140. See also Bjorge (2014)—for an analysis of the evolutionary principle at international courts and tribunals.

Nevertheless, equally significant to the interpretative act in *US – Shrimp/Turtle* is the principle of effectiveness. The Appellate Body recalls that its task is also 'to interpret the language of the chapeau, seeking additional interpretative guidance, as appropriate, from the general principles of international law'.[144] It supports this proposition by invoking again the ICJ's precedents when the principle of effectiveness was expressly applied to similar treaty interpretative difficulties, such as in the *Border and Transborder Armed Actions Case* (1988), *Rights of Nationals of the United States in Morocco Case* (1952), *Anglo-Norwegian Fisheries Case* (1951).[145] Based on these ICJ precedents, the Appellate Body finds that 'in line with the principle of effectiveness in treaty interpretation, measures to conserve exhaustible natural resources ... may fall within Article XX (g)'.[146] In this context, the Appellate Body acknowledges also the important role of the 'good faith' principle, expressly admitting that the 'chapeau of Article XX is, in fact, but one expression of the principle of good faith'.[147]

The Appellate Body appears to rely further on the 'supplementary means of interpretation' to shed more light on, and confirm, the common intention of the contracting parties (drafters) in respect of Article XX, an approach compatible with the subjective method, which asks what intention was in the mind of a treaty's drafters. The Body holds that the chapeau 'is confirmed by its negotiating history' and that '[t]he language initially proposed by the United States in 1946 for the chapeau of what would later become Article XX was unqualified and unconditional'.[148] However, one could say that this approach, especially analysing the history, is somehow less compatible with the 'evolutionary interpretation' that the Appellate Body promotes in this case. But the decision of the Appellate Body to look at the 'negotiating history' of Article XX appears to acknowledge and confirm important aspects: that 'the paragraphs of Article XX set forth limited and conditional exceptions from the obligations of the substantive provisions of the GATT',[149] and also that 'certain other developments have occurred since the original language of the GATT's Preamble 1947 was negotiated', which help in

[144]*US – Shrimp/Turtle* (1998), para 158.

[145]*Border and Transborder Armed Actions Case* (1988) I.C.J. Rep. 105; *Rights of Nationals of the United States in Morocco Case* (1952) I.C.J. Rep. 176; *Anglo-Norwegian Fisheries Case* (1951) I.C.J. Rep. 142.

[146]*US – Shrimp/Turtle* (1998), para 131. The Appellate Body supports its finding by relying on extensive reference to international environmental instruments, e.g., the Convention on International Trade in Endangered Species of Wild Fauna and Flora (CITES).

[147]*Id*, para 158. The Appellate Body reiterates the role of *good faith* when it states: 'One application of this principle, the application widely known as the doctrine of *abuse de droit*, prohibits the abusive exercise of a state's rights and enjoins that whenever the assertion of a right impinges on the field covered by [a] treaty obligation, it must be exercised bona fide, that is to say, reasonably.'

[148]*Id*, para 157.

[149]*Id*.

elucidating the objectives of WTO members with respect to the relationship between trade and the environment.[150]

In sum, despite an emphasis on the textualist approach in *US – Shrimp/Turtle*, the whole focus of the Appellate Body appears to be directed, actually, towards 'the specific language of the preamble to the WTO Agreement', described as giving 'color, texture and shading to the rights and obligations of Members under the WTO Agreement, generally, and under the GATT 1994, in particular'.[151] Relying on this purposive (teleological) approach the Appellate Body finds a strong indication in the Preamble that the term 'sustainable development' is susceptible to an 'evolutionary interpretation'. The Body justifies this reasoning by stating that the language of the Preamble of the WTO Agreement 'demonstrates recognition by WTO negotiators that optimal use of the world's resources should be made in accordance with the objective of *sustainable development*'.[152] Therefore, the Appellate Body performs in *US – Shrimp/Turtle* a *holistic* interpretation of the provision at issue, consistent with the requirements of Article 3.2 of the DSU. This case demonstrates that the WTO adjudicative body clearly relies on the general methodology of interpretation reflected in VCLT, general international law, as well as on the ICJ's practice—as a framework for interpreting the provisions of the WTO Agreements.

The following section and the subsequent sections will provide additional examples of interpretative approaches performed by the Appellate Body on different other provisions of the WTO Agreement. These analyses will clearly show furthermore how this Body approaches the interpretative tools in patterns resembling those used by the ICJ.

### 6.3.6 Reliance on the VCLT Rules, ICJ's Practice and Also Principles

As the GATT/WTO case analyses above can show, panels (even prior to the adoption of the VCLT) and the Appellate Body have stated either directly or indirectly, explicitly or implicitly, that each of the customary rules of treaty and also principles has value and weight in the treaty interpretative process, depending on the circumstances that require their application. In addition, despite an emphasis on a rule/principle or another, these adjudicative bodies have shown tendency to adopt a *holistic* approach to interpretation, similarly to the ICJ.

---

[150] *Id*, para 154. In this regard the Appellate Body found that the most significant was the Decision of Ministers at Marrakesh to establish a permanent Committee on Trade and Environment (the "CTE").

[151] *Id.*

[152] *Id.*

Since the VCLT rules of interpretation appear as a necessary reasoning means in clarifying the meaning of the WTO Agreement's provisions, particularly in revealing the specific inherent normative element of their construction, they clearly complement and not substitute the WTO's special doctrines, rules or principles used in the interpretation and application of the GATT/WTO Agreements. So given that such special doctrines, rules or principles (e.g., 'mandatory/discretionary' law, 'product process', 'Special and Differential Treatment' of developing countries, non-discrimination (most-favoured-nation treatment obligation and the national treatment obligation), market access (reduction of tariff and non-tariff barriers to trade), harmonisation of national regulation) appear to resolve only the normative problems inherent in the GATT/WTO Agreements, so a reliance only on them would not be sufficient, and the existence of Article 3.2 of the DSU in itself confirms it. Moreover, the WTO adjudicative bodies often seem to appeal confidently to the ICJ's practice on treaty interpretation, especially, when they need to confirm or to strengthen a certain interpretative aspect and indeed, when there is really a need to find inspiration from the ICJ's jurisprudence to solve a difficult issue of treaty interpretation. It shows that the WTO's interpretative practice is highly influenced by the ICJ's long experience on treaty interpretation matter.

In addition to all of the above, another point of scholarly debate is related to the existence in international law of other principles of interpretation ancillary to the VCLT. Similar to Van Damme, some authors have admitted that in the process of interpretation, both panels and the Appellate Body have recourse to some general principles of interpretation not expressly stated in the Vienna Convention's 'general rule of interpretation'.[153] For example, Mitchell argues that the WTO adjudicative bodies resort not only to *rules* when deciphering the intentions of the drafters but also to *general principles of international law* such as good faith, evolutionary meaning, the effectiveness principle, due process, proportionality or special and differential treatment, which operate in a normative manner and assist the WTO adjudicators in interpreting the WTO provisions.[154] Although WTO panels and the Appellate Body do not always spell out whether they refer to general principles of law (stemming from national law or of public international law) in their interpretation and application of WTO dispute settlement rules and procedures, the number of WTO dispute settlement reports referring to such principles (expressly or implicitly) is perceived as continuing to increase steadily (Petersmann 2004, pp. 1:12 and 1:27). And such 'basic principles underlying this multilateral trading

[153]Van Damme (2009). Van Damme argues that, generally, the critics of the VCLT do not demonstrate on what base these non-codified interpretative maxims/principles are applied in the interpretative process, and that such critics neglect to formulate new principles.

[154]Mitchell (2007), pp. 798–803. Other principles revealed by the WTO case law analysis are: *expresio unius es exclusion alterius* (the expression of one thing is the exclusion of another), presumption of consistency, precautionary principle, *in dubio mitius* (the reasonable meaning is to be preferred to the unreasonable), legitimate expectation, *lex specialis*, evolutionary meaning, *actori incumbit probatio* (the (burden of) proof weights on the plaintiff).

system',[155] described by Lennard as 'the most interesting area of the WTO interpretative jurisprudence', clearly evidentiate the relation of interdependence between *trade law* and *general international law* (Lennard (2002, p. 77).

Furthermore, the recourse to extra WTO sources such as general principles of law might be simply required to fill inescapable gaps in the WTO law (Mavroidis 2008, p. 36). So the fact that non-WTO international law is relevant as an interpretative element, an aspect upon which most commentators agreed, as observed by Mavrotidis, it simply confirms the rapport between the WTO and general international law.[156] Such an example is provided by the *lex specialis* principle, which is not explicitly included in the WTO law.[157] Mavrotidis claims that *lex specialis* is compatible with the principle of effective treaty interpretation—*ut res magis valeat quam pereat*, 'the cornerstone of the VCLT', which, however, an interpreter should start with.[158] Analogously, relying on the WTO's practice Marceau observes that the interpretative principle of effectiveness has tremendous impact on the interpretation and application of several WTO provisions (Marceau 2006, p. 30). Most importantly Marceau advocates the idea that within the WTO trade regime, there are no closed boxes and that all provisions must be interpreted and applied together *harmoniously*.[159]

Thus, further cases analysed in the present author's view, highlighting various interpretative issues, are used to illustrate and support the aforementioned theoretical aspects. In this scope, Sect. 6.3.6.1 will look at a case showing a clear holistic approach and emphasis of the 'object and purpose', Sect. 6.3.6.2 focuses on the use and emphasis on the *ut res magis valeat quam paereat* principle, Sect. 6.3.6.3 shows a clear emphasis and reliance on the 'ordinary meaning' and 'context of the treaty' rules, Sect. 6.3.6.4 shows an emphasis on the 'good faith' and 'intention' elements, Sect. 6.3.6.5 shows a strong reliance on the 'supplementary means' rule and Sect. 6.3.6.6 illustrates an instance of deviance from the VCLT established standard of treaty interpretation.

---

[155]Petersmann (2004), pp. 1:12 and 1:27. Petersmann observes that, since 'the procedural rules of WTO dispute settlement are designed to promote . . . the fair, prompt and effective resolution of trade disputes,' many principles of (municipal) law (e.g. rules on the distribution of the burden of proof, *jura novit curia*) and of international law (e.g. the interpretive principle of in *dubio mitius* as a corollary of respect for state sovereignty) may be classifiable as 'basic principles underlying this multilateral trading system' that are 'implicit in, or required by, the WTO dispute settlement rules and procedures in order to realise their respective objectives (such as "providing security and predictability to the multilateral trading system")'.

[156]Mavroidis (2008), p. 19.

[157]*Id.*

[158]*Id*, p. 16. See also for the 'good faith' principle discussion, Mercurio and Tyagi (2010), p. 318. These authors assert that the *good faith principle*, provided in Article 31(1) of the VCLT, is amorphous and "operates with little guidance", fact that enable the dispute settlement bodies to "infuse" "good faith" into their deliberation by resorting to certain international rules of interpretation, which are not explicitly provided by the VCLT framework's general rule of interpretation.

[159]Marceau (2006), p. 30.

#### 6.3.6.1 Clear Holistic Approach and Emphasis on the 'Object and Purpose' Rule

As noted in Chap. 3 of this book, it was the ILC's recognition of the fundamental principle underlying the Vienna rules that a proper interpretation must give meaning to every element of the text of the treaty/agreement ('The Principle of Including All Strategic Acts'). In particular, the scholarship admits that 'good faith' is being derived from the jurisprudence of the PCIJ/ICJ, and it is reflected in the principles of interpretation formulated by Fitzmaurice, among which the 'principle of integration' and 'principle of effectiveness' (*ut res magis valeat quam pereat*) are relevantly linked to 'good faith'.[160] As observed by Gardiner, the principle of effectiveness has dual aspects. First, it bears out the suggestion that *an interpretation gives a term some meaning rather than none*. And second, *it suggests guidance for the interpreter towards an interpretation that realizes the aims of the treaty*, which constitutes, nevertheless, 'an aspect of the *object and purpose of a treaty*'.[161] Although the effectiveness principle is not specified as such in the ILC's text formulation of Article 31 of the VCLT, its meaning is reflected in this provision's requirements. This principle is thought to have a tremendous interpretive guiding function, as the case analyses at the ICJ (Chap. 4), ECtHR (Chap. 5) and WTO (in the above and further analysis of this chapter) clearly can show.

The next case: ***Korea – Dairy (EC v. Korea)* (1999)**[162] can illustrate a clear holistic approach adopted by the WTO's Appellate Body in the light of the textualist, teleological and subjective methods, as also the interpretive principle of effectiveness (*ut res magis valeat quam pereat*). This approach is supported by the WTO's past decisions and, additionally, by relevant ICJ decisions on treaty interpretation. Although in this case the Appellate Body places on the same footing the rules of interpretation set forth in Articles 31 and Article 32 of the VCLT, it, nevertheless, appraises each of the interpretive rules more or less, depending on the circumstances required by the case. The Appellate Body had to determine in *Korea – Dairy* whether the definitive safeguard measures in the form of quantitative

[160]See Gardiner (2008), p. 149—commenting on the Third Report on the Law of Treaties (1964), paras 13–14. Gardiner explains the origin of 'good faith' meaning, history and preparatory work in the relevant documents, and also as it is reflected in the VCLT. Formulated in the Third Report on the Law of Treaties (1964), the *Principle of integration* provided that 'Treaties are to be interpreted as a whole, and particular parts, chapters or sections also as a whole'. Also, the *Principle of effectiveness* provided that: 'Treaties are to be interpreted with reference to their declared or apparent objects and purposes; and particular provisions are to be interpreted as to give them their fullest weight and effect consistent with the normal sense of the words and with other parts of the text, and in such a way that reason and meaning can be attributed to every part of the text.'

[161]*Id*, p. 160.

[162]*Korea – Definitive Safeguard Measure On Imports of Certain Dairy Products*, WT/DS98/AB/R, 14 December 1999.

restrictions imposed by Korea on the European Communities on imports of skimmed milk powder preparations (SMPP)[163] complied with the requirement contained in Article XIX (1) (a) of the GATT 1994, respectively, to apply safeguard measures only where the alleged increase in imports is 'as a result of unforeseen developments'.[164] The main provision under interpretation is Article XIX of the GATT 1994 and, subsequently, Articles 4, 5, 12 of the Agreement on Safeguards. The Appellate Body proceeds first with expressly recalling that the guideline of interpretation applicable to the dispute is provided by Article 3.2 of the DSU, respectively the rules of interpretation set forth in Articles 31 and 32 of the VCLT.[165] Then the Body makes an explicit reference to the principle of effectiveness (*ut res magis valeat quam paereat*), which requires that an interpreter 'must give meaning and effect to all terms of the treaty', and also that '[a]n interpreter is not free to adopt a reading that would result in reducing whole clauses or paragraphs of a treaty to redundancy or inutility'.[166] This approach is applied by the Appellate Body, for example, in respect of Article 12.2 of the Agreement on Safeguards, and finds accordingly that 'if such had been the intention of the drafters ... they would have simply referred back to Article 3 and 4 when requiring "evidence of serious injury" in Article 12. 2'.[167] The Body adds in this regard that '[a]n important corollary of this principle is that *a treaty should be interpreted as a whole*, and, in particular, its sections and parts should be read as a *whole*'.[168] Further, the Appellate Body strengthens this approach by direct reference to its own case law,[169] and also

---

[163] *Id.* In principle, the Appellate Body had to determine whether the clause in Article XIX 1(a) of the GATT 1994: 'if, as a result of unforeseen developments and of the effect of the obligation incurred by a Member under this Agreement, including tariff concessions ...' did add conditions for any safeguard measure to be applied to Article XIX.

[164] *Id.* Article XIX of the GATT 1994 (Emergency Action on Imports of Particular Products) provides:

> 1. (a) If, as a result of unforeseen developments and of the effect of the obligations incurred by a contracting party under this Agreement, including tariff concessions, any product is being imported into the territory of that contracting party in such increased quantities and under such conditions as to cause or threaten serious injury to domestic producers in that territory of like or directly competitive products, the contracting party shall be free, in respect of such product, and to the extent and for such time as may be necessary to prevent or remedy such injury, to suspend the obligation in whole or in part or to withdraw or modify the concession.

[165] *Id*, para 80.

[166] *Id.*

[167] *Id*, para 109.

[168] *Id*, para 81 (emphasis added).

[169] *Id.* The Appellate Body relies on *Gasoline*, *supra* note 32, p. 23, where it invoked the ICJ's *Corfu Channel* and *Territories Dispute* cases as to illustrate the effectiveness principle; *Japan – Alcoholic Beverages II*, *infra* note 186, p. 12; *Canada – Measures Affecting the Importation of Milk and the Exportation of Dairy Products*, WT/DS103/AB/R, WT/DS113/AB/R, adopted 27 October 1999, para 133; *Argentina – Safeguard Measures on Imports of Footwear*, WT/DS121/AB/R, circulated 14 December 1999, para 88.

to the relevant practice of the PCIJ/ICJ,[170] in which the World Court clarified the duty to interpret a treaty as a whole when dealing with *unclear or ambiguous* terms of a treaty. Such references are to the *Competence of the ILO to Regulate Agricultural Labour* (1922),[171] *Ambatielos* (1953),[172] *Reservations to the Convention on the Prevention and Punishment of the Crime of Genocide* cases (1951)[173] and the *Case Concerning Rights of United States in Morocco* (1952).[174]

Further, the Appellate Body indicates that it looks to the ordinary meaning of these words, and that based on the dictionary definitions it will clarify the terms, such as 'unforeseen', 'developments' or 'unexpected' in Article XIX.[175] The textualist approach is clearly underlined, for example, when the Appellate Body specifies that '[t]he ordinary meaning of the language in Article 11.1(a) "unless such action conforms with the provisions of that Article applied in accordance with this Agreement" – is that any safeguard action *must conform* with the provisions of Article XIX of the GATT 1994 as well as with the provisions of the Agreement on Safeguards'.[176] As it can be observed, this interpretation is supported by the contextualist approach that the Appellate Body explicitly adopts when interpreting the mentioned provision in the context of the whole treaty.[177] The 'context' is also clearly revealed by the logical grammatical construction within the provision at issue. For example, with reference to the first clause of Article XIX, the Appellate Body states that there 'is a dependent clause which, in our view, is linked

[170]*Id.* See footnote 44 of the Appellate Body's report. The Appellate Body makes also reference to the most relevant publications of international law such as Brownlie (1998), p. 634; Fitzmaurice (1957), p. 211; McNair (1961), pp. 381–382; Sinclair (1984), pp. 127–129; Hudson (1936), pp. 654–659; Costa and Ruda (1985), p. 105.

[171]*Competence of the ILO to Regulate Agricultural Labour*, PCIJ, Series B, Nos. 2 and 3, 1922, p. 23. The PCIJ held in this case: 'In considering the question before the Court upon the language of the Treaty, it is obvious that the Treaty must be read as a *whole*, and that its meaning is not to be determined merely upon particular phrases which, if detached from the context, may be interpreted in more than one sense.' (emphasis added).

[172]*Ambatielos Case*, ICJ Reports, 1953, p. 23.The ICJ held in *Ambatielos* that 'the provisions of the Declaration are in the nature of an interpretation clause, and, as such, should be regarded as an integral part of the Treaty, even if this was not stated in terms.'

[173]*Reservation to the Convention of the Prevention and Punishment of the Crime of Genocide*, ICJ Reports, 1951, pp. 15–16. The ICJ held that: 'the common duty of the contracting States to be guided in their judgment by the compatibility or incompatibility of the reservation with the object and purpose of the Convention. It must clearly be assumed that the contracting States are desirous of preserving intact at least what is essential to the object of the Convention; should this desire be absent, it is quite clear that the Convention itself would be impaired both in its principle and in its application.'

[174]*Case Concerning Rights of United States in Morocco*, ICJ Reports, 1952, pp. 196–199. The Court held that 'the interpretation of the provisions of the Act must take into account its purposes, which are set forth in the Preamble . . .'

[175]*Korea – Dairy* (1999), para 84.

[176]*Id.*

[177]*Id*, para 86.

grammatically to the verb phrase "is being imported" in the second clause of that paragraph'.[178]

Despite a clear insistence on the textualist approach,[179] which indubitably involves in this case heavy reliance on the dictionary definitions, the Appellate Body appears to give equal account to the teleological approach. It makes clear further that the 'object and purpose' of the GATT/WTO Agreement is necessary to support a *holistic* interpretation. The 'object and purpose' results to be the key in the present case in keeping the balance of all the interpretative elements when the Appellate Body states that '[t]his reading of the clauses is also confirmed by the object and purpose of Article XIX of GATT 1994'.[180] Nevertheless, the *holistic* approach can be even more revealed when the Appellate Body, by acknowledging an interpretation in consideration of the effectiveness principle (which realises the aims of the provisions at issue), holds that '[o]ur reading of these prerequisites makes certain that all the relevant provisions of Article XIX of the GATT 1994 and the *Agreement on Safeguards* relating to safeguard measures are given their full meaning and their full legal effect'.[181]

Furthermore, it appears that the Appellate Body does not neglect either the subjective method of interpretation. Despite an implicit, vague reference to supplementary means, the Appellate Body appears to rest its decision also on the evidence of 'intention' derived from the circumstances of the conclusion of the WTO Agreement. It notes in this regard that '[o]ur reading, too, is consistent with the desire expressed by Uruguay Round negotiators in the *Preamble to the Agreement on Safeguards*', as 'to clarify and reinforce the disciplines of GATT 1994, and *specifically* those of its Article XIX ... , to re-establish *multilateral control* over safeguards and eliminate measures that escape such control ..."'.[182]

In sum, by approaching all the provisions at issue in the light of the textualist, teleological and subjective methods and the effectiveness principle, the Appellate Body performs in *Korea – Dairy* a *holistic* interpretation, in a way that gives full meaning and effect to the (WTO Agreement) provisions at issue, 'harmoniously',[183] in compliance with the VCLT's general rule of interpretation, particularly Articles 31(1), (2), and 32. This approach is expressly supported by reference to ICJ precedents.

[178] *Id*, para 85.

[179] *Id*, para 75.

[180] *Id*, para 87.

[181] *Id*, para 88.

[182] *Id*.

[183] *Id*, para 81.

#### 6.3.6.2 Clear Holistic Approach and Emphasis on the 'Ut Res Magis Valeat Quam Pereat' Principle[184]

In Chap. 4 of this book (particulalry in Sect. 4.3.1.3), it was discussed, *inter alia*, the basic idea, widely admitted in law, that if a piece of law seems unclear, one should try to understand that piece of law in a way that it will have effect rather than not ('better the thing should function than that it should perish'). This idea is clearly reflected in the role and goal of the *effectiveness principle*, which is admitted as a *fundamental tenet of treaty interpretation*, explained by the International Law Commission as follows:

> When a treaty is open to two interpretations one of which does and the other does not enable the treaty to have appropriate effects, *good faith* and the *objects and purposes* of the treaty demand that the former should be adopted.[185]

As it has been admitted in the scholarship, 'the ICJ has in its case law consistently "harnessed" the principle of effectiveness to the purposive interpretation of treaties'; thus, the purposive interpretation (teleological) is closely linked to the principle of effectiveness (Devaney 2016, p. 190). The empirical analysis at the PCIJ/ICJ provided in Chap. 4 of this book can show that the principle of effectiveness has been applied with consistency by the PCIJ/ICJ (starting with its earliest practice) on any type of difficulty in the construction of treaty text, playing a vital role in this Court's interpretation of treaties. Generally, by approaching *holistically* the customary rules of interpretation and *taking the treaty as a whole*, the ICJ has made the treaty most effective, to work and have appropriate effects. The example of the ***Japan – Alcoholic Beverages II (EC, Canada, US v. Japan)*** **(1996)** case[186] is an illustration of the Appellate Body's explicative resort not only to the customary rules of interpretation when deciphering the intentions of the drafters (on *ambiguous* text), similarly to the ICJ, but also to the fundamental effectiveness principle of international law, which is here, however, even more articulated than in the above case, or others discussed in this chapter. Thus, after reiterating that the 'general rule of interpretation' has attained the status of a rule of customary or general international law and is applicable to the case, the Appellate Body

---

[184]See discussion on this principle in Chap. 3 of this book (Sect. 2.3.2.1). As it was initially drawn up and proposed by G. G. Fitzmaurice as a distinct article in the Third Draft on the Law of Treaties, the *effectiveness principle* proposed that: 'Treaties are to be interpreted with reference to their declared or apparent objects and purposes; and particular provisions are to be interpreted so as to give them their fullest weight and effect consistent with the normal sense of the words and with other parts of the text, and in such a way that a reason and a meaning can be attributed to every part of the text.'

[185]Yearbook of the International Law Commission (1966), p. 219.

[186]*Japan-Taxes on Alcoholic Beverage* II, WT/DS8/AB/R; WT/DS10/AB/R; WT/DS11/AB/R, 4 October, 1996, pp. 7–8. The dispute concerned the European Communities, Canada and the United States' complaints against Japan relating higher rates of taxation on imports alcoholic beverages including whiskies, brandies, other distilled alcoholic beverages and liquor than on Japanese shochu imposed pursuant to the Liquor Tax Law.

concentrates on explaining in this case one of the corollaries of the 'general rule of interpretation' in the Vienna Convention, which 'is that interpretation must give meaning and effect to all the terms of the treaty'.[187] This approach is supported by a rich reference to the ICJ jurisprudence, which expressly attests to the 'dialogue' between the WTO and ICJ. The Appellate Body was requested in *Japan – Alcoholic Beverages II* to establish whether Japan's Liquor Tax Law (Shuzeiho) was applied 'so as to afford protection to domestic production' and discriminated against 'like domestic' or 'directly competitive or substitutable' products (such as whiskies, brandies, other distilled alcoholic beverages and liquor), in violation of Article III of the GATT 1994.[188]

First, by declaring Article 3.2 of the DSU as the interpretative guide applicable to the case,[189] the Appellate Body points out that, according to Article 31 of the Vienna Convention, 'interpretation must be based above all upon the text of the treaty'.[190] This rule is supported by the Appellate Body's direct reference to the ICJ's practice, in particular to the *Territorial Dispute* (1994)[191] case, when the ICJ (as the WTO in the case at hand) had to clarify an *ambiguous* treaty provision, and also to the *Maritime Delimitation and Territorial Questions between Qatar and Bahrain* (1995) case.[192] Then the Appellate Body recalls the relevancy of the

[187]*Id*, p. 10. Also the Body states that 'there can be no doubt that Article 32 of the Vienna Convention, dealing with the role of supplementary means of interpretation, has also attained the same status.'

[188](Specifically in violation of Article III, paragraphs 1 and 2, of the GATT 1994). Article III provides:

> 1. The contracting parties recognize that internal taxes and other internal charges, and laws, regulations and requirements affecting the internal sale, offering for sale, purchase, transportation, distribution or use of products, and internal quantitative regulations requiring the mixture, processing or use of products in specified amounts or proportions, should not be applied to imported or domestic products so as to afford protection to domestic production.
> 2. The products of the territory of any contracting party imported into the territory of any other contracting party shall not be subject, directly or indirectly, to internal taxes or other internal charges of any kind in excess of those applied, directly or indirectly, to like domestic products. Moreover, no contracting party shall otherwise apply internal taxes or other internal charges to imported or domestic products in a manner contrary to the principles set forth in paragraph 1.

[189]*Japan – Alcoholic Beverages II* (1996), p. 10.

[190]*Id*, p. 11.

[191]*Libyan Arab Jamahiriya v. Chad*, *supra* note 75, p. 20. The ICJ held in this case a similar approach: 'interpretation must be based above all upon the text of the treaty.'

[192]*Maritime Delimitation and Territorial Questions between Qatar and Bahrain, Jurisdiction and Admissibility*, Judgment (1995) I.C.J. Reports, p. 12. The Court held: '[t]he Court will first enquire into the nature of the texts upon which Qatar relies before turning to an analysis of the content of those texts.'

'context' rule when stating that '[t]he provisions of the treaty are to be given their ordinary meaning in their context'.[193] It strengthens this approach by invoking the ICJ's *Second Admissions Case* (1950).[194]

Further, the teleological method is expressly adopted when, for example, in clarifying the provisions of Article III of the GATT 1994, the Appellate Body outlines that their meaning must be found in 'their context and in the light of the overall object and purpose of the WTO'.[195] The Body enforces and supports this approach with reference to the relevant publications of international law materials and documents and, again, with reference to the relevant ICJ case law,[196] such as the *Competence of the ILO to Regulate the Personal Work of the Employer* (1926)[197] and *International Status of South Africa* (1962)[198] cases.

The key aspect of the interpretative approach adopted in the present case appears, however, when the Appellate Body recalls that '[a] fundamental tenet of treaty interpretation flowing from the general rule of interpretation set out in Article 31 is the principle of effectiveness: *ut res magis valeat quam pereat*'.[199] Explicitly, here, the Appellate Body admits that '[o]ne of the corollaries of the "general rule of interpretation" in the Vienna Convention *is that interpretation must give meaning and effect to all the terms of the treaty*. An interpreter is not free to adopt a reading that would result in reducing whole clauses or paragraphs of a treaty to redundancy or inutility.'[200]

Comparing with the above cases in which the effectiveness principle was seen employed (either expressly or implicitly), in the present case, the Appellate Body feels to insist further on this principle's meaning and role. Relying on the ILC's findings, the Body reiterates that '[w]hen a treaty is open to two interpretations one of which does and the other does not enable the treaty to have appropriate effects, *good faith* and the *objects and purposes* of the treaty

[193] *Japan – Alcoholic Beverages II* (1996), p. 10. The Appellate Body holds: 'the first duty of a tribunal which is called upon to interpret and apply the provisions of a treaty, is to endeavour to give effect to them in their natural and ordinary meaning and in the context in which they occur.'

[194] *Id. Competence of the General Assembly for the Admission of a State to the United Nations (Second Admissions Case)*, *supra* note 97, p. 4.

[195] *Japan – Alcoholic Beverages II* (1996), p. 19.

[196] *Id.* The Appellate Body finds a similar illustration of this rule in the practice of the ICJ, specifically in *Competence of the ILO to Regulate the Personal Work of the Employer* (at pp. 6–18), and *International Status of South Africa* (p. 128, para 336), *supra* note 77. The AB relies in addition on other sources of international law such as scholarly work of prominent jurists: Harris (1991), p. 770; de Arechaga (1978), p. 1; Sinclair (1984), p. 130; Jennings and Watts (1992), p. 1273.

[197] *Competence of the ILO to Regulate the Personal Work of the Employer*, *supra* note 79, p. 15. The ICJ held: 'Article 387 of the Treaty declares that the Organization was "established for the promotion of the objects set forth in the Preamble"'. The ICJ applied a teleological approach to an ambiguous provision of the ILO.

[198] *International Status of South Africa*, *supra* note 79.

[199] *Japan – Alcoholic Beverages II* (1996), pp. 11–12 (emphasis added).

[200] *Id*, p. 23. The Appellate Body relies on the approach adopted in *Gasoline* (emphasis added).

demand that the former should be adopted'.[201] It applies this rule as, for example, in respect of Article III, stating that the purpose of this provision is to establish the general guiding principle for understanding the specific obligations contained in Article III: 2 while 'respecting, and not diminishing in any way, the meaning of the words actually used in the texts of the others paragraphs'.[202] The Body adds that any other reading would render the words of this provision meaningless, violating the fundamental principle of effectiveness.[203] This approach is supported by the Appellate Body's reliance on the *Gasoline* case, where, as it has been seen above, the Body cited relevant cases of the ICJ's practice,[204] and also on the ILC's commentaries on treaty interpretation.[205]

In addition, the Appellate Body looks to 'any subsequent practice in the application of the treaty which establishes the agreement of the parties regarding its interpretation',[206] pursuant to Article 31(3)(b) of the VCLT. Although the Appellate Body assumes that an isolated act is generally not sufficient to establish subsequent practice,[207] however, the Body appears to admit that 'adopted panel reports are an important part of the GATT acquis' and 'are often considered by subsequent panels'.[208] The Appellate Body supports this conclusion by reference to the Statute of the ICJ, which has an explicit provision, Article 59, to the same effect.[209]

One could admit in the case at hand that it is difficult to appreciate how much weight is assigned to the drafting history of the WTO Agreement (supplementary

[201] *Id*, p. 12. The Appellate Body cites in this support the findings of the ILC in the Yearbook of the International Law Commission (1966), p. 219 (emphasis added).

[202] *Id*, p. 18.

[203] *Id*.

[204] *Id*, p. 23.

[205] *Id*, p. 11.

[206] *Id*, p. 10.

[207] *Id*, p. 10. In its further analysis the Appellate Body makes clear the meaning of the 'subsequent practice' in Article 31(3)(b) of the VCLT, as: "a concordant, common and consistent' sequence of acts or pronouncement which is sufficient to establish a discernible pattern implying the agreement of the parties regarding its interpretation.'

[208] *Id*. The Body adds: 'However, they are not binding, except with respect to resolving the particular dispute between the parties to that dispute.'

[209] *Id*. Article 59 of Statute of the ICJ provides: 'The decision of the Court has no binding force except between the parties and in respect of that particular case.' The Appellate Body states further that '[t]his has not inhibited the development by that Court (and its predecessor) of a body of case law in which considerable reliance on the value of previous decisions is readily discernible.' See for a similar approach at the ICJ, the *Interpretation of Peace Treaties with Bulgaria, Hungary and Romania* case (ICJ, Advisory Opinion of Jul. 18, 1950, para 229), or *Application for Revision and Interpretation of the Judgment of 24 February 1982 in the Case Concerning the Continental Shelf; Land, Island and Maritime Frontier Dispute (El Sal. v. Hond.)*, Application for Permission to Intervene, ICJ, February 28, 1990, pp. 3–4.

means) to determine the intention of the drafters as to the meaning of the term 'so as to afford protection' under Article III: 2,[210] since the Appellate Body concludes in respect of this term that '[t]his is not an issue of intent ... It is not necessary for a panel to sort through the many reasons legislators and regulators often have for what they do and weigh the relative significance of those reasons to establish legislative or regulatory intent'.[211] Yet the Appellate Body appears to confirm, based implicitly on the *travaux preparatoire*, that '[*t*]*he intention of the drafters* of the Agreement was clearly to treat the imported products in the same way as the like domestic products...'.[212]

Like in the other cases discussed above, the temptation would be to assume that by reading the Appellate Body's statements such as 'interpretation must be based above all upon the text of the treaty';[213] '[g]iving full meaning to the text and to its context...';[214] '[t]he ordinary meaning of the words of Article III: 2, first sentence leads inevitably to this conclusion...',[215] the Body attaches a greater weight to the textualist method than to others. The reason of showing such an emphasis, similarly to the ICJ in the majority of cases on treaty interpretation (irrespective of the type of difficulties in interpreting the text of treaties), could be understood as the Appellate Body's need to clarify for the parties in the dispute that '[t]he *WTO Agreement is a treaty* – the international equivalent of a contract'[216] and that the parties 'have agreed to exercise their sovereignty according to the commitments they have made in the *WTO Agreement*'.[217]

In sum, the Appellate Body in *Japan – Alcoholic Beverages II* deconstructs the provision at issue (Article III) in its parts; interprets it textually, contextually and teleologically; and, when having confirmed the intention of the drafters, recomposes back the provision, reassembling its pieces, not adding, not diminishing the rights and obligations provided therein. In this process, the reliance of the Appellate Body on the ICJ's practice throws light on the WTO's linkage with general international law. By giving full meaning and effect to the WTO provisions at issue, the Appellate Body's approach to interpretation in this case is clearly *holistic*, consistent with the Vienna customary rules of treaty interpretation as required by Article 3.2 DSU, and with the principle of effectiveness, as a general guiding

[210]*Id* (to determine whether 'directly competitive or substitutable products are "not similarly taxed" in a way that affords protection').

[211]*Id*, p. 27.

[212]*Id*, p. 17 (emphasis added).

[213]*Id*, p. 11. In this support, the Appellate Body invokes two ICJ cases: *Libyan Arab Jamahirya/Chad*, *supra* note 75, p. 20; and *Maritime Delimitation and Territorial Questions between Qatar and Bahrain*, *supra* note 192, p. 18.

[214]*Id*, p. 24.

[215]*Id*, p. 17.

[216]*Id*, p. 13.

[217]*Id*, p. 14.

principle of international law that enables the treaties to work and have appropriate effects.

#### 6.3.6.3 Clear Holistic Approach and Emphasis on the 'Ordinary Meaning' and 'Context of the Whole Treaty' Rules

The case analyses in this chapter can also evidence that panels and the Appellate Body have given a great deal to the textualist approach and frequently resorted to dictionary definitions to elucidate the meanings of a provision's terms in the context of their immediate use. However, just as in the case of the ICJ, this textual emphasis appears, in principle, to be intended by the GATT/WTO adjudicative bodies to convey the notion that the *text is the presumed manifestation of the authentic and common intention (will) of the treaty's framers* (the contracting parties) and, thus, the reasonable basis of commencing the interpretative act. It is to be recalled that, unlike the textualist method, which bases its interpretation mainly on the text, presuming it the authentic expression of the parties, the subjective method, which stresses the need to interpret a treaty text according to the common intention of the contracting parties, admits that no disputed text is ever completely clear.[218] So the case law analyses provided in this chapter can show a clear reliance of the WTO adjudicative bodies on the rule of 'context', regardless of whether the treaty text is clear or not, which implies an application of the subjective method (intentions) among the other methods. The 'context' of both the provision in question and the whole treaty appears to be fundamentally important for the WTO Panels and Appellate Body in establishing the real intention of the contracting parties when they interpret the WTO Agreement. According to Fitzmaurice and Merkouris, the concept 'context of a treaty' must be understood as 'any instrument that is of relevance to the conclusion of a treaty, as well as the preamble to the treaty and its annexes' (Fitzmaurice and Merkouris 2010, p. 157). Essentially, in respect of which method of interpretation governs the interpretative act, the generally accepted view is that 'the wording of the general rule of interpretation as contained in the 1969 VCLT is phrased in such a manner as to give comfort to supporters of both intentions and the object and purpose schools' (Fitzmaurice and Merkouris 2010, p. 157). Thus, the textualist method, which simply coexists with the subjective and teleological methods, all being reflected in the VCLT's 'general rule of interpretation', cannot be treated as governing the act of interpretation.

The recent case of ***China – Raw Materials (US v. China)* (2012)**[219] supports the argument that even when the WTO adjudicator's reliance is mainly on one rule, as is the 'text', and the text of the provisions at issue is declared by the WTO adjudicative bodies as *sufficiently clear*, this rule is, nevertheless, necessarily

---

[218] See Chap. 3 for this aspect.

[219] *China – Measures related to the exportation of various raw materials*, WT/D394/AB/R; WT/D395/AB/R; WT/DS398/AB/R, 30 January 2012.

assisted by other rules of interpretation (and principles of international law). Among such other rules is the 'context of the whole treaty' as a mandatory interpretative rule that helps the adjudicator to render a proper interpretation. As stated above, in its wider sense, the 'context of the treaty', which is provided by the VCLT in Article 31 (2), implies the whole text of the treaty, its preamble and annexes. In *China – Raw Materials*, the Appellate Body was requested to clarify whether the export quotas and export duties on certain forms of 'raw materials' (such as bauxite, coke, fluorspar, magnesium, manganese, silicon carbide, silicon metal, yellow phosphorous and zinc), imposed by China against the complaining members,[220] constituted violations of China's WTO obligations. The main treaty provisions to be interpreted were Articles XX, VIII and XI of the 1994 GATT/WTO, together with paragraph 11.3 of China's Accession Protocol, which provides for China's elimination of 'all taxes and charges applied to exports, unless specifically provided for in Annex 6 of this Protocol or applied in conformity with the provisions of Article VIII of the GATT 1994'.

The Appellate Body recalls here the key principles that govern the interpretation: 'the customary rules of interpretation of public international law, as codified in: Articles 31 and 32 of the Vienna *Convention on the Law of Treaties* (the "*Vienna Convention*") ... pursuant to Article 3.2 of the DSU'.[221] After establishing that paragraph 1.2 of China's Accession Protocol provides that the Protocol 'shall be an integral part of the WTO Agreement', the Appellate Body reiterates that 'the *Vienna Convention*' is the applicable norm in interpreting paragraph 11.3 of that Protocol.[222] Then, based on its own relevant case law, the Body recalls that 'the text' is the starting point,[223] under the customary rule laid down by Article 31(1) of the VCLT. This approach was confirmed by the ICJ, for example, in the *Territorial Dispute* (1994)[224] case, when having to interpret *sufficiently clear* terms of a treaty; as the Court itself declared that it had no difficulties in ascertaining their meaning,[225] the ICJ acknowledged that 'the text', as the starting point, attained the status of customary rule of international law. It held that an interpretation 'must be based above all upon the text of the treaty'.[226] Another similar example could be the

[220]The complaining party was the United States and the third Parties were Argentina; Brazil; Canada; Chile; Colombia; Ecuador; European Union; India; Japan; Korea, Republic of; Mexico; Norway; Chinese Taipei; Turkey; Saudi Arabia.

[221]*China – Raw Materials* (2012), para 278.

[222]*Id.* Paragraph 11.3 of China's Accession Protocol provides that:

> China shall eliminate all taxes and charges applied to exports unless specifically provided for in Annex 6 of this Protocol or applied in conformity with the provisions of Article VIII of the GATT 1994.

[223]*Id.* The Appellate Body invokes *Gasoline* (1996), para 16; *Japan – Alcoholic Beverages II* (1996), para 104.

[224]*Libyan Arab Jamahiriya v. Chad*, *supra* note 75, p. 6.

[225]*Id*, p. 20.

[226]*Id.*

*Kasikili/Sedudu* (1999) case, where the ICJ had the occasion to clarify this key principle under Article 31(1) of the VCLT.[227]

Although frequent, the resort of the Appellate Body in the present case to the dictionary for the meaning of the multitude of terms at issue attests only to the starting point in interpretation. For example, based on the ordinary meaning of the word 'temporarily' used in its context (textualist approach),[228] the Appellate Body finds in respect of the 'temporarily applied' expression within Article XI: 2 (a) that it 'permits measures that are applied for a "limited time frame"'.[229] The 'ordinary meaning' rule is supported by the adoption of the 'context' rule, which clearly manifests at two levels. First is when the Appellate Body interprets the terms of the provision at issue in their context, as the above example shows ('temporarily applied'). Second is when the Appellate Body interprets the provision in the context of the GATT/WTO Agreement taken as a whole, as, for example, in respect of paragraph 11.3 of China's Accession Protocol. The Body finds that this provision 'expressly refers to Article VIII of the GATT 1994, but does not contain any reference to other provisions of the GATT 1994, including Article XX'.[230]

Furthermore, the Appellate Body's interpretation extends as to the inclusion of the teleological method when analysing the provisions at issue in the light of the Preamble of the WTO Agreement. The Body appears to give a clear *holistic* perspective to interpretation when it stresses that '[t]he preamble concludes with the resolution "to develop an integrated, more viable and durable trading system". Based on this language, we understood the WTO Agreement, *as a whole*, to reflect the balance struck by WTO Members between trade and non-trade-related concerns'.[231] In the attempt to further ascertain the real intention of the parties with regard to paragraph 11.3 of China's Accession Protocol, the Appellate Body applies the subjective method by looking for 'any subsequent practice' in the application of the treaty which establishes the agreement of the parties regarding its interpretation, under Article 31 (3) (b) of the VCLT. The Body upholds the Panel's finding that there is a measure indicating that the export restriction is annually reviewed and reserved and that an export between the parties existed.[232]

The test of the effectiveness principle is also applied here, as, for example, in determining whether China may have recourse to Article XX to justify a breach of its commitment to eliminate export duties under paragraph 11.3. The Appellate Body finds on this basis that 'if there had been a common intention to provide

---

[227] *Kasikili/Sedudu (Botswana v. Namibia)*, ICJ Judgment of 13 December, 1999, p. 32.

[228] *China-Raw Materials* (2012), para 213. The Appellate Body resorts to the *Shorter Oxford English Dictionary* (Trumble and Stevenson 2002), p. 3204.

[229] *Id*, para 310. For example "temporary" is defined as '[l]asting or meant to last for a limited time only; not permanent; made or arranged to supply a passing need.'

[230] *Id*, para 303. See for Article XX of the GATT, *supra* note 68.

[231] *Id*, para 306.

[232] *Id*, para 240.

access to Article XX of the GATT 1994 in this respect, the drafters would have included language to that effect in Paragraph 11.3 or elsewhere in China's Accession Protocol'.[233] The indication by the Appellate Body of the circumstances of China's accession to the WTO Agreement shows an implied reliance of this Body on the 'supplementary means' rule of interpretation.[234] Again, by not insisting on the use of 'supplementary means' in interpreting the provision in question (paragraph 11.3 of China's Accession Protocol), it could be understood as the Appellate Body's intent to clarify to the parties in the dispute that the *text* of the Protocol, as 'an integral part' of the WTO Agreement, is *clear* so it does not leave way to doubts. And that the '*WTO Agreement*' (always emphasized in the course of the judgments) is concluded by virtue of the *bona fide* and *pacta sunt servanda* principles, which require members of the WTO *to abide by their treaty obligations, thus to fulfil in good faith the obligations assumed by them under the treaties.* In sum, by interpreting the terms of the provision in their ordinary meaning in the context, seeking light from the object and purpose of the WTO Agreement and its *context* (the Agreement *taken as a whole*), as also from the 'supplementary means',[235] the Appellate Body performs an interpretation, as itself admits, in accordance with 'the customary rules of interpretation of public international law as codified in the Vienna Convention in a *holistic* approach'.[236]

#### 6.3.6.4 Emphasis on the 'Good Faith' and 'Intention' Elements

There are other instances when the Appellate Body shows a stronger emphasis on the 'good faith' and/or 'intention' than on other terms/elements of the treaty in interpreting the WTO covered agreements, while giving interpretative value to each of the terms/elements employed. As the case analyses at the ICJ (Chap. 4) can show, 'good faith' is a principle *sine qua non* in concluding a treaty/agreement. Reflecting a general principle of law of the treaties, *good faith* is referred in Article 26 of the 1969 VCLT, providing that '*[e]very treaty in force is binding upon the parties to it and must be performed by them in good faith*'.[237] According to Gardiner, besides a general application in the law of treaties, *good faith* has also one *specific* application in the interpretation of treaties as reflected in the

[233]*Id.*

[234]*Id*, para 298.

[235]See a similar approach taken by the ICJ in *Libyan Arab Jamahiriya v. Chad*, *supra* note 75, p. 27. As the text of the treaty was considered sufficiently clear, the ICJ declared it "may" 'refer to the *travaux preparatoire* to elucidate the context of the 1955 Treaty … to confirm its reading of the text.'

[236]*China-Raw Materials* (2012), para 307 (emphasis added).

[237]Article 26 of the VCLT is entitled '*Pacta sunt servanda*' (emphasis added).

requirement of Article 31(1) VCLT, that 'a treaty is to be interpreted in good faith'.[238] Thus, Article 31, paragraph 1, of the VCLT embodies the *good faith* element, which, as concisely put by the Gardiner, simply indicates '*how* the task of interpretation is to be undertaken'.[239] Given this, 'good faith' within the mentioned provision relates to all the component terms of the treaty (text, context, object and purpose), ensuring a balance of the terms in the process of interpretation. For example, in respect of the reference of Article 31(1) to the 'object and purpose', Gardiner observes that 'the combination of good faith and taking account of object and purpose results in an outcome that is more likely to reflect effectively the true intentions recorded in the text than would a purely literal approach'.[240]

By placing sometimes a strong emphasis on the *good faith*, similarly to the ICJ (especially when dealing with, e.g., *unclear, doubtful, ambiguous, vague, or silent* treaty text), the WTO appears to underline the importance of the role that this principle has in ensuring a balance of all the treaty (WTO Agreement) elements (text, context, object and purpose) and in performing (in good faith by the parties) the legal obligations enshrined therein. An illustration of this aspect can be found, for example, in the ***EC – Computer Equipment (EC v. US)*** **(1998)** case.[241] The main issue of interpretation in this case was to establish whether the tariff treatment

[238]Gardiner (2008), p. 152. Citing Oppenheim, Gardiner explains that the concept of good faith as reflected in Article 31(1) 'strongly implies an element of reasonableness and that the requirement that a treaty is to be interpreted in good faith, as well as being necessary 'as a matter of general principle ... follows from article 26...'

[239]*Id.*

[240]*Id.*

[241]*European Communities – customs classification of certain computer equipment*, T/DS62/AB/RWT/DS67/AB/R; WT/DS68/AB/R, 5 June 1998. In the first phase of this case, the complaints of the United States were in respect of the alleged reclassification by the European Communities, for tariff purposes, of certain Local Area Network (LAN) adapter equipment and personal computers with multimedia capability. The US alleged that these measures violated Article II of GATT 1994. In appeal, the European Communities requested the Appellate Body to review a number of errors of law and certain legal interpretations developed by the Panel. The Appellate Body reversed the Panel's conclusion that the EC tariff treatment of LAN equipment is inconsistent with Article II:1 of GATT 1994.

Article II: 1 of GATT/WTO 1994 provides for "Schedules of Concessions":

> 1. (a) Each contracting party shall accord to the commerce of the other contracting parties treatment no less favorable than that provided for in the appropriate Part of the appropriate Schedule annexed to this Agreement. b) The products described in Part I of the Schedule relating to any contracting party, which are the products of territories of other contracting parties, shall, on their importation into the territory to which the Schedule relates, and subject to the terms, conditions or qualifications set forth in that Schedule, be exempt from ordinary customs duties in excess of those set forth and provided therein. Such products shall also be exempt from all other duties or charges of any kind imposed on or in connection with the importation in excess of those imposed on the date of this Agreement or those directly and mandatorily required to be imposed thereafter by legislation in force in the importing territory on that date.

accorded by the custom authorities in the European Communities to the Local Area Network (LAN) equipment and personal computers with multimedia capability imported from the United States was less favourable than that provided for tariff concessions for ADP machines and telecommunication equipment, in Schedule LXXX (as part of the GATT), in violation of Article II of the GATT 1994.[242]

The key point for the Appellate Body in this case is to determine the meaning of the term 'reasonable expectations' in the interpretation of a Schedule, which the Panel referred to as 'legitimate expectations' of an exporting member.[243] Having established that '[a] Schedule is made an integral part of the GATT 1994 by Article II: 7' and that 'the concessions provided for in that Schedule are part of the terms of the treaty',[244] the Appellate Body makes clear that 'the only rules which may be applied in interpreting the meaning of a concession are the general rules of treaty interpretation set out in the *Vienna Convention*'.[245] Confronted here with an *unclear meaning*, considering that 'Schedule LXXX does not contain any explicit reference to "LAN equipment"',[246] the Appellate Body feels to commence its interpretation reassuring that it will follow the requirements of the Vienna rules of interpretation, pursuant to Article 3.2 of the DSU. It reiterates the role and the scope of the Vienna rules in the interpretation of treaties and, certainly, of the WTO covered agreements, by invoking the *India – Patents* (1998) case, where the Appellate Body held that 'these principles of interpretation neither require nor condone the imputation into a treaty of words that are not there or the importation into a treaty of concepts that were not intended'.[247]

The Appellate Body's approach identifies several steps. First, it specifically relies on the textualist method when stating that the terms of the provision are 'to be determined in accordance with the ordinary meaning', in their 'context' (adding: 'and in the light of the object and purpose of the treaty', implying also a teleological approach).[248] For example, the Body holds on this rule: '[i]t is clear from the wording of Article II: 5 that it does not support the Panel's view'.[249] Second, since the 'ordinary meaning' of the term 'reasonable expectations' in its context

[242]Schedule LXXX of the European Communities (in Final Act Embodying the Results of the Uruguay Round of Multilateral Trade Negotiations, done at Marrakesh, 15 April 1994). The Appellate Body notes that 'Schedule LXXX provides tariff concessions for ADP machines under headings 84.71 and 84.73 and for telecommunications equipment under heading 85.17. The customs duties set forth in Schedule LXXX on telecommunications equipment are generally higher than those on ADP machines.'

[243]*EC – Computer Equipment* (1998), para 80.

[244]*Id*, para 64.

[245]*Id*, para 50.

[246]*Id*, para 75. From the provision results that 'the European Communities currently treats LAN equipment as telecommunications equipment', and thus not ADP machines, as the United States expected.

[247]*India – Patents*, WT/DS 50/AB/R, 16 January 1998.

[248]*EC – Computer Equipment* (1998), para 84.

[249]*Id*, para 81.

does not yield an unambiguous answer, the Appellate Body attributes further significance to the intention of the parties by relying on the subjective method of interpretation. The Body stresses on this basis that '[t]he purpose of treaty interpretation under Article 31 of the *Vienna Convention* is to ascertain the common intentions of the Parties'.[250] It stresses moreover in this connection the 'good faith' element, necessary for a reasonable interpretation, when stating that the Appellate Body does 'not agree with the Panel that interpreting the meaning of a concession in a Member's Schedule in the light of the "legitimate expectations" of exporting Members is consistent with the principle of good faith interpretation under Article 31 of the *Vienna Convention*'.[251] Underlying further the importance of the 'intention' element in revealing the real meaning of the terms at issue, the Appellate Body adds: '[t]hese common intentions cannot be ascertained on the basis of the subjective and unilaterally determined "expectation" of one of the parties to a treaty'.[252] The Appellate Body clarifies that the prior practice of only *one* of the parties does not suffice to establish the *common* intention of the parties, though it is relevant, and then the Body stresses again that '[t]he purpose of treaty interpretation is to establish the *common intention* of the parties to the treaty'.[253]

Third, the Appellate Body makes specific use of the teleological method of interpretation when setting 'the context of Schedule LXXX in the light of the *object and purpose* of the WTO Agreement and the GATT 1994, in accordance with the rules of treaty interpretation set out in the *Vienna Convention*'.[254] Fourth, to ensure that the interpretation reached on the basis of the rules provided in Article 31 of the VCLT does not leave room for misinterpretation, the Appellate Body appeals to the 'supplementary means'. It explicitly recalls that 'if after applying Article 31 the meaning of the term remains ambiguous or obscure, or leads to a result which is manifestly absurd or unreasonable, Article 32 allows a treaty interpreter to have recourse to: . . . supplementary means of interpretation, including preparatory work of the treaty and the circumstances of its conclusion'.[255] Invoking Sinclair's opinion on 'supplementary means', the Appellate Body points out that 'the reference in Article 32 of the Convention to the circumstances of the conclusion of a treaty may have some value in emphasizing the need for the interpreter to bear constantly in mind the historical background against which the treaty has been negotiated'.[256]

The resort to 'supplementary means' as determinative and/or confirmatory tool for the drafters' intention has been applied by the ICJ, either expressly or implicitly, especially when dealing with *unclear, inconclusive, ambiguous, vague, silent treaty*

[250] *Id*, para 84.
[251] *Id*, para 83.
[252] *Id*, para 84.
[253] *Id*, para 93.
[254] *Id*.
[255] *Id*, para 86.
[256] Sinclair (1984), p. 141.

*text* but also on a *sufficiently clear or clear* text of the treaty as, for example, in the more recently decided *Territorial Dispute* (1994) case. The ICJ held in this case that 'it is not necessary to refer to the *travaux preparatoire* to elucidate the context of 1955 Treaty, but as in previous cases, it finds it possible to confirm its reading of the text . . .'.[257] Although the 'supplementary means' of interpretation can be implied from the Appellate Body's wording in the *EC – Computer Equipment* case as only eventually necessary, they appear to be acquiring greater force in the final result, confirming therefore the intention of the drafters in respect of Schedule LXXX.[258] The Body finds in this regard that 'classification practice in the European Communities during the Uruguay Round is part of the "circumstances of [the] conclusion" of the WTO Agreement and may be used as supplementary means of interpretation within the meaning of Article 32 of the Vienna Convention'.[259]

Fifth, in the attempt to throw more light upon the intention of the parties, the Appellate Body recalls another important interpretative rule: the 'subsequent practice', meant to have weight in elucidating the meaning of a treaty term, an approach that supports directly the subjective method ('intentions'). The Body reiterates that '[a] proper interpretation also would have included an examination of the existence and relevance of subsequent practice'.[260] Consequently, the Appellate Body finds that 'in interpreting the tariff concessions in Schedule LXXX, decisions of the WTO may be relevant; and, therefore, they should have been examined by the Panel'.[261] The 'subsequent practice' rule was confirmed by the ICJ as instrumental in revealing the real intention of the parties to a treaty, especially on *ambiguity* or *vagueness* in treaty text but also on all types of treaty text's difficulties, as, for example, in *The Interpretation of Article 3, Paragraph 2, of the Treaty of Lausanne* (1925) case. The ICJ held in this case that the subsequent practice to the conclusion of the treaty could only concern the Court in so far as it was throwing light on the intention of the parties they had at the conclusion of that Treaty.[262]

Finally, the Appellate Body supplements its interpretation by resort to 'any relevant rules of international law applicable in relations between the parties', although without a specific, technical reference to Article 31(3)(c) of the VCLT. Thus, under the systemic integration principle, which this provision promotes, the Appellate Body admits that to determine the obligations of the European

---

[257] *Libyan Arab Jamahirya/Chad, supra* note 75, p. 27.

[258] *EC – Computer Equipment* (1998), para 109.

[259] *Id.*

[260] *Id*, para 90. Based subsequent practice rule, the AB finds that: in interpreting the tariff concessions in Schedule LXXX, decisions of the WTO may be relevant; and, therefore, they 'should have been examined by the Panel.'

[261] *Id*, p. 24.

[262] *Interpretation of Article 3, Paragraph 2, of the Treaty of Lausanne*, Advisory Opinion of 21 November 1925, PCIJ, Ser. B, No 12, p. 24. The PCIJ ruled in this case that: '[t]he facts subsequent to the conclusion of the Treaty of Lausanne can only concern the Court in so far as they are calculated to throw light on the intention of the Parties at the time of the conclusion of that Treaty.'

Communities under Schedule LXXX *vis-à-vis* the WTO members, a proper interpretation of Schedule LXXX should include an examination of the *Harmonized System and its Explanatory Notes* to which the European Community and the United States are parties.[263] In sum, the Appellate Body adopts in *EC – Computer Equipment* a clear *holistic* approach, which is based on an explicit methodology of interpretation, pursuant to Articles 31 and 32 of the VCLT. It gives full meaning and effect to the provision at issue, however, strongly relying on the subjective method (intentions), with emphasis on the good faith principle of interpretation.

#### 6.3.6.5 Reliance on the 'Supplementary Means' Rule

It is to be recalled that Article 32 of the VCLT provides that in order to deduce the parties' intention, an interpreter may take into account 'supplementary means of interpretation, including the preparatory work of the treaty and circumstances of its conclusion' (VCLT 1969). In Chap. 3 of this book it was mentioned that the preparatory work (*travaux preparatoire* or *travaux*) was intended by the VCLT drafters 'to be an integral component of interpretation'.[264] It was also mentioned that all the schools of (treaty) interpretation admit recourse to supplementary means, particularly to the *travaux preparatoire*, but they disagree about the circumstances that justify such resort (Fitzmaurice 1951, p. 7). However, as correctly asserted by Mortenson, in any serious effort to understand a treaty text, thus the real meaning of its drafters' intention, interpreters should rely on drafting history in addition to other tools (provided by Articles 31) in 'every plausibly contestable case', as well as 'in some cases even to override what had initially seemed like its clear import'.[265] Some of the case analyses in this chapter can also evidence that panels and the Appellate Body have shown a tendency to rely on the 'preparatory work' or/and 'circumstances of the conclusion of the treaty' (Article 32 of the VCLT), even when they have declared (or apparently treated) the text of the provision at issue as *clear*, or *sufficiently clear*. Similarly to the ICJ, the WTO (panels and the Appellate Body) has resorted, in general, to 'supplementary means' as a necessary test to determine the meaning of a treaty provision or to confirm it after it was obtained on the basis of rules contained in Article 31 of the VCLT. As it was already shown, this resort manifests in the WTO approaches similarly to the ICJ, either expressly (by spelling it out) or implicitly (by suggesting but not making a technical reference to it), however, with even more caution than does the ICJ, by vague indications or deduced from a language that points towards an implicit admission of the 'supplementary means' rule. The cautious resort of the Appellate

---

[263] *EC – Computer Equipment* (1998), para 89. Explanatory Notes to the Harmonized Commodity Description and Coding System, Customs Cooperation Council, Brussels, 1986. The European Communities are Members of the World Customs Organization (the 'WCO').

[264] Mortenson (2013), p. 821.

[265] *Id.*

Body, and also panels, to the 'supplementary means' appears to be due to these bodies' tendency/preference to adopt a dynamic or evolutive interpretation of the WTO Agreement, in the light of the actual trade law's developments.

In the approach taken by the Appellate Body in the ***EC – Poultry (Brazill v. EC) (1998)*** case,[266] unlike in other examples discussed above, the Body makes an explicit resort to the 'supplementary means' of interpretation, which proved to be subtantially valuable in shedding light on the intention o the drafters in respect of the provision at issue. As the other cases discussed above, the present case also constitutes an illustration of a clear abidance of the Appellate Body by the *holistic* approach promoted by the VCLT's 'general rule of interpretation'. The main issue of interpretation in *EC – Poultry* was to determine whether the tariff quota for frozen poultry meat in Schedule LXXX was exclusively for the benefit of Brazil, on the basis of an existing agreement between Brazil and the European Community on the allocation of the tariff quota under the GATT 1994,[267] and whether the EC violated the Agreement on Import Licensing Procedures by distorting trade in frozen poultry meat through its licensing procedure.[268]

The Appellate Body proceeds in this case with a step-by-step approach of interpretation, following the patterns it has already used. It finds first that Schedule LXXX[269] is annexed to the Marrakesh Protocol, and therefore it is an integral part of the GATT and WTO Agreement.[270] For this reason, the Appellate Body considers Schedule LXXX as the legal basis for this dispute, 'which must be interpreted in accordance with "customary rules of interpretation of public international law" under Article 3.2 of the DSU'.[271] The 'ordinary meaning' and the 'context' rules apparently constitute, here, the focus of interpretation. The Appel-

[266]*European Communities – Measures Affecting the Importation of Certain Poultry Products*, WT/DS69/AB/R, 13 July 1998, p. 31, para 86. In the first phase of this case, the European Communities authorised by GATT Contracting Parties to enter into negotiations under Article XXVIII of GATT- Modification of Schedules, with interested parties. Such negotiations were entered into with Brazil, as well with nine other contracting parties. The Appellate Body upheld most of the Panel's findings and conclusions, but reversed the Panel's finding that the EC had acted inconsistently with Article 5.1(b) of the Agreement on Agriculture. It, however, concluded that the EC had acted inconsistently with Article 5.5 of the Agreement on Agriculture.

[267]Under Article XIII: 2(a) of the GATT.

[268]*EC-Poultry* (1998), *supra* note 266. The bilateral agreement set out in the "Oilseeds Agreement" provided inter-alia a duty—free global annual tariff rate quota. Brazil complained that the tariff-rate quota on frozen poultry meat should have been allocated by the EC exclusively to Brazil, and not shared on an MFN basis, and that the EC had improperly invoked a special safeguard provision under the Agreement on Agriculture.

[269]Schedule LXXX of the European Communities provides for a duty-free tariff–rate quota for up to 15,500 tonnes of frozen poultry meat in Part I—Most Favored Nation Tariff, Section I Agricultural Products (Section I-B Tariff Quotas, with out-of-quota base duty rates of 1600 ECU/tonne, 940 ECU/tonne, and 1575/tonne).

[270]*EC – Poultry* (1998), para 86.

[271]*Id*, para 81.

late Body states, for example, that 'on the basis of ordinary meaning of the terms', the tariff-rate quota for frozen poultry meat was intended to be allocated on the most-favoured-nation-tariff (MFN-tariff) basis and that 'there are no other terms and conditions' specified regarding the tariff quota in Schedule LXXX.[272] However, to confirm this result and thus the intention of the parties in respect of Schedule LXXX, the Appellate Body expressly resorts to 'supplementary means' of interpretation. It finds, pursuant to Article 32 of the VCLT, that the Oilseeds Agreement serves 'as supplementary means of interpretation of the concession made by the European Communities in Schedule LXXX'.[273] Reliance on the *travaux preparatoire* and the circumstances of the GATT/WTO Agreement's conclusion is suggested several times in this case. Furthermore, in establishing whether Brazil's claim that the tariff-rate quota for frozen poultry meat set forth in Schedule LXXX was intended to be a country-specific tariff-rate quota with Brazil as the sole beneficiary, the Appellate Body finds that '[t]he bilateral character of the Oilseeds Agreement does not, by itself, constitute evidence of a common intent that the tariff-rate quota was for the exclusive benefit of Brazil'.[274] Furthermore, in checking out the meaning of the term 'global annual tariff quota' in the *travaux preparatoire* of the *Oilseeds Agreement*, the Appellate Body finds confirmation that 'the "tariff quota" for frozen poultry was not intended to be allocated on an MFN', and that the term 'global annual tariff quota', describing the '15,500 tonnes',[275] is, in addition, according to the GATT/WTO practice, a quota 'that is to be administered on non-discriminatory basis pursuant to Article XIII of the GATT 1994'.[276] The Appellate Body finds further confirmation of this result in the (Havana Conference in 1947) discussions (as *travaux*) of the provisions of what later became Article XIII of the GATT.[277]

One could assume, however, that similarly to other cases analysed above, also in the present case, the Appellate Body appears to favour the textualist method, and it rests its decision substantially on the evidence of the common intention of the parties resulting from the 'text' alone. Nevertheless, by expressions such as 'the ordinary meaning of the text of Article 5.5 *is clear*,'[278] or '[t]here is no qualifying language, and there is no language that permits any method other than that set out in

[272] *Id*, paras 81–90.

[273] *Id*, para 91.

[274] *Id*, para 94.

[275] *Id*, paras 91–92.

[276] *Id*.

[277] *Id*, para 92.

[278] *Id* (emphasis added). The textualist-contextualist approach could be clearly observed in examining the Agreement on Agriculture, Article 5.1(b), when the Appellate Body recalls a long recognised customary rule of interpretation. It holds: '[t]his reading of the text of Article 5.1 (b) is supported by our reading of the context of that provision in accordance with Article 31 of the Vienna Convention, which specifies that the ordinary meaning of the terms of a treaty should be interpreted in their context'.

the schedule in Article 5.5 as a basis for the calculation of additional duties',[279] the Appellate Body seems to project the idea that the 'text' offers naturally the basis of interpretation. Such an approach with a strong emphasis on the 'ordinary meaning' rule can be seen similarly adopted by the ICJ, for example in the *Territorial Dispute* (1994) case; when having to interpret a *sufficiently clear* text of a treaty, the Court stressed that '[i]nterpretation must be based above all upon the text of the treaty'.[280] However, despite the fact that the Appellate Body in *EC – Poultry* declared the provisions at issue as *clear enough* to reflect the intention of the parties, similarly to the ICJ in *Territorial Dispute*, the Body resorted to other rules and methods of interpretation in order to confirm it.[281]

Thus, the interpretative process is extended in the case at hand as to include other rules of interpretation, either in an express or only suggested way, an approach I described in Chap. 4 as 'overbuilding'. A further instance shows that when examining the meaning of the term 'c.i.f. import price' in the *Agreement on Agriculture*, the Appellate Body appeals to general international law by virtue of Article 31(3) (c) of the VCLT to elucidate the meaning of that term. It finds in the *Incoterms 1990 of the International Chamber of Commerce* that the acronym 'c.i.f.' means 'cost, insurance and freight' and that 'in customary usage in international trade, the c.i.f. import price does not include any taxes, customs duties, or other charges that may be imposed on a product by a Member upon entry into its customs territory'.[282]

Furthermore, the 'object and purpose' rule is employed when the Appellate Body needs to determine the meaning of Schedule LXXX in the context of the GATT/WTO as a whole. It finds in this regard that the Preamble to the *Licensing Agreement* stresses that the Agreement aims at ensuring that import licensing procedures 'are not utilized in a manner contrary to the principles and obligations of GATT 1994' and that they are 'implemented in a transparent and predictable manner'.[283] The result reached is tested further by an implicit resort to the effectiveness principle when the Appellate Body differentiates the term 'global quotas', used in contrast with quotas allocated on a country-specific basis. The Appellate

[279] *Id*, para 165.

[280] *Libyan Arab Jamahiriya/Chad*, *supra* note 75, p. 22.

[281] See the analysis of this case in Chap. 4 of this book.

[282] *EC-Poultry* (1998), para 146. The Appellate Body looks to the 'the Incoterms 1990 of the International Chamber of Commerce' which 'explains what the acronym "c.i.f." means "cost, insurance and freight"', and finds that it 'does not give a definition of "c.i.f. import price". This definition may also be inferred from paragraph 2 of the Attachment to Annex 5 of the Agreement on Agriculture.'

[283] *Id*, para 89. Article 1.2 of the Licensing Agreement states in relevant part:

> Members shall ensure that the administrative procedures used to implement import licensing regimes are in conformity with the relevant provisions of GATT 1994 including its annexes and protocols as interpreted by this Agreement trade distortions that may arise from an inappropriate operation of those procedures, taking into account the economic development purposes and financial and trade needs of developing country Members.

Body asserts that because there is no persuasive evidence of such a 'country-specific rate quota' on frozen poultry meat, it cannot construe the term 'global annual tariff quota', as used in the *Oilseeds Agreement*, to mean a country-specific quota allocated exclusively to Brazil, as Brazil claimed.[284] In sum, the Appellate Body's language used here clarifies that its interpretation gives meaning and effect to all the terms of the WTO provisions at issue, without diminishing the rights and obligations stated therein, so not adding something that was not there. The Appellate Body adopts in *EC – Poultry* a *holistic* interpretative approach in compliance with the customary rules of interpretation provided in Articles 31 and 32 of the VCLT and, thus, in compliance with Article 3.2 of the DSU.

#### 6.3.6.6 Compliance with or Deviance from the VCLT?

As correctly observed by Fitzmaurice and Merkouris, the importance of *the VCLT interpretative rules lies in the fact that these rules would always lead to an unambiguous result*, *a singular interpretation* of the provision in question, in any given dispute (Fitzmaurice and Merkouris 2010, p. 185). What the authors underline here is the clear intention of the VCLT's drafters for a *general rule of interpretation*, and that by its application the interpretation of a treaty should achieve some result and not render it ineffective. Therefore, 'any interpretation that would make the text ineffective is suspect'.[285] Since all the provisions of a treaty must be admitted 'as intended to have significance and to be necessary to contain the intended meaning',[286] a treaty interpreter is then justly required to consider *that treaty as a whole*. It involves, according to Fitzmaurice and Merkouris, taking into account all elements of treaty interpretation: text, context, object and purpose, intention, as well as *travaux preparatoire*.[287] In other words, because all these treaty elements connect and complement each other, they are necessary for, and ensure, a proper interpretation of a treaty.[288] Therefore, only when being combined into *a single logical operation* can these elements confer objectivity to the legal norms' interpretation.

If the above case analyses have illustrated approaches of interpretations in compliance with the requirements of the VCLT's standard of interpretation, other instances could show deviance from such standard. The requirement of the 'basic rule of interpretation' under Article 31(1) (2) of the VCLT is that interpretation

[284] *Id*, para 92. A similar illustration of this rule could be seen in the *Question Concerning the Acquisition of Polish Nationality* (Advisory opinion), PCIJ, 15 September 1923, p. 21. In referring to Article 4 of the Peace Treaty, the PCIJ held that the provision must be accepted "in the present meaning" for the purpose of applying the Treaty, and that by imposing an additional condition in the acquisition of Polish nationality would lead 'not to interpreting the Treaty, but to reconstructing it.'

[285] Fitzmaurice and Merkouris (2010), p. 180.

[286] *Id*, p. 160.

[287] *Id*, p. 182.

[288] *Id*.

must give meaning and effect to all the terms of the treaty and functions as standard for any treaty interpretation. By not following such standard, the interpretation could not attain the level of objectivity required for the legal norm at issue to be effective. Such an example is the ***Brazil Aircraft (Canada v. Brazil)*** **(1999)** case,[289] where the Appellate Body displays an interpretation on an apparent *clear* text, mainly relying on the 'ordinary meaning' approach, with the exclusion of other equally important rules within Article 31(1) (2) of the VCLT, respectively the 'object and purpose' and 'context of the treaty' (taken as a whole). Although such an interpretation seems to limit the relevance of the non-WTO rules (Vienna rules), it does not appear to be a regular pattern in the practice of the WTO. Nevertheless, such an instance[290] shows that the WTO interpretative approach does not always go in one direction: that of being consistent with the VCLT rules of interpretation, but also it sometimes goes in the other direction: that of deviation from the standard of

[289] *Brazil Export Financing Programme for Aircraft*, WT/DS 46/AB/R, 2 August, 1999. In the first phase, the panel concluded that Brazil failed to establish that the payments subsidies fell within the first paragraph of item (k) of the Illustrative List of Export Subsidies of Annex 1 of the SCM Agreement (Agreement on Subsidies and Countervailing Measures), and that the PROEX payments were prohibited export subsidies under Article 3.1(a) of the SCM Agreement.

[290] See other similar examples of deviation of the WTO adjudicative bodies from the general *standard of treaty interpretation*, e.g., in Babu (2010)—discussing some cases of improper and excessive use of power by the Panels and Appellate Body, e.g., in: *India-Quantitative Restrictions*, Appellate Body and the Panel Report, WT/DS 90/AB/R, 23 August 1999 and WT/DS 90/R, 6 April 1999; *US-Section 301-310 of the Trade Act of 1974*, Panel Report, WT/DS 152/R of 22 December *1999; India – Patent Protection for Pharmaceutical and Agricultural Chemical Products*, Appellate Body and Panel Report, WT/DS 50/AB/R, 19 December 1997 and WT/DS 50, 5 September 1997. See also Gruszczynski (2012)—for a discussion on WTO cases (of deviation from international law) analysed from the perspective of the fragmentation of international law due to the WTO's *overreliance on dictionaries* (of specific terms in the WTO Agreements) in, e.g., *European Communities – Anti-Dumping Duties on Malleable Cast Iron Tube or Pipe Fittings from Brazil* WT/DS219/AB/R, 18 August 2003; or *European Communities-Measures Concerning Meat and Meat Products (Hormones)*, WT/DS26/AB/R, WT/DS48/AB/R WTO, 16 January 1998; or other examples of deviation (from the substantive international law, i.e., customary international law) under Article 31(3)(c) VCLT such as: Report of the Panel, *United States – Restrictions on Imports of Tuna*, DS21R/-39S/155 (Sept. 3, 1991), GATT B.I.S.D. (39th Supp.), and Report of the Panel, *Thailand – Restrictions on Importation of and Internal Taxes on Cigarettes*, ¶ 75, DS10/R—37S/200 (Oct. 5, 1990)—These cases are discussed in the scholarship as illustrations where the GATT panels generally did not favour trade restrictive measures, and where they approached narrowly interpretations of the exceptions to free trade. In this regard, see, e.g., McInerney (2009); *European Communities-Measures Concerning Meat and Meat Products (Hormones)*, WT/DS26/AB/R, WT/DS48/AB/R WTO, 16 January 1998, para 123—where the Appellate Body refused to take the precautionary principle in international law, and to treat it as 'customary' under Article 31(3)(3) VCLT. The AB held: 'We consider, however, that it is unnecessary, and probably imprudent, for the Appellate Body in this appeal to take a position on this important, but abstract, question.' Also, *European Communities – Measures Affecting the Approval and Marketing of Biotech Products*. WT/DS291/R, WT/DS292/R, WT/DS293/R, 21 November 2006—This case reviewed the jurisprudence and doctrine related to the precautionary principle, noting many uncertainties in the status of this principle. The Panel held (at para 7.88): 'The Panel finally declined to uphold the European Communities' contention that the precautionary principle has "by now becomes a fully-fledged and general principle of international law".'

interpretation mandated by the VCLT's general rule of interpretation and, therefore, from Article 3.2 DSU's requirements to interpret the WTO covered agreements according to the VCLT customary rules of treaty interpretation.

The Appellate Body had to determine in *Brazil Aircraft* whether Brazil's measures of export subsidies for regional aircraft granted under the Brazilian *Programa de Financiamento às Exportações (PROEX)* on sales of aircraft to foreign purchasers of Brazil's 'Embraer' aircraft[291] were used to secure for Brazil 'a material advantage in the field of export credit terms' in violation of the SCM Agreement (part of the GATT/WTO Agreement). The main provision under interpretation is Article 27 of the SCM Agreement (Agreement on Subsidies and Countervailing Measures), Item (k) of the Illustrative List. In this case, the Appellate Body deals with the principle of 'special and differential treatment' within Article 27 of the SCM Agreement.[292] Without any technical reference to the Vienna Convention's rules of interpretation, however, the Appellate Body suggests in the present case the application of these rules. It first concentrates on the terms of the provision at issue, for example, when referring to 'the ordinary meaning of the text of Article 27.2',[293] admitting it as being 'clear'.[294] In the next step, the Appellate Body applies the 'context' rule, predominantly by implying it, as the following statement can illustrate: 'the phrase in item (k), *"in so far as they are used to secure a material advantage"*, would have no meaning if it were simply to be equated with the term "benefit" in the definition of "subsidy". As a matter of treaty interpretation, this cannot be so. Therefore, we consider it an error to interpret the "material advantage" clause in item (k) of the Illustrative List as meaning the same as the term "benefit" in Article 1.1(b) of the SCM Agreement.'[295] As it could be observed, this approach implies also a resort to the effectiveness principle that the Appellate Body

[291] Empresa Brasileira de Aeronáutica S.A. ("Embraer") refers to a Brazilian manufacturer of regional aircraft.

[292] *Brazil Aircraft* (1999), *supra* note 289, para 40. Article 27 entitled: 'Special and Differential Treatment of Developing Country Members.'

[293] Article 27. 2 (b) of the SCM Agreement provides:

> The prohibition of paragraph 1(a) of Article 3 shall not apply to: ... (b) other developing country Members for a period of eight years from the date of entry into force of the WTO Agreement, subject to compliance with the provisions in paragraph 4.

Article 27.4 of the SCM Agreement provides in its relevant part:

> Any developing country Member referred to in paragraph 2(b) shall phase out its export subsidies within the eight-year period, preferably in a progressive manner. However, a developing country Member shall not increase the level of its export subsidies (55), and shall eliminate them within a period shorter than that provided for in this paragraph when the use of such export subsidies is inconsistent with its development needs.

[294] *Brazil Aircraft* (1999), para 139.

[295] *Id*, para 80.

supports by invoking the use of it in the *Gasoline* and *Japan – Alcoholic Beverages II* cases (discussed above).

Further in the judgment, the Appellate Body explicitly applies the 'context' rule, for example, when it upholds the Panel's conclusion that it considered the context of the 'material advantage' clause, in general, in the SCM Agreement.[296] Then the Appellate Body suggests that the 'text' and 'context' cannot be detached from the 'object and purpose'. Therefore, the Body supplies its interpretation by adopting the teleological approach.[297] Support for this suggestion can be found, for example, in regard to Article 27, when the Appellate Body concludes that paragraph 1 of this Article provides that 'Members recognize that subsidies may play an important role in economic development programmes of developing country Members' and that '[b]oth from its title and from its terms, it is clear that Article 27 is intended to provide special and differential treatment for developing country Members, under certain specified conditions'.[298] A clearer disclosure of the 'object and purpose' rule appears when the Appellate Body specifies that '[t]he Panel also discussed its view of the object and purpose of the SCM Agreement', which 'is to impose multilateral disciplines on subsidies which distort international trade'.[299]

Again, it can be observed that the Appellate Body approaches this interpretation without any express or technical reference to the VCLT articles on rules of interpretation (Vienna rules). A closer reading of the Appellate Body's language reveals an over-reliance on the textualist approach, notably on the plain, literal or ordinary meaning rule. This over-reliance can be evidenced by the Appellate Body's emphasis on the actual text of the provisions at issue, such as in the phrases '[t]he ordinary meaning of the text of Article 27.2(b) is clear',[300] '[b]oth from its title and from its terms, it is clear that Article 27 is intended to provide special and differential treatment for developing country Members, under certain specified conditions',[301] or '[w]e look first to the ordinary meaning of the language used. We agree with the Panel's statement that the ordinary meaning of the word "advantage" is "a more favourable or improved position" or a "superior position"'.[302] However, despite an express recognition of the inclusion of the 'object and purpose' rule in the interpretation of Article 27, the Appellate Body appears, actually, to disregard an interpretation of this provision such as in the light of the 'object and purpose' of the GATT/WTO Agreement, and in its 'context', so to consider *the Agreement as a whole*. Since

---

[296] *Id*, para 174.

[297] *Id*, para 173.

[298] *Id*, para 174.

[299] *Id*. The Panel added: 'It is for this reason that the SCM Agreement prohibits two categories of subsidies – subsidies contingent upon exportation and upon the use of domestic over imported goods – that are specifically designed to affect trade.'

[300] *Id*, para 139.

[301] *Id*, para 140.

[302] *Id*, para 78.

the Appellate Body does not refer to any other evidence to support its position, this leads the reader to the conclusion that the interpretation is predominantly textualist, thus mainly based on the dictionary for the meaning of the terms at issue. It can be argued that such an interpretation does not give meaning and effect to all the terms of the treaty,[303] here the GATT/WTO Agreement, under the requirements of Article 31(1)(2) of the VCLT—basic rule of interpretation. The provisions under these (VCLT) article's two paragraphs, reflecting a corollary principle of interpretation, requires that the 'object and purpose' may be sought not only in the preamble of a particular agreement (i.e., the SCM Agreement in this case) but also in the light of the 'object and purpose' (objectives) of the WTO treaty (Marrakesh Agreement) as a whole.[304] Applied compulsorily by the Appellate Body, the basic rule under Article 31(1)(2) was confirmed in the *US – Shrimp/Turtle* case,[305] when holding that:

> A treaty interpreter must begin with, and focus upon, the text of the particular provision to be interpreted. It is in the words constituting that provision, read in their context, that the object and purpose of the states parties to the treaty must first be sought. Where the meaning imparted by the text itself is equivocal or inconclusive, or where confirmation of the correctness of the reading of the text itself is desired, *light from the object and purpose of the treaty as a whole* may usefully be sought.[306]

Yet this rule has been employed by the Appellate Body on many occasions, either expressly or implying, and in all the cases discussed above, even when the text of the provision at issue was declared as being clear, sufficiently clear or clear enough, as it is suggested to be the provision at issue in the present case.[307] Therefore, one could draw the conclusion that the Appellate Body fails to interpret the provisions regarding the special and differential treatment[308] in the light of the Preamble of the GATT/WTO Agreement (giving effect to the 'object and purpose' of the WTO Agreement), which provides for 'a need for positive efforts designed to ensure that developing countries, and especially the least developed among them, secure a share in the growth of international trade commensurate with the needs of their economic development'.[309] Actually, the Appellate Body appears to overlook in *Brazil Aircraft* 'a fundamental rule of treaty interpretation', which 'has received its most authoritative and succinct expression in the Vienna Convention of the Law of the Treaties', as stated in *Gasoline*,[310] and it was applied constantly by the WTO adjudicative bodies, sometimes being supported by reference to the ICJ's practice. Such an approach also differs from the ICJ's approaches adopted usually when the

---

[303] *Id.*

[304] Marrakesh Agreement Establishing the World Trade Organisation (1999).

[305] See *US Shrimp/Turtle*, *supra* note 114.

[306] *Brazil Aircraft* (1999), para 114.

[307] See the other cases in this chapter.

[308] For Article 27 of the SCM Agreement, *supra* note 293.

[309] See Preamble of the Marrakesh Agreement Establishing the World Trade Organization.

[310] *Gasoline*, *supra* note 32, p. 16.

text of a treaty was considered to be *clear*, or *sufficiently clear*.[311] Just to give an example in this respect, it could be the *Conditions of Admission* (1948) case. As it was shown in Chap. 4, in this case despite an admission that the conditions were exhaustive because the 'natural' or 'ordinary' meaning of the terms of the treaty revealed the real intention of the parties, the ICJ adopted in parallel a teleological and contextualist approach. It interpreted Article 4 of the Charter in the light of its 'object and purpose' and in the context of the Charter, as a whole.[312] As admitted in the scholarship, the 'ordinary meaning' of the terms can only be assessed in the *context*. And the term 'context' involves the entire article at issue and the remainder of the treaty, its text, preamble and any annexes, as also the other means mentioned in paragraphs 2 and 3 of Article 31 of the VCLT.[313]

Furthermore, by upholding the Panel's finding that the clause in Article 27.4 is mandatory,[314] and 'a conclusion that this clause was not susceptible of application by a panel would be inconsistent with the principle of effective treaty interpretation',[315] the Appellate Body appears to promote in *Brazil Aircraft* rather a restrictive interpretation of this provision. It actually fails to provide further inquiry into the context and in the light of the Preamble of the GATT/WTO Agreement as to whether export subsidies under Article 27.4 of the SCM Agreement are inconsistent with the 'development needs' of a developing country member, here Brazil.[316] Therefore, it could be concluded that the Appellate Body's failure to obtain proper guidance *from the object and purpose of the WTO Agreement as a whole* under the basic rule of interpretation mandated by Article 31 of the VCLT resulted in a deviation from its holistic understanding.[317]

---

[311]See examples of cases where the ICJ stated that the text of the provision at issue is *clear*, and adopted the teleological method of interpretation in addition to the textualist method, e.g., the *Case of S.S. Wimbledon*, PCIJ, Ser. A, No. 1, 1923; *Corfu Channel (U.K. and N. Ir. v. Alb.)*, (Preliminary Objection), 1948, I.C.J; *Ambatielos Case (Greece v. U.K.)*, 1953 I.C.J. (Merits: Obligation to Arbitrate); *Temple of Preah Vihear (Cambodia v. Thailand)*, 1961, I.C.J. (Preliminary Objections); *Aegean Sea Continental Shelf (Greece v. Turk.)*, 1978 I.C.J.

[312]*Conditions of Admission of a State to Membership in the United Nations (Article 4 of the Charter)*, *supra* note 54, p. 62.

[313]Villiger (2009), pp. 434–436. See discussion on this point in Chap. 3 of this book.

[314]Notably, that a developing country Member 'shall eliminate [its export subsidies] within a period shorter than that provided for in this paragraph when the use of such export subsidies is inconsistent with its development needs'.

[315]See the Panel's report of this case, at para 7.89. The Panel justified this approach stating that it 'is an inquiry of a peculiarly economic and political nature, and notably ill-suited to review by a panel whose function is fundamentally legal', moreover as 'the SCM Agreement provides panels with no guidance with respect to the criteria to be applied in performing this examination'.

[316]*Brazil Aircraft* (1999), para 140. It is to be noted that Brazil defended itself invoking (at para 7.37, in Panel's report) that the PROEX measure was an attempt of Brazil to reduce the disadvantage 'as a result of the differences in interest rates between developed and developing countries ... especially when government financial institutions were involved'.

[317]However later, in the Second Recourse made by Canada in 2001 (*Brasil-Export Financing Programme for Aircraft*, Second Recourse by Canada to Article 21.5 of the DSB, WT/DS46/RW/2, 26 July 2001), the Panel was able to correct the decision, this time in favour of Brazil. It

## 6.4 Conclusions

The criticism advanced by McDougal on the ILC's final draft of the Vienna Convention, that the textualist approach relies on artificial, hierarchical distinctions between primary and secondary sources of interpretation, helps in starting to draw the conclusions on the above comparative case analysis.[318] According to McDougal, the established hierarchical distinctions between certain primary means of interpretation, described as 'a general rule of interpretation' and 'certain allegedly supplementary means of interpretation', as well as 'the predominant emphasis which the Vienna Convention ascribed to the text of the treaty',[319] are rigidities and restrictions, which 'have never in the past been international law' and 'cannot successfully be made international law in the future if adopted in the Convention'.[320]

The comparison between the WTO and ICJ approaches of interpretation based on the general rules of treaty interpretation provided in this chapter and Chap. 4 could show that, similarly to the ICJ, the WTO adjudicative bodies have generally tended to value all the rules and methods of treaty interpretation, whether admitting them explicitly or implicitly or displaying an emphasis on one of the rules/methods or another. Despite the specificity and nature of the treaties the WTO and ICJ are called to interpret, the criterion of analysis given by the interpretative treatment of the text of treaties (difficulties encountered in the construction of the language of treaty provisions), and the general methodology of treaty interpretation enables a comparative analysis between these two different adjudicative bodies. Although far from being exhaustive, the case law analyses presented in this chapter support the argument that the WTO adjudicative bodies, generally, use *patterns* of reasoning that resemble those of the ICJ when applying the general rules/methods and principles of interpretation to solve treaty interpretation difficulties (e.g., insufficient clarity, ambiguity, obscurity, inconsistency, vagueness or silence in the text). The analyses also show that the ICJ's treaty interpretative practice could have very well played an influential role upon the practice of the GATT/WTO on treaty interpretation prior to and after the 1969 VCLT's adoption periods.

---

concluded that Canada had failed to establish that PROEX III mandated that the Brazilian government conferred a "benefit" on producers of regional aircraft, and that there was no prohibited export subsidy and no violation of Article 3.1(a) and 27.4 of the SCM Agreement so that the Brazil's measures were not inconsistent with these GATT/WTO provisions and the object and purpose of the GATT/WTO Agreement.

[318] McDougal (1968), pp. 1021–1023.

[319] *Id.* McDougal specifies that '[a]mong the primary means a predominant emphasis is ascribed to the text of the treaty, which is to be interpreted in accordance with the ordinary meaning to be given to the terms . . .' The author adds that these rules (as presented in the former Articles 27 and 28, which correspond to the actual Articles 31 and 32 of the VCLT), 'should not be made international law in the future even if we possessed the omnipotence so to make them'.

[320] *Id.*

However, the majority of the case analyses presented here in this author's opinion could also suggest that the WTO adjudicative bodies display rather an emphasis on the textualist approach/method than on others. Thus, the frequent resort to dictionary definitions in order to elucidate the meanings of the terms at issue appears to project the idea, similarly to the ICJ, that the 'text' of the treaty is the reasonable starting point of the interpretative act and it should be first explored by virtue of the 'ordinary meaning' rule because the text is the presumed manifestation of the authentic and common intention of the treaty's framers. Also, it appears to be the constant intention of (panels and) the Appellate Body to remind and clarify for the parties in the dispute that *the WTO Agreement* is an international written agreement, similar to a contract, based on the *pacta sunt servanda* customary principle and that, according to this principle, the contracting parties are bound to fulfil in good faith the obligations assumed by them under the WTO Agreement; thus, this treaty must be respected (by the parties) as it stands. However strong this emphasis appears to be displayed, the case analyses in this chapter can show that, actually, panels and the Appellate Body do not, overall, qualify the textualist approach as dominant. Just as in the case of the ICJ, this argument could be refuted by all those instances where, for example, the Appellate Body has similarly stressed a greater emphasis on other interpretative rules, such as the 'context of the treaty'(the treaty taken as a whole); 'intention'; 'good faith'[321]; 'object and purpose'[322] or, at times, an emphasis on the 'supplementary means'; the principle of effectiveness or the evolutive interpretation,[323] while equally qualifying the 'text'.

Thus, the case analyses show that the overall attitude of the WTO to treaty interpretation conveys the message that *interpretation must give meaning and effect to all the terms of a treaty*, as the fundamental rule under Article 31(1)(2) of the VCLT demands.[324] However, it does not necessarily imply that the other means of interpretation under Articles 31, 32 or 33 of the VCLT have a negligible interpretative value. As it has been shown in Chaps. 4, 5 and this chapter, similarly to the ICJ and ECtHR, the GATT/WTO panels (even prior to the adoption of the VCLT) and the Appellate Body have consistently stated, directly or indirectly, explicitly or implicitly, that each of these customary rules has its own interpretative value and weight, depending on the circumstances that require their application, as each matters and has relevance in rendering a proper interpretation. By appraising to each rule or principle its own weight and place, generally imprinting a *holistic* character to interpretation similarly to the ICJ, the WTO adjudicative bodies reach the level of objectivity required for an interpretation to be in conformity with the

[321]See *EC – Computer Equipment*, *supra* note 241.

[322]E.g. *Gasoline*, *supra* note 32; *US – Shrimp/Turtle*, *supra* note 114; *Korea – Dairy*, *supra* note 162.

[323]*Japan – Alcoholic Beverages II*, *supra* note 186.

[324]E.g. *Korea – Dairy*, *supra* note 162. This corollary was best expressed in the *Gasoline* case, under the: 'basic international law rule of treaty interpretation . . .' that is 'the terms of a treaty are to be given their ordinary meaning, in context, so as to effectuate its object and purpose . . .'

VCLT's established methodology of interpretation under Article 3.2 of the DSU. In addition, the viewpoint which the WTO seems to promote in respect of its general approach to interpretation of the *WTO Agreement* is that there is a constant interplay between the customary rules/principles of treaty interpretation and the special WTO doctrines/rules/principles.

Similarly to the ICJ, it can also be observed that panels and the Appellate Body do not always spell out the rule or principle they resort to in their interpretative act, many times applying them implicitly/tacitly (by suggesting). However, even panels before the inception of the WTO in 1995, and panels and the Appellate Body after it, have tended to resort with *consistency* (explicitly or implicitly) and *in patterns* to more than one method, and so to more than one customary rule in a dispute, irrespective of whether a text provision was declared *clear* and, in general, irrespective of the difficulties encountered on the text construction of the GATT/ WTO Agreement provisions. The ICJ case law analyses in Chap. 4 have shown that such an approach, which I termed 'overbuilding', has been commonplace also for the ICJ in its practice on treaty interpretation.

In addition, differences in the patterns of treaty interpretation between the ICJ and WTO dispute settlement bodies are also to be observed in regard to their application of the general rules of treaty interpretation. Especially, in respect of the 'supplementary means' of interpretation, the case law analyses presented in this chapter can show that the WTO adjudicative bodies tend to resort to, and rely on, 'supplementary means', but with less vigour than the ICJ. This attitude could be explained by the fact that, overall, the WTO regime appears to promote rather a dynamic or evolutive interpretation, based on the actual 'text', and predominantly in the light of the object and purpose (teleological interpretation) of the WTO Agreement. Such an approach implies rather taking into consideration the international law's developments (in interpreting the WTO Agreement) than the WTO Agreement's negotiating history.[325] In this interpretative picture, it is important not to ignore the relevance of the principle of effectiveness and its impact on the interpretation of the WTO Agreement provisions. The cases analysed in this chapter can clearly show the valuable function that this interpretative principle has in the guidance of the WTO adjudicative bodies towards an interpretation that realises the aims of the GATT/WTO Agreement.

Returning to McDougal's view on the basic, generally, admitted rule of treaty interpretation, it can be argued that the practice of the WTO adjudicative bodies suggests that the customary rules reflected in Article 31(1) of the VCLT constitute

[325] An approach which also could be seen in the ICJ's practice, e.g, *Namibia (Legal Consequences)*, Advisory Opinion (1971) I.C.J. Rep., p. 31; *Aegean Sea Continental Shelf Case (Greece v. Turkey)*, 1978 I.C.J., p. 34. The ICJ preferred to take in such cases an 'evolutive interpretation' approach, in the light of the relevant international law's development and the object and purpose of the treaty at issue.

the logical guideline for commencing the act of interpretation and that the 'ordinary meaning' so much emphasised is not at all (and should not be) an 'inexorable command foreclosing further inquiry'.[326] Thus, the repeated emphasis of the WTO adjudicative bodies on the 'text' (textualist approach) appears to indicate that the 'text' is the manifested intention of the parties that should be considered first, but further *needs* to be inquired into and confirmed. The analyses on cases can show that panels and the Appellate Body have applied the customary rules of interpretation in a holistic, unitary exercise, not mechanically subdivided into rigid components.

Furthermore, the case law analysis in this chapter offers the possibility to reach additional conclusions. The VCLT rules of interpretation appear as necessary tools in clarifying the meaning of the WTO provisions, particularly in revealing the specific inherent normative element of their construction. Then it could be said that the reliance of panels (even before the adoption of the WTO) and the Appellate Body on the specific (trade) rules or doctrines would not be sufficient since they tend to resolve only the normative problems inherent to the GATT/WTO Agreements' provisions. Thus, in principle, such special rules/doctrines address (as in the case of the human rights context) a different analytical level (normative) than that strictly related to the legal reasoning and procedural level to which the act of interpretation refers by virtue of the general rules of treaty interpretation. In addition, similarly to the ECtHR, also the WTO adjudicative bodies appear to perceive the Vienna rules of interpretation as flexible, permissible since they can be adapted to the special context of the WTO trade regime. Thus, the Vienna rules appear as necessary since they assist in the interpretation and clarification of the WTO covered agreements, complementing and not substituting the WTO's special doctrines and rules used in the clarification of the trade covered agreements.[327]

However, there could also be instances[328] when panels or the Appellate Body fail to obtain further guidance in the interpretation of the provisions at issue from the 'object and purpose' of the WTO Agreement, as also from the context of this treaty as a whole, and not only from the preamble of a particular agreement. The bodies perform in this way rather a restrictive, 'ordinary meaning' (textualist), or dictionary-based interpretation. An instance, such as *Brazil Aircraft*, is presented in this chapter to illustrate (just as in the case of the ECtHR) that the WTO's interpretative approaches do not always go in one direction. It refutes an absolute claim that the WTO always complies with the customary rules of interpretation when clarifying the WTO's Agreements by virtue of Article 3.2 of the DSU. Since the international trade regime deals with conflicting interests of the states involved in trade relations, and the attempt of the WTO regime to adjust other various conflicting interests that may collide with the economic ones, inconsistencies in the interpretation of the WTO Agreements may appear unavoidable. And those deviations from the general

[326] Statement of Professor McDougal (1968), pp. 1021–1023.

[327] Which rather addresses a different normative level, respectively how economic law ought to be.

[328] *Brazil Aircraft*, *supra* note 289.

standard of treaty interpretation, as the *Brazil Aircraft* case illustrates, inasmuch as such deviations cannot be ignored, if occurring frequently, they may have an impact on the coherence/unity of international law.[329] However, such instance/s, clearly, cannot 'prove' either that the WTO dispute settlement regime tends to go in the other direction—that of deviating from general international law. And this is so because the number of such cases appears statistically insignificant compared with the cases where the WTO applied the customary rules of treaty interpretation with consistency. Another reason could be because the WTO, after delivering a decision, appears in general to be able to correct a deviation, such as that seen in the *Brazil Aircraft* case discussed in this chapter,[330] as also to balance the WTO's normative goals of its economic system. In addition, the analysis provided in this chapter shows that a relation between (the practice on treaty interpretation of) the ICJ and WTO exists, and it clearly indicates that the WTO is not an isolated, 'self-contained regime' that functions independently of international law.[331] That the WTO dispute settlement practice appears to be highly influenced by the ICJ's long experience on treaty interpretation,[332] and, generally, by the ICJ's practice on international law,[333] can

[329]See also, e.g., the *EC-Biotechnical Products* (2006) and *Beef Hormones* (1998) cases (briefly discussed in Chap. 3 of this book) as illustrations of deviation from general international law and limitation of the use of the 'systemic integration' principle reflected in Article 31(3)(c) of the VCLT.

[330]For example, when the WTO returned to the *Brazil Aircraft* case, in the Second Recourse by Canada (*Brazil-Export Financing Programme for Aircraft*, Second Recourse by Canada to Article 21.5 of the DSB, WT/DS46/RW/2, 26 July 2001), the Panel was able to correct the decision.

[331]Also in relation with other international regime(s)—realising the so-called cross-fertilization.

[332]See examples of cases in which the WTO makes an express reference to the ICJ such as: *US Shrimp/Turtle*, *Japan Beverages II* cases, or *Gasoline*, where the WTO emphasised the relation between trade and international law, stating that 'the General Agreement is not to be read in clinical isolation from public international law'.

[333]It should be recalled that there are more cases than those strictly related to *treaty interpretation* matter in which the Panels and the Appellate Body refer directly to PCIJ/ICJ case law (or to other international judicial bodies) in order to resolve questions of trade law. Notably, these bodies refer to substantive aspects of *international law* that have, at best, been applied as part of the interpretation and application of trade rules. For example: the Appellate Body Report in *EC Measures Concerning Meat and Meat Products* (*Hormones*), (*EC – Hormones*) WT/DS26/AB/R, WT/DS48/AB/R, (AB-1997-4), 16 January 1998, DSR 1998: I, 135; 1998 WL 25520 (W.T.O.), at paras 123–165, and footnotes 93 and 154—for references to the ICJ's *Case Concerning the Gabcikovo-Nagymaros Project (Hungary/Slovakia)* (1997)—when establishing the level of recognition of the precautionary principle in international law, respectively to the ICJ's *Nuclear Tests Case (Australia v. France)* (1974), and to the PCIJ's *Access of Polish War Vessels to the Port of Danzig* (1931) case, among other relevant international arbitral bodies cases, in establishing the acceptance in international law of the interpretative principle: *in dubio mitius*, among the 'supplementary means of interpretation'; Appellate Body Report in *Canada-Measures Affecting the Export of Civilian Aircraft (Canada – Aircraft)*, 2 August 1999, WT/DS70/AB/R, DSR 1999: III, 1377 (1999 WL 591866 (W.T.O.)), at para 202—for reference to the PCIJ/ICJ practice in determining the meaning of authority of an international judicial body to include drawing inferences from States actions and inactions; Panel Report in *United States-Section 211 Omnibus Appropriation Act of 1998 (US – Section 211 Appropriations Act)*, WT/DS176/R, submitted 6 August 2001, paras 8.79 and subseq., and footnote 122—for direct reference to the ICJ practice, specifically to the *Corfu Channel Case and Territorial Dispute Case (Libyan Arab Jamahiriya v. Chad)* (1994)—for

be better evidenced by the Appellate Body's resort to the ICJ's precedents. On matter of treaty interpretation, the WTO (in particular, the Appellate Body) appears to resort to the ICJ's jurisprudence, especially when it needs to confirm or to strengthen a certain interpretative aspect and when it deals with difficult or non-routine issues of treaty interpretation. Moreover, the relationship between the WTO trade regime and international law can also be strongly evidenced by those cases analysed in this chapter, in which the WTO adjudicative bodies resorted to 'any relevant rules of international law applicable in the relations between the parties' as reflected in Article 31(3)(c) of the VCLT.[334] Actually, the relationship between international law and international trade law could not be underestimated since, after all, '[t]rade is to be found at the origin of entire segments of public international law, and it accounts for one of its main sources: *the treaty*',[335] as the former general director of the WTO, Pascal Lamy, eloquently and memorably stated.

---

establishing the principle of effective treaty interpretation (Latin: *ut res magis valeat quam pereat*) in a dispute related to the conformity of trademark registration in national law with the obligations assumed under WTO and other multilateral treaties; Report of the Panel in *Guatemala-Definitive Anti-Dumping Measures on Grey Portland Cement from Mexico (Guatemala – Cement I)*, WT/DS60/R, circulated 24 October 2000, at para 6.386, and FN 372—for reference, *inter-alia*, to the ICJ case law (Appeal relating to the jurisdiction of the *ICOA Council (India v. Pakistan)* (1972) I.C.J. 46 (18 August) (Separate Opinion of Judge Dillard)—when establishing the large recognition in international law of the principle of "harmless error" applicable in the *Guatemala* case; Panel Report in *Korea-Measures Affecting Government Procurement (Korea – Procurement)*, WT/DS163/R, circulated 1 May 2000, adopted 19 June 2000, DSR 2000:VIII, 3541, 2000 WL 559176 (W.T.O.), at para 7.123—for reference to the PCIJ *(Legal Status of Eastern Greenland)* (1933) and ICJ *(Temple of Preah Vihear)* (1962) practice in developing the concept of "error" in respect to a treaty, in customary international law; Panel Report in *United States Countervailing Measures Concerning Certain Products from the European Communities (US – Countervailing Measures on Certain EC Products)*, WT/DS212/R (July 2002), para 7.124, and FN 380—for reference to ICJ *Brazilian Loans*, PCIJ, Series A, Nos. 20/21, p. 124 cited in *Elettronica Sicula S.p.A. (ELSI)*, Judgment, ICJ Reports 1989, p. 47, para 62—for examination of case law of *municipal courts*, when the determination of a question of municipal law appear before an international Court; Panel Report in *China – Measures Related to the Exportation of Various Raw Materials (China – Raw Materials)*, 5 July 2011, WT/DS394/R, WT/DS395/R, WT/DS398/R, at pp. 111–112—for reference to the PCIJ case law for establishing the principle of state sovereignty in international law; Panel Report in *United States – Certain Measures Affecting Imports of Poultry from China*, WT/DS392/R, 29 September 2010, at p. 109; 2010 WL 3835614 (W.T.O.), at p. 126—for reference to the PCIJ: *Certain German Interests in Polish Upper Silesia*, (PCIJ, 1926, Rep., Series A, No. 7, p. 19)—in order to establish that for international courts 'municipal law is to be approached as a "factual issue"'. See also e.g. Lindroos and Mehling (2005)—for a discussion related to the WTO's resort to substantive aspects of international law. These authors observe that 'several panels and the Appellate Body have applied rules and principles of general international law, such as representation, legal interest, *compétence de la compétence*, burden of proof, the treatment of municipal law, acceptability of amicus *curiae briefs*, *lex specialis*, and the authority to draw adverse inferences, and judicial economy, all of which are by nature procedural rules. Finally, in the area of general international law, the judicial bodies of the WTO have also referred to the rules of state responsibility.'

[334]See e.g. *US – Shrimp/Turtle, EC-Poultry, Gasoline* discussed in this chapter.

[335]Lamy (2006), p. 969.

In summary, the ICJ's practice on treaty interpretation appears to draw upon the WTO's economic thinking in its decisions, as Lennard has envisaged, clearly playing an important role in cementing the relationship between *trade law* and *general international law*.[336] It could be concluded that the application with consistency by the WTO of the general rules of interpretation in interpreting its covered agreements in patterns resembling those of the ICJ, as well as the use by this specialised adjudicative body of the ICJ's precedents on treaty interpretation, constitute tools that work against the fragmentation of international law. Since the WTO has emerged out of necessity in the context of the expansion of international law that must respond to the needs of an increasingly diversified and constantly changing world, it could be admitted that this regime, through its adjudicative practice, has gained its own place and legitimacy in the international legal order.

## References


Babu, R. R. (2010). Interpretation of the WTO agreements, democratic legitimacy and developing nations. *Indian Journal of International Law, 50*, 45–83.

Beckford, D. S. (2008). *Power and judicial activism in the WTO: The Appellate Body's interpretation of trade remedy agreements*. Saarbrücken, Germany: VDM Publishing.

Bermann, G. A., Goebel, R. J., Davey, W. J., & Fox, E. M. (2002). *Cases and materials on European Union law, American casebook series*. St. Paul, MN: West Group.

Bjorge, E. (2014). *The evolutionary interpreation of treaties*. Oxford University Press.

Brownlie, I. (1998). *Principles of public international law*. Oxford, England: Clarendon Press.

Cameron, J., & Gray, K. R. (2001). Principles of international law in the WTO dispute settlement body. *International and Comparative Law Quarterly, 50*(2), 248–298.

Costa, L. A. P., & Ruda, J. M. (1985). *Derecho Internacional Público*. Buenos Aires: Tipográfica Editora Argentina.

de Arechaga, J. (1978). International law in the past third of a century. *Recueil Des Cours, 159*(9), 64–67.

Devaney, J. G. (2016). *Fact-finding before the international court of justice*. Cambridge, England: Cambridge University Press.

Fitzmaurice, G. G. (1951). Law and procedure of the International Court of Justice: Treaty interpretation and certain other treaty points. *British Year Book of International Law, 28*, 1.

Fitzmaurice, G. G. (1957). Law and procedure of the International Court of Justice 1951-4: Treaty interpretation and other treaty points. *British Year Book of International Law, 33*, 203.

Fitzmaurice, M., & Merkouris, M. (2010). Canons of treaty interpretation: Selected case studies from the World Trade Organization and the North American Free Trade Agreement. In *Treaty interpretation and the Vienna Convention on the Law of Treaties: 30 years on* (pp. 153–238). Leiden, The Netherlands: Brill.

Gardiner, R. K. (2008). *Treaty interpretation*. New York: Oxford University Press.

Gruszczynski, L. (2012). Customary rules of interpretation in the practice of WTO dispute settlement bodies. In A. Nollkaemper & K. O. Fauchald (Eds.), *The practice of international and national courts and (de) fragmentation of international law*. Oxford, England: Hart Publishing.

Harris, D. J. (1991). *Cases and materials on international law*. Sweet and Maxwell Publishers.


[336] Lennard (2002).

Hudson, M. O. (1936). *La Cour permanente de Justice internationale – Traité*. Paris: Ed. Pédone.
International Law Commission. (2006). *Fragmentation of international law: Difficulties arising from the diversification and expansion of international law*. Geneva, Switzerland: United Nations.
Jackson, J. H. (1998). Fragmentation or unification among international institutions: The World Trade Organization. *New York University Journal of International Law and Politics, 31*, 823.
Jackson, J. H. (2006). *Sovereignty, the WTO, and changing fundamentals of international law* (Vol. 18). Cambridge, England: Cambridge University Press.
Jennings, M. (2004). The World Trade Organization and international law. Mapping the Relationship between WTO and other fields of international law. In *A.N.Z.S.I.L. conference*.
Jennings, R., & Watts, A. (1992). *Oppenheim's international law (Vol. 1): Peace* (9th ed.). Longman Higher Education, Longman Group UK Ltd.
Kelly, J. P. (2002). Judicial activism at the World Trade Organization: Developing principles of self-restraint. *Northwestern Journal of International Law & Business, 22*, 353–388.
Kelly, J. P. (2005). The seduction of the Appellate Body: Shrimp/sea turtle I and II and the proper role of states in WTO governance. *Cornell International Law Journal, 38*, 459–491.
Kelly, J. P. (2008). International law and the shrinking space for politics in developing countries. In *Law and rights: Global perspectives on constitutionalism and governance*. Vandeplas Publishing. Widener Law School Legal Studies Research Paper No. 08-31. https://papers.ssrn.com/sol3/papers.cfm?abstract_id=1104694.
Kuyper, P. J. (1994). The law of GATT as a special field of international law: Ignorance, further refinement or self-contained system of international law? *Netherlands Yearbook of International Law, 25*, 227–257.
Lamy, P. (2006). The place of the WTO and its law in the international legal order. *European Journal of International Law, 17*(5), 969–984.
Lennard, M. (2002). Navigating by the stars: Interpreting the WTO agreements. *Journal of International Economic Law, 5*(1), 17–89.
Lindroos, A., & Mehling, M. (2005). Dispelling the chimera of 'self-contained regimes' international law and the WTO. *European Journal of International Law, 16*(5), 857–877.
Marceau, G. (2006). The WTO is not a closed box. *Proceedings of the Annual Meeting, American Society of International Law, 100*, 29–31.
Mavroidis, P. C. (2008). No outsourcing of law? WTO law as practiced by WTO courts. *American Journal of International Law, 102*, 421–474.
McDougal, M. S. (1968). Statement of Professor Myres S McDougal, United States delegation, to the Committee of the Whole, April 19, 1968. *American Journal of International Law, 62*, 1021.
McInerney, C. P. (2009). From shrimps and dolphins to retreaded tyres: An overview of the World Trade Organization disputes, discussing exceptions to trading rules. *New York International Law Review, 22*, 153–158.
McNair, B. A. D. M. (1961). *The law of treaties*. Oxford, England: Clarendon Press.
McRae, D. (2004). What is the future of WTO dispute settlement? *Journal of International Economic Law, 7*(1), 3–21.
Mercurio, B. C., & Tyagi, M. (2010). Treaty interpretation in WTO dispute settlement: The outstanding question of the legality of local working requirements. *Minnesota Journal of International Law, 19*(2), 275–326.
Merrills, J. G. (2005). *International dispute settlement*. Cambridge, England: Cambridge University Press.
Mitchell, A. D. (2007). The legal basis for using principles in WTO disputes. *Journal of International Economic Law, 10*(4), 795–835.
Mortenson, J. D. (2013). Is the Vienna Convention hostile to drafting history? *American Journal of International Law, 107*, 780.
Panitchpakdi, S. (2006). The WTO at ten: Building on ten years of achievements. In G. Sacerdoti, A. Yanovich, & J. Bohanes (Eds.), *The WTO at ten: The contribution of the dispute settlement system*. Cambridge University Press.

Pauwelyn, J. (2003). *Conflict of norms in public international law: How WTO law relates to other rules of international law* (Vol. 29). Cambridge, England: Cambridge University Press.
Petersmann, E. U. (2004). Ten years of the WTO dispute settlement system: Past, present and future. *Journal of International Law and Policy, 3*, 1–48.
Sheeran, S. (2014). The relationship of international human rights and general international law; hermeneutic constraint, or pushing the boundaries? In S. Sheeran & N. Rodley (Eds.), *Routledge handbook of international human rights law*. London: Routledge.
Simma, B., & Pulkowski, D. (2006). Of planets and the universe: Self-contained regimes in international law. *European Journal of International Law, 17*(3), 483–529.
Sinclair, I. M. (1984). *The Vienna Convention on the Law of Treaties*. Manchester, England: Manchester University Press.
Smith, F. (2010, November). *Treaty interpretation in the WTO: Beyond the Vienna Convention on the Law of Treaties*. Public International Law Discussion Group/University of Oxford
The Structure of WTO. Retrieved from http://www2.econ.iastate.edu/classes/econ355/choi/wtoworks.htm
The WTO guide: "Understanding the WTO". Retrieved from http://www.wto.org
Trachtman, J. P. (1999). Domain of WTO dispute resolution. *Harvard International Law Journal, 40*, 333.
Trumble, W. R., & Stevenson, A. (Eds.). (2002). *Shorter Oxford English Dictionary: On historical principles*. Oxford, England: Oxford University Press.
Van Damme, I. (2009). *Treaty interpretation by the WTO Appellate Body*. Oxford, England: Oxford University Press.
Van Damme, I. (2010). Treaty interpretation by the WTO Appellate Body. *European Journal of International Law, 21*(3), 605–648.
Villiger, M. E. (2009). *Commentary on the 1969 Vienna Convention on the Law of Treaties*. Leiden, The Netherlands: Brill.
Waldock, H. (1964). Third report on the law of treaties by Sir Humphrey Waldock, Special Rapporteur. *Yearbook of the International Law Commission, 2*, 62–65.

## *Documents*

International Law Commission. (1966). Draft articles on the law of treaties with commentaries. In *Yearbook of the International Law Commission* (Vol. 2).
Vienna Convention on the Law of Treaties, opened for signature May 23, 1969, 1155 UNTS 331, available at http://untreaty.un.org/ilc/texts/instruments/english/conventions/1_1_1969.pdf.

# Chapter 7
# Conclusions

The process of adjudication in international law is thought to involve a wide range of activities and institutions. Some of the judicial institutions adjudicating treaty disputes have been perceived as 'self-contained regimes' and more politically active than others (especially the WTO, ECtHR and CJEU), promoting judicial activism and thus becoming a potential threat to the global unity and efficacy of the international legal order. This judicial activism of some international courts and tribunals has generated a fear of fragmentation of international law and a wide ongoing debate.[1] However, in order to admit or reject the theoretical proposition advanced in the legal scholarship that the proliferation of international judicial bodies may create chaos in the international legal system, leading to fragmentation of international law,[2] I considered it essential to examine comparatively in this book practices of general (ICJ) and specialised courts (ECtHR and WTO) on the application of *general rules of treaty interpretation of public international law* as reflected in *the 1969 Vienna Convention on the Law of the Treaties*. What I did not purport, however, to provide in this book was an extensive argument/discussion or contribution to the debate related to the fragmentation of international law. My goal was to provide several specific key findings related to the *treaty interpretative trends* of two different international specialised courts, the ECtHR and WTO, compared with the ICJ, as a general international court, and to assess the impact of the two specialised courts' practices on treaty interpretation upon international law.

[1] See Chap. 2 of this book.

[2] *Id.*



L.E. Popa, *Patterns of Treaty Interpretation as Anti-Fragmentation Tools*,
DOI 10.1007/978-3-319-65488-1_7

## 7.1 Consistency in Interpretative Practices

Specifically, this work set out to respond to the question of whether the general rules and methods of treaty interpretation applied by the ICJ, as an international court of universal character and general jurisdiction, are applied in a similar fashion by the ECtHR and WTO in their special context (human rights and trade), respectively, whether these two specialised courts, when confronted with similar difficulties of interpreting the text of treaties (e.g., insufficient, doubtful, ambiguous, vague or silent), solve these difficulties in patterns resembling those of the ICJ. In this connection, one of the statements of the former judge and president of the ICJ, Gilbert Guillaume, deserves attention. Guillaume expressed the concern that fragmentation of international law might occur as a result of the proliferation of international judicial forums. He suggests that, due to the proliferation of autonomous jurisdictions, it is 'necessary to investigate the extent to which each court or tribunal makes use of precedent that other courts and tribunals create'[3] and that the judges 'must inform themselves more fully of the case-law developed by their colleagues, conduct more sustained relationships with other courts and, in a word, engage in constant inter-judicial dialogue' to avoid fragmentation in international law.[4] Thus, a first conclusion that emerges from the empirical analysis provided in Chaps. 4–6 of this book is that the ECtHR and WTO (Appellate Body) make use of the ICJ's precedents in respect of the application of the customary rules of treaty interpretation as reflected in the 1969 VCLT; thus, these specialised courts appear influenced by the ICJ's practice and experience in treaty interpretation.

Further, it is known that, by virtue of Article 3.2 of the DSU, the WTO clearly establishes the methodology of interpretation based on the 1969 VCLT applicable to the GATT/WTO Agreements. Yet, despite the fact that the ECtHR has no similar provision or guidance in its core treaty, the case analyses in Chap. 5 show that the ECtHR has indeed developed its practice of *treaty interpretation* in reliance upon customary rules and principles of interpretation used by the ICJ and codified in the VCLT. In this regard, it is important to mention that the ECtHR relied on these rules even before the entry into force of the VCLT, and the *Golder* case is one of the cases that evidence this aspect, however, most strongly.[5] *Golder* explicitly attests to the recognition of the 'customary' nature of the rules of interpretation by the ECtHR. However, *Golder* was not an isolated case in which the Strasbourg Court acknowledged the application of the customary rules of treaty interpretation since the ECtHR already applied with consistency these rules long before the *Golder* case analogously to the ICJ (in *similar patterns*) when dealing with similar difficulties of

[3]Guillaume (2011), pp. 7 and 23. In the author's view, such utilisation of the precedent is a guarantor of certainty and foreseeability in the application of law by any dispute settlement system, and plays an important role in 'the organisation of a decentralised jurisdictional system, such as the one existing in international law'.

[4]Guillaume (2000).

[5]The ECtHR often referred to *Golder* in other cases.

interpreting the text of treaty. Thus, the ECtHR was aligning its treaty interpretative practice with that of the ICJ, and so did the WTO. The further frequent reference of the ECtHR to *Golder* in other cases decided by the Strasbourg Court also attests to its use of the customary rules of interpretation after the codification of these rules in the 1969 VCLT. *Golder* taken singularly and also other cases often invoked by the ECTHR in its interpretative practice, nevertheless, support and expand those theories that admit the adherence and application by the ECtHR of the Vienna rules of interpretation into its special context. The same can be said about the *Gasoline* case or other important cases referred to by the WTO in many of its following cases on treaty interpretation.

The case analyses provided in the empirical part of this book show furthermore that the influence of the ICJ upon the ECtHR's human rights interpretation could be perceived even when the ECtHR has not made a direct reference to the ICJ's practice,[6] and despite the general preference of the ECtHR to rely on its own judgments as precedents. The ECtHR case analyses in Chap. 5 indicate that this Court has shaped its own path of interpretation of the European Convention on Human Rights by adopting the general rules of treaty interpretation into its *lex specialis* context (ECHR), in addition to those that it has itself developed as 'doctrines' and techniques of human rights interpretation. Also, even if an express resort to the customary rules (by explicitly describing them as such) is not always visible in the ECtHR's practice on treaty interpretation,[7] nevertheless, this Court appears to resort to such rules implicitly, and with consistency, in the traditional fashion of application of the canons of interpretation, mainly developed by the PCIJ/ICJ. Arguably, this implicit resort to customary rules could be reflected in the ECtHR's desire to develop a flexible approach of interpretation so, at least, as to avoid the problem characterised by Lauterpacht as follows: '[t]he absence of an agreed rule is a greater evil than the adoption of a rule which is perhaps not as good as the one which could have been adopted'.[8] Moreover, such resort to customary rules of interpretation points directly to the *unity of international law*; it attests to the recognition of human rights as merely part of international law system and thus of the international legal order.

In respect of the GATT/WTO interpretative practice, the case analyses in Chap. 6 show that the WTO panels and the Appellate Body approach the VCLT rules of interpretation with greater vigour than the ECtHR, frequently providing detailed explicative models of treaty interpretation.[9] However, just as in the case of

[6]See Chap. 5 of the book. A direct reference to the ICJ practice (although scarcely in the ECtHR's practice), could be seen, e.g., in the *Case of Mamatkulov* and *Askarov v. Turkey*, *Case of Stoll v. Switze*rland.

[7]Prior to the VCLT entered into force, e.g., the *Vagrancy* case, and also after it, see, e.g., the *Catan* case (Chap. 5 of this book).

[8]Lauterpacht (1955), p. 24.

[9]See Crawford (2014). As observed by Crawford, the WTO is admitted as 'one of the most influential users of the VCLT on matter of treaty interpretation'. Crawford's main argument is that conflicts between general and specific norms of international law 'may be prevented, and a workable compromise reached'.

the ECtHR, the resort by GATT (panels) to the customary rules of interpretation was evident even before the adoption of the VCLT in 1969, and before the DSU adopted Article 3.2 (1995) as the interpretative guide for the GATT/WTO Agreements. The case analyses also show that when confronted with difficulties of treaty interpretation, the GATT/WTO's adjudicative bodies found within the ICJ's authoritative forum a rich source of inspiration, displaying it more frequently than the ECtHR and successfully adapting the ICJ's findings on treaty interpretation difficulties to the interpretation involved in trade disputes.[10] Furthermore, even before the adoption of the 1969 VCLT, the GATT's patterns of approaching the customary rules, methods and principles of treaty interpretation appear to resemble those applied by the ICJ. But in particular, the WTO's Appellate Body appears to display a clear resort to the ICJ's techniques and practice when it feels the need to reiterate and strengthen aspects regarding the interpretative value and effectiveness of the customary rules in interpreting the GATT/WTO Trade Agreements, especially when dealing with unclear, vague, obscure or ambiguous formulation in this treaty's language. This aspect, clearly, points toward enhancing the effective operation of the general rules of international law in the WTO's special context and, consequently, toward keeping the coherence and unity of international law.

In addition, the case analyses in Chaps. 5 and 6, which provide approaches adopted by the ECtHR and WTO based on the VCLT's customary rules of interpretation, help in expanding and generalising the theory of the application by the international specialised judicial bodies of the universal methodology of treaty interpretation (Articles 31–33 of the VCLT). Also, the empirical analysis of this book (Chaps. 4–6) evidences that, similar to the ICJ, the ECtHR and the GATT/WTO's adjudicative bodies show predilection to approach *holistically* the treaties they are called to interpret. It signifies that these courts adopt in a given case more than one interpretative rules and methods in combination (either stating them directly, or indirectly, in *similar patterns*), in their quest to give full meaning and effect to the provisions at issue. This aspect implies that both the ECtHR and WTO tend to employ, in addition to the general rule/s and method/s they declare (or suggest that they adopt) as sufficient for interpretation, other general rules and methods of interpretation in the course of the judgment, just as the ICJ usually does, a process which I termed: 'overbuilding'. Once employed by the courts, all the general rules and methods have admittedly different weight, some as to ascertain/determine, others just as to confirm/verify a meaning already reached, but, nevertheless, an equal interpretative value since they all proved to matter and have relevance in reaching a final interpretation in any given case.[11] Thus, perceived as flexible, permissible and necessary, these customary rules of treaty interpretation (codified in the VCLT), applied in both human rights and trade adjudication regimes, come to assist in clarifying the meaning of their treaty provisions,

[10]See Chap. 6 of this book, in, e.g., *US-Shrimp* (WTO, 1998); *Japan-Alcoholic Beverages* (WTO, 1996); *Korea – Dairy Products* (WTO, 1999) cases.

[11]Even if some of rules only confirm the result found initially on other method/s and rules' basis.

particularly in revealing that specific inherent normative element of their construction. These customary rules clearly complement and not substitute the human rights and, respectively, the trade special (autonomous) doctrines/rules that the ECtHR and WTO developed. In other words, the special doctrines/rules of interpretation, developed by both human rights and trade courts, address a normative analytical level that is different than that strictly related to the act of legal reasoning in the procedural interpretation of treaties performed by virtue of the general rules of interpretation. These general rules only instruct judges as to *how technically they should argue to arrive at a conclusion about the meaning of the interpreted provision.*[12] The case law analyses provided in the empirical part of this book evidence that the general rules of interpretation of treaties (Vienna rules) are procedural/methodological means, used by the ECtHR, WTO and ICJ as guidelines and so as rules of construction that help judges to analyse and determine the internal structure of a treaty text (the conventional meanings of the terms used in the treaty), in the quest to ascertain the intention of the treaty's drafters (parties) that they had at the time of concluding it.

However, what appears to differentiate more evidently the ICJ's from the ECtHR's and WTO's resort to the same general rule of treaty interpretation is in principle the use of the 'supplementary means'. While the ICJ, generally, appears to rely more on this determinative and confirmatory tool, especially on the *travaux preparatoire* in interpreting treaties, both the ECtHR and the WTO tend to rely on, and promote, rather a *dynamic* or *evolutive interpretation*, in the light of the 'object and purpose' of their treaties and the present-day conditions, however with a different emphasis. Thus, the case analyses in the empirical part of the book can clearly show that, despite the ECtHR's and WTO's overall imprint of a *holistic* character to interpretation, similar to the ICJ, these specialised courts' interpretative approaches vary also in respect of the emphasis they put on the teleological method. The ECtHR, for example, shows more evidently than the WTO an emphasis on the teleological approach due to the specific nature of the Convention it interprets (the ECHR). In particular, the non-reciprocal nature of human rights, and the idea that their meaning is influenced by changes in beliefs and evolution in the field of human rights knowledge, compels the ECtHR to promote a strong teleological approach.[13] However, the case analyses in Chap. 5 can show that the adjustment of the meaning of human rights to the present-day circumstances is usually performed by the ECtHR with the belief in *the moral objectivity and universality of human rights.* In this context, the resort to the *travaux preparatoire*, which is also a means of interpretation used by the ECtHR, but not with the weight given by the ICJ, nevertheless indicates the desire of the ECtHR to interpret the Convention in accordance with the ECHR drafters' intention.[14]

[12]See on this aspect, e.g., Linderfalk (2007).

[13]See discussion on this point in Chap. 5 of this book, e.g., Fitzmaurice (2013).

[14]See on this aspect Letsas (2010), p. 267. As observed by Letsas, an approach which adapts the meaning of human rights to contemporary circumstances could not contradict the abstract belief of

Another interpretative similarity between the ECtHR, WTO and ICJ, perceived in the cases analysed in this book, is indicated by the fact that all these three adjudicative regimes (irrespective of the specific treaties they interpret) have overall approached the general rules and principles of interpretation with *consistency*, both prior to and after the VCLT's adoption. It can then be admitted that a *coherency* at the micro-level within each of the courts analysed exists in respect of the application of customary rules of treaty interpretation. Indeed, it could be admitted that the ECtHR and WTO specialised regimes have also had a contribution on the formation and crystallisation of these rules as *customary*. A reference of the international judicial bodies to principles and maxims/canons of interpretation, even long before the adoption of the Vienna Convention, is to be found, for example, in the commentaries of the 1966 Draft Articles on the Law of Treaties.[15]

## 7.2 Deviation in Interpretative Practices

As it has been shown in Chaps. 5 and 6, on occasion, the ECtHR has taken different stances and deviated from its own practice of application of the VCLT customary rules of interpretation (e.g., *Bankovic*, *Stoll*), as has the GATT/WTO (e.g., *Brazil Aircraft*).[16] The examples of cases of deviation I used and analysed in the book are to be taken and regarded not as 'samples' that illustrate the frequency of deviations in the practice of the ECtHR and WTO but as *analytic generalisations*. As it was mentioned in the introduction of this book, according to Yin's theory, the purpose of a *case study* is 'to expand and generalise theories (analytic generalisation) and not to enumerate frequencies (statistical generalisation)'.[17] So even if overall such examples do not appear to constitute a pattern of deviation from the standard of interpretation provided by the VCLT in these courts' practice, they could not be ignored. Such deviations can show that the Law of Treaties (VCLT) has been at times disregarded.

The mentioned case examples indicate that both the ECtHR and WTO can deviate from the standard of interpretation provided by the VCLT, thus, arguably, weakening the authority of that standard. For example, the ECtHR's *Bankovic* or *Stoll* case can show, on the one hand, a deviation from its own practice of

the drafters in the moral objectivity and universality of human rights, since they intended 'to protect the *fundamental* rights that people are entitled to'.

[15]Draft Articles on the Law of Treaties with commentaries (1966), p. 200.

[16]See Chap. 6 of this book, e.g., the *Brazil Aircraft* case.

[17]Yin (2003), p. 11. According to Yin: 'case studies like experiments are generalisable to theoretical propositions and not to populations of universes. In this sense, the case study, like experiment, does not represent a "sample", and in doing a case study [the] goal will be to expand and generalise theories (analytic generalisation) and not to enumerate frequencies (statistical generalisation)'.

interpretation of the Convention as a 'living instrument', in the light of the present-day conditions.[18] On the other hand, these cases show a clear deviation from the standard of interpretation of a treaty, required by Article 31(1)(2) of the VCLT. According to this standard, when interpreting a treaty, *an interpreter must give full meaning and effect to all the terms of the treaty* (text, context, object and purpose), thus taking the treaty as a *whole*.[19] So this fundamental principle of interpretation[20] implies that an interpreter (e.g., court, tribunal) should take into account, together with the *text*, also the *context*, *object and purpose* and *context of the whole treaty* and not restrict the rights and obligations of the treaty under interpretation, by overlooking such standard. As it was clearly explained by Fitzmaurice and Merkouris, the treaty must be taken 'as a *whole* and each of its provisions must be taken as intended to achieve some end'[21] and that the essence of interpretation is that 'no part of a treaty can be interpreted out of context'.[22] In consequence, as the authors aptly point out, 'an interpretation that would make the text ineffective to achieve its object is ... suspect'.[23] An analogous deviation from this interpretative standard could also be illustrated at the WTO, in the *Brazil Aircraft* case analysed in Chap. 6. The analysis of this case, likewise the cases of deviation mentioned at the ECtHR, can evidence rather a *restrictive interpretation* that the WTO (similarly to the ECtHR) adopted, mainly based on the textualist method (terms of the provision at issue interpreted in their ordinary meaning in the context in which they occur). As it was shown, an interpretation could be restrictive when it is mainly based on the 'plain' and 'ordinary meaning' rule, with the exclusion of other rules, in principle of the 'object and purpose', 'good faith' and 'context of the treaty as a whole', which support the 'intention' element. Such cases could show that restrictive interpretations (accounting to rather a grammatical interpretation), which render treaties ineffective, as also changes in the interpretation of the same provision/s of a treaty (in different cases), present the danger of developing greater variations in a specialised court's application of the general rules of interpretation and, consequently,

---

[18] See *Bankovic* and *Stoll* cases analysed in Chap. 5 of this book, or *Al-Adsani* in respect of the application of Article 31(3)(c) VCLT- as illustration of a deviation from substantive (international) law.

[19] Which also implies resort to the *travaux preparatoire*. See discussion on this aspect in Chap. 3 of the book.

[20] It is regarded as the effectiveness principle. See on this important aspect Fitzmaurice and Merkouris (2010).

[21] Fitzmaurice and Merkouris (2010), p. 155 (emphasis added).

[22] *Id*, the rest of comments remain. The authors note that 'treaties are to be interpreted as a whole, and particular parts, chapters or sections also as a whole' (it was regarded as *the principle of integration*).

[23] *Id*. The authors admit that according to the effectiveness principle—*ut res magis valeat quam pereat*—, treaties must be 'interpreted with reference to their declared or apparent object and purpose, and particular provisions are to be interpreted as to give fullest effect consistent with the normal sense of the words and with other parts of the text, in such a way that a reason and meaning are to be attributed to every part of the text'. See also Sir Fitzmaurice (1957) for a discussion on the principles of treaty interpretation.

variations in their *lex specialis*' application.[24] More evident in this sense at the ECtHR is the situation whereby the same provision (e.g., Article 1 of the ECHR) has been the subject of numerous different interpretations (at different times).[25] Thus, the case analyses in Chap. 5 can show that ECtHR appears to display two trends in its practice of interpreting the European Convention. Overall, this Court has interpreted a treaty provision by circumscribing the application of the 'margin of appreciation', favouring the individual *vis-à-vis* the respondent state.[26] And at other times, the ECtHR has refused to do so, granting too wide a 'margin of appreciation' to governments,[27] limiting therefore the individual rights and freedoms provided by the Convention. Such instances of deviation from the VCLT's general standard of interpretation could indicate that the consistency in the application of the general rules and principles of treaty interpretation is affected and that a degree of 'fragmentation' (at the methodological/procedural level) admittedly occurs in the practice of the ECtHR and WTO. Thus, because such level of 'fragmentation' is perceived as a matter of the fragmentation of the interpretation of international law norms (customary rules of interpretation),[28] it could, arguably, be seen as potentially having an impact on the coherence and unity of general international law when occuring frequently. As it was mentioned in Chap. 2 of this book, many authors admit that *consistency* in the case law, which supposes correct interpretations of norms and application of principles, is what gives *coherence* to international law. And this *coherence* could be admitted as being more or less a counterbalance to any process of fragmentation in international law.[29] It follows that a uniform application of general international law principles by all the adjudicative bodies is at the core of the *unity* of international law.[30] Although both the ECtHR and WTO appear as institutions that generally avoid deviance from the customary rules of treaty interpretation, the fact that such deviation does occur sometimes makes the jurisprudence emanating from these courts somehow

[24]See Chaps. 5 and 6 of this book.

[25]See e.g. Article 1 of the European Convention of Human Rights (discussed in Chap. 5 of this book), entitled: 'Obligations to respect Human Rights', or Article XX of the WTO Agreement (discussed in Chap. 6 of this book), entitled 'General Exceptions', in particular paragraph (g).

[26]E.g. *Loizidou, Catan, Golder, Lawless, Mamatkulov* (Chap. 5 of this book).

[27]E.g. *Bankovic, Stoll, Witold* (Chap. 5 of this book).

[28]See also other examples, e.g., *Al Adsani* (2001), *EC-Biotechnical Products* (2006), *Beef Hormones* (1998) which show a deviation from general international law rules (under 'systemic integration' reflected in Article 31(3)(c) VCLT) (Chap. 3 of this book).

[29]See e.g. Wellens (2003), Abi-Saab (1998), Pauwelyn and Salles (2009), Charney et al. (2002), Letsas (2012). According to Letsas (at p. 23) the ECtHR must be *consistent* with itself in applying the Convention's rights, which implies that this Court simply 'cannot rely on one principle to decide a case and then offend that very same principle to decide the next case'.

[30]See Chap. 2 of this book for more on this argument, authors, e.g., John Finnis, Jean-Marie Dupuy, Jonathan I. Charney, George Abi-Saab, Sang Wook Daniel Han, etc.

unpredictable.[31] As it has been shown in the empirical part of this book, a deviation from the VCLT's standard of interpretation could end up not just as a deviation from general international law alone[32] but also as a deviation from the *lex specialis* provided by the European Convention of Human Rights and WTO Agreements, respectively.[33] However, this deviation from *lex specialis* as a result of the application of the general rules of interpretation, both in respect of the ECtHR and WTO, reveals even more the role and the value that the VCLT customary rules should have as guidelines for specialised regimes to interpret their *lex specialis* properly.

Thus, despite a clear adherence and reliance of the ECtHR and WTO on the universal methodology of interpretation, cases such as *Bankovic*, *Stoll* or *Brazil Aircraft* can show, arguably, that the customary rules of interpretation are not always applied with consistency.[34] Such divergences reveal the dark side of the interpretative process at both the ECtHR and WTO, respectively, the occurrence of a degree of deviation (at micro-level) from the interpretative standard mandated by the VCLT. While such examples of deviation cannot be ignored, they could not, on the other hand, 'prove' either that these courts go, or tend to go, in the other direction, notably that of deviation from the customary rules of interpretation of public international law. In principle, what the case analyses provided in Chaps. 5 and 6 can clearly show is that these courts do not always go in one direction. But, certainly, they do not predominantly deviate from the standard of treaty interpretation provided by the VCLT.[35] And this is evidenced by the fact that, usually, after delivering a case that deviates from the universally admitted standard of interpretation, these specialised courts tend to 'return' then to a path that is more in line with that standard.[36] Therefore, because such deviations are not frequent, and the ECtHR and WTO adjudicative bodies show that they are able to 'correct' an approach that deviates from that standard of interpretation when in other further cases they encounter the same issue/s of interpretation, it can be assumed that such deviations *cannot link closely enough to the fragmentation of international law so as to affect*

[31] Although inconsistencies in approaches to interpretation on the same issue exist, it is less likely that such deviations become a pattern in these courts' practice.

[32] See also those examples of deviation in international law by application of Article 31(3)(c) of the VCLT, such as *Al Adsani* (2001) at the ECtHR, or *EC-Biotechnical Products* (2006) and *Beef Hormones* (1998) at the WTO.

[33] E.g., the *Stoll*, *Brazil Aircraft* cases.

[34] See also *Al Adsani* (2001), *EC-Biotechnical Products* (2006), and *Beef Hormones* (1998).

[35] The number of such cases, both at the ECtHR and WTO appears statistically insignificant in relation to the cases in which these courts apply the customary rules of treaty interpretation with consistency.

[36] See, e.g., the recent cases: *Catan*, or *Al-Skeini* at the ECtHR as to the issue of 'jurisdiction' under Article 1 of the ECHR (Chap. 5), where the Court applies the exception to the principle that jurisdiction under Article 1 is limited to a State's own territory, a different approach than in *Bankovic*. Also in regard to the *Brazil Aircraft* case (discussed in Chap. 6) at the WTO, later, in the Second Recourse by Canada (*Brazil-Export Financing Programme for Aircraft*, Second Recourse by Canada to Article 21.5 of the DSB, WT/DS46/RW/2, 26 July 2001), the panel corrected the decision in favour of Brazil.

*it fundamentally*. In particular, as it has been shown also in this book both empirically and theoretically, the practices of the ECtHR and WTO *are not outside the framework of general international law, since these regimes clearly take into account the rules of international law* (customary law and general principles of law recognised by civilised nations), generally, conforming to them.[37] Moreover, these regimes *are not outside the framework of general international law*, even if their special context (the human rights and trade) requires an adaptation of *general law* (the general methodology of interpretation) to their own *lex specialis*' application.

## 7.3 Treaty Interpretation as a Tool for Harmonisation?

The case analyses in the empirical part of this study can show in addition that the VCLT's general rule of interpretation appears to be clearly received by the ECtHR and WTO into their special context as a guideline that complements their autonomous means of interpretation. Since the VCLT provides guiding principles also for interpreting special treaties, conventions and agreements (such as the ECHR and WTO Agreements), it can be stated that these interpretative means/guidelines, by being applied to special contexts, clearly contribute to preserving the general rules and principles of international law, as also to expanding their role and perception. Moreover, the comparative perspective offered in Chaps. 5 and 6 shows that, in general, the ICJ's practice does not appear to be losing its importance and central place as the authority in matters of treaty interpretation, even if its jurisprudence is not frequently and/or expressly invoked by these specialised courts, especially by the ECtHR. This perspective indicates that the ECtHR and WTO, overall, respond to the question of treaty interpretation by reconciling the normative requirements of their respective Convention/Agreements with the requirements of general international law. These specialised bodies' relationship with international law is reinforced also by their resort, although not with great frequency, to Article 31(3)(c) of the VCLT, which provides a tool for harmonisation between *lex specialis* and

[37]See for this discussion (Chaps. 5 and 6 of this book), e.g., International Law Commission Report (2006). In brief, the ILC admits (at p. 85) the compliance, in general, of treaty bodies in human rights (such as the European and Inter-American Courts), and also in trade (WTO panels and the Appellate Body) with rules and principles of general international law (relating to, e.g., treaty interpretation, statehood, jurisdiction, immunity, as well as a wide variety of principles of procedural propriety). See also in this regard: Koskenniemi (2004), Simma and Pulkowski (2006), or Charney (1998a, b). Generally, both the ECtHR and WTO are admitted in the scholarship as specialised regimes that do not lose track of one another, creating norms which may be in conflict with norms emanating from other specialised regimes (, i.e., norms emanating from the WTO take into account environmental rules, or the ECtHR sometimes invoke the practice of the IACHR, or of the ICTY's).

*lex generalis*, and a way to integrate human rights practice and, respectively, trade, into general international law.

Since the ECtHR[38] and the WTO adjudicative bodies resort to the VCLT's rules of interpretation, this fact provides in itself a way to relate to international law,[39] and it, nevertheless, constitutes evidence that these specialised bodies are not promoting 'self-contained' regimes. To the contrary, their practices appear overall as tools of maintaining a coherent international law. By giving, in general, a *holistic* approach to interpretation and reading their *lex specialis* pursuant to Article 31(3)(c), thus in the context of other rules/norms within the international law system, and also keeping account of precedents (legal practice) or past uses of the law,[40] both the ECtHR and WTO adjudicative bodies, moreover, enhance their authority and legitimacy. Therefore, at the present time, the common language of the VCLT's general methodology of treaty interpretation which the human rights and trade regimes use, and the source of inspiration provided by the ICJ's developed treaty interpretation methodology can all attest to holding a clear connection of these regimes with international law. These aspects allow these regimes' practice to integrate better into the wider system of international law. So the ECtHR's and WTO's practices on treaty interpretation are nonetheless part of the broader body of decisions based on international law, which are authoritative.[41] As correctly observed by Sheeran, the relationship of 'special regimes', such as human rights and trade, with general international law is conceived as *one of unity* and is *not one characterized by fragmentation*.[42] Thus, since the special regimes' implementation and their very existence depends on general international law, it results that all general and special regimes are undeniably part of a *unified system of law*.[43]

Nevertheless, like a painting needs light and shadow, some 'deviations' of the ECtHR and WTO from their own practice (of treaty interpretation) could be seen, at most, as those *shadows* that reveal much of the shape and extension of international law in the human rights and trade's environments. So such deviations can be seen as heightening not only how international law *should* be properly applied by the two specialised courts in their own (special) context but also the limits of their application of the *lex specialis*—the treaties—due to their partial incompleteness, in

[38]However, the ECtHR makes an express reference to the ICJ less than the WTO, but this reference to the ICJ is increasingly, as, for example, Judge Higgins observes (see Chap. 2 of this book, the concept of 'self-contained regime').

[39]More than the ECtHR, the WTO adjudicative bodies tend to emphasize the application of customary rules of treaty interpretation in their disputes, given the express demand of Article 3.2 of the DSU as the guideline for interpretating the GATT/WTO Agreements.

[40]Such an approach is explained in the scholarship through notions as *legal history of the community; interpretative community* (the existence of an already assumed interpretation on a text, what other authoritative interpreters have held similar texts to mean); or 'common standard justifications'.

[41]See for such argument, e.g., Charney (1998a, b), p. 705.

[42]Sheeran (2013), p. 82.

[43]*Id.*

relationship with general international law. However, as the cases of deviation mentioned in this book can also show, such deviations do not appear merely as errors resulting from a misunderstanding or misinterpretation of the meaning and role of the rules and principles of treaty interpretation, but as a matter of policy that these courts sometimes choose to adopt.[44]

As recognised in the scholarship, the ICJ is a leading court with vast experience in matters of treaty interpretation. It is also known that the ICJ has mostly contributed to the development and clarification of the rules and principles of international law.[45] Thus, in respect of the ECtHR and WTO, the cases analysed in the empirical part of the book show the ICJ as clearly having an influence upon the human rights and economic thinking, respectively, of these specialised courts, realising a bond between these regimes and general international law. What Judge Guillaume suggested then as being of crucial importance for 'fragmentation' not to happen was the use by each court or tribunal of the precedent of other courts or tribunals.[46] He recommended, moreover, the use of the ICJ's advisory opinions to avoid fragmentation, as also *the creation of a dialogue among judicial bodies*.[47] Then *the use of the ICJ's precedents* of treaty interpretation by both the ECtHR and WTO, and equally important the use of *common patterns of interpretation* as were identified in these bodies' practices analysed in this book, can constitute therefore an important aspect that contributes to impeding international law to fragment.

As a secondary matter, Judge Guillaume suggested, for example, that there must be consideration 'as in domestic law of the methods followed by each of the judicial and arbitration bodies in the use of its own precedent'[48] in order to provide consistency in case law and avoid fragmentation. The case analyses in Chaps. 4–6 can illustrate that such consideration of the methods followed by the ICJ, ECtHR and WTO in the use of their own precedents (past decisions) appears also to be respected by these courts in their interpretative practices. So these courts' frequent resort to their own precedents constitutes, in addition, an important aspect in keeping the *coherence* of international law. By frequently invoking certain past decisions,[49] these adjudicative bodies (general: the ICJ, specialised: ECtHR and WTO), generally, decide in a way that is consistent with the methods and rules of interpretation they adopted in those invoked decisions, reducing therefore the risk of deviating from the standard of treaty interpretation and, consequently, from the *lex specialis* (in the case of the ECtHR and the WTO).

[44]See for this opinion, e.g., Koskenniemi (2007).

[45]Lauterpacht (1982), p. 282.

[46]Guillaume (2011).

[47]*Id.*

[48]*Id.*

[49]The frequent use by the courts (ECtHR and WTO) of some of their leading cases, such *as Golder, Loizidou, Mamatkulov* at the EctHR; or *Gasoline, US-Shrimp/Turtle, Japan Alcoholic Beverages II* at the WTO, indicate the tendency of these courts to rely on their own precedents.

## 7.4 Treaty Interpretation and the Fragmentation of International Law? Broader Dimensions

Chapters 2 and 3 of this book have shown that, since the proliferation and elaboration of highly detailed treaties are admitted by some scholars to be a source of fragmentation of international law, and ultimately of the international legal order, the subject of *treaty interpretation* appears to be at the core of understanding of the dialectic of the *scope and role of international treaties* within the international legal order. Since treaties are the main tool in creating/establishing international and regional institutions, the foremost source of international law, or principal means of establishing relations between states on various matters and interests, which aim is to promote peaceful cooperation among nations, it could be admitted that *treaties play a key role in maintaining the coherence and unity of international law* and controlling the international legal order. From the perspective of the proliferation of judicial bodies/forums and its related 'fragmentation' issue approached *vis-à-vis* the treaty interpretative practice of three different courts, some additional conclusions could be drawn. Keeping in mind the risks that the proliferation of international courts and tribunals poses, the evidence provided by the activity of the ECtHR and WTO forums shows that they are more beneficial than harmful,[50] given the multitude of disputes before them in which claimants were able to obtain and seek peaceful resolution of their disputes.

A question that undoubtedly arises out of the 'proliferation' phenomenon discussion[51] is whether there was a true 'legal order' before the recognition of individuals' rights. For example, before the Second World War, an individual's basic and inalienable human rights were not recognised as such. So the individual was not a subject of international law, and there was no mechanism for ensuring human rights protection.[52] By taking the example of human rights that were not developed at the time when the PCIJ was functioning or, indeed, when the ICJ began its judicial activities, the expansion of human rights and the mechanisms of enforcing and protecting them have fully shown their importance. Thus, human rights have become emblematic to the contemporary international legal order. As the case analyses at the ECtHR (Chap. 5) can evidence from the perspective of human rights, most international political issues today involve an aspect of human rights.[53]

---

[50]For the idea that proliferation of disputes settlement bodies is beneficial for international law, see (in Chap. 2 of this book), e.g., Boyle (1997), Han (2006), Charney et al. (2002), Pauwelyn and Salles (2009), Spelliscy (2001), Kingsbury (1998), Abi-Saab (1998).

[51]See detail on this subject in Chap. 2 of this book.

[52]Lauterpacht (1950), p. 61.

[53]As is for example: the right: to life, liberty, to a fair trial, to privacy; freedom of: speech, thought, education, conscience and religion; use of torture; when states crack down on dissent; clandestine mass data-collection/surveillance on internet; terrorism, etc.

It is to be recalled that the practice of the human rights mechanisms for dispute settlement can function in terms of human rights and not in terms of general international law,[54] which, naturally, could not suffice in solving human rights matters. Nevertheless, while the membership in European institutions has expanded proportionally with the need for regional human rights protection, which is unquestioned in Europe, concern about enforcing uniform human rights standard is indeed expressed in scholarship.[55] In this regard, the ECtHR struggles to achieve, as it stated, 'common European standard' based upon domestic law and practice, other international or European instruments and the Court's own case law.[56] By following such an approach, as it is argued in the scholarship, the active and influential European Court of Human Rights has proved to contribute to the development of judicial settlement and international law, moving the world with an important step toward peace.[57]

In essence, international human rights must frequently respond to *threats to human dignity* associated with modern markets and authoritarian states that become universal across the globe.[58] Given this, the scholarship admits that functional universality of human rights depends on the *effectiveness of human rights mechanisms* to provide attractive remedies for some of the most pressing systemic threats to human dignity.[59] The ECtHR case law analysis in Chap. 5 of this book could illustrate the variety of such threats to human dignity that this Court has been called upon to resolve. Although not always consistent with itself in respect of the Convention's interpretation, the overall position of the ECtHR has been to protect the rights and freedoms of different individuals or group of individuals, thus enhancing its *legitimacy*. It could be stated that the ECtHR's *activity is part of a more general struggle towards achieving consensus in human rights practice and thinking*, by shedding more light on the purpose of that list of rights (the ECHR), which Donnelly concisely captured as reflecting a society's understanding of the principal '*standard threats*' *to human dignity*.[60]

Indeed, in the matter of trade, it is well known that the GATT/WTO emerged out of necessity generated by the horrors of war, in the aftermath of the World War II, with the scope of expanding the trade in goods and services, to raise standards of living around the globe and to prevent and eliminate the causes of war. Also, like human rights, the WTO multilateral agreements appear to be susceptible to democratic changes, struggling to achieve universality through their move towards identical trade structures and rules. Suffice it to mention here that at the centre of the present-day political economy stands the idea of expanding the scope and

[54]See more on this aspect Khrebtukova (2008).

[55]Shelton (2003), p. 95.

[56]*Id.*

[57]Carter (1999), p. 319.

[58]Donnelly (2013), p. 97.

[59]*Id.*

[60]*Id.*

powers of the WTO and that almost any issue can now be related to trade, which the WTO lawmaking process may cover.[61] Furthermore, WTO rules are invoked occasionally and are applied by various international judicial bodies such as the CJEU, NAFTA, EFTA, the Andean, Caribbean, and Central American Courts of Justice, 'MERCOSUR' Permanent Court of Review, the Economic Court of the Commonwealth of Independent States ('CIS' Court) or various regional economic courts in Africa.[62] Also, the Law of the Sea Convention includes explicit reference to GATT rules,[63] and vice versa, the LOS Convention rules may be relevant for the interpretation of various WTO exceptions.[64] Such arguments can show that the WTO dispute settlement is viewed not in isolation from the broader international system of dispute settlement regimes since the trade regime forum is part and belongs to it.[65] Moreover, the WTO is considered a pillar of the multilateral world trading system, having a unique role in the global economic stability.[66]

However, an international legal system could arguably not function properly without all the range of mechanisms capable to resolve an increasing multitude of different issues and disputes resulting from a dynamic world community.[67] In fact, as it is widely admitted by scholars, the diversification of international mechanisms for dispute settlement resolution appears as an answer to the overwhelming changes occurring in the international community, since they have emerged out of necessity and to better accommodate the myriad of interests in the post-war era of the international legal order. So multiplication and diversification of international law (e.g., human rights law, trade law, criminal aw, environmental law, humanitarian law, maritime law), as also of adjudicative mechanisms, could only be seen as necessary for the development of the body of international law and international legal system.

Therefore, it could be stated that general international law, in the context of proliferation and diversification of international law bodies, is more alive than ever since it is applied and tested in different (special) law contexts, and it often serves

[61]Patomäki (2008), p. 222. The author clearly captures this phenomenon as an existing struggle over which treaties should prevail in any given context, notably, whether the norms of human rights should prevail over the rules and principles of the WTO.

[62]Petersmann (2006), p. 273.

[63]This reference is to be found in the Annex Relating to the Implementation of Part XI of the Convention (UNCLOS), in Section 6 concerning Production Policy, which provides: '(b) The provisions of the General Agreement on Tariffs and Trade, its relevant codes and successor or superseding agreements shall apply with respect to activities in the Area.'

[64]*Id.*

[65]Jackson (2006), p. 87.

[66]Understanding WTO: A unique contribution, paper available at: http://www.wto.org/english/thewto_e/whatis_e/tif_e/disp1_e.htm (last visited May, 2012).

[67]Consequently, the international legal system should absorb all kind of issues, in the forms of disputes between States, individual and State, interpretation of treaties/agreements, states responsibility; prosecution of individuals for wars, genocide, or crimes against humanity; international trade disputes and others. See on this argument, e.g., Han (2006), Rao (2003), Charney et al. (2002).

for clarifying and filling gaps in *lex specialis*.[68] Moreover, the interplay between *lex specialis* and *lex generalis* implies a normative and procedural diversification of international law that comes as a necessity to respond to the constant socio-economic and political changes of a dynamic world. It follows that the substantive and procedural divergences that the 'proliferation' phenomenon generates should be seen, however, as shaping even more the movement toward an evolution and development of international law, in general. As any other system or phenomenon, also general international law could be seen as governed by the law of physics that functions on the dynamics of 'contraries' ('opposites', 'contrary'/'opposing qualities', 'opposing tendencies') as inherent features that contribute to its development. In addition, as one thing is changing around to another, general international law clearly functions in relation to other 'systems' of law. So it could similarly be said for the special law (sub-)systems, such as that of the ECtHR and WTO, that they exist and function in relation to general international law system, and also to other (sub-)systems of law (e.g., environmental, maritime, criminal). As it is argued in the scholarship, for example, that though the interplay and checks and balance between the human rights and trade fields remain highly exceptional in practice, the link between them clearly exists.[69] At least, since fundamental rights warrant in many ways support for freedom of economic players, or protecting from undue government intervention, human rights therefore interplay with the trade field.[70] However, a relation between human rights and trade is also reflected in a number of free trade agreements, bilateral or regional, in the explicit clauses introduced within them concerning, for example, transparency, good governance or anti-corruption, which point out in the human rights direction.[71]

Furthermore, the case analyses of the present work can show that, since the ICJ appears to draw upon the ECtHR's human rights and WTO's trade thinking, it helps in keeping a balance between these different law (sub-)systems. One can admit that if the ICJ, ECtHR, and WTO adopt the same general treaty interpretative methodology, which is applied in *similar patterns*, and a dialogue between them exists (exchanges of views between the ICJ and ECtHR; between the ICJ and WTO), then these human rights and trade regimes do not exist as *sub-systems*.[72] It follows that the notion of *sub-system* could be admitted, actually, as being used as an analytical theoretical concept (tool) that does, or does not, have any link with reality and is discussed by scholars as to differentiate and compare various perceived trends derived from patchy observations of international law. So as any analytical concept

[68]See more on the argument that specialised regimes relate to international law, e.g., Simma and Pulkowski (2006), ILC Report (2006), Lamy (2006), Cameron and Gray (2001), Marceau (2006).

[69]Cottier et al. (2005), p. 5.

[70]*Id.*

[71]Jackson (2006). Also, the Law of the Sea Convention includes explicit reference to GATT rules, and vice-versa, as the LOS Convention rules may be relevant for the interpretation of various WTO exceptions.

[72]See in this respect, e.g., Klabbers (2010), p. 31.

with loose links with reality, the utility of the notion of *sub-system* could, arguably, be questioned. In sum, because international judicial forums emerge out of *necessity* and *specialism*, the changes in the structure of the body of international law brought by such specialised forums should be viewed not just as a diversification but more as a 'maturisation' of international law, which must adapt to an evolving world community, or, as concisely expressed by the ILC, a necessary form of 'experimentation in the collective struggle to find the best rule to serve the international community as a whole'.[73]

The focus of this book was to determine whether *common patterns of treaty interpretation* emerge in the practice of the ICJ and two of the most prolific specialised courts, the ECtHR and WTO, and the implication of this aspect *vis–àvis* international law. As the analysis provided in this book has shown, the two specialised courts apply similarly the VCLT universal methodology of treaty interpretation, in patterns resembling those developed by the ICJ. Analysing critically and comparatively decisions of the ECtHR, WTO and ICJ, it was concluded that such *common patterns of interpretation function as anti-fragmentation (of international law) tools*. Therefore, the analysis provided in this book contributes to expanding the general theory on treaty interpretation topic and supports the view of those scholars who argue that proliferation of international judicial forums does not lead to fragmentation of international law. However, since difficulties that may arise from multiplication and diversification of international judicial forums manifest in many ways, the 'fragmentation' versus 'unity' of international law remains inevitably an open subject. It invites further empirical investigation into other matters of international law, on different levels (either at the same international courts or others), and from different perspectives, which could confirm the findings of this work and offer much-needed insights into the strengths and weaknesses of the theories on 'fragmentation'/'unification' of international law.

## References

Abi-Saab, G. (1998). Fragmentation or unification: Some concluding remarks. *New York University Journal of International Law and Politics, 31*, 919.

Boyle, A. E. (1997). Dispute settlement and the law of the sea convention: Problems of fragmentation and jurisdiction. *International and Comparative Law Quarterly, 46*(1), 37–54.

Cameron, J., & Gray, K. R. (2001). Principles of international law in the WTO dispute settlement body. *International and Comparative Law Quarterly, 50*(2), 248–298.

Carter, B. E. (1999). International law's contributions to peace, 32 J. Marshall L. Rev. 319 (1999). *The John Marshall Law Review, 32*(2), 4.

Charney, J. I. (1998a). *Is international law threatened by multiple international tribunals?* Dordrecht, The Netherlands: Martinus Nijhoff.

Charney, J. I. (1998b). Impact on the international legal system of the growth of international courts and tribunals. *New York University Journal of International Law and Politics, 31*, 697.

[73]International Law Commission Report (2006), p. 578 (emphasis added).

Charney, J. I., Bilder, R. B., Oxman, B. H., & Wald, P. M. (2002, March). The "horizontal" growth of international courts and tribunals: challenges or opportunities? In *Proceedings of the Annual Meeting* (pp. 369–380). Washington, DC: American Society of International Law.

Cottier, T., Pauwelyn, J., & Bürgi, E. (2005). Linking trade regulation and human rights in international law: An overview. In T. Cottier, J. Pauwelyn, & E. Bürgi (Eds.), *Human rights and international trade* (p. 1). Oxford, England: Oxford University Press.

Crawford, J. (2014). *Chance, order, change: The course of international law, general course on public international law*. Leiden, The Netherlands: Brill.

Donnelly, J. (2013). *Universal human rights in theory and practice*. Ithaca, NY: Cornell University Press.

Fitzmaurice, G. G. (1957). Law and procedure of the International Court of Justice 1951-4: Treaty interpretation and other treaty points. *British Year Book of International Law, 33*, 203.

Fitzmaurice, M. (2013). Interpretation of human rights treaties. In D. Shelton (Ed.), *The Oxford handbook of international human rights law* (pp. 739–772). Oxford University Press. www.oxfordhanbooks.com, https://doi.org/10.1093/law/970199640133.003.0032.

Fitzmaurice, M., & Merkouris, P. (2010). Canons of treaty interpretation: Selected case studies from the World Trade Organization and the North American Free Trade Agreement. In *Treaty interpretation and the Vienna Convention on the Law of Treaties: 30 years on* (pp. 153–238). Leiden, The Netherlands: Brill.

Guillaume, G. (2000). *The proliferation of international judicial bodies: The outlook for the international legal order*. Speech by his excellency Judge Gilbert Guillaume, President of the International Court of Justice, to the Sixth Committee of the General Assembly of the United Nations.

Guillaume, G. (2011). The use of precedent by international judges and arbitrators. *Journal of International Dispute Settlement, 2*(1), 5–23.

Han, S. W. D. (2006). Decentralized proliferation of international judicial bodies. *Journal of Transnational Law & Policy, 16*, 101.

International Law Commission. (1966). Draft articles on the law of treaties with commentaries. In *Yearbook of the International Law Commission* (Vol. 2).

Jackson, J. H. (2006). *Sovereignty, the WTO, and changing fundamentals of international law* (Vol. 18). Cambridge, England: Cambridge University Press.

Khrebtukova, A. (2008). Call to freedom: Towards a philosophy of international law in an era of fragmentation. *Journal of International Law and International Relations, 4*, 51.

Kingsbury, B. (1998). Foreword: Is the proliferation of international courts and tribunals a systemic problem. *New York University Journal of International Law and Politics, 31*, 679.

Klabbers, J. (2010). Virtuous interpretation. In *Treaty interpretation and the Vienna Convention on the Law of Treaties: 30 years on* (pp. 15–38). Leiden, The Netherlands: Brill.

Koskenniemi, M., & Leino, P. (2002). Fragmentation of international law? Postmodern anxieties. *Leiden Journal of International Law, 15*(3), 553–579.

Koskenniemi, M. (2004). *Study on the function and scope of the Lex Specialis Rule and the question of 'Self-Contained Regimes'*. Preliminary report by the Chairman of the Study Group submitted for consideration during the 2004 session of the International Law Commission (unpublished, on file with the author).

Koskenniemi, M. (2007). The fate of public international law: Between technique and politics. *Modern Law Review, 70*(1), 1–30.

Lamy, P. (2006). The place of the WTO and its law in the international legal order. *European Journal of International Law, 17*(5), 969–984.

Lauterpacht, H. (1950). *International law and human rights*. North Haven, CT: Shoe String Press.

Lauterpacht, H. (1955). Codification and development of international law. *American Journal of International Law, 49*, 16.

Lauterpacht, H. (1982). *The development of international law by the international court*. Cambridge, England: Cambridge University Press.

Letsas, G. (2010). Intentionalism and the interpretation of the ECHR. In *Treaty interpretation and the Vienna Convention on the Law of Treaties: 30 years on* (pp. 255–272). Leiden, The Netherlands: Brill.

Letsas, G. (2012). *The ECHR as a living instrument: Its meaning and its legitimacy*. https://papers.ssrn.com/sol3/papers.cfm?abstract_id=2021836.

Linderfalk, U. (2007). *On the interpretation of treaties: The modern international law as expressed in the 1969 Vienna Convention on the law of treaties* (Vol. 83). Springer Science & Business Media.

Marceau, G. (2006). The WTO is not a closed box. *Proceedings of the Annual Meeting, American Society of International Law, 100*, 29–31.

Patomäki, H. (2008). Rethinking Global Democracy/World Parlament: Towards determining what international cosmopolitical law is. In P. Korkman & V. Mäkinen (Eds.), *Studies across disciplines in the humanities and social sciences, vol. 4: Universalism in international law and political philosophy*. Helsinki: Collegium for Advanced Studies.

Pauwelyn, J., & Salles, L. E. (2009). Forum shopping before international tribunals: (Real) concerns, (im)possible solutions. *Cornell International Law Journal, 42*, 77–118.

Petersmann, E. U. (2006). Justice as conflict resolution: Proliferation, fragmentation, and decentralization of dispute settlement in international trade. *University of Pennsylvania Journal of International Economic Law, 27*, 273.

Rao, P. S. (2003). Multiple international judicial forums: A reflection of the growing strength of international law or its fragmentation. *Michigan Journal of International Law, 25*, 929.

Sheeran, S. (2013). The relationship of international human rights and general international law hermeneutic constraint, or pushing the boundaries? In S. Sheeran & N. Rodley (Eds.), *Routledge handbook of international human rights law* (pp. 79–109). London: Routledge.

Shelton, D. (2003). Boundaries of human rights jurisdiction in Europe. *Duke Journal of Comparative & International Law, 13*, 95.

Simma, B., & Pulkowski, D. (2006). Of planets and the universe: Self-contained regimes in international law. *European Journal of International Law, 17*(3), 483–529.

Spelliscy, S. (2001). Proliferation of international tribunals: A chink in the armor. *Columbia Journal of Transnational Law, 40*, 143.

Wellens, K. (2003). Fragmentation of international law and establishing an accountability regime for international organizations: The role of the judiciary in closing the gap. *Michigan Journal of International Law, 25*, 1159.

Yin, R. K. (2003). *Case study research design and methods, Applied social research methods series* (Vol. 5, 3rd ed.). Thousand Oaks, CA: Sage Publications.

## *Document*

International Law Commission, 2006. Fragmentation of international law: Difficulties arising from the diversification and expansion of international law. *Geneva: United Nations*.

# Bibliography


Abi-Saab, G. (1998). Fragmentation or unification: Some concluding remarks. *New York University Journal of International Law and Politics, 31*, 919.

Abi-Saab, G. (2010). The Appellate Body and treaty interpretation. In *Treaty interpretation and the Vienna convention on the law of treaties: 30 years on* (pp. 97–110). Leiden: Brill.

Arangio-Ruiz, G. (1991). *Third report on state responsibility*. New York: United Nations, General Assembly.

Arato, J. (2010). Two perspectives on the rules of treaty interpretation: A review of Richard Gardiner, treaty interpretation. *New York University Journal of International Law and Politics 43*(2).

Arato, J. (2011). *The constitutional transformation of international organizations through treaty interpretation: The ECtHR's use of VCLT 31(3)(c)*. Working Paper. http://papers.ssrn.com/sol3/papers.cfm?abstract_id=1951547

Austin, J. (1995). In W. E. Rumble (Ed.), *The province of jurisprudence determined*. Cambridge: Cambridge University Press.

Bakircioglu, O. (2007). Application of the margin of appreciation doctrine in freedom of expression and public morality cases. *German Law Journal, 8*, 711.

Basch, F. F. (2007). Doctrine of the Inter-American Court of Human Rights regarding states' duty to punish human rights violations and its dangers. *American University International Law Review, 23*, 195.

Bassiouni, M. C. (1996). International crimes: jus cogens and obligatio erga omnes. *Law and Contemporary Problems, 59*, 63.

Baudenbacher, C. (2003). Foreword: Globalization of the judiciary. *Texas International Law Journal, 38*, 397.

Beckett, E. (1950). Comments by Sir E. Beckett. *Annuaire de L'institut de Droit International, 43*, 435.

Bederman, D. J. (2001). Grotius and his followers on treaty construction. *Journal of the History of International Law, 3*(1), 18–37.

Benvenisti, E., & Downs, G. W. (2007). The empire's new clothes: Political economy and the fragmentation of international law. *Stanford Law Review, 60*, 595–631.

Bermann, G. A., Goebel, R. J., Davey, W. J., & Fox, E. M. (2002a). *Cases and materials on European Union law*. Saint Paul: West Group.

Bermann, G. A., Goebel, R. J., Davey, W. J., & Fox, E. M. (2002b). *Cases and materials on European Union law, American casebook series*. Saint Paul: West Group.

Bernhardt, R. (1997). *Encyclopedia of public international law* (Vol. 3). Amsterdam: North Holland Publishing Company.




L.E. Popa, *Patterns of Treaty Interpretation as Anti-Fragmentation Tools*,
DOI 10.1007/978-3-319-65488-1

Bjorge, E. (2014). *The evolutionary interpretation of treaties*. Oxford: Oxford University Press.

Blome, K. (2010). Wallflower or essential constituent? The Inter-American Court of Human Rights' role in an emerging International judicial human rights system. In *SGIR 7th, Pan European international relations conference*.

Boyle, F. A. (1987). Determining US responsibility for contra operations under international law. *American Journal of International Law, 81*(1), 86–93.

Boyle, A. E. (1997). Dispute settlement and the law of the sea convention: Problems of fragmentation and jurisdiction. *International and Comparative Law Quarterly, 46*(1), 37–54.

Brierly, J. L. (1955). *The law of nations: An introduction to the international law of peace*. Oxford: Clarendon Press.

Brown, C. (2002). The proliferation of international courts and tribunals: Finding your way through the maze. *Melbourne Journal of International Law, 3*, 453.

Brownlie, I. (1998). *Principles of public international law*. Oxford: Clarendon Press.

Buergenthal, T. (2001). Proliferation of international courts and tribunals: Is it good or bad? *Leiden Journal of International Law, 14*(2), 267–275.

Buffa, D. G. (2010). Proposed remedy for the dilemma of innumerable futures: Ukraine, Russia, and NATO Membership. *Brooklyn Journal of International Law, 35*, 593.

Cameron, J., & Gray, K. R. (2001). Principles of international law in the WTO dispute settlement body. *International and Comparative Law Quarterly, 50*(2), 248–298.

Cannizzaro, E., & Arsanjani, M. H. (2011). *The law of treaties beyond the Vienna convention*. Oxford: Oxford University Press.

Carozza, P. G. (2008). Human dignity and judicial interpretation of human rights: A reply. *European Journal of International Law, 19*(5), 931–944.

Carozza, P. (2009, January). *Fifty years of the European court of human rights viewed by its fellows international courts, Strasbourg*. Retrieved from http://www.echr.coe.int/NR/rdonlyres/3B662702-FFDB-4187-AAC56B926725DF35/0/30012009PresidentCarozzaSeminar_eng_.pdf

Carter, B. E. (1999). International law's contributions to peace, 32 J. Marshall L. Rev. 319 (1999). *The John Marshall Law Review, 32*(2), 4.

Casanovas, O., & La Rosa, O. C. (2001). *Unity and pluralism in public international law* (Vol. 39). The Hague: Martinus Nijhoff Publishers.

Charney, J. I. (1998a). The impact on the international legal system of the growth of international courts and tribunals. *New York University Journal of International Law and Politics, 31*, 697.

Charney, J. I. (1998b). *Is international law threatened by multiple international tribunals?* Dordrecht: Martinus Nijhoff Publishers.

Charney, J. I., Bilder, R. B., Oxman, B. H., & Wald, P. M. (2002). The "horizontal" growth of international courts and tribunals: Challenges or opportunities? In *Proceedings of the Annual Meeting* (pp. 369–380). Washington, DC: American Society of International Law.

Cho, S. (2006). Defragmenting world trade. *Northwestern Journal of International Law and Business, 27*, 39.

Ciobanu, D. (1991). *Introducere in Studiul Dreptului* [Introduction in the study of law]. Bucuresti: Ed. Hyperion XXI.

Constantinou, C. M. (2005). *Treaty. New York new dictionary of the history of ideas* (Vol. 6). Charles Scribner Publisher. http://works.bepress.com/costas_constantinou/24/

Costa, L. A. P., & Ruda, J. M. (1985). *Derecho Internacional Pu´blico*. Buenos Aires: Tipográfica Editora Argentina.

Cottier, T., Pauwelyn, J., & Bürgi, E. (2005). Linking trade regulation and human rights in international law: An overview. In T. Cottier, J. Pauwelyn, & E. Bürgi (Eds.), *Human rights and international trade* (p. 1). Oxford: Oxford University Press.

Crawford, J. (2014). *Chance, order, change: The course of international law, general course on public international law*. Leiden: Brill.

Curran, V. G. (2001). Fear of formalism: Indications from the fascist period in France and Germany of judicial methodology's impact on substantive law. *Cornell International Law Journal, 35*, 101.

Curtis, C. P. (1949). Better theory of legal interpretation. *Vanderbilt Law Review, 3*, 407.

De Arechaga, J. (1978). International law in the past third of a century. *Recueil Des Cours, 159*(9), 64–67.

De Frouville, O. (2010). Attribution of conduct to the state: Private individuals. In *The law of international responsibility* (pp. 257–280). Oxford: Oxford University Press.

De Vattel, E. (1758). *The law of nations or the principles of natural law*. Washington, DC: Carnegie Institution of Washington.

Desierto, D. A. (2010). Necessity and supplementary means of interpretation of non-precluded measures in bilateral investment treaties. *University of Pennsylvania Journal of International Law, 31*, 827.

Detter, I. (1994). *The international legal order*. Aldershot: Dartmouth.

Devaney, J. G. (2016). *Fact-finding before the International Court of Justice*. Cambridge: Cambridge University Press.

Donnelly, J. (2013). *Universal human rights in theory and practice*. Ithaca, NY: Cornell University Press.

Dupuy, P. M. (1998a). *Droit international public*. Paris: Dalloz.

Dupuy, P. M. (1998b). Danger of fragmentation or unification of the international legal system and the International Court of Justice. *New York University Journal of International Law and Politics, 31*, 791.

Dupuy, P. M. (2007). Unity of application of international law at the global level and the responsibility of judges. *European Journal of Legal Studies, 1*, 29.

Dworkin, R. (1978). *Taking rights seriously* (Vol. 136). Cambridge: Harvard University Press.

Dworkin, R. (2013). A new philosophy for international law. *Philosophy and Public Affairs, 41*(1), 2–30.

Eikema Hommes, H. J. (1978). *Legal order and legal principles*. 1978 Working paper. Retrieved May 5, 2011, from http://biblio.juridicas.unam.mx/libros/1/468/5.pdf

El Sheemy, S. (2007). International law-making, problems of coherence and fragmentation, a summary of the Chatham House International Law discussion group meeting held on 23 March 2007, Chatham House. *Independent thinking on international affairs*. Retrieved from https://www.chathamhouse.org/sites/files/chathamhouse/public/Research/International%20Law/il230307.pdf

Endicott, T. A. O. (2000). *Vagueness in law*. Oxford: Oxford University Press.

Engelen, F. A. (2004). *Interpretation of tax treaties under international law* (Vol. 7). Amsterdam: IBFD.

Falk, R. A. (1967). On treaty interpretation and the New Haven approach: Achievements and prospects. *Virginia Journal of International Law, 8*, 323.

Finnis, J. (1992). Natural law theory. In R. P. George (Ed.), *Contemporary essays*. Oxford: Clarendon Press.

Fish, S. E. (1980). *Is there a text in this class? The authority of interpretive communities*. Cambridge: Harvard University Press.

Fitzmaurice, G. G. (1957). Law and procedure of the International Court of Justice 1951–1954: Treaty interpretation and other treaty points. *British Year Book of International Law, 33*, 203.

Fitzmaurice, M. (2013). Interpretation of human rights treaties. In D. Shelton (Ed.), *The Oxford handbook of international human rights law* (pp. 739–772). Oxford: Oxford University Press. www.oxfordhanbooks.com, https://doi.org/10.1093/law/970199640133.003.0032

Fitzmaurice, M., Elias, O. A., & Merkouris, P. (Eds.). (2010). *Treaty interpretation and the Vienna Convention on the Law of Treaties: 30 years on* (Vol. 1). Leiden: Brill.

Fitzmaurice, M., & Merkouris, P. (2010). Canons of treaty interpretation: Selected case studies from the World Trade Organization and the North American Free Trade Agreement. In *Treaty interpretation and the Vienna Convention on the Law of Treaties: 30 years on* (pp. 153–238). Leiden: Brill.

Forowicz, M. (2010). *The reception of international law in the European court of human rights*. New York, NY: Oxford University Press.

French, D. (2006). Treaty interpretation and the incorporation of extraneous legal rules. *International and Comparative Law Quarterly, 55*(2), 281–314.

Fry, J. D. (2007). International human rights law in investment arbitration: Evidence of international law's unity. *Duke Journal of Comparative and International Law, 18*, 77.

Gardiner, R. K. (2008). *Treaty interpretation*. Oxford: Oxford University Press.

Gardiner, R. K. (2009, March 4). Beyond the Vienna rules. *Opinio Juris Blog*. Retrieved August 31, 2011, from http://opiniojuris.org/2009/03/04/beyond-the-vienna-rules/

Gentili, A. (1933). *De iure belli libri tres*. Oxford: Clarendon Press. (1612, No. 16).

Ghandhi, S. (2011). Human rights and the International Court of Justice: The Ahmadou Sadio Diallo case. *Human Rights Law Review, 11*(3), 527–555.

Gordon, E. (1995). Book review. *American Journal of International Law, 89*, 461–463.

Greer, S. (2006). *The European convention on human rights: Achievements, problems and prospects*. Cambridge: Cambridge University Press.

Gross, L. (1971). The International Court of Justice: Consideration of requirements for enhancing its role in the international legal order. *American Journal of International Law, 65*(2), 253–326.

Grotius, H. (1901). *The rights of war and peace* (A. C. Campbell, AM, Trans. Rev., p. 293). Washington, DC: M. Walter Dunne Publisher.

Grotius, H. (1925). *De Jure Belli ac Pacis Libri Tres. Vol. 2: The classics of international law* (J. B. Scott, Ed. & F. W. Kelsey, Trans.). Oxford: Clarendon Press.

Grotius, H. (2005). *De Jure Belli ac Pacis* [The rights of war and peace] (Jean Barbeyrac, Ed.). Amsterdam. (1724).

Gruszczynski, L. (2012). Customary rules of interpretation in the practice of WTO dispute settlement bodies. In A. Nollkaemper & K. O. Fauchald (Eds.), *The practice of international and national courts and (de) fragmentation of international law*. Oxford: Hart Publishing.

Guillaume, G. (1995). The future of international judicial institutions. *International and Comparative Law Quarterly, 44*(4), 848–862.

Guillaume, G. (2000a, October 27). *The proliferation of international judicial bodies: The outlook for the international legal order*. Speech by his excellency Judge Gilbert Guillaume, President of the International Court of Justice, to the Sixth Committee of the General Assembly of the United Nations.

Guillaume, G. (2000b, October 26). Address by HE Judge Gilbert Guillaume, President of the International Court of Justice to the United Nations General Assembly, New York. Retrieved from http://www.icj-cij.org/court/index.php?pr=84&pt=3&p1=1&p2=3&p3=1

Guillaume, G. (2004). Advantages and risks of proliferation: A blueprint for action. *Journal of International Criminal Justice, 2*, 300.

Guillaume, G. (2011). The use of precedent by international judges and arbitrators. *Journal of International Dispute Settlement, 2*(1), 5–23.

Hagle, T. M. (1990). So many cases, so little time: Judges as decision makers. In *American politics in the heartland*. Dubuque, IA: Kendall Hunt.

Han, S. W. D. (2006). Decentralized proliferation of international judicial bodies. *Journal of Transnational Law and Policy, 16*, 101.

Harris, D. J. (1991). *Cases and materials on international law*. London: Sweet and Maxwell Publishers.

Harris, J. D., O'Boyle, M., Bates, P. E., & Buckley, M. (2014). *Law of the European convention on human rights*. Oxford: Oxford University Press.

Hart, H. L. A., Raz, J., & Bulloch, P. A. (1994). *The concept of law* (2nd ed.). with a Postcript. Oxford: Oxford University Press.

Heard, A. (1997). *Human rights: Chimeras in sheep's clothing*. Simon Fraser University. http://www.sfu.ca/-aheard/intro.html

Henckaerts, J. M. (1993). The compulsory jurisdiction of the International Court of Justice, by Renata Szafarz. Dordrecht, The Netherlands: Martinus Nijhoff Publishers, 1993. *George Washington Journal of International Law and Economics, 27*, 265–573.

Henkin, L., Neuman, G. L., Orentlicher, D. F., & Leebron, D. W. (1999). *Human rights*. New York: Foundation Press.

Hernandez, J. G. (2014). Interpretation. In J. Kammerhofer & J. d'Aspremont (Eds.), *International legal positivism in a post-modern world*. Cambridge: Cambridge University Press.

Higgins, R. (2007). Human rights in the International Court of Justice. *Leiden Journal of International Law, 20*(4), 745–751.

Hoof, G. J. (1983). *Rethinking the sources of international law*. Deventer: Kluwer.

Hossain, K. (2005). Concept of Jus Cogens and the obligation under the UN charter. *Santa Clara Journal of International Law, 3*, i.

Houchins, D. L. (2002). Extending the application of the ICJ's July 8, 1996, advisory opinion to environment-altering weapons in general: What is the role of international environmental law in warfare. *Journal of Land, Resources and Environmental Law, 22*, 463.

Hudson, M. O. (1936). *La Cour permanente de Justice internationale—Traité*. Paris: Ed. Pédone.

Irwin, J. C. (1997). Alternative role for the International Court of Justice: Applied to Cameroon v. Nigeria. *Denver Journal of International Law and Policy, 26*, 759.

Jackson, J. H. (1998). Fragmentation or unification among international institutions: The World Trade Organization. *New York University Journal of International Law and Politics, 31*, 823.

Jackson, J. H. (2006). *Sovereignty, the WTO, and changing fundamentals of international law* (Vol. 18). Cambridge: Cambridge University Press.

Jacobs, F. G. (1969). Varieties of approach to treaty interpretation: With special reference to the draft convention on the law of treaties before the Vienna Diplomatic Conference. *The International and Comparative Law Quarterly, 18*(2), 318–346.

Jacobs, F. G. (2003). Judicial dialogue and the cross-fertilization of legal systems: The European Court of Justice. *Texas International Law Journal, 38*, 547.

Jacobs, D. (2010). The Al Bashir appeals Chamber Judgment on genocide: A critical appraisal in law and in context. *Hague Justice Portal*. Retrieved from http://www.haguejusticeportal.net/index.php?id=10761

Janis, M. W. (1987). Somber reflections on the compulsory jurisdiction of the international court. *American Journal of International Law, 81*(1), 144–146.

Janis, M. W. (1999). *An introduction to international law*. Gaithersburg, MD: Aspen Publishers.

Janis, M. W. (2010). *America and the law of nations 1776–1939*. Oxford: Oxford University Press on Demand.

Jennings, M. (2004). The WTO and international law. In ANZSIL conference. *International and Comparative Law Quarterly, 18*, 318.

Jennings, R., & Watts, A. (1992). *Oppenheim's international law (Vol. 1): Peace* (9th ed.). London: Longman Higher Education, Longman Group UK Ltd.

Jonas, D. S., & Saunders, T. N. (2010). Object and purpose of a treaty: Three interpretive methods. *Vanderbilt Journal of Transnational Law, 43*, 565.

Kammerhofer, J. (2004). Uncertainty in the formal sources of international law: Customary international law and some of its problems. *European Journal of International Law, 15*(3), 523–553.

Kamminga, M. T. (2008). *Final Report on the impact of international human rights law on general international law*. Report of the 73d Conference of the International Law Association, pp. 663–685. SSRN: https://ssrn.com/abstract=1150664

Kamminga, M. T., & Scheinin, M. (Eds.). (2009). *The impact of human rights law on general international law*. Oxford: Oxford University Press.

Kaufman, Z. D. (2011). The human element: The impact of regional trade agreements on the human rights and the rule of law: Comment. *University of Miami Inter-American Law Review, 42*, 253–443.

Kelly, J. P. (2001). Judicial activism at the World Trade Organization: Developing principles of self-restraint. *Northwestern Journal of International Law and Business, 22*, 353.

Kelly, J. P. (2005). The seduction of the Appellate Body: Shrimp/sea turtle I and II and the proper role of states in WTO governance. *Cornell International Law Journal, 38*, 459–491.

Kelly, J. P. (2008). International law and the shrinking space for politics in developing countries. In *Law and rights: Global perspectives on constitutionalism and governance*. Vandeplas Publishing. Widener Law School Legal Studies Research Paper No. 08-31. https://papers.ssrn.com/sol3/papers.cfm?abstract_id=1104694

Kelsen, H. (1970). *Pure theory of law*. Translation from the 2d (Revised and Enlarged) German Edition by Max Knight.

Kelsen, I. (2003). *Principles of international law*. Clark, NJ: The Lawbook Exchange, Ltd. (Third Print 1959).

Khrebtukova, A. (2008). Call to freedom: Towards a philosophy of international law in an era of fragmentation. *Journal of International Law and International Relations, 4*, 51.

Kingsbury, B. (1998). Foreword: Is the proliferation of international courts and tribunals a systemic problem. *New York University Journal of International Law and Politics, 31*, 679.

Klabbers, J. (2010). Virtuous interpretation. In *Treaty interpretation and the Vienna Convention on the Law of Treaties: 30 years on* (pp. 15–38). Leiden: Brill.

Koskenniemi, M. (2001). *The gentle civilizer of nations: The rise and fall of international law 1870–1960 (Hersch Lauterpacht memorial lectures)*. Cambridge: Cambridge University Press.

Koskenniemi, M. (2004). *Study on the function and scope of the Lex Specialis Rule and the question of 'Self-Contained Regimes'*. Preliminary report by the Chairman of the Study Group submitted for consideration during the 2004 session of the International Law Commission.

Koskenniemi, M. (2006). *From apology to utopia: The structure of international legal argument*. Cambridge: Cambridge University Press.

Koskenniemi, M. (2007). The fate of public international law: Between technique and politics. *Modern Law Review, 70*(1), 1–30.

Koskenniemi, M., & Leino, P. (2002). Fragmentation of international law? Postmodern anxieties. *Leiden Journal of International Law, 15*(3), 553–579.

Kuyper, P. J. (1994). The law of GATT as a special field of international law: Ignorance, further refinement or self-contained system of international law? *Netherlands Yearbook of International Law, 25*, 227–257.

Lamy, P. (2006). The place of the WTO and its law in the international legal order. *European Journal of International Law, 17*(5), 969–984.

Lauterpacht, H. (1949). Restrictive interpretation and the principle of effectiveness in the interpretation of treaties. *British Year Book of International Law, 26*, 48.

Lauterpacht, H. (1950). *International law and human rights*. North Haven, CT: Shoe String Press.

Lauterpacht, H. (1955). Codification and development of international law. *American Journal of International Law, 49*, 16.

Lauterpacht, H. (1982). *The development of international law by the international court* (p. 282). Cambridge: Cambridge University Press.

Leal-Arcas, R. (2010). Proliferation of regional trade agreements: Complementing or supplanting multilateralism. *Chicago Journal of International Law, 11*, 597.

Lennard, M. (2002). Navigating by the stars: Interpreting the WTO agreements. *Journal of International Economic Law, 5*(1), 17–89.

Letsas, G. (2007). *A theory of interpretation of the European convention on human rights*. Oxford: Oxford University Press.

Letsas, G. (2010a). Strasbourg's interpretive ethic: Lessons for the international lawyer. *European Journal of International Law, 21*(3), 509–541.

Letsas, G. (2010b). Intentionalism and interpretation of human rights. In M. Fitzmaurice, O. A. Elias, & P. Merkouris (Eds.), *Treaty interpretation and the Vienna Convention on the Law of Treaties: 30 years on* (Vol. 1, pp. 257–272). Leiden, The Netherlands: Brill.

Letsas, G. (2012). *The ECHR as a living instrument: Its meaning and its legitimacy*. https://papers.ssrn.com/sol3/papers.cfm?abstract_id=2021836

Lévesque, J. F. (2006). Traites de Verre: Reflexions sur l'Interpretation. *Revue quebecoise de droit international, 19*, 53.

Linderfalk, U. (2007). *On the interpretation of treaties: The modern international law as expressed in the 1969 Vienna Convention on the law of Treaties* (Vol. 83). Dordrecht: Springer Science and Business Media.

Lindroos, A., & Mehling, M. (2005). Dispelling the chimera of 'self-contained regimes' international law and the WTO. *European Journal of International Law, 16*(5), 857–877.

Linton, S., & Tiba, F. K. (2009). The international judge in an age of multiple international courts and tribunals. *Chicago Journal of International Law, 9*(2), 407.

Llamzon, A. P. (2007). Jurisdiction and compliance in recent decisions of the International Court of Justice. *European Journal of International Law, 18*(5), 815–852.

Lu, B. (2004). Reform of the international court of justice—A jurisdictional perspective. *Perspectives, Overseas Young Chinese Forum 5*(2).

Macdonald, R. S. J. (1993). The margin of appreciation. In R. S. J. Macdonald, F. Matscher, & H. Petzold (Eds.), *The European system for the protection of human rights*. Dordrecht: Martinus Nijhoff.

Mahoney, P. (1998). The doctrine of the margin of appreciation under the European Convention of Human Rights: Its legitimacy in theory and application in practice. *Human Rights Law Journal, 19*(1), 3.

Mann, F. A. (1984). The doctrine of jurisdiction in international law, twenty years later. *Rec des Cours, 1*, 9.

Marceau, G. (2006). The WTO is not a closed box. *Proceedings of the Annual Meeting, American Society of International Law, 100*, 29–31.

Martineau, A. C. (2009). The rhetoric of fragmentation: Fear and faith in international law. *Leiden Journal of International Law, 22*(1), 1–28.

Mavroidis, P. C. (2008). No outsourcing of law? WTO law as practiced by WTO courts. *American Journal of International Law, 102*, 421–474.

McConville, M., & Chui, W. H. E. (Eds.). (2007). Research methods for law. Edinburgh University Press: Edinburgh.

McDougal, M. S. (1967). The international law commission's draft articles upon interpretation: Textuality redivivus. *American Journal of International Law, 61*(4), 992–1000.

McDougal, M. S. (1968). Statement of Professor Myres S McDougal, United States delegation, to the Committee of the Whole, April 19, 1968. *American Journal of International Law, 62*, 1021.

McDougal, M. S., & Gardner, R. N. (1951). The Veto and the Charter: An interpretation for survival. *Yale Law Journal, 60*(2), 258–292.

McDougal, M. S., Lasswell, H. D., & James Clifford Miller, J. C. (1994). *The interpretation of international agreements and world public order*. Leiden: Martinus Nijhoff Publishers.

McInerney, C. P. (2009). From shrimps and dolphins to retreaded tyres: An overview of the World Trade Organization disputes, discussing exceptions to trading rules. *New York International Law Review, 22*, 153–158.

McInerney-Lankford, S. (2012). Fragmentation of international law redux: The case of Strasbourg. *Oxford Journal of Legal Studies, 32*(3), 609–632.

McLachlan, C. (2005). The principle of systemic integration and article 31 (3)(c) of the Vienna Convention. *International and Comparative Law Quarterly, 54*(2), 279–320.

McNair, B. A. D. M. (1961). *The law of treaties*. Oxford: Clarendon Press.

McRae, D. (2004). What is the future of WTO dispute settlement? *Journal of International Economic Law, 7*(1), 3–21.

Mechlem, K. (2009). Treaty bodies and the interpretation of human rights. *Vanderbilt Journal of Transnational Law, 42*, 905.

Meng, W. (1987). Extraterritorial effects of administrative, judicial and legislative acts. *Encyclopedia of Public International Law, Instalment, 10*(1987), 155.

Mercurio, B. C., & Tyagi, M. (2010). Treaty interpretation in WTO dispute settlement: The outstanding question of the legality of local working requirements. *Minnesota Journal of International Law, 19*(2), 275–326.
Merkouris, P. (2010a). Introduction: Interpretation is a science, is an art, is a science. In *Treaty interpretation and the Vienna Convention on the Law of Treaties: 30 years on* (pp. 1–14). Leiden: Brill.
Merkouris, P. (2010b). *Article 31(3)(c) of the VCLT and the principle of systemic integration.* Study submitted for the degree of Ph.D., Queen Mary University of London School of Law.
Merrills, J. G. (1968). Two approaches to treaty interpretation. *Australian Year Book of International Law, 4*, 55.
Merrills, J. G. (2005). *International dispute settlement.* Cambridge: Cambridge University Press.
Michaels, R., & Paulwelyn, J. (2011). Conflict of norms or conflict of laws: Different techniques in the fragmentation of public international law. *Duke Journal of Comparative and International Law, 22*, 349.
Milanovic, M. (2011). *Extraterritorial application of human rights treaties: Law, principles, and policy.* Oxford: Oxford University Press.
Mitchell, A. D. (2007). The legal basis for using principles in WTO disputes. *Journal of International Economic Law, 10*(4), 795–835.
Moore, J. N. (1987). The Nicaragua case and the deterioration of world order. *American Journal of International Law, 81*(1), 151–159.
Morgenthau, H. J. (1940). Positivism, functionalism, and international law. *American Journal of International Law, 34*(2), 260–284.
Morgenthau, H. J. (1948). *Politics among nations: The struggle for power and peace* (p. 51973). New York: Alfred A. Knopf.
Morigiwa, Y., Stolleis, M., & Halpérin, J. L. (Eds.). (2011). *Interpretation of law in the age of enlightenment: From the rule of the king to the rule of law* (Vol. 95). Dordrecht: Springer Science and Business Media.
Mortenson, J. D. (2013). Is the Vienna Convention hostile to drafting history? *American Journal of International Law, 107*, 780.
Mosler, H. (1980). Supra-national judicial decisions and national courts. *Hastings International and Comparative Law Review, 4*, 425.
Mowbray, A. (2005). The creativity of the European Court of Human Rights. *Human Rights Law Review, 5*(1), 57–79.
Nicolaidis, K., & Tong, J. L. (2003). Diversity or Cacophony—The continuing debate over new sources of international law. *Michigan Journal of International Law, 25*, 1349.
O'Boyle, M. (1998). The margin of appreciation and derogation under Article 15: Ritual incantation or principle? *Human Rights Law Journal, 19*, 23–29.
Oppenheim, L. F. (1921). In R. F. Roxburgh (Ed.), *International law: A treatise* (Vol. 2, p. 2) (1923). London: Longmans/Green & Co.
Orakhelashvili, A. (2003). Restrictive interpretation of human rights treaties in the recent jurisprudence of the European Court of Human Rights. *European Journal of International Law, 14* (3), 529–568.
Orakhelashvili, A. (2008). *The interpretation of acts and rules in public international law.* Oxford: Oxford University Press.
Panitchpakdi, S. (2006). The WTO at ten: Building on ten years of achievements. In G. Sacerdoti, A. Yanovich, & J. Bohanes (Eds.), *The WTO at ten: The contribution of the dispute settlement system.* London: Cambridge University Press.
Patomäki, H. (2008). Rethinking global democracy/world parlament: Towards determining what international cosmopolitical law is. In P. Korkman & V. Mäkinen (Eds.), *Studies across disciplines in the humanities and social sciences, vol. 4: Universalism in international law and political philosophy.* Helsinki: Collegium for Advanced Studies.
Patterson, D. (2001). Normativity and objectivity in law. *William and Mary Law Review, 43*, 325.
Patterson, D. (2005). Interpretation in law. *San Diego Law Review, 42*, 685.

Pauwelyn, J. (2003). *Conflict of norms in public international law: How WTO law relates to other rules of international law* (Vol. 29). Cambridge: Cambridge University Press.

Pauwelyn, J., & Elsig, M. (2011). *The politics of treaty interpretation: Variations and explanations across international tribunals*. https://ssrn.com/abstract=1938618 or https://doi.org/10.2139/ssrn.1938618

Pauwelyn, J., & Elsig, M. (2013). In L. J. Dunoff & A. M. Pollack (Eds.), *Interdisciplinary perspectives on international law and international relations: The state of the art*. Cambridge: Cambridge University Press.

Pauwelyn, J., & Salles, L. E. (2009). Forum shopping before international tribunals: (Real) concerns, (im)possible solutions. *Cornell International Law Journal, 42*, 77–118.

Payandeh, M. (2010). The concept of international law in the jurisprudence of HLA Hart. *European Journal of International Law, 21*(4), 967–995.

Peczenik, A. (1985). Moral and ontological justification of legal reasoning. *Law and Philosophy, 4* (2), 289–309.

Pegorier, C. (2013). *Ethnic cleansing: A legal qualification*. New York: Routledge.

Petersmann, E. U. (2004). Ten years of the WTO dispute settlement system: Past, present and future. *Journal of International Law and Policy, 3*, 1–48.

Petersmann, E. U. (2006). Justice as conflict resolution: Proliferation, fragmentation, and decentralization of dispute settlement in international trade. *University of Pennsylvania Journal of International Economic Law, 27*, 273.

Petsche, M. (2010). Jus Cogens as a vision of the international legal order. *Penn State International Law Review, 29*, 233.

Phillimore, R. (1856). Commentaries upon international law. *Law Library Journal, 88*, i.

Posner, E. A., & De Figueiredo, M. (2004). Is the International Court of Justice biased? *University of Chicago Law & Economics*, Olin Working Paper, 234.

Pound, R. (1923). The theory of judicial decision. *Harvard Law Review, 36*, 802.

Prost, M. (2012). *The concept of unity in public international law*. Oxford: Bloomsbury Publishing.

Prost, M., & Clark, P. K. (2006). Unity, diversity and the fragmentation of international law: How much does the multiplication of international organizations really matter? *Chinese Journal of International Law, 5*(2), 341–370.

Pufendorf, S. (1934). *De jure naturae et gentium libri octo* (C. H. Oldfather & W. A. Oldfather, Trans., Vol. 2). Oxford: Clarendon Press.

Pulkowski, D. (2005). *Narratives of fragmentation: International law between unity and multiplicity*. Paper presented at 'Agora' 2005 florence founding conference of the European Society of International Law (ESIL).

Ramberg, B., & Gjesdal, K. (2009). *"Hermeneutics", the Stanford Encyclopedia of Philosophy* (E. N. Zalta, Ed.). Retrieved December 2012, from http://plato.stanford.edu/archives/sum2009/

Rao, P. S. (2003). Multiple international judicial forums: A reflection of the growing strength of international law or its fragmentation. *Michigan Journal of International Law, 25*, 929.

Rayfuse, R. (2005). Future of compulsory dispute settlement under the law of the sea convention. *Victoria University of Wellington Law Review, 36*, 683.

Reed, L., & Jacovides, A. (2002). Great expectations: Where does the proliferation of international dispute resolution tribunals leave international law? In *Proceedings of the Annual Meeting (American Society of International Law)* (pp. 219–237). Washington, DC: The American Society of International Law.

Ris, M. (1991). Treaty interpretation and ICJ recourse to Travaux Préparatoires: Towards a proposed amendment of Articles 31 and 32 of the Vienna Convention on the Law of Treaties. *Boston College International and Comparative Law Review, 14*, 111.

Romano, C. P. (1998). Proliferation of international judicial bodies: The pieces of the puzzle. *New York University Journal of International Law and Politics, 31*, 709.

Romano, C. P. (2001). The southern bluefin tuna dispute: Hints of a world to come... like it or not. *Ocean Development and International Law, 32*(4), 313–348.

Romano, C. P. (2006). Shift from the consensual to the compulsory paradigm in international adjudication: Elements for a theory of consent. *New York University Journal of International Law and Politics, 39*, 791.

Romano, C. P. (2011). A taxonomy of international rule of law institutions. *Journal of International Dispute Settlement, 2*(1), 241–277.

Rozakis, C. L. (2005). European judge as Comparatist. *Tulane Law Review, 80*, 257.

Runersten, M. (2008). *Defining 'Self-contained Regime'—A case study of the international covenant on civil and political rights*. Lund: University of Lund.

Sands, P. (1998). Treaty, custom and the cross-fertilization of international law. *Yale Human Rights and Development Law Journal, 1*, 85.

Sands, P., & Commission, J. (2010). Treaty, custom and time: Interpretation/application? In *Treaty interpretation and the Vienna Convention on the Law of Treaties: 30 years on* (pp. 39–58). Leiden: Brill.

Schermers, H. G., & Blokker, N. M. (2011). *International institutional law: Unity within diversity*. Leiden, The Netherlands: Martinus Nijhoff Publishers.

Scheinin, M. (2009). Impact on the law of treaties. In M. T. Kamminga & M. Scheinin (Eds.), *The impact of human rights law on general international law* (p. 33). Oxford: Oxford University Press.

Schwelb, E. (1967). Some aspects of international jus cogens as formulated by the International Law Commission. *American Journal of International Law, 61*(4), 946–975.

Scott, J. B. (1925). Grotius' De Jure Belli ac Pacis Libri Tres: The work of a lawyer, stateman and theologian. *American Journal of International Law, 19*, 461.

Scott, J. B. (1935). *Hugo Grotius De Jure Belli Ac Pacis Libri Tres*. Washington, DC: Carnegie Endowment for International Peace.

Scott, G. L., Bothwell, H. M., & Pennell, J. (1996). Recent activity before the International Court of Justice: Trend or cycle. *ILSA Journal of International and Comparative Law, 3*, 1.

Shaw, M. N. (2008). *International law*. Cambridge: Cambridge University Press.

Sheeran, S. (2014). The relationship of international human rights and general international law: A hermeneutic constraint, or pushing the boundaries? In S. Sheeran & N. Rodley (Eds.), *Routledge handbook of international human rights law*. London: Routledge.

Shelton, D. (2002). Hierarchy of norms and human rights: Of trumps and winners. *Saskatchewan Law Review, 65*, 301.

Shelton, D. (2003). Boundaries of human rights jurisdiction in Europe. *Duke Journal of Comparative and International Law, 13*, 95.

Simma, B. (1985). Self-contained regimes. *Netherlands Yearbook of International Law, 16*, 111–136.

Simma, B. (2009). Universality of international law from the perspective of a practitioner. *European Journal of International Law, 20*(2), 265–297.

Simma, B., & Pulkowski, D. (2006). Of planets and the universe: Self-contained regimes in international law. *European Journal of International Law, 17*(3), 483–529.

Sinclair, I. M. (1984). *The Vienna Convention on the Law of Treaties*. Manchester: Manchester University Press.

Slaughter, A. M., & Ratner, S. R. (1999). Appraising the methods of international law: A prospectus for readers. *American Journal of International Law, 93*, 291.

Smith, F. (2010, November). *Treaty interpretation in the WTO: Beyond the Vienna Convention on the Law of Treaties*. Oxford: Public International Law Discussion Group/University of Oxford.

Sornarajah, M. (2010). *The international law on foreign investment*. Cambridge: Cambridge University Press.

Spelliscy, S. (2001). Proliferation of international tribunals: A chink in the armor. *Columbia Journal of Transnational Law, 40*, 143.

Spiermann, O. (2007). Judge Max Huber at the permanent court of international justice. *European Journal of International Law, 18*(1), 115–133.

Stein, P. (1994). Interpretation and legal reasoning in Roman law. *Chicago-Kent Law Review, 70*, 1539.

Stevenson, A. (Ed.). (2010). *Oxford Dictionary of English* (3rd ed.). Oxford: Oxford University Press.

Stone, J. (1953). Fictional elements in treaty interpretation—A study in the international judicial process. *Sydney Law Review, 1*, 344.

Sweet, A. S. (2000). *Governing with judges: Constitutional politics in Europe*. Oxford: Oxford University Press.

Tate, C. N., & Vallinder, T. (1995). *The global expansion ofjudicial power*. New York: New York University Press.

Teitel, R., & Howse, R. (2008). Cross-judging: Tribunalization in a fragmented but interconnected global order. *New York University Journal of International Law and Politics, 41*, 959.

The Structure of WTO. Retrieved from http://www2.econ.iastate.edu/classes/econ355/choi/wtoworks.htm

The WTO Guide: "Understanding the WTO". Retrieved from http://www.wto.org

Tittemore, B. D. (2005). Ending impunity in the Americas: The role of the inter-american human rights system in advancing accountability for serious crimes under international law. *Southwestern Journal of Law and Trade in the Americas, 12*, 429.

Toufayan, M. (2005). *Human rights treaty interpretation: A postmodern account of its claim to "speciality"*. NYU Centre for Human Rights and Global Justice Working Paper.

Trachtman, J. P. (1999). Domain of WTO dispute resolution. *Harvard International Law Journal, 40*, 333.

Trumble, W. R., & Stevenson, A. (Eds.). (2002). *Shorter Oxford English Dictionary: On historical principles*. Oxford: Oxford University Press.

Tzevelekos, V. P. (2009). Use of Article 31 (3)(C) of the VCLT in the case law of the ECtHR: An effective anti-fragmentation tool or a selective loophole for the reinforcement of human rights teleology-between evolution and systemic integration. *Michigan Journal of International Law, 31*, 621.

Van Damme, I. (2009). *Treaty interpretation by the WTO Appellate Body*. Oxford: Oxford University Press.

Van Hoecke, M. (Ed.). (2011). Methodologies of legal research: Which kind of method for what kind of discipline? Oxford: Hart Publishing.

Venzke, I. (2012). *How interpretation makes international law: On semantic change and normative twists*. Oxford: Oxford University Press.

Verdross, A. (1949). On the concept of international law. *American Journal of International Law, 43*, 435.

Verdross, A. (1966). Jus dispositivum and jus cogens in international law. *American Journal of International Law, 60*(1), 55–63.

Villiger, M. E. (2009). *Commentary on the 1969 Vienna Convention on the Law of Treaties*. Leiden: Brill.

Villiger, M. E. (2011). The rules on interpretation-misgivings, misunderstandings, miscarriage? The "Crucible" intended by the International Law Commission. In E. Cannizzaro (Ed.), *The law of treties beyond the Vienna Convention*. Oxford: Oxford University Press.

Vitányi, B. (1983). Treaty interpretation in the legal theory of Grotius and its influence on modern doctrine. *Netherlands Yearbook of International Law, 14*, 41–67.

Voeten, E. (2010). Borrowing and nonborrowing among international courts. *The Journal of Legal Studies, 39*(2), 547–576.

Waibel, M. (2011). Demystifying the art of interpretation. *European Journal of International Law, 22*(2), 571–588.

Webb, P. (2013). *International judicial integration and fragmentation*. Oxford: Oxford University Press.

Weisburd, A. M. (2009). International Court of Justice and the concept of state practice. *University of Pennsylvania Journal of International Law, 31*, 295.

Wellens, K. C. (1994). Diversity in secondary rules and the unity of international law: Some reflections on current trends. *Netherlands Yearbook of International Law, 25*, 3–37.
Wellens, K. C. (2003). Fragmentation of international law and establishing an accountability regime for international organizations: The role of the judiciary in closing the gap. *Michigan Journal of International Law, 25*, 1159.
Wilde, R. (2005). The 'legal space' or 'espace juridique' of the European Convention on Human Rights: Is it relevant to extraterritorial state action? *European Human Rights Law Review, 10*, 115–124.
Wróblewski, J. (1985). Legal language and legal interpretation. *Law and Philosophy, 4*(2), 239–255.
Yin, R. K. (2003). *Case study research design and methods, Applied social research methods series* (Vol. 5, 3rd ed.). Thousand Oaks, CA: Sage Publications.
Zemanek, K. (2009). Vienna Convention on the Law of Treaties. *United Nations Audiovisual Library of International Law*. Retrieved from http://untreaty.un.org/cod/avl/pdf/ha/vclt/vclt-e.pdf
Zhang, Y. (1933). *The interpretation of treaties by judicial tribunals (No. 389)*. New York: Columbia University Press.

## *Documents*

Assembly, U. G. (1948). *Universal declaration of human rights*. UN General Assembly.
Charter, U. N. (1945, June 26). *Charter of the United Nations*.
Harvard Research in International Law. (1957). Draft convention of the law of treaties (1935). *American Journal of International Law, 29*(Suppl), 938.
International Law Commission. (1966). Draft articles on the law of treaties with commentaries. In *Yearbook of the International Law Commission* (Vol. 2).
International Law Commission. (2001). *Draft articles on responsibility of states for internationally wrongful acts*. Report of the International Law Commission on the Work of Its Fifty-third Session.
International Law Commission. (2006). *Fragmentation of international law: Difficulties arising from the diversification and expansion of international law*. Geneva: United Nations.
Report of International Law Commission. (2003). Fifty-fifth session, Supplement No. 10 (A/58/10).
Summary Records of the Sixteenth Session. (1964, May 11–July 24). Vol. I, UN. UN Doc A/CN.4/SER A/1964.
The European Convention on Human Rights—Convention for Protection of Human Rights and Fundamental Freedoms. (1950). Retrieved from http://conventions.coe.int/Treaty/en/Treaties/Html/005.htm
The European Court of Human Rights. Projects on International Courts and Tribunals. Retrieved from http://www.pict-pcti.org/courts/ECHR.html
The Work of International Law Commission. (2007). *Office of legal affairs* (7th ed., p. 1). New York: United Nations.
Vienna Convention on the Law of Treaties, opened for signature May 23, 1969, 1155 UNTS 331. Retrieved from http://untreaty.un.org/ilc/texts/instruments/english/conventions/1_1_1969.pdf
Waldock, H. (1964). Third report on the law of treaties, by Sir Humphrey Waldock, Special Rapporteur. *Yearbook of the International Law Commission, 2*, 49.

FSC
www.fsc.org
MIX
Papier | Fördert
gute Waldnutzung
FSC® C083411

Kolibri 360 GmbH
Ferdinand-Jühlke-Straße 7
99095 Erfurt, Deutschland
produktsicherheit@kolibri360.de